Fodor's 94
Hawaii

W9-BXZ-770

Fodor's Travel Publications, Inc.
New York • Toronto • London • Sydney • Auckland

Grateful acknowledgement is made to the following for permission to reprint previously published material: Alfred A. Knopf, Inc. and Garrett Hongo: "Village: Kahuku-*mura*" from *The River of Heaven* by Garrett Hongo. Rights in the British Commonwealth administered by Garrett Hongo. Rights in all other territories administered by Alfred A. Knopf, Inc. Copyright © 1987 by Garrett Hongo. Reprinted by permission of Alfred A. Knopf, Inc. and Garrett Hongo. "The Aloha Shirt: A Colorful Swatch of Island History" by DeSoto Brown reprinted from *Aloha Magazine;* copyright © Davick Publications. Dive information adapted from "The Underwater World," copyright © 1989 by Barbara Brundage. Originally printed in *Pleasant Hawaii: The Aloha State Magazine.*

Fodor's Hawaii

Editor: Larry Peterson
Editorial Contributors: Robert Blake, Gary Diedrichs, Donnë Florence, Michael Flynn, Betty Fullard-Leo, Linda Kephart, Valerie Martone, Robert Norton, Marty Wentzel
Creative Director: Fabrizio La Rocca
Cartographer: David Lindroth
Illustrator: Karl Tanner
Cover Photograph: Paul Chesley/Photographers/Aspen

Design: Vignelli Associates

Special Sales

Contents

Maps and Plans

Foreword

We wish to express our gratitude to the offices of the Hawaii Visitors Bureau on Oahu, the Big Island, Maui, and Kauai for their assistance in the preparation of this guidebook. We also would like to thank Nancy Daniels, Tom Herman, and Sonia Franzel for their help.

While every care has been taken to assure the accuracy of the information in this guide, the passage of time will always bring change, and consequently, the publisher cannot accept responsibility for errors that may occur.

All prices and opening times quoted here are based on information supplied to us at press time. Hours and admission fees may change, however, and the prudent traveler will avoid inconvenience by calling ahead.

Fodor's wants to hear about your travel experiences, both pleasant and unpleasant. When a hotel or restaurant fails to live up to its billing, let us know and we will investigate the complaint and revise our entries where the facts warrant it.

Send your letters to the editors of Fodor's Travel Publications, 201 E. 50th Street, New York, NY 10022.

Highlights'94 and Fodor's Choice

Highlights '94

Oahu

Waikiki Waikiki's massive multi-million-dollar renovation has refurbished the area from top to bottom. With sidewalks widened, street signs improved, and clutter removed, the place has never looked better.

At the same time, the **Waikiki Improvement Association** remains focused on the constant upkeep of Waikiki. The 25-year-old organization recently spruced up several parks in the area, including the Waikiki Triangle, Gateway Park, Kuhio Beach Park, and Kaiulani Triangle. The WIA also plans to put cultural markers throughout Waikiki to help visitors appreciate its fascinating history.

Plans to build a **convention center** in Waikiki stalled in the spring of 1993 when the state legislature failed to agree on a site for the facility. Two locations are in the running: one is at the corner of Kalakaua Avenue and Kapiolani Boulevard, and the other at a block called Ala Wai Gateway, on Ala Moana Boulevard. Nonetheless, legislators remained confident that a decision would be made sometime in 1993, with completion of the center—at whichever site—by 1997.

Some $100 million has already been spent on the **Hilton Hawaiian Village** for renovations and additions, and they're still spending and adding. In 1992, the 20-acre Waikiki destination created a new **Executive Club** on the top two floors of its 31-story Rainbow Tower, where guests get such extra touches as butler service, preferred dining reservations, daily newspaper delivery, and free limousine service in the Waikiki and Ala Moana areas. The latest word is that the hotel will be developing a complete health-spa complex including tennis courts and a gourmet health-food restaurant.

Every Friday evening the Hilton Hawaiian Village stages its **King Kalakaua Jubilee,** poolside, with the beach as a backdrop. It's a monarchy-era musical presentation complete with pomp, song, hula, a fire swallower, a painless history lesson, and culminating in a spectacular fireworks show. It's one of the best pageants in Waikiki—and it's free.

From 1935 to 1975, a musical program called **"Hawaii Calls"** aired on radio stations across the mainland, Europe, and Asia, and was known as the voice of Hawaii. In 1992 the tradition was revived, and today the show is broadcast weekly to some 45 cities worldwide. Each week "Hawaii Calls" features a contemporary Hawaiian group as well as vocalists and musicians who were regulars on the original show. Interviews with local and visiting celebrities and interesting facts about Hawaii round out the half-hour broadcast, which originates from the Hilton Hawaiian Village on Saturday afternoons, three Saturdays each month. (The fourth week, the show travels to a different Neighbor Island locale.) Visitors can attend the Hilton show for $22; the price includes a buffet luncheon (tel. 808/947–7993).

Two of Waikiki's most famous attractions have recently changed for the better. The **Honolulu Zoo's new African savanna** houses rhinos, cheetahs, and other exotic creatures in an environment which lets them wander freely rather than sit in cages. Designed with trees, grasses, ponds, and hilly terrain, the 7.5-acre habitat convincingly creates the illusion that there are no barriers between the animals and the zoo guests. A second $8.3 million phase of 5.4 acres is scheduled to open in 1993. Up the street at the **Waikiki Aquarium,** a $2 million renovation was scheduled to be finished by the end of 1993, with an overhaul of five exhibit areas. The aquarium has already brightened its appearance with the new 32-seat **Sea Visions Theater** and adjacent exhibit areas.

Around the Island **Honolulu International Airport** is undergoing major renovations, and all terminals will be overhauled or rebuilt by the late 1990s. A new inter-island terminal is being built and is scheduled for completion sometime in 1994. The state is also building a new four-level international terminal, scheduled to open in the mid-1990s.

The long-awaited **Pacific Aerospace Museum** has opened in the airport's main concourse. Hawaii's first museum devoted to technology, the 7,500-square-foot facility is also the first of its kind in the world to be housed in a major airport. It commemorates aviation and aerospace achievements in Hawaii and throughout the Pacific with its interactive exhibits, computer and laser technology, and three-dimensional multi-media theater.

Mega-resorts may be the mega-trend, but small boutique hotels are continuing to spring up in Waikiki, offering intimate, personalized alternatives. First, in 1988, came the Waikiki Joy, placing an emphasis on high-tech amenities, followed by the Coconut Plaza with its chic decor and low rates. Most recently, Aston Hotels & Resorts opened the refurbished **Aston Waikiki Beachside,** an Island boutique hotel with a decidedly European flair.

A new attraction called **Hawaii's Plantation Village** traces the history of the sugar plantations, which were the touchstones for the islands' ethnic diversity. Set in the historic plantation town of Waipahu in central Oahu, about a 30-minute drive from Honolulu, the three-acre site has been designed as a living museum with buildings, artifacts, and demonstrations that bring the plantation era of the late 19th and early 20th century alive.

Despite the economic recession of 1991 and 1992, the lack of space for expansion within Waikiki encouraged the construction of **Ko Olina**, a vast $3 billion (yes, *billion*) resort along the dry Ewa Coast west of Honolulu International Airport. It will include seven hotels, having a total of 4,000 rooms, 5,200 condominium units, a 44-acre marina, its own 18-hole golf course, a tennis complex, and a shopping center. Set on 642 acres, it will be the largest resort in the state. Some 3,000 coconut palms have already been planted on the property. The first hotel to open will be the **Ihilani Resort & Spa**, scheduled to begin operations in the Fall of 1993. The 15-story, 390-room hotel will cater to the upscale crowd with luxurious furnishings, four restaurants, two pools, meeting facilities, health spa, tennis club, beauty salon, and year-round child care.

Hawaiian Regional Cuisine is all the rage in the islands these days, thanks to an influx of talented chefs who are keen on working with locally grown products. A leader in this movement is **Roy Yamaguchi**, who opened a new Waikiki restaurant in 1992. Dubbed **Roy's Park Bistro**, it showcases fresh, home-grown ingredients prepared in innovative and unusual ways. Yamaguchi also runs **Roy's restaurant** in Hawaii Kai and the even newer **Roy's Kahana Bar & Grill** on Maui. For more samples of Hawaii Regional Cuisine at its best, stop by **La Mer** at the Halekulani Hotel and the **Prince Court** at the Hawaii Prince Hotel.

The Big island of Hawaii

Hawaiians seem congenitally disposed to look for the hidden blessing in every calamity, from a rain-delayed outdoor wedding to a hurricane. When Hurricane Iniki forced Kauai-bound vacationers to pick another island in the fall of 1992, many chose the Big Island of Hawaii and gave the Volcano Isle a much-needed economic boost. The resort-dotted **Kona** and **Kohala Coasts** saw some hotel occupancy rates jump to as high as 95 percent in the last months of the year—not quite enough to reverse the annual visitor count decline that began in 1989, but it prompted sighs of relief nevertheless.

Despite the active volcano, historic sites, ski facilities, and cowboy cachet that make it unique, the Big Island is still overlooked by many vacationers. Informal Hawaii Visitors Bureau questioning reveals that many tourists who have stayed in Waikiki believe they have "been to Hawaii." HVB's George Applegate hopes promotion of the longer name—The Big island of Hawaii—will help end the confusion between a visit to the state and a visit to its largest island.

Mount Kilauea continues to cooperate with the HVB, putting on an astonishing show for visitors who do find their way to the Big Island. Small New Year's earthquakes prompted speculation that the lava flow would change direction again, but Madame Pele had already closed the bottom of Chain of Craters Road and didn't seem inclined to make any more sudden moves, so sightseers were soon allowed back to the close-up viewing sites along the beach.

Both **Aloha Airlines** and **Hawaiian Airlines** announced cutbacks in their interisland schedules in January. A smaller number of fuller planes will be landing at Keahole Airport on the Kona Coast and at Hilo in the east. Aloha's subsidiary, **Aloha IslandAir,** which offers the only commercial service to Waimea's Kamuela airport, raised its prices by adding $10–$20 surcharges for passengers using Aloha interisland coupons.

The slow economy has stalled resort construction and planned expansion on the island's west coast. Developers have gone back to the drawing board to create plans for a smaller, low-rise **Four Seasons Resort** and its projected opening has now been put off to at least 1995. Conversion of the still-closed Kona Lagoons Hotel into a 250-suite facility, which would then become part of the adjoining **Keauhou Beach Hotel,** have been tabled, with no new target date announced.

Condo developments are blooming on parcels of former ranch land in Kohala's paniolo (cowboy) region. Short-term rental units here are likely to be the next ones added to the accommodations mix. At least some of these will offer spectacular ocean views but no beach access.

Maui

Conventional wisdom has it that "Nobody goes to Maui to eat," but then, nobody goes to Maui to starve, either, and the island's continuing allure (it was the only island whose visitor count rose during lean years 1991 and 1992) has brought star-quality chefs—and the diners who love them—to the restaurants of **Wailea, Kaanapali,** and **Kapalua** resorts. Oahu's celebrated Roy Yamaguchi opened his first Neighbor Island venue, **Roy's Kahana Bar & Grill** (Kahana Gateway, on Honoapiilani Highway between Kaanapali and Kapalua, tel. 808/669–6999) in January. And **David Paul's Lahaina Grill** broke through the wall of its former gallery neighbor to double in size.

Malama ka aina—protect the land—has become an anthem as developers attempt to counter local fears that they will "overrun" Maui while local interests, including preservation of habitat and lifestyle, are ignored. Longtime Hana residents were horrified when rumor spread in 1992 that a shopping mall was being planned for the secluded East Maui community, but some local merchants hoped a mall might tempt more customers to travel the long and winding **Road to Hana,** The mall seems for now to have fallen victim to the same economic doldrums that afflicted merchants.

Nevertheless, Maui hoteliers and other tourism-dependent operators are making highly visible efforts to preserve Maui's natural and historic sites if only to fend off tough restrictions on further resort and golf-course development. Plans for the new **Ritz-Carlton, Kapalua,** for example, were revised, and the building was moved back from an ocean-side bluff, when an ancient Hawaiian burial ground was discovered on the intended site. The hotel took on the responsibility of maintaining the beautiful site—believed to contain the remains of royal children—and local Hawaiians held a blessing ceremony there before the hotel opened in October 1992.

The new resort scored still more points with Valley Isle residents when it decided to break with Ritz-Carlton tradition by commissioning local artists to create some of its art collection. And an annual **spring art festival** aims to bring local artists together with imported talent—and hotel guests— for some creative quality time. Bring your paintbox.

Getting to Maui is not quite as easy as it used to be. Both **Aloha Airlines** and **Hawaiian Airlines** trimmed their interisland schedules in January 1993, in hopes of flying fewer but fuller planes around the state. Aloha's subsidiary, **Aloha IslandAir,** which offers the only commercial service to the smaller airports, raised its prices by adding surcharges for passengers using the parent airline's interisland coupons, still the most economical way to travel interisland. Better news: Although coupons are still offered in six-packs, some Hawaii travel agents will fill requests for just one or two Aloha or Hawaiian Airlines coupons without raising the per-trip cost.

Purely economic decisions ended, at least temporarily, the debate over expanding Maui's **Kahului Airport** to accommodate larger jets and more Maui-bound nonstops from the U.S. mainland. The lull may give jumbo-jet supporters time to devise solutions for the environmental-impact problems their opponents fear before a reviving economy makes this a hot issue again. Meanwhile, the anti-expansionists have a chance to gather evidence for their theory that too-easy access was making Maui seem less exotic to tourists.

At tiny **Napalua Airport,** which serves the West Maui resorts north of Lahaina, the rental car companies have all replaced their on-site service counters with courtesy phones. A shuttle arrives to transport renters to pickup and return sites in nearby Kaanapali. The new routine is still easier and more convenient than picking up a rental car at, say, Los Angeles International Airport.

Molokai

Molokai is thought to be the **birthplace of the hula,** and since 1991 Destination Molokai has hosted a special annual celebration to honor the famous dance. Held in May, the outdoor bash is comprised of musicians, singers, craftspeople, foods, and, of course, hula dancers, and thousands of residents and visitors have attended the event, which gets bigger each year.

Molokai Ranch has launched a new visitor program that combines the popular Wildlife Park Camera Safari with a west end beach excursion, water sports, and a picnic. Called the **Molokai Ranch Wildlife and Beach Adventure,** it was created by safari chief Pilipo Solatorio, who has been associated with the wildlife preserve since it opened to visitor tours in 1977. Highlights of the new excursion include the giraffe picnic, in which visitors have a chance to feed the park's giraffes and be photographed while doing so. Most of the beach sites in the tour are isolated and reachable only by Ranch roads.

Lanai

It seems almost a natural phenomenon that with commercial growth comes a self-promotion organization. **Destination Lanai** was formed in 1991 to get the word out about this tiny, remote, beautiful, and under-visited island, through brochures, advertisements, and other promotional efforts.

As tourism replaces the pineapple as the mainstay of Lanai's economy, the island is looking to upgrade and expand its airport. Construction of a new **$7.5 million passenger terminal** got underway in late 1992 and was scheduled to be finished in a year. It will be five times larger than the old terminal, and it will have more counter space as well as more square footage for concession operators. A new parking area and access road are also part of the plan.

After months of the trials and errors of learning what could be grown with Lanai's soil and weather conditions, **Rockresorts' 10-acre organic garden** is now the envy of island chefs. Vegetables can be harvested on the spot and served to hotel guests the same evening, ensuring ultimate freshness. Lanai's chefs draw inspiration by taking a jaunt into the fields, where white and black beauty eggplant thrive beside Chinese water spinach.

Kauai

Since **Hurricane Iniki** devestated Kauai on September 11, 1992, the rebuilding process has been slow but steady. Most hotel, restaurant, and activity operators were anticipating a return to full operation by the end of 1993. Those properties **hardest hit** included the **Princeveille Hotel** to the north and, to the south, the **Stouffer Waiohai Beach Resort** and **Sheraton Kauai Resort & Towers**. Officials at the three hotels expect to re-open by 1994, but travel planners are advised to call ahead of time for updates on the reconstruction process.

Kauai's various travel promoters have discovered the benefits of joint marketing. In 1992, the island's destination associations joined forces with the County of Kauai and the Hawaii Visitors Bureau's Kauai Chapter to sing the island's praises, and it came up with the marketing theme of **"Kauai—Hawaii's Treasured Island."** Among the group's efforts is an official **32-page vacation planner** with information about the island and its four resort destinations: Princeville to the north, **Royal Coconut Coast** to the east, **Kalapaki Bay** near Lihue, and **Poipu Beach Resort** to the south. The group's new cooperative ad campaign got an extra boost when United Airlines kicked in $1 million worth of support.

The Kauai Hilton and Beach Villas is now called the **Outrigger Kauai Beach Hotel**, thanks to a switch in management on January 1, 1993. Located on the eastern shores just outside of Lihue, the property is currently operated by Outrigger Hotels in Hawaii, the largest hotel chain in the islands. Outrigger spokespeople said there will be no other immediate changes made to the property.

Kauai's residents have long awaited the completion of a new three-mile, two-lane rural roadway which would bypass the bustling little burg of Koloa and ease congestion in the Poipu area. Plans for the $7.6 million project were moving forward until Hurricane Iniki hit the island, but officials predicted that the work would be back on track and finished by the mid-1990s.

Thanks to its lush tropical beauty, Kauai has played starring and supporting roles in a variety of Hollywood films over the years. Screen credits include *South Pacific, The Wackiest Ship in the Army, Raiders of the Lost Ark, Indiana Jones and the Temple of Doom, King Kong, Blue Hawaii, Uncommon Valor, Islands in the Stream,* and *Honeymoon in Vegas.* Most recently, Kauai was the backdrop for Steven Spielberg's *Jurassic Park.*

Fodor's Choice

No two people will agree on what makes a perfect vacation in the Aloha State, but it's fun and helpful to know what others think. We hope you'll have a chance to experience some of Fodor's Choices yourself while visiting Hawaii. For detailed information about each entry, refer to the appropriate chapters in this guidebook.

Beaches

Oahu Hanauma Bay in the morning (it gets too crowded in the afternoon)

Kailua Beach

Waikiki in front of the Royal Hawaiian Hotel

Waimea Bay in summer (the best time to swim there)

The Big Island Anaehoomalu Beach, especially for windsurfing

Hapuna Beach

Kaunaoa Beach at Mauna Kea Beach Resort

Spencer Beach, especially for children

Punaluu Black Sand Beach to watch the turtles

Maui Wailea Beach in the morning as the sun comes over Haleakala

Hookipa Beach to watch world-class windsurfing

Kapalua Beach for sheer class

Hana Beach for that Old Hawaii experience

Molokai Halawa Beach Park

Kawakiu Beach

Kepuhi Beach

Papohaku Beach

Lanai Hulopoe Beach

Shipwreck Beach

Kauai Hanakapiai Beach

Lumahai Beach

Polihale Beach State Park

Tunnels Beach

Best Buys

Oahu Aloha shirts—Liberty House for quality; F.W. Woolworth for price

Fine jewelry—Maui Divers

Hawaiian arts and crafts—Little Hawaiian Craft Shop

Most fun—Shirokiya

Variety—Ala Moana Shopping Center

The Big Island Ethnic finds—Woodblock prints by Dietrich Varez at Volcano Art Center; woven lauhala baskets, hats, and mats at Kimura's Lauhala Store in Holualoa

Gifts—Wooden bowls by Jack Straka, boxes or cutting boards

Hawaiian arts and crafts—Alapaki's at the Keauhou Shopping Center

Most fun—Ira Ono's Trashface earrings at Volcano Art Center

Orchid corsages and cut anthuriums from Volcano Store

Maui Fine art in Lahaina

Hawaiian quilts

Made on Maui crafts and food

Tedeschi wine at the vineyards in Kula

Molokai Aloha shirts and muumuus—Molokai Gift Shop

Jewelry—Imports Gift Shop

Hawaiian arts and crafts—Molokai Island Creations

Most fun—Big Wind Kite Factory

Lanai Lanai T-shirts at Richard's Shopping Center

Kauai Art—Wyland Galleries; Kauai Images Gallery

Flowers—Shimonishi Orchids

Hawaiian arts and crafts—Kapaia Stitchery;

Jim Saylor Jewelers; Remember Kauai

Variety—Coconut Plantation Market Place; Koloa Town

Drives

Oahu From Hawaii Kai to Waimanalo

Likelike Highway on the windward side

Pali Highway on the leeward side

The Big Island From Hilo to Waipio Valley along the Hamakua coast

From Kona to Waimea to stop-and-shop in cooler weather

Maui The road to Hana

From Lahaina to Maalaea during whale season

Coming down Haleakala

Molokai Shoreline route east to Halawa Valley Overlook

Lanai Lanaihale in a jeep

Kauai North Shore—The oceanside drive from Hanalei to Ke'e Beach Park

Waimea Canyon Road from Waimea to the Kalalau Lookout

For Kids

Oahu Children's Touch and Feel Museum

Honolulu Zoo, especially the petting zoo

Sea Life Park

Waikiki Aquarium

The Big Island Thomas Jaggar Museum, Volcanoes National Park

Swimming with dolphins at the Hyatt Regency Waikoloa

Hiking through the Thurston Lava Tube or into Kilauea Iki Crater

Watching monkeys and tigers at Panaewa Zoo

Maui Haleakala Crater

Lahaina Sugar Cane Train

Maui Tropical Plantation

Whale watching

Molokai Molokai Ranch Wildlife Safari

Kauai Kamokila

Smith's Tropical Paradise

Snorkeling excursion along the south shore

Hotels

Oahu Halekulani (*Very Expensive*)

Kahala Hilton (*Very Expensive*)

Royal Hawaiian Hotel (*Very Expensive*)

Manoa Valley Inn (*Moderate*)

Royal Grove Hotel (*Inexpensive*)

The Big Island Hyatt Regency Waikoloa (*Very Expensive*)

Kona Village Resort (*Very Expensive*)

Mauna Kea Beach Hotel (*Very Expensive*)

Mauna Lani Bay Hotel (*Very Expensive*)

Ritz-Carlton, Mauna Lani (*Expensive*)

Maui The Four Seasons (*Very Expensive*)

Hotel Hana-Maui (*Very Expensive*)

Kapalua Bay Hotel (*Very Expensive*)

Coconut Inn (*Moderate*)

Plantation Inn (*Moderate*)

Molokai Paniolo Hale (*Expensive*)

Hotel Molokai (*Moderate*)

Pau Hana Inn (*Inexpensive*)

Lanai Lodge at Koele (*Very Expensive*)

Kauai Princeville Hotel (*Very Expensive*)

Sheraton Kauai Hotel (*Very Expensive*)

Hanalei Bay Resort (*Expensive*)

Kauai Resort (*Expensive*)

Kokee Lodge (*Inexpensive*)

Kamaaina (Islanders') Favorites

Oahu Manapua from any lunch wagon

Morning snorkel at Hanauma Bay

Poi luncheon at the Willows

Shave ice with vanilla ice cream and azuki beans at Matsumoto's in Haleiwa

Sunset jog around Diamond Head

The Big Island Edelweiss in Waimea for dinner

Kona Inn for cocktails or dinner at sunset

Liliuokalani Park in Hilo on a Sunday afternoon

Ohelo berry picking at Volcano

Suisan Fish Auction in Hilo

Maui The Makawao Rodeo

People-watching at Avalon and the Hard Rock Cafe

People-watching at Longhi's

Sunrise from Haleakala

Wine-tasting at Tedeschi

Molokai Family swimming at Pohakuloa Beach

Hiking the Halawa Valley Trail

Watching the Molokai-to-Oahu Canoe Race

Lanai Cocktails on the porch of Hotel Lanai

Hamburgers from the Blue Ginger Cafe

Snorkeling in Hulopoe Bay

Kauai Bodysurfing at Brennecke's Beach, Poipu

Eggs Benedict at the Eggberts in Lihue

Sunday lunch at the Green Garden Restaurant, Hanapepe

Sunset picnic at Hanalei Beach Park

Local Dining

Oahu Haupia at Ono Hawaiian Foods

"Mile High" pie at the Willows

Mahimahi in any preparation, at Bali by the Sea

Portuguese sausage omelette at Eggs 'n Things

The Big Island Breakfast or lunch at Ocean View Inn, Kailua-Kona

Loco-moco (eggs, rice, and hamburger dish that originated at Cafe 100 in Hilo)

Luau at Haile Church, Hilo

Teshima's at Honalo

Maui Lahaina's trendy "nouvelle Hawaiian" cuisine at Chez Paul's or Avalon

Fresh fish at Mama's

Maui onion rings at the Maui Onion

Shaved ice from any roadside stand

Molokai Beef adobo from Oviedo's

Lilikoi sundaes at Jojo's Cafe

Plate lunch from Molokai Drive Inn

Molokai bread from Kanemitsu Bakery

Lanai Filipino-style doughnuts from Blue Ginger Cafe

Kauai Kalua pig and lomilomi salmon at Tahiti Nui

Lilikoi chiffon pie at the Green Garden Restaurant

Sashimi and poke at Club Jetty

Shave ice from carry-out trucks at Haena Beach Park

Nightlife

Oahu Aikane Catamaran Sunset Dinner Cruise

Brothers Cazimero Show, Royal Hawaiian Hotel

Danny Kaleikini Show, Kahala Hilton

Royal Hawaiian Luau

Rumours, Ala Moana Hotel

The Big Island d'Angoras in Hilo for dancing

Spats at the Hyatt Regency Waikoloa

Vanda Lounge at the Royal Waikoloan for mellow music and dancing

Maui Blackie's Bar

Inu Inu Lounge at the Maui Inter-Continental

Old Lahaina Luau

Banana Moon at the Marriott

Molokai Weekend dancing at Hotel Molokai and Pau Hana Inn

Kauai Club Jetty

Kuhio's Nightclub, Hyatt Regency Kauai

Legends Nightclub

Tahiti Nui Luau

Restaurants

Oahu La Mer, Halekulani Hotel (*Very Expensive*)

Maile, Kahala Hilton Hotel (*Expensive*)

Orchids, Halekulani Hotel (*Moderate*)

Roy's (*Moderate*)

Eggs 'n Things (*Inexpensive*)

The Big Island The Dining Room at the Ritz-Carlton, Mauna Lani (*Expensive*)

CanoeHouse at Mauna Lani Bay Hotel (*Moderate-Expensive*)

La Bourgogne (*Moderate*)

Merriman's in Waimea (*Moderate*)

Roussel's (*Moderate*)

Edelweiss (*Inexpensive*)

Maui Raffles at the Stouffer Wailea (*Very Expensive*)

Gerard's (*Expensive*)

David Paul's LaHaina Grill (*Moderate-Expensive*)

Haliimaile General Store (*Inexpensive-Moderate*)

Lahaina Coolers (*Inexpensive*)

Molokai Ohia Lodge (*Moderate*)

Hop Inn (*Inexpensive*)

Kualapuu Cookhouse (*Inexpensive*)

Lanai Lodge at Koele (*Very Expensive*)

Hotel Lanai (*Moderate*)

Blue Ginger Cafe (*Inexpensive*)

Kauai La Cascata at the Princeville Hotel (*Expensive*)

A Pacific Cafe (*Moderate*)

Casa di Amici (*Moderate*)

Gaylord's (*Moderate*)

Hanamaulu Cafe (*Inexpensive*)

Romantic Hideaways

Oahu Breakfast at Michel's at the Colony Surf

Dinner at Nick's Fishmarket

Picnic lunch at the top of Diamond Head

Picnic dinner at the Waikiki Shell

Room in the old section of the Royal Hawaiian Hotel

The Big Island Kilauea Lodge at Volcano (light a fire in the bedroom fireplace)

Kona Village Resort in a thatched hale beside the sea

Candlelight dinner at Palm Café

Mauna Lani Bay Resort's luxury bungalows

Maui Kula Lodge chalets with fireplaces

Royal Lahaina cottages with private pools

Waianapanapa cabins

Molokai Condo with a hot tub on the lanai at Paniolo Hale

Moaula Falls, at the back of Halawa Valley

Papohaku Beach

Lanai Lanaihale

Shipwreck Beach

Kauai Cottage at Kokee State Park

Horse-drawn carriage ride at Kilohana

Picnic at Lumahai Beach

Sunset cruise on the *Na Pali Queen*

Sunsets

Oahu Diamond Head Lighthouse

Sunset Beach, North Shore

The Big Island From the end of Kona Pier or from the lounges at Kona Inn or the Kona Hilton

From deckside on Captain Beans' Booze Cruise

From Keauhou lookout

In the Kohala mountains

Maui From Kimo's in Lahaina

From Kapalua's Bay Club

From the beach at Kaanapali

From the beach at Wailea

Molokai Kepuhi Beach

Ohia Room, Kaluakoi Resort

Lanai Hulopoe Beach

Kauai Kekaha Beach, west shore

Polihale Beach State Park

Views

Oahu Makapuu Point

Nuuanu Pali Lookout

Top of the Ilikai Waikiki Hotel

Upper ocean-view rooms at the Hilton Hawaiian Village and the Halekulani

The Big Island Upper ocean-view rooms of Mauna Kea Beach and Mauna Lani resorts

Horizon and flanks of Mauna Kea from the observatories

Kealakekua Bay from upcountry Kona

Waipio Valley and Pololu Valley from the overlooks at road's end

Maui All of Maui from Haleakala

Islands of Molokai, Lanai, Kahoolawe, and Molokini

Underwater at Wailea

Waterfalls along the Hana Highway

Molokai Halawa Valley Overlook

Kalaupapa Overlook

Lanai Lanaihale

Molokai from Shipwreck Beach

Kauai Hanalei Valley Overlook

Kalalau Lookout

Na Pali coast from a boat

Nihau by helicopter tour

Waimea Canyon

The Hawaiian Islands

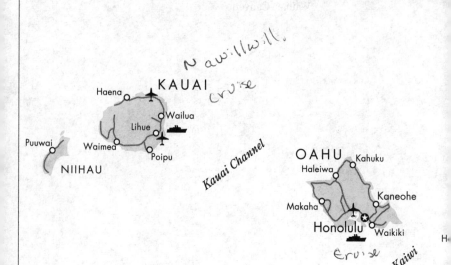

Nawilliwili Cruise

KAUAI

Haena

Wailua

Lihue

Puuwai

Waimea

Poipu

NIIHAU

Kauai Channel

OAHU   Kahuku

Haleiwa

Kaneohe

Makaha

Honolulu   Waikiki

Cruise   *Kaiwi*

P A C I F I C O C E A N

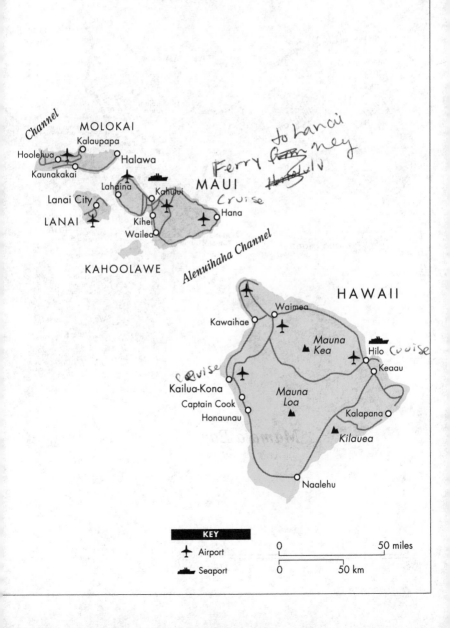

Honolulu Including Waikiki

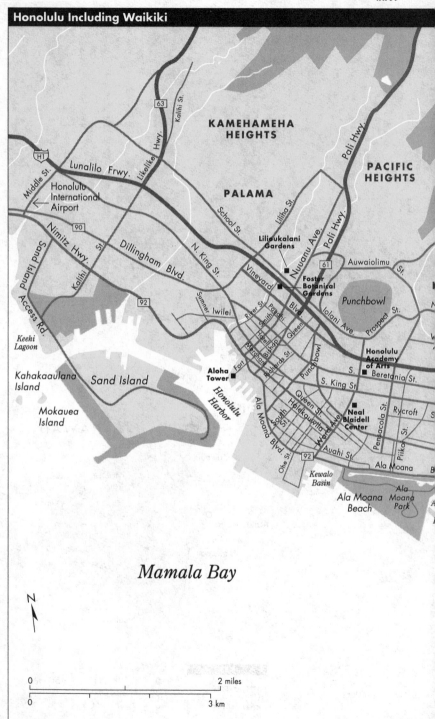

KAMEHAMEHA HEIGHTS

PALAMA

PACIFIC HEIGHTS

63

H1

Lunalilo Frwy.

Likelike Hwy.

Kalihi St.

Pali Hwy.

Middle St.

Honolulu International Airport

School St.

Liliha St.

Nuuanu Ave.

Pali Hwy.

Auwaiolimu St.

90

Nimitz Hwy.

Dillingham Blvd.

N. King St.

Vineyard

Liliaukalani Gardens

61

Foster Botanical Gardens

Iolani Ave.

Punchbowl

Prospect St.

Kalihi St.

Sand Island Access Rd.

92

Sumner

Iwilei

River St.

Smith

Hotel

Beretania Blvd.

Queen

Punchbowl

Honolulu Academy of Arts

Beretania St.

Keehi Lagoon

Aloha Tower

Fort

Maunakea

Bishop

Richards St.

Punchbowl

S. King St.

Kahakaaulana Island

Sand Island

Honolulu Harbor

Ala Moana Blvd.

South St.

Queen St.

Halekauwila

Ward Ave.

S.

Neal Blaidell Center

Pensacola St.

Rycroft

Mokauea Island

Ohe St.

92

Auahi St.

Ala Moana

Piikoi St.

Kewalo Basin

Ala Moana Beach

Ala Moana Park

Mamala Bay

N

0   2 miles

0   3 km

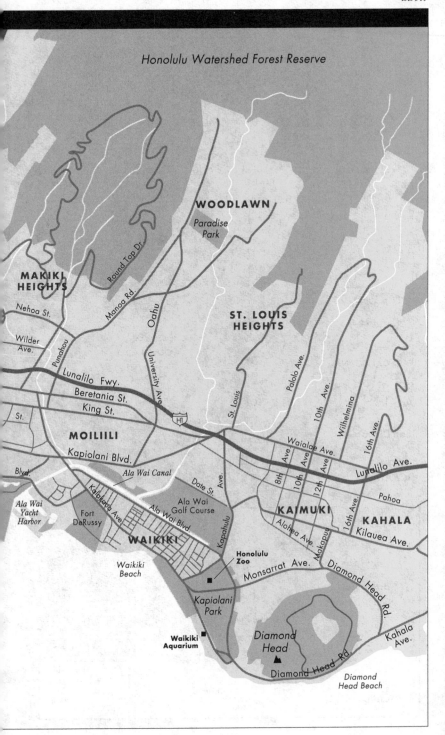

Honolulu Watershed Forest Reserve

WOODLAWN

Paradise Park

MAKIKI HEIGHTS

Round Top Dr.

Manoa Rd.

Nehoa St.

Oahu

Wilder Ave.

Punahou

University Ave.

ST. LOUIS HEIGHTS

St. Louis

Palolo Ave.

10th Ave.

Wilhelmina

16th Ave.

Lunalilo Fwy.
Beretania St.
King St.

St.

MOILIILI

Kapiolani Blvd.

Waialae Ave.

Lunalilo Ave.

Blvd.

Ala Wai Canal

Date St.

Ave.

8th Ave.

10th Ave.

12th Ave.

16th Ave.

Pahoa

Ala Wai Yacht Harbor

Kalakaua Ave.

Ala Wai Blvd.

Fort DeRussy

Ala Wai Golf Course

Kapahulu

KAIMUKI

Alohea Ave.

Makapuu

KAHALA

Kilauea Ave.

WAIKIKI

Waikiki Beach

Honolulu Zoo

Monsarrat Ave.

Diamond Head Rd.

Kapiolani Park

Waikiki Aquarium

Diamond Head

Diamond Head Rd.

Kahala Ave.

Diamond Head Beach

The United States

World Time Zones

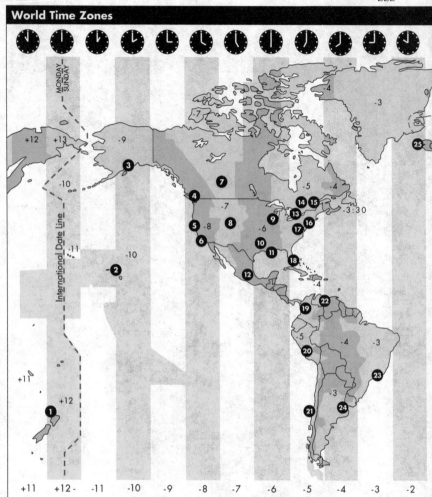

Numbers below vertical bands relate each zone to Greenwich Mean Time (0 hrs.).
Local times frequently differ from these general indications,
as indicated by light-face numbers on map.

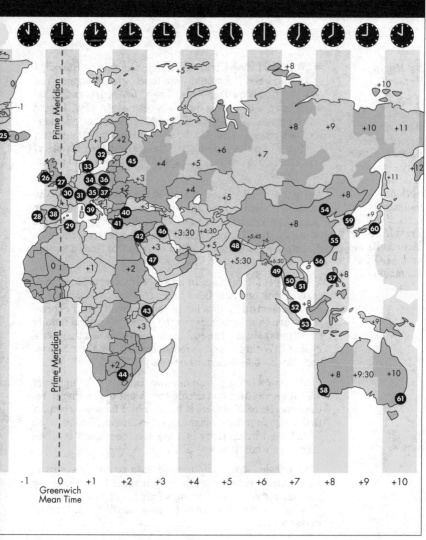

Introduction

By Marty Wentzel

A resident of Honolulu, Marty Wentzel is a free-lance writer whose articles have appeared in several local and national magazines, including TravelAge West, Modern Bride, *and* ALOHA Magazine.

The first time I traveled from California to Hawaii, I wondered if I would ever touch ground again. The flight seemed endless. Then, 5½ hours and 2,390 miles later, a landscape new to me came into view. I could see the green spires of the Koolau Mountains, the glimmering high rises of Waikiki, the aqua intensity of the water, the fleets of white sails dotting the sea, and the network of crisscrossing freeways, pineapple plantations, and sugarcane fields.

A trip to Hawaii from anywhere else in the world makes you aware of its remoteness. It waits in the middle of the Pacific Ocean like a crossroads as well as a cloister; although it is influenced by all its neighbors, it remains very much its own destination. As a state, it often seems as exotic as a foreign land.

Visitors get off the plane in Hawaii with a sort of dizzy, uncertain look on their faces after spending as many as 18 hours cooped up inside a jumbo jet. Gradually their expressions turn to astonishment as the scents of tropical flowers surround them and the cool trade winds freshen their weary limbs. Within hours, paradise has smitten their hearts, and they become determined to stay forever.

That's how a lot of people discover Hawaii. Like me, they visit it on vacation and decide they want to live there. Yet the experience of Hawaii is broader and far more complex than those first few enchanting impressions. Moving to the Islands and living there is a big step because it involves learning a whole new way of life.

Even simple Island customs can take a visitor by surprise. For instance, residents remove their shoes before entering a home, a tradition that springs from the Japanese culture. (It also makes a lot of sense, because less dirt gets tracked in that way.)

People operate on Hawaiian time, which means that if you're late for a party, an appointment, a meeting, a dinner party, or any other social function, you don't worry about it. Sure, there is rush-hour traffic, and there are schedules for movies and airplanes. But on Hawaiian time, people take a more laid-back approach to everything, which may be why residents live longer than those in other states.

Living in Hawaii teaches you to respect nature. You stay out of the water when the huge winter waves come up on the north shores of the islands. You avoid hiking in the valleys during rainy days because flash floods have been known to race down out of the mountains and wash people away. You tape your windows before a hurricane (the last one, Hurricane Iniki in 1992, hit Kauai with such intensity that it damaged nearly every building on the island). And when the sun starts to make its descent to the horizon, you stop what you're doing to enjoy the sunset, a guaranteed spectacle almost every day of the year.

Islands of Discovery

Today Hawaii offers much of the same mystique that it presented to the earliest Polynesian explorers. The Hawaiian Islands amazed them back in the 6th century AD; that magnificent landscape has been preserved, and if anything, it has improved over the centuries.

Fortunately, Hawaii's six major islands are readily and rapidly accessible to each other. A flight from the northernmost island (Kauai) to the southernmost (the Big Island, Hawaii) takes no more than an hour. Each island has its own personality and warrants your attention, time, and exploration.

For instance, the Garden Island, Kauai, is so green and lush that it has served as a backdrop for Hollywood movies. On the other hand, much of Lanai is a dry and windswept panorama of red soil and rocky coastlines. Oahu is cosmopolitan, with its world-famous tourist mecca, Waikiki, while Molokai consists mostly of family-run businesses and natural attractions.

There are incredible heights on Maui, such as its 10,023-foot-high dormant volcano, Haleakala, as well as on the Big Island, with 13,796-foot-high Mauna Kea and 13,677-foot-high Mauna Loa (the world's largest shield volcano). On the other hand, Kauai boasts amazing depths, such as Waimea Canyon, a 3,657-foot-deep chasm, while Molokai has the 4-mile-long and ½-mile wide Halawa Valley.

Traveling from one island to the next, you will most likely find yourself doing things you never dreamed of back on the mainland. Imagine this: On the least populated island, Lanai, you're riding a mountain bike through pineapple fields, intoxicated by the sweet fragrance of the ripening fruit surrounding you. You pedal through groves of ironwood trees along bumpy dirt roads, then climb steadily until you come to the clearing at the Garden of the Gods, a breathtaking assemblage of rocks and boulders that are scattered across a barren landscape overlooking the sea. You catch your breath and think, surely some greater being reached out its arm to create this work of natural art on such a wild island.

Picture yourself on Kauai, the oldest island, hiking the Kalalau Trail on the Na Pali coast. You meander through ancient landscapes and along 1,000-foot-high cliffs, great walls of sheer rock that rise above untamed surf. The trail winds up and down the edges of those cliffs, past exceptionally beautiful Pacific vistas, through groves of guava and *lilikoi* (passion fruit) trees, until you reach your destination: Kalalau Valley. You stand under a fresh, bracing waterfall off the beach; then you relax in a sea cave and gaze upon little birds with long legs skittering along the mile-long expanse of isolated sand.

Or imagine yourself on Maui, the Valley Isle. At 3:30 AM you stumble out of bed and join the dozens of sun worshipers who are driving up Haleakala in time to see the sunrise. The clouds part before you as the sun makes its grand entrance and fills the crater with colors of every hue and shadows of every size. Then you walk down into the crater, so big, they say, that all of Manhattan could fit into it. You wander through lunar landscapes along lava and sand, and you get the once-over from a flock of *nene* (Hawaiian geese), the now-endangered state birds. Then you discover enormous purple berries growing by the cabin at Paliku, an Edenesque setting at the far end of the crater.

If you visit Oahu, you just might find yourself following a road that runs right through a tunnel in the wall of Diamond Head. Once inside that famous crater, you see a trail that leads you on a half-hour walk up its inner cliffs. Near the top, you lumber up steep steps and hold onto a railing while wandering through the dark bunkers where U.S. soldiers once kept a watch for enemy forces. Climbing up the lookout at the 760-foot-high summit, you can see what appears to be the entire southern coast of the island. To the east, a cratered cone called Koko Head rises over Hanauma Bay, while to the west stretch the Waianae Mountains. When you turn around you can gaze upon the interior, with its green-gilded Koolau Mountains, and below you is the majestic shoreline of Waikiki, with its shiny high rises, Ala Wai Canal, and Kapiolani Park.

Natural Beauty

Hawaii is America's most exotic and unusual state, with 132 islands and atolls stretching across some 1,600 miles of ocean. It is blessed with a uniform climate of predictably warm temperatures and cool trade winds; except for the occasional squalls of December, January, and February, the rains pass quickly.

It's hard to believe that such a gentle place sprang from such a violent beginning, as islands were forced up from the ocean by mighty volcanic explosions. For centuries, the fiery heights steamed and sizzled, after which they were worked on by the elements; crashing surf, mighty sea winds, and powerful rivers carved and chiseled the great mountains and lush valleys that are visible today.

Each year, nearly 7 million visitors come to Hawaii to see the results of nature's handiwork. While most of them used to head straight for Waikiki, more and more people are bypassing Oahu altogether and making the Neighbor Islands (as the rest of Hawaii is called) their final destination. What they find on any island is a combination of the wild and the tame, the simple and the slick.

Sun worshippers can't go wrong in Hawaii. On Oahu alone there are more than 50 miles of beaches. Among the beaches on Molokai is Papohaku, which measures a whopping 3 miles long, and Lumahai Beach on Kauai is so splendid that it was featured in the movie *South Pacific*. The Big Island's sands, a photographer's delight, include the black-sand beaches that are formed when hot lava touches cold seawater. Even more unusual is the Big Island's green-sand beach, which was created long ago when a cinder cone of the mineral olivine collapsed into a bay.

Throughout Hawaii, nature lovers find countless delights to satisfy the senses. On an easy hike in the Tantalus hills above Waikiki, you pass by tropical plants with leaves 10 times the size of ordinary house plants. Birds with bright yellow wings and unusual names, such as *o'o'a'a*, flit in the highlands of Kauai and come into view if you're in the right place at the right time. Perhaps most miraculous of all, as you walk along the bleak, steaming floor of Kilauea Iki Crater on the Big Island, you can see new life growing up from the cracks in the lava: ferns, grasses, and ohia trees with scarlet lehua blossoms.

This rich natural environment now needs special protection. The people of Hawaii are aware of their fragile surroundings, and they have joined forces in order to take care of it. In the forefront of this movement is the Nature Conservancy of Hawaii, a dedicated group of volunteers who manage lands on most every island. They oversee such projects as protecting endangered birds, as well as Pepeopae, Hawaii's most ancient bog, and Molokai's Moomomi Dunes, one of the few remaining coastal dune areas in Hawaii.

As Hawaii's people give to the earth, so it has given to them. Millions of acres of this generous land have produced pineapple and sugarcane, the Islands' two most famous exports. If anything, Hawaii is growing increasingly prolific as its farmers become more diversified, first with macadamia nut farms and coffee plantations, then with orchid and anthurium nurseries, along with such fruits and vegetables as guava, mango, bananas, corn, and sweet onions. Farmers on Kauai are growing baby vegetables for use in Hawaii's upscale restaurants, which have come to rely more and more on local products. On the Big Island, Excelsior Dairy is making its own butter from the milk of local herds and creating a fresher, more flavorful product. And Maui is becoming well-known for its upcountry farms, which cultivate such fresh herbs as fennel, basil, and thyme.

Painters, sculptors, weavers, photographers, and other artists have responded to their beautiful island environment in innovative ways. With a flash of fingers and a flick of the wrist, crafts people can handily turn lau hala leaves into a basket, or plumeria blossoms into a fresh, fragrant lei. An entourage of backwoods artists can be found at the volcano's edge on the Big Island, including photographer Boone Morrison and wood-print carver Deitrich Varez. On Maui, world-famous poet W.S. Merwin lives and writes about the inspiration he receives from his delicate island home. Robert Lyn Nelson creates colorful paintings of the humpback whales that each winter make their pilgrimage to the channels between the islands. On Oahu, photographer Joe Carini dedicates himself to documenting the hula. These and many other islanders share their vision of Hawaii in a heartfelt outpouring of creativity, as if they were nature's own spokespeople.

Hawaii's magnificent environment also encourages sports, the number-one pastime in the islands. A veritable regatta of vessels takes to the sea each day, from snorkeling-cruise boats to ocean liners. People hit the tennis courts, the golf courses, the running routes, the bridle paths, and the bike trails. Most of the major hotels offer some sort of fitness program, be it aerobics classes, nature walks, weightlifting rooms, or guided hikes to nearby outdoor attractions.

The superstars of sports love Hawaii's climate as well. Robbie Naish, one of the world's best windsurfers, wows folks with his 360-degree flips in the waves of Hookipa on Maui. Outstanding ocean paddlers, such as Marshall Rosa, brave the waves of the Pacific for the grueling Molokai-to-Oahu kayak race, a 38-mile contest that is similar to the annual Molokai-to-Oahu outrigger canoe race.

Hawaii is also famous for its endurance tests. Two such events that have thrust Hawaii into the international sports spotlight are the grueling Ironman Triathlon (combination swim-bike-run) on the Big Island and the annual 26.2-mile road race called the Honolulu Marathon on Oahu. Why do people do these crazy things? Simply put, there's something about Hawaii that makes people want to push themselves to do their very best.

The Past in the Present

The natural beauty of the Islands has allowed for a variety of accommodations, from the countrified to the chic. You might find yourself on Kauai, staying at a bed-and-breakfast spot and hearing stories about the Garden Island from a sprightly resident in her 70s. Or you might wind up on the Big Island in a posh South Kohala hotel decorated with fish ponds, waterfalls, tropical gardens, gondolas, and a multimillion-dollar collection of international art. The cosmopolitan side of Hawaii has become more visible, with the backcountry options less easy to track down. The east side of Maui has become a seaside parade of luxury resorts, and there are fantasyland hotels on Kauai and the Big Island, plus a new resort being built in west Oahu. Even little Lanai has seen big changes as two very classy new hotels opened their doors in the past few years.

However, the old will never completely disappear in Hawaii because traditions are paramount. To this day, the locals have a custom of blessing all things that are new by paying tribute to the past, with a dance, a chant, a lei, or even just a few words spoken by a minister. They respect the legends of their ancestors and honor the gods as they see fit. Dancers return reverently to the huge hula pavilion on the north shore of Kauai, a site that is dedicated to the goddess of the dance, Laka. Hikers leave rocks wrapped in ti leaves to thank the gods for their smooth passage. On the Big Island, those who visit the steaming Halemaumau pit toss in flowers and other gifts to the volcano goddess, Pele, to appease her unpredictable wrath.

Many island traditions can be learned and enjoyed by guests. In fact, as soon as you step off the plane you encounter your first island custom, as a fresh plumeria lei is draped around your neck. Centuries ago, garlands of leaves, nuts, or flowers were offered to the gods, and today the practice continues as they are given to family and friends on special occasions. It is said that the idea of bestowing a kiss along with a lei dates back to World War II, when during a show a female entertainer smooched a soldier after draping him with a flower lei. Then she justified it by saying, "It's tradition in Hawaii." It has been ever since.

The past endures, thanks to several concerned organizations that have been fighting to save the visible remnants of days gone by. For instance, a nonprofit group called the Historic Hawaii Foundation works to preserve the unique decades-old structures of the state despite the enormous new high rises that are springing up around them.

The results are within plain view. Just look around downtown Honolulu and you can see such historic masterpieces as Iolani Palace, which dates back to 1882. King Kalakaua commissioned this colonial-style building for his short but dynamic reign. The only royal palace built on American soil, it is slowly but carefully being put back together inside and out, complete with the restored furnishings from its original days. Down the street from the palace is the Mission Houses Museum, whose restored buildings hark back to the 1820s, when they were the homes of the first missionaries on Oahu.

They now sit near one of the busiest intersections in downtown Honolulu and serve as quiet yet effective representations of the past.

The old also blends with the new in the form of the Hawaii Theatre, another Honolulu landmark, which dates from 1922 and is now being restored as 1,700-seat center of performing arts. The project will take several years during which time the theater can be used for fund-raisers, fashion shows, private parties, and meetings.

The Neighbor Islands offer further examples of architectural restoration. In Kona you can see the charming Mokuaikaua Church, constructed in 1837 of coral and lava rock; on Kauai, one of the most popular visitor attractions is Kilohana Estate, a gracious sugar plantation dating back to 1835. In Hana on Maui stands Wananalua Church, built in 1838 out of native lava rock, timbers from the surrounding mountains, and coral from the sea. Molokai features the historic 19th-century churches built by the caring priest Father Damien. On Lanai, during construction of the Lodge at Koele in the late 1980s, the developers actually took the time to relocate the historic Kalokahi O Ka Malamalama Church and the former homes of two old cowboys in order to preserve them.

Perhaps even more crucial to the restoration and preservation of Hawaiiana is the upkeep of its *heiau*, or ancient sacred sites. On the Big Island, you can visit Mookini Heiau, the birthplace of King Kamehameha the Great and now a National Historic Landmark. On Molokai awaits Iliiliopae, the largest outdoor shrine in the islands, which is as big as a football field. In Pupukea on Oahu is Pu'u o Mahuka, a "hill of escape" where Hawaiians still leave offerings to the gods, while on Lanai is another time-honored gathering place called Halulu Heiau, near the summer home of that great king.

Cultural Potpourri

At the heart of Hawaii are the people who live there every day and who turn life into a rewarding experience for both visitors and residents. From its earliest days the Islands have beckoned to races from around the world, beginning way back when Polynesian kings and queens ruled its lands. Along the way, Russia and France both tried to claim Hawaii for their own, as did Great Britain. Many people came from the Orient to work on the island's sugar and pineapple plantations. From Japan, China, the Philippines, Korea, Vietnam, Samoa, Thailand, and Portugal they have come, bringing with them their beliefs, their thoughts, and their traditions and turning Hawaii into what many people call a melting pot of cultures.

You can witness Hawaii's multicultural diversity in the way people dress. Go on a shopping spree and you'll encounter everything from designer Pierre Cardin blouses and classically casual Reyn's island fashions to shocking pink muumuus and Oriental-style slippers, the ubiquitous island footwear. There are kimonos from Japan, saris from India, and other exotic imports from China, the Philippines, and Korea. Most popular of all is the aloha shirt, which has become synonymous with Hawaii around the world and which has been worn with pride by such celebrities as Arthur Godfrey, Robin Williams, and Tom Selleck.

You can taste the local color in Hawaii's foods, a wonderful stew of cuisines from around the globe. On any given night you can dine on Japanese sashimi, Indian curry, Hawaiian lomilomi salmon, or Chinese roast duck, not to mention French, German, Korean, American, Mexican, Thai, Italian, Moroccan, and Greek dishes.

There are, of course, tastes that are uniquely tropical, especially when it comes to fruit. Hawaii's trademark bananas, papayas, and pineapple grow throughout the year, while the prized mangos, watermelons, and lychees appear only in the summer. Island seafood is equally splashy, with Pacific delicacies as exotic as their names: *mahimahi* (dolphin fish), *opakapaka* (pink snapper), *ulua* (crevelle), and *ahi* (yellowfin tuna), to name a few.

Hawaii is making headway in the international dining scene, thanks to a recent influx of talented chefs from around the world. These culinary masters are coming to Hawaii primarily to cater to the ever-growing visitor population, and the results of their craft can be savored in the finer restaurants throughout the state.

In Hawaii, meals are presented in environments as diverse as the menus. As you sip the finest champagne, you can enjoy an oceanside, candlelit dinner of fresh *opakapaka* fish that has been lavished with a sauce of three caviars. Or you can have just as much fun at a beachside carryout, munching on a lunch of teriyaki beef over rice served on paper plates with plastic utensils, then topping off your meal with a "shave ice" (snow cone) flavored with coconut, mango, and *lilikoi* (passion fruit) syrups.

Hawaii's ethnic mix is also evident on the cultural calendar, which is a wonderful hodgepodge of events, such as Japanese *bon* dances, Filipino festivals, Samoan shindigs, Chinese New Year celebrations, Scottish Highland flings, Greek galas, and the yearly Aloha Festival.

Standing out among the international din is that which is uniquely Hawaiian, as best exemplified by the dance and music of the Islands. Highly cherished are the hula and chants, which find their roots in ancient island history and have been handed down for centuries. Today they are praticed almost religiously; in fact, children can learn hula in school. Each year enthusiastic audiences applaud performances at such events as the Merrie Monarch Hula Festival on the Big Island, the Prince Lot Hula Festival on Oahu, and the Keiki Hula Festival, in which Hawaii's children carry on the tradition of Hawaiian poetry in motion.

Along with the swaying hips and stamping feet of the hula, the strumming sound of the ukulele has become innately associated with Hawaii. The ukulele (the name means "jumping flea") was brought from Portugal by sugar-plantation workers. Today most every musical group that plays old-time Hawaiian songs has a ukulele in the band. Some of Hawaii's most cherished songsters play it, too, such as old-timer Andy Cummings, who wrote the hit song "Waikiki" and who still strums and sings beloved standards each week in a Honolulu restaurant called Buzz's.

While many of Hawaii's performers faithfully strive to re-create the songs and dances of the past, a renaissance of the Hawaiian culture has spurred on a new generation of composers. Leading the wave of entertainers who make new music in the old tradition are the Brothers Cazimero, who perform at the Royal Hawaiian Hotel on Oahu, and Peter Moon, who plays at various clubs around the Islands. Their sounds are upbeat and easy to relate to for audiences unfamiliar with Hawaiian musical history.

The Aloha Spirit

Since the earliest days, island hospitality has played a key role in Hawaiian lifestyle. In fact, in ancient times members of the community who were not friendly to incoming guests were shunned by the rest of society. Since then it has been a revered island custom that when people come to call, they are not treated like tourists but instead are embraced as cherished guests or long-lost friends. In this very special way, Hawaii becomes everyone's home, and each visitor is a new and welcome member of the family.

Hawaii has a precious asset in its people. They go out of their way to help each other. On the freeway during rush hour, drivers often smile and wave you into their lane of traffic when you signal. At your hotel, a bellman carries your bag as if it's an honor, and your waitress seems genuinely excited that you're about to taste your first mai tai. Goodwill is not just a job to those in the visitor industry; it's their nature.

That sort of spirit just naturally rubs off on the people who visit Hawaii. Perhaps you first feel it as you smell the floral perfume in the air, that fragrance of the tropics. Dissected, it's a blend of plumeria, ginger, mock-orange blossoms, freshly clipped hedges, newly mown lawns, and the salt air from the Pacific surf. Together it presents an alluring essence that turns the most level-headed traveler into a giddy aficionado of Hawaii. The name for the way it makes you feel? Why, aloha spirit, of course!

The undeniable aloha spirit permeates each island with such strength that it is impossible to ignore. It keeps people in Hawaii much longer than they originally planned to stay. It's also the best reason to pay a visit to the 50th state. Enjoy your trip, and remember that you are invited to stay as long as you like.

1 Essential Information

Before You Go

Visitor Information

The source of all information on Hawaii is the **Hawaii Visitors Bureau** (HVB, Waikiki Business Plaza, 2270 Kalakaua Ave., Suite 801, Honolulu, 96815, tel. 808/923–1811). The bureau publishes an official state travel guide, *The Islands of Aloha*, as well as various brochures, a comprehensive annual calendar of events, an accommodations guide (which includes everything from a property's distance from the beach to its amenities), a list of budget properties, and a restaurant listing containing one-line descriptions of bureau members. The bureau also maintains representative and regional offices in **New York** (350 5th Ave., Suite 808, NY 10118, tel. 212/947–0717), **Los Angeles** (3440 Wilshire Blvd., Suite 610, CA 90010, tel. 213/385–5301), **Chicago** (180 N. Michigan Ave., Suite 2210, IL 60601, tel. 312/236–0632), **San Francisco** (50 California St., Suite 450, CA 94111, tel. 415/ 392–8173), **the United Kingdom** (14 The Green, Richmond, Surrey, TW9 1PX, England, tel. 081/332–6969), **Japan** (Hibiya Kokusai Bldg., 11th floor, 22-3 Uchisaiwaicho, Chiyodaku, Tokyo 100, tel. 81/33–597–7951), and **Hong Kong** (W. Tower, Suite 3702A, Bond Centre, Queensway Central, tel. 852/526–0387).

Tours and Packages

Should you buy your travel arrangements to Hawaii packaged or do it yourself? There are advantages either way. Buying packaged arrangements saves you money, particularly if you can find a program that includes exactly the features you want. You also get a pretty good idea of what your trip will cost from the outset. Generally, you have two options: fully escorted tours and independent packages. Escorted bus tours mean having limited free time and traveling with strangers. Escorted tours are most often via motorcoach, with a tour director in charge. Your baggage is handled, your time rigorously scheduled, and most meals planned. An escorted tour is therefore the most hassle-free way to see a destination, as well as generally the least expensive. But more flexibility is available through independent packages. They generally include airline travel and hotels, with certain options available, such as sightseeing, car rental, and excursions. Independent packages are usually more expensive than escorted tours, but your time is your own.

Travel agents are your best source of recommendations for both tours and packages. They will have the largest selection, and the cost to you is the same as buying direct. Whatever program you ultimately choose, be sure to find out exactly what is included: taxes, tips, transfers, meals, baggage handling, ground transportation, entertainment, excursions, sports or recreation (and rental equipment for any sports you may plan to pursue). Ask about the level of hotel used, its location, the size of its rooms, the kind of beds, and its amenities, such as pool, room service, or programs for children, if they're important to you. Another important point: If the beach is the centerpiece of your vacation, ask exactly where the nearest is with respect to your hotel: The words "beach nearby" can mean many things.

Find out the operator's cancellation penalties. Nearly everyone charges them, and the only way to avoid them is to buy trip-cancellation insurance (*see* Trip Insurance, *below*). Also ask about the single supplement, a surcharge assessed to solo travelers. Some operators do not make you pay it if you agree to be matched up with a roommate of the same sex, even if one is not found by departure time. Remember that a program that has features you won't use, whether for rental of sporting equipment or discounted museum admissions, may not be the most cost-wise choice for you.

Fully Escorted Tours Escorted tours to Hawaii are plentiful. They are usually sold in three categories: deluxe, first-class, and tourist or budget class. The most important differences are the price, of course, and the level of accommodations. Some operators specialize in one category, while others offer a range. A deluxe operator such as **Maupintour** (Box 807, Lawrence, KS 66044, tel. 913/843–1211 or 800/255–4266) has several Hawaiian programs that combine Oahu with Maui, Kauai and the Big Island. Also try **Tauck Tours** (11 Wilton Rd., Westport, CT 06881, tel. 800/468–2825), another deluxe operator, which uses luxurious hotels such as the Hyatt Regency and the Four Seasons on Maui. First-class tours are available from **Cartan Tours** (2809 Butterfield Rd., Oakbrook, IL 60521, tel. 800/422–7826), which has an enormous choice, and **Globus-Gateway** (95-25 Queens Blvd., Rego Park, NY 11374, tel. 800/221–0090); Globus's sister company, **Cosmos** (at the same address and telephone number), offers budget programs.

Most itineraries are jam-packed with sightseeing, so you see a lot in a short amount of time (usually one place per day). To judge just how fast-paced the tour is, review the itinerary carefully. If you are in a different hotel each night, you will be getting up early each day to head out, travel to your next destination, do some sightseeing, have dinner, and go to bed, then you'll start all over again. If you want some free time, make sure it's mentioned in the tour brochure; if you want to be escorted to every meal, confirm that any tour you consider does that. Also, when comparing programs, be sure to find out if the motorcoach is air-conditioned and has a rest room on board. Make your selection based on price and stops on the itinerary.

Independent Packages Independent packages are offered by airlines, tour operators who may also do escorted programs, and any number of other companies from large, established firms to small, new entrepreneurs. Their programs come in a wide range of prices based on levels of luxury and options. Note that when pricing different packages, it sometimes pays to purchase the same arrangements separately, as when a rock-bottom promotional airfare is being offered, for example. Again, base your choice on what's available at your budget for the destinations you want to visit.

Among major operators packaging round-trip airfare with a wide choice of resorts from budget to deluxe are **American Airlines Fly AAway Vacations** (tel. 800/321–2121), **Continental Airlines' Grand Destinations** (tel. 800/634–5555), **Delta Dream Vacations** (tel. 800/872–7786), and **United's Vacation Planning Center** (tel. 800/328–6877). Others include **American Express Vacations** (300 Pinnacle Way, Norcross, GA 30093, tel. 800/

241–1700); **Pleasant Hawaiian Holidays** (2402 Townsgate Rd., Westlake Village, CA 91361, tel. 800/2–HAWAII), a supermarket of independent packages; **Cartan Tours** (*see above*), which has independent as well as escorted programs); and **Classic Hawaii** (1 N. First St., 3rd floor, San Jose, CA 95113, tel. 800/221–3949). Independent packages are also available from escorted tour operators **Globus** and **Cosmos** (*see above*).

Special-Interest Travel Special-interest programs may be fully escorted or independent. Some require a certain amount of expertise, but most are for the average traveler with an interest and are usually hosted by experts in the subject matter. When the program is escorted, it enjoys the advantages and disadvantages of all escorted programs; because your fellow travelers are apt to be passionate or knowledgeable about the subject, they can prove as enjoyable a part of your travel experience as the destination itself. The price range is wide, but the cost is usually higher— sometimes a lot higher—than for ordinary escorted tours and packages, because of the expert guiding and special activities.

Golf **Trieloff Tours** (24031 El Toro Rd., Suite 140, Laguna Hills, CA 92653, tel. 800/248–6877 or 800/432–7125 in CA) has programs for all levels with tournaments and trophies.

Hiking On a **Mountain Travel Sobek** (6420 Fairmount Ave., El Cerrito, CA 94530, tel. 800/227–2384) program, travelers stay in huts along the trails traversing the various islands' coastlines.

Natural History **Oceanic Society Expeditions** (Ft. Mason Center, Bldg. E, San Francisco, CA 94123, tel. 415/441–1106 or 800/326–7491) has programs that include whale-watching, seal-watching, and snorkeling. **Questers Worldwide Nature Tours** (257 Park Ave. S, New York, NY 10010, tel. 212/673–3120 or 800/468–8668) are led by experts in ornithology, botany, and the environment.

U.K. Tour Operators For tours and packages from the United Kingdom, contact **Albany (Manchester) Travel Ltd.** (Central Buildings 196 Deansgate, Manchester M3 3NF, tel. 061/833–0202), **The Hawaiian Dream** (17 Station Chambers, High St. N, London E6 1JE, tel. 081/470–1181), **Jetsave** (Sussex House, London Rd., East Grinstead, West Sussex RH19 1LD, tel. 0342/312–033), or **Kuoni Travel** (Kuoni House, Dorking, Surrey RH5 4AZ, tel. 0306/742–222). **Poundstretcher** (Airline House, Hazelwick Ave., Three Bridges, Crawley, West Sussex RH10 1Y5, tel. 0293/518022). Many Hawaii packages include stopovers in California or other mainland destinations.

Passports and Visas

Canadian Citizens Canadian citizens need only proof of citizenship and identity (a passport, birth certificate with raised seal, or voter registration card).

U.K. Citizens Citizens of the United Kingdom need a valid 10-year passport to enter the United States. A visa is not necessary unless (1) you are planning to stay more than 90 days; (2) your trip is for purposes other than vacation; (3) you have at some time been refused a visa, or refused admission, to the United States or have been required to leave by the U.S. Immigration and Naturalization Service; or (4) you do not have a return or onward ticket. You will need to fill out the Visa Waiver Form, 1–94W, supplied by the airline.

To apply for a visa or for more information, call the U.S. Embassy's Visa Information Line (tel. 0891/200–290; calls cost 48p per minute or 36p per minute cheap rate). If you qualify for the visa-free travel but want a visa anyway, you must apply in writing, enclosing a self-addressed envelope, to the U.S. Embassy's Visa Branch (5 Upper Grosvenor St., London W1A 2JB), or, for residents of Northern Ireland, to the U.S. Consulate General (Queen's House, Queen St., Belfast BT1 6EO). Submit a completed Nonimmigrant Visa Application (Form 156), a valid passport, a photograph, and evidence of your intended departure from the United States after a temporary visit. If you require a visa, call 0891/234–224 to schedule an interview.

Applications for new and renewal passports are available from main post offices as well as at the six passport offices, located in Belfast, Glasgow, Liverpool, London, Newport, and Peterborough. You may apply in person at all passport offices, or by mail to all except the London office; Londoners should mail applications to the Glasgow office (3 Northgate, 96 Milton St., Cowcaddens, Glasgow G4 0BT, tel. 041/332–0271). For your first passport, you must submit the completed form plus the original of your birth or adoption certificate; two recent, identical photographs measuring 45 millimeters by 35 millimeters; and, if you're a married or divorced woman, the original of your marriage certificate or divorce documents. The form and one of the photographs must be countersigned by a Commonwealth citizen who has known you personally for at least two years and is a minister, judge, doctor, lawyer, teacher, civil servant, member of parliament, police officer, or person of similar standing. For a renewal passport, you may submit the renewal application along with your old passport and new photos; the application and photographs must be countersigned as above only if your appearance has changed so much that you no longer look like the same person. The fee is £18 for a 32-page passport, £27 for a 48-page document. If applying by mail, send a postal order or check made out to "Passport Office," crossed "Account Payee," and with your name and address written on the back; if applying in person, you must pay cash or support the check with a bank card. Children under 16 may travel on a parent's passport when accompanying them. All passports are valid for 10 years. Allow a month for processing.

Customs

Restrictions on Import and Export

Plants Plants and plant products are subject to regulation by the Department of Agriculture, both on entering and leaving Hawaii. Pineapples and coconuts pass freely; papayas must be treated. All other fruits are banned for export to the U.S. mainland. Flowers pass except for gardenia, rose leaves, jade vine, and mauna loa. Also banned are insects, snails, coffee, cotton, cacti, sugarcane, all berries, and soil.

Pets Leave dogs and other pets at home. A strict 120-day quarantine is imposed to keep out rabies, which is nonexistent in Hawaii. For full details, contact the **Animal Quarantine Station, Department of Agriculture** (State of Hawaii, 951 Halawa Valley St., Aiea, HI 96701, tel. 808/483–7171).

Returning Home
Canadian Customs Once per calendar year, when you've been out of Canada for at least seven days, you may bring in $300 worth of goods duty-

free. If you've been away less than seven days but more than 48 hours, the duty-free exemption drops to $100 but can be claimed any number of times (as can a $20 duty-free exemption for absences of 24 hours or more). You cannot combine the yearly and 48-hour exemptions, use the $300 exemption only partially (to save the balance for a later trip), or pool exemptions with family members. Goods claimed under the $300 exemption may follow you by mail; those claimed under the lesser exemptions must accompany you on your return.

Alcohol and tobacco products may be included in the yearly and 48-hour exemptions but not in the 24-hour exemption. If you meet the age requirements of the province through which you reenter Canada, you may bring in, duty-free, 1.14 liters (40 imperial ounces) of wine or liquor *or* two dozen 12-ounce cans or bottles of beer or ale. If you are 16 or older, you may bring in, duty-free, 200 cigarettes, 50 cigars or cigarillos, and 400 tobacco sticks or 400 grams of manufactured tobacco. Alcohol and tobacco must accompany you on your return.

Gifts may be mailed to friends in Canada duty-free. These do not count as part of your exemption. Each gift may be worth up to $60—label the package "Unsolicited Gift—Value under $60." There are no limits on the number of gifts that may be sent per day or per addressee, but you can't mail alcohol or tobacco.

For more information, including details of duties on items that exceed your duty-free limit, ask the Revenue Canada Customs and Excise Department (Connaught Bldg., MacKenzie Ave., Ottawa, Ont., K1A OL5, tel. 613/957–0275) for a copy of the free brochure "I Declare/Je Déclare."

U.K. Customs From countries outside the EC such as the United States, you may import duty-free 200 cigarettes, 100 cigarillos, 50 cigars, or 250 grams of tobacco; 1 liter of spirits or 2 liters of fortified or sparkling wine; 2 liters of still table wine; 60 milliliters of perfume; 250 milliliters of toilet water; plus £36 worth of other goods, including gifts and souvenirs.

For further information or a copy of "A Guide for Travellers," which details standard customs procedures as well as what you may bring into the United Kingdom from abroad, contact HM Customs and Excise (New King's Beam House, 22 Upper Ground, London SE1 9PJ, tel. 071/620–1313).

When to Go

Hawaii's long days of sunshine, fairly mild year-round temperatures, and activities throughout each season allow for 12 months of pleasurable island travel. In resort areas near sea level, the average afternoon temperature during the coldest winter months of December and January is 80°F; during the hottest months of August and September the temperature often reaches 90°F. Cold weather (30°F) can occur in Hawaii during the winter, but only near the summit of the Big Island's Mauna Kea crater, where snow skiers occasionally find enough accumulation for a run or two.

Slight differences exist when it comes to monthly rainfall, high- and low-season travel rates, and the number of fellow travelers you'll find upon arrival. Winter is the season when most travelers prefer to head for the islands. From mid-December through mid-April, visitors from the mainland and other areas covered with snow find Hawaii's sun-splashed beaches and balmy trade winds particularly appealing. Not surprisingly, this high season also means that fewer travel bargains are available; room rates average 10%–15% higher during this season than the rest of the year.

The only weather change most areas experience during the December–February span is a few more days of rainfall, though the sun is rarely hidden behind the clouds for a solid 24-hour period. Visitors should remember that regardless of the season, the northern shores of each island usually receive more rain than those on the south. And Kauai and the Big Island's northern sections get more annual rainfall than the rest of Hawaii.

Rain or shine, the Aloha State offers more than the weather to think about during the winter months. December ranks as the best time to see the magnificent crashing surf on Oahu's North Shore, where surfers gather from around the world to participate in competitions.

Climate The following are average maximum and minimum temperatures for certain areas of the Hawaiian Islands:

Waikiki, Oahu

Jan.	81F	27C	**May**	83F	28C	**Sept.**	88F	31C
	63	17		70	21		70	21
Feb.	81F	27C	**June**	85F	29C	**Oct.**	86F	30C
	63	17		70	21		70	21
Mar.	83F	28C	**July**	86F	30C	**Nov.**	85F	29C
	68	20		72	22		70	21
Apr.	83F	28C	**Aug.**	88F	31C	**Dec.**	83F	28C
	67	19		72	22		65	18

Hilo, the Big Island

Jan.	79F	26C	**May**	81F	27C	**Sept.**	83F	28C
	63	17		65	18		67	19
Feb.	79F	26C	**June**	83F	28C	**Oct.**	83F	28C
	63	17		67	19		67	19
Mar.	79F	26C	**July**	83F	28C	**Nov.**	81F	27C
	63	17		67	19		67	19
Apr.	79F	26C	**Aug.**	83F	28C	**Dec.**	79F	26C
	65	18		68	20		65	18

Lahaina, Maui

Jan.	85F	29C	**May**	86F	30C	**Sept.**	88F	31C
	61	16		63	17		70	21
Feb.	83F	28C	**June**	88F	31C	**Oct.**	88F	31C
	59	15		65	18		68	20
Mar.	85F	29C	**July**	88F	31C	**Nov.**	86F	30C
	63	17		65	18		67	19
Apr.	85F	29C	**Aug.**	88F	31C	**Dec.**	83F	28C
	63	17		68	20		65	18

Molokai Airport, Molokai	Jan.	79F 63	26C 17	May	81F 67	27C 18	Sept.	85F 70	29C 21
	Feb.	77F 63	25C 17	June	83F 68	28C 20	Oct.	85F 68	29C 20
	Mar.	79F 63	26C 17	July	85F 70	29C 21	Nov.	81F 67	27C 19
	Apr.	79F 65	26C 18	Aug.	85F 70	29C 21	Dec.	79F 65	26C 18

Lanai City, Lanai	Jan.	76F 58	24C 14	May	79F 63	26C 17	Sept.	81F 63	27C 17
	Feb.	76F 59	24C 15	June	79F 63	26C 17	Oct.	81F 63	27C 17
	Mar.	76F 58	24C 14	July	81F 65	27C 18	Nov.	79F 63	26C 17
	Apr.	77F 61	25C 16	Aug.	83F 65	28C 18	Dec.	76F 61	24C 16

Lihue, Kauai	Jan.	79F 61	26C 16	May	81F 67	27C 19	Sept.	85F 70	29C 21
	Feb.	79F 61	26C 16	June	83F 70	28C 21	Oct.	83F 68	28C 20
	Mar.	79F 63	26C 17	July	83F 70	28C 21	Nov.	81F 67	27C 19
	Apr.	79F 65	26C 18	Aug.	83F 70	28C 21	Dec.	79F 65	26C 18

Information Sources For current weather conditions for cities in the United States and abroad, plus the local time, helpful travel tips, and hurricane, foliage, and ski reports, call the **Weather Channel Connection** (tel. 900/WEATHER; 95¢ per minute) from a touch-tone phone. For month-by-month weather information and clothing suggestions, obtain the 24 **World Climate Charts** published by the International Association for Medical Assistance to Travellers (no charge, but a $25 donation is requested). *See* Staying Healthy, *below,* for more on this organization.

Festivals and Seasonal Events

Hawaii has a busy calendar of holidays and special events; listed below are some of the most important or unusual ones.

January **Hawaii Formula 40 World Cup** (Oahu). Twelve 40-foot catamarans and trimarans participate in a challenging race that starts and ends at the Ala Wai Yacht Harbor, Honolulu.
Kodak Hula Bowl (Oahu). This annual college all-star football game is played at Aloha Stadium, Honolulu.
Morey Boogie World Body Board Championships (Oahu). Thirty-six of the world's best body-boarders compete; the exact date depends on the best wave action.
Kilauea Volcano Wilderness Marathon and Rim Runs (the Big Island). More than 1,000 athletes from Hawaii, the mainland, and Japan run 26.2 miles across Kau desert, 10 miles around the Kilauea Caldera rim, and 5.5 miles into Kilauea Iki Crater. The event takes place in Hawaii Volcanoes National Park.

January–February **Narcissus Festival** (Oahu). Welcoming the Chinese New Year are a queen pageant, coronation ball, cooking demonstrations, and a noisy evening of fireworks in Chinatown.

February **NFL Pro Bowl** (Oahu). This annual pro football all-star game is played at Aloha Stadium.
Hawaiian Open Golf Tournament (Oahu). Top golf pros tee off for $1.2 million or more in prizes at the Waialae Country Club.
Punahou Carnival (Oahu). Hawaii's most prestigious school stages an annual fund-raiser with rides, arts and crafts, local food, and a great flea market.
Captain Cook Festival (Kauai). Honoring the British explorer who came to the island in 1778, Kauai offers a reenactment of the captain's landing, canoe races, and a three-day fair at Waimea.
Sand-castle Building Contest (Oahu). The students of the University of Hawaii School of Architecture take on Hawaii's professional architects in a friendly competition; the result is some amazing and unusual sand sculpture at Kailua Beach Park.

February–March **Cherry Blossom Festival** (all islands). This popular celebration of all things Japanese includes a run, cultural displays, cooking demonstrations, music, and the inevitable queen pageant and coronation ball.

March **Buffalo's Annual Big Board Surfing Classic** (Oahu). The event features surfing as it used to be, on old-fashioned 12- to 16-foot boards, plus food and entertainment.
Opening Day of Polo Season (Oahu). Games are held every Sunday through August at 2 PM at the Hawaii Polo Club, Mokuleia, and every Saturday at Honolulu Polo Club, Waimanolo.
Prince Kuhio Day (all islands). March 26, a local holiday, honors Prince Kuhio, who might have been king if Hawaii had not been granted statehood. Instead, he became a congressman.
Art Maui (Maui). This prestigious annual event highlights the best of a wide variety of media.

March or April **Merrie Monarch Festival** (the Big Island). A full week of ancient and modern hula competition begins with a parade the Saturday morning following Easter Sunday. Tickets must be purchased months in advance; the competition is held at the Edith Kamakaole Auditorium in Hilo.

April **Buddha Day** (all islands). Flower pageants are staged at temples throughout the islands to celebrate the birth of Buddha.

May **Carole Kai International Bed Race and Parade** (Oahu). Big names in town turn out for this wild event centered in Waikiki. The race and parade are part of a charity fund-raiser.
Lei Day (all islands). The annual flower-filled celebration on May 1 includes music, hula, food, and lots of leis on exhibit and for sale, some of them exquisite floral masterpieces.

May–June **50th State Fair** (Oahu). Produce exhibits, food booths, entertainment, and amusement rides mark this Hawaiian-style bit of Americana held at Aloha Stadium.

June **Festival of the Pacific** (Oahu). This week-long affair of sports, music, songs, and dances highlights regional ethnic culture.
Pro Surf Championships (Oahu). Body- and skim-board surfing highlight this summer surfing event held at Sandy Beach.
King Kamehameha Day (all islands). Kamehameha united all the islands and became Hawaii's first king, making Hawaii the only state to have a royal background. In addition to parades and fairs, twin statues of the king—in Honolulu, Oahu, and Hawi on the Big Island—are draped in giant leis.

June–July **Hawaii State Farm Fair** (Oahu). Farm products, agricultural exhibits, arts and crafts, a petting zoo, contests, and a country market are featured at one of Hawaii's best farm fairs.

July **Makawao Statewide Rodeo** (Maui). This old-time upcountry rodeo, held at the Oskie Rice Arena, includes the annual Makawao Rodeo Parade.

Independence Day (all islands). The national holiday on July 4 is celebrated with a tropical touch, including fairs, parades, and, of course, fireworks. Special events are the Walter J. MacFarlane Regatta and Surf Race, an outrigger canoe regatta featuring 30 events held on and off Waikiki Beach.

Prince Lot Hula Festival (Oahu). A whole day of hula unfolds beneath the towering trees of Oahu's Moanalua Gardens.

International Festival of the Pacific (the Big Island). The event features music, dance, and food from Japan, China, Korea, Portugal, Tahiti, New Zealand, and the Philippines.

July–August **Bon Odori Season** (all islands). Buddhist temples invite everyone to festivals that honor ancestors and feature Japanese dancing.

August **Hawaii International Billfish Tournament** (the Big Island). Billed as the world's leading international marlin fishing tournament, the event, held in Kailua-Kona, includes a parade with amusing entries.

Queen Liliuokalani Keiki Hula Competition (Oahu). The crowds turn out to see the children's hula competition, which is held over three days. Tickets are usually available at the end of June and sell out soon after.

Admission Day (all islands). The state holiday, on August 18, recognizes Hawaii's statehood.

September **Waikiki Rough Water Swim** (Oahu). Swimmers of all ages and skill levels can compete in this 2-mile outing.

September–October **Aloha Festivals** (all islands). This traditional celebration, started in 1946, preserves Hawaiian native culture. Crafts, music, dance, pageantry, street parties, and canoe races are all part of the festival.

Bankoh Molokai Hoe. Two annual canoe races from Molokai to Oahu finish in Waikiki. The women's race is in September; the men's is in October.

October **Gatorade Ironman Triathlon World Championships** (the Big Island). This popular annual sporting event is limited to 1,250 competitors who swim, run, and bicycle.

November **Pearl Harbor Aloha Festival** (Oahu). This event is the largest military festival of its kind in Hawaii. Major concerts, from rock to country and traditional Hawaiian, are common during the fair.

King Kalakaua Kupuna and Keiki Hula Festival (the Big Island). Another big, popular hula contest, this one features both a children's competition and one for *kupuna*—adults 55 years and older.

Kona Coffee Festival (the Big Island). A week-long celebration follows the coffee harvest. The Miss Kona Coffee contest and a coffee-cupping (tasting) contest are capped by a parade and family day with ethnic foods and entertainment at Hale Halawai Recreation Pavilion.

Mission Houses Museum Annual Christmas Fair (Oahu). Artists and craftspeople sell their creations in an open market.

November–December   **Hawaii International Film Festival** (Oahu). The visual feast showcases films from the United States, Asia, and the Pacific.

December   **Triple Crown of Surfing** (Oahu). The world's top pro surfers gather for the big winter waves and some tough competition.

Honolulu Marathon (Oahu). Watch or run in one of the country's most popular marathons.

Bodhi Day (all islands). The traditional Buddhist Day of Enlightenment is celebrated at temples throughout the islands. Visitors are welcome to the services.

Eagle Aloha Bowl (Oahu). Two top college football squads meet in this annual contest held at Aloha Stadium.

Christmas (all islands). The hotels outdo each other in extravagant exhibits and events such as Santa arriving by outrigger canoe.

What to Pack

You can pack lightly because Hawaii is casual. Bare feet, bathing suits, and comfortable, informal clothing are the norm.

The Man's Suitcase   In the Hawaiian Islands, there's a saying that when a man wears a suit during the day, he's either going for a loan or he's a lawyer trying a case. Only a few upscale restaurants require a jacket for dinner, and none requires a tie. Hawaii regulars wear their jackets on the plane—just in case—and many don't put them on again until the return flight. The aloha shirt is accepted dress in Hawaii for business and most social occasions. A visitor can easily buy one after arriving in Hawaii.

Shorts are acceptable daytime attire, along with a T-shirt or polo shirt. If you want to be marked as a tourist, wear your shorts with dark shoes and white socks. Local-style casual footwear consists of tennis or running shoes, sandals, or rubber slippers. You'll also see a lot of bare feet, but state law requires that footwear be worn in all food establishments.

Pack your toiletries, underwear, and a pair or two of easy-care slacks to wear with those aloha shirts, and you're all set.

The Woman's Suitcase   During the winter months, bring a sweater or wrap for the evening because the trade winds cool things off when the sun goes down. If you have an elaborate coiffure, a scarf will help keep it from getting windblown. Sundresses, shorts, and tops are fine for daytime. If you have a long slip, bring it for the muumuu you say you won't buy, but probably will. As for shoes, sandals and tennis or running shoes are fine for daytime, and sandals are perfect for the evening. If you wear boots, you'll wish you hadn't.

If you don't own a *pareu*, buy one in Hawaii. It's simply a length of light cotton (about 1½ yards long), usually in a tropical motif, that can be worn as a beach wrap, a skirt, or a dozen other wrap-up fashions. A pareu is useful wherever you go, regardless of climate. It makes a good bathrobe, so you don't have to pack one. You can even tie it up as a handbag or sit on it at the beach.

For Everyone   In summer, synthetic slacks and shirts, although easy to care for, can get uncomfortably warm.

Don't forget your bathing suit. Sooner or later, the crystal clear water tempts even the most sedentary landlubber. Of course, bathing suits are easy to find in Hawaii. Shops are crammed with the latest styles. If you wear a bathing cap, bring one; you can waste hours searching for one.

Probably the most important thing to tuck in your suitcase is sunscreen. This is the tropics, and the ultraviolet rays are much more powerful than those to which you are accustomed. Doctors advise putting on sunscreen when you get up in the morning. Women can wear it as a moisturizer under makeup. The upper chest area of a woman is hypopigmented and should be protected. Don't forget to reapply sunscreen periodically during the day, since perspiration can wash it away. Consider using sunscreens with a sun protection factor (SPF) of 15 or higher. There are many tanning oils on the market in Hawaii, including coconut and kukui oils, but doctors warn that they merely sauté your skin. Too many Hawaiian vacations have been spoiled by sunburn.

If you're planning to visit a volcano area, bring along a light-weight jacket, especially in the winter months.

It's a good idea to tuck in a few jumbo zip-top plastic bags when you travel—they're ideal for wet swimsuits or food souvenirs that might leak. All major hotels in Hawaii provide beach towels. Some hotels provide hair dryers and some don't. Unless you know for sure, bring your own.

Visitors who wear glasses are wise to pack an extra pair. Eyeglasses are easy to lose, and you can waste days of your precious Hawaiian holiday replacing them. If you have a health problem that may require you to purchase a prescription drug, take enough to last the duration of the trip. And don't forget to pack a list of the addresses of offices that supply refunds for lost or stolen traveler's checks.

Luggage
Regulations
Free baggage allowances on an airline depend on the airline, the route, and the class of your ticket. In general, on domestic flights and on international flights between the United States and foreign destinations, you are entitled to check two bags—neither exceeding 62 inches, or 158 centimeters (length + width + height), or weighing more than 70 pounds (32 kilograms). A third piece may be brought aboard as a carryon; its total dimensions are generally limited to less than 45 inches (114 centimeters), so it will fit easily under the seat in front of you or in the overhead compartment. There are variations, so ask in advance. The only rule, a Federal Aviation Administration safety regulation that pertains to carry-on baggage on U.S. airlines, requires only that carryons be properly stowed and allows the airline to limit allowances and tailor them to different aircraft and operational conditions. Charges for excess, oversize, or overweight pieces vary, so inquire before you pack.

Safeguarding Your
Luggage
Before leaving home, itemize your bags' contents and their worth; this list will help you estimate the extent of your loss if your bags go astray. To minimize that risk, tag them inside and out with your name, address, and phone number. (If you use your home address, cover it so that potential thieves can't see it.) At check-in, make sure that the tag attached by baggage handlers bears the correct three-letter code for your destination. If your bags do not arrive with you, or if you detect damage, do not leave the airport until you've filed a written report with the airline.

Getting Money from Home

Cash Machines Automated-teller machines (ATMs) are proliferating; many are tied to international networks such as **Cirrus** and **Plus.** You can use your bank card at ATMs away from home to withdraw money from your checking account and get cash advances on a credit-card account (providing your card has been programmed with a personal identification number, or PIN). Check in advance on limits on withdrawals and cash advances within specified periods. Remember that finance charges apply on credit-card cash advances from ATMs as well as on those from tellers. And note that transaction fees for ATM withdrawals outside your home turf will probably be higher than for withdrawals at home.

For specific Cirrus locations in Hawaii, call 800/424–7787 (for U.S. Plus locations, 800/843–7587), and press the area code and first three digits of the number you're calling from (or the calling area where you want an ATM).

American Express Cardholder Services The company's **Express Cash** system lets you withdraw cash and/or traveler's checks from a worldwide network of 57,000 American Express dispensers and participating bank ATMs. You must *enroll first* (call 800/CASH–NOW for a form and allow two weeks for processing). Withdrawals are charged not to your card but to a designated bank account. You can withdraw up to $1,000 per seven-day period on the basic card, more if your card is gold or platinum. There is a 2% fee (minimum $2.50, maximum $10) for each cash transaction, and a 1% fee for traveler's checks (except for the platinum card), which are available only from American Express dispensers.

At AmEx offices, cardholders can also cash personal checks for up to $1,000 in any seven-day period; of this, $200 can be in cash, more if available, with the balance paid in traveler's checks, for which all but platinum cardholders pay a 1% fee. Higher limits apply to the gold and platinum cards.

Wiring Money You don't have to be a cardholder to send or receive an **American Express MoneyGram** for up to $10,000. To send one, go to an American Express MoneyGram agent, pay up to $1,000 with a credit card and anything over that in cash, and phone a transaction reference number to your intended recipient, who need only present identification and the reference number to the nearest MoneyGram agent to pick up the cash. There are MoneyGram agents in more than 60 countries (call 800/543–4080 for locations). Fees range from 5% to 10%, depending on the amount and how you pay. You can't use American Express, which is really a convenience card—only Discover, Master-Card, and Visa credit cards.

You can also use **Western Union.** To wire money, take either cash or a check to the nearest office. (Or you can order money sent by phone, using a credit card.) Money sent from the United States or Canada will be available for pickup at agent locations in Hawaii within minutes, and fees are roughly 5%–10%. (Note that once the money is in the system it can be picked up at *any* location. You don't have to miss your train waiting for it to arrive in City A, because if there's an agent in City B, where you're headed, you can pick it up there, too.)

Insurance

Most tour operators, travel agents, and insurance agents sell specialized health-and-accident, flight, trip-cancellation, and luggage insurance as well as comprehensive policies with some or all of these features. But before you make any purchase, review your existing health and homeowner policies to find out whether they cover expenses incurred while traveling.

For U.S. Residents
Health-and-Accident Insurance

Supplemental health-and-accident insurance for travelers is usually a part of comprehensive policies. Specific policy provisions vary, but they tend to address three general areas, beginning with reimbursement for medical expenses caused by illness or an accident during a trip. Such policies may reimburse anywhere from $1,000 to $150,000 worth of medical expenses; dental benefits may also be included. A second common feature is the personal-accident, or death-and-dismemberment, provision, which pays a lump sum to your beneficiaries if you die, or to you if you lose one or both limbs or your eyesight. This is similar to the flight insurance described below, although it is not necessarily limited to accidents involving airplanes or even other "common carriers" (buses, trains, and ships) and can be in effect 24 hours a day. The lump sum awarded can range from $15,000 to $500,000. A third area generally addressed by these policies is medical assistance (referrals, evacuation, or repatriation and other services). Some policies reimburse travelers for the cost of such services; others may automatically enroll you as a member of a particular medical-assistance company.

Flight Insurance

This insurance, often bought as a last-minute impulse at the airport, pays a lump sum to a beneficiary when a plane crashes and the insured dies (and sometimes to a surviving passenger who loses eyesight or a limb); thus it supplements the airlines' own coverage as described in the limits-of-liability paragraphs on your ticket (up to $75,000 on international flights, $20,000 on domestic ones—and that is generally subject to litigation). Charging an airline ticket to a major credit card often automatically signs you up for flight insurance; in this case, the coverage may also embrace travel by bus, train, and ship.

Baggage Insurance

In the event of loss, damage, or theft on international flights, airlines limit their liability to $20 per kilogram for checked baggage (roughly about $640 per 70-pound bag) and $400 per passenger for unchecked baggage. On domestic flights, the ceiling is $1,250 per passenger. Excess-valuation insurance can be bought directly from the airline at check-in but leaves your bags vulnerable on the ground.

Trip Insurance

There are two sides to this coin. **Trip-cancellation-and-interruption insurance** protects you in the event you are unable to undertake or finish your trip. **Default** or **bankruptcy insurance** protects you against a supplier's failure to deliver. Consider the former if your airline ticket, cruise, or package tour does not allow changes or cancellations. The amount of coverage to buy should equal the cost of your trip should you, a traveling companion, or a family member get sick, forcing you to stay home, plus the nondiscounted one-way airline ticket you would need to buy if you had to return home early. Read the fine print carefully; pay attention to sections defining "family member" and "preexisting medical conditions." A characteristic quirk of default policies is that they often do not cover default by travel agencies or default by a tour operator, airline, or cruise line if you bought your tour and the coverage directly from the firm in question. To reduce your need for default insurance, give preference to tours packaged by members of the United States Tour Operators Association (USTOA), which maintains a fund to reimburse clients in the event of member defaults. Even better, pay for travel arrangements with a major credit card, so that you can refuse to pay the bill if services have not been rendered—and let the card company fight your battles.

Comprehensive Policies Companies supplying comprehensive policies with some or all of the above features include **Access America, Inc.,** underwritten by BCS Insurance Company (Box 11188, Richmond, VA 23230, tel. 800/284–8300); **Carefree Travel Insurance,** underwritten by The Hartford (Box 310, 120 Mineola Blvd., Mineola, NY 11501, tel. 516/294–0220 or 800/323–3149); **Tele-Trip** (Mutual of Omaha Plaza, Box 31762, Omaha, NE 68131, tel. 800/228–9792), a subsidiary of Mutual of Omaha; **The Travelers Companies** (1 Tower Sq., Hartford, CT 06183, tel. 203/277–0111 or 800/243–3174); **Travel Guard International,** underwritten by Transamerica Occidental Life Companies (1145 Clark St., Stevens Point, WI 54481, tel. 715/345–0505 or 800/782–5151); and **Wallach and Company, Inc.** (107 W. Federal St., Box 480, Middleburg, VA 22117, tel. 703/687–3166 or 800/237–6615), underwritten by Lloyds, London. These companies may also offer the above types of insurance separately.

U.K. Residents Most tour operators, travel agents, and insurance agents sell specialized policies covering accident, medical expenses, personal liability, trip cancellation, and loss or theft of personal property. Some policies include coverage for delayed departure and legal expenses, winter-sports, accidents, or motoring abroad. You can also purchase an annual travel-insurance policy valid for every trip you make during the year in which it's purchased (usually only trips of less than 90 days). Before you leave, make sure you will be covered if you have a preexisting medical condition or are pregnant; your insurers may not pay for routine or continuing treatment, or may require a note from your doctor certifying your fitness to travel.

The **Association of British Insurers,** a trade association representing 450 insurance companies, advises extra medical coverage for visitors to the United States.

For advice by phone or a free booklet, "Holiday Insurance," that sets out what to expect from a holiday-insurance policy and gives price guidelines, contact the Association of British Insurers (51 Gresham St., London EC2V 7HQ, tel. 071/600–3333; 30 Gordon St., Glasgow G1 3PU, tel. 041/226–3905; Scottish Provincial Bldg., Donegall Sq. W, Belfast BT1 6JE, tel. 0232/249176; call for other locations).

Car Rentals

Finding rental cars during your Hawaii visit is about as difficult as finding palm trees in paradise. They're everywhere. Not only do bustling Oahu and Maui have more than their fair share of U-drive outlets; even the tiny island of Lanai, with only 32 miles of paved roadway, has two rental agencies. You can find yourself driving anything from a $28-a-day econobox to a $1,100-a-day Ferrari. It's wise to make reservations in advance.

Major car rental agencies all have branches in Hawaii, including **Avis** (tel. 800/331–1212 or 800/879–2847 in Canada), **Budget** (tel. 800/527–0707 or 800/268–8900 in Canada), **Dollar** (tel. 800/800–4000 in the U.S. and Canada), and **USA** (tel. 800/678–6000) rent on Oahu, the Big Island, Kauai, Maui, and Molokai. **Alamo** (tel. 800/327–9633), **Hertz** (tel. 800/654–3131 or 800/263–0600 in Canada), and **National** (tel. 800/CAR–RENT in the U.S. and Canada), offer cars on each of the major islands except Molokai. **Thrifty** (tel. 800/367–2277) offers cars on Oahu, Maui, the Big Island, and Kauai. **Aloha Funway Rentals** (tel. 808/942–9696), on Oahu, and **VIP Car Rentals** (tel. 808/922–4605) rent on Maui and the Big Island. If you decide to drive on Lanai, call **Lanai City Service** (tel. 808/565–7227), or **Dollar** (tel. 800/800–4000).

Unlimited-mileage rates range from $30.99 per day for an economy car to $51.99 for a large car; weekly unlimited-mileage rates range from $140 to $238. This does not include tax, which in Hawaii is 4.17%. In addition, $2 per day is added for the state highway fund.

Cutting Costs If you know you will want a car for more than a day or two, you can save by planning ahead. Major international companies have programs that discount their standard rates by 15%–30% if you make the reservation before departure (anywhere from two to 14 days), rent for a minimum number of days (typically three or four), and prepay the rental. Ask about these advance-purchase schemes when you call for information. More economical rentals are those that come as part of fly/drive or other packages, even those as bare-bones as the rental plus an airline ticket (*see* Tours and Packages, *above*).

One last tip: Remember to fill the tank when you turn in the vehicle, to avoid being charged for refueling at what you'll swear is the most expensive pump in town.

Insurance and Collision Damage Waiver The standard rental contract includes liability coverage (for damage to public property, injury to pedestrians, etc.) and coverage for the car against fire, theft (not included in certain countries), and collision damage with a deductible—most commonly $2,000–$3,000, occasionally more. In the case of an accident, you are responsible for the deductible amount unless you've purchased the collision damage waiver (CDW), which costs an average $12 a day, although this varies depending on what you've rented, where, and from whom.

Because this adds up quickly, you may be inclined to say "no thanks"—and that's certainly your option, although the rental agent may not tell you so. Planning ahead will help you make the right decision. By all means, find out if your own insurance covers damage to a rental car while traveling (not simply a car to drive when yours is in for repairs). And check whether charging car rentals to any of your credit cards will get you a CDW at no charge. Note before you decline that deductibles are occasionally high enough that totaling a car would make you responsible for its full value. In many states, laws mandate that renters be told what the CDW costs, that it's optional, and that their own auto insurance may provide the same protection.

Traveling with Cameras, Camcorders, and Laptops

About Film and Cameras If your camera is new or if you haven't used it for a while, shoot and develop a few rolls of film before leaving home. Pack some lens tissue and an extra battery for your built-in light meter, and invest in an inexpensive skylight filter, to both protect your lens and provide some definition in hazy shots. Store film in a cool, dry place—never in the car's glove compartment or on the shelf under the rear window.

Films above ISO 400 are more sensitive to damage from airport security X-rays than others; very high speed films, ISO 1,000 and above, are exceedingly vulnerable. To protect your film, don't put it in checked luggage; carry it with you in a plastic bag and ask for a hand inspection. Such requests are honored at American airports, up to the inspector abroad. Don't depend on a lead-lined bag to protect film in checked luggage—the airline may very well turn up the dosage of radiation to see what you've got in there. Airport metal detectors do not harm film, although you'll set off the alarm if you walk through one with a roll in your pocket. Call the Kodak Information Center (tel. 800/242–2424) for details.

About Camcorders Before your trip, put new or long-unused camcorders through their paces, and practice panning and zooming. Invest in a skylight filter to protect the lens, and check the lithium battery that lights up the LCD (liquid crystal display) modes. As for the rechargeable nickel-cadmium batteries that are the camera's power source, take along an extra pair, so while you're using your camcorder you'll have one battery ready and another recharging. Most newer camcorders are equipped with the battery (which generally slides or clicks onto the camera body) and, to recharge it, with what's known as a universal or worldwide AC adapter charger (or multivoltage converter) that can be used whether the voltage is 110 or 220. All that's needed is the appropriate plug.

About Videotape Unlike still-camera film, videotape is not damaged by X-rays. However, it may well be harmed by the magnetic field of a walk-through metal detector. Airport security personnel may want you to turn the camcorder on to prove that's what it is, so make sure the battery is charged when you get to the airport.

About Laptops Security X-rays do not harm hard-disk or floppy-disk storage. Most airlines allow you to use your laptop aloft but request that you turn it off during takeoff and landing so as not to interfere with navigation equipment. Make sure the battery is charged when you arrive at the airport, because you may be asked to turn on the computer at security checkpoints to prove that it is what it appears to be. If you're a heavy computer user, consider traveling with a backup battery.

Traveling with Children

Getting There On domestic flights, children under 2 not occupying a seat trav-
Airfares el free, and older children currently travel on the "lowest applicable" adult fare.

Baggage The adult baggage allowance applies for children paying half or more of the adult fare. Check with the airline for particulars.

Safety Seats The FAA recommends the use of safety seats aloft and details approved models in the free leaflet "**Child/Infant Safety Seats Recommended for Use in Aircraft**" (available from the Federal Aviation Administration, APA–200, 800 Independence Ave. SW, Washington, DC 20591, tel. 202/267–3479). Airline policy varies. U.S. carriers must allow FAA-approved models, but because these seats are strapped into a regular passenger seat, they may require that parents buy a ticket even for an infant under 2 who would otherwise ride free.

Facilities Aloft Airlines do provide other facilities and services for children, such as children's meals and freestanding bassinets (to those sitting in seats on the bulkhead, where there's enough legroom to accommodate them). Make your request when reserving. The annual February/March issue of *Family Travel Times* gives details of the children's services of dozens of airlines (*see below*). "Kids and Teens in Flight" (free from the U.S. Department of Transportation, tel. 202/366–2220) offers tips for children flying alone.

Publications *Family Travel Times,* published 10 times a year by Travel With
Newsletter   Your Children (TWYCH, 45 W. 18th St., 7th Floor Tower, New York, NY 10011, tel. 212/206–0688; annual subscription $55), covers destinations, types of vacations, and modes of travel; an airline issue comes out every other year (the last one, February/March 1993, is sold to nonsubscribers for $10). On Wednesday, the staff answers subscribers' questions on specific destinations.

Books *Great Vacations with Your Kids,* by Dorothy Jordan and Marjorie Cohen ($13; Penguin USA, 120 Woodbine St., Bergenfield, NJ 07621, tel. 800/253–6476), helps you plan your trip with children, from toddlers to teens. Traveling with Children—And Enjoying It, by Arlene K. Butler ($11.95 plus $3 shipping per book; Globe Pequot Press, Box 833, Old Saybrook, CT 06475, tel. 800/243–0495 or 800/962–0973 in CT), also geared to travel in general rather than specific destinations, discusses car, plane, and train travel, has useful pretrip checklists, and offers tips on how to cut costs and keep kids healthy and happy en route; its focus is largely domestic, but the information included would serve equally well abroad. From the same publisher is *Recommended Family Resorts in the United States, Canada, and the Caribbean,* by Jane Wilford with Janet Tice ($12.95), which describes 100 resorts at length and includes a "Children's World" section describing activities and facilities as part of each entry. *Innocents Abroad: Traveling with Kids in Europe,* by Valerie Wolf Deutsch and Laura Sutherland ($15.95 or $4.95 paperback, Penguin USA, *see above*), is a guide to child- and teen-friendly activities, food, and transportation in Britain and on the Continent, with sections on individual countries.

Tour Operators GrandTravel (6900 Wisconsin Ave., Suite 706, Chevy Chase, MD 20815, tel. 301/986–0790 or 800/247–7651) offers international and domestic tours for grandparents traveling with their grandchildren. The catalogue, as charmingly written and illustrated as a children's book, positively invites armchair traveling with lap-sitters aboard. **Rascals in Paradise** (650 5th St., Suite 505, San Francisco, CA 94107, tel. 415/978–9800 or 800/872–7225) specializes in programs for families.

Hints for Travelers with Disabilities

The Society for the Advancement of Travel for the Handicapped has named Hawaii the most accessible vacation spot for the disabled; the number of ramped visitor areas and specially equipped lodgings in the state attests to its desire to make everyone feel welcome.

Getting Around Several transportation options are available to Hawaii travelers with disabilities. For $1 a ride, city-run **Handi Vans** provides curb-to-curb service (tel. 808/924–VANS; pick up applications for service at satellite city halls or at the municipal office, 711 Kapiolani Blvd., Suite 275, Honolulu, HI 96813, tel. 808/523–4083). A private company, **HandiCabs of the Pacific** (Box 22428, Honolulu 96823, tel. 808/524–3866), offers van service on Oahu for a $9 curbside pickup charge plus $2.25 per mile. For both, 24-hour notice is required.

Those who prefer to do their own driving may rent hand-controlled cars from **Avis** (tel. 800/331–1212; reserve 24 hrs ahead) and **Hertz** (tel. 800/654–3131; 48-hr notice required). You can use the windshield car from your own state, or obtain a special local handicapped-parking pass at the accommodating **Department of Transportation Services** (650 S. King St., Honolulu 96813, tel. 808/523–4021), which is open weekdays 8–4.

Services Travelers may rent wheelchairs, walkers, oxygen, lifts, and overbed tables from **Abbey Medical** (500 Ala Kawa St., Honolulu 96817, tel. 808/845–5000). The company should be contacted in advance.

Organizations In Hawaii Several agencies and companies make helping travelers with disabilities their number one priority, including the **Commission on Persons with Disabilities** (5 Waterfront Plaza, 500 Ala Moana Blvd., Suite 210, Honolulu 96813, tel. 808/586–8121). Its *Aloha Guide for Persons with Disabilities* (pick it up for free in person or send $3 for postage and handling) includes addresses and telephone numbers of those providing support services, and rates the island's hotels, beaches, shopping centers, entertainment, and major visitor attractions for accessibility. For accessibility information about the Neighbor Islands, contact the commission on the Big Island (1190 Waianuenue Ave., Box 1641, Hilo 96820, tel. 808/933–4747); on Kauai (3060 Eiwa St., Room 207, Lihue 96766, tel. 808/241–3308); and on Maui (54 High St., Wailuku 96793, tel. 808/243–5441).

General Travel Assistance The **Information Center for Individuals with Disabilities** (Fort Point Pl., 27–43 Wormwood St., Boston, MA 02210, tel. 617/727–5540 or 800/462–5015 in MA between 11 and 4, or leave message; TDD/TTY tel. 617/345–9743) helps with problem-solving and publishes a monthly newsletter and numerous fact sheets, including the 10-page "Tips for Planning a Vacation" (with airlines' toll-free TDD numbers and sections on auto and van, bus, train, ship, and plane travel) and the state-by-state list of "Tour Operators, Travel Agencies, and Travel Resources for People with Disabilities" (23 pages at present). On out-of-state orders, enclose $2 per sheet for postage. **Mobility International USA** (Box 3551, Eugene, OR 97403, voice and TDD tel. 503/343–1284) is the U.S. branch of an international organization based in Britain (*see below*) and present in 30 countries. It coordinates exchange programs for disabled people, especially programs with an educational, work, or community-service component; provides travel information; and publishes and sells *A World of Options for the '90s*, a guide to travel for people with disabilities ($16). Annual membership costs $20 and includes a quarterly newsletter and access to a referral service. **MossRehab Hospital Travel Information Service** (1200 W. Tabor Rd., Philadelphia, PA 19141, tel. 215/456–9603, TDD tel. 215/456–9602) tries to get people started with their travel plans;

for a nominal postage and handling fee, it will send information on tourist sights, transportation, and accommodations in destinations around the world. The **Society for the Advancement of Travel for the Handicapped** (SATH, 347 5th Ave., Suite 610, New York, NY 10016, tel. 212/447–7284, fax 212/725–8253) provides lists of tour operators specializing in travel for the disabled, information sheets on traveling with specific disabilities and to specific countries, and a quarterly newsletter. Annual membership is $45, $25 for students and senior citizens. Nonmembers may send $3 and a self-addressed, stamped envelope for information on specific destinations. **Travel Industry and Disabled Exchange** (TIDE, 5435 Donna Ave., Tarzana, CA 91356, tel. 818/368–5648) supplies travel information and publishes a quarterly newsletter. Annual membership is $15; most members are travel suppliers (travel agents, cruise lines, etc.), but consumers are welcome. **Travelin' Talk** (Box 3534, Clarksville, TN 37043, tel. 615/552–6670) is a network of disabled people worldwide ready to provide the lowdown on accessibility in their area. To join, there is a one-time registration fee (on a sliding scale of $1–$10 for individuals, $15–$50 for organizations) that also entitles you to a quarterly newsletter.

In the United Kingdom Main sources include the **Royal Association for Disability and Rehabilitation** (RADAR, 25 Mortimer St., London W1N 8AB, tel. 071/637–5400), which publishes travel information for the disabled in Britain, and **Mobility International** (228 Borough High St., London SE1 1JX, tel. 071/403–5688), the headquarters of an international membership organization that serves as a clearinghouse of travel information for people with disabilities.

Travel Agencies and Tour Operators Directions Unlimited (720 N. Bedford Rd., Bedford Hills, NY 10507, tel. 914/241–1700), a travel agency, has expertise in tours and cruises for the disabled. Evergreen Travel Service (4114 198th St. SW, Suite 13, Lynnwood, WA 98036, tel. 206/776–1184 or 800/435–2288) operates Wings on Wheels Tours for those in wheelchairs, White Cane Tours for the blind, and tours for the deaf and makes group and independent arrangements for travelers with any disability. Flying Wheels Travel (143 W. Bridge St., Box 382, Owatonna, MN 55060, tel. 800/535–6790 or 800/722–9351 in MN), a tour operator and travel agency, arranges international tours, cruises, and independent travel itineraries for people with mobility disabilities. Nautilus, at the same address as TIDE (*see above*), packages tours for the disabled internationally.

Publications In addition to the fact sheets, newsletters, and books mentioned above are several free publications available from the Consumer Information Center (Pueblo, CO 81009): "New Horizons for the Air Traveler with a Disability," a U.S. Department of Transportation booklet describing changes resulting from the 1986 Air Carrier Access Act and those still to come from the 1990 Americans with Disabilities Act (include Department 608Y in the address), and the Airport Operators Council's Access Travel: Airports (Dept. 5804), which describes facilities and services for the disabled at more than 500 airports worldwide.

Twin Peaks Press (Box 129, Vancouver, WA 98666, tel. 206/694–2462 or 800/637–2256) publishes the *Directory of Travel Agencies for the Disabled* ($19.95), listing more than 370 agencies worldwide; *Travel for the Disabled* ($19.95), listing some

500 access guides and accessible places worldwide; the *Directory of Accessible Van Rentals* ($9.95) for campers and RV travelers worldwide; and *Wheelchair Vagabond* ($14.95), a collection of personal travel tips. Add $2 per book for shipping.

The **National Park Service** provides a **Golden Access Passport** free of charge to those who are blind or who have a permanent disability; the passport covers the entry fee for the holder and anyone accompanying the holder in the same private, noncommercial vehicle and a 50% discount on camping, boat launching, and parking. All charges are covered except lodging. Apply for the passport in person at any national recreation facility that charges an entrance fee; proof of disability is required. For additional information, write to the National Park Service (Box 37127, Washington, DC 20013-7127).

Hints for Older Travelers

Organizations The **American Association of Retired Persons** (AARP, 601 E St. NW, Washington, DC 20049, tel. 202/434–2277) provides independent travelers the Purchase Privilege Program, which offers discounts on hotels, car rentals, and sightseeing, and the AARP Motoring Plan, provided by Amoco, which furnishes domestic trip-routing information and emergency road-service aid for an annual fee of $39.95 per person or couple ($59.95 for a premium version). AARP also arranges group tours, cruises, and apartment living through AARP Travel Experience from American Express (400 Pinnacle Way, Suite 450, Norcross, GA 30071, tel. 800/927–0111); these can be booked through travel agents, except for the cruises, which must be booked directly (tel. 800/745–4567). AARP membership is open to those 50 and over; annual dues are $8 per person or couple.

Two other membership organizations offer discounts on lodgings, car rentals, and other travel products, along with such nontravel perks as magazines and newsletters. The **National Council of Senior Citizens** (1331 F St. NW, Washington, DC 20004, tel. 202/347–8800) is a nonprofit advocacy group with some 5,000 local clubs across the United States; membership costs $12 per person or couple annually. **Mature Outlook** (6001 N. Clark St., Chicago, IL 60660, tel. 800/336–6330), a Sears Roebuck & Co. subsidiary with 800,000 members, charges $9.95 for an annual membership.

Note: When using any senior-citizen identification card for reduced hotel rates, mention it when booking, not when checking out. At restaurants, show your card before you're seated; discounts may be limited to certain menus, days, or hours. If you are renting a car, ask about promotional rates that might improve on your senior-citizen discount.

Educational Travel **Elderhostel** (75 Federal St., 3rd floor, Boston, MA 02110, tel. 617/426–7788) is a nonprofit organization that has inexpensive study programs for people 60 and older since 1975. Programs take place at more than 1,800 educational institutions in the United States, Canada, and 45 countries overseas, and courses cover everything from marine science to Greek myths and cowboy poetry. Participants generally attend lectures in the morning and spend the afternoon sightseeing or on field trips; they live in dorms on the host campuses. Fees for programs in the United States, which usually last one week, run about $300, not including transportation.

Interhostel (University of New Hampshire, 6 Garrison Ave., Durham, NH 03824, tel. 800/733–9753), a slightly younger enterprise than Elderhostel, caters to a slightly younger clientele—that is, 50 and over—and runs programs overseas in some 25 countries. But the idea is similar: Lectures and field trips mix with sightseeing, and participants stay in dormitories at cooperating educational institutions or in modest hotels. Programs are usually two weeks in length and cost $1,500–$2,100, not including airfare from the United States.

Tour Operators **Saga International Holidays** (222 Berkeley St., Boston, MA 02116, tel. 800/343–0273), which specializes in group travel for people over 60, offers a selection of variously priced tours and cruises covering five continents. If you want to take your grandchildren, look into GrandTravel (*see* Traveling with Children, *above*).

Publications *The International Health Guide for Senior Citizen Travelers,* by W. Robert Lange, MD ($4.95 plus $1.50 for shipping; Pilot Books, 103 Cooper St., Babylon, NY 11702, tel. 516/422–2225), advises on pretrip planning and on traveling with specific medical conditions. It includes a list of what to pack in a basic medical travel kit and a chart showing how to adjust insulin dosages when flying across multiple time zones. *Get Up and Go* ($10.95 plus $1.75 postage, Gem Publishing Group, Box 50820, Reno, NV 89513, tel. 702/786–7419) is a 325-page handbook of travel tips and deals for Americans over 49; the same organization publishes the monthly *Mature Traveler* newsletter ($24.50 annually), covering senior travel bargains and programs.

Further Reading

Hawaii, by James A. Michener, ranks as one of the best novels from which to gain an overall historical perspective of the Islands. *Hawaii: An Uncommon History*, by Edward Joesting, gives a behind-the-scenes look at the factual side of some of the same events in the Michener novel. *A Voyage to the Pacific Ocean*, by Captain James Cook, ranks as one of the first guidebooks to the islands and still contains many valid insights; *Shoal of Time*, by Gavan Daws, chronicles Hawaiian history from Cook's time to the 1960s. Information concerning the gods and goddesses once thought to inhabit the region can be found in *Hawaiian Mythology*, by Martha Warren Beckwith. *Chanting the Universe*, by John Charlot, examines Hawaiian culture through its poetry and chants. Another level of early island spiritual life is recorded in the missionary memoirs titled *A Residency of Twenty-one Years in the Sandwich Islands*, by Hiram Bingham.

More recent history comes to life in the pages of *Travels in Hawaii*, by Robert Louis Stevenson, while *Stevenson in Hawaii*, by Sister Mary Martha McGaw, makes an interesting story of the traveling storyteller himself. *History Makers of Hawaii*, by A. Grove Day, provides a biographical dictionary of the key people who shaped the territory from past to present. A more recent view (1984) of the state comes from the text and photographs of *A Day in the Life of Hawaii*, by Rick Smolen and David Cohen.

Those interested in the physical attractions of the islands may want to read *A Guide to Tropical and Semitropical Flora*, by Loraine Kuck and Richard Tongg. The *Handbook of Hawaiian*

Fishes, by W. A. Gosline and Vernon Brock, is a must for snorkelers; *Hawaii's Birds* by the Hawaii Audubon Society is perfect for bird-watchers.

The athletic-minded might consider *Hawaiian Hiking Trails,* by Craig Chisholm, just the guide for day hikers and backpackers. *Surfing: The Ultimate Pleasure,* by Leonard Lueras, covers everything about the sport from its early history to the music and films of its later subculture.

If you want to prepare your palate for an upcoming Hawaiian visit, or have returned from the islands in love with haute Hawaiian cuisine, get Jean-Marie Josselin's *A Taste of Hawaii: New Cooking from the Crossroads of the Pacific,* published by Stewart, Tabori & Chang. This beautifully designed and photographed book features recipes for innovative Pacific Rim cooking.

The bimonthly *ALOHA Magazine* (subscription $17.97 per year; Box 3260, Honolulu 96801), a colorful magazine devoted to the 50th State, contains scenic photo essays and articles about history, arts, culture, sports, food, and fashion, as well as visitor attractions and a calendar of events. A sister publication, *Aloha Travelers' Newsletter* ($14.95 per year), contains travel tips and savings specifically aimed for Hawaii visitors. The beautifully rendered bimonthly *Hawaii Magazine* (U.S. subscription $12.99 per year; 3 Burroughs, Irvine, CA 92718) features articles about culture, customs, resorts, and dining in the islands.

Arriving and Departing

By Plane

Flights are either nonstop, direct, or connecting. A **nonstop** flight requires no change of plane and makes no stops. A **direct** flight stops at least once and can involve a change of plane, although the flight number remains the same; if the first leg is late, the second waits. This is not the case with a **connecting** flight, which involves a different plane and a different flight number. Note: PADI recommends that you not scuba dive and fly within a 24-hour period.

Airports Hawaii's major airport is **Honolulu International** (tel. 808/836–
Oahu 6411), about a five-hour flight from West Coast cities and a 20-minute drive from Waikiki. The facility was renovated in 1993 to help ease congestion. The Honolulu Airport is packed with shops perfect for last-minute buying: places where you can get a lei, a pineapple, T-shirts, and even Gucci bags. If you're flying from Honolulu to another island, you'll need to locate one of the two separate interisland terminals (one for Aloha Airlines and one for Hawaiian Airlines) to the left of the main terminal as you exit. A free Wiki Wiki Shuttle will take you to and from the interisland terminals; however, it's an easy five-minute walk between the international and the interisland terminals.

Maui Maui's efficient **Kahului Airport** (tel. 808/872–3803), in Maui's central town of Kahului, will spend the next several years undergoing renovation. Maui's other airport, the **Kapalua-West Maui Airport** (call either Aloha IslandAir or Hawaiian Airlines, *see* Interisland Flights, *below*) opened in 1987 and capably handles the traffic it gets. For visitors to West Maui, landing at the Kapalua facility is the easiest way to arrive. It saves about an hour's drive from the Kahului airport. The tiny town of **Hana** in east Maui also has an airstrip (tel. 808/248–8208), but it is only serviced by one commuter airline and one charter airline.

Kauai   On Kauai, visitors have a choice between the recently expanded **Lihue Airport** (tel. 808/246–1400), on the east side of the island, and **Princeville Airport** (tel. 808/826–3040), near the north shore. The main facility in Lihue has finished a major portion of its renovation, making it a dramatically new and clean airport, while the airstrip in Princeville is partly maintained by private funds and is the best way to reach hotels on Kauai's northern shore.

The Big Island of   Those flying to the Big Island can land at one of three fields.
Hawaii   Kona's **Keahole Airport** (tel. 808/329–2484), on the west side, best serves Kailua-Kona, Keauhou, and the Kohala Coast. **Hilo International Airport** (tel. 808/933–4782), formerly General Lyman Field, also is a large, new airport but is more appropriate for those going to the east side.

Lanai and Molokai   Nearby **Lanai** (tel. 808/565–6757) and **Molokai** (tel. 808/567–6140) airports are centrally located on those islands. Both are small, rural airports that can handle only a limited number of flights and planes per day.

From Mainland   Flying into Honolulu International Airport are **America West**
U.S.   (tel. 800/247–5692); **American** (tel. 800/433–7300); **Continental** (tel. 800/525–0280); **Delta** (tel. 800/221–1212); **Hawaiian** (tel. 800/ 367–5320); **Northwest** (tel. 800/225–2525); **TWA** (tel. 800/ 221–2000); and **United** (tel. 800/241–6522). Many of those flights originate in Los Angeles and San Francisco, but it's also possible to fly from Dallas, Chicago, St. Louis, New York, Seattle, Minneapolis, San Diego, and other gateways. United Airlines—which boasts some 50% of the airline traffic to Hawaii—flies directly into the Big Island's Keahole Airport, Maui's Kahului Airport, and Kauai's Lihue Airport.

International   Foreign air carriers are prohibited by law from serving Hawaii
Flights   from American cities. From other parts of the world, **Air New Zealand** (tel. 800/262–1234), **Canadian Airlines** (tel. 800/426–7000), **China Air Lines** (tel. 800/421–1289 or 800/227–5118), **Japan Air Lines** (tel. 800/525–3663), **Qantas** (tel. 800/227–4500), and others, fly to Honolulu.

From the United   **American, Continental, Delta,** and **TWA** are among the airlines
Kingdom   that fly from Britain to Honolulu. An APEX ticket is generally the least expensive way to fly, excluding bargain fares that are offered from time to time. Check the back pages of *Time Out* and the Sunday papers for good offers. **Trailfinders** (42–50 Earl's Court Rd., Kensington, London W8 6EJ, tel. 071/937–5400) can arrange flights.

Interisland Flights   While some national airlines make it possible to fly directly into Kauai, Maui, and the Big Island, most travelers still fly to Honolulu and connect with interisland shuttle flights. Aircraft vary in size from Boeing 737 jets to twin prop Cessna 402s. One advantage of the smaller planes is that they can land at some of the state's more remote airfields.

Aloha Airlines (tel. 800/367–5250) and **Hawaiian Airlines** (tel. 800/367–5320) serve Honolulu International (Oahu), Keahole and Hilo International Airport (the Big Island), Kahului

(Maui), and Lihue (Kauai). In addition, Hawaiian serves the Kapalua-West Maui, Molokai, and Lanai airports. **Island Air** (tel. 800/323–3345) serves Honolulu International, Kahului, and Hana (Maui), Kapalua (West Maui), Princeville (Kauai), Hoolehua and Kalaupapa (Molokai), and Lanai.

Cutting Flight Costs The Sunday travel section of most newspapers is a good source of deals. When booking, particularly through an unfamiliar company, call the Better Business Bureau to find out whether any complaints have been registered against the company, pay with a credit card if you can, and consider trip-cancellation and default insurance (*see* Insurance, *above*). *The Airline Passenger's Guerrilla Handbook*, by George Albert Brown ($14.95; Slawson Communications, Inc., 165 Vallecitos de Oro, San Marcos, CA 92069, tel. 619/744–2299 or 800/752–9766), may be out of date in a few areas but remains a solid source of information on every aspect of air travel, including finding the cheapest fares; it can turn a neophyte into a veteran in short order.

Promotional Airfares Most scheduled airlines offer three classes of service: first class, business class, and economy or coach. To ride in the first-class or business-class sections, you pay a first-class or business-class fare. To ride in the economy or coach section—the remainder of the plane—you pay a confusing variety of fares. Most expensive is full-fare economy or unrestricted coach, which can be bought one-way or round-trip and can be changed and turned in for a refund.

All the less expensive fares, called promotional or discount fares, are round-trip and involve restrictions. The exact nature of the restrictions depends on the airline, the route, and the season and on whether travel is domestic or international, but you must usually buy the ticket—commonly called an APEX (advance purchase excursion) when it's for international travel—in advance (seven, 14, or 21 days are usual). You must also respect certain minimum- and maximum-stay requirements (for instance, over a Saturday night or at least seven and no more than 30, 45, or 90 days), and you must be willing to pay penalties for changes. Airlines generally allow some changes for a fee. But the cheaper the fare, the more likely the ticket is nonrefundable; it would take a death in the family for the airline to give you any of your money back if you had to cancel. The cheapest fares are also subject to availability; because only a certain percentage of the plane's total seats will be sold at that price, they may go quickly.

Consolidators Consolidators or bulk-fare operators—also known as bucket shops—buy blocks of seats on scheduled flights that airlines anticipate they won't be able to sell. They pay wholesale prices, add a markup, and resell the seats to travel agents or directly to the public at prices that still undercut the airline's promotional or discount fares. You pay more than on a charter but ordinarily less than for an APEX ticket, and, even when there is not much of a price difference, the ticket usually comes without the advance-purchase restriction. Moreover, although tickets are marked nonrefundable so you can't turn them in to the airline for a full-fare refund, some consolidators sometimes give you your money back. Carefully read the fine print detailing penalties for changes and cancellations. If you doubt the reliability of a company, call the airline once you've made your booking and confirm that you do, indeed, have a reservation on the flight.

The biggest U.S. consolidator, C.L. Thomson Express, sells only to travel agents. Well-established consolidators selling to the public include **UniTravel** (Box 12485, St. Louis, MO 63132, tel. 314/569–0900 or 800/325–2222); **Council Charter** (205 E. 42nd St., New York, NY 10017, tel. 212/661–0311 or 800/800–8222), a division of the Council on International Educational Exchange and a longtime charter operator now functioning more as a consolidator; and **Travac** (989 6th Ave., New York, NY 10018, tel. 212/563–3303 or 800/872–8800), also a former charterer.

Charter Flights Charters usually have the lowest fares and the most restrictions. Departures are limited and seldom on time, and you can lose all or most of your money if you cancel. (Generally, the closer to departure you cancel, the more you lose, although sometimes you will be charged only a small fee if you supply a substitute passenger.) The charterer, on the other hand, may legally cancel the flight for any reason up to 10 days before departure; within 10 days of departure, the flight may be canceled only if it becomes physically impossible to operate it. The charterer may also revise the itinerary or increase the price after you have bought the ticket, but if the new arrangement constitutes a "major change," you have the right to a refund. Before buying a charter ticket, read the fine print for the company's refund policy and details on major changes. Money for charter flights is usually paid into a bank escrow account, the name of which should be on the contract. If you don't pay by credit card, make your check payable to the escrow account (unless you're dealing with a travel agent, in which case, his or her check should be payable to the escrow account). The Department of Transportation's Consumer Affairs Office (I–25, Washington, DC 20590, tel. 202/366–2220) can answer questions on charters and send you its "Plane Talk: Public Charter Flights" information sheet.

Charter operators may offer flights alone or with ground arrangements that constitute a charter package. Well-established charter operators include **Council Charter** (205 E. 42nd St., New York, NY 10017, tel. 212/661–0311 or 800/800–8222), now largely a consolidator, despite its name, and **Travel Charter** (1120 E. Long Lake Rd., Troy, MI 48098, tel. 313/528–3570 or 800/521–5267), with Midwestern departures. **DER Tours** (Box 1606, Des Plains, IL 60017, tel. 800/782–2424), a charterer and consolidator, sells through travel agents.

Discount Travel Travel clubs offer their members unsold space on airplanes, *Clubs* cruise ships, and package tours at nearly the last minute and at well below the original cost. Suppliers thus receive some revenue for their "leftovers," and members get a bargain. Membership generally includes a regular bulletin or access to a toll-free telephone hot line giving details of available trips departing anywhere from three or four days to several months in the future. Packages tend to be more common than flights alone, so if airfares are your only interest, read the literature before joining. Reductions on hotels are also available. Clubs include **Discount Travel International** (114 Forrest Ave., Suite 203, Narberth, PA 19072, tel. 215/668–7184; $45 annually, single or family), **Moment's Notice** (425 Madison Ave., New York, NY 10017, tel. 212/486–0503; $45 annually, single or family), **Travelers Advantage** (CUC Travel Service, 49 Music Sq. W, Nashville, TN 37203, tel. 800/548–1116; $49 annually, single or family), and **Worldwide Discount Travel Club** (1674 Meridian Ave., Miami Beach, FL 33139, tel. 305/534–2082; $50 annually for family, $40 single).

Smoking Smoking is banned on all domestic flights of less than six hours' duration; the ban also applies to domestic segments of international flights aboard U.S. and foreign carriers. On U.S. carriers flying overseas, a seat in a no-smoking section must be provided for every passenger who requests one, and the section must be enlarged to accommodate such passengers if necessary as long as they have complied with the airline's deadline for check-in and seat assignment. If smoking bothers you, request a seat far from the smoking section.

Foreign airlines are exempt from these rules but do provide no-smoking sections, and some nations, including Canada as of July 1, 1993, have gone as far as to ban smoking on all domestic flights; other countries may ban smoking on flights of less than a specified duration. The International Civil Aviation Organization has set July 1, 1996, as the date to ban smoking aboard airlines worldwide, but the body has no power to enforce its decisions.

Lei Greeting When you walk off a long flight from the mainland, perhaps a bit groggy and stiff from at least 4½ hours in the air, nothing quite compares with a Hawaiian lei greeting. The casual ceremony ranks as one of the fastest ways to make the transition from the worries of home to the joys of your vacation. Unfortunately, the state of Hawaii cannot bedeck each of its 6-million-plus annual visitors. Still, it's possible to arrange for a lei ceremony for yourself or your companions before you arrive. At least 10 companies make lei greetings all or at least part of their businesses. Try contacting **Greeters of Hawaii** (Box 29638, Honolulu 96820, tel. 808/834–7667, fax 800/736–5665), the oldest greeting company in the islands, or one of the more recent arrivals, such as **Aloha Lei Greeters** (Box 29133, Honolulu 96820, tel. 800/367–5255) or **Kamaaina Leis, Flowers & Greeters** (Aloha Reservations, 3159B Koapaka St., Honolulu 96819, tel. 800/367–5183). Prices for the flower necklaces range from about $10 to $40; 24 hours' notice is suggested.

By Ship

When Pan Am's amphibious *Hawaii Clipper* touched down on Pearl Harbor's waters in 1936, it marked the beginning of the end of regular passenger ship travel to the islands. From that point on, the predominant means of transporting visitors would be by air, not by sea. Today, however, cruising to Hawaii still holds a special appeal for those with the time and money to afford sailing, and with a bit of work, you can arrange passage aboard the luxury liners that call on Honolulu when traveling the seven seas.

No regularly scheduled American ships steam between the mainland and Hawaii. Although foreign-owned vessels often ply the Pacific, the Jones Act of 1896 prohibits them from carrying passengers between two U.S. ports unless the ships first stop at an intervening foreign port or carry the passengers to a foreign destination. What that means to those wishing for the relaxing ways of ship travel is that they'll have to book with one of the major lines passing through Honolulu. For details, check with such lines as **Cunard** (tel. 800/221–4770), **Hol-**

land American (tel. 800/426–0327), and Royal Viking (tel. 800/ 422–8000).

Cruises within the islands are available on the 800-passenger twin ships the SS *Constitution* and the SS *Independence*, under the direction of American Hawaii Cruises (550 Kearny St., San Francisco, CA 94108, tel. 800/765–7000). Both ships offer seven-day cruises that originate in Honolulu and visit the Big Island, Maui, and Kauai. American Hawaii also sells three and four-day packages with fewer stops.

Staying in Hawaii

Getting Around by Car

Your mainland driver's license is valid in Hawaii for up to 90 days. Be sure to buckle up. Hawaii has a strictly enforced seat-belt law for front-seat passengers. Children under age 3 must be in a car seat (available for a fee from car-rental agencies). Highway speeds are 55 mph; in-town traffic moves from 25 to 40 mph. Jaywalking is very common, so be particularly watchful for pedestrians, especially in congested areas such as Waikiki.

It's difficult to get lost in most of Hawaii. Roads and streets, although they may challenge the visitor's tongue (Kalanianaole Highway, for example), are well-marked. Keep an eye open for the Hawaii Visitor Bureau's red-caped warrior signs that mark major visitor attractions and scenic spots. Free visitor publications that contain good-quality maps can be found on all islands. Pick up several and choose the route that best suits your needs and destination.

Asking for directions will almost always produce a helpful explanation from the locals, but you should be prepared for an island term or two. Instead of compass directions, Hawaii residents refer to places as being either *mauka* (toward the mountains) or *makai* (toward the ocean) from one another. Other directions depend on your location: in Honolulu, for example, people say to "go Diamond Head," which means toward the famous landmark, or to "go *ewa*," meaning the opposite direction. A shop on the mauka-Diamond Head corner of a street is on the mountain side of the street on the corner closest to Diamond Head. It all makes perfect sense once you get the lay of the land.

Technically, the Big Island of Hawaii is the only island you can completely circle by car, but each island offers plenty of sightseeing from its miles of roadways. Oahu can be circled except for the roadless west-shore area around Kaena Point. Elsewhere, major highways follow the shoreline and traverse the island at two points. Rush-hour traffic (6:30–8:30 AM and 3:30–6 PM) can be frustrating around Honolulu and the outlying areas. Parking along many streets is curtailed during those times, and towing is strictly practiced. Read the curbside parking signs before leaving your vehicle, even at a meter.

Kauai has a well-maintained highway running south from Lihue to Barking Sands Beach; a spur at Waimea takes you along Waimea Canyon to Kokee State Park. A northern route also winds its way from Lihue to end at Haena, the beginning of the rugged and roadless Na Pali Coast. Maui also has its share of impenetrable areas, although four-wheel-drive vehicles rarely run into problems on the island. Saddle roads run between the east and west land masses composing Maui. Although Molokai and Lanai have fewer roadways, car rental is still worthwhile and will allow plenty of interesting sightseeing. Opt for a four-wheel-drive vehicle if dirt road exploration holds any appeal.

Radio Stations

Most Hawaiians wake up with Perry and Price on **KSSK AM 590** or **FM 92**. The lively duo provide news, traffic, and weather reports between "easy listening music" and phone calls from listeners from 5 AM to 10 AM.

For contemporary hits, turn to **KIKI/HOT 94 FM, KQMQ AM 690** or **FM 93.1**; both stations also regularly report surf conditions. If it's high-voltage rock-and-roll you're after, tune into **KPOI FM 98**. Country-western sounds come from **KDEO AM 94**, and contemporary Hawaiian music is on **KCCN AM 1420**.

Hawaii's Public Radio stations on Oahu are **KIFO FM 1380** (news); **KIPO FM 89.3** (jazz); **KHPR FM 88.1** (classical music); and on Maui, **KKUA FM 90.7** (classical).

Shopping

Next to relaxing on the beach and eating, shopping is probably the most popular activity among Hawaii tourists. That may be less of a reflection on the visitors themselves than on the variety of products available in the islands. Where else in the world, for example, could you find a strip of shops, all in one place, that sells rare black coral jewelry, University of Waikiki T-shirts, and intricately etched scrimshaw pieces?

Retail outlets abound in the Aloha State. You'll find someone selling something whether you're in the large city of Honolulu on Oahu or the town of Hanalei on Kauai. One-stop shopping malls are prevalent, although not in the same numbers as those in many mainland destinations. On Oahu, Ala Moana Center is one of the largest shopping spots; it's within easy walking distance of Waikiki. The Royal Hawaiian Shopping Center is centrally located in Waikiki itself. Farther away, you'll find Ward Warehouse, the Kahala Mall, and Pearlridge Center.

The Neighbor Islands offer more in the way of smaller strips of shops. Still, it's possible to find larger stores grouped in areas such as Kauai's Kukui Grove Center in Lihue, Maui's Kahului Shopping Center, and the Big Island's Prince Kuhio Mall in Hilo. Exclusive shops can often be found in the lobbies of the luxury hotels on all islands.

See the individual island chapters for more specific shopping information.

Aloha Wear Aloha shirts and muumuus are standard businesswear on Friday of every work week, so you're sure to find plenty of shops selling high-quality prints. In fact, it's nearly impossible to walk through any shopping area without coming upon at least one store selling the clothing. Liberty House, Sears, and JC Penney department stores offer a wide selection of the latest styles. A number of new designers sell their originals from small shops in Waikiki, Lahaina, and other major destinations.

Great deals on slightly worn older styles can be picked up in secondhand stores throughout the state.

Coral Jewelry "Going to great depths for the customer" is no exaggeration when it comes to coral jewelry. Island divers bring up the raw materials for the black, pink, and gold coral trinkets from the bottom of the sea. Honolulu's Maui Divers of Hawaii (*see* Shopping in Chapter 3) offers tours of its design center, as well as a large showroom of rings and necklaces. Shops throughout the islands carry this jewelry.

Kona Coffee The country's only commercial coffee plantations are found on the western slopes of the Big Island, which is also the best place in the state to buy the rich roasted Kona coffee beans. If you want the strongest java, go for pure Kona coffee; Kona blends are often sold, with little distinction made for the buyer.

Macadamia Nuts Also grown on the Big Island, macadamia nuts are among the richest and most delicious foodstuffs in Hawaii. You'll find them everywhere and in every way—from chocolate-covered to chopped for cookie filling. Supermarkets and convenience stores statewide sell the nuts in small tins and larger cans.

Pineapples Nothing, visitors claim, evokes the real Hawaii like the taste of a locally grown pineapple. Taking the fruit of the islands home with you is simple: You may either purchase the fruit in a shop or grocery store, or buy it preboxed, for a slightly higher price, from the vendors at Honolulu International Airport.

T-shirts Hawaii must surely be the T-shirt capital of the Pacific, providing plenty of inexpensive souvenirs and gifts for island visitors. Everything from "Hang Loose" to "Don't Worry—Be Happy" can be found in local shops. Sidewalk artists in Waikiki and smaller Neighbor Island towns will airbrush a custom T-shirt design for a higher price. The least expensive shirts can be found in convenience stores and F. W. Woolworth, which often sell them two- and three-for-the-price-of-one.

Wood Products Attractive trays, bowls, furniture, and other products are among the wonderful creations wrought from island woods. Shops in towns around the state have a wide selection and can put you in touch with woodworkers who specialize in custom pieces. Rich koa (the wood favored for outrigger canoes), mango, milo, and monkeypod are the favorites of local craftsmen. Because the great koa forests are dwindling, visitors might consider buying only antique koa products.

Beaches

Ask people why they vacation in Hawaii and most of them will tell you they go there for the beaches. The 50th State boasts some of the most beautiful stretches of sand and surf in the world, and with the short travel distances, they are never far away. All beaches are open to the public.

Oahu's **Waikiki Beach** is nearly synonymous with Hawaii. Stretching from the Hilton Hawaiian Village to the foot of Diamond Head, the strip still ranks as the premier place to soak up the sun. Waikiki Beach, as most people know it, is actually a collection of smaller areas such as Fort De Russy, Gray's, and Queen's Surf beaches. By whatever name, though, it's tough to beat Waikiki in terms of convenience to the hotels, restaurants, and shopping.

Oahu offers an array of other sandy seashores. The North Shore's **Sunset Beach** is famous in the surfing world; **Kailua Beach Park** has hosted windsurfing athletes for international competition; and **Makapuu Beach,** near Sea Life Park, has some of the best bodysurfing to be found in the state.

Neighbor Island beaches hold equal attraction. The Big Island lures beach bums and beauties with its unique and diverse collections of sand. There visitors can wiggle their toes in everything from the sparkling white sands of **Hapuna Beach** to the green- and black-sand beaches near the southeastern town of **Kalapana.** The Big Island also has the newest beaches in the state—black-sand stretches that form as hot lava from the active Kilauea volcano flows into the sea.

The nearby luxury hotels of Maui's **Kaanapali Beach** make it a fine place to get a tan while watching for movie stars and other celebrities. **Hookipa Beach Park,** near the town of Paia, has become known as the Mecca of windsurfing, and is as likely to be full of European and Japanese sailors as Hawaiians.

Molokai has several uncrowded beaches, but perhaps the most sensational on the island is the 3-mile-long **Papohaku Beach,** the largest white-sand beach in the state. Across the Kalohi Channel, the south shore of Lanai offers **Hulopoe Beach,** with its excellent snorkeling opportunities.

Kauai's south shore has **Poipu Beach Park,** popular with bodysurfers and sunbathers. On the opposite side of the island is **Lumahai,** a small beach rimmed in black lava and vegetation that proved the perfect setting for the movie *South Pacific.*

Families and singles alike use all of Hawaii's beaches together, and seldom will anyone feel out of place at any area. What can be found in the way of facilities, however, will vary greatly from place to place. Most areas have fresh running water, bath and changing rooms, and outside showers. Picnic tables are less common. Hawaii's beaches are clean compared to other coastal areas, and visitors are asked to do their part in keeping them that way.

As with any sort of water-related activity, swimming and wading from Hawaii's beaches should be approached with caution until you are familiar with the local conditions. Forceful waves and undertows can surprise even experienced swimmers. Swimming is always at your own risk, and prudence should be the rule. Those guidelines extend to other ocean activities as well. More popular areas offer equipment rentals for windsurfing, snorkeling, sailing, and parasailing, but participants should be well aware of the dangers present in venturing into unknown waters.

See the individual island chapters for detailed information on beaches.

Sports and the Outdoors

Bicycling   Hawaii's near-perfect climate makes for ideal cycling conditions. Match that with the well-maintained coast-hugging roadways, and you come up with an exciting place for a cycling vacation. All of Hawaii is accessible to cyclists, but the Big Island, with its extra mileage, offers the best bet when it comes to long-distance tours. On Maui, a number of firms offer down-hill rides from the top of Haleakala.

Fishing Hawaii residents know how to take advantage of the waters surrounding their state, and they'll pass on their fishing secrets to anyone with an interest in hooks, lines, and sinkers. The biggest lure to visiting fishing enthusiasts is the deep-sea fishing for marlin, especially off the shores of the Big Island. Each morning an entire fleet of sportfishing boats leaves Kona in search of the elusive gamefish. If the marlin aren't biting, reels are often whining with catches of local *ahi* (tuna) or *opakapaka* (blue snapper).

Golf The large number of luxury hotels and resorts in the 50th State provide an instant tip about the prevalence of golf courses. One cruise-ship company even goes so far as to offer its passengers a round of golf at a course on a different island each day of the sail. Whether you want to tee off on the latest course designed by Arnold Palmer or play 18 holes overlooking wave-crashing coastline, Hawaii has the course for you. Some of Hawaii's top spots for golfing include the courses at the Sheraton Makaha Resort and the Turtle Bay Hilton on Oahu; the courses at the Mauna Kea Beach Resort and the Mauna Lani Resort on the Big Island; the Royal Kaanapali Golf Course and the Kapalua Golf Club on Maui; and the Princeville Makai Course on Kauai.

Hiking The ancient Hawaiians blazed a wide variety of trails across their island domains, and many of these paths can still be hiked today. The state offers trails through rain forests, along palm-lined beaches, and around volcanic landscapes, such as Diamond Head on Oahu, Hawaii Volcanoes National Park on the Big Island, and Haleakala National Park on Maui.

Horseback Riding Riders may saddle up on all the major islands for guided horseback trips through a range of terrain. Two recommended rides explore Maui's Haleakala Crater or Kauai's south shore.

Hunting Deer, wild boar, bighorn sheep, mountain goat, turkey, and a variety of game birds can be hunted in Hawaii. The Big Island and Lanai are the two prime hunting grounds, where a number of guide services offer day trips. Rifles, shotguns, and archery equipment may be rented on-site.

Snow Skiing Believe it or not, you can ski in Hawaii—atop the Big Island's Mauna Kea volcano. Because of the fickleness of the snowfall, guide companies melt away faster than a snowball in Hana. As soon as one operator fades from the scene, however, another seems to come along for a shot at running what has to be one of the world's most unique ski areas. December–February is your best bet for skiing Hawaiian-style.

Surfing Hawaii names such as the Bonzai Pipeline and Sunset Beach are to surfers what the Super Bowl and the Astrodome are to football players. Little surprise then that surf enthusiasts from around the world come to Hawaii to ride the waves. Waikiki Beach is probably the best spot for first-time surfers to pick up the basics; Oahu's North Shore makes for excellent viewing of the veterans, especially during the December–January period of high surf.

Tennis The court sport is popular at many island hotels and condominiums. Forget your racquet? No problem. The accompanying pro shops and retail centers will be happy to rent the latest to you and will even offer a brushup lesson if you need it.

Waterskiing   Skimming across the water's surface in Hawaii usually translates into surfing, but waterskiing also has its fans in the state.
Oahu and Maui offer ocean skiing; companies on Kauai offer ski
trips up and down the Wailua River near Lihue.

Windsurfing   Hawaii's steady winds and surf conditions have helped to make
it one of the premier windsurfing spots around the globe. To-
day, the world's fastest growing sport can be seen and experienced throughout the state, with Oahu and Maui attracting
the best athletes. Beginning, intermediate, and advanced
equipment can be rented from a variety of shops, and lessons
abound.

Diving

Hawaii is now rated the fourth most popular scuba diving destination worldwide. Some 60,000 certified divers visit the islands
each year, and another 55,000 experience their first dive here.
Snorkeling is also extremely popular, and more than 125,000
people arrange snorkeling charters annually. More than 60
dive operations have emerged in response to the increasing de-
mands of visiting divers seeking underwater adventure.

Those who've peered beneath the ocean's surface around the
world say that the Hawaiian Islands have some of the most
spectacular underwater scenery anywhere. As the islands
emerged many millions of years ago, molten lava spilled into
the sea, cooling instantly to form huge cavernous rooms, mammoth archways, tall pinnacles needling skyward, and networks
of tunnels called lava tubes. Corals developed, beginning the
food chain for many other marine organisms. Today, more than
600 species of tropical fish thrive in Hawaiian waters. Nearly a
third of these fish can be found *only* in Hawaii.

A number of marine preserves scattered throughout the islands provide safe homes for marine life. No fishing or taking of
shells is allowed in these areas. Fish have become extremely
tame and will follow divers and snorkelers for handouts of
bread or frozen peas. Several areas are common ground for
green sea turtles who spend much of their time sleeping under
ledges but will wake to the passing sound of bubbles.

Because of the islands' remoteness from other land masses, Hawaii is an oasis in the sea for larger pelagic (ocean-going) marine life. Spinner dolphins often trailblaze ahead of the boat
bow en route to dive sites. Several species of shark inhabit Hawaiian waters. White tip sharks rest under ledges and in lava
tubes. Rarely seen whale sharks exceeding 50 feet in length
come into shallower depths to bask in the sun-warmed surface,
and manta rays and spotted eagle rays sail gracefully through
the sunlight-shafted waters.

Hawaiian waters are well known for the humpback whales that
make their seasonal trek from Alaska to the islands between
November and May. These are most often spotted from dive
boats, and divers can hear their haunting songs underwater.

Hawaii's numerous shipwrecks make for great diving, as do the
wrecks of airplanes and World War II tanks that sit as watery
monuments to islands' war years.

Although hundreds of sites have become dive favorites, much
of the water around the islands remains rarely seen and ripe for

exploration. The most popular dive sites tend to be on the south and west shores—the lee sides—protected from the trade winds. Dive sites along the north and east shorelines become accessible during the summer months when the large winter surf subsides. Throughout the islands, water visibility often exceeds 100 feet and water temperature remains a comfortable 75–80 degrees year-round.

For More Information A comprehensive 24-page guide to dive spots also lists dive shops. To obtain the guide, send $2 to University of Hawaii (Seagrant Extension, MSB, 1000 Pope Rd., Honolulu, HI 96822).

National and State Parks

Like many other states, Hawaii has sought to protect some of its natural beauty by designating portions of its property national and state parkland. The islands have seven national parks, national historic parks, and national memorials. There are also 76 state parks and historic sites throughout the chain.

National Parks Hawaii's two national parks are the Big Island's **Hawaii Volcanoes National Park,** with 207,643 acres, and Maui's 27,350-acre **Haleakala National Park.** Both offer excellent views and opportunities to learn about volcanoes and their role in the formation of the islands. As of January 1993, Kilauea volcano in Hawaii Volcanoes National Park was continuing on its eleventh year of uninterrupted eruption. Helicopter tours over the active volcano represent the best way to see the action. Several of the roads into the area have been closed because they were overrun with flowing lava. Maui's Haleakala, which means "house of the sun," draws a large number of tours and individuals who make the two-hour drive to the summit to see the sun rise each morning. Any time of day, however, will find plenty of sights on, in, and around the dormant volcano.

The Big Island encompasses three other national areas: **Kaloko-Honokohau National Historical Park,** a royal fish pond area; **Puuhonua o Honaunau National Historical Park,** better known as the City of Refuge; and **Puukohola Heiau National Historic Site,** an ancient worship place. Molokai's **Kalaupapa National Historical Park,** site of Father Damien's leper colony, and the USS *Arizona* **Memorial** at Pearl Harbor on Oahu round out the national selection.

Federal park information may be obtained from the **National Park Service** (300 Ala Moana Blvd., Suite 6305, Box 50165, Honolulu, 96850, tel. 808/541–2693).

State Parks State parks range in size from the 2½-acre wayside stop at Oahu's **Nuuanu Pali Lookout** to the 6,175-acre **Na Pali Coast State Park** on Kauai. Falling somewhere in between are other popular state areas including Maui's haunting **Iao Valley State Monument,** Kauai's **Kokee State Park** and the **Wailua River State Park,** and the Big Island's **Hapuna Beach State Recreation Area**—site of what is often claimed to be the prettiest beach on that island.

Details of state parks and historic areas come from the **District Office of the Hawaii Department of Land and Natural Resources,** Division of State Parks (1151 Punchbowl St., Room 310, Honolulu 96813, tel. 808/587–0300).

Dining

Honolulu ranks in the top five cities nationally in the propensity of its residents to dine out, and restaurateurs there and throughout the islands have been quick to take the hint and fulfill the need for good food. The result is a large number of restaurants, cafés, and other eateries, which makes it easy to find food service but difficult to decide among all the options.

Hawaii's melting-pot population also accounts for its great variety of epicurean delights. In addition to American and Continental cuisines, you can choose from Hawaiian, Thai, Korean, Japanese, Chinese, Philippine, Vietnamese, and other kinds of cooking as well. Such diversity need not cause indigestion; it just means you'll have that much more to sample from the international buffet Hawaii offers.

Hawaiian food, obviously, has a loyal following among visitors to the state. Many rate their trip to a luau among the highlights of their stay. Delicacies you're likely to find at one of these outdoor feasts include the traditional *kalua*—pig, often roasted underground in an *imu* (oven); *poi*, the starchy, bland paste made from the taro root; and *laulau*—fish, meat, and other ingredients wrapped and steamed in ti leaves. Luaus are presented at many hotels and visitor attractions around the state, or you can ask most any local for directions to a favorite Hawaiian-style feast.

With the heavy influx of Japanese into Hawaii, you'll find ample opportunity to sample foodstuffs from the land of the rising sun. Sushi (sliced raw fish and seafood served on balls of vinegared rice) and sashimi (raw fish without the rice) make the biggest hits. Other favorites include miso soup and tempuras, a variety of fish and vegetables deep fried with a light batter coating. Thai cuisine also has its fans in Hawaii. First-timers will be amazed at the interesting sauces and flavors—as well as such dish names as Evil Jungle Prince—that the cooks can concoct from a few simple ingredients.

Rest assured you'll also find plenty in the way of Continental offerings. Nearly every European country is represented in island dining circles, from Austria to Spain, Italy to Switzerland. Almost all luxury hotels have at least one gourmet dining spot for Continental cuisine, and a healthy number of independent operations can be found as well.

A word of caution concerning the origins of the seafood served in Hawaii: Although the state's surrounded by water, don't be surprised to find that many of the *fruits de mer* come to the islands the same way you did—by airplane. Several varieties of local tuna, dolphin (not porpoise), and snapper can be found under such names as *ahi*, *mahimahi*, and *opakapaka*, respectively; and lobster, the clawless species known as spiny lobster, is also taken from the local reefs. Trout, oysters, and other ocean dwellers, however, have most likely been caught somewhere else, although some of these species are now commercially raised at Keahole on the Big Island.

Lodging

Hotels Hawaii hosts most of the nationwide and worldwide hotel operators within its chain of islands. Hilton, Sheraton, Westin,

Hyatt, Four Seasons, Marriott, Ritz-Carlton, Embassy Suites, and others operate or have plans to open resorts within the state. A number of large, locally based operators, such as Aston Hotels and Resorts and Outrigger Hotels Hawaii, round out the accommodations scene, and a number of independents also have loyal followings. The result is an extensive range of rooms, from rock-bottom economy units to suites fit for, and occasionally used by, kings.

Condominiums Hawaii is known for developing the resort condominium concept in the early 1970s, and the destination continues to maintain its status as a leader in the field. Condominiums, from simple studios to multiroom spreads, are now available on all islands. Besides large living areas and full kitchens, many condos have recently begun offering front-desk and daily maid services just like their hotel counterparts. Nearly 100 companies in Hawaii and around the United States rent out condominium space in the islands. Your travel agent will be the most helpful in finding the condo you desire.

Bed-and-Breakfasts B&Bs have made heavy inroads into the Hawaiian market in the past several years. It's now possible to find the combination room-and-meal lodgings throughout the state. Operations range from beachside rooms on Maui to comfortable accommodations bordering the Big Island's Hawaii Volcanoes National Park. Most operators advertise their own lodgings, but three centralized booking services, **Bed and Breakfast Hawaii** (Box 449, Kapaa 96746, tel. 800/733–1632), **Pacific Hawaii Bed and Breakfast** (19 Kainani Pl., Kailua, HI 96734, tel. 808/262–6026 or 800/999–6026), and **Bed and Breakfast Honolulu** (statewide) (3242 Kaohinani Dr., Honolulu 96817, tel. 800/288–4666), list a variety of properties.

Apartment, Villa, and House Rentals If you want a home base that's roomy enough for a family and comes with cooking facilities, a furnished rental may be the solution. It's generally cost-wise, too, although not always—some rentals are luxury properties (economical only when your party is large). Home-exchange directories do list rentals—often second homes owned by prospective house swappers—and there are services that will not only look for a house or apartment for you (even a castle if that's your fancy), but also handle the paperwork. Some send an illustrated catalogue and others send photographs of specific properties, sometimes at a charge; up-front registration fees may apply.

More than 15 companies act as rental agents for Hawaii houses; some, such as **Villas of Hawaii** (4218 Waialae Ave., Suite 203, Honolulu 96816, tel. 800/522–3030) offer accommodations on Oahu, Maui, the Big Island, and Kauai, while such others as **Hawaiian Properties Ltd.** (1784 Ala Moana Blvd., Honolulu 96815, tel. 808/955–3341) offer listings only on Oahu.

In addition, there are a number of international companies, including **Rent a Home International** (7200 34th Ave. NW, Seattle, WA 98117, tel. 206/789–9377 or 800/488–7368); **Vacation Home Rentals Worldwide** (235 Kensington Ave., Norwood, NJ 07648, tel. 201/767–9393 or 800/633–3284); **Villa Leisure** (Box 209, Westport, CT 06881, tel. 407/624–9000 or 800/526–4244); and **Villas International** (605 Market St., Suite 510, San Francisco, CA 94105, tel. 415/281–0910 or 800/221–2260).

Camping and RV Facilities Camping offers an inexpensive alternative to high-priced accommodations and allows the opportunity to appreciate Hawaii's great outdoors. A variety of national, state, and county parks are available, some with bathroom and cooking facilities, others a bit more primitive. The National Park Service and Division of State Parks of the Hawaii Department of Land and Natural Resources (*see above*) can provide more information; details on county camping are available from the individual counties. The **City and County of Honolulu** (tel. 808/523–4525) can provide addresses and telephone numbers for the neighboring counties. You can pack up your own sleeping bag and bring it along, or you can rent camping equipment at companies such as **Omar the Tent Man** (650A Kakoi St., Honolulu 96819, tel. 808/836–8785), on Oahu; **Pacific Rent-All** (1080 Kilauea Ave., Hilo 96720, tel. 808/935–2974), on the Big Island; and **Jungle Bob's** (Box 1245, Hanalei 96714, tel. 808/826–6664), on Kauai.

Home Exchange This is obviously an inexpensive solution to the lodging problem, because house-swapping means living rent-free. You find a house, apartment, or other vacation property to exchange for your own by becoming a member of a home-exchange organization, which then sends you its annual directories listing available exchanges and includes your own listing in at least one of them. Arrangements for the actual exchange are made by the two parties to it, not by the organization. Principal clearinghouses include **Intervac U.S./International Home Exchange** (Box 590504, San Francisco, CA 94159, tel. 415/435–3497), the oldest, with thousands of foreign and domestic homes for exchange in its three annual directories; membership is $62, or $72 if you want to receive the directories but remain unlisted. The **Vacation Exchange Club** (Box 650, Key West, FL 33041, tel. 800/638–3841), also with thousands of foreign and domestic listings, publishes four annual directories plus updates; the $50 membership includes your listing in one book. **Loan-a-Home** (2 Park La., Apt. 6E, Mount Vernon, NY 10552, tel. 914/664–7640) specializes in long-term exchanges; there is no charge to list your home, but the directories cost $35 or $45 depending on the number you receive.

Credit Cards

The following credit card abbreviations are used in this guide: AE, American Express; D, Discover; DC, Diners Club; MC, MasterCard; V, Visa.

39

2 Portraits of Hawaii

Hawaiian History at a Glance: A Chronology

c. AD 500 The first human beings to set foot on Hawaiian shores are Polynesians, who travel 2,000 miles in 60- to 80-foot canoes to the islands they name *Havaiki* after their legendary homeland. Researchers today believe they were originally from Southeast Asia, and that they discovered the South Pacific Islands of Tahiti and the Marquesas before ending up in Hawaii.

c. 1750 Kamehameha, the Hawaiian chief who unified the Islands, is born.

1778 In January, British Captain James Cook, commander of the HMS *Resolution* and the consort vessel HMS *Discovery*, lands on the island of Kauai and "discovers" it for the Western world. He names the archipelago the Sandwich Islands after his patron, the Earl of Sandwich. In November, he returns to Hawaii for the winter, anchoring at Kealakekua Bay on the Big Island.

1779 In February, Cook is killed in a battle with Hawaii's indigenous people at Kealakekua.

1786 The isolation of the Islands ends abruptly as British, American, French, and Russian fur traders and New England whalers come to Hawaii. Tales spread of thousands of acres of sugarcane growing wild, and farmers come in droves from the United States and Europe.

1790 Kamehameha begins his rise to power through a series of bloody battles to unify the Islands of Hawaii.

1791 Kamehameha builds Puukohola Heiau temple and dedicates it by killing a rival chief.

1794 Using Western arms, Kamehameha completes his conquest of the Islands.

1810 The chief of Kauai acknowledges Kamehameha's rule, uniting the Islands under one chief. Kamehameha becomes known as King Kamehameha I, and he rules the unified Kingdom of Hawaii with an iron hand.

1819 Kamehameha I dies, and his eldest son, Kamehameha II, begins his short reign, notable for the official demise of pagan religion and ancient taboos. The first whaling ships land at Lahaina on Maui.

1820 By the time the first missionaries arrive from Boston, Hawaii's social order is beginning to break down. The Hawaiians are disillusioned with their own gods and are receptive to the ideas of Christianity. The influx of Western culture also introduces Hawaii to Western disease, liquor, and what some view as moral decay.

1824 King Kamehameha II and his queen die of measles. His younger brother becomes King Kamehameha III, a wise and gentle sovereign who reigns for 30 years.

1835 The first commercial sugar plantation is established on Kauai, financed by American merchants in Honolulu.

1840 The Wilkes Expedition, sponsored by the U.S. Coast and Geodetic Survey, pinpoints Pearl Harbor as a potential Naval Base.

1845 Kamehameha III and the Legislature move Hawaii's seat of government from Lahaina, on Maui, to Honolulu, on Oahu.

1849 Kamehameha III turns Hawaii into a constitutional monarchy and wins official recognition of Hawaii as an independent country by the United States, France, and Great Britain.

1852 As Western diseases depopulate the Islands, a labor shortage occurs in the sugarcane fields. For the next nine decades, a steady stream of foreign labor pours into Hawaii, beginning with the Chinese. The Japanese begin arriving in 1868, followed by Filipinos, Koreans, Portuguese, and Puerto Ricans.

1872 Kamehameha V dies without heirs, ending the direct descendants of the first king. A power struggle ensues between the adherents of David Kalakaua and William Lunalilo.

1873 Lunalilo is elected Hawaii's sixth king in January. The bachelor rules only 13 months before dying of tuberculosis.

1874 Kalakaua vies for the throne with the Dowager Queen Emma, half-Caucasian widow of Kamehameha IV. Kalakaua is elected by the Hawaii Legislature, against protests by supporters of Queen Emma. American and British marines are called in to restore order, and Kalakaua begins his reign as the "Merry Monarch."

1875 The United States and Hawaii sign a treaty of reciprocity assuring Hawaii a duty-free market for sugar in the United States.

1882 After a visit to the United States, King David Kalakaua builds Iolani Palace, an Italian Renaissance–style structure, on the site of the previous royal palace.

1887 The reciprocity treaty of 1875 is renewed, giving the United States the exclusive use of Pearl Harbor as a coaling station.

1891 King Kalakaua dies and is succeeded by his sister, Queen Liliuokalani, the last monarch of Hawaii.

1893 In trying to eliminate the restrictions that have been placed on the monarchy, Liliuokalani brings on a bloodless revolution. After reigning only two years, she is removed from the throne by American business interests led by Sanford B. Dole (son of a missionary). Liliuokalani is imprisoned in Iolani Palace for nearly eight months.

1894 The provisional government converts Hawaii into a republic and proclaims Sanford Dole president.

1898 The outbreak of the Spanish-American War and Hawaii's strategic military importance in the Pacific lead the next U.S. president, William McKinley, to move toward Hawaii's annexation. On August 12, Hawaii is officially annexed by a joint resolution of Congress.

1901 Sanford Dole is appointed first governor of the territory of Hawaii. The first major tourist hotel, the Moana (now called the Sheraton Moana Surfrider), is built on Waikiki Beach.

1903 James Dole (a cousin of Sanford Dole) produces nearly 2,000 cases of pineapple, marking the beginning of Hawaii's pineapple industry. Pineapple eventually surpasses sugar as Hawaii's number-one crop.

1907 Fort Shafter Base, headquarters for the U.S. Army, becomes the first permanent military post in the Islands.

1908 Dredging of the channel at Pearl Harbor begins.

1919 Pearl Harbor is formally dedicated by the U.S. Navy.

1927 Army Lieutenants Lester Maitland and Albert Hegenberger make the first successful nonstop flight from the Mainland to the Islands. Hawaii begins to increase efforts to promote tourism, the industry that eventually dominates development of the Islands. The Matson Navigation Company builds the Royal Hawaiian Hotel as a destination for its cruise ships.

1929 Hawaii's commercial interisland air service begins.

1936 Pan American World Airways makes history as the first to start regular commercial passenger flights to Hawaii from the Mainland.

1941 Pearl Harbor becomes a tragic part of U.S. history when the U.S. Pacific Fleet is attacked by the Japanese, causing the U.S. to enter World War II. Nearly 4,000 casualties result from the surprise attack.

1942 James Jones, with thousands of others, trains at Schofield Barracks on Oahu. He later writes about it in *From Here to Eternity*.

1959 Congress passes legislation granting Hawaii statehood. Later in the year, the first Boeing 707 jets make the flight from San Francisco in a record five hours. By year's end, 243,216 tourists visit Hawaii, and tourism becomes Hawaii's major industry. Today it draws more than 6 million visitors a year.

Volcano Country

By Gary
Diedrichs

A former editor
for Los Angeles
magazine, Gary
Diedrichs has
written
previously on
Jamaica and
Maui for Fodor's.

Dawn at the crater on horseback. It's cold at 10,023 feet above the warm Pacific—maybe 45°. The horses' breath condenses into a smoky cloud, and the riders cling against their saddles. Eerily quiet except for the creak of straining leather and the crunch of volcanic cinders under hooves, those sounds magnify absurdly in the vast and empty space that yawns below. . . .

This is Haleakala, which literally means "house of the sun." It's the crown of east Maui and the largest dormant volcano crater in the world. Every year thousands of visitors to Maui shake themselves awake at three in the morning to board vans that take them from their comfortable hotels, up the world's most steeply ascending auto route to the summit of Haleakala National Park. Sunrise is the show of shows here, from the palest pink to the most fiery red spreading across the lip of the summit. Mark Twain called it "the sublimest spectacle" he had ever witnessed.

But sunrise is only the beginning of the spectacle that this volcano offers. The park encompasses 28,665 acres, and the valley itself is 21 miles in circumference and 19 square miles in area. At its deepest, it measures 3,000 feet from the summit. The two towers of Manhattan's World Trade Center could be stood end to end and not reach the top. While Haleakala is, of course, a dormant volcano, the vast, wonderous valley here isn't by itself a single crater created by some devastating eruption. Misnamed by the first European explorers, Haleakala's huge depression would be more properly called an "erosional valley," the result of eons of wind and rain wearing down what was likely a small crater at the mountain's original summit. The small hills within the valley are volcanic cinder cones, each the site of an eruption.

More than anything, entering Haleakala is like descending to the moon. Trails for hiking and horseback riding crisscross the crater for some 32 miles. The way is strewn with volcanic rubble, crater cones, frozen lava flows, vents, and lava tubes. The colors that surround the descent are muted yet dramatic—black, yellow, russet, orange, lavender, browns, and grays, even a pinkish-blue. It seems as if nothing could live here, but in fact this is an ecosystem that sustains, among other, more humble life forms, the surefooted mountain goat, the rare nene goose (no webbing between its toes, to better negotiate the rugged terrain), and the strange and delicate silversword. The silversword, a spiny, metallic-leafed plant, once proliferated on Haleakala's slopes. Today it survives in small numbers at Haleakala and at high elevations on the Big Island of Hawaii. The plants live up to 20 years, bloom only once, scatter their seeds, and die.

The valley's starkness is overwhelming. Even shadows cast in the thin mountain air are flinty and spare. It's easy to understand why, in the early days of this nation's space program, moon-bound astronauts trained in this desolate place.

It is also not difficult to see this place as a bubbling, sulfurous cauldron, a direct connection not to the heavens but to the core of the Earth and to the origins of this island. Haleakala's last—and probably final—eruption occurred in 1790, a few years after a Frenchman named La Perouse became the first European to set foot on Maui. That fiery outburst was only one of many in Hawaii over the millennia, just as Maui and its now-cold crater are just one facet of the volcanic variety of the Aloha State.

Large and small, awake or sleeping, volcanoes embody Hawaii's history and its heritage; behind their beauty is the story of the flames that created this ethereal island chain. This tale began some 25 million years ago, yet it is still unfinished.

The islands in the Hawaiian archipelago are really only the very crests of immense mountains rising from the bottom of the sea. Formed by molten rock known as magma, the islands were slowly pushed up from the Earth's volatile, uneasy mantle, forced through cracks in the thin crust that is the ocean floor.

The first ancient eruptions cooled and formed pools on the Pacific bottom. Then, as more and more magma spilled from the vents over millions of years, the pools became ridges and grew into crests; the latter built upon themselves over the eons, until finally, miles high, they at last towered above the surface of the sea.

As the islands cooled in the Pacific waters, the stark lava slopes slowly bloomed, over centuries, with colorful flora— exotic, jewel-like species endemic only to these islands, with their generous washings of tropical rain and abundant sunshine. Gradually, as seeds, spores, or eggs of living creatures were carried by the winds and currents to this isolated area, more than 2,000 miles from the closest continental land mass, the bare and rocky atolls became a paradise of greenery, with the occasional new eruption expanding their domain.

This type of volcano, with its slowly formed, gently sloping sides, is known as a shield volcano, and each of the Hawaiian isles is composed of them. As long as the underwater vents spew the lifeblood lava out from the Earth's core and into the heart of the mountain, a shield volcano will continue to grow.

The Hawaiian Islands rest upon an area called the Pacific Plate, and this vast shelf of land is making its way slowly to the northwest, creeping perhaps 2 to 3 inches every year. The result is that contact between the submarine vents and the volcanoes' conduits for magma is gradually disrupted and closed off. Slowly, the mountains stop growing, one by one. Surface eruptions slow down and finally halt completely, and these volcanoes ultimately become extinct.

That, at least, is one explanation. Another—centuries older and still revered in Hawaiian art and song—centers upon Pele, the beautiful and tempestuous daughter of Haumea, the Earth Mother, and Wakea, the Sky Father. Pele is the Hawaiian goddess of fire, the maker of mountains, melter of rocks, eater of forests, and burner of land—both creator and destroyer. Legend has it that Pele came to the Islands long ago to flee from her cruel older sister, Na Maka o Kahai, goddess of the sea. Pele ran first to the small island of Niihau, making a crater home there with her digging stick. But Na Maka found her and destroyed her hideaway, so Pele again had to flee. On Kauai she delved deeper, but Na Maka chased her from that home as well. Pele ran on—from Oahu to Molokai, Lanai to Kahoolawe, Molokini to Maui—but always and ever Na Maka pursued her.

Pele came at last to Halemaumau, the vast firepit crater of Kilauea, and there, on the Big Island, she dug deepest of all. There she is said to remain, all-powerful, quick to rage, and often unpredictable; the mountain is her impenetrable fortress and domain—a safe refuge, at least for a time, from Na Maka o Kahai.

Interestingly, the chronology of the old tales of Pele's flight from isle to isle matches closely with modern volcanologists' reckonings on the ages of the various craters. Today, the Big Island's Kilauea and Mauna Loa retain the closest links with the Earth's superheated core and are active and volatile, though three other volcanoes that shaped the island are not. The remainder of the Hawaiian volcanoes have been carried beyond their magma supply by the movement of the Pacific Plate. Those farthest to the northwest in the island chain are completely extinct. Those at the southeasterly end of the island chain—Haleakala, Mauna Kea, and Hualalai—are dormant and slipping away, so that the implacable process of volcanic death has begun.

Eventually, experts say, in another age or so, the same cooling and slow demise will overtake all of the burning rocks that are the Hawaiian Islands. Eventually, the sea will claim their bodies and, to Pele's rage, Na Maka o Kahai will win in the end. Or will she? Off the Big Island of Hawaii, a new island is forming. It's still a half mile below the water's surface. Several thousand years more will be required for it to break into the sunlight. But it already has a name: Loihi.

At this time, it's hard to imagine the demise of that burgeoning Grand Canyon of fire that is Pele's current home on the Big Island. Kilauea is today very much the living center of volcanic activity in the Hawaiian islands.

By far the largest island of the archipelago, the Big Island of Hawaii, measured at the summit of Mauna Kea, is some 13,796 feet above sea level, with the tip of Mauna Loa nearly as lofty at 13,667 feet. Taken as a whole, from their bases on the ocean floor, these shield volcanoes are the largest mountain masses on the planet. Geologists believe it required more than 3 million years of steady volcanic activity to bring these peaks up above the waters of the Pacific.

Mauna Loa's little sister, Kilauea, at about 4,077 feet, is the most active volcano in the world. Between the two of them, they have covered nearly 200,000 acres of land with their red-hot lava flows over the past 200 years or so. In the process, they have ravished trees, fields, meadows, villages, and more than a few unlucky human witnesses. For generations, Kilauea, in a continually eruptive state, has pushed molten lava up from the earth's magma at 1,800° and more. But as active as she and Mauna Loa are, their eruptions are comparatively safe and gentle, producing continuous small and especially liquid lava flows rather than dangerous bursts of fire and ash. The exceptions were two violently explosive displays during recorded history—one in 1790, the other in 1924. During these eruptions, Pele came closest to destroying the Big Island's largest city, Hilo, although she gave residents another scare as recently as 1985.

It is around these major volcanoes that the island's Hawaii Volcanoes National Park is located. A sprawling natural preserve, the park attracts geology experts, volcanologists, and ordinary wide-eyed visitors from all over the world. They come for the park's unparalleled opportunity to view, up close and in person, the visual wonders of Pele's kingdom of fire and fantasy. They come to study and to improve methods for predicting the times and sites of eruptions. They have done so for a century or more. It has not been unusual for tourists to send back postcards with edges deliberately scorched by Kilauea's heat, or for the more adventurous to wander into the firepit when the volcano was quiet, with an egg and frying pan in hand, to cook breakfast in nature's most sizzling cauldron.

Thomas Augustus Jaggar, the preeminent volcanologist and student of Kilauea, built his home on stilts wedged into cracks in the volcanic rock of the crater rim. Harvard-trained and universally respected, he was the driving force behind the establishment of the Hawaiian Volcano Observatory at Kilauea. When he couldn't raise research funds from donations, public and private, he raised pigs to keep the scientific work going. After his death, his wife surreptitiously scattered Jaggar's ashes over the great fiery abyss.

The park is located on the Big Island's southeastern flank, about 30 minutes out of Hilo on the aptly named Volcano Highway. Wear sturdy walking shoes and carry a warm sweater. It can be a long hike across the lava flats to see Pele in action, and at 4,000 feet above sea level, temperatures can be brisk, however hot the volcanic activity. So much can be seen at close range along the road that circles the crater that Kilauea has been dubbed the "drive-in volcano."

At the park's Visitor Center sits a large display case. It contains dozens of lava-rock "souvenirs"—removed from Pele's grasp and then precipitantly returned, accompanied by letters of apology. They are sent back by visitors who say they regret having broken the *kapu* (taboo) against removing even the smallest grain of native volcanic rock from Hawaii. A typical letter might say: "I never thought Pele would miss just one little rock, but she did, and now I've wrecked two cars . . . I lost my job, my health is poor, and I know it's because I took this stone." Some of the letters are humorous, but more are poignant, full of remorse and requests for Pele's forgiveness. They are replaced, at frequent intervals, by a whole new batch.

I t is surprisingly safe at the crater's lip. Unlike Japan's Mount Fuji or Washington State's Mount St. Helens, Hawaii's shield volcanoes spew their lava downhill, along the sides of the mountain. Still, the clouds of sulphur gas and fumes produced during volcanic eruptions are noxious and heady and can make breathing unpleasant, if not difficult. It has been pointed out that the chemistry of volcanoes—sulfur, hydrogen, oxygen, carbon dioxide—closely resembles the chemistry of the egg.

It's an 11-mile drive around the Kilauea crater, via the Crater Rim Road, and the trip takes about an hour. But it's better to walk a bit. There are at least eight major trails in the park, ranging from short 15-minute strolls to the three-day, 18.3-mile (one-way) Mauna Loa Trail, which is, as you might expect, only for the seasoned hiker. A comfortable walk is Sulfur Banks, with its many vast, steaming vents creating halos of clouds around the rim of Kilauea. The route passes through a seemingly enchanted forest of sandalwood, flowers, and ferns.

Just ahead is the main attraction: the center of Pele's power, Halemaumau. This yawning pit of flame and burning rock measures some 3,000 feet wide and is a breathtaking sight. When Pele is in full fury, visitors come here in droves, on foot and by helicopter, to see her crimson expulsions coloring the dark earth and smoky sky.

Recently, however, Kilauea's most violent activity has occurred along vents in the mountain's sides instead of at its summit crater. Known as rift zones, they are lateral conduits that often open in shield volcanoes. Kilauea has two rift zones, one extending from the summit crater toward the southwest, through Kau. The other extends east-northeast through Puna, past Cape Kumakahi and into the sea. In the last two decades, repeated eruptions in the east rift zone have blocked off 12 miles of coastal road—some under more than 300 feet of rock—and have covered a total of 10,000 acres with lava. Where the flows entered the ocean, roughly 200 acres have been added to the Big Island.

Farther along the Crater Rim Road (about 4 miles from the Visitor Center) is the Thurston Lava Tube, an example of a strangely beautiful volcanic phenomenon common on the islands. Lava tubes are formed when lava flows rapidly downhill; the sides and top of this river of molten rock cool, while the fluid center flows on. Most of these formations are short and shallow, but some measure 30 to 50 feet high and hundreds of yards long. Dark, cave-like places, lava tubes were often used to store remains of the ancient Hawaiian royalty—the *alii*. All around the site of the Thurston Lava Tube is the justly famed Fern Jungle, a beautiful prehistoric fern forest.

Throughout the park, new lava formations are continually in the process of being created. Starkly beautiful, these volcanic deposits demonstrate the different types of lava produced by Hawaii's volcanoes: *'a'a*, the dark, rough lava that solidifies as cinders of rock; and the more common *pahoehoe*, the smooth, satiny lava that forms the vast plains of black rock in ropy swirls known as lava flats, which in some areas go on for miles. Other terms that help identify what may be seen in the park include *caldera*, which are the open, bowl-like lips of a volcano summit; *ejecta*, the cinders and ash that float through the air around an eruption; and *olivine*, the semiprecious chrysolite (greenish in color) found in volcanic ash.

But it isn't all fire and flash, cinders, and devastation in Volcano Country. Hawaii Volcanoes National Park is also a repository for some of the most beautiful of the state's black-sand beaches; humid forest glens full of lacy butterflies and colorful birds like the dainty flycatcher called the *'elepaio;* and exquisite grottoes sparked with bright wild orchid sprays and crashing waterfalls. Even as the lava cools, still bearing a golden, glassy skin, lush, green native ferns—the *amaumau* and *kupukupu* and *okupukupu*—spring up in the midst of Pele's fallout, as if defying her destructiveness or simply confirming the fact that after fire, she brings life.

Some 12 centuries ago, in fact, Pele brought mankind himself to her verdant islands: The fiery explosions that lit Kilauea and Mauna Loa like twin beacons in the night probably led to Pele's side the first stout-hearted explorers to Hawaii from the Marquesas Islands, some 2,400 miles away across the trackless, treacherous ocean.

Once summoned, they worshiped her from a discreet distance. Great numbers of religious *heiau* (temples) dot the landscapes near the many older and extinct craters scattered throughout Hawaii, demonstrating the great reverence the native islanders have always held for Pele and her creations. But the ruins of only two heiau are to be found near the very active crater at Halemaumau. There, at the center of the capricious Pele's power, native Hawaiians caution one even today to "step lightly, for you are on holy ground."

For all the teeming tourism and bustle that is modern Hawaii, no man today steps on the ground that Pele may one day claim for her own. In future ages, when mighty Kilauea is no more, this area will still be Volcano Country. Beneath the blue Pacific waters, fiery magma flows, and new mountains form and grow. Just below the surface, Loihi waits.

The Aloha Shirt: A Colorful Swatch of Island History

By DeSoto Brown

A fourth-generation Islander of part-Hawaiian ancestry, DeSoto Brown is the author of two books, Hawaii Recalls *and* Aloha Waikiki.

Elvis Presley had an entire wardrobe of them in the '60s films *Blue Hawaii* and *Paradise, Hawaiian Style*. During the '50s, entertainer Arthur Godfrey and bandleader Harry Owens often sported them on television shows. John Wayne loved to lounge around in them. Mick Jagger felt compelled to buy one on a visit to Hawaii in the 1970s. Dustin Hoffman, Steven Spielberg and Bill Cosby avidly collect them.

From gaudy to grand, from tawdry to tasteful, aloha shirts are Hawaii's gift to the world of fashion. It's been more than 50 years since those riotously colored garments made their first appearance as immediately recognizable symbols of the Islands.

The roots of the aloha shirt go back to the early 1930s, when Hawaii's garment industry was just beginning to develop its own unique style. Although locally made clothes did exist, they were almost exclusively items for plantation workers, which were constructed of durable palaka or plain cotton material.

Out of this came the first stirrings of fashion: Beachboys and schoolchildren started having sport shirts made from colorful Japanese kimono fabric. The favored type of cloth was the kind used for children's kimonos—bright pink and orange floral prints for girls; masculine motifs in browns and blues for boys. In Japan, such flamboyant patterns were considered unsuitable for adult clothing, but in the Islands, such rules didn't apply, and it seemed the flashier the shirt, the better—for either sex. Thus, the aloha shirt was born.

It was easy and inexpensive in those days to have garments tailored to order; the next step was moving to mass production and marketing. In June 1935, Honolulu's best-known tailoring establishment, Musa-Shiya, advertised the availability of "Aloha shirts—well tailored, beautiful designs and radiant colors. Ready-made or made to order . . . 95¢ and up." This is the first known printed use of the term that would soon refer to an entire industry. By the following year, several local manufacturers had begun full-scale production of "aloha wear." One of them, Ellery Chun of King-Smith, registered as local trademarks the terms "Aloha

"The Aloha Shirt: A Colorful Swatch of Island History" first appeared in ALOHA, The Magazine of Hawaii and the Pacific. *Reprinted with permission of Davick Publications.*

Sportswear" and "Aloha Shirt" in 1936 and 1937, respectively.

These early entrepreneurs were the first to create uniquely Hawaiian designs for fabric as well—splashy patterns that would forever symbolize the Islands. A 1939 *Honolulu Advertiser* story described them as a "delightful confusion (of) tropical fish and palm trees, Diamond Head and the Aloha Tower, surfboards and leis, ukuleles and Waikiki beach scenes."

The aloha wear of the late 1930s was intended for—and mostly worn by—tourists, and interestingly, a great deal of it was exported to the Mainland and even Europe and Australia. By the end of the decade, for example, only 5% of the output of one local firm, the Kamehameha Garment Company, was sold in Hawaii.

World War II brought this trend to a halt, and during the postwar period, aloha wear really came into its own in Hawaii. A strong push to support local industry gradually nudged Island garb into the workplace, and kamaainas began to wear the clothing that previously had been seen as attire for visitors.

In 1947, for example, male employees of the City and County of Honolulu were first allowed to wear aloha shirts "in plain shades" during the summer months. Later that year, the first observance of Aloha Week started the tradition of "bankers and bellhops . . . mix(ing) colorfully in multihued and tapa-designed Aloha shirts every day," as a local newspaper's Sunday magazine supplement noted in 1948. By the 1960s, "Aloha Friday," set aside specifically for the wearing of aloha attire, had become a tradition. In the following decade, the suit and tie practically disappeared as work attire in Hawaii, even for executives.

Most of the Hawaiian-themed fabric used in manufacturing aloha wear was designed in the Islands, then printed on the Mainland or in Japan. The glowingly vibrant rayons of the late '40s and early '50s (a period now seen as aloha wear's heyday) were at first printed on the East Coast, but manufacturers there usually required such large orders, local firms eventually found it impossible to continue using them. By 1964, 90% of Hawaiian fabric was being manufactured in Japan—a situation that still exists today.

Fashion trends usually move in cycles, and aloha wear is no exception. By the 1960s, the "chop suey print" with its "tired clichés of Diamond Head, Aloha Tower, outrigger canoes (and) stereotyped leis" was seen as corny and garish, according to an article published in the *Honolulu Star-Bulletin*. But it was just that outdated aspect that began to appeal to the younger crowd, who began searching out old-fashioned aloha shirts at the Salvation Army and Goodwill thrift stores. These shirts were dubbed "silkies," a name by which they're still known, even though most of them were actually made of rayon.

Before long, what had been 50-cent shirts began escalating in price, and a customer who had balked at paying $5 for a shirt that someone had already worn soon found the same item selling for $10—and more. By the late 1970s, aloha wear designers were copying the prints of yesteryear for their new creations.

The days of bargain silkies are now gone. The few choice aloha shirts from decades past that still remain are offered today by specialized dealers for hundreds of dollars apiece, causing many to look back with chagrin to the time when such treasures were foolishly worn to the beach until they fell apart. The best examples of vintage aloha shirts are now rightly seen as art objects worthy of preservation for the lovely depictions they offer of Hawaii's colorful and unique scene.

Village: Kahuku-*mura*

By Garrett Hongo

Born in Volcano, Hawaii, Garrett Hongo is the author of two poetry collections, Yellow Light *and* The River of Heaven.

I'm back near the plantation lands of cane and mule trails
and narrow-gauge track rusting in the rainbow distance
against the green cliffs and bridal veils of the *pali*.

I know the mill is just beyond my sight,
around the sand point, past old caneland
cleared now for prawn farms and melon patches,
and that the village is beyond them, Quonset huts
and barracks in clusters arranged without pattern.

I remember someone—Iiyama-*san*—kept a carp pond,
and someone else made bean curd, fresh,
every day, and my chore was to fetch it,
in a bucket or a shallow pail or a lunchbox,
and I'd rush through the dusty, unpaved streets
winding past the rows of tiny shotguns,
thrilled with my job, anxious to get to
the low, barnlike building all in shadow
and cool as a cave in the middle of the day.

I'd knock or call—*Tadaima!*—as I was taught,
in Japanese for this Japanese man (other words
for the Portuguese or Chinese or Hawaiian),
and he'd slide the grey door back, *shōji*-like,
on its runner, opening up, and I'd see,
under dim lab-lights, long sinks like flumes
in three rows all brimming with a still water
lustrous and faintly green in the weak light.

There was an odor too, stark as dawnlight,
of fermentation I'd guess now, the cool paste
curdling in the damp, cold dark, silting
clear water milky under the coarse wire screens,
the air gaseous and fragrant and sharp.

It must have been a dime or a nickel—
I remember its shine and the coin's neat fit
in my hand—and he'd take it, drop it in
a slotted coffee can, then reach a slick palm,
small spade of flesh, into the supple water,
draw the raw, white cube, delicate and new,
drenched in its own strange juice, and place it,
without words or ceremony, into the blank pail
I held before me like a page to be written on.

How did I know it would all recede into nothing,
derelict shacks unpainted and overgrown
with morning glories, by canefields fringed
with *ekoa* and castor beans, swinging
their dark, brittle censers over the road?
How did I know my own joy's beginning
would be relic in my own lifetime?

I turn up the dirt road that took me in,
the green cane all around me, flush by the roadside,
a parted sea of masts and small sails scissoring the air,
whispering their sullen history on a tuneless wind.

3 Oahu

More and more Hawaiians are stepping forward to say that Oahu is their favorite island, and many claim that it has the most spectacular scenery of all Hawaii. Part of its dramatic appearance can be attributed to its majestic highlands: the western Waianae Mountains, which rise 4,000 feet above sea level, and the verdant Koolaus, which cross the island's midsection at elevations of more than 3,000 feet. After eons of erosion by wind and weather, these ranges now have sculptured, jagged peaks, deep valleys, sheer green cliffs, and dynamic vistas. Below the mountains, Oahu is a gathering place of beach parks, with more than 50 draped around its edges like a beautiful lei. Many of the parks include restrooms, showers, and picnic tables sprinkled along the shoreline. Each beach is known for a different ocean activity, such as snorkeling, bodysurfing, swimming, or windsurfing.

The center of the island is carpeted in pineapple plantations. Acres of waving sugarcane go down almost to the sea. There are ranches, banana farms, and fields of exotic flowers grown for export. The plantation towns are small. Some have become cute with boutiques and little art galleries. Others are just themselves—old, wooden, and picturesque—the small homes surrounded by a riot of flowers and trees heavy with mango, pomelo, and lychee.

Third largest of the Hawaiian Islands, Oahu's 608 square miles were formed by two volcanoes that erupted 4 million to 6 million years ago and, over time, eventually created the peaceable kingdom we see today. Honolulu is located on the island of Oahu, and though 75% of Hawaii's 1.1 million residents live on Oahu, somehow there is enough room for wide-open spaces and sufficient time to take a deep breath and relax.

Hawaii's kings and queens ruled from Honolulu's Iolani Palace, near the present downtown. It was at Iolani that the American flag first flew over the Islands. Even in those days of royalty, the virtues of Waikiki as a playground were noticed. Long processions of *alii* (nobility) would make their way across the streams and swamps, past the duck ponds, to the coconut groves and the beach.

By the 1880s, guest houses were sprinkled along the beach like confetti. The first hotel, the Moana (now the refurbished Sheraton Moana Surfrider), was built at the turn of the century. At that time, Waikiki was connected to the rest of Honolulu by a tram, bringing townspeople to the shore. In 1927, the "Pink Palace of the Pacific," the Royal Hawaiian Hotel, was built by Matson Navigation Company to accommodate travelers arriving on luxury liners. It was opened with a grand ball, and Waikiki was launched as a first-class tourist destination: duck ponds, taro patches, and all. The rich and famous came from around the world. December 7, 1941, brought that era to a close, with the bombing of Pearl Harbor and Hawaii's entry into the war in the Pacific. The Royal Hawaiian was turned over to American servicemen. Hundreds of war-weary soldiers and sailors found a warm welcome in Waikiki.

With victory came the boom. By 1952, Waikiki had 2,000 hotel rooms. In 1969, there were 15,000 rooms. Today, that figure has more than doubled. Hundreds of thousands of visitors now sleep in the more than 33,000 rooms of Waikiki's nearly 129 hotels and condominiums. To this 1½-square-mile Pacific playground come sun bunnies, honeymooners, Marines on holiday, long-staying Europeans and Canadians, Japanese, and every other type of tourist imaginable. Waikiki vibrates with international excitement and offers more to see, do, and eat than all the other Hawaiian islands combined.

Bordered by the ocean on the south, Waikiki sparkles along 2½ miles of spangled sea from the famous Diamond Head landmark on the east to the Ala Wai Yacht Harbor on the west. Separated from the sprawling city of Honolulu by the broad Ala Wai Canal on its northern boundary, Waikiki is 3½ miles from downtown Honolulu and worlds apart from any other city in the world. Nowhere else is there such a salad of cultures so artfully tossed, each one retaining its distinct flavor and texture. McDonald's offers burgers and *saimin*, the ubiquitous noodle soup of Nippon. You'll find yourself saying things like *aloha* and *mahalo* (thank you). You'll come across almost as many sushi bars as ice cream stands.

Waikiki sits on the sunny, dry side of Oahu, one of the eight major Hawaiian islands, seven of which are inhabited. In all, there are 132 Hawaiian isles and atolls, stretched across 1,600 miles of ocean. Hawaii is America's most exotic, most unusual state, and Waikiki is its generator, keeping everything humming. It incorporates all the natural splendors of the Islands and synthesizes them with elegance and daring into an international resort city in the middle of the vast blue Pacific.

Essential Information

Arriving and Departing by Plane

From the Mainland United States
Honolulu International Airport is one of the busiest in the nation. It is under complete renovation and is only 20 minutes from Waikiki. Flying time from the West Coast is 4½–5 hours.

American carriers serving Hawaii include **United, Northwest, American, Continental, Delta, TWA, Hawaiian,** and **America West.** Most flights to Hawaii originate in Los Angeles or San Francisco, which, of course, means they are nonstop. There are also nonstop flights from Dallas/Fort Worth, Chicago, Seattle, San Diego, and St. Louis. There are direct flights (which means there are one or more stops along the route, but you don't have to change planes) from Anchorage, New York, and other cities in the East, Southwest, and Midwest. Connecting flights are available from almost every American city.

By law, foreign carriers serving Hawaii may not carry passengers from other American cities. Bringing passengers from foreign destinations are **Qantas, Air Canada, Japan Air Lines, Philippine Air Lines, Air New Zealand, China Airlines, Korean Air, Singapore Airlines, All Nippon Airways, Air Micronesia, Canadian Airlines International, Garuda Indonesia, Aero Peru, Scandinavian Airlines, Lufthansa German Airlines, Varig Brazilian Airlines,** and **Malaysia Airlines.**

From the United Kingdom
American, Continental, Delta, and **TWA** are among the airlines that fly to Honolulu. An APEX ticket costs about £559 for a midweek flight, plus taxes. Ring around for the best offer.

Discount Flights
Charter flights are the least expensive and the least reliable—with chronically late departures and occasional cancellations.

They also tend to depart less frequently (usually once a week) than do regularly scheduled flights. If the savings are worth the potential annoyance, charter flights serving Honolulu International Airport include **American Trans Air** (tel. 800/225–9920) and **Hawaiian Airlines** (tel. 808/537–5100 or 800/367–5320). Consult your local travel agent for further information.

Smoking Smoking is banned on all routes within the 48 contiguous states; within the states of Hawaii and Alaska; to and from the U.S. Virgin Islands and Puerto Rico; and on flights of less than six hours to and from Hawaii and Alaska. The rule applies to both domestic and foreign carriers.

On a flight where smoking is permitted, you can request a nonsmoking seat during check-in or when you book your ticket. If the airline tells you there are no seats available in the nonsmoking section, insist on one: Department of Transportation regulations require carriers to find seats for all nonsmokers, provided they meet check-in time restrictions. These regulations apply to all international flights on domestic carriers; however, the Department of Transportation does not have jurisdiction over foreign carriers traveling out of, or into the United States.

Lei Greeting Many visitors are disappointed to find that everyone arriving in Hawaii is not automatically given a lei. With the visitor count at nearly 7 million, doing so would bankrupt the state. If you have booked through a tour company and are being met at the airport, you will probably be given a lei by the person who meets you. If you have friends meeting you, most definitely they will have a lei for you. If you are traveling independently, you can arrange for a lei greeting from **Greeters of Hawaii** (Box 29638, Honolulu 96820, tel. 808/836–0161); it requires 48 hours' notice. Cost: $14.95 to $39.95 per person, add $10 for late notification. The standard $14.95 lei usually contains orchids or an orchid-carnation mixture. You might also try **Aloha Lei Greeters** (tel. 808/836–0249 or 800/367–5255). Being draped in flowers is definitely one of the pleasures of arriving in the Islands.

Between the Airport and Waikiki There are taxis right at the airport baggage claim exit. At $1.50 start-up plus $1.50 for each mile, the fare will run approximately $20 plus a tip. Drivers are also allowed to charge 30¢ per suitcase. **Terminal Transportation** (tel. 808/836–0317) runs an airport shuttle service to Waikiki for $6. The municipal bus is only 60¢, but you are allowed only one bag that must fit on your lap. Some hotels have their own pickup service. Check when you book your reservations.

If you have extra time at the airport, be sure to visit the new **Pacific Aerospace Museum** (tel. 808/531–7747) in the central waiting lobby of the main terminal. It includes a 1,700-square-foot, 3-dimensional, multi-media theater tracing the history of flight in Hawaii, and a full-scale space shuttle flight deck. Hands-on exhibits include a mission control computer program tracing flights in the Pacific. *Donation: $4 adults, $1 children 6–12.*

Arriving and Departing by Ship

Boat Day used to be the biggest day of the week. Jet travel has almost obscured that custom, and it's too bad, because arriving in Hawaii by ship is a great experience. If you have the time, it is one sure way to unwind. Many cruises are planned a year or more in advance and fill up fast. Because of customs regulations, if you sail on a foreign ship from any U.S. port, you must return with that ship to that port. If you arrive in Hawaii from a foreign port, you may disembark in Honolulu. Most cruiseship companies today offer a fare that includes round-trip air travel to the point of embarkation.

Cunard/N.A.C. Line, Royal Cruises, P & O/Princess Cruises, and **Royal Viking** have cruise ships passing through Honolulu once or twice a year. The S.S. *Constitution* and the S.S. *Independence* stop in Honolulu each Saturday morning on their week-long interisland sails. You can also book three- and four-day packages on one of these Hawaii-based luxury liners. *American Hawaii Cruises, 550 Kearny St., San Francisco, CA 94108, tel. 800/765–7000.*

Getting Around

Waikiki is only 2½ miles long and a ½-mile wide, which means you can usually walk to where you are going. There are plenty of places to stop and rest, the shop windows are interesting, and people-watching is fun, and free.

By Bus You can go all around the island or just down Kalakaua Avenue for 60¢ on Honolulu's municipal transportation system, affectionately known as The Bus (tel. 808/848–5555). You are also entitled to one free transfer per fare if you ask for it when boarding. Board at the front of the bus. Exact change is required. The student fare (grades 1–12) is 25¢ and children under 6 ride free. Monthly bus passes are available at $15 for adults, $7.50 for students. In Waikiki, get them at the 7-11 store (2999 Kuhio Ave.) or the Foodland at Ala Moana Center.

There are no official bus-route maps, but you can find privately published booklets at most drugstores and other convenience outlets. The important route numbers for Waikiki are 2, 4, 8, 19, 20, and 58. If you venture afield, you can always get back on one of those.

There are also a number of brightly painted private buses, many free, that will take you to such commercial attractions as dinner cruises, garment factories, and the like.

By Trolley An open trolley cruises Waikiki, the Ala Moana area, and downtown, making 27 stops along a 90-minute route. The trolley ride provides a good orientation. The conductor narrates, pointing out sights, as well as shopping, dining, and entertainment opportunities along the way. *Tel. 808/526–0112. Departs from the Royal Hawaiian Shopping Ctr. every 30 min. Buy an all-day pass from the conductor for $15 and for children under 12, $5. Daily 8AM–4:30PM.*

By Taxi You can usually get one right at the doorstep of your hotel. Most restaurants will call a taxi for you. Rates are $1.50 at the drop of the flag, plus $1.50 per mile. Drivers are generally courteous, and the cars are in good condition, many of them air-conditioned. The two biggest taxicab companies are **Charley's** (tel. 808/531–1333), a fleet of company-owned cabs; and **SIDA of Hawaii, Inc.** (tel. 808/836–0011), an association of individually owned cabs.

By Car   Your Mainland driver's license is valid in Hawaii for 90 days. If you plan to stay in the Islands for extended periods, apply for a Hawaii driver's license for $8.50 at the Honolulu Department of Motor Vehicles (1370 Maunakea St., tel. 808/532–7700).

Be sure to buckle up. Hawaii has a seat-belt law for front-seat passengers. Children under age 3 must be in a car seat, available from your car-rental agency.

It's hard to get lost in Hawaii. Roads and streets, although they may be unpronounceable to the visitor (Kalanianaole Hwy., for example), are at least well marked. Major attractions and scenic spots are marked by the distinctive Hawaii Visitors Bureau sign with its red-caped warrior.

You can usually orient yourself by the mountains and the ocean. North, south, east, and west are less important than the local references. To go **mauka** means to go *toward the mountains* (north from Waikiki); go **makai** means to go *toward the ocean* (south); go toward **Diamond Head** means to go *in the direction of that famous landmark* (east); and go **ewa** (pronounced *ehva*) means to go *away from Diamond Head* (west). You may be told that a shop is on the mauka–Diamond Head corner of the street, meaning it is on the mountain side of the street on the corner closest to Diamond Head. When giving directions, most local people state the highways by name, not by number.

Hawaii's drivers are generally courteous, and you rarely hear a horn. People will slow down and let you into traffic with a wave of the hand. A friendly wave back is appreciated and customary.

Driving in rush-hour traffic (6:30–8:30 AM and 3:30–5:30 PM) can be frustrating, not only because of the sheer volume of traffic but because left turns are forbidden at many intersections. Parking along many streets is curtailed during these hours, and towing is strictly enforced. Read the curbside parking signs before leaving your vehicle, even at a meter.

Don't leave valuables in your car. Tourists are targets for thieves because they probably won't be here by the time the case comes to trial, even if the crooks are caught.

Car Rentals   The cost of shipping a car by freighter is at least $500. We advise leaving your car at home and renting one.

There's absolutely no need to rent a car if you don't plan to leave Waikiki. In fact, it will be a nuisance with all the one-way streets and the difficulty in parking. If you plan to do some sightseeing outside Waikiki, a number of highly competitive rental-car companies offer special deals and discount coupons. When you're booking your hotel or plane reservations, ask if there is a car tie-in. The Hawaii State Consumer Protection Office also suggests that on fly/drive deals, you ask (1) whether the company will honor a reservation rate if only larger cars are available when you arrive, and (2) whether only certain credit cards will be accepted. **Alamo, Tropical, Avis, National,** and **Dollar** have tie-ins with Hawaiian and Aloha Airlines; Aloha also ties in with **Budget.**

During peak seasons—summer, Christmas vacation, and February—car rental reservations are necessary.

Rental agencies abound in and around the Honolulu Airport and in Waikiki. Often it is cheaper to rent in Waikiki than at the airport. Expect to pay around $35–$45 daily at the airport and $30–$40 in Waikiki, with lower rates at local budget companies. On Oahu, unlimited mileage is often the rule. At press time, Dollar had the best daily rate and Budget the best weekly rate.

Avis (tel. 800/331–1212), **Hertz** (tel. 800/654–3131), **Budget** (tel. 800/527–0700), **National** (tel. 800/227–7368), and **Dollar** (tel. 800/800–4000) have airport and downtown offices. Local budget and used-rental-car companies include **USA** (tel. 800/678–6000), which serves other islands, too; **Five-O** (tel. 808/836–1028), with passenger vans available; **VIP** (tel. 808/732–3327); **United** (tel. 800/922–4605); **Apollo** (tel. 808/926–8336), which rents convertibles; and **Maxi Car Rental** (tel. 808/923–7381).

Find out a few essentials *before* you arrive at the rental counter. (Otherwise a sales agent could talk you into additional costs you don't need.) The major added cost in renting cars is usually the so-called collision damage waiver (CDW). Find out from the rental agency you're planning to use what the waiver will cover. Your own employee or personal insurance may already cover the damage to a rental car. If so, bring along a photocopy of the benefits section of your insurance policy.

More and more companies—Hertz leading the way—now hold renters responsible for theft and vandalism if they don't buy the CDW. In response, some credit card and insurance companies are extending their coverage to rental cars. These include **Chase Manhattan Bank Visa Cards** (tel. 800/441–2753), and **Access America** (tel. 800/284–8300).

You should also find out before renting if you must pay for a full tank of gas whether you use it all or not. In addition, you should make sure the rental agency gives you a reservation number for the car you are planning to rent.

By Limousine **Crown Limousine** (tel. 808/536–9066) has Cadillacs and Lincoln Presidential stretches from $55 an hour, with a two-hour minimum. **Cloud Nine Limousine Service** (tel. 808/524–7999) will provide red-carpet treatment in its chauffeur-driven Rolls Royce limousines. Riding in such style costs $60 an hour with a two-hour minimum service required.

By Moped/ **Aloha Funway Rentals** (tel. 808/946–2766) has mopeds for $15–
Motorcycle $20 a day. It rents motorcycles for $60–$150 a day. **Island**
and Bicycle **Scooters** (tel. 808/924–9331) rents bicycles for $10 per half day.

By Pedicab You may have heard about them, but they have been banned, and no longer operate on the main streets. You may still find some cruising the side streets. Be sure to settle on the fare ahead of time, and don't buy anything else from the operator.

Important Addresses and Numbers

Hawaii Visitors 2270 Kalakaua Ave., 8th Floor, Honolulu 96815, right in Waiki-
Bureau ki, tel. 808/923–1811.

Emergencies **911** will get you the police, the fire department, an ambulance, or the suicide center.
Honolulu County Medical Society (tel. 808/536–6988)—information on doctors.
Coast Guard Rescue (tel. 808/541–2450).
Doctors on Call. A doctor, laboratory/radiology technician, and nurses are on duty. Appointments are recommended but not necessary. Services include diagnosis and treatment of illness

and injury, laboratory testing and X-ray on site, and referral, when necessary. More than 150 kinds of medical insurance are accepted, including Medicare, Medicaid, and most kinds of travel insurance. *Outrigger Waikiki, 2335 Kalakaua Ave., Suite 207, tel. 808/971–6000. Open 8–4:30.*

Hospitals **Straub Clinic,** 888 S. King St., Honolulu, tel. 808/522–4000; **Queen's Medical Center,** 1301 Punchbowl St., Honolulu, tel. 808/538–9011; **Kapiolani Medical Center for Women and Children,** 1319 Punahou St., Honolulu, tel. 808/973–8511; **Castle Medical Center,** 640 Ulukahiki, Kailua, tel. 808/263–5500.

Pharmacies **Kuhio Pharmacy** (Outrigger West Hotel, 2330 Kuhio Ave., tel. 923–4466).

Longs Drug Store (Ala Moana Shopping Center, 1450 Ala Moana Blvd., 2nd level, tel. 808/949–4010).

Surf Report Dial 808/836–1952.

Weather Dial 808/833–2849.

Marine Forecast Dial 808/836–3921.

Time of Day Dial 808/983–3211.

Opening and Closing Times

Most Oahu banks are open Monday through Thursday 8:30–3 or 4:30, Friday 8:30–6. Most financial institutions are closed on weekends and holidays.

Major museums are open daily 9 or 10–4:30 or 5. The Honolulu Academy of Arts is closed Sunday morning and all day Monday. Most museums are closed on Christmas.

Major shopping malls are generally open daily 10–9, although some shops may close at 4 or 5. Ala Moana Center is open weekdays 9:30–9, Saturday 9:30–5:30, Sunday 10–5, with extended hours leading up to Christmas.

Guided Tours

Types of Tours **Circle Island Tour.** There are several variations on this theme. Read Scenic Drives around Oahu in the Excursions from Waikiki chapter to decide what's important to you and then see which tour comes the closest to matching your desires. Some of these all-day tours include lunch. Cost: $47–$52, depending on number of stops, whether lunch is included or whether you go by bus or minibus, the latter being slightly more expensive.

Little Circle Tour. These tours cover the territory discussed in the East Oahu Ring section of Scenic Drives around Oahu in the Excursions from Waikiki chapter. Most of these tours are the same, no matter what the company. This is a half-day tour. Cost: $22–$25.

Pearl Harbor, City, and Punchbowl Tour. This comprehensive tour includes the boat tour to Pearl Harbor run by the National Park Service. (*See* Tour 5: Circle Island Driving Tour, *below*, for particulars on the attractions.) Cost: $22–$25.

Polynesian Cultural Center. *See* Tour 5: Circle Island Driving Tour, *below*, for details on the center. The only advantage of the tour is that you don't have to drive yourself back to Waikiki after dark if you take in the evening show. Cost: $60–$70.

Tour Companies Many "ground" companies handle these excursions. Some herd you onto an air-conditioned bus and others use smaller vans. Vans are recommended because less time is spent picking up passengers and you get to know your fellow passengers and your tour guide. Whether you go by bus or van, you'll probably be touring in top-of-the-line equipment. The competition among these companies is fierce, and everyone has to keep up. If you're booking through your hotel travel desk, ask whether you'll be on a bus or a van and exactly what the tour includes in the way of actual "get-off-the-bus" stops and "window sights."

Most of the tour guides have been in the business for years. Many have taken special Hawaiiana classes to learn their history and lore. They expect a tip ($2 per person at least), but they're just as cordial without one.

There are many tour companies. Here are some of the most reliable and popular:

American Express (tel. 808/921–6300). American Express books through several tour companies and can help you choose which tour best suits your needs.
Diamond Head Tours (tel. 808/922–0544). Guides must complete the Bishop Museum's Hawaiiana classes.
E Noa Tours (tel. 808/599–2561). This company uses mini-buses exclusively and likes to get you into the outdoors.
Gray Line Hawaii (tel. 808/833–8000) has air-conditioned motorcoaches, vans, and mini-buses.
Polynesian Adventure Tours (tel. 808/922–0888). Some tours are action-oriented. Charters are also available.
Roberts Hawaii (tel. 808/523–8860). Equipment ranges from vans to Presidential limousines.
Trans Hawaiian Services (tel. 808/735–6467 or 800/533–8765). Multi-lingual services are offered.

Walking Tours **Chinatown Walking Tour.** Meet at the Chinese Chamber of Commerce (42 N. King St.) for a fascinating peek into herbal shops, an acupuncturist's office, open-air markets, and specialty stores. The two-hour tour is sponsored by the Chinese Chamber of Commerce. Reservations required. *Tel. 808/533–3181. Cost: $5. Tues. only, 9:30 AM.*
Historic Downtown Walking Tour. Volunteers from the Mission Houses Museum (553 S. King St.) take you on a two-hour walk through Honolulu, where the historic sites are side by side with the modern business towers. If it's Friday, end the tour by picking up a fast-food lunch and enjoying the noontime concert on the Iolani Palace lawn. *Tel. 808/531–0481. Reservations required. Cost: $4. Wed. 10:30AM.*
Clean Air Walks. Volunteers from this environmental action group conduct a variety of interesting walks, such as the "Wealthy Residential Walk" (Sun.), the "Secluded Tropical Paradise Walk" in Manoa Valley (Fri.), and a Diamond Head summit hike (Sat.). Call for schedule. *Tel. 808/948–3299. Donation: $3 to the Clean Air Fund. 9 AM.*

Great Outdoor Tours **Action Hawaii Adventures.** This company manages to compress into one day adventures the tourist rarely gets to do in a week. You'll go on guided hikes through rain forests and valleys, swim beneath waterfalls, and snorkel at "insider" spots. Boogieboarding and spearfishing are also available. A sandwich lunch plus samples of local food are included in the all-day tours. *Tel. 808/732–4453. Cost: $79.*

Helicopter Tours **Papillon.** If you've never tried a whirlybird and can afford to, this company has a 20-minute bird's-eye introductory view of Waikiki and Diamond Head for $79 per person. The 30-minute flight for $99 through the dramatic Nuuanu Pali and over the sunken crater of Hanauma Bay is beautiful, or you can circle the entire island for one hour for $187. All of Papillon's helicopter tours take off from Honolulu International Airport, and the company picks you up from your Waikiki hotel in a courtesy shuttle, so you don't have to bother with the confusion of airport traffic. *Waikiki Business Plaza, 2270 Kalakaua Ave., Suite 1104, tel. 808/836–1566.*

Flightseeing Tours Several air tour companies offer the chance to see Hawaii from the skies. Even if your itinerary does not include stays on the Neighbor Islands, a flightseeing tour can give you an overview, so to speak, of the entire Aloha State. **Scenic Air Tours Hawaii** offers a full-day, eight-island tour from Honolulu, with stops on Maui, where you get a picnic lunch and Kauai, for the boat trip up to Fern Grotto. Trips are made aboard twin-engine nine-passenger Beechcrafts and cost $260. *100 Iolana Pl., Honolulu International Airport, tel. 808/836–0044.*

Exploring

Oahu is a mixed bag, with enough sightseeing attractions and adventures to fill an entire vacation. Most of the time it's just too warm and sunny to spend all day exploring in the car or on a walking tour. So plan ahead, see only what you are interested in, and relax the rest of the time.

Whether you're driving, taking a tour, or riding the bus, this section will give you an idea of what you want to see. Ready? If you're driving, KCCN 1400 on your AM radio dial plays Hawaiian music exclusively, to set the right mood.

Directions on Oahu are often given as *mauka*—toward the mountains (north), and *makai*—toward the ocean (south). In Honolulu and Waikiki, you may also hear people referring to "Diamond Head"—toward that landmark (east); and *ewa*—away from Diamond Head (west). You'll find these terms used throughout this section.

Highlights for First-time Visitors

Arizona Memorial, Tour 5
Bishop Museum, Tour 3
Diamond Head Crater, Tour 4
Honolulu Zoo, Tour 1
Iolani Palace, Tour 2
Pali Lookout, Tour 4
Polynesian Cultural Center, Tour 5
Sea Life Park, Tour 4
Waikiki Aquarium, Tour 1
Waimea Falls Park, Tour 5

Tour 1: Waikiki

Numbers in the margin correspond to points of interest on the Waikiki map.

❶ The **Ilikai Waikiki Hotel** (1777 Ala Moana Blvd.) is a good place to start a walking tour. From the second-floor pool deck,
❷ there's a fine view of the **Ala Wai Yacht Harbor,** home berth to an armada of pleasure boats and two yacht clubs, both of which are open to members only. America's Cup champion skipper Dennis Conner hung his binnacle at the Waikiki Yacht Club when training for his victorious race against the Australians in 1987. Stroll the docks and check out the variety of craft, from tiny catamarans to luxury cruisers.

Head toward the main intersection of Ala Moana Boulevard and
❸ Kalia Road. Take a little detour to the **Hilton Hawaiian Village** (2005 Kalia Rd.), a 20-acre complex with gardens and waterfalls. The hotel fronts the pretty Kahanamoku Lagoon and beach, which looks the part of a quintessential tropical setting, complete with a little island in the lagoon and palm trees all around. Look for the penguin pond in the back of the main lobby.

The village is a hodgepodge of Oriental architecture, with a Chinese moon gate, a pagoda, and a Japanese farmhouse with a water wheel, all dominated by a tall mosaic mural of the hotel's Rainbow Tower. Dubbed the Rainbow Bazaar, this is a good place to browse and pick up souvenirs.

❹ Across the street on Kalia Road is the U.S. Army's **Fort DeRussy.** On Saturday evenings during the summer, there are Catholic masses on the lawn by the beach, with the setting sun as a backdrop and a lot of Hawaiian pageantry as part of the service. (For the schedule, call 808/263–8844.) Battery Randolf (Building 32) was built in 1909 as a key in the defense of Pearl Harbor and Honolulu. Within its walls, which measure 22 feet thick in places, is the **Army Museum,** housing an intimidating collection of war paraphernalia. The major focus is World War II memorabilia, but exhibits range from ancient Hawaiian weaponry to displays relating to the Vietnam War. *Tel. 808/ 438–2821. Group guided tours can be arranged. Admission free. Open Tues.–Sun. 10 AM–4:30 PM; closed Mon.*

❺ Across the street from Fort DeRussy, nestled snugly amid the commerce of Waikiki, is an oasis of tranquility: the **Tea House of the Urasenke Foundation.** Take part in a Japanese tea ceremony; you'll be served tea and sweets by ladies in kimonos. The Urasenke Foundation is a centuries-old institution based in Kyoto, Japan. It has set the etiquette for the tea ceremony based on the Zen philosophy that has influenced Japanese art and taste. The Waikiki teahouse was donated by the Kyoto foundation and was the first to be built outside Japan. The teahouse is a good, basic introduction to Japanese culture. Wear something comfortable enough for sitting on the floor (but no shorts, please). *245 Saratoga Rd., tel. 808/923–3059. Minimum donation: $2. Open Wed. and Fri., 10 AM.*

❻ With a little zip from the tea and a little Zen for the road, head mauka (toward the mountains, north) toward Kalakaua Avenue and turn toward Diamond Head. At **First Hawaiian Bank** (2181 Kalakaua Ave.) on the corner of Lewers Street, look in the lobby for six massive murals depicting the various ethnic groups that make up the population of Hawaii. They also deal with the evolution of Hawaiian culture—from Hawaiian arts before contact with the Western world to the introduction of the first printing press to the islands in 1872. The impressive

Waikiki

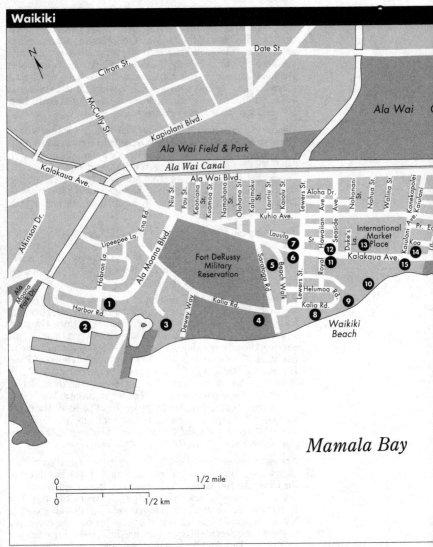

Mamala Bay

```
0          1/2 mile
0          1/2 km
```

Ala Wai Yacht
Harbor, **2**

Damien Museum, **18**

Diamond Head, **27**

First Hawaiian
Bank, **6**

Fort De Russy, **4**

Gump Building, **7**

Halekulani Hotel, **8**

Hawaii Visitors
Bureau, **12**

Hilton Hawaiian
Village (Rainbow
Bazaar) , **3**

Honolulu Zoo, **19**

Hyatt Regency
Waikiki, **14**

Ilikai Waikiki Hotel, **1**

International Market
Place, **13**

Kahuna (or Wizard)
Stones, **15**

Kapiolani
Bandstand, **23**

Kapiolani Park, **20**

Kapiolani Park Rose
Garden, **26**

Kodak Hula Show, **22**

Pacific Beach
Hotel, **16**

Royal Hawaiian
Hotel, **10**

Royal Hawaiian
Shopping Center, **11**

Saint Augustine's, **17**

Sheraton Moana
Surfrider, **15**

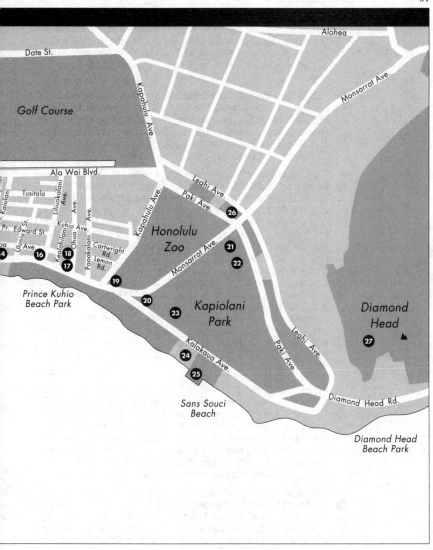

Sheraton Waikiki, **9**

Tea House of the
Urasenke
Foundation, **5**

Waikiki Aquarium, **24**

Waikiki Business
Plaza, **12**

Waikiki Shell, **21**

Waikiki War Memorial
Natatorium, **25**

panels were painted in 1951–1952 by Jean Charlot (1898–1979), whose work is represented in the Uffizi Gallery in Florence, the British Museum in London, and the Metropolitan Museum and the Museum of Modern Art in New York. The murals are beautifully lit at night, with some panels visible from the street.

Across the street, at 2200 Kalakaua Avenue, is one of Waikiki's architectural landmarks, the blue-tile roof of the **Gump Building.** Built in 1929 in the Hawaiian colonial style, and featuring Oriental architectural motifs, it was once the premier store of Hawaii and was known for the quality of its Asian and Hawaiian objects. Now it houses a Louis Vuitton store.

Walk down Lewers Street toward the ocean, to the impressive **Halekulani Hotel** (2199 Kalia Rd.). One of the most interesting things about the hotel, aside from its famed restaurants, is the gigantic floral arrangement in the lobby. While you're there, take a peek at the swimming pool with its huge orchid mosaic at the bottom. Incorporated into the relatively new Halekulani Hotel is a portion of its old (1917) structure, which was the setting for the first of the Charlie Chan detective novels, *The House without a Key.*

Time Out If it's lunchtime, you should enjoy dining at **Orchids** restaurant in the Halekulani with a view of Diamond Head from most every table. The lunch menu includes light entrées and tasty salads. But if you're looking for eye-boggling quantity, wait a few minutes until you reach the **Royal Hawaiian Hotel** and try its famous lunch buffet in the Surf Room, $17.75, served Monday–Saturday noon–2:30 PM.

From the Halekulani, treat yourself to a stroll along the ocean on the paved walkway leading past the **Sheraton Waikiki** (2255 Kalakaua Ave.) to the gracious old **Royal Hawaiian Hotel** (2259 Kalakaua Ave.). The lovely lobby, with its pink decor, is reminiscent of another era. A stroll through the old gardens, with their tall swaying coconut palms and vivid flowers, is like stepping through a time warp to a period when Waikiki was a sleepy, tropical paradise with a couple of gracious old hotels.

The illusion is only momentary, for the path leads to the modern **Royal Hawaiian Shopping Center** (2201 Kalakaua Ave.), a four-story, open-air arcade with hundreds of shops. A tasty treat here is the local favorite, shave ice, the Hawaiian version of a snow cone, which comes in exotic fruit flavors like *lychee* and *li hing mui.* Have it with ice cream and *azuki* beans at the Island Snow stand (tel. 808/926–3067).

Across the street from the Royal Hawaiian Shopping Center is the **Waikiki Business Plaza** (2270 Kalakaua Ave.), recognizable by its fish mosaic mural and little fountain. The **Hawaii Visitors Bureau** (tel. 808/923–1811) is on the eighth floor. Pick up free booklets on hotels, buses, and restaurants, as well as a calendar of events. On the 10th floor are some wholesale fashion outlets open to the public. This is a good place to end a day's walking tour, or to take a break before moving on.

Walking toward Diamond Head, in the middle of the same block as the Waikiki Business Plaza, you can't miss the **International Market Place** (2330 Kalakaua Ave.) with its spreading banyan and Swiss Family Robinson–style treehouse. There's usually a lot of activity here, with wood-carvers, basket-weavers, and other artisans from various Pacific islands creating and selling their handicrafts. Most of the souvenir stuff, both tacky and 24-karat, is sold from little Asian-style pushcarts.

Time Out The **Food Court** in the **Market Place** is a collection of individual food concessions with a central outdoor seating area. It includes inexpensive Japanese, Chinese, Korean, Filipino, Greek, Italian, and American kitchens.

If you take a short walk from King's Village in the direction of Diamond Head, you'll reach the **Hyatt Regency Waikiki** (2424 Kalakaua Ave.). To help visitors become acquainted with Hawaiian arts and crafts, Auntie Malia Solomon, resident Hawaiian authority for the Hyatt Regency, has assembled what she calls her "sharing place." The hotel calls the small second-floor museum of artifacts, quilts, and crafts **Hyatt's Hawaii.** It's a charming collection.

Time Out If you need to rest your feet, stop at **Harry's Bar,** which is right in the Hyatt Regency's atrium by the big waterfall (on the ground floor). Open from 2:30 PM, Harry's is a fun place to have a drink and watch the passing parade of people.

Across the way, the oldest hotel in Waikiki, the venerable **Moana,** has undergone a major historical renovation. Wander through the breezy lobby to the wide back porch that overlooks the beach. They've done a beautiful job on this historic building. The Moana is now merged with the neighboring Surfrider Hotel and is renamed the **Sheraton Moana Surfrider** (2365 Kalakaua Ave.). There are period furnishings, historical exhibits, and plenty of nostalgia. The Beaux Arts–style hotel has been placed on the National Register of Historic Places. Visit the **Historical Room** in the rotunda just above the main entrance, and enjoy a collection of old photographs and memorabilia dating from the opening of the hotel in 1901.

Next to the Sheraton Moana Surfrider are the four **Kahuna (or Wizard) Stones of Waikiki,** which, according to legend, were placed there in tribute to four prophets from Tahiti, who came to Hawaii sometime before the 16th century. Before disappearing, the prophets are said to have transferred their healing powers to the stones. They're by the beach showers, and, more often than not, are irreverently draped in wet towels. Nearby is the **Duke Kahanamoku Statue,** raised in honor of Hawaii's famed Olympic swimmer.

Two blocks away at 2490 Kalakaua Avenue, with an entrance on Liliuokalani Avenue, is the **Pacific Beach Hotel,** with its huge 280,000-gallon aquarium. The aquarium is two stories high and harbors a thousand fish. The **Oceanarium Restaurant** is on the lobby level, and the hotel's fine dining room, **Neptune,** is directly above it. Both wrap around the aquarium. *Tel. 808/ 922–1233. Admission free. Daily feeding times are 9 and 11:30 AM; 12:30, 5:30, 6:30, and 7:30 PM.*

If you walk two blocks toward Diamond Head, you'll find the only church in Waikiki with its own building, the Roman Catholic **Saint Augustine's** (130 Ohua Ave., tel. 808/923–7024).

Just around the corner, in back of the church, is the **Damien Museum,** a small but fascinating two-room exhibit centering on the life and work of the Belgian priest Father Joseph Damien de Veuster, who came to Hawaii and labored and died among the victims of Hansen's disease (leprosy) on the island of Molokai. Ask to see the museum's 20-minute videotape. It is low-budget, but well done and emotionally gripping. *Tel. 808/923–2690. Admission free. Open weekdays, 9–3, Sat. 9–noon.*

This is a good place to end a tour of Waikiki. The area in and around Kapiolani Park, next on the list, is worth a day's outing by itself to allow plenty of time to smell the flowers—and the fresh clean surf.

⑲ The **Honolulu Zoo** (151 Kapahulu Ave., on the corner of Kalakaua Ave. and Kapahulu Ave.), is just a two-block walk toward Diamond Head from the Damien Museum. The zoo is 40 green acres of lush foliage and home to 2,000 furry and finned creatures. There are bigger and better zoos, but this one is pretty, and where else can you see a *nene*, Hawaii's state bird? On Wednesday evenings in the summer, the zoo offers "The Wildest Show in Town," a free program of singing, dancing, and other entertainment. Check the local newspaper, either the *Honolulu Advertiser* or *Star Bulletin*, for what's playing. In 1992, the zoo opened its impressive 7 ½-acre African savanna, where animals roam freely on the other side of hidden rails and moats. *Tel. 808/971–7171. Admission: $3, children free. Open daily 8:30–4.*

On Saturdays and Sundays, look for the **Zoo Fence Art Mart,** on Monsarrat Avenue outside the zoo, on the Diamond Head side. There's some affordable work by good contemporary artists and craftspeople that make better souvenirs of Hawaii than junky ashtrays and monkeypod Hawaiian gods carved in the Philippines.

Across Monsarrat Avenue between Kalakaua Avenue and Paki
⑳ ㉑ Street, in **Kapiolani Park,** is the **Waikiki Shell,** Honolulu's outdoor concert arena. Check the newspaper to see what's playing. Local people bring a picnic and get "grass" seats (lawn seating). Here's a chance to have a magical night listening to some of the world's best musicians while lying on a blanket with the moon shining over Diamond Head. *Most concerts are held between May 1 and Labor Day.*

㉒ In bleachers adjacent to the Waikiki Shell, the famous **Kodak Hula Show** has been wowing crowds for more than 50 years. It's colorful, lively, and fun. For the best seats, get there by 9:30 AM for the 10 AM one-hour show. Naturally, it's a great opportunity to take photographs. *Tel. 808/833–1661. Admission free. Shows Tues.–Thurs. only.*

Kapiolani Park's other major entertainment area is the
㉓ **Kapiolani Bandstand.** There's usually a free show of some kind on Sunday afternoons at 2, often a concert by the Royal Hawaiian Band. Check the newspaper for particulars. Some excellent hula dances are performed here by local groups that don't frequent the hotels.

㉔ To save steps, cut diagonally across the park to the **Waikiki Aquarium** (2777 Kalakaua Ave.). Recently renovated, the amazing little aquarium harbors more than 300 species of Hawaiian and South Pacific marine life, including the giant clam, the chambered nautilus, and sharks. It's the third oldest aquarium in the United States. Check out the newly opened Sea Visions Theater, whose 10-minute-or-so films highlight the current exhibits. *Tel. 808/923–9741. Admission: $3, children under 15 free. Open daily 9–5. Closed Thanksgiving and Christmas.*

㉕ A little farther along Kalakaua Avenue toward Diamond Head is the **Waikiki War Memorial Natatorium.** This pale stone-colored concrete open-air swimming stadium was built to commemorate lives lost in World War II. Although it's fallen into disrepair and is no longer open to the public, it stands proudly, its outer wall lit at night, showing off what's left of the pair of eagle statues that sit atop the entrance. Narrowly saved from the wrecker's ball, there is a drive to restore it.

Time Out Close by, at the **New Otani Kaimana Beach Hotel** (2863 Kalakaua Ave.), you can dine outdoors beside the sand in the shade of a *hau* tree. This spot is not well known to tourists, but it's one of the nicest oceanfront dining options on the island.

㉖ You could walk over to the **Kapiolani Park Rose Garden** at Paki Street and Monsarrat Avenue, but it's a long walk, and if you come from an area where roses thrive, you've probably seen better. There are picnic tables, and the admission is free.

㉗ For those willing to do more strenuous walking, the hike to the summit of **Diamond Head** offers a marvelous view. Drive along Diamond Head Road, on the Waikiki side of the extinct volcano. The entrance to the crater is marked by a sign. Drive through the tunnel to the inside of the crater, once a military fortification.

You can also take a bus from Waikiki. Bus 58, "Hawaii Kai–Sea Life Park," stops near the entrance. A sign points the way.

The trail begins at the parking lot. Signs tell you that the hike takes an hour, but you can probably do it in 40 minutes or less, even with a child in tow. Most guidebooks also say there are 99 steps on the trail to the top. That's true of one flight, but there are four flights altogether. Bring a flashlight to see your way through a narrow tunnel. The view is worth it when you get there, sweeping across Waikiki and Honolulu in one direction and out to Koko Head in the other, with Diamond Head Lighthouse and surfers and windsurfers scattered like confetti on the cresting waves below. *Park hours daily 6 AM–6 PM.*

You can also walk the 2.3 miles from the zoo to the crater and then climb the additional .7 mile to the 760-foot summit. A group meets Saturdays at 9 AM by the rainbow windsock at the zoo entrance. All but the last part of the hike is escorted and narrated by volunteer guides. Everyone gets a free souvenir "I Climbed Diamond Head" badge. *Tel. 808/944–0804. Donation: $3, free for children.*

Tour 2: Historic Downtown Honolulu

Numbers in the margin correspond to points of interest on the Downtown Honolulu map.

Honolulu's past and present play a delightful counterpoint throughout the downtown sector. Modern skyscrapers stand directly across the street from a series of piers where huge ocean liners come to call, as they have for decades. To reach this area from Waikiki by car, take Ala Moana Boulevard to Alakea

Street. Turn left to find the public parking in the Aloha Tower parking lot, across Ala Moana Boulevard from Alakea Street. You could also park at various public lots in the office buildings downtown, but be warned that they are quite expensive.

If you travel by public transportation, take Bus 2 from Waikiki. Get off at Alapai Street and walk makai (toward the ocean) to King Street. Most of the historic sites are clustered within easy walking distance.

❶ Begin this tour at the **Hawaii Maritime Center,** which is across Ala Moana Boulevard from Alakea Street in downtown Honolulu. Opened in late 1988, it features such attractions as the *Falls of Clyde,* a century-old, four-masted, square-rigged ship now used as a museum. Pier 7 was the international steamship pier in turn-of-the-century Honolulu. Aloha Tower, built in 1926 and once the tallest building in Hawaii, provides a panoramic view of the city and coastline. The Kalakaua Boat House includes exhibits covering Hawaii's whaling days, the history of Honolulu Harbor, and canoes, plus the Pacific Ocean Theater and open-air restaurants. *The Hokule'a* is a double-hulled canoe used on the Polynesian Voyaging Society's "Voyage of Rediscovery" to the South Pacific. *Pier 7, Ala Moana Blvd., Honolulu, tel. 808/536–6373. Admission: $7. Open daily 9–5.*

The **Children's Touch and Feel Museum** is also part of the Hawaii Maritime Center. At this 1,000-square-foot aquatic attraction, kids can play captain of a mock submarine complete with periscope, engine, steering and diving controls, and crew's quarters. A lifeboat and the deck of a 19th-century sailing vessel with steering wheel, capstan, and cargo winch, are also here to explore. A cassette tour narrated by William Conrad guides you through the museum. *Pier 7, Ala Moana Blvd., Honolulu, tel. 808/536–6373. Admission: $7 adults, $4 ages 6–17. Open daily 9–5.*

❷ Cross Ala Moana Boulevard, walk a block ewa (away from Diamond Head) and turn mauka (toward the mountains) on newly renovated **Fort Street Mall,** a pedestrian walkway that passes buildings historic and new. Sit on a bench for a few minutes and watch the fascinating parade of everyone from businesspeople to street preachers.

❸ Turn left on King Street, and in a few blocks you'll reach **Chinatown,** the old section of downtown Honolulu, which is crammed with interesting shops. Slightly on the tawdry side, it has lately been getting a piecemeal face-lift as little art galleries open in renovated structures. There are lei stands, herb shops, acupuncture studios, noodle factories, Chinese and Thai restaurants, and the colorful Oahu Market, an open-air emporium with hanging pig heads, display cases of fresh fish, row after row of exotic fruits and vegetables, and plenty of smiling vendors of all ethnic backgrounds.

Time Out   There are plenty of fun Chinese restaurants in Chinatown, but **Wo Fat** (115 N. Hotel St., one block north of King St., tel. 808/ 537–6260) is a great lunchtime stop on your walking tour. Reputed to be Hawaii's oldest restaurant, this Hotel Street landmark has been doing business since 1882, with no indication of slowing down. Authentic Cantonese food is the fare in this three-story establishment with tile floors, and the meals are a

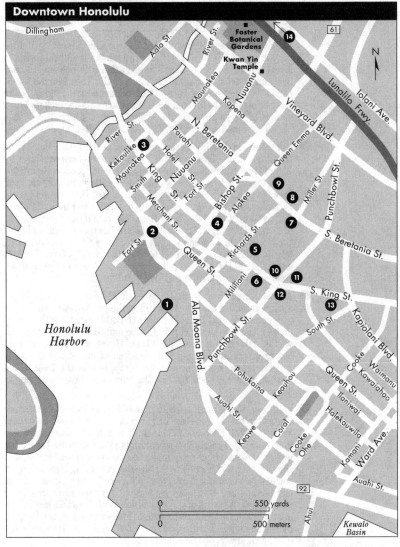

Downtown Honolulu

Dillingham

Aala St.

River St.

Maunakea

Foster
Botanical
Gardens

Kwan Yin
Temple

14

61

Iolani Ave.

Lunalilo Frwy.

N

River St.

Ketaulike

Maunakea

3

Pauahi

Nuuanu

Kapena

N. Beretania

Vineyard Blvd.

Queen Emma

Punchbowl St.

Smith

King

Hotel St.

Nuuanu St.

Fort St.

Bishop St.

Alakea

9

8

Miller St.

S. Beretania St.

2

Merchant St.

4

Richards St.

7

Fort St.

Queen St.

5

Milliani

10

6

11

12

S. King St.

13

Kapiolani Blvd.

1

Ala Moana Blvd.

*Honolulu
Harbor*

Punchbowl St.

South St.

Cooke

Waimanu

Kawaiahao

Queen St.

Iloniwai

Pohukaina

Keauhou

Halekauwila

Kamani

Ward Ave.

Auahi St.

Keawe

Coral

Cooke

Ohe

92

Auahi St.

0 ──── 550 yards

0 ──── 500 meters

Ahui

*Kewalo
Basin*

Aliiolani Hale
(Kamehameha I
statue), **6**

Bishop Museum, **14**

Chinatown, **3**

Fort Street Mall, **2**

Hawaii Maritime
Center, **1**

Hawaii State
Capitol, **7**

Hawaii State
Library, **10**

Honolulu Hale, **11**

Iolani Palace, **5**

Kawaiahao Church, **12**

Mission Houses
Museum, **13**

Saint Andrew's
Cathedral, **9**

Tamarind Park, **4**

Washington Place, **8**

great bargain. Be sure to order some of Wo Fat's special fried noodles with beef in oyster sauce.

Walk back toward Diamond Head along King Street until it intersects with Bishop Street. On the mauka (mountain) side is ❹ lovely **Tamarind Park,** where folks gather at lunchtime to hear live music, from jazz and Hawaiian to the U.S. Marine band. Check the newspaper to find out the schedule. Friday is the most likely day to catch an act. Do as the locals do: Pick up lunch at one of the many carryouts bordering the park, pull up a bench or some lawn, and enjoy. *Admission free. Open all day.*

❺ Continue along King Street until you reach **Iolani Palace,** on the mauka side. This graceful Victorian structure was built by King David Kalakaua on the site of an earlier palace. Beautifully restored, it is America's only royal palace and contains the thrones of King Kalakaua and his successor (and sister) Queen Liliuokalani. Also on the palace grounds is the **Kalakaua Coronation Bandstand,** where the Royal Hawaiian Band performs at noon most Fridays. Stop at the **Iolani Barracks,** built to house the Royal Guard and now a gift shop. *King St. at Richards St., tel. 808/522-0832. Reservations required. Admission: $4 adults, $1 children 5-12; children under 5 are not permitted. Open only for guided tours, Wed.-Sat. 9-2:15.*

❻ Across King Street from the palace is **Aliiolani Hale,** the old judiciary building that once served as the parliament hall during the monarchy era. In front of it is the gilded **statue of Kamehameha I,** the Big Island chieftain who united all the warring Hawaiian Islands into one kingdom. He stands with one arm outstretched in welcome. The original of this statue is on the Big Island, in Kapaau, near the birthplace of the king. Each year on June 11, his birthday, the Honolulu statue is draped in leis.

❼ Walk one block mauka up Richards Street to see the **Hawaii State Capitol** (S. Beretania St. between Punchbowl and Richards Sts., tel. 808/586-2211). Built in 1969, this architectural gem is richly symbolic: The columns look like palm trees, the legislative chambers are shaped like volcanic cinder cones, and the central court is open to the sky, representing Hawaii's open society. The capitol is surrounded by reflecting pools, just as the Islands are embraced by water. Between the capitol and the palace is a statue of Queen Liliuokalani, Hawaii's last reigning monarch. In front is a statue of Father Damien, the Belgian priest who gave his life caring for the victims of Hansen's disease, or leprosy, on the island of Molokai.

❽ Almost across the street from the state capitol is **Washington Place** (320 S. Beretania St.). This graceful 1846 mansion is currently the home of Hawaii's governor. Queen Liliuokalani lived here until her death in 1917. You can only peer through the wrought-iron gates, since the residence is not open to the public.

❾ Next to Washington Place is **Saint Andrew's Cathedral** (S. Beretania St. at Queen Emma St.), Episcopal headquarters in Hawaii. Queen Emma, widow of Kamehameha IV, supervised the construction of the church and was baptized in the sanctuary. The building was designed in England, and parts of it were shipped from there.

Time Out Walk back to King Street and continue one block farther, to Merchant Street. Turn right and you'll discover a charming open-air restaurant ideal for lunch, a snack, or a cool drink. True to its name, the **Croissanterie** (222 Merchant St., tel. 808/533-3443) features fresh-baked breads, muffins, and croissants, great for sandwiches or on their own. Order a beer or a cup of Hawaii's own Lion Coffee, get a salad with your sandwich, and enjoy the relaxed atmosphere of this homey indoor-outdoor spot. In the restaurant's basement, you'll find a used book store, complete with bargain volumes on Hawaii and the Pacific.

Return to King Street, stay on the mauka side, and proceed in a Diamond Head direction. Past the palace is the massive, stone, 1913 **Hawaii State Library,** which was renovated in 1992 and is now a showcase of architectural restoration. Its "Asia and the Pacific" room has a fascinating collection of books old and new about Hawaii. *478 King St., tel. 808/586-3500. Open Tues. and Thurs. 9-8; Mon., Wed., Fri., and Sat. 9-5.*

Next on the mauka side is **Honolulu Hale,** or City Hall (530 S. King St. at Punchbowl St.), a Mediterranean/Renaissance-style building constructed in 1929. You can walk into the cool, open-ceiling lobby, which sometimes displays works by local artists.

Across the street, on the corner of King and Punchbowl, is **Kawaiahao Church,** Hawaii's most famous religious structure. Fancifully called Hawaii's Westminster Abbey, the coral-block church witnessed the coronations, weddings, and funerals of generations of Hawaiian royalty. The graves of missionaries and of King Lunalilo are in the yard. The upper gallery has an exhibit of paintings of the royal families. *957 Punchbowl St. at King St., tel. 808/522-1333. Services in English and Hawaiian each Sun. morning at 8 and 10:30. Free tours weekdays 9-1 and Sun. after the service. Call ahead to schedule one.*

On the Diamond Head side of the church is the **Mission Houses Museum,** a historic complex where the first American missionaries in Hawaii lived. Arriving in 1820, the stalwart band gained royal favor and influenced every aspect of island life. Their descendants have become leaders in government and business. The white frame house was prefabricated in New England and shipped around the Horn. *553 S. King St., tel. 808/531-0481. Admission: $3.50 adults, $1 children 6-15. Museum can be seen only on a guided tour, which is held once an hour, with the last tour at 3. Open Tues.–Sat. 9-4, Sun. 12:30-4. Closed New Year's Day, Easter, Thanksgiving, and Christmas.*

Tour 3: A Side Trip to the Bishop Museum and Planetarium

Anyone who is interested in any facet of Hawaiian or Pacific culture should make the time to take this special tour. The building alone, with its huge Victorian turrets and immense stone walls, is a sight worth seeing.

Founded in 1889 by Charles R. Bishop as a memorial to his wife, Princess Bernice Pauahi, the **Bishop Museum** began as a repository for the royal possessions of this last direct descendant of King Kamehameha the Great. It has since achieved world fame as a center of Polynesian archaeology, ethnology, and history.

There are lustrous feather capes, scary god images, the skeleton of a giant sperm whale, an authentic, well-preserved grass house, and changing displays of old photographs and ethnic crafts. The planetarium next door spotlights "Polynesian Skies," a narrated show that helps you unravel the mysteries of the tropical skies. Arts and crafts demonstrations take place regularly. *1525 Bernice St., tel. 808/848–4129. Admission: $7.95 adults; $6.95 children 6–17, senior citizens, and military; children under 6 free, including the planetarium. Open daily 9–5. Closed Christmas. By car, take Lunalilo Fwy. to Houghtailing exit. Make an immediate right on Houghtailing St., then a left onto Bernice St. By public transportation, take Bus 2 ("School Street") from Waikiki. Get off at the Kamehameha Shopping Center, walk makai (toward the ocean) 1 block to Bernice St., then go left.*

Tour 4: A Driving Tour of the East Oahu Ring

Numbers in the margin correspond to points of interest on the Oahu map.

From Waikiki, there are two routes to Lunalilo Freeway (H-1). On the Diamond Head end, go mauka (toward the mountains) on Kapahulu Avenue and follow the signs to the freeway. On the ewa (away from Diamond Head) end, take Ala Wai Boulevard and turn mauka at Kalakaua Avenue, staying on it until it ends at Beretania Street, which is one-way going left. Turn right off Beretania at Piikoi Street, and the signs will direct you onto the freeway heading west.

Take the freeway exit marked **Pali Highway,** one of two roads that cut through the Koolau Mountains.

❶ On the right is the **Queen Emma Summer Palace.** The colonial-style white mansion, which once served as the summer retreat of King Kamehameha IV and his wife, Queen Emma, is now a museum maintained by the Daughters of Hawaii. It contains many excellent examples of koa furniture of the period, including the beautiful cradle of Prince Albert, heir to the throne, who died at age 4. *2913 Pali Hwy., tel. 808/595–3167. Admission: $4. Guided tours daily 9–4. Closed Thanksgiving, Christmas, New Year's Eve, Easter, and July 4.*

As you drive toward the summit of the highway, the road is lined with sweet ginger during the summer and red poinsettias during the winter. If it has been raining, waterfalls will be tumbling down the sheer, chiseled cliffs of the Koolaus, creating a veritable wonderland in green.

❷ Watch for the turn to the **Pali Lookout** (Nuuanu Pali). There is a small parking lot and a lookout wall from which you can see all the way up and down the windward coast—a view that Mark Twain called the most beautiful in the world. It was in this region that King Kamehameha I drove defending forces over the edges of the 1,000-foot-high cliffs, thus winning the decisive battle for control of Oahu.

As you descend the highway on the other side of the mountain, continue straight along what becomes Kailua Road. If you are interested in Hawaiian history, look for the YMCA at the Cas-

tle Hospital junction of Kalanianaole Highway and Kailua
❸ Road. Behind it is **Ulu Po Heiau.** Though it may look like a pile
of rocks to the uninitiated, Ulu Po Heiau is a sacred platform for
the worship of the gods that dates back to ancient times.

❹ If you're ready for a detour to **Kailua Beach,** which many people
consider the best on the island, continue straight on Kailua
Road. It twists and turns, so watch the signs. Eventually Kailua Road forms a "T" with Kalaheo Avenue and Kawailoa Road.

At the intersection you will see the **Kalapawai Market.** Generations of children have gotten their beach snacks here, and you
might like to as well, since there's no concession stand at Kailua
Beach. Across the street is the **Kailua Beach Center** (130 Kailua
Rd.), where you can rent windsurfing equipment and arrange
for lessons at **Kailua Sailboards** (tel. 808/262–2555; *see* Sports,
below, for further information). **Naish Hawaii** (tel. 808/262–
6068 or 808/261–3539) and **Windsurfing Hawaii** (tel. 808/261–
3539) also offer rental equipment in nearby Kailua.

Turn right past the market. The road crosses a little bridge. On
your left is Kailua Beach Park, where there are showers and
picnic areas, plus a small parking lot (*see* Beaches, *below*). On a
windy day, you'll see scores of windsurfing enthusiasts rigging
their sails on the grass. At the beach, everyone from beginners
to international pro Robbie Naish can be seen boardsailing on
the aqua waters of Kailua Bay.

Retracing your route back to Castle Junction, turn left at the
intersection onto Kalanianaole Highway. Soon you will come to
❺ the town of **Waimanalo,** traditionally a depressed area. Down
the side roads, heading mauka, are little farms that grow a variety of fruits and flowers. Toward the back of the valley,
flanked by cliffs, are small ranches with grazing horses. In the
small Waimanalo Shopping Center on the makai (ocean) side of
the road, there's a **Dave's Ice Cream** (41-1537 Kalanianaole
Hwy., tel. 808/259–8576), which has some of the best ice cream
in the islands, including such exotic, tropical flavors as lychee
and mango.

If you see any trucks selling corn on the cob and you're staying
at a place where you can cook it, be sure to get some. It may be
the sweetest you'll ever eat, and the price is the lowest on Oahu.

❻ **Bellows Beach** (off Kalanianaole Hwy. in Bellows Air Force
Station) is open weekends and holidays. The entrance is on the
makai (ocean) side of the highway. The beach is uncrowded and
great for swimming and bodysurfing. There's shade as well as
picnic areas (*see* Beaches, *below*).

Time Out Just past the entrance to Bellows Beach, on the makai side of
the highway, is **Bueno Nalo** (41-865 Kalanianaole Hwy., tel.
808/259–7186), a funky Mexican eatery with fantastic south-of-
the-border specialties at low prices. The space is small and unpretentious, but the food is terrific. It's BYOB; stop next door
at Jimmy's Market if you'd like a cold one.

For dessert (if you're still hungry), go next door to **Ken's,** a no-
frills bakery with delicious cinnamon rolls (tel. 808/259–9084).

❼ A block farther and you reach **Waimanalo Beach Park,** on the
makai side of the road. The beach is safe for swimming, al-

Oahu

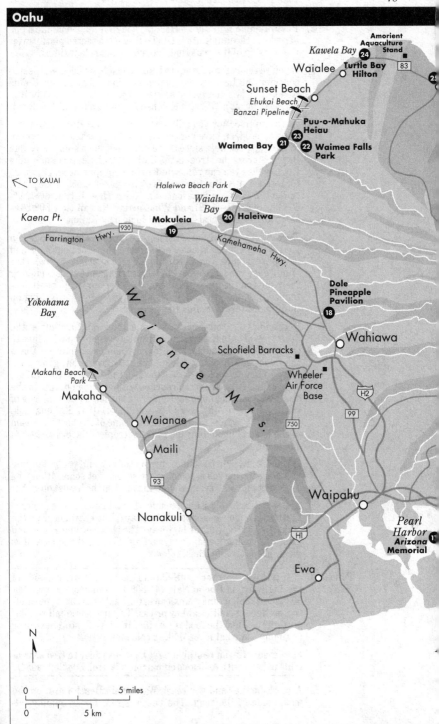

Amorient
Aquaculture
Stand

Kawela Bay **24**

Waialee **Turtle Bay**
Hilton

83

Sunset Beach
Ehukai Beach
Banzai Pipeline
Puu-o-Mahuka
Heiau

Waimea Bay **21** **23** **22** **Waimea Falls**
Park

← TO KAUAI

Haleiwa Beach Park

Waialua
Bay
20 **Haleiwa**

Kaena Pt.
Farrington
Hwy.
930
Mokuleia
19
Kamehameha Hwy.

Yokohama
Bay

Dole
Pineapple
Pavilion
18

W a i a n a e

Schofield Barracks

Makaha Beach
Park
Makaha

Wheeler
Air Force
Base

Wahiawa

Waianae

M t s.

750

99

H2

Maili

93

Nanakuli

Waipahu

H1

Ewa

Pearl
Harbor
Arizona
Memorial
1

N

0   5 miles

0   5 km

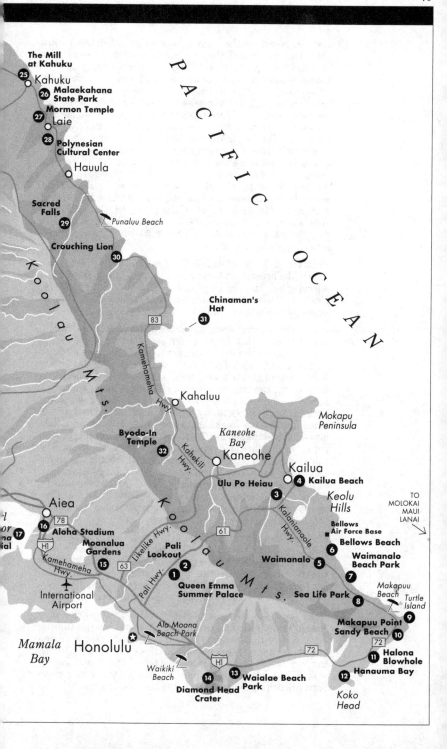

though the park area often draws young toughs (*see* Beaches, *below*).

8 Another mile down the highway on the right is **Sea Life Park,** a marine attraction definitely worth a stop. Its finned menagerie includes the world's only "wholphin," the offspring of a romance between a whale and a dolphin. Children will especially enjoy watching dolphins leap and spin, penguins frolic, and a killer whale perform impressive tricks at the shows in the outdoor amphitheater. There's also a 300,000-gallon Hawaiian reef tank where you can come nose-to-nose with hundreds of marine creatures. The Pacific Whaling Museum teaches you about the fascinating history of whaling in Hawaii. Snacks and sodas are available, and there's a souvenir shop. Even if you've seen trained cetaceans at other marine parks, the distinctively Hawaiian flavor makes this place special. The setting alone, right across from the ocean and Rabbit Island, is worth the price of admission. *Makapuu Point, Waimanalo, tel. 808/259–7933. Admission: $14.95 adults, $7.95 6–12, children 5 and under free. Open Sat.–Thurs. 9:30–5, Fri. 9:30–10 PM. Live local music Fri. 8:30 PM. Cost: $5.25.*

From the cliffs above Sea Life Park, colorful hang gliders often soar in the breezes. It takes a lot of daring to leap from these imposing heights, and there have been several fatalities here. Nestled in the cliff face above the water is the Makapuu Lighthouse (not open to the public).

Across the highway from Sea Life Park is **Makapuu Beach,** a beautiful cove that is great for seasoned bodysurfers but treacherous for the weak swimmer (*see* Beaches, *below*). Parking may be difficult to find, but the beach with offshore views of Rabbit Island makes a wonderful picnic spot. If you decide to keep going, the road winds up a hill, at the top of which is a **9** turnoff on the makai side of the road. This is **Makapuu Point,** a fabulous photo opportunity, with breathtaking views of the mountains and bay, ocean and islands, including the large Rabbit Island and the smaller Turtle Island. The peninsula jutting out in the distance is Mokapu, site of a U.S. Marine base. The spired mountain peak is Mount Olomana. In front of you on the long pier is part of the Makai Undersea Test Range, a research facility that is closed to the public. The facility has launched a manned submersible to study Loihi, the active undersea volcano that is forming another Hawaiian island. Loihi should surface in about 1,000 years.

Continue along the highway past the **Hawaii Kai Championship Golf Course** (tel. 808/395–2538), on the mauka side of the road (*see* Sports, *below*). Across the highway is the area known as **Queen's Beach.** In recent years, developers and conservationists have fought over the shoreline here. During the 1988 elections the people of Oahu voted to make it conservation land.

10 Next you'll see a long stretch of inviting sand called **Sandy Beach.** Tempting as this beach looks, it is not advisable to swim here. Notice that the only people in the water are local and young. They know the powerful and tricky waves well. Even so, the fierce shore break lands many of them in the hospital every year with back and neck injuries. The steady winds make Sandy Beach a popular place to fly kites (*see* Beaches, *below*).

Time Out Across Kalanianaole Highway from Sandy Beach you might see a fleet of **carryout trucks** offering fast-food specialties ideal for a break from the car. They sometimes line up along the shoulder, with colorful banners and enormous signs boasting their menus. On any given day they'll be selling shave ice (snow cones), plate lunches, cold sodas, and such dim sum goodies as *manapua* (dough wrapped around diced pork) and pork hash. Indulge yourself. You still have some traveling to do.

After Sandy Beach, the road takes you along the **Koko Head shoreline**—untamed and open to the ocean. This is a favorite stretch of coastline for visitors and residents alike, because the road twists and turns next to steep cliffs. Offshore, the islands of Molokai and Lanai call like distant sirens, and every once in a while, Maui is visible in blue silhouette. Pull into at least one scenic turnoff.

⓫ One stop features the famous **Halona Blowhole,** a lava tube that sucks in the ocean and then spits it out in lofty plumes. The blowhole may or may not perform, depending on the currents. Nearby is the tiny beach used to film the wave-washed love scene in *From Here to Eternity*. If you do get out here, lock up, because the spot is frequented by thieves.

At the top of the hill on the makai side of the road you will see a ⓬ sign for **Hanauma Bay.** If you make only one stop during your drive, this one should be it. Even from the overlook, the horseshoe-shaped bay is a beauty, and you can easily see the reefs through the clear aqua waters. You can also see the crowds of people snorkeling and sunbathing, but it's still worth a visit (*see* Beaches and Sports, *below*).

From here back to Waikiki the highway passes several residential communities. First there is the sprawling **Hawaii Kai** development. Ancient Hawaiian fish ponds once flourished in this valley, but now the waterways are lined with suburban homes with two cars in the garage and a boat out back. The next communities are **Niu Valley** and **Aina Haina,** each of which has a small shopping center with a food store if you need a soda or a snack. Best to keep driving, however, because during rush hour, Kalanianaole Highway becomes choked with commuter traffic.

Right before you turn off from Kalanianaole Highway you'll notice a long stretch of green on the makai side. This is the private **Waialae Country Club** (4997 Kahala Ave., tel. 808/734–2151), scene of the annually televised Hawaiian Open golf tournament (*see* Sports, *below*). Take the Kahala exit, right before the highway becomes the freeway. Turn left at the stoplight onto Kilauea Avenue. Here you'll see **Kahala Mall** (4211 Waialae Ave.), an upscale shopping complex with yuppie eateries, high-fashion stores, and eight movie theaters.

Take a left on Hunakai Street and follow it to Kahala Avenue. If you want to hit one more beach, turn left and drive several ⓭ blocks to **Waialae Beach Park,** where there is a shower house, beach pavilion, and nice sand for strolling. Windsurfers enjoy sailing here, though the reefs can be tricky. Just down the road is the fancy Kahala Hilton Hotel, where movie stars and royalty stay when they're in town.

Turn around and follow Kahala Avenue toward Waikiki through **Kahala,** Oahu's wealthiest neighborhood. Here the oceanfront homes have been selling for more than $15 million, mostly to Japanese investors. At intervals along this tree-lined street are narrow lanes that provide public access to the beach.

As you reach a small, triangular park on the right, you have the option of continuing straight on what becomes Diamond Head Road or turning right on Monsarrat Avenue. A right turn will take you up to the top of a hill, where there is a sign pointing ⑭ left to **Diamond Head Crater.** The famous extinct volcano got its common name from sailors who thought they had found precious gems on the slope; the diamonds proved to be volcanic refuse. If you're feeling energetic, drive through the tunnel to the inside of the crater and take the half-hour (one-way) hike to the lookout at the top. From 760 feet, you'll get a tremendous view of where you've been and where you're going. *Monsarrat Ave. near 18th Ave., tel. 808/587–0300. Admission free. Open daily 6–6.*

If you continue straight along Diamond Head Road from the triangular park, you will crest a hill next to Diamond Head Crater. Pull off at one of the two scenic turnouts on the makai side of the road for a pretty view of the multicolored sails of the windsurfers below. A bit farther on the makai side is the picturesque **Diamond Head Lighthouse,** one of the oldest in the Pacific.

Drive along the road to Kapiolani Park, and stay on the right side of the park until you hit Kapahulu Avenue. Take a left, and you're back in Waikiki.

Tour 5: Circle Island Driving Tour

Numbers in the margin correspond to points of interest on the Oahu map.

Follow the directions to the H-1 Freeway heading west that appear at the beginning of the East Oahu Ring Tour. The freeway will diverge into Moanalua Freeway (Route 78). Stay on this ⑮ past **Moanalua Gardens,** a lovely park with huge, spreading monkeypod trees. A hula festival is held on the ancient hula mound during the third weekend in July. Hikes are offered into historic Moanalua Valley; call for specific times. *1401 Mahiole, Honolulu, tel. 808/833–1944. Admission free. Open weekdays 8–4.*

⑯ On your left you'll pass **Aloha Stadium.** This 50,000-seat park has movable stands, and the seating configuration changes at the touch of a switch to conform to the type of event, be it a football or baseball game or a rock concert. There's no reason to stop here unless there's a game you plan to attend or, if you happen to see the unmistakable **Aloha Flea Market** in progress in the parking lot on a weekend. For 50¢ a head, Flea Market–goers can browse around the booths for hours. Operations range from slick tents with rows of neatly stacked, new wares to blankets spread on the pavement, covered with rusty tools and cracked china. You'll find gold trinkets, antique furniture, digital watches, Japanese fishing floats, T-shirts, muumuus, and palm-frond hats. Price haggling—in moderation—is the order of the day.

As you approach the stadium on the freeway, bear right at the sign to Aiea, then merge left onto Kamehameha Highway (Route 90) going south to Pearl Harbor. Turn right at the

⓱ Halawa Gate for a tour of the *Arizona* **Memorial,** a must-see stop. The gleaming white memorial shields the hulk of the USS *Arizona,* which sank with 1,102 men aboard when the Japanese attacked Pearl Harbor on December 7, 1941. The tour includes a 20-minute documentary and a shuttle-boat ride to the memorial. *USS Arizona Memorial and Visitor Center, U.S. Naval Reservation, Pearl Harbor, tel. 808/422–0561. Admission free. Open daily 8–3. Tues. is the most crowded, with afternoon waits sometimes as long as 2 hrs. Late in the week and early in the day are your best bets. For safety reasons, no children under 45 in. tall are permitted aboard the shuttle or the memorial. Also prohibited are people in bathing suits or with bare feet.*

Afterward you may also want to take a self-guided tour of the USS *Bowfin,* a World War II submarine moored near the Visitor Center. *11 Arizona Memorial Pl., Pearl Harbor, tel. 808/ 423–1341. Admission: $6 adults, $1 children 6–12. Tours daily 8–5. Closed Thanksgiving, Christmas, and New Year's Day.*

After Pearl Harbor, retrace your steps and take either Kamehameha Highway or the H-2 Freeway to Wahiawa, home of the U.S. Army base at **Schofield Barracks.** This old plantation town has a distinctly military flavor.

If you're really into plants, stop by the 27-acre **Wahiawa Botanical Gardens.** *1396 California Ave., Wahiawa, tel. 808/621– 7321. Admission free. Open daily 9–4.*

For a modest glimpse of ancient Hawaiiana, take Kamehameha Highway, now Route 80, just over the bridge and turn onto the dirt road on the left. It's a short ride to the **Hawaiian Birth Stones,** once a sacred site for royal births.

Back on the main road, there is a scrubby-looking patch ambitiously called the **Del Monte Pineapple Variety Garden.** Unpromising as it looks, it's actually quite interesting, with varieties of the ubiquitous fruit ranging from thumb-size pink ones to big golden ones.

⓲ Turn left on Kamehameha Highway and you'll see the **Dole Pineapple Pavilion,** a big hit with Oahu sightseers since 1951. It has become even bigger with a new visitor pavilion, pineapple variety garden, 10,000-square-foot plantation gift shop, and restaurant. All of this, along with tram tours of an agricultural field, is a vast improvement over the old Dole Visitor Center. *64-1550 Kamehameha Hwy., tel. 808/621–8408. Admission free. Open daily 9–5:30.*

From here, Kamehameha Highway (now Route 99) cuts through pineapple and sugarcane fields. Once you hit the traffic circle, you have some choices to make. If you go around the circle and continue 7 miles to **Mokuleia** on Route 82, you'll come to **⓳** the **polo fields** (*see* Sports, *below*). Beyond that is **Dillingham Airfield,** where you can watch the gliders or book a sailplane ride and try it yourself. *Dillingham Airfield, Mokuleia, tel. 808/677–3404. Cost: $45 for one passenger, $70 for two. Open daily 10:30–5. No reservations, with 20-min flights every 20 min.*

⓴ Another option at the circle is to follow the signs to **Haleiwa,** a sleepy old plantation town that has come of age. In the 1920s it was a fashionable retreat at the end of a railroad line that no longer exists. During the '60s, the hippies gathered here. Now, Haleiwa is a fun mix of old and new. Old general stores peacefully co-exist with contemporary boutiques, art galleries, and eateries.

Time Out For a real slice of Haleiwa color, stop at **Matsumoto's** (66-087 Kamehameha Hwy., tel. 808/637–4827). Many sources claim that this place serves the best shave ice—a tropical snow cone, only better. They shave the ice right before your eyes and offer every flavor imaginable, including banana, mango, papaya, coconut, or combinations thereof. If you want to do it right, get it with vanilla ice cream and sweet azuki beans.

Leaving Haleiwa and continuing along Kamehameha Highway (Route 83), you'll pass the famous north shore beaches, where ㉑ the winter surf comes in size large. The first of these is **Waimea Bay**, a popular family picnic spot with a big, broad beach and fine facilities.

Across the street, on the mauka (mountain) side of the road, is ㉒ **Waimea Falls Park**. An ancient Hawaiian community once thrived in Waimea Valley and today you can see remnants of that early civilization, as well as more than 2,500 species of flora from around the world. The garden trails are well marked, and the plants are labeled. An interesting assortment of animals roams the grounds, including the Hawaiian nene (goose), and there's a spectacular cliff-diving show at the 45-foot-high falls. Hawaiian games and dances are presented, there's a restaurant and picnic areas, and two evenings a month during the full moon, the park is open for free "moonwalks." *59-864 Kamehameha Hwy., Haleiwa, tel. 808/638–8511. Admission: $14.95 adults, $7.95 children 6–12, children 5 and under free. Open daily 10–5:30.*

If you're interested in seeing a fine example of an ancient Hawaiian heiau (sacred stone platform for the worship of the gods), turn mauka (toward the mountains) at the Foodland store and take the Pupukea Road up the steep climb, not quite a ㉓ mile, to the dirt road on the right, leading to the **Puu-o-Mahuka Heiau**. Once a site of human sacrifice, it is now on the National Register of Historic Places. The views are spectacular.

Continue along the coastal road past more famous surfing beaches, including **Ehukai** and **Sunset** (*see* Beaches, *below*). If it's wintertime, keep clear of those waves, which sometimes rise as high as 30 feet. Leave the sea to those daring (some say crazy) surfers who ride the towering waves with astounding grace.

The only hotel of any consequence in these parts is your next ㉔ landmark: the **Turtle Bay Hilton** (57-091 Kamehameha Hwy., tel. 808/293–8811). If it's Sunday between 9 AM and 2 PM, you might want to stop for its incredibly extensive champagne brunch, served in a pretty oceanside dining room ($24.95 for adults, $12.50 for children under 12). Reservations are not accepted.

Time Out Down the road from Turtle Bay is the **Amorient Aquafarm Stand**, a fascinating example of what has become an extremely successful venture for Oahu. Amorient (Kamehameha Hwy., Kahuku, tel. 808/293–8661) is one of several companies that grow prawns, shrimp, and other fish and sea creatures in controlled environments. The results are as tasty as their natural counterparts. Stop by this stand on the makai side of the road and take a cup of carryout shrimp cocktail to one of the picnic benches. The stand also sells fresh prawns, shrimp, and fish that you can take back to your condominium and cook for dinner.

Across the road, there is often a small lean-to set up with **Kahuku watermelons** for sale. By all means, buy one. They're the juiciest, sweetest melons you'll find on the islands.

㉕ The old Kahuku Sugar Mill on Kamehameha Highway, which shut down in 1971 and then enjoyed a brief stint as a tourist attraction, has reopened as **The Mill Market Place** (56-565 Kamehameha Hwy., tel. 808/293–8747), with a restaurant and businesses. Visitors may take a free self-guided tour from 9 to 5 of parts of the turn-of-the-century mill, with its steam engines and enormous gears. There's also a gift shop and a crafts area, and Chuchos Restaurant serves Mexican food daily from 4–9:30.

㉖ As you approach the town of Laie, on the makai (ocean) side is a long stretch of pine trees. Look for the entrance to **Malaekahana State Park,** a lovely place to take a break from driving. You can park in the big lot and wander the shady grounds or stroll on the long beach. At low tide you can even wade to Goat Island. *Admission free. Open Oct.–Mar., daily 7–6:45; Apr.–Sept. 7–7:45.*

㉗ Coming up on the makai side is a road that leads to the **Mormon Temple** (55-415 Iosepa St., tel. 808/293–9167), a white structure made of pulverized volcanic rock and coral. It is a house of worship, not a visitor attraction. The Mormons run Brigham Young University's Hawaii campus, in Laie as well.

㉘ The Mormons also operate the sprawling **Polynesian Cultural Center,** next on the makai side of the road. A visit to the center isn't cheap, but it's worth the money to see the 40 acres of lagoons and seven re-created South Pacific villages representing Hawaii, Tahiti, Samoa, Fiji, the Marquesas, New Zealand, and Tonga. Shows and demonstrations enliven the area, and there's a spectacular evening dinner show. If you're short on time, you can try to sandwich this attraction into a driving tour, but you'll miss much of what makes it so popular. If you're staying in Honolulu, it's better to see the center as part of a van tour, so you won't have to drive home after the evening show. *55-370 Kamehameha Hwy., Laie, tel. 808/293–3333 or 808/923–1861. Cost: Standard Package (general admission to all villages and daytime shows plus American dinner) $40.50 adults, $23.50 children 5–11; Luau Package (general admission, afternoon shows, and the luau) $50.50 adults, $30.50 children 5–11; Ambassador Passport (this VIP ticket includes standard shows and attractions, plus a kukui-nut-lei greeting, an escorted tour, a special dinner, prime show seating, and more) $80.50 adults, $50.50 children 5–11. Open Mon.–Sat. 12:30–9.*

㉙ About 4 miles down the highway on the mauka (toward the mountains) side of the road, look for the Hawaii Visitors Bureau sign for **Sacred Falls.** This wild state park, with a strenuous 2-mile hike to an 80-foot-high waterfall, is Hawaiian country as you dreamed it would be. A swim in the pool beneath the falls is a welcome refresher after the hike. Be sure to hike with someone else, and don't attempt the trail if there has been rain; the valley is subject to flash flooding, and the trail can be slippery. *Admission free. Open Oct.–Mar., daily 7–6:45; Apr.–Sept., daily 7–7:45.*

The next thing to look for, although it's not spectacular, is the **③⓪ Crouching Lion** mountain formation on the ridge line behind an inn of the same name. If someone tells you it has a deeply significant Hawaiian legend attached to it, don't believe them. The lion was an idea thought up by modern-day promoters. As you continue driving along the shoreline, you'll notice a pictur-
③① esque little island called, for obvious reasons, **Chinaman's Hat.**

At the town of Waiahole is a little market with an unlikely name, Hygienic Store. Here, continue straight on Kahekili Highway (Route 83) and look on your right for the Valley of the **③② Temples** and its lovely **Byodo-In Temple.** This replica of a 900-year-old temple in Kyoto, Japan, dramatically set against the sheer green cliffs of the Koolau Mountains, is surrounded by Japanese gardens and a two-acre lake stocked with prize carp. A two-ton statue of Buddha presides over all. *47-200 Kahekili Hwy., Kaneohe, tel. 808/239–8811. Admission: $2 adults, $1 children under 12. Open daily 8–4:30.*

Continue on Kahekili Highway to the Likelike Highway, where you turn mauka and head back toward Honolulu through the Wilson Tunnel. The highway leads to the Lunalilo Freeway going east. Exit at Pali Highway and go south through downtown Honolulu to Nimitz Highway, then turn left on Ala Moana Boulevard, which leads to Kalakaua Avenue in Waikiki.

Oahu for Free

Aside from the obvious things like sunshine and sand, there are many attractions and events in Waikiki and around the island of Oahu that are free.

This section includes both attractions that are covered elsewhere in the book and additional attractions that are described here for the first time. They are divided into those that are in Waikiki and those that are beyond Waikiki, and they are listed alphabetically. Also, many hotels provide free hula lessons, lei-making classes, exercise sessions, and other entertainment for their guests. Be sure to check your hotel's activities desk or concierge.

In Waikiki **Aerobics on the Beach.** Gold's Gym sponsors morning aerobics classes led by television fitness guru Gilad Janklowicz, host of ESPN's "Bodies in Motion" (filmed in Hawaii). *Waikiki Beach, across from the Pacific Beach Hotel, 2490 Kalakaua Ave., tel. 808/922–1233. Daily 8 AM.*

Bandstand Concerts (*see* Tour 3, *above*).

Damien Museum (*see* Tour 1, *above*).

Exercise class. Bring a towel or mat for an outdoor session on the lawn. *Fort De Russy Beach, in front of the Hale Koa Hotel, 2055 Kalia Rd., Mon.–Sat 9 AM.*

Honolulu marathon clinic. Lectures and instructions on running are given by experts, then participants break into groups, depending on level of ability and experience, for a run around the park and beyond. *Kapiolani Bandstand, Kapiolani Park, tel. 808/734–7200. Sun. 7:30 AM.*

Hula lessons. Learn the real hula from a certified hula teacher. *Royal Hawaiian Shopping Center, 2201 Kalakaua Ave., Bldg. C, 3rd floor, tel. 808/922–0588. Mon., Wed., and Fri. 10 AM.*

Karate. Take a lesson in one of the Asian martial arts. *Waikiki Community Center, 310 Paokalani Ave., tel. 808/923–1802. T'ai chi lessons (another martial art) are given Wed. and Fri. 11 AM.*

King's Village (*see* Shopping, *below*).

Polynesian Cultural Center Mini Show. The enthusiastic young entertainers from Hawaii's number-one paid visitor attraction stage a freebie miniproduction. Of course they're hoping you'll rush right into their Waikiki ticket office and sign up for the complete package, but there's no pressure. *Royal Hawaiian Shopping Center, 2201 Kalakaua Ave., Bldg. C, 1st floor, tel. 808/922–0588. Tues., Thurs., Sat. 9:30 AM.*

Porpoise Feeding. Kahala Hilton (*see* What to See and Do with Children, *below*).

Tennis courts. For public courts in Waikiki, *see* Participant Sports, *below.*

Wildest Show in Town. The zoo, which normally charges admission, is free after 4 PM in summer, when a free show is staged under the banyan tree. The bill includes a wide variety of entertainment from rock to puppet shows. *Honolulu Zoo, 151 Kapahulu Ave., tel. 808/971–7171. June, July, and Aug. only, Wed. 6PM.*

Zoo Fence Art Mart (*see* Tour 1, *above*).

Beyond Waikiki *Arizona* Memorial (*see* Tour 5).

East-West Center. Located on the University of Hawaii campus, the center was founded to promote understanding among the people of Asia, the Pacific, and the United States. There are some fascinating buildings and gardens, especially the Japanese garden. The center offers free tours. Reservations are not required, except for groups. Meet at Jefferson Hall. *1777 East-West Rd., tel. 808/944–7691. Bus No. 4 "Nuuanu-Dowsett" from Waikiki. Wed. 1:30 PM.*

Evening at City Hall. A free concert is offered on the fourth Thursday of each month in the courtyard of City Hall. *King and Punchbowl Sts., tel. 808/527–5666. Concerts start at 7 PM.*

Humanities Conversation. A lecture and discussion on history, literature, philosophy, or culture is held by the Hawaii Committee for the Humanities. *3599 Waialae Ave., Rm. 23, Honolulu, tel. 808/732–5402. First Wed. of each month, 4 PM. No meetings in Jan. Shuttle Bus 17 from Ala Moana Shopping Center.*

Helemano Plantation. Five acres of flowers, fruits, and vegetables are maintained by mentally disabled citizens working in a vocational training program. A gift shop, bake shop, silk flower shop, and restaurant are on the site. *64-1510 Kamehameha Hwy., adjacent to the Dole Pineapple Pavilion, tel. 808/622–3929. Daily 7:30–4:30. Bus 8, 19, or 20 from Waikiki to Ala Moana Shopping Center, then transfer to Bus 55, "Circle Island," going west.*

Honolulu Hale. The lovely Spanish Colonial–style building is Honolulu's city hall. There are often art exhibits showing the work of local artists. At Christmas, the lobby is filled with decorated trees and becomes one of Honolulu's prime attractions. A free booklet describing the building is available from the mayor's office on the third floor. *Corner of King and Punchbowl Sts., tel. 808/523–4385. Bus 2 from Waikiki.*

Hoomaluhia Botanic Garden Guided Nature Walk. Exotic flora from around the world grow in this 400-acre garden. Bring light rain gear, insect repellent, and lunch. Reservations are necessary. *End of Luluku Rd., Kaneohe, tel. 808/235–6636. Guided tours Sat. 10 AM and Sun. 1 PM. Bus 55 "Kaneohe" from Ala Moana Shopping Center.*

Iolani Palace grounds. The Royal Hawaiian Band holds a free concert every Friday from 12:15 to 1. Pick up a picnic lunch, sit on the lawn, and enjoy the music. This series is popular with the downtown office workers. *King and Richards Sts., tel. 808/ 527–5666.*

Kaneaki Heiau. An impressive ancient Hawaiian temple has been partially restored and includes a prayer tower and several thatched buildings on massive stone platforms. It is beyond the Sheraton Makaha Resort. *Phone Sheraton's guest services desk, tel. 808/695–9511, to be sure it's open before the long ride out. 84-626 Makaha Valley Rd. Tues.–Sun. 10–2; closed Mon. Bus 51 "Makaha" from Ala Moana Shopping Center.*

Kawaiahao Church (*see* Tour 2).

Keaiwa Heiau State Park. This temple of the old religion of Hawaii was used as a place of healing. Labeled medicinal plants are maintained by the state parks division. The park also contains the Aiea Loop Trail, an easy 4.8-mile mountain hike. Look for the remains of a Japanese plane that crashed into the mountain during the attack on Pearl Harbor. *Aiea Heights Dr., tel. 808/488–6626. Open 7–4. Bus 11 "Aiea Heights" from Ala Moana Shopping Center.*

Koko Head Shoreline (*see* Tour 4).

Lyon Arboretum. Affiliated with the University of Hawaii, this 200-acre garden is tucked in lush Manoa valley, adjacent to the popular (and paying) tourist attraction, Paradise Park. It features a wide variety of tropical flora. *3860 Manoa Rd., tel. 808/ 988–3177. Open weekdays 9–3, Sat. 9–noon; closed Sun. Free guided tours first Fri. and third Wed. at 1 PM, third Sat. at 10 AM. Bus 5 from Ala Moana Shopping Center to the end of the line, a 45-min ride.*

Mayor's Aloha Friday Music Break. Downtown office workers gather around the fountains at lunch to enjoy a concert. The entertainment is varied and may be anything from a school choir to one of the big-name Hawaii groups. There are several fastfood restaurants bordering the square, so you can pick up a picnic. *Tamarind Park, corner of Bishop and King Sts., tel. 808/ 527–5666. Fri. only, noon. Bus 2 from Waikiki.*

Royal Hawaiian Mint. Pure gold, silver, and bronze coins are created here, the only private mint on exhibition in the world. Coins are available for purchase, but just wandering around and watching a royal tradition continue is free. *1421 Kalakaua Ave., tel. 808/949–6468. Weekdays 10–5.*

Royal Mausoleum. Six of Hawaii's eight monarchs are buried in this 3-acre plot: Kings Kamehameha II, III, IV, V, Kalakaua, and Queen Liliuokalani. *2261 Nuuanu Ave., Honolulu. Weekdays 8–4. Bus 4 "Nuuanu" from Waikiki.*

Tennent Art Foundation Gallery. The works of celebrated island artist Madge Tennent are displayed here. Her subjects are Polynesian and her interpretations are massive in stature, conveying both power and a sensuous softness. *203 Prospect St., tel. 808/531–1987. Tues.–Sat. 10–2, Sun. 2–4. Bus 15 from the main depot.*

Young People's Hula Show. The Kapiolani Butterworth children's hula group presents the songs and dances of various Pacific islands. The young dance students are delightful. *Ala Moana Shopping Center, Ala Moana Blvd. and Atkinson Dr., tel. 808/946–2811. Sun. 9:30 AM. Bus 8, 19, or 20 from Waikiki.*

What to See and Do with Children

The Hawaiian word for child is *keiki* (CAKE-ee). Many restaurants offer special keiki menus. There are keiki events and keiki admissions to attractions at reduced rates or for free.

Hawaii is a family-centered society, and Waikiki, surprisingly, is a family kind of place. When you need time on your own, many hotels have excellent baby-sitting services and exciting summer and holiday programs to keep your children entertained.

The beach is the big draw. With a shallow, sandy bottom, reef-protected waters, and gentle waves, **Waikiki Beach** is safe. There are concessions all along the strand for snacks, and umbrella and raft rental (*see* Beaches, *below*). You can sign up the children for surfing lessons to learn Hawaii's sport of kings. Catamaran sails take the family to sea for an hour, a half-day snorkel trip, or a sunset cruise. There are outrigger canoe rides and aqua-bikes. The best swimming spots for children are the walled-in area in front of the Holiday Inn and the lagoon at the Hilton Hawaiian Village. There are playground fixtures at **Queen's Surf Beach.** All beaches in Hawaii are open to the public. Be sure to use sunscreen on young skin, and reapply often.

Other Waikiki attractions especially for children include:

Honolulu Zoo. There's a petting zoo, an elephant show, a farm, and a tower to climb to look the giraffes right in the eye (*see* Tour 1, *above*).

Zoo Fence Art Mart. On weekends there's usually an artist who will do while-you-wait pastel portraits of children (*see* Tour 1, *above*).

Waikiki Aquarium. (*see* Tour 1, *above*).

Kapiolani Park. Adjacent to the zoo, it offers 140 acres in which to run free. There's good family fun at the Kodak Hula Show, including children's hula lessons (*see* Tour 1, *above*). *Admission: $2.50 adults.*

Diamond Head Hike. It takes a 6-year-old hiker 40 minutes to get to the top. Bring a flashlight for the tunnel (*see* A Waikiki Hike, *above*).

U.S. Army Museum at Fort DeRussy. This is for young Rambo fans (*see* Tour 1, *above*).

Pacific Beach Hotel. One thousand fish live in the lobby of this hotel, housed in a 280,000-gallon aquarium (*see* Tour 1, *above*).

Hilton Hawaiian Village Hotel. The newly landscaped grounds are practically a bird park with macaws, flamingoes, penguins, and more. *2005 Kalia Rd., tel. 808/949-4321.*

Hawaii IMAX Theatre. This film image–maximization concept immerses you in what's on a screen 5 stories high and 70 feet wide. Shows' subjects and times vary. *325 Seaside Ave., tel. 808/923-4629. Admission $7.50 adults, $5 children 3-11. Open daily 9-9.*

Beyond Waikiki **Hawaii Children's Museum.** The theme here is "You the Child," with opportunities to learn about the body, tracing a family tree, and ethnic heritage, plus a Bug Zoo. *Dole Cannery Sq., 650 Iwilei Rd., Honolulu 96817, tel. 808/522-0040. Admission: $5 adults, $3 children 2-17. Open Tues.–Fri. 9-1, weekends 10-4.*

Hawaii Maritime Center. Many of the center's exhibits are targeted for children. Climb aboard a reproduction of a Matson liner, see a whaling film, explore a real four-masted sailing ship (*see* Tour 2).

Kahala Hilton Hotel. A lagoon with porpoises is the feature. *5000 Kahala Ave., tel. 808/734-2211. Feeding times: daily 11 AM; 2 and 4 PM.*

Paradise Park. The highlight is the performing bird show, 10:25 AM and 1:30 and 3:30 PM. Other attractions: nature walks, "Dancing Waters" lighted fountain show, having your picture taken with magnificent macaws.

Polynesian Cultural Center. You get around this 40-acre park by tram, canoe, or on foot. Children will have so much fun they won't even notice they're getting an education (*see* Tour 5).

Sea Life Park (*see* Tour 4).

Waimea Falls Park. Bring along swimsuits for the children— they'll enjoy a dunk under the falls (*see* Tour 5).

Off the Beaten Track

An authentic submarine operates just off Waikiki. *Atlantis,* which has been taking tourists down to the sea in ships at Caribbean sites for many years, now does Waikiki dives aboard a 65-foot, 80-ton sub carrying up to 46 passengers. Price includes a catamaran ride aboard the *Hilton Rainbow I* to the dive site and a tour of the Waikiki and Diamond Head shoreline. The sub dives up to 100 feet to see a sunken Navy yard oiler and an artificial reef populated by brilliant fish. While the man-made concrete reef looks more like a fish tenement, it is drawing reef fish back to the area. You get a one-hour, 45-minute cruise with informative narration. The dive itself lasts about 50 minutes. *1600 Kapiolani Blvd., Suite 1630, Honolulu 96814, tel. 808/973-9811. $79 adults, $48 children 4-12. Children must be at least 3 feet tall. Note: Flash photography will not work. Use film speed 200 or above without flash.*

Dole Cannery Square. Oahu boasts the biggest pineapple in the world, weighing in at 28.5 tons and standing 199.3 feet tall, with 46 leaves sticking out of its crown. This mega-pineapple is actually a 100,000-gallon water tower built in 1928 by Hawaii Pineapple Company, the predecessor to Dole. More important, it marks the location of the cannery, at whose visitor center you can learn all about the century-old business history of Hawaii's fruit export. The center has a 27-projector film, exhibits, specialty shops, a food court, and a fascinating factory tour lasting 35 minutes. Complimentary Dole products are served at the end of the tour. *650 Iwilei Rd., Honolulu, tel. 808/531–8855. Free "Pineapple Transit" buses leave from Waikiki hotels on a regular schedule; ask at your hotel front desk for times. Entrance to the square is free; admission to tour and film, $5 adults and children 13–17. There are continuous cannery tours daily every 15 min, 9–4.*

Hawaii's Plantation Village. This "living museum" opened in 1992 in the historic sugar plantation town of Waipahu, 30 minutes from downtown Honolulu. Displays and authentically furnished buildings re-create Hawaii's plantation era. Tour a Chinese social hall, Japanese shrine, sumo ring, saimin stand, old-time garage and dental office, and historic homes. *94–695 Waipahu St., Waipahu, tel. 808/676–6727. Take the H-1 freeway west. Exit at 8B (Waipahu) on to Farrington Hwy., then turn right at Depot Rd. and left onto Waipahu St. $5 donation. Open daily 8:30–5.*

Journey to Old Waikiki. This unique walking tour takes you back in time courtesy of historian and master storyteller Glen Grant who, dressed in turn-of-the-century garb, tells tales of the late 1800s and early 1900s, when island royalty surfed and tourists arrived only by boat. *Sponsored by Passport Hawaii, 2330 Kalakaua Ave., 2nd floor, tel. 808/924–1191. Tour begins at the Duke Kahanamoku Statue at Kuhio Beach. Admission: $7 adults, $5 children 5–12. Open Tues., Thurs., and Sat. at 9 AM. Reservations recommended.*

Senator Fong's Plantation and Gardens. Though Fong hasn't been a senator for many years, this enterprising 83-year-old exlegislator hosts an agricultural attraction showcasing the splendors of Hawaii's rich soil and climate. Flowering vines, ethnic gardens, edible bushes, and tropical fruit trees cover 725 acres of windward Oahu. Guests get a 40-minute guided tour of the plantation and gardens in an open-air minibus. The visitor center includes a snack bar, rest rooms, and a gift shop. *47-285 Pulama Rd., Kahaluu, tel. 808/239–6775. 35 min from Honolulu on the way to the Polynesian Cultural Center, 2 mi past Byodo-In Temple. Admission: $6.50 adults, $3 children 5–12. Open daily 9–4.*

Shopping

Locals used to complain about the lack of shopping options in the islands. Some even went so far as to hop on a plane and fly to the mainland to find the latest fashions or that perfect gift. Happily, those days are past, and Hawaii (particularly Oahu) has assumed its place as an international crossroads of the shopping scene.

As the capital of the 50th state, Honolulu is the number one shopping town in the islands. It features sprawling shopping malls, spiffy boutiques, hotel stores, family-run businesses, and a variety of other enterprises selling brand-new merchandise as well as priceless antiques and one-of-a-kind souvenirs and gifts. What makes shopping on Oahu so interesting is the rich cultural diversity of its products and the many items unique to Hawaii.

As you drive around the island, you'll find souvenir stands and what appear to be discount stores for island products. Watch out, because you could end up buying something tacky and expensive. Start with the reliable stores listed below; they're bound to have what you're looking for, and more.

Major shopping malls are generally open daily from 10 to 9, although some shops may close at 4 or 5.

Shopping Centers

Oahu's many fine shopping malls assemble a little of everything at a wide range of prices. Be sure to wander to the upper levels, where the rents are cheaper and the shops are usually smaller and more original.

In Waikiki **The Royal Hawaiian Shopping Center** (2201 Kalakaua Ave., tel. 808/922–0588), fronting the Royal Hawaiian and Sheraton Waikiki hotels, is three blocks long and contains 120 stores on three levels. There are such Paris shops as **Chanel** (tel. 808/923–0255) and **Louis Vuitton** (tel. 808/926–0621), as well as local arts and crafts from the **Little Hawaiian Craft Shop** (tel. 808/926–2662), which features Bishop Museum reproductions, Niihau shell leis (those superexpensive leis from the island of Niihau), feather hatbands, and South Pacific art. **Bijoux Jewelers** (tel. 808/926–1088) has a fun collection of baubles, bangles, and beads for your perusal. **Royal Hawaiian Gems** (tel. 808/926–2722) fashions gold bracelets, necklaces, and rings with Hawaiian names engraved in them. These popular accessories are often given to local women on special occasions. You can get a refreshing shave ice at Island **Snow Hawaii** (tel. 808/926–3067) and buy a kite at **High As a Kite** (tel. 808/924–2775).

The Waikiki Shopping Plaza (2270 Kalakaua Ave., tel. 808/923–1191) is across the street; its landmark is a 75-foot-high water-sculpture gizmo, which looks great when it's working. Two clothing shops worth checking out are **Chocolates for Breakfast** (tel. 808/923–4426), with its trendy, fairly expensive items from the high-fashion scene; and its sister store, **Villa Roma** (tel. 808/923–4447), equally trendy but younger and less pricey.

The **Waikiki Trade Center** (at the corner of Kuhio and Seaside Aves., tel. 808/922–7444) is slightly out of the action and features shops only on the first floor. **Bebe Sport** (tel. 808/926–7888), which leans to the leather look, is for the slim and affluent. **C. June Shoes** (tel. 808/926–1574) offers European designer shoes, clothing, handbags, belts, and accessories, featuring Carlo Fiori of Italy.

Waikiki also boasts three theme-park-style shopping centers. Right in the heart of the area is the **International Market Place** (2330 Kalakaua Ave., tel. 808/923–9871), a tangle of souvenir stalls under a giant banyan tree. It spills into adjacent **Kuhio**

Mall (2301 Kuhio Ave., tel. 808/922–2724), which has more of the same beads, beach towels, and shirts. **King's Village** (131 Kaiulani Ave., tel. 808/944–6855) looks like a Hollywood stage set of monarchy-era Honolulu, complete with a changing-of-the-guard ceremony every evening at 6:15.

Around Honolulu **Ala Moana Shopping Center** (1450 Ala Moana Blvd., tel. 808/946–2811) is a gigantic open-air mall just five minutes from Waikiki on Bus 8. The 50-acre center is on the corner of Atkinson and Ala Moana boulevards. All the main Hawaiian department stores are here, including **Sears** (tel. 808/947–0211) and **J. C. Penney** (tel. 808/946–8068). **Liberty House** (tel. 808/941–2345) is highly recommended for its selection of stylish Hawaiian wear. Hawaii's first **Neiman-Marcus** is also planned for the center. For stunning Hawaiian prints, try the **Art Board** (tel. 808/946–4863), and buy your local footwear at the **Slipper House** (tel. 808/949–0155).

Also at Ala Moana is **Shirokiya** (tel. 808/941–9111), an authentic Japanese department store where someone is usually demonstrating the latest state-of-the-art kitchen gadget in at least two languages, one of them Japanese. The upper-level food section is like a three-ring circus of free samples, hawkers, and strange Japanese specialties, both fresh and canned. The toy department whirls and clinks with wind-up wonders.

Ala Moana also features a huge assortment of local-style souvenir shops, such as **Hawaiian Island Creations** (tel. 808/941–4491) and **Irene's Hawaiian Gifts** (tel. 808/946–6818). Its **Makai Market** is a food bazaar, with central seating and 20 kitchens serving everything from pizza to health food, poi, ribs, sushi, and Thai food. Stores open their doors daily between 7 and 9:30 AM. The shopping center closes weekdays at 9 PM; Saturday it closes at 5:30, and Sunday at 5, with longer hours during the Christmas holidays.

Heading west, toward downtown Honolulu, you'll run into **Ward Centre** (1200 Ala Moana Blvd., tel. 808/531–6411) and **Ward Warehouse** (1050 Ala Moana Blvd., tel. 808/531–6411). Both are eclectic mixes of boutiques and restaurants. Two of their best-loved shops are **Thongs 'N Things** (tel. 808/524–8229), notable for its huge collection of casual footwear, and **Neon Leon** (tel. 808/545–7666), which features racks and racks of outrageous cards.

Farther west is **Restaurant Row** (500 Ala Moana Blvd. between South and Punchbowl Sts., tel. 808/538–1441), a newer conglomeration of fun retailers and eateries. Stop by **Whalers General Store** (tel. 808/521–2255) for some souvenirs with nautical overtones.

Kahala Mall (4211 Waialae Ave., tel. 808/732–7736) is 10 minutes by car from Waikiki in the chic residential neighborhood of Kahala, near the slopes of Diamond Head. This mall features such clothing stores as **Liberty House** (tel. 808/941–2345; *see* listing in Ala Moana Shopping Center, *above*) and **Ethel's** (tel. 808/732–3844), which offers high-level fashions for those evenings out. **Reyn's** (tel. 808/737–8313) is the acknowledged place to go for men's resort wear; its aloha shirts have muted colors and button-down collars, suitable for most social occasions. **Banana Republic** (tel. 808/737–4747) has designer outdoor wear. Along with a fun assortment of gift shops, Kahala Mall also features eight movie theaters (tel. 808/733–6233) for post-shopping entertainment.

Specialty Stores

Aloha Shirts and Muumuus For stylish Hawaiian wear, the kind worn by local men and women, look in **Liberty House** at 2314 Kalakaua Avenue, and other locations throughout the islands; **Carol & Mary,** at the Halekulani, Royal Hawaiian, and Hilton Hawaiian Village hotels; and **Andrade,** at the Princess Kaiulani, and Sheraton Waikiki hotels. For menswear, try **Reyn's** at the Kahala Hilton and Sheraton Waikiki hotels and at Ala Moana and Kahala Mall shopping centers. If you want something bright, bold, and cheap, there are any number of "garment factory to you" outlets and street stalls. Don't bother with free buses that offer to take you to a factory. They're a waste of limited vacation time and the factory bargains aren't exceptional. For vintage aloha shirts, try **Bailey's Antique Clothing and Thrift Shop** (758 Kapahulu Ave., tel. 808/734–7628), just beyond Waikiki.

High Fashion **Liberty House** is again recommended. **Carol & Mary** has been known for high quality and designer labels since 1937. **Altillo** (Ala Moana Shopping Center and Kahala Mall) carries a line of European menswear, with shirts ranging from $20 to over $200. **Chocolates for Breakfast,** in Ala Moana and the Waikiki Shopping Plaza, is the trendy end of the high-fashion scene. For the latest in shoes and bags, **C. June Shoes,** in the Waikiki Trade Center, displays an elegant array of pricey styles. Elegant international fashions for men and women are available at **Mandalay** (Halekulani Hotel), home of Star of Siam silks and cottons, Anne Namba couture, and designs by Choisy, who works out of Bangkok. On the same floor, **Leather of the Sea** has the best prices on eel-skin purses, wallets, and attaché cases.

Resort Wear Clothing **Liberty House** has the widest selection. **Chapman's** at the Hyatt Regency Waikiki, Royal Hawaiian, Hilton Hawaiian Village hotels and other island locations, is a fine men's specialty shop. **McInerny** has shops in the Royal Hawaiian Shopping Center, Ala Moana Center, and in the Halekulani, Hilton Hawaiian Village, Hyatt Regency Waikiki, and Royal Hawaiian hotels. **Andrade** has a compact but good inventory of both men's and women's resort fashions in its hotel shops.

Food Take home fresh pineapple, papaya, or coconut and you'll be a hit with friends and family. Jam comes in flavors like poha, passion fruit, and guava. Kona coffee has an international following. There are dried food products such as *saimin* (Japanese noodle soup), *haupia* (a firm coconut pudding), and teriyaki barbecue sauce. All kinds of cookies are available, as well as exotic teas, drink mixes, and pancake syrups. And don't forget the macadamia nuts. By law, all fresh-fruit products must be inspected by the Department of Agriculture. The following stores carry only inspected fruit, ready for shipment:

The best place to shop for all these delicacies is the second floor of **F. W. Woolworth** (2224 Kalakaua Ave., tel. 808/923–2331). It accepts credit-card (MC, V) telephone orders and ships directly to your home. So do **ABC stores,** with 24 locations in Waikiki (tel. 808/538–6743; MC, V). An outfit called **Tropical Fruits Distributors of Hawaii** (429 Waiakamilo Rd., Honolulu, tel. 808/847–3234) specializes in inspected, packed pineapple and papaya. It will deliver to your hotel and to the airport baggage check-in counter or ship to the mainland United States and Canada. **Pacific Tropical Products** (tel. 808/836–2792) offers a similar service, including shipments to Japan; telephone credit-card orders are also accepted (MC, V).

Gifts **Robyn Buntin's Galleries** in downtown Honolulu (900 Maunakea St., tel. 808/523–5913) presents Chinese nephrite jade carvings, Japanese lacquer and screens, Buddhist sculptures, and other international pieces. At the Halekulani Hotel, **Takenoya Arts** (tel. 808/926–1939) specializes in intricately carved netsuke (small Japanese ornaments), both antique and contemporary, and one-of-a-kind ivory necklaces, some reasonably priced. **Following Sea** (Kahala Mall, tel. 808/734–4425) sells beautiful handmade jewelry and pottery.

Hawaiian Arts and Crafts One of the nicest gifts is something hand-crafted of native Hawaiian wood. Some species of trees grow only in Hawaii. Koa and milo each have a beautiful color and grain. The great koa forests are disappearing because of environmental factors, so the wood is becoming valuable. There are also framed arrangements of delicate *limu* (seaweed), feather leis and polished kukui nut leis, wooden bowls, and hula implements.

The best selection and best prices are at the **Little Hawaiian Craft Shop** in the Royal Hawaiian Shopping Center. The manager is a former librarian and enjoys talking about the ancient arts. Some items are Bishop Museum reproductions, with a portion of the profits going to the museum. The shop also has a good selection of Niihau shell leis (those superexpensive leis from Niihau Island), feather hatbands, and South Pacific arts. Both traditional Hawaiian and more contemporary arts and crafts are featured at the **Kuhio Mall Craft Court.** It's upstairs and hard to find but worth the search. For collector's items, head downtown to **Martin & MacArthur** (tel. 808/524–4434), specialists in koa furniture.

Jewelry You can buy gold chains by the inch on the street corner, and jade and coral trinkets by the dozen. **Bernard Hurtig's** has a fine jewelry department, specializing in 18K gold and antique jade. Hurtig's boutique jewelry is a collection of fabulous fakes, many of them reproductions of famous pieces and priced from $35. Hurtig's is a recognized authority on *netsuke*, the small Japanese sword ornaments carved in jade, ivory, and other precious materials. Waikiki shops are at the Kahala Hilton Hotel (5000 Kahala Ave.) and Hilton Hawaiian Village (2005 Kalia Rd.). **Haimoff & Haimoff Creations in Gold,** in the Halekulani Hotel and Kahala Hilton, features the original work of award-winning jewelry designer Harry Haimoff.

Beaches

Waikiki Beaches

The 2½-mile strand called Waikiki Beach is actually a lei of beaches extending from the Hilton Hawaiian Village on one end to Diamond Head on the other. All of Hawaii's beaches are public, so you can plunk down with aplomb in front of the most elegant hotel. We've listed them from east to west.

There are some words of caution to keep in mind when approaching any Hawaiian beach. Take notice of the signs. If they warn of dangerous surf conditions or currents, pay attention. Before you stretch out beneath a swaying palm, check it for coconuts. The trade winds can bring them tumbling down on top of you with enough force to cause serious injury. And don't forget the sunscreen. The sun-protection factor in some new preparations now goes higher than 29. It's a good idea to reapply sunscreen after swimming. Waikiki is only 21 degrees north of the equator, and the ultraviolet rays are much more potent than they are at home. Also, no alcoholic beverages are allowed on the beaches.

Kahanamoku Beach and Lagoon. The lagoon's calm waters are safe for small children, and you can lazily paddle around it in a little boat. The beach offers decent snorkeling and swimming and gentle surf. The area is named for Hawaii's famous Olympic swimming champion, Duke Kahanamoku. There's a snack concession, a surfboard and beach-equipment rental shop, showers, catamaran cruises, and a sand volleyball court. *Fronting the Hilton Hawaiian Village.*

Fort DeRussy Beach. Sunbathers and bikini-watchers enjoy this beach, the widest in Waikiki. It trails off to a coral ocean bottom with interesting snorkeling sights. The beach is frequented by military personnel but is open to everyone. There are volleyball courts, food stands, picnic tables, dressing rooms, showers, and snack concessions. *Fronting Fort DeRussy and the Hale Koa Hotel.*

Gray's Beach. Named for a little lodging house called Gray's-by-the-Sea that once stood here, this beach is best known for the two good surfing spots called Paradise and Number Threes just beyond its reef. High tides often cover the narrow beach. The Hawaiians used to consider this a place for spiritual healing and baptism and called it *Kawehewehe* (the removal). You'll find food concessions, surfboard and beach-equipment rental shops, and canoe and catamaran rides. *Fronting the Halekulani Hotel.*

Kahaloa and Ulukou Beaches. Probably the best swimming, and certainly the most activity, is at this little stretch of Waikiki Beach. There are catamaran rides and outrigger-canoe rides, and you can sign up for a surfing lesson at the Waikiki Beach Center. The Royal Hawaiian Hotel cordons off a small section of sand for its guests, bringing to mind a rich kid's sandbox. Facilities include public rest rooms, changing rooms, showers, and a snack stand. The police station is located here. *Fronting the Royal Hawaiian Hotel and Sheraton Moana Surfrider.*

Kuhio Beach Park. A seawall jutting into the ocean acts as a breakwater to keep shoreside waters calm. The area is deceptive, though, and children should be watched closely, because there are unpredictably deep holes in spots. (There have been several drownings here.) Beyond the wall, surfers and bodysurfers ride the waves. The wall is a great place for sunset-watching, but be careful of your footing. *Extending from the Waikiki Beach Center to the wall.*

Queen's Surf. This is a great place for a sunset picnic. It's beyond the seawall, toward Diamond Head, at what is known as the "other end of Waikiki," and named for once having been the site of Queen Liliuokalani's beach house. The sand is softer than by the hotels, and the beach slopes gently to the water. A mix of families and gays gathers here, and it seems as if someone is always playing a bongo drum. There are good shade trees, picnic tables, and a changing house with showers. *Across from the entrance to the Honolulu Zoo.*

Sans Souci. This small rectangle of sand is nicknamed Dig-Me Beach because of its outlandish display of skimpy bathing suits. However, it's a good beach for all ages. Children enjoy playing in its shallow, safe waters, and the spot draws many ocean kayakers and outrigger canoers. Serious swimmers and triathletes also swim in the channel here, beyond the reef. The beach wall is a good vantage point for sunset-watching. There's no food concession, but adjacent to one end of the beach is the Hau Tree Lanai, a wonderful open-air eatery that is part of the hotel. Sans Souci also has a pair of outdoor showers (no changing house) and a grassy area that is popular with picnickers and volleyball buffs. *Makai side of Kapiolani Park, between the New Otani Kaimana Beach Hotel and the Waikiki War Memorial Natatorium.*

Beaches Around Oahu

Here are Oahu's finer beaches, listed clockwise around the island from Waikiki.

Ala Moana Beach Park. Ala Moana has a protective reef, which keeps the waters calm and perfect for swimming. Waikiki aside, this is the most popular beach for tourists. The sand is hard and packed, and bodies are everywhere, tanning, listening to radios, practicing acrobatics, eating picnics, and watching the surf action outside the reef. To the Waikiki side is a peninsula called Magic Island, with picnic tables, shady trees, and paved sidewalks ideal for jogging; residents flock here on weekends. Ala Moana also features playing fields, changing houses, indoor and outdoor showers, lifeguards, concession stands, and tennis courts. This is a beach for everyone; don't expect to find easy parking. *Honolulu, makai side of Ala Moana Shopping Center and Ala Moana Blvd. For public transportation from Waikiki, take Bus 8, get off at the shopping center, and walk across Ala Moana Blvd.*

Bellows Field Beach. The waves here are great for bodysurfing, and the sand is soft for sunbathing. Locals come here for the fine swimming on the weekends, when the Air Force opens the beach to civilians. There are showers, abundant parking, and plenty of places for picnicking underneath shady ironwood trees. There are no food concessions here, but right outside the entrance gate is a McDonald's and some other carryouts. *Entrance is on Kalanianaole Hwy., near Waimanalo town center. It is marked with signs on the makai side of the road. Open to the public on weekends and holidays.*

Ehukai Beach Park. Ehukai is part of a series of beaches running for many miles along the north shore. What sets it apart is the view of the famous Banzai Pipeline, site of international surfing competitions. The winter waves are fierce, and the lifeguards are constantly shooing people away from the shorebreak. There's a grassy area above the beach and a steep dune dropping down to it. The long, wide, and generally uncrowded beach has a changing house with showers and an outdoor shower and water fountain. Bring along a cooler with sodas, because there is virtually no shade here, and the nearest store is a mile away. *North shore, 1 mi north of the Foodland store at Pupukea. Turn makai off Kamehameha Hwy. onto the dirt road that parallels the highway. The small Ehukai parking lot is about 2 blocks away.*

Haleiwa Beach Park. The winter waves are impressive here, but in the summertime the ocean is like a lake, ideal for family swimming. The beach itself is big and pleasant and often full of locals. Broad lawns between the highway and the beach are busy with volleyball action, Frisbee games, and groups of barbecuers. There is a changing house with showers. There are no food concessions, but Haleiwa has everything you need for provisions. *North shore, makai side of Kamehameha Hwy., north of Haleiwa town center and just past the boat harbor.*

Hanauma Bay. The main attraction here is snorkeling. The coral reefs are clearly visible through the turquoise waters of this sunken crater, a designated marine preserve. Crowds flock to its palm-fringed shores and fill the water and the narrow crescent of packed sand. Beyond the reef is a popular site for scuba-diving classes. The bay is best early in the morning (7 AM), before the crowds arrive. There is a busy food and snorkel equipment rental concession on the beach, plus changing houses and showers. *Makai of Kalanianaole Hwy., at the top of the hill just east of Hawaii Kai. A big sign points to the parking lot. A jitney runs down the steep slope to the beach for 50¢, one-way. Hanauma Bay Taxi and Tours (tel. 808/941-5555) runs to and from Waikiki and costs $17 round-trip, including snorkeling gear and lessons.*

Kahana Bay Beach Park. Parents often bring their children to wade in safety at this pretty beach cove with very shallow, protected waters. A grove of tall ironwood and pandanus trees keeps the area cool, shady, and ideal for a picnic. An ancient Hawaiian fish pond, which was in use until the 1920s, is visible nearby. There are changing houses, showers, and picnic tables. Across the highway is Kahana Valley, burgeoning with banana, breadfruit, and mango trees. *On the windward side of the island, makai of Kamehameha Hwy., just north of Kualoa Park.*

Kualoa Regional Park. This is one of the island's most beautiful picnic, camping, and beach areas. Grassy expanses border a long, narrow stretch of beach with spectacular views of Kaneohe Bay and the Koolau Mountains. The highlight of the landscape/seascape is an islet called Mokoli'i (more commonly known as Chinaman's Hat), which rises like the cone-shaped headgear 206 feet above the water. At low tide you can wade out to the island on the reef. The one drawback is that it's usually windy. Bring a cooler; no refreshments are sold here. There are places to shower, change, and picnic in the shade of palm trees. *On the windward side, makai of Kamehameha Hwy., just north of Waiahole.*

Kailua Beach Park. Steady breezes attract windsurfers by the dozens to this long, palm-fringed beach with gently sloping sands. You can rent equipment in Kailua and try it yourself. Young athletes and members of the military enjoy this beach, as do local families, so it gets pretty crowded on the weekend. There are showers, changing houses, picnic areas, and a concession stand. You can also buy your picnic provisions at the Kalapawai Market nearby. *On the windward side, makai of*

Kailua town. Turn right on Kailua Rd. at the market, cross a bridge, then turn left into the beach parking lot.

Makaha Beach Park. Because it's off the beaten tourist path this beach provides a slice of local life most visitors don't see. Families string up tarps for the day, fire up hibachis, set up lawn chairs, get out the fishing gear, and strum ukuleles while they "talk story," or chat. The swimming is generally decent in the summer, but avoid the big winter waves. The quarter-mile-long beach has a changing house and showers and is the site of a yearly big-board surf meet. *On the Waianae coast, 1½ hours west of Honolulu on the H-1 Fwy. and Farrington Hwy. On the makai side of the highway.*

Makapuu Beach. Swimming at Makapuu should be reserved for strong strokers and bodysurfers, because the swells can be overwhelmingly big and powerful. Instead, consider this tiny crescent cove as a prime sunbathing spot. It's set at the base of high sea cliffs, and if you look up you just might see a hang glider launching from the cliffs above. From the beach you can see Rabbit Island, a picturesque cay so named because some think it looks like a swimming bunny. Makapuu is a popular beach with the locals. Because the lot is small, parking can be tricky, and you may have to park on the narrow shoulder and walk down to the beach. There is a changing house with indoor and outdoor showers. *Makai of Kalanianaole Hwy., across from Sea Life Park, 2 mi south of Waimanalo.*

Malaekahana Beach Park. The big attraction here happens only at low tide when the waters are shallow enough to wade out to tiny Goat Island, a bird sanctuary just offshore. The water never gets much more than waist high. If you decide to wade, be sure to wear sneakers so you don't cut yourself on the coral. Families love to camp at Malaekahana State Park, because there are groves of ironwood trees that provide lots of shade during the heat of the day. The beach itself is fairly narrow but long enough for a 20-minute stroll, one-way. The waves are never too big to swim in, and sometimes they're just right for the beginning bodysurfer. There are several changing houses and indoor and outdoor showers, plus picnic tables. *On the windward side. Entrance gates are makai of Kamehameha Hwy., ½ mi north of Laie. They're easy to miss, because you can't see the beach from the road.*

Sandy Beach. Strong, steady winds make "Sandy's" a kite-flyer's paradise. But the shorebreak is vicious here, and there's generally a rescue truck parked on the road, which means that people are swimming where they shouldn't and getting hurt. That should stop *you* from jumping in. Sandy's is a popular spot for the high school and college crowd. There's a changing house with indoor and outdoor showers here, and food trucks across the highway. *Makai of Kalanianaole Hwy., 2 mi east of Hanauma Bay.*

Sunset Beach. This is another link in the chain of north shore beaches, which extends for miles. It is popular for its gentle summer waves and crashing winter surf. The beach is broad, and the sand is soft. It's a fun place to look for puka shells. Sunset has a tiny parking lot, so it's easy to miss. Across the street are usually carryout trucks selling shave ice, plate lunches, and sodas. There are no facilities except a portable outhouse. *On* *the north shore, 1 mi north of Ehukai Beach Park, on the makai side of Kamehameha Hwy.*

Waimanalo Beach Park. Boogie-boarders and bodysurfers enjoy the predictably gentle waves of this beach. The lawn at Waimanalo plays host to hundreds of local people who set up minicamps for the weekend, complete with hibachis, radios, lawn chairs, coolers, and shade tarps. Sometimes these folks are not very friendly to tourists. However, the beach itself is more welcoming, and from here you can walk a mile along the shore for fantastic windward and mountain views. The grassy, shady grounds have picnic tables and shower houses. *On the windward side. Look for the signs makai of Kalanianaole Hwy., just south of Waimanalo town.*

Waimea Bay. Made popular in that old Beach Boys song, "Surfin' U.S.A.," Waimea Bay is a slice of hang-ten heaven. Winter is when you should stand well away from the shore break and leave the 25-foot-high waves to the hotdogs. Try walking near the water and the lifeguards will shoo you away through their bullhorns. Summer is the time to swim and snorkel in the calm waters. The beach is a broad crescent of soft sand, backed by a shady area with tables, a changing house, and showers. Parking is almost impossible in the lot on weekends, so folks just park along the road and walk down. *On the north shore. Across the street from Waimea Falls Park, 3 mi north of Haleiwa, on the makai side of Kamehameha Hwy.*

Yokohama Bay. You'll be one of the few tourists at this Waianae-coast beach at the very end of the road. It feels and looks remote and untouched, which may explain its lack of crowds. Locals come here to fish and swim in waters that are calm enough for children during the summer. The beach is narrow, and rocky in places. Bring provisions, because the nearest town is a 15-minute drive away. There's a changing house and showers, plus a small parking lot, but most folks just pull over and park on the side of the bumpy road. *On the Waianae coast, at the northern end of Farrington Hwy., about 7 mi north of Makaha.*

Sports and the Outdoors

Participant Sports

Biking The good news is that the coastal roads are flat and well paved. On the downside, they're also awash in vehicular traffic. Frankly, biking is no fun in either Waikiki or Honolulu, but things are a bit better outside the city. Be sure to take along a nylon jacket for the frequent showers on the windward side and remember that Hawaii is Paradise After the Fall: Lock up your bike, or be prepared to hike back.

Mountain bikes are available for rent at **Aloha Funway Rentals** (2025 Kalakaua Ave., Waikiki, tel. 808/946–2766). Rates for a 5-speed: $14.90 (7 hours) and $19.90 (24 hours). You can buy a bike or, if you brought your own, you can get it repaired at **Eki Cyclery Shop** (1603 Dillingham Blvd., Honolulu, tel. 808/847–2005). If you want to find some biking buddies, write ahead to the **Hawaii Bicycling League** (Box 4403, Honolulu 96813, tel.

808/735–5756). This organization can tell you about upcoming races, which are frequent on all the islands.

Fitness Centers **Clark Hatch Physical Fitness Center** has complete weight-training facilities, an indoor pool, a racquetball court, aerobics classes, treadmills, and indoor running apparatus. *745 Fort St., Honolulu, tel. 808/536–7205. Daily, weekly, and monthly guest rates work out to approximately $10 a day. Open weekdays 6 AM–8 PM, Sat. 7:30 AM–5:30 PM.*

Gold's Gym is Waikiki's most accessible fitness center. The 11,217-square-foot facility has weight-training machines, cardiovascular equipment, free weights, and a pro shop. *Pacific Beach Hotel, 2nd floor, 2490 Kalakaua Ave., tel. 808/971–4653. $5 daily for hotel guests, $20 nonguests. Open daily 24 hrs.*

Among the hotels that have established fitness centers are:

Halekulani Hotel (2199 Kalia Rd., Waikiki, tel. 808/923–2311) has aerobics classes three times a week. Universal weight machines, a treadmill, two exercise bikes, and a massage room are available for guests only.

Hilton Hawaiian Village (2005 Kalia Rd., Waikiki, tel. 808/949–4321) has an extensive fitness center open to those staying in the hotel's Alii Tower, including a Nautilus weight room and a Jacuzzi.

Kahala Hilton (5000 Kahala Ave., Kahala, tel. 808/734–2211) has an excellent, sophisticated fitness center available for its guests. The hotel is affiliated with Maunalua Bay Club, which has tennis courts, a swimming pool, aerobics classes, Nautilus machines, rowing machines, and treadmills. The Kahala offers a shuttle to the club, which is only five minutes away.

Golf Oahu is honeycombed with golf holes. It has more golf courses than any other Hawaiian island—more than two dozen—most of them open to the public. One of the most popular facilities is the **Ala Wai Golf Course** (404 Kapahulu Ave., tel. 808/296–4653) on Waikiki's mauka (north) end, across the Ala Wai Canal. It's par 70 on approximately 6,424 yards and has a pro shop and a restaurant. Greens fees: $30; carts $11. The waiting list is long, so if you plan to play, call the minute you land.

You'll stand a better chance of getting to play at the 6,350-yard **Hawaii Kai Championship Course** or the neighboring 2,386-yard **Hawaii Kai Executive Course** (8902 Kalanianaole Hwy., Honolulu, tel. 808/395–2358 for either). Fees are $80 with a cart for the former and $35 with a cart for the latter. The 27-hole **Hawaii Prince Golf Club** (91-1200 Ft. Weaver Rd., Ewa Beach, tel. 808/944–4567) opened in 1992. Fees for 18 holes are $85 (guests), $135 (nonguests), both with cart. The **Sheraton Makaha Resort and Country Club** (84–626 Makaha Valley Rd., Waianae, tel. 808/695–9544) has an exceptional course in a beautiful valley setting. Rates, including cart: $75 for guests, $140 for nonguests. At the **Turtle Bay Hilton** (57–091 Kamehameha Hwy., Kahuku, tel. 808/293–8811) the 18-hole **Links at Kuilima,** designed by Arnold Palmer, opened in 1992. Fees are $75 (guests) and $125 (nonguests). Fees for the 9-hole course are $50 (guests) and $65 (nonguests), with cart.

Horseback Riding **Kualoa Ranch** (49–560 Kamehameha Hwy., Kaaawa, tel. 808/237–8515 or 808/538–7636 in Honolulu), on the windward side, across from Kualoa Beach Park, features trail rides in Kaaawa, one of the most beautiful valleys in all Hawaii. (Cost: $20 per 45 minutes.) For $105 a day, you can go horseback riding, fly in a helicopter, ride a dune buggy, go snorkeling, try the shooting range, and have lunch (weekdays only). **Sheraton Makaha Lio Stables** (84-626 Makaha Valley Rd., Makaha, tel. 808/695–9511 ext. 7646) offers escorted rides into Makaha Valley; a one-hour guided trail ride costs $20 per person for guests, $25 per person for nonguests. **Turtle Bay Hilton** (57–091 Kamehameha Hwy., Kahuku, tel. 808/293–8811) has 75 acres of hotel property (including a private beach) for exploring on horseback, at $24 per guest, $25.50 per nonguest, per 50 minutes.

Jogging In Honolulu, the most popular places are the two parks, **Kapiolani** and **Ala Moana,** at either end of Waikiki. In both cases, the loop around the park is just under 2 miles. You can also run a 4.6-mile ring around **Diamond Head Crater,** past scenic views, luxurious homes, and herds of other joggers. If you jog along the 1½-mile **Ala Wai Canal,** you'll probably glimpse outrigger-canoe teams practicing on the canal. If you're looking for jogging companions, show up for the free **Honolulu Marathon Clinic** that starts at the Kapiolani Park Bandstand (Mar.–Nov., Sun. 7:30 AM).

Once you leave Honolulu, it gets trickier to find places to jog that are scenic as well as safe. Best to stick to the well-traveled routes, or ask the experienced folks at the **Running Room** (768 Kapahulu Ave., Honolulu, tel. 808/737–2422) for advice.

Tennis In the Waikiki area, there are four free public courts at **Kapiolani Tennis Courts** (2748 Kalakaua Ave., tel. 808/971–2525); nine at the **Diamond Head Tennis Center** (3908 Paki Ave., tel. 808/971–7150); and 10 at **Ala Moana Park** (tel. 808/522–7031). Several Waikiki hotels have tennis facilities open to nonguests, but guests have first priority. The **Ilikai** (1777 Ala Moana Blvd., tel. 808/949–3811) has seven courts, one lighted for night play, plus a pro shop, tennis clinics, and a ball machine. The hotel also offers special tennis packages. There's one court at the **Hawaiian Regent Hotel** (2552 Kalakaua Ave., tel. 808/922–6611), with lessons by Peter Burwash International. The two courts at the **Pacific Beach Hotel** (2490 Kalakaua Ave., tel. 808/922–1233) also offer instruction. The new **Hawaii Prince Golf Club** (91-1200 Ft. Weaver Rd., Ewa Beach, tel. 808/944–4567) has two courts.

Water Sports The seemingly endless ocean options can be arranged through any hotel travel desk or beach concession or at the **Waikiki Beach Center,** next to the Sheraton Moana Surfrider.

Deep-Sea Fishing For fun on the high seas, try **Coreene-C Sport Fishing Charters** (tel. 808/536–7472), **Island Charters** (tel. 808/536–1555), or **Tradewind Charters** (tel. 808/973–0311). Another reliable outfit is **ELO–1 Sport Fishing** (tel. 808/947–5208). All are berthed in Honolulu's Kewalo Basin. Plan to spend $100 per person to share a boat for a full day (7 AM–3:30 PM). Half-day rates are $50–$65. Boat charters run $450–$500 for a full day and $375–$400 for a half-day. All fishing gear is included, but lunch is not. The captain usually expects to keep the fish. Tipping is customary, and $20 to the captain is not excessive, especially if you keep the fish you caught.

Sailing Lessons may be arranged through **Tradewind Charters** (1833 Kalakaua Ave., Honolulu 96815, tel. 808/973–0311). Instruction follows American Sailing Association standards. Cost: $35 per hour for the first student, $15 for each additional student, up to four. Transportation from Waikiki is available. Tradewinds specializes in intimate three-hour sunset sails for a maximum of six people at $59 per person, including hors d'oeuvres, champagne, and other beverages. The same price will buy you a half-day snorkel or scuba sail.

Cloud Nine Limousine Service (Box 8603, Honolulu 96830, tel. 808/524–7999) arranges private yacht charters, complete with limousine pickup at your hotel. A three-hour sail for one to six passengers is $500, and a seven-hour sail is $800.

Scuba Diving and Snorkeling For scuba diving, **South Seas Aquatics** (2155 Kalakaua Ave., Suite 112, Honolulu 96815, tel. 808/735–0437) offers two-tank boat dives for $70. A beginning course costs $75, with equipment.

The most famous snorkeling spot in Hawaii is Hanauma Bay. **Hanauma Bay Snorkeling Excursion** (Hawaiian Monarch Hotel, 444 Niu St., Honolulu 96815, tel. 808/944–8828) has a half-day Hanauma Bay excursion for $16 adults, $14 children under 12, including transportation and equipment. That leaves you about two hours of actual snorkeling time.

Dive Sites **Maunalua Bay,** east of Diamond Head, has several sites, including Turtle Canyon, with lava flow ridges and sandy canyons teeming with green sea turtles of all sizes; *Kahala Barge* a penetrable, 200-foot sunken vessel; Big Eel Reef with many variety of moray eels; and Fantasy Reef, a series of lava ledges and archways populated with barracuda and eels.

Mahi Waianae is a 165-foot minesweeper sunk in 1982 to create an artificial reef. It's intact and penetrable. Goatfish, tame lemon butterfly fish, blue-striped snapper, and a six-foot moray eel can be seen hanging about. Depths are from 50 to 90 feet.

Hanauma Bay, east of Koko Head, is an underwater state park and a popular dive site. The shallow inner reef gradually drops from 10 to 70 feet at the outer reef. Among the tame, colorful tropical fish you'll see here are butterfly fish, goatfish, parrot fish, and surgeon fish; there are also sea turtles.

Shark's Cove, on the north shore, is diveable in the summer months only, and should be explored only by experienced divers. There are large, roomy caverns where sunlight from above creates a stained-glass effect. Easily accessible from shore, the cove's depths range from 15 to 45 feet. This is the most popular cavern dive on the island.

Three Tables, on the north shore, is named for the trio of flat rocks that break the surface near the beach. Beneath the waves are large rock formations, caverns, and ledges. Diveable only in the summer months, the site has easy access from shore.

Ocean Kayaking This dynamic sport is catching on fast in the islands. You sit on top of a board and paddle on both sides; it's great fun for catching waves or just exploring the coastline. Bob Twogood, a name that is synonymous with Oahu kayaking, runs a shop called **Twogood Kayaks Hawaii** (171 Hamakua Dr., Kailua, tel. 808/262–5656), which makes and sells the fiberglass craft and runs free demonstrations on Kailua Beach at least every two weeks.

Twogood rents solo kayaks for $20 a half-day, and $25 for a full day; tandems are $35 a half-day and $45 for a full day.

Surfing To rent a board, contact **Aloha Beach Services** (tel. 808/922–3111 ext. 2341), next to the Sheraton Moana Surfrider. Rentals cost $8 per hour, $12 for two hours. Lessons are $25 per hour with board, and they promise to have you riding the waves by lesson's end.

Windsurfing This sport was born in Hawaii, and Oahu's Kailua Beach is its cradle. World champion Robby Naish and his family build and sell boards, rent equipment, run "windsurfari" tours, and offer instruction. **Naish Hawaii** (155A Hamakua Dr., Kailua 96734, tel. 808/261–6067). A three-hour beginner's group lesson costs $35 per person, with equipment. **Windsurfing Hawaii** (155A Hamakua Dr., Kailua 96734, tel. 808/261–3539) carries a complete line of boardsailing equipment and accessories. Or consider **Kailua Sailboard Company** (130 Kailua Rd., Kailua 96734, tel. 808/262–2555). This shop rents equipment and provides carts to roll it to the waterfront five minutes away.

Spectator Sports

Football The **Pro Bowl,** featuring the NFL elite, is played here in early February, a week after the Super Bowl. In December, collegiate football hits the stadium during the **Aloha Bowl.** The **Hula Bowl,** held each January at Aloha Stadium in Honolulu (tel. 808/486–9300), is a sports classic bringing together All-American college stars and presenting a field full of hula girls at halftime. For local action, the **University of Hawaii Rainbows** take to the field at Aloha Stadium in season, with a big local following. There are often express buses from Kapiolani Park (tel. 808/956–6508 for details).

Golf The giants of the greens return to Hawaii every January or February (depending on television scheduling) to compete in the **Hawaiian Open Golf Tournament** (tel. 808/526–1232), a PGA tour regular with a $1 million purse. It is held at the exclusive Waialae Country Club near Waikiki, and it's always mobbed.

Polo Mokuleia on the North Shore is a picturesque oceanside setting for weekly polo matches. Local teams compete against international players during the season, which runs from March to August. *68–411 Farrington Hwy., tel. 808/637–7795. Admission: $6 adults and children 12–17. Food concession available, or pack a tailgate picnic. Game: 2 PM.*

Running **The Honolulu Marathon** is a thrilling event to watch as well as to participate in. Join the throngs who cheer at the finish line at Kapiolani Park as internationally famous and local runners tackle the 26.2-mile challenge. It's held on a Sunday in early December and is sponsored by the Honolulu Marathon Association (tel. 808/734–7200).

Surfing For two weekends each March, **Buffalo's Annual Big-Board Surfing Classic** fills Makaha Beach with Hawaiian entertainment, food booths, and the best in big-board surfing (tel. 808/696–3878 or consult the newspaper). In the winter, you can head out to the north shore and watch the best surfers in the world hang ten during the **Triple Crown Hawaiian Pro Surfing Championships.** This two-day event, scheduled according to the wave conditions, is generally held at the Banzai Pipeline and Sunset Beach during November and December. Watch the newspapers for details.

Triathlon Swim-bike-run events are gaining in popularity and number in Hawaii. Most fun to watch (or enter) is the **Tinman Triathlon** (tel. 808/942–9764), held in mid-July in Waikiki.

Volleyball This is an extremely popular sport in the islands, and no wonder. The **University of Hawaii Rainbow Na Wahine** (women's team) has blasted to a number-one league ranking in years past. Crowded, noisy, crazy, and very exciting home games are played during the September–December season in Klum Gym (1337 Lower Campus Rd., Honolulu, tel. 808/956–6376). Admission: $5.

Windsurfing Watch the pros as they jump and spin on the waves during July's **Pan Am Hawaiian Windsurfing World Cup** off Kailua Beach. There are also windsurfing competitions off Diamond Head point, including August's **Wahine Classic,** featuring the world's best female boardsailors. Consult the sports section of the daily newspaper for details on these events.

Dining

The strength of Hawaii's tourist industry has allowed Oahu's hotels to attract and pay for some of the best culinary talent in the world. Consequently, Honolulu is a city where the best dining in town is in the hotels, and Waikiki is the area where you will pay the highest prices for dinner.

A wide variety of restaurants serve excellent ethnic food, especially Chinese and Japanese. So pervasive is the Eastern influence that even the McDonald's menu is posted in both English and *kanji*, the universal script of the Orient. In addition to its regular fare, McDonald's serves saimin, a Japanese noodle soup that ranks as the local favorite snack. Thai and Vietnamese cuisines are also catching on rapidly.

Honolulu is much, but not all, of the Oahu dining picture. As you head away from town there are a handful of culinary gems sparkling among many lesser eateries not worth a second look. Treat yourself to some of these rare finds, which are often less expensive than the city restaurants. So diverse is the island's dining scene that on successive nights you may eat with silver and fine linen napkins, from monkey-pod dishes, with chopsticks, or with your fingers. There may be candlelight, moonlight, or neon light. You can choose from some of the most delectable fish, including *opakapaka* (blue snapper) and mahimahi (white dolphin fish, not to be confused with Flipper). Or you may want to tackle a bowl of brown paste called *poi*, the traditional starch that Hawaiians lap up with love.

For snacks and fast food around the island, look for the *manapua* wagons, the food trucks usually parked at the beaches; and *okazu-ya* stores, the local version of delis, which dispense tempura, sushi, and plate lunch, Hawaii's unofficial state dish. A standard plate lunch has macaroni salad, "two scoops rice," and an entrée that might be curry stew, kalua (roasted) pig and cabbage, or sweet-and-sour spareribs.

New dining spots keep opening their doors at Restaurant Row (500 Ala Moana Blvd., tel. 808/538–1441) in downtown Honolulu. To get there from Waikiki, take Bus 19 or 20 marked "Airport."

Few restaurants require men to wear jackets. Still, as casual as Hawaii is, most restaurants will turn away the shirtless, the shoeless, and those in bathing suits. An aloha shirt and pants for men and a simple dress or pants for women are acceptable in all but the fanciest establishments. Restaurants are open daily, unless otherwise noted.

The following credit card abbreviations are used: AE, American Express; DC, Diners Club; MC, MasterCard; and V, Visa.

Highly recommended restaurants are indicated by a star ★.

Category	Cost*
Very Expensive	over $60
Expensive	$40–$60
Moderate	$20–$40
Inexpensive	under $20

per person excluding drinks, service, and sales tax (4%)

Waikiki

American
★ **Orchids.** You can't beat the setting, right beside the sea, with Diamond Head looming in the distance and fresh orchids everywhere. Seating is available indoors and outdoors, with the best views from the lanai. The popovers are huge, and the salads are light and unusual. The most popular meals of the week here is the special Sunday brunch and dinner buffets, featuring table after table of all-you-can-eat buffet delights; one spread features an impressive variety of island sashimi. Chafing dishes give you a range of options, from eggs Benedict to chicken curry. Desserts, such as warm poha-berry bread pudding, are all made in the Halekulani's own kitchen. *Halekulani Hotel, 2199 Kalia Rd., tel. 808/923–2311. Reservations advised. Dress: casual. AE, DC, MC, V. Moderate.*

Eggs 'N Things. This breakfast-only eatery with unusual hours is popular in part for its waitresses, and their breezy, chatty style that makes you feel right at home. Late-night revelers often stop here after a night on the town. Omelets are as huge as your plate and come with a variety of fillings; chili and cheese is a favorite. Blackened Cajun-style fish is great with scrambled eggs, and the macadamia nut waffle topped with whipped cream is rich enough to be dessert. The best bargain is the $2.75 Early Riser Special (two eggs any style and three huge pancakes) served 5–9 AM, 1–2 PM, and 1–2 AM. *1911 Kalakaua Ave., tel. 808/949–0820. No reservations. Dress: casual. No credit cards. Open 11 PM–2 PM. Inexpensive.*

Hau Tree Lanai. Renovations have made this restaurant right beside the sand at Kaimana Beach more charming than ever. It is often overlooked and shouldn't be. At breakfast, lunch, or dinner, you can dine under graceful hau trees and hear the whisper of the waves. Breakfast offerings include a huge helping of eggs Benedict, a fluffy Belgian waffle with your choice of toppings (strawberries, bananas, or macadamia nuts), and a tasty fresh salmon omelet. Two standout entrées are the jumbo tiger prawns stir-fried in a spicy black-bean sauce, and a classic

Waikiki Dining

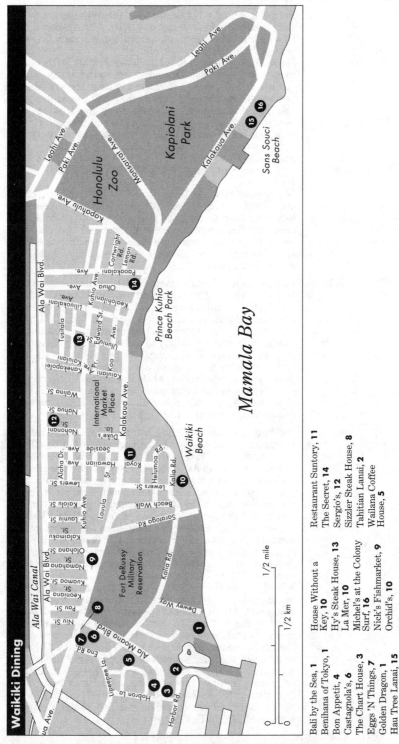

Mamala Bay

Honolulu Zoo

Kapiolani Park

Sans Souci Beach

Prince Kuhio Beach Park

Waikiki Beach

Fort DeRussy Military Reservation

Ala Wai Canal

1/2 mile

1/2 km

Bali by the Sea, **1**
Benihana of Tokyo, **1**
Bon Appetit, **4**
Castagnola's, **6**
The Chart House, **3**
Eggs 'N Things, **7**
Golden Dragon, **1**
Hau Tree Lanai, **15**

House Without a
 Key, **10**
Hy's Steak House, **13**
La Mer, **10**
Michel's at the Colony
 Surf, **16**
Nick's Fishmarket, **9**
Orchid's, **10**

Restaurant Suntory, **11**
The Secret, **14**
Sergio's, **12**
Sizzler Steak House, **8**
Tahitian Lanai, **2**
Wailana Coffee
 House, **5**

fettuccine Alfredo. For dessert, try the fresh papaya cheese-cake. *New Otani Kaimana Beach Hotel, 2863 Kalakaua Ave., tel. 808/921-7066. Reservations required at dinner. Dress: casual. AE, DC, MC, V. Moderate.*

House Without a Key. One of the jewels of Waikiki, this casual seaside spot serves salads, sandwiches, and hearty meals. Special meat, fish, pasta, and chicken entrées are available for lunch or dinner. Favorites include the Joy Sandwich (crabmeat salad, bacon, and avocado on whole-wheat bread) and the hamburger on a kaiser roll. With the ocean and Diamond Head in view, this is a mesmerizing place for *pupus* (hors d'oeuvres) at sunset, with live entertainment. A breakfast buffet is served daily 7–10:30 AM *Halekulani Hotel, 2199 Kalia Rd., tel. 808/923-2311. No reservations necessary. Dress: casual. AE, DC, MC, V. Inexpensive.*

Wailana Coffee House. If you like coffee shops, this is a reliable one. Nothing fancy—just booths and tables, waitresses who look like a favorite aunt, and all the coffee you can drink. Pancakes, waffles, omelets, and everything else that goes with breakfast are among the specialties of this budget diner. *1860 Ala Moana Blvd., tel. 808/955-1764. Dress: casual. AE, DC, MC, V. Inexpensive.*

Chinese **Golden Dragon.** Local Chinese people consider this the best.
★ New chef Steve Chiang is rigorously maintaining his predecessor's high standard of excellence. The tasty bill of fare includes Szechuan, Cantonese, and unconventional nouvelle Chinese cuisine. Set by the water, the restaurant has a stunning red-and-black decor, with big lazy susans in the middle of each table for easy sharing of food. Among the best items are stir-fried lobster with *haupia* (coconut), and Szechuan beef. The Peking duck and beggar's chicken (whole chicken baked in a clay pot) must be ordered 24 hours in advance. *Hilton Hawaiian Village, 2005 Kalia Rd., tel. 808/946-5336. Reservations required. Dress: casual. AE, DC, MC, V. Moderate.*

Continental **Bali by the Sea.** Like the island it's named for, this restaurant is
★ breeze-swept and pretty, with an oceanside setting offering glorious views of Waikiki Beach. But don't be fooled by the name. This is not an Asian ethnic eatery but an internationally acclaimed restaurant featuring such entrées as roast duck with papaya puree and macadamia nut liqueur. Another favorite is the poached mahimahi and opakapaka, a pair of island fish served with two sauces. American pastry chef Gale O'Malley is so talented that he has been decorated by the French government. His magnificent tarts, cakes, and sweets are displayed on the rolling pastry cart. *Hilton Hawaiian Village, 2005 Kalia Rd., tel. 808/941-2254. Reservations advised. Dress: casual. AE, DC, MC, V. Expensive.*

★ **Michel's at the Colony Surf.** With mirrors, candlelight, piano music, crystal, and chandeliers, this is easily the most romantic restaurant in town. One wall opens up to panoramas of the sea, lovely by day or night. The service is superb, and the waiters' mastery of tableside cooking is impressive. For starters, try the lobster bisque, flamed with cognac and laced with lobster chunks and homemade croutons. Pepper steak flamed with Jack Daniels whiskey is another winner. Breakfast, an insider's secret, features crepes suzette sautéed with fruit. *Colony Surf Hotel, 2895 Kalakaua Ave., tel. 808/923-6552. Reservations required. Dress: casual at breakfast, jacket required at dinner. AE, DC, MC, V. Expensive.*

The Secret. Formerly known as The Third Floor, this elegant restaurant feels like Europe—maybe Spain—with extravagant food displays and huge wicker chairs in which to hide. Try the abalone sautéed with lemon and served with capers on basmati rice, or consider such other fine entrées as lamb chops with *ohelo* berry sauce and sun-dried tomatoes, or the mussels and basil on pasta. Complimentary bon-bons served atop a minivolcano of dry ice follows the five-tier dessert cart. *Hawaiian Regent Hotel, 2552 Kalakaua Ave., tel. 808/922–6611. Reservations required. Dress: casual. AE, DC, MC, V. Expensive.*

French **La Mer.** In the exotic, elegant atmosphere of a Mandalay man-
★ sion, you'll be served a unique blend of French and nouvelle Hawaiian regional cuisine that many connoisseurs consider the finest dining experience in Hawaii. Portions are delicate and beautifully presented. A standout among the entrées is onaga (a local fish) baked in a thyme and rosemary rock salt crust with a sauce of fresh herbs. A favorite dessert is the lemon symphony (lemon tart, lemon caramel, confit of lemon zest, and lemon candy). Each evening there are two complete dinner menus, which run $75–$98, soup through dessert. Highly recommended is the cheese and port course, offered in lieu of dessert. *Halekulani Hotel, 2199 Kalia Rd., tel. 808/923–2311. Reservations required. Jacket required. AE, DC, MC, V. Very Expensive.*

Bon Appetit. Country French cuisine is presented in a cozy atmosphere reminiscent of a European bistro. Elegantly decorated in pink and black with French-style paintings on the wall, this restaurant is the brainchild of owner-chef Guy Banal, who has created a fascinating menu. Appetizers include a Scandinavian plate of Norwegian salmon and trout marinated in champagne with Gravlak sauce (cream, mustard, horseradish, lemon juice, and dill). Tempting entrées include broiled fresh fillet of fish with ginger-lobster butter, and broiled lamb with sweet pimientos, fresh basil, mint, and garlic. The fixed-price dinner goes for $21–$26. The recently added tapas selection has become a hit with regulars. *Discovery Bay, 1778 Ala Moana Blvd., tel. 808/942–3837. Reservations required. Dress: casual. AE, DC, MC, V. Closed Sun. Moderate.*

Italian **Castagnola's.** Opened by a New Jersey transplant who missed his home state's hearty Italian cooking, this spot has become wildly popular. The restaurant takes great pride in the excellence of its ingredients; makes its own bread daily; and imports olive oil, peppers, cheeses, sausages, tomatoes, and olives directly from Italy. Favorites of the traditional family fare served here are veal Sorrentino, baked stuffed eggplant, and chicken Siciliano. The strict reservation schedule is followed to the nanosecond, and no amount of power, influence, or money will get you to the front of the line any sooner. *Inn-On-The-Park, 1920 Ala Moana Blvd., tel. 808/949–6277. Reservations strongly recommended. Dress: casual. MC, V. Moderate.*

Sergio's. Sergio Battistetti's popular dining room offers a tantalizing taste of Italy in the heart of Waikiki. The atmosphere is sophisticated and romantic, with dark booths providing plenty of intimacy. The menu offers nearly two dozen hot and cold appetizers, including shiitake mushrooms in white wine, butter, and garlic or spicy calamari (squid) marinara. Among the 16 pasta dishes is the *bugili puttanesca*, whose wide noodles swim in a tomato sauce spiced by anchovies and capers. Other fine entrées include saltimbocco, osso bucco, veal marsala, and Dover sole, pan-fried or broiled. The wine list is extensive and impressive. *445 Nohonani St., tel. 808/926-3388. Reservations advised. Dress: casual. AE, DC, MC, V. Moderate.*

Japanese **Benihana of Tokyo.** These restaurants are as famous for their theatrical knife work at the *teppan* (iron grill) tables as they are for their food. You are seated at a long table with other diners and together you watch as steak, chicken, seafood, and a variety of vegetables are sliced, diced, tossed, and sautéed before your eyes. There's not much variety to the menu, but it's still a lot of fun. Finish off the meal with some green-tea ice cream, a Benihana tradition. *Hilton Hawaiian Village, 2005 Kalia Rd., tel. 808/955-5955. Reservations required. Dress: casual. AE, DC, MC, V. Moderate.*

Restaurant Suntory. This unique restaurant offers Japanese dining at its most elegant. You can choose to eat in four areas: a sushi bar, a *teppanyaki* room (with food prepared on an iron grill), a *shabu shabu* room (thinly sliced beef boiled in broth), or a private dining room. The waiters and waitresses are stiff, and the atmosphere formal, but the food is very good. Beef sashimi and assorted shellfish top the shabu shabu entrées. A complete *teishoku* dinner served teppanyaki-style includes miso soup, vegetable and fish tempura, rice, and dessert. The sushi chef is a wizard to watch as he creates inventive morsels of delicate raw seafood and rice. *Royal Hawaiian Shopping Center, 2233 Kalakaua Ave., 3rd floor, tel. 808/922-5511. Reservations advised. Dress: casual. AE, DC, MC, V. Moderate.*

Polynesian **Tahitian Lanai.** Polynesian with a capital *P* in setting and
★ menu, it's an indoor-outdoor, poolside spot with thatched huts. There's serious talk of tearing down the hotel that houses this Waikiki institution, so stop by soon. When you do, try the landmark eggs Benedict. *Waikikian Hotel, 1811 Ala Moana Blvd., tel. 808/946-6541. Reservations advised. Dress: casual. AE, DC, MC, V. Inexpensive.*

Seafood **Nick's Fishmarket.** It's a little old-fashioned, perhaps, with its
★ black booths, candlelight, and formal table settings, but for a romantic diner, you just can't beat Nick's. A longtime fixture on the Waikiki dining scene, it's a popular place for celebrating special occasions. A favorite dish at Nick's is the bouillabaisse, but there are many other wonderful offerings, as well. Nick's special salad with spinach cream dressing is special indeed. This restaurant is also one of the few places you'll find Monterey abalone, served here with a Ricci sauce containing morsels of tender fish. For dessert, ask for the vanbana pie, a decadent combination of bananas, vanilla ice cream, and hot caramel sauce. *Waikiki Gateway Hotel, 2070 Kalakaua Ave., tel. 808/955-6333. Reservations required. Dress: casual. AE, DC, MC, V. Expensive.*

The Chart House. On the second floor overlooking the Ala Wai Yacht Harbor and the sunset is this popular cocktail spot. (Salty dogs may want to visit the Yacht Harbor Pub first, just to the right and below the Chart House, where sailors of all sorts gather to quaff a few and swap tales.) The Chart House decor ranges from varnished wood to saltwater aquariums, glass fishing floats to racing sailboat photos. Dinner specialties include Hawaiian lobster and other seafood, as well as steak. The Dungeness crab is remarkable. *Ilikai Waikiki Hotel, Ma-*

rina Bldg., 1765 Ala Moana Blvd., tel. 808/941-6669. Reservations advised. Dress: casual. AE, DC, MC, V. Moderate.

Steak **Hy's Steak House.** Things always seem to go well at Hy's, from
★ the steak tartare and oysters Rockefeller right through to the
flaming desserts, such as cherries jubilee. The atmosphere is
snug and librarylike, and you can watch the chef perform behind glass. Tuxedoed waiters, catering to your every need,
make helpful suggestions about the menu. Hy's is famous for its
broiled lobster tail, *kiawe*-broiled rack of lamb ("kiawe" is a
mesquite-type wood), and glazed New York peppercorn steak.
The Caesar salad is excellent, as are the potatoes O'Brien. *Waikiki Park Heights Hotel, 2440 Kuhio Ave., tel. 808/922-5555.
Reservations required. Dress: casual. AE, DC, MC, V. Moderate.*

Sizzler Steak House. This neon-and-chrome, low-budget steak
and seafood eatery is designed for people who are stopping in
for a quick meal. There's generally an all-you-can-eat special,
with soup, salad, and hot bread. You walk through a cafeteria-
style line to place your order for such items as fried shrimp,
steak, and lobster. Breakfast here is pretty good, and the pancakes are substantial. The salad bar is a popular stop. *1945
Kalakaua Ave., tel. 808/955-4069. No reservations. Dress: casual. No credit cards. Inexpensive.*

Honolulu

American **Hala Terrace.** This restaurant has an open-air setting that stars
unusual salads and vegetarian dishes. Highly recommended is
the spicy, Thai-style chicken salad. There is also a full low-calo-
rie menu, with calories listed, along with more substantial offerings, such as a corned beef sandwich on rye with sauerkraut
or the excellent homemade lobster ravioli. The Hala Terrace is
the site of the long-running Danny Kaleikini Show, a delightful
Polynesian revue performed Monday–Saturday during the dinner hour. On Sundays, there's a seafood buffet instead. *Kahala
Hilton Hotel, 5000 Kahala Ave., tel. 808/734-2211. Reservations required. Dress: casual. AE, DC, MC, V. Moderate.*

Sunset Grill. The sweet smell of wood smoke greets you as you
enter the Sunset Grill, which specializes in kiawe-broiled
foods. The place is supposed to feel unfinished, with the marble
bar top and white tablecloths contrasting nicely with the concrete floors. The salade niçoise, big enough for a whole dinner,
includes red-top lettuce, beans, tomato, egg, potatoes, and olives, as well as marinated grilled *ahi* (tuna). The trout and scallops, cooked in a wood oven, are both very good. *Restaurant
Row, 500 Ala Moana Blvd., tel. 808/521-4409. Reservations
advised. Dress: casual. AE, DC, MC, V. Moderate.*

Tripton's American Cafe. Local residents love this place as
much for its spare, Napa Valley ambience—a real change of
pace from the relentless glitz of Waikiki, only a five-minute
drive away—as for its menu of inventive American cuisine.
Seasonal specialties are emphasized here, and the ocean-sweet
Australian rock lobster tails are massive and delicious. The
marinated Southwest grilled chicken, "blackened" orange
chicken, and zesty lemon-herb chicken are strongly recommended. For a lighter meal, try the "Green Grocery" of lettuce,
tomatoes and choice of 10 salad ingredients, served with the
soup of the day. The knockout desserts are made fresh daily.
Diamond Head Center, 449 Kapahulu Ave., tel. 808/737-3819.

112

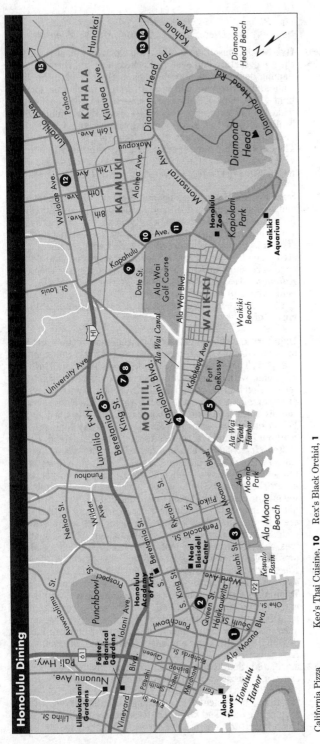

California Pizza
Kitchen, **5, 15**
Columbia Inn, **2**
Compadres Mexican
Bar and Grill, **3**
Hala Terrace, **13**
Hard Rock Cafe, **4**

Keo's Thai Cuisine, **10**
Kim Chee Two, **12**
Maile, **13**
Maple Garden, **7**
Ono Hawaiian
Foods, **9**
Phillip Paolo's, **6**

Rex's Black Orchid, **1**
Ruth's Chris Steak
House, **1**
Sunset Grill, **1**
Swiss Inn, **14**
Tripton's American
Cafe, **11**
The Willows, **8**

Reservations advised. Dress: casual. AE, DC, MC, V. Moderate.

★ **The Willows.** Thatched dining pavilions set amid koi, or carp, ponds full of prize fish make this a cherished landmark on Oahu's dining scene. The jungle elegance of the setting makes the perfect backdrop for American meals with an international flavor. Curries are particularly good here, and the "mile-high" lemon and coconut meringue pies have been top sellers since the 1950s. The sautéed opakapaka with spinach sauce is excellent, as are the lamb medallions in brandy and honey. Hawaiian curry salad is another good choice. For a glimpse of real down-home Hawaii, reserve a space at the Kamaaina Luncheon, held every other Thursday. You'll discover lots of local food, music, and spontaneous hula. *901 Hausten St., tel. 808/946–4808. Reservations required. Dress: casual. AE, DC, MC, V. Moderate.*

Columbia Inn. "At the top of the boulevard" sits this well-established, recently renovated coffee shop with a tradition of offering three square meals, low prices, and plenty of camaraderie. Solo diners sit at the long counter, while others take up the booths. The walls are covered with sports memorabilia and caricatures of personalities who have stopped by over the years. The banana pancakes are a good breakfast choice. At lunch, go for the Reuben sandwich. Dinner specials include such American standards as roast chicken, along with such local fare as saimin and broiled teriyaki pork chops. *645 Kapiolani Blvd., tel. 808/531–3747. No reservations. Dress: casual. AE, DC, MC, V. Inexpensive.*

Hard Rock Cafe. The Honolulu branch of this international chain features the signature rock-and-roll memorabilia, including an outfit once worn by John Lennon, platinum and gold records donated by Tina Turner and Michael Jackson, guitars autographed by rock stars, and for local color, a Tom Selleck aloha shirt. The Hard Rock has always sold more T-shirts than T-bones, so don't expect any culinary surprises on its formula menu. The portion-controlled quarter-pound burgers hold sway, but don't overlook the ahi steak sandwiches or baby back ribs as alternatives. French fries are, of course, a must with any choice. The decibel level of the oldies playing over the sound system is set at "too loud." *1837 Kapiolani Blvd., tel. 808/955–7583. No reservations. Dress: casual. AE, MC, V. Inexpensive.*

Chinese **Maple Garden.** The fine reputation of Maple Garden is founded on spicy Mandarin cuisine, not on decor. There are some booths, some tables, an Oriental screen or two, and lights that are a little too bright at times. It's comfortable, however, and that's all that matters, because the food is delicious. A consistent favorite is the eggplant in a tantalizing hot garlic sauce. *909 Isenberg St., tel. 808/941–6641. Reservations advised. Dress: casual. AE, DC, MC, V. Inexpensive.*

Continental **Maile.** The signature restaurant in this "hotel of the stars" is
★ glamorous and glimmering. Situated on the lower level, the Maile has no view but instead casts an indoor spell with magic all its own. Trickling waterfalls, tropical flowers and greenery, and soft live music create a lovely background to the exceptional dishes, which include both Continental favorites and island cuisine. Steaks and meats are the pride of the restaurant. Roast duckling Waialae has long been its most famous entrée, prized for its sauce of lychees, bananas, and mandarin orange slices. The gingerbread soufflé laced with cinnamon ice and

fresh strawberry compote is a must-try dessert. *Kahala Hilton, 5000 Kahala Ave., tel. 808/734-2211. Reservations required. Jacket advised. AE, DC, MC, V. Expensive.*

Rex's Black Orchid. When it opened in 1988 as the Black Orchid, it was a stratospherically upscale restaurant with prices to match. But since restaurateur Rex Chandler took it over in 1992, the dining room has loosened up and lowered its prices, although the dark wood and art deco decor still make this a trendy place for lunch or dinner. Black-and-blue ahi, cooked with Cajun spices, seared on the outside and left raw inside, is one of the top-selling appetizers, and deservedly so. *Restaurant Row, 500 Ala Moana Blvd., tel. 808/521-3111. Reservations required. Dress: casual. AE, DC, MC, V. Moderate.*

Hawaiian **Ono Hawaiian Foods.** Locals frequent this no-frills hangout for a regular hit of their favorite foods. You can tell it's good, because there's usually a line outside after about 5 PM. Housed in a plain storefront site and furnished simply with tables and booths, this small (it seats about 40) restaurant is a good place to do some taste testing of such Island innovations as *poi* (taro paste), *lomilomi* salmon (massaged until tender and served with minced onions and tomatoes), *laulau* (steamed bundle of ti leaves containing pork, butterfish, and taro tops), *kalua* (roasted) pig, and *haupia* (dessert made from coconut). Appropriately enough, the Hawaiian word *ono* means delicious. *726 Kapahulu Ave., tel. 808/737-2275. No reservations. Dress: casual. No credit cards. Inexpensive.*

Italian **Phillip Paolo's.** The talented Phillip Paolo creates Southern Italian cuisine with a flair all his own. The restaurant is set in an old colonial-style house, with rooms of different sizes, wooden floors, and high ceilings. The outdoor garden is a charming place for casual dinners under the trees. The lobster parmigiana is a classic dish, and the steak Capri is served with fresh crab legs and shrimp, all covered with béarnaise sauce. There are always specials here. For dessert, try vanilla cheesecake with a sauce of mangoes from Paolo's own tree (in season, May–July). *2312 S. Beretania St., tel. 808/946-1163. Reservations advised. Dress: casual. AE, MC, V. Moderate.*

Korean **Kim Chee Two.** Here's an unassuming little carryout and sit-down restaurant featuring Korean food. The prices are low and the portions are big. You get little side dishes of spicy *kimchee* (pickled vegetables) with your meal. This is a fun place to try such specialties as *bi bim kook soo* (noodles with meat and vegetables), meat *jun* (barbecued beef coated with egg and highly seasoned), *chop chae* (fried vegetables and noodles), and fried *man doo* (plump meat-filled dumplings). *3569 Waialae Ave., tel. 808/737-0006. No reservations. Dress: casual. No credit cards. BYOB. Inexpensive.*

Mexican **Compadres Mexican Bar and Grill.** The after-work crowd gathers here for frosty pitchers of potent margaritas and yummy ★ pupus. An outdoor terrace with patio-style furnishings is best for cocktails and chips. Inside, the wooden floors, colorful photographs, and lively paintings create a festive setting for imaginative Mexican specialties. Fajitas, chili rellenos, baby back ribs, and grilled shrimp are just a few of the many offerings. *The Ward Centre, 1200 Ala Moana Blvd., tel. 808/523-1307. No reservations. Dress: casual. AE, MC, V. Inexpensive.*

Pizza **California Pizza Kitchen.** This pair of dining and watering holes for young fast-trackers is worth the more-than-likely wait for a table. At the Kahala site, a glass atrium with tiled and mirrored walls and one side open to the shopping mall creates a sidewalk-café effect. The pizza features toppings you'd never expect, such as Thai chicken, Peking duck, and Caribbean shrimp. The pastas, made fresh daily on the premises, include angel hair, fettuccine, rigatone, fusilli, and linguine. *Kahala Mall, 4211 Waialae Ave., tel. 808/737–9446; 1910 Ala Moana Blvd., Waikiki, tel. 808/955–5161. No reservations. Dress: casual. AE, MC, V. Inexpensive.*

Steak **Ruth's Chris Steak House.** At last, a steak joint that doesn't look like one. This pastel-hued place with sophisticated decor serves generous salads and hefty steak cuts. The charbroiled fish serves as an excellent alternative to the meat dishes. A rich bread pudding is the house dessert. *Restaurant Row, 500 Ala Moana Ave., tel. 808/599–3860. Reservations recommended. Dress: casual. AE, MC, V. Moderate.*

Swiss **Swiss Inn.** Waitresses in dirndls and color photos of Alpine villages create a Swiss setting for the concoctions of Swiss-born
★ chef Martin Wyss. Appetizers include *bundnerfleisch* (thinly sliced air-dried beef) and *croûte emmental* (creamed mushrooms on toast with ham and Swiss cheese). Dinners come complete with soup, salad, vegetables, and coffee or tea. Veal medallions Florentine, served on a bed of spinach and covered with sliced bacon and Swiss cheese, is an outstanding entrée. With her sparkling aloha spirit, Martin's wife, Jeanie, does an excellent job of keeping things running smoothly. *Niu Valley Shopping Center, 5730 Kalanianaole Hwy., tel. 808/377–5447. Reservations advised. Dress: casual. AE, DC, MC, V. Moderate.*

Thai **Keo's Thai Cuisine.** Hollywood celebrities have discovered this
★ twinkling nook with tables set amid lighted trees, big paper umbrellas, and sprays of orchids everywhere. In fact, Keo has a whole wall devoted to photos of himself with a variety of stars. Favorite dishes include Evil Jungle Prince (shrimp, vegetables, or chicken in a sauce flavored with fresh basil, coconut milk, and red chili) and *chiang mai* salad (chicken salad seasoned with lemongrass, red chili, mint, and fish sauce). Ask for your food mild or medium; it'll still be hot, but not as hot as it *could* be. The crispy Thai noodles have a wonderful, barely-there sauce. The food comes in serving dishes Chinese-style, to share. For dessert, the apple-bananas in coconut milk are wonderful. *625 Kapahulu Ave., tel. 808/737–8240. Reservations required. Dress: casual. AE, DC, MC, V. Moderate.*

Around the Island

Haleiwa **Steamer's.** Whether you're seated at a comfortable booth or a
Seafood table, you'll have the finest meal available on the north shore amid this restaurant's mirrored walls and ceiling fans. The emphasis is on seafood, including a chowder with fresh fish chunks. Pastas and salads are also quite good. *Haleiwa Shopping Plaza, 66-165 Kamehameha Hwy., tel. 808/637–5071. Reservations advised. Dress: casual. AE, MC, V. Moderate.*

Hawaii Kai **Roy's.** Roy Yamaguchi, a widely acclaimed Los Angeles chef,
Hawaii Regional has brought his talents to Hawaii. His Hawaii Kai venture (he has a bistro in Waikiki) is a noisy two-story restaurant. Two

Bueno Nalo, **4**
The Chart House, **2**
Pearl City Tavern, **3**
Roy's, **5**
Steamer's, **1**

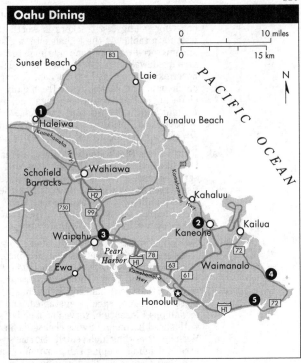

Oahu Dining

0   10 miles

0   15 km

Sunset Beach

Laie

PACIFIC OCEAN

N

Haleiwa

Punaluu Beach

Kamehameha Hwy

Schofield Barracks

Wahiawa

Kahaluu

Kaneohe

Kailua

Waipahu

Pearl Harbor

Ewa

Waimanalo

Kamehameha Hwy

Honolulu

walls of windows offer views of Maunalua Bay and Diamond Head in the distance, and a glassed-in kitchen affords views of what's cooking. Roy's cuisine combines the best of island flavors with French, Italian, Japanese, Thai, and Chinese accents. *Hawaii Kai Corporate Plaza, 6600 Kalanianaole Hwy., tel. 808/396-7697. Reservations advised. Dress: casual. AE, DC, MC, V. Moderate.*

Kaneohe
Steak and Seafood

The Chart House. Set in the lush surroundings of Haiku Gardens, this restaurant is one in a chain on Oahu. The decor is rustic but pretty, with views of tropical plants and flowers. The food is predictable but good, and includes New York steak, sweet-and-sour chicken, and fresh fish. *46-336 Haiku Rd., tel. 808/247-6671. Reservations not necessary. Dress: casual. AE, MC, V. Moderate.*

Pearl City
American/Japanese

Pearl City Tavern. Be forewarned: This is a real local hangout. Established in 1944, it boasts the world-famous Monkey Bar, with *live* monkeys who frolic behind glass panels, plus a bonsai garden upstairs and Japanese decorations everywhere. Japanese and American dinners are the fare, including very good beef sukiyaki, ahi (tuna) sashimi and *tonkatsu* (pork cutlet served over rice). *905 Kamehameha Hwy., tel. 808/455-1045. No reservations. Dress: casual. AE, DC, MC, V. Inexpensive.*

Waimanalo
Mexican

Bueno Nalo. Don't blink or you'll drive right by this hole-in-the-wall that serves authentic Mexican food. The decor is a riot of colors, with velvet paintings, piñatas, and year-round Christmas tinsel. The lack of air-conditioning can sometimes make the rooms uncomfortably warm. The food, however, is reliably good, and it's worth standing in the line that sometimes forms outside in the evening. Topopo salad is a heap of greens, tomatoes, onions, tuna, olives, cheese, and beans on top of a tortilla. Combination plates with tacos, enchiladas, and tamales are bargains. The chili rellenos are expertly seasoned. *41-865 Kalanianaole Hwy., tel. 808/259-7186. No reservations. Dress: casual. No credit cards. BYOB. Inexpensive.*

Lodging

Oahu boasts a huge variety of accommodations, so it takes some planning ahead to find your perfect vacation home-away-from-home.

When considering the options, first decide if you want to get away from the everyday hustle and bustle. If your answer is yes, then you should look at the accommodations listed in the "Around the Island" category. If you prefer proximity to the action, go for a hotel or condominium in Honolulu or near Waikiki, where the majority of the island's lodgings are located.

Tiny as it is, Waikiki offers you everything from tidy, simple accommodations (bed, bath, room service, and telephone) away from the beach to elegant oceanside suites furnished with all your heart's desires. There are bed-and-breakfast establishments and condominiums with fully equipped kitchens. If you want a hotel right on the beach in Waikiki, just ask for it. However, Waikiki is small enough that you don't have to pay a premium for a hotel *near* the beach. You can rent a little room three blocks from the ocean and still spend your days on the sand rubbing elbows with the rich and famous.

Some people look at a hotel as simply a place to sleep at night. Others prefer a bit of ambience. The hotels that are recommended in each price category offer a good range of options. A place doesn't have to be expensive to be clean, friendly, and attractive. For a complete list of every hotel and condominium unit on the island, write to the Hawaii Visitors Bureau for the free *Accommodation Guide*. It details amenities and gives each hotel's proximity to the beach.

One asset Oahu's hotels have in common is the service—in other words, the people with whom you come in contact every day. Their hospitality is part of the aloha spirit, a spirit you can find at the simplest boarding houses as well as at the top-of-the-line properties. Hawaii's hotel personnel often receive their training at the college level, and tourism is their profession; they take pride in what they do.

Except for the peak months of January, February, and August, you'll have no trouble getting a room if you call ahead of time. When making your reservations, either on your own or through a travel agent, ask about packages and extras. Some hotels have special tennis, golf, or honeymoon deals. Others have periodic room-and-car packages. Oahu hotel prices usually follow a European plan, meaning no meals included.

The following credit card abbreviations are used: AE, American Express; DC, Diners Club; MC, MasterCard; and V, Visa.

Highly recommended hotels are indicated by a star ★.

Category	Cost*
Very Expensive	over $170
Expensive	$120–$170
Moderate	$75–$120
Inexpensive	under $75

All prices are for a standard double room, excluding 9¼% tax and service charges.

Waikiki

Very Expensive   **Halekulani Hotel.** Today's sleek, modern, and luxurious
★ Halekulani was built around the garden lanai and historic 1931 building of the gracious old Halekulani Hotel. Throughout its colorful history, it has attracted visitors looking for an elegant oceanside retreat. The tidy marble-and-wood rooms have accents of white, beige, blue, and gray. All have lanais, sitting areas, refrigerators, bathrobes, and dozens of little touches that are sure to pamper. The in-room check-in service means no waiting in the lobby. The hotel has two of the finest restaurants in Honolulu and an oceanside pool with a giant orchid mosaic. Try to get a room with an ocean view, looking toward Diamond Head. *2199 Kalia Rd., Honolulu 96815, tel. 808/923–2311 or 800/367–2343. On the beach. 456 rooms with bath. Facilities: pool, shops, meeting rooms, 3 restaurants, 3 lounges. AE, DC, MC, V.*

Hawaii Prince Hotel Waikiki. Waikiki's newest hotel is also the final hotel zoned for the heavily developed resort area. On the site of the Old Kaiser Medical Center—adjacent to the well-known "Whaling Wall" mural—the Hawaii Prince opened in April 1990 to enthusiastic reviews. The hotel's architecture and interior design are a departure from the traditional Hawaiian motif, but the businesslike feel of the city hotel works well with views of the nearby Ala Wai Yacht Harbor. Each guest room in the 32-story towers overlooks the boats and the ocean. Every Friday at 5:30 PM yachtsmen raise their sails for a spectacular race out of the channel. Harbor views can be had from the elegant Prince Court Restaurant; the Hakone Japanese Restaurant offers dining thrills of another kind. Jazz lovers will find the Captain's Room lounge one of Waikiki's hottest musical venues. *100 Hololmoana St., Honolulu, 96815, tel. 808/956–1111 or 800/321–6248. Free shuttle to beach and downtown for guests. 521 rooms with bath. Facilities: pool, shop, meeting rooms, 4 restaurants, 1 lounge. AE, DC, MC, V.*

★ **Hilton Hawaiian Village.** Hilton spent $100 million to remake this complex into a brand-new, lavishly landscaped resort, the largest in the state. There are four towers, 22 restaurants, three swimming pools, cascading waterfalls, colorful fish and birds, and even a botanical garden of labeled flora. Rooms are decorated in attractive raspberry or aqua colors, with rattan and bamboo furnishings. The top two floors of the Rainbow Tower have been transformed into an executive club with butler service, the pricey suites of the Ocean Tower offer all the amenities. Ask for an ocean view. The hotel has a private dock for its catamaran and a fine stretch of oceanfront. *2005 Kalia Rd., Honolulu 96815, tel. 808/949–4321 or 800/445–8667. On the beach. 2,523 rooms with bath. Facilities: 2-tier superpool*

119

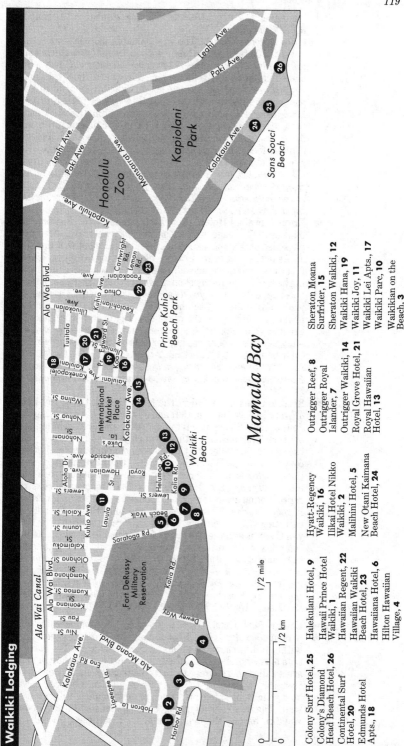

Waikiki Lodging

Colony Surf Hotel, **25**
Colony's Diamond Head Beach Hotel, **26**
Continental Surf Hotel, **20**
Edmunds Hotel Apts., **18**

Halekulani Hotel, **9**
Hawaii Prince Hotel Waikiki, **1**
Hawaiian Regent, **22**
Hawaiian Waikiki Beach Hotel, **23**
Hawaiiana Hotel, **6**
Hilton Hawaiian Village, **4**

Hyatt-Regency Waikiki, **16**
Ilikai Hotel Nikko Waikiki, **2**
Malihini Hotel, **5**
New Otani Kaimana Beach Hotel, **24**

Outrigger Reef **8**
Outrigger Royal Islander, **7**
Outrigger Waikiki, **14**
Royal Grove Hotel, **21**
Royal Hawaiian Hotel, **13**

Sheraton Moana Surfrider, **15**
Sheraton Waikiki, **12**
Waikiki Hana, **19**
Waikiki Joy, **11**
Waikiki Lei Apts., **17**
Waikiki Parc, **10**
Waikikian on the Beach, **3**

(10,000 sq. ft.), 2 additional pools, 22 restaurants, 11 lounges. AE, DC, MC, V.

Hyatt Regency Waikiki. The focal point of this twin-tower beauty is the 10-story atrium lobby with its two-story waterfall and mammoth metal sculpture. Shops, live music, and Harry's Bar make this one of the liveliest lobbies anywhere, though you may get lost in it. Each guest room has an Oriental art print to complement the warm earth tones, wall-to-wall carpeting, private lanai, color TV, air-conditioning, and combination desk/game table and chairs. Spats is the hotel's fun Italian restaurant and disco, and the Ciao Mein restaurant serves both Italian and Chinese food. Since the hotel has two towers, there are two Regency Clubs and eight penthouses. *2424 Kalakaua Ave., Honolulu 96815, tel. 808/923–1234 or 800/233–1234. Across the street from the beach and a short walk from Kapiolani Park. 1,230 rooms with bath. Facilities: 7 restaurants; 6 lounges, including a disco; a pool; 70 shops. AE, DC, MC, V.*

★ **Royal Hawaiian Hotel.** This "Pink Palace of the Pacific" was built in 1927, an age of gracious and leisurely travel when people sailed on Matson luxury liners and spent months at the Royal. As befits that grand era, the hotel has high ceilings, period furniture, and flowered wallpaper. People who have been coming here for 30 years insist on a favorite chair or bureau, but the hotel appeals to newlyweds as well as old-timers. Dreams are made of breakfast at the beachside Surf Room, the pink telephones in each room, the corridors of pink carpeting, and the great crystal chandeliers tinkling in the wind. The modern wing is more expensive, but for charm, the original building can't be beat. *2259 Kalakaua Ave., Honolulu 96815, tel. 808/923–7311 or 800/325–3535. On the beach. 526 rooms with bath. Facilities: pool, meeting rooms, 3 restaurants, 2 lounges. AE, DC, MC, V.*

★ **Sheraton Moana Surfrider.** The Moana Hotel, the "First Lady of Waikiki," was built in 1901 and restored to her original grandeur in 1989. Sheraton has taken great pains and spent millions on this landmark structure, which has been merged with the newer Surfrider next door. Accommodations retain their cozy charm, and, as in the old days, the furnishings on each floor are made of a different kind of wood: mahogany, oak, maple, cherry, and rare Hawaiian koa. Each room has a colonial-reproduction armoire and such modern amenities as a minibar, in-room movies, Hawaiian soaps and toiletries, a hair dryer, daily newspaper delivery, and 24-hour room service. The Banyan Court is still the focal point for beachside activity, and you can relax on the gracious veranda, sip tea, and tune yourself in to turn-of-the-century living. *2365 Kalakaua Ave., Honolulu 96815, tel. 808/922–3111 or 800/325–3535. On the beach. 790 rooms with bath. Facilities: pool, recreation deck, shops, meeting rooms, 3 restaurants, 3 lounges, poolside snack stand, beach bar. AE, DC, MC, V.*

Expensive ★ **Colony Surf Hotel.** This small hotel with impeccable and personal service is like a condominium; each unit is equipped with a full kitchen and an attractive living area. The same is true of the hotel's annex, the **Colony Surf East,** although units are smaller there. Wealthy patrons like to keep this one a secret; they appreciate the fine points, such as a staff that will hold your aloha shirts and beach paraphernalia until your next visit. The hotel is way up on the Diamond Head (east) end of Waikiki, beyond the mainstream. Its restaurant, Michel's, is

French, fashionable, open to the sea, and considered the most romantic dining room in town. *2895 Kalakaua Ave., Honolulu 96815, tel. 808/923–5751 or 800/252–7873, fax 808/922–8433. On the beach. Of 171 units, 50 are available for booking. There are an additional 50 units in the Colony Surf East. Facilities: 2 restaurants, 2 cocktail lounges in the 2 buildings. AE, DC, MC, V.*

Colony's Diamond Head Beach Hotel. Right on the ocean, but at the quiet end of Waikiki, is this smaller hotel that appeals to those in search of peaceful accommodations that are still close to the action of Waikiki. Irwin Stroll & Associates, a popular Los Angeles design firm, has decorated many of the rooms with mirrors, glass, and fine fabrics. Some rooms have kitchenettes. Continental breakfast is served to all guests. *2947 Kalakaua Ave., Honolulu 96815, tel. 808/922–1928 or 800/777–1700. Of 61 units, 53 are available for booking. AE, DC, MC, V.*

Hawaiian Regent Hotel. The huge lobbies and courtyards, open to the breezes, are sunlit and contemporary in feel. With two towers and two lobbies, the layout is a bit confusing, but if you can get past that, this is an outstanding hotel. It has several dining choices, including the award-winning Secret (formerly The Third Floor) and two Japanese restaurants, Regent Marushin and Kobe Fogetsudo. A complimentary breakfast is served each morning, and your bed will be turned down and an orchid left for you each evening. *2552 Kalakaua Ave., Honolulu 96815, tel. 808/922–6611 or 800/367–5370. Across the street from the beach. 1,346 rooms with bath. Facilities: shops, meeting rooms, 2 pools, tennis court, 2 lounges, disco, 6 restaurants. AE, DC, MC, V.*

Ilikai Hotel Nikko Waikiki. It's not on the beach, but it's one of the closest hotels to the Ala Moana Shopping Center and Ala Moana Beach Park. It's also the acknowledged tennis center of Waikiki. There are three towers and a huge esplanade, which is always busy, and crowds usually gather for the hula-dancing demonstrations and local musicians. You can get a good look at the Ala Wai Yacht Harbor from here. *1777 Ala Moana Blvd., Honolulu 96815, tel. 808/949–3811 or 800/367–8434. 800 rooms with bath. Facilities: 2 pools, 7 tennis courts, meeting rooms, shops, 4 restaurants, 2 lounges. AE, DC, MC, V.*

Outrigger Waikiki Hotel. A total renovation in 1992 transformed the Outrigger's star property. Located on Kalakaua Avenue in the heart of the shopping and dining action, it has some of the nicest sands in Waikiki. Rooms are newly redecorated with a Polynesian motif, and each has a lanai. Some have kitchenettes, for a higher price. For more than 20 years, the main show room has been the home of the sizzling Society of Seven and the group's Las Vegas–style production. *2335 Kalakaua Ave., Honolulu 96815, tel. 808/923–0711 or 800/462–6262, fax 800/622–4852. 530 rooms with bath. Facilities: pool, shops, 6 restaurants, 6 lounges. AE, DC, MC, V.*

Sheraton Waikiki. Towering over its neighbors, this hotel recently underwent a $4 million renovation and updated all its room furnishings. The porte cochere has a new slate floor, teak furniture, and a copper backdrop of Hawaiian design. The rooms are spacious, and many have a grand view of Diamond Head. The hotel is just steps away from the multilevel Royal Hawaiian Shopping Center and next to the Royal Hawaiian Hotel. Be sure to take the glass elevator up to the Hanohano Room, an elegant dining room with breathtaking panoramas of the sea and Waikiki. Thirty-minute room service is guaranteed. *2255 Kalakaua Ave., Honolulu 96815, tel. 808/922–4422 or 800/325–3535. On the beach. 1,852 rooms with bath. Facilities: 2 pools, shops, meeting rooms, 5 restaurants, 3 lounges. AE, DC, MC, V.*

Waikiki Joy. With rooms ranging in price from moderate to very expensive, this lodging has something for everybody. Some rooms have full kitchens, and others have complete wet bars. One tower has all suites, and another has standard hotel rooms. Bed sizes range from double to king, and you can also ask for ocean or partial ocean views. The common denominators: Each room has a lanai, a Jacuzzi, a deluxe stereo system with Bose speakers, and a control panel by the bed. A $1 million investment has transformed the second floor into 15 state-of-the-art karaoke sing-along rooms that can be rented by the hour, and hold from 2 to 30 people. *320 Lewers St., Honolulu 96815, tel. 808/923–2300 or 800/733–5569, fax 808/924–4010. 93 rooms with bath. Facilities: pool, sauna, restaurant, lounge. AE, DC, MC, V.*

★ **Waikiki Parc.** Billing itself as offering "affordable luxury," this hotel lives up to that promise in all essentials except the main entrance, which is down a narrow side street, and the location, which is not on the beach. The lobby is light and airy, with mirrors and pastel tones. Guest rooms are done in cool blues and whites, with lots of rattan, plush carpeting, conversation areas, tinted glass lanai doors, and shutters. Each room features a lanai, a refrigerator, central air-conditioning, an electronic in-room safe, and a high-security electronic-card entry system. The hotel has a fine Japanese restaurant called Kacho and the lovely Parc Café. *2233 Helumoa Rd., Honolulu 96815, tel. 808/921–7272 or 800/422–0450, fax 808/923–1336. 298 rooms with bath. Facilities: pool, recreation deck, 2 restaurants, 2 shops. AE, DC, MC, V.*

Moderate **Hawaiian Waikiki Beach Hotel.** The location—almost next to Kapiolani Park, the zoo, and other attractions—is excellent, and the seawall in front of the hotel offers the best sunset views. The mauka (north) tower has been completely refurbished and offers mainly ocean views. The rooms have nice rattan furniture, right down to the headboards. Each room is equipped with a color TV, private lanai, and air-conditioning. The Captain's Table serves meals in surroundings modeled after old-time luxury liners. *2570 Kalakaua Ave., Honolulu 96815, tel. 808/922–2511 or 800/877–7666. Across the street from the beach. 715 rooms with bath. Facilities: pool, 2 restaurants, 3 lounges, shops. AE, DC, MC, V.*

Hawaiiana Hotel. One of the cherished old-timers of Waikiki, this hotel has definitely improved with age. The aloha spirit permeates the place. When you arrive you are offered fresh pineapple, and when you leave you get a flower lei. Two- and three-story sections are arranged around a gorgeous tropical garden, and the sands of Fort DeRussy Beach are a short walk away. Open your door, and the gardens and pools are right there. The decor is simple and basic, and rooms come with electronic safes, air-conditioning, phones, and kitchens. Many have lanais as well. Complimentary newspapers, juice, and coffee are offered each morning on the patio. *260 Beach Walk, Honolulu 96815, tel. 808/923–3811 or 800/367–5122, fax 808/926–5728. ½ block from the beach. 95 rooms with bath. Facilities: pool, free washers and dryers. AE, MC, V.*

★ **New Otani Kaimana Beach Hotel.** Extensive renovations have taken this establishment a long way. The ambience is cheerful and charming, and the lobby has happily maintained its unpretentious feel. Polished to a shine, it is open to the trade winds and furnished with big, comfortable chairs and good magazines. Best of all, the hotel is right on the beach at the quiet end of Waikiki, practically at the foot of Diamond Head. Hotel manager Steve Boyle has received national recognition for his efforts to preserve the beauty of Diamond Head, and he often leads hikes to the summit. The staff is also friendly and helpful. Rooms are smallish but very nicely appointed, with soothing pastels, off-white furnishings, and color TV. Get a room with an ocean view, if possible, and dine at least once at the Hau Tree Lanai. *2863 Kalakaua Ave., Honolulu 96815, tel. 808/ 923–1555 or 800/421–8795, fax 808/922–9404. 125 rooms with bath. Facilities: 2 restaurants, lounge, shops, meeting rooms. AE, DC, MC, V.*

Outrigger Reef Hotel. The big recommendations here are the location right on the beach and the price—which is right. Fashion and souvenir boutiques grace the lobby, and the rooms are done in soft mauves and pinks; many have lanais, and all have air-conditioning and color TVs. Ask for an ocean view; the other views are decidedly less delightful. The seventh floor is for nonsmokers. *2169 Kalia Rd., Honolulu 96815, tel. 808/923– 3111 or 800/462–6262, fax 800/622–4852. 885 rooms with bath. Facilities: pool, 2 restaurants, 4 lounges, nightclub, shops, meeting rooms. AE, DC, MC, V.*

Waikikian on the Beach. It's one of the few low-rise hotels left, although it does have a newer, air-conditioned Tiki Tower. This hotel is a little gem, decidedly unpolished in spots, but the romance of old Hawaii is definitely here in the South Seas architecture, high-pitched roofs, and jungle-like gardens. Rooms are decorated in old Polynesian style, very different from more modern accommodations, and windows and doors open onto a garden path. The hotel is not technically on the beach, but it fronts the Duke Kahanamoku Lagoon, which has a sandy shore. The Tahitian Lanai restaurant has a faithful local following. *1811 Ala Moana Blvd., Honolulu 96815, tel. 808/949– 5331, 800/922–7866, 800/445–6633 in Canada. 135 rooms with bath. Facilities: pool, shops, restaurant, cocktail lounge. AE, DC, MC, V.*

Waikiki Hana. Behind the Hyatt Regency sits this little-known secret, a moderately priced hotel in a superb location. Although the building is not new, it has been renovated, and the lobby is charmingly furnished with wicker furniture. The rooms are attractively decorated, with pink walls, blue quilted bedspreads, and light wood. Each room has a color TV, a telephone, and air-conditioning. Some have kitchenettes. All that, and it's just a block to the beach (the hotel has no pool). Go during the off-season, and the prices are $10 lower. *2424 Koa Ave., Honolulu 96815, tel. 808/926–8841 or 800/367–5004. 73 rooms with bath. AE, DC, MC, V.*

Inexpensive **Continental Surf Hotel.** One of the great budget hotels of Waikiki, this appealing high rise is located along the Kuhio Avenue strip, two blocks from the ocean and convenient to tons of shopping and dining options. The lobby is large and breezy, and the comfortable rooms are decorated in standard Polynesian hues of browns and golds. Each room has a color TV, a telephone, and air-conditioning. However, the units have limited views and no lanais. Some rooms have a well-equipped kitchenette.

*2426 Kuhio Ave., Honolulu 96815, tel. 808/922–2755 or 800/
367–5004, fax 808/533–0472. 2 blocks from the beach. 140
rooms with bath. Facilities: guests may use the facilities of
its sister hotel, the Miramar, 1½ blocks away. AE, DC, MC,
V.*

Edmunds Hotel Apartments. Located on the Ala Wai Canal,
four blocks from the ocean, this has been a budget gem for more
than 20 years. Long lanais wrap around the building, so each
room has its own view of the pretty canal and glorious Manoa
Valley beyond—views that look especially lovely at night, when
lights are twinkling up the mountain ridges. The rooms are
small, nondescript studios, but they have all the basics: kitchenette, toaster, ironing board, and TV set. If you can put up
with the occasional sounds of traffic on the boulevard, this is a
real bargain. *2411 Ala Wai Blvd., Honolulu 96815, tel. 808/
923–8381. 4 blocks from the beach. 12 rooms with bath. No credit cards.*

Malihini Hotel. There's no pool, it's not on the beach, none of
the units has a television or air-conditioning, and the rooms are
spartan. Still, the atmosphere of this low-rise complex is cool
and pleasant, and the gardens are well maintained. All rooms
are either studios or one-bedrooms, and all have kitchenettes,
daily maid service, and fans. The low prices and good location
make this a popular place, so be sure to book well in advance.
*217 Saratoga Rd., Honolulu 96815, tel. 808/923–9644. 28
rooms with bath. Facilities: shop. No credit cards.*

Outrigger Royal Islander. The location—only two minutes from
a very nice section of Waikiki Beach—is the key to this inexpensive link in the Outrigger hotel chain. The rooms have tapa-
print bedspreads and ceramic lamps with matching patterns,
and there are island-inspired pictures on the walls. Each room
also has a private lanai, color TV, and air-conditioning. Choose
from studios, one-bedroom apartments, or suites. The staff is
helpful in arranging activities, such as golf and scuba packages
and sightseeing tours. *2164 Kalia Rd., Honolulu 96815, tel.
808/922–1961 or 800/462–6262, fax 808/923–4632. 101 rooms
with bath. Facilities: use of pools at other Outrigger Hotels.
AE, DC, MC, V.*

Royal Grove Hotel. You won't go wrong with this flamingo-pink
hotel, reminiscent of Miami. With just six floors, it is one of
Waikiki's smaller hotels. The lobby is comfortable; the rooms,
though agreeably furnished, have no real theme and no views.
They do, however, have kitchens, air-conditioning, color TVs,
and telephones. The pool area is bright with tropical flowers
(the hotel is not on the beach). Most people enjoy the family atmosphere. *15 Uluniu Ave., Honolulu 96815, tel. 808/923–7691.
87 rooms with bath. Facilities: pool. AE, DC, MC, V.*

Waikiki Lei Apartments. A favorite with repeat guests looking
for affordable lodging in the heart of the action, this four-story
pink establishment is one-of-a-kind. There's no elevator;
guests use the outside staircase. Everything is well maintained, and the studio units have a kitchen and refrigerator.
You need to ask ahead if you want a room with a TV and air-
conditioning, and there is no maid service. The decor is dark
wood and light-colored spreads, with tile floors. The longer you
stay, the lower the daily price. *241 Kaiulani Ave., Honolulu
96815, tel. 808/923–6656 or 808/734–8588. 2 blocks from the
beach. 19 units with bath. Facilities: pool, coin-operated washers and dryers. No credit cards.*

Honolulu

Very Expensive **Kahala Hilton.** Minutes away from Waikiki, on the quiet side of
★ Diamond Head, this elegant and understated hotel is in the
wealthy neighborhood of Kahala. This is the place where kings,
Hollywood stars, and presidents stay when they come to Oahu.
The Kahala Hilton's impressive lobby features chandeliers,
tropical flower displays, and a musician playing a grand piano.
The very large, recently refurbished rooms, decorated in earth
and natural tones and have his and her dressing rooms and par-
quet floors. The hotel also has a porpoise pond and three restaurants, including Maile, with Continental cuisine, and the
Hala Terrace supper club, featuring local star Danny Kaleikini.
The hotel is affiliated with the Maunalua Bay Club, a fitness
center just a short shuttle away. *5000 Kahala Ave., Honolulu
96816, tel. 808/734–2211 or 800/367–2525. On the beach. 309
rooms and suites with bath, plus 60 cottage-style units in the
Lagoon Terrace. Facilities: pool, tennis court, shops, meeting
rooms, 3 restaurants, 2 lounges. AE, DC, MC, V.*

Expensive **Ala Moana Hotel.** This 20-year-old landmark boasts an excellent location, right next to the popular Ala Moana Shopping Center (they're connected by a pedestrian ramp) and one
block from Ala Moana Beach Park. A $30 million renova-
tion has turned this 36-floor hotel into a gorgeous showcase,
and the rooms have been refurbished to include color TVs,
air-conditioning, AM/FM radios, electronic-card door locks,
and private safes. Each has a lanai with a view of the ocean, the
Koolau Mountains, or Diamond Head. Preferred floors with
special suites feature complete bar service, a spa, and free
newspaper and breakfast delivery each morning. The Mahina
Lounge, a sleek lobby bar with a white grand piano, hosts live
entertainment, and Rumours is one of the city's best discos. *410
Atkinson Dr., Honolulu 96814, tel. 808/955–4811 or 800/367–
6025. 1,174 rooms with bath. Facilities: 5 restaurants, 2
lounges, nightclub, shops, pool, pool bar. AE, DC, MC, V.*

Moderate **Manoa Valley Inn.** Here's an intimate surprise tucked away in
Manoa Valley, just 2 miles from Waikiki. Built in 1919, this
stately hotel features a complimentary Continental-breakfast
buffet on a shady lanai, and fresh tropical fruit and cheese in
the afternoon. Rooms are furnished in country-inn style, with
antique four-poster beds, marble-topped dressers, patterned
wallpaper, and fresh flowers. *2001 Vancouver Dr., Honolulu
96822, 808/947–6019, or 800/634–5115. 8 guest rooms, 4 with
private bath; 1 cottage with bath. Facilities: TV and VCR in the
reading room. MC, V.*

Inexpensive– **Pagoda Hotel.** Minutes away from the Ala Moana Shopping
Moderate Center and from Ala Moana Beach Park, the Pagoda has a convenient location. A free shuttle bus makes the trip between the
hotel and its sister property, the Pacific Beach in Waikiki. The
location, along with the moderate rates, makes this a good
choice if you're simply looking for a place to sleep and to catch a
couple of meals. Studio rooms include a full-size refrigerator, a
stove, and cooking utensils. No real views are available here,
since the hotel is pretty much surrounded by high rises. However, the rooms are all air-conditioned, and each has a color TV.
The hotel features the Pagoda floating restaurant, notable for
its Japanese gardens and waterways filled with colorful carp.
1525 Rycroft St., Honolulu 96814, tel. 808/941–6611 or 800/

*367–6060. 361 rooms with bath. Facilities: pool, shops, 2 res-
taurants. AE, DC, MC, V.*

Around the Island

Very Expensive | **Turtle Bay Hilton.** This is the only place to stay for miles and miles along the island's north shore. Though it's not swanky, this oceanside retreat has everything it takes for a relaxing stay away from town. The rooms, in three separate wings, have private lanais and are furnished with basic wicker, brass, pastels, and light woods, with pastel prints on the walls. Many people like the hotel for its golf course and horseback-riding facilities. Others drive out just to enjoy its mammoth Sunday champagne brunch, where you dine next to huge windows with a view of the crashing surf. The sunsets are wonderful, so try to get a room with a view of the water. The cottages adjacent to the hotel are pricier but offer more privacy. *Box 187, Kahuku 96731, tel. 808/293–8811 or 800/445–8667. On the beach. 486 rooms, suites, and cottages with bath. Facilities: pool, golf, tennis, horses, shops, restaurants. AE, DC, MC, V.*

Expensive | **Sheraton Makaha Resort and Country Club.** It takes more than
★ | an hour by car to get from Waikiki to this country resort set in glorious Makaha Valley, and the trip is worth it. Clusters of low-rise cottages and open-air pavilions keep this place simple and sweet. The Polynesian architecture and steep A-frame roofs look a little dated, but the interiors are done in a lovely combination of natural colors and woods. Each room has a private lanai with chairs and a table, plus a refrigerator, air-conditioning, a telephone, and a color TV. Most of the guests here play golf on one of the two highly acclaimed Makaha courses. Makaha Beach, popular with the locals, is about a mile away. Be sure to sign up for the horseback ride to the valley's restored ancient heiau (sacred Hawaiian site). *84-626 Makaha Valley Rd., Makaha 96792, tel. 808/695–9511 or 800/325–3535. 189 rooms with bath. Facilities: golf, tennis, horseback riding, pool, shops, lounge, 2 restaurants. AE, DC, MC, V.*

Inexpensive | **Laniloa Lodge.** Situated on the main road right next to the Polynesian Cultural Center, this plain, two-story establishment is the only hotel in Laie. That means you can break your round-the-island driving tour in two and spend the night here in basic comfort. The rooms are all studios, with color TVs and air-conditioning. The motif is Polynesian. Five separate wings form a circle around the swimming pool, and all the lanais face inward. *55109 Laniloa St., Laie 96762, tel. 808/293–9282 or 800/526–4562. 46 rooms with bath. Facilities: pool. AE, DC, MC, V.*

Schrader's Windward Marine Resort. Here is another rural resort with fewer luxuries than you would find in Waikiki but with perhaps a little more personalized attention from the staff. Some of the one-, two-, and three-bedroom apartments have kitchens and refrigerators. Each unit has a color TV, air-conditioning, a couch and coffee table; beds are turned down for the guests at night. The fancier rooms include full cooking facilities and remote-control TV. Some rooms open onto Kaneohe Bay, which is so close that people have been known to fish right off their lanais. Other rooms face the Koolau Mountains. Set on a peninsula, this is a popular spot for water activities. Jet skiing, snorkeling, windsurfing, and other excursions are offered to guests at special rates. *47-039 Lihikai Dr., Kaneohe 96744,*

Ala Moana Hotel, **7**

Aston at the Waikiki Banyan, **9**

Kahala Hilton, **11**

Kailua Kottages, **12**

Laniloa Lodge, **2**

Manoa Valley Inn, **8**

Pagoda Hotel, **6**

Pat's at Punaluu, **3**

Polynesian Plaza, **10**

Schrader's Windward Marine Resort, **5**

Sheraton Makaha Resort and Country Club, **4**

Turtle Bay Hilton, **1**

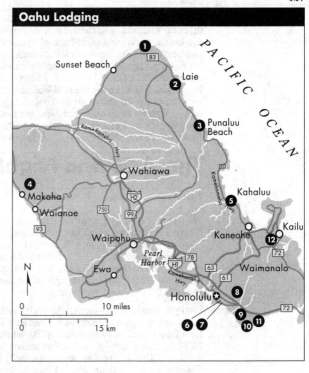

Oahu Lodging

tel. 808/239–5711 or 800/735–5711. On the beach. 55 rooms with bath. Facilities: water sports, pool, spa. AE, DC, MC, V.

Other Accommodations

Bed-and-Breakfasts **Bed and Breakfast Hawaii.** This reliable booker offers home-stays around Oahu, as well as on the other islands. *Box 449, Kapaa 96746, tel. 808/822–7771 or 800/733–1632.*

Bed and Breakfast Honolulu. This company has an especially good selection of rooms in Honolulu, including a place to stay in one of the few remaining private homes in Waikiki. *3242 Kaohinani Dr., Honolulu 96817, tel. 808/595–7533 or 800/288–4666.*

Condominiums **Aston at the Waikiki Banyan.** Families enjoy this 876-unit high-rise condominium resort near Diamond Head, one block from Waikiki Beach and close to Kapiolani Park. One-bedroom suites have full kitchens, daily maid service, and private lanais. There's also a pool, sauna, tennis facilities, barbecues, and a children's playground. *201 Ohua Ave., Honolulu 96815, tel. 808/922–0555 or 800/922–7866. Moderate–Expensive.*

Pat's at Punaluu. This unpretentious condo is located between the windward side and the North Shore. The mood is decidedly country, and the building is on a reef-protected beach whose calm waters are good for most water sports. Fully furnished apartments include kitchens; many have washer-dryers. *53-567 Kamehameha Hwy., Hauula 96717, tel. 808/293–8111 or 800/845–8799. Inexpensive.*

Vacation Rentals **Kailua Kottages.** The windward side of Oahu provides a restful rural vacation, and these three cottages, three blocks from the beach, serve as a good base of operations. Choose from a two-person studio, four-person cottage, or four-person one-bedroom suite, all with cooking facilities. *362 Kailua Rd., Kailua 96734, tel. 808/262–2212. Inexpensive.*

Polynesian Plaza. In the heart of Waikiki, this apartment building offers fully furnished studios with kitchenettes and private lanais. There's also a pool, sun deck, garden, and laundry facilities. Weekly and monthly rentals only. *2131 Kalakaua Ave., Honolulu 96815, tel. 808/923–4818. Inexpensive.*

The Arts and Nightlife

The Arts

The arts thrive right alongside the tourist industry in Oahu's balmy climate. The island has a symphony orchestra, an opera company, chamber-music groups, and theater troupes. Major ballet companies and rock stars also make their way to Honolulu from time to time. Check the local newspapers, the morning *Honolulu Advertiser,* and the afternoon *Honolulu Star-Bulletin* for the latest happenings.

Dance Every autumn, the Honolulu Symphony (tel. 808/537–6191) imports one or other of mainland America's finer ballet troupes for a joint effort. A local company, **Ballet Hawaii** (tel. 808/988–7578), is active during the holiday season with its annual production of **The Nutcracker,** which is usually held at the Mamiya Theater (3142 Waialae Ave., Chaminade University, Honolulu).

Film Art, international, classic, and silent films are screened at the little theater at the **Honolulu Academy of Arts.** *900 S. Beretania St., Honolulu 96814, tel. 808/538–1006. Tickets: $4. Dinner in the garden courtyard (tel. 808/532–8734) is served Thurs. at 6:15 PM.*

The Hawaii International Film Festival (1777 East–West Rd., Honolulu 96822, tel. 808/944–7007) may not be Cannes, but it is unique and exciting. The week-long festival, held from the end of November to early December, is based on the theme "When Strangers Meet." Top films from the United States, Asia, and the Pacific are aired day and night at several theaters on Oahu. Many local people plan their vacations around this time and spend days viewing free films and attending lectures, workshops, and social events with visiting film experts.

The Varsity Theater (1106 University Ave., tel. 808/973–5833) is a two-theater art house that brings internationally acclaimed motion pictures to Honolulu.

Waikiki generally gets the first-run films at its trio of theaters dubbed, appropriately, the **Waikiki 1, Waikiki 2,** and **Waikiki 3** (tel. 808/971–5033). Check newspapers for what's playing.

The Kahala Mall (4211 Waialae Ave., tel. 808/733–6233) has a complex of eight movie theaters that presents Honolulu's most diverse range of films in one location. It's a 10-minute drive from Waikiki.

Music **Chamber Music Hawaii** (tel. 808/528–2578) gives 25 concerts a year at the Honolulu Lutheran Church (1730 Punahou St.), Honolulu Academy of Arts (900 S. Beretania St.), and other locations around the island.

The Hawaii Opera Theater's season spans February and March, and includes such works as Saint-Saens' *Samson & Delilah*, Strauss's, *Die Fledermaus*, and Puccini's *Madama Butterfly*. Neal Blaisdell Concert Hall, Ward Ave. and King St., tel. 808/521–6537. Tickets: $18–$57 at the box office. To charge on credit cards, tel. 808/521–2911. MC, V.

The Honolulu Symphony's season runs September to April, Tuesday evenings and Sunday afternoons at Blaisdell Concert Hall (Ward Ave. at King St.). The Symphony on the Light Side series is on Friday evenings during the same season. Well-known island musicians often play with the symphony, and occasionally international performers are headlined. Write or call for a complete schedule. *1441 Kapiolani Blvd., Suite 1515, Honolulu 96814, tel. 808/942–2200. Tickets: $10–$30.*

During the school year, the faculty of the **University of Hawaii Music Department** (tel. 808/956–8742) gives concerts at Orvis Auditorium on the Manoa campus.

Rock concerts are usually performed at the cavernous **Neal Blaisdell Center Arena** (tel. 808/521–2911). Internationally famous stars also pack them in at **Aloha Stadium** (tel. 808/486–9300). Check newspapers for upcoming events.

Theater Because the islands are so expensive to get to and stay on, major touring companies seldom come to Hawaii. As a result, Oahu has developed several excellent local theater troupes, which present first-rate entertainment on an amateur and semiprofessional level all year long.

The **Diamond Head Theater** is in residence five minutes away from Waikiki, right next to Diamond Head. Its repertoire includes a little of everything: musicals, dramas, experimental, contemporary, and classics. *520 Makapuu Ave., Honolulu 96816, tel. 808/734–0274. Tickets: $20.*

The **Honolulu Theater for Youth** stages delightful productions for children around the islands from July to May. Write or call for a schedule. *2846 Ualena St., Honolulu 96819, tel. 808/839–9885. Tickets: $7.50 adults, $5 youth.*

The **John F. Kennedy Theater** at the University of Hawaii's Manoa campus is the setting for eclectic dramatic offerings—everything from musical theater to Kabuki, Noh, and Chinese opera. *1770 East–West Rd., Honolulu 96822, tel. 808/956–7655. Prices vary.*

Kumu Kahua is the only troupe presenting shows and plays written on and about the islands. It offers five productions a year in Tenney Theatre, on the grounds of St. Andrew's Cathedral. *224 St. Emma Sq., Honolulu 96813, tel. 808/737–4161. Tickets: $7 adults, $4 students and seniors.*

The **Manoa Valley Theater** gives wonderful nonprofessional productions in an intimate theater in Manoa Valley. Its season is September–June. Write or call for a schedule. *2833 E. Manoa Rd., Honolulu 96822, tel. 808/988–6131. Tickets $16–$20.*

The **Windward Theater Guild** is now in its 35th year of offering live family entertainment on the windward side of Oahu. Since it has no theater of its own, check the newspapers for location. *Box 624, Kailua 96734, tel. 808/247–9777. Tickets: $8–$10.*

Nightlife

Nightlife on Oahu can be as simple as a barefoot stroll in the sand or as elaborate as a dinner show with all the glittering choreography of a Las Vegas production. You can view the vibrant hues of a Honolulu sunset during a cocktail cruise, or hear the melodies of ancient chants at a luau on a remote west-shore beach.

Waikiki is where nearly all Oahu's night action takes place, and what action there is! Kalakaua and Kuhio avenues come to life when the sun goes down and the lights go on. It's fun just to watch the parade of people. Some strollers walk purposefully, knowing they have dinner reservations. Others wander along the strip reading every sign, every posted menu, looking for something to strike their fancy, whether it's the right atmosphere, the right price, or the catchiest tune.

Outside Honolulu, the offerings are slimmer but equally diverse. You can dance the two-step at a waterfront café one night and the next night boogie to live bands in a tiny second-story windward bar. The north shore is more conducive to settling back to the music of a slack-key guitar and lilting falsetto voice, while the ranch country of Waimanalo lends itself to country tunes and fiddle playing.

Wafting through the night air of Oahu is the sound of music of every kind—from classical to contemporary. Music has been the language of Hawaii from the beginning, and Oahu has the best selection of any island. Along with the music of the ancients, there's a new music in the soul of Hawaii. Traditional Hawaiian music has absorbed or fused with rock and disco to create a distinctively Hawaiian contemporary sound. Strong currents of jazz, country, and reggae also run through the local music pool.

Meanwhile, hula dancers wear sequined skirts in Waikiki and authentic ti-leaf skirts at Paradise Cove; they are accompanied by everything from *ipu* drums to electric guitars, mercifully not on the same stage in most cases. The latest high-tech, multimedia video discos may also be found on Oahu, but then, so are acoustic ukulele trios.

Bars/Cabarets/Clubs The drinking age is 21 on Oahu and throughout Hawaii. Many bars will admit younger people but will not serve them alcohol. By law, all establishments that serve alcoholic beverages must close at 2 AM. The only exceptions are those with a cabaret license, which have a 4 AM curfew. These may be billed as discotheques, but they are required to have live music. Most of the places listed below have a cover charge of $2–$5.

Waikiki **Bobby McGee's Conglomeration** (2885 Kalakaua Ave., tel. 808/922–1282). The club has disco dancing for adults in the 21–30 age group. It's located at the far Diamond Head end of Waikiki. Nightly 7–2.

Cilly's (1909 Ala Wai Blvd., basement, tel. 808/942–2952). This is another place where the fast-moving younger-adult crowd goes for disco dancing. Evening drink specials come as cheap as you'll find in Waikiki. Nightly 9–4.

Cupid's Lobby Bar (Prince Kuhio Hotel, 2500 Kuhio Ave., tel. 808/922–0811). Singer Carol Atkinson takes the stage Tuesdays–Thursdays, and on Fridays and Saturdays Leon Siu steps forward for some local-style guitar entertainment. Open daily 11–11 with live music Tuesday–Saturday 7–11.

Esprit (Sheraton Waikiki Hotel, 2255 Kalakaua Ave., tel. 808/922–4422). The Love Notes croon oldies Monday–Thursday at 8 and 9:45, and at 8 on weekends. Nohelani Cypriano sings Friday and Saturday at 9:30, and Woody the Disco Man does his thing on Sunday 8–midnight.

Jazz Cellar (205 Lewers St., tel. 808/923–9952). Live rock every night and 25¢ drinks on Monday make this a popular spot with the young-adult set. Music nightly 9–4. Late-night happy hour 2–4 AM.

Lewers Lounge (Halekulani Hotel, 2199 Kalia Rd., tel. 808/923–2311). Contemporary jazz and standards by singer Loretta Ables, Tuesday–Saturday 9–12:30. Vocalist/pianist Billy Kurch sits in Sunday and Monday 9–12:30. A dessert menu is offered.

Maile Lounge (Kahala Hilton Hotel, 5000 Kahala Ave., tel. 808/734–2211). A band called Kit Samson's Sound Advice has kept folks swinging on the small dance floor for more than 15 years, playing everything from contemporary hits to '40s favorites. Tuesday–Saturday 8–1.

Monarch Room (Royal Hawaiian Hotel, 2255 Kalakaua Ave., tel. 808/923–7311). Tea dancing is a tradition at this historic hotel. Dancers spill out onto the grassy area near the ocean to dance to music by the Del Courtney Orchestra with guest vocalists. Sunday 4:30–7:30.

Moose McGillycuddy's Pub and Cafe (310 Lewers St., tel. 808/923–0751). A variety of bands play for the beach-and-beer gang in a casual setting. Nightly 9–1:30.

Nick's Fishmarket (Waikiki Gateway Hotel, 2070 Kalakaua Ave., tel. 808/955–6333). This is probably the most comfortable of the Waikiki dance lounges, with an elegant crowd, inspiring music, and an intimate, dark atmosphere. There's some singles action here. Nightly 9–1:30.

Nicholas Nickolas (Ala Moana Hotel, 410 Atkinson Dr., tel. 808/955–4466). The view is splendid, the music is good, and the crowd dresses well, but the place is a bit on the stuffy side. Dancing Sunday–Thursday nights 9:30–2, Friday and Saturday 10–3.

Oasis Nightclub (2888 Waialae Ave., tel. 808/734–3772). On the mauka edge of Waikiki, the Oasis has dancing to live music amid high-tech, hard-edged decor. Nightly 11–3:30.

Paradise Lounge (Hilton Hawaiian Village, 2005 Kalia Rd., tel. 808/949–4321). It's expensive, which is reflected in the crowd's appearance. A piano player sets the tone for the dancing, nightly 5:30–11. One of Honolulu's top jazz crooners, Jimmy Borges, headlines with the Betty Loo Taylor Trio Friday and Saturday 8–midnight.

Pink Cadillac (478 Ena Rd., tel. 808/942–5282). The hard-rock music draws a rowdy crowd. You can dance by yourself or with your partner. Nightly 9–2.

Point After (Hawaiian Regent Hotel, 2552 Kalakaua Ave., tel. 808/922–6611). This club, with video dancing for young adults, is a cut above most. Nightly 7–4.

Rumours (Ala Moana Hotel, 410 Atkinson St., tel. 808/955–

4811). The after-work crowd loves this spot, which offers video and disco dancing with all the lights and action. Wednesday–Friday nights 5–2, Saturday nights 8–4. On Big Chill nights each Friday, the club plays oldies from the '60s and '70s and serves free pupus, or hors d'oeuvres. There's also ballroom dancing on Sundays, 5–9.

Scruples (Waikiki Market Place, 2310 Kuhio Ave., tel. 808/923–9530). The club features disco dancing to Top 40 tunes, with a young adult, mostly local crowd. Nightly 8–4.

Shore Bird Beach Broiler (Outrigger Reef Hotel, 2169 Kalia Rd., tel. 808/922–2887). This beachfront disco that spills right out to the sand features a large dance floor and 10-foot video screen. Karaoke sing-alongs are held nightly 9–2.

Wave Waikiki (1877 Kalakaua Ave., tel. 808/941–0424). Dance to live rock-and-roll until 1:30, recorded music after that. It can be a rough scene, but the bands are tops. Nightly 9–4.

Honolulu **Anna Bannana's** (2440 S. Beretania St., tel. 808/946–5190). At this two-story, smoky dive, the live music is fresh, loud, and sometimes experimental. Local favorites the Pagan Babies perform ultracreative reggae music regularly, but the likes of blues singer Taj Mahal have been known to slip in for a set or two. Open nightly 11:30–2. Live music Wednesday–Sunday 9–2.

Black Orchid (Restaurant Row, 500 Ala Moana Blvd., tel. 808/521–3111). A very upscale atmosphere pervades this restaurant and club. A variety of singers perform jazz weeknights 6:30–9:30 and Sundays 8:30–1:30. Live dance bands play Tuesday–Saturday nights 9:30–3:30.

Buzz's Original Steak House (2535 Coyne St., tel. 808/944–9781). The lounge area of this comfortable restaurant is the forum for mellow folk/jazz singers on Friday and Saturday nights 8–11:30. For a real treat, old-time songwriter Andy Cummings strolls around strumming his ukulele and telling stories about the old days, some Sunday nights 6–9. (Call ahead first to be sure he's appearing.)

Jubilee Nightclub (1007 Dillingham Blvd., tel. 808/845–1568). If you can see through the smoke and hear over the noise, this local hangout is a great spot to experience live, authentic Hawaiian music. It's not fancy, so don't dress up. Nightly 8–4.

Studebakers (Restaurant Row, 500 Ala Moana Blvd., tel. 808/526–9888). Exhausting "nonstop bop" revives the early rock-and-roll era with an all-American '50s and '60s look. Free pupus weekdays 4–8. Open Monday–Saturday 11 AM–2 AM, Sunday noon–2 AM. Minimum age: 23.

Around the Island **Pecos River Cafe** (99–016 Kamehameha Hwy., tel. 808/487–
Aiea 7980). Billing itself as Hawaii's premier country and western nightclub, this easygoing establishment features nightly performances by one or other of two bands that split the week between them. Nightly 9–1:20.

Kahuku **Bayview Lounge** (Turtle Bay Hilton, tel. 808/293–8811). A beautiful place to watch the sun set over the north-shore water. Regulars the Ohana Trio play contemporary Hawaiian tunes Thursday nights 6–9.

Kailua **Fast Eddie's** (52 Oneawa St., tel. 808/261–8561). If you want to boogie, visit this hot spot for live local and national bands playing everything from rock to Top 40 songs. Nightly 8–4. Attention, ladies: The Fast Eddie's Male Revue is a longstanding tradition not to be missed. Friday and Saturday nights 8:30–10:30.

Makaha **Lobby Lounge** (Sheraton Makaha Resort and Country Club, tel. 808/695–9511). If you're staying at this tranquil resort, stop in the Lobby Lounge for Karaoke Night, when you can try your hand at performing, Friday–Saturday 8:30–12:30.

Makapuu **The Galley** (Sea Life Park, Makapuu Point, tel. 808/259–7933). Some of the top names in island entertainment play at this relaxed restaurant in the popular marine park. Friday nights 8:30–10, with park admission.

Cocktail and Dinner Shows Some Oahu entertainers have been around for years, and others have just arrived on the scene. Either way, the dinner-show food is usually acceptable, but certainly not the main reason for coming. If you want to dine on your own and then take in a show, sign up for a cocktail show. Dinner shows are all in the $40–$55 range, with the cocktail shows running $25–$30. The prices usually include one cocktail, tax, and gratuity. In all cases, reservations are required.

Brothers Cazimero (Monarch Room, Royal Hawaiian Hotel, 2259 Kalakaua Ave., tel. 808/923–7311). Robert and Roland Cazimero put on a class act, complete with their own hula dancers and a splendid blend of traditional and contemporary Hawaiian tunes. The Monarch Room is a lovely oceanside setting. Dinner show Tuesday–Saturday at 8:30, cocktail show Friday and Saturday at 10:30.

Charo (Tropics Surf Club, Hilton Hawaiian Village, 2005 Kalia Rd., tel. 808/949–4321 or 942–7873). The "coochie-coochie" girl's latest venture is a live act in one of Waikiki's flashiest showrooms, located beachside. Latin rhythms, flamenco dancing, songs of the islands, and international music add up to a fiery evening with an explosive performer. Dinner seating at 6:30; cocktail seating at 7:30 for the show at 8.

Danny Kaleikini (Kahala Hilton Hotel, 5000 Kahala Ave., tel. 808/734–2211). This mellow fellow has been serenading guests for more than 25 years with songs, stories, and an occasional tune on the nose flute. Kaleikini's a gentleman, and a very gifted one. He performs an interesting mix of songs from Hawaii and Japan, where he's also a major star. Book early, because there's rarely an empty table. Dinner and cocktail show Monday–Saturday at 9.

Don Ho (Hula Hut Theater Restaurant, 286 Beachwalk, tel. 808/923–8411). Waikiki's old pro still packs them in with his glitzy Las Vegas–style Polynesian revue. His memorable show features a cast of attractive performers from around the South Pacific, led by the "King of Hawaiian Entertainment" himself. The Aliis warm up the crowd. Dinner seating Sunday to Friday at 8, cocktail seating at 8:30 for a 9 PM show.

Frank DeLima (Polynesian Palace, Reef Towers Hotel, 247 Lewers St., tel. 808/923–9861). Local funny man Frank DeLima places a heavy accent on the ethnic humor of the islands and does some pretty outrageous impressions. By the end of the evening he's poked fun at everyone in the audience—and folks eat it up. A word of caution: Reserve a stage-side table only if you're up for a personal ribbing. Tuesday–Saturday nights at 9.

The Krush (Polynesian Palace, Reef Towers Hotel, 247 Lewers St., tel. 808/923–9861). Back on stage after a hiatus of several years, this musical ensemble puts on an energetic show of pop,

Broadway, and jazz numbers with a heavy emphasis on its island roots. Tuesdays–Saturdays at 10:30 and midnight.

Magic of Polynesia (Hilton Hawaiian Village Dome, 2005 Kalia Rd., tel. 808/949–4321). Magician John Hirokawa displays mystifying sleight-of-hand in this highly entertaining show, which also includes the requisite hula dancers and island music. Shows nightly at 6:30 and 8:45.

Polynesian Cultural Center (55–370 Kamehameha Hwy., Laie, tel. 808/293–3333). Easily one of the best shows on the islands. The actors are students from Brigham Young University's Hawaii campus. The production has soaring moments and an "erupting volcano." Dinner served from 4:30 on for the 7:30 show. During peak seasons (Christmas–March and June–August) there are two shows, at 6 and 7:45.

Sheraton's Spectacular Polynesian Revue (Ainahau Showroom, Sheraton Princess Kaiulani Hotel, 120 Kaiulani Ave., tel. 808/971–5300). From drumbeats of the ancient Hawaiians to Fijian war dances and Samoan slap dances, this show takes audiences on a musical tour of Polynesia. The highlight is a daring Samoan fire knife dancer. Nightly dinner seating at 5:15 or 8, cocktail seating at 5:45 or 8:15. A fashion show and magic presentation precede the shows, which start at 6 and 8:30.

Society of Seven (Outrigger Waikiki Hotel, 2335 Kalakaua Ave., tel. 808/923–0711). This lively, popular septet has great staying power and, after 20 years, continues to put on one of the best shows in Waikiki. They sing, dance, do impersonations, play instruments, and above all, entertain with their contemporary sound. Monday–Saturday nights, 8:30 and 10:30. No 10:30 show on Wednesday.

Dinner Cruises The fleet of boats gets bigger every year. Most set sail daily from Fisherman's Wharf at Kewalo Basin, just beyond Ala Moana Beach Park, and head along the coast toward Diamond Head. There's usually dinner, dancing, drinks, and a sensational sunset. Dinner cruises cost approximately $45–$55, except as noted.

Aikane Catamarans (677 Ala Moana Blvd., Honolulu 96813, tel. 808/522–1533). The table seating for dinner is a plus. This is one of the veteran outfits, with catamarans based on an ancient Hawaiian design. Also offered: a package that takes you to the Outrigger Waikiki Hotel after the cruise to spend the rest of the evening with the Society of Seven entertainers. Dinner cruises nightly at 5:15 and moonlight sails at 7:45.

Alii Kai Catamarans (Pier 8, street level, Honolulu 96813, tel. 808/524–6694). Patterned after an ancient Polynesian vessel, the huge *Alii Kai* catamaran casts off from historic Aloha Tower with 1,000 passengers. The deluxe dinner cruise features two open bars, a huge dinner, and an authentic Polynesian show full of colorful hulas and upbeat music. The food is good, the after-dinner show loud and fun, and everyone dances to the Alii Kai musicians on the way back to shore. Nightly at 5:30.

Hawaiian Cruises (Box 29816, Honolulu 96820, tel. 800/852–4183). The sleek *Navatek* is a revolutionary craft designed to sail smoothly in rough waters. That allows it to power farther along Waikiki's coastline than its competitors. Its nightly dinner cruise from 5:30 to 8 costs $145; entertainment is by singer Nohelani Cypriano.

Star of Honolulu (350 Ward Ave., Honolulu 96814, tel. 800/334–6191). New to the cruise circuit in 1992, this $7 million, four-deck, 1,600-person ship offers a $180 five-star dinner cruise package complete with limousine service, captain's VIP reception, dinner, and dancing on the top deck. Less expensive dinner cruise options are available on the lower decks of the ship. **Tradewind Charters** (1833 Kalakaua Ave., Suite 612, Honolulu 96815, tel. 808/973–0311). This is a real sailing experience, a little more expensive and a lot more intimate than the other cruises mentioned. The three-hour sunset sail carries no more than six people. Champagne and hors d'oeuvres are extra. **Windjammer Cruises** (2222 Kalakaua Ave., 6th Floor, Honolulu 96814, tel. 808/922–1200). The pride of the fleet is the 1,500-passenger *Rella Mae*, done up like a clipper ship. It was once a Hudson River excursion boat in New York. Cocktails, dinner, a Polynesian revue, and dancing to a live band are all part of the package. Prices vary from $50 for a dinner buffet to $125 for the deluxe steak and lobster spread.

Luaus   Just about everyone who comes to Hawaii goes to at least one luau. Traditionally, the luau would last for days, with feasting, sporting events, hula, and song. But at today's scaled-down and, for the most part, inauthentic version, you're as likely to find macaroni salad on the buffet as *poi* (taro paste) and big heaps of fried chicken beside the platter of *kalua* (roasted) pig. Traditional dishes that visitors actually enjoy include *laulau* (steamed bundles of ti leaves containing pork, butterfish, and taro tops), *lomilomi* salmon (massaged until tender and served with minced onions and tomatoes), and *haupia* (dessert made from coconut). As for the notorious poi, the clean, bland taste goes nicely with something salty, like bacon or kalua pig.

If you want authenticity, look in the newspaper to see if a church or civic club is holding a luau fund-raiser. You'll not only be welcome, you'll experience some down-home Hawaiiana.

Here are some other good luaus that emphasize fun without giving much thought to tradition. They generally cost $40–$55 adults, $25 children. Reservations are required.

Germaine's Luau (tel. 808/941–3338). You and a herd of about 1,000 other people are bused to a private beach near the industrial area, 35 minutes from Waikiki. The bus ride is actually a lot of fun, and the beach and the sunset are pleasant. The service is brisk in order to feed everyone on time, and the food is so-so, but the show is warm and friendly. The bus collects passengers from 13 different Waikiki hotels; luaus start daily at 6. **Paradise Cove Luau** (tel. 808/945–3571). Another mass-produced event for 1,000 or so. Once again, a bus takes you from one of six Waikiki hotel pickup points to a remote beach beside a picturesque cove on the western side of the island, 27 miles from Waikiki. There are palms and a glorious sunset, and the pageantry is fun, even informative. The food—well, you didn't come for the food, did you? Luaus begin daily at 5:30 (doors open at 5). **Polynesian Cultural Center Luau** (tel. 808/923–2911). An hour's drive from Honolulu, this North Shore Oahu attraction takes place amid seven re-created villages of Polynesia. Dinner is all-you-can-eat, followed by an entertaining revue. Monday–Saturday at 5:30. **Royal Hawaiian Luau** (tel. 808/923–7311). This is a notch above the rest of the commercial luaus on Oahu, perhaps because it takes place at the wonderful pink palace. With the setting sun, Diamond Head, the Pacific Ocean, and the enjoyable entertainment, who cares if the luau isn't totally authentic? Monday at 6.

4 The Big Island of Hawaii

*By Betty
Fullard-Leo*

*A Hawaii resident
since 1962, Betty
Fullard-Leo is
editor of* Pacific
Art & Travel
*magazine.
Previously, she
wrote and edited
for* ALOHA
*magazine and for
the* Aloha
Travelers'
Newsletter.

Nearly twice as large as all the other Hawaiian Islands combined, this youngest island of the chain is still growing, with lava adding black-sand beaches and more than 70 acres of land in the last decade on its southeast side. As a matter of fact, the Big Island has the world's most active volcano: The east rift zone below Halemaumau on Kilauea has been spewing lava intermittently since January 3, 1983.

The Big Island is accustomed to setting records. It is hyped as having the tallest mountain in the world (if you measure from Mauna Kea's origins some 32,000 feet beneath the ocean's surface to its lofty 13,796-foot peak). The island's southern tip extends farther south than any other state in the United States. To the southeast, far beneath the surface of the ocean, Loihi, a sea mount bubbling lava, is slowly building another Hawaiian Island, due to emerge in about a thousand years. On a higher plane, the Big Island has the world's most powerful telescope (at Keck Observatory), which searches the universe from the summit of Mauna Loa, the clearest place on earth for peering into the heavens.

The most diverse of all the islands, Hawaii offers skiing (but only for experts) in the winter and year-round sunshine on its southern and western shores, where the average temperature range is 69–84 degrees in July and 53–75 degrees in January. Yet there is so much rain near Hilo, its major city, that its only zoo is situated right in the middle of a rain forest.

Two of the Big Island's golf courses, the Mauna Kea Beach Resort course and the Francis H. I'i Brown Course at Mauna Lani Resort, are repeatedly chosen by golfing magazines as the best, the most spectacular, and the favorite of businesspeople and others. If locals were the bragging type, they could give Texans a run for their money—particularly since the Parker Ranch is touted as the largest privately owned ranch in the United States (though the folks at the King Ranch in Texas might justifiably say that's open to debate).

Yet visitors have been known to lack appreciation for, or to miss completely, the spiritual, sensual, untamed feel of this vast island. One Oahuan returned home after three days in Kailua-Kona to report, "I got bored. I couldn't find the beach, the shopping wasn't any different from Waikiki, and I walked the length of the town the first day!"

The first secret to enjoying the Big Island to the max is: Rent a car! The second secret is: Stay more than three days, or return again and again until you've seen all the facets of this fascinating place.

With 266 miles of coastline made up of white-coral, black-lava, and a dusting of green-olivine beaches, and with its cliffs of lava and emerald gorges slashing into jutting mountains, the Big Island is so large and so varied that it is easiest to split it up when planning a visit, in the same way former mayor Dante Carpenter divided it to discuss the exciting changes taking place. "Kona," he said, "is where the jobs are. Hilo and the Puna District are where the people are." Unfortunately, it's a bumpy 60 miles along Saddle Road, which runs between the Big Island's two largest volcanos, Mauna Kea and Mauna Loa, to travel from Hilo to the fancy resorts along the Kona–Kohala coast. This latter area, however, is where you'll find growth.

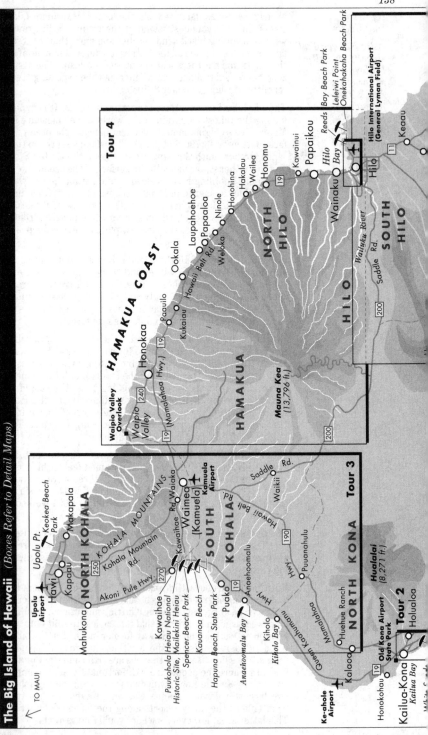

The Big Island of Hawaii (Boxes Refer to Detail Maps)

← TO MAUI

NORTH KOHALA

Upolu Pt.
Upolu Airport
Keokea Beach Park
Hawi
Kapaau
Makapala

KOHALA MOUNTAINS

Mahukona

Akoni Pule Hwy.

Kohala Mountain Rd.

250

270

Kawaihae
Puukohola Heiau National Historic Site, Mailekini Heiau
Spencer Beach Park
Kauanoa Beach
Hapuna Beach State Park
Puako

Kawaihae Rd—Waioka

Waimea [Kamuela]

Kamuela Airport

SOUTH KOHALA

19

Anaehoomalu

Anaehoomalu Bay

Kiholo

Kiholo Bay

Queen Kaahumanu Hwy.

Mamalahoa Hwy.

Puuanahulu

190

Saddle Rd.

Waikii

Tour 3

Huehue Ranch

Kalaoa

NORTH KONA

Hualalai (8,271 ft.)

Honokohau

Ke-ahole Airport

Old Kona Airport State Park

Tour 2

Kailua-Kona
Kailua Bay

Holualoa

White Sands

HAMAKUA COAST

Waipio Valley Overlook

Waipio Valley

240 (Mamalahoa Hwy.)

19

19

HAMAKUA

Honokaa

Paauilo

Kukaiau

Ookala

Laupahoehoe

Papaaloa

Ninole

Weloka

Hawaii Belt Rd.

Mauna Kea (13,796 ft.)

Saddle Rd.

200

Tour 4

Kawainui

Honohina

Hakalau

Wailea

Honomu

Papaikou

Reeds

Wainaku

NORTH HILO

Hilo Bay

Waiakea

Wailuku River

Saddle Rd.

200

SOUTH HILO

HILO

Hilo

11

Keaau

Bay Beach Park
Leleiwi Point
Onekahakaha Beach Park

Hilo International Airport (General Lyman Field)

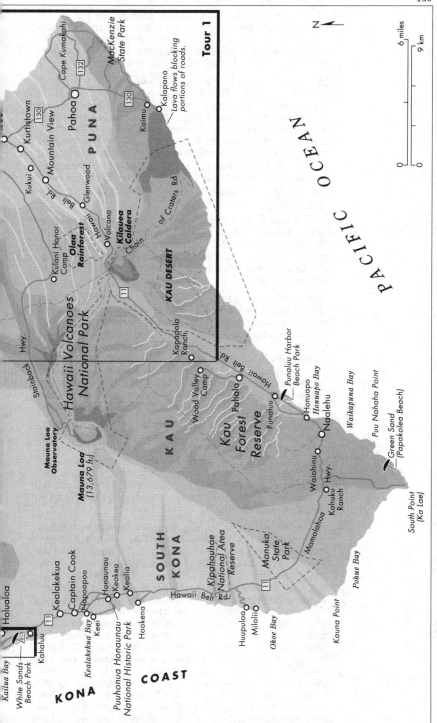

Tour 1

N

PACIFIC OCEAN

0 ─── 6 miles
0 ─── 9 km

Cape Kumukahi

MacKenzie State Park

[132]

Pahoa

PUNA

Kurtistown

[130]

Mountain View

Kukui

Glenwood

Kaimu

Kalapana
Lava flows blocking
portions of roads.

[130]

Kulani Honor
Camp

Bell Rd.

Hawaii

Volcano

Olaa Rainforest

Kilauea Caldera

Chain of Craters Rd.

Stainback Hwy.

Hawaii Volcanoes National Park

[11]

KAU DESERT

Mauna Loa Observatory

Mauna Loa
(13,679 ft)

Kapapala Ranch

KAU

Wood Valley Camp

Kau Forest Reserve

Pahala

Punaluu

Punaluu Harbor Beach Park

Honuapo
Honuapo Bay

Naalehu

Waiohinu

Mamalahoa Hwy.

Waikapuna Bay

Puu Nahaha Point

Green Sand
(Papakolea Beach)

South Point
(Ka Lae)

Kahuku Ranch

Manuka State Park

Kipahoehoe National Area Reserve

[11]

Hawaii Belt Rd.

SOUTH KONA

Kealakekua

Captain Cook

Napoopoo

Honaunau

Keokea

Kealia

Keei

Kealakekua Bay

Puuhonua Honaunau National Historic Park

Hookena

Huupuloa

Miloliii

Okoe Bay

Kauna Point

Pohue Bay

KONA COAST

Holualoa

[11]

Kailua Bay

White Sands Beach Park

Kahaluu

Luckily, there is plenty of room to grow on the Big Island. Land along the Kona–Kohala coast is generally dry, uninhabited stretches of lava. When a developer snakes a road to the ocean across a barren flow and supplies the water that creates a green oasis, many of us think it's an improvement.

In earlier times, Hawaii's kings and queens lived and played along this coastline. King Kamehameha I was born close to its northern shore, near the 500-year-old Mookini *Heiau* (a sacred stone platform for the worship of the gods). All along the water's edge are reminders of earlier inhabitants. At Kawaihae, two heiaus, Puukohola and Mailekini, mark the site of the final victory in Kamehameha's battle to unite the Hawaiian Islands in 1810. At Puako Petroglyph Park, an easy 15-minute walk from the road, are abundant examples of petroglyphs, the carvings that depict everyday events etched into lava flows by early Hawaiians.

In 1812 King Kamehameha I chose to build his principal residence, Kamakahonu, in Kailua-Kona. From this site, now on the grounds of the Hotel King Kamehameha, he ruled Hawaii in his later years, in a large enclosure bordered on one side by the Ahuena Heiau. Today the hotel offers free tours of these historic structures.

Most developers are aware of the reverence the Hawaiian people feel for their *aina* (land), and they attempt to preserve and restore the bits and pieces of Hawaiian history that come to light when a bulldozer rakes the land. Such modern resorts as the Royal Waikoloan and Kona Village conduct tours of the petroglyph fields on their grounds. The Royal Waikoloan at Anaehoomalu Bay and the Mauna Lani Resort have restored the fish ponds that once supplied the tables of Hawaiian royalty and have placed tasteful signs so that a stroll around the beachfront ponds is an interesting and informative experience.

In the calm tranquility of the Kohala Mountains to the north, where *paniolos* (cowboys) ride the range, or in the windswept isolation of South Point, which is thought to have been populated as early as AD 750, you wonder about the early Hawaiians who crossed this land on foot. Did they bring their gods and goddesses from their ancient homeland in the Tahitian islands? Or was the goddess Pele conceived as an explanation for some violent volcanic eruption?

Five volcanos formed the Big Island perhaps a half-million years ago: Kohala, Hualalai, Mauna Kea (white mountain), Mauna Loa (long mountain), and Kilauea, which is currently active. Early Hawaiians believed that Pele lived in whichever crater was erupting. Even today, eerie stories are repeated as fact; they tell of a woman hitchhiker who dresses in red and wanders the volcano area, accompanied by a small white dog. "My neighbor gave her a ride, but when he looked in the mirror she was gone!" is how one oft-repeated tale goes. As far as volcanic eruptions, those Pele has caused in recent years have been relatively nondestructive, flowing from rift zones through ohia forests on Kilauea's gentle slopes. Lava has flowed through Kalapana and the remote Royal Gardens subdivision repeatedly since 1983, however, destroying nearly 200 housing units and blocking Chain of Craters Road; but no lives have been lost. You can drive almost to the end of the road, follow park rangers' instructions about where to park, and walk to where the molten lava flows into the ocean. Helicopters carry passengers to view the 2.5-mile lava lake called Kupaianaha, an 800-foot cinder cone, and the clouds of steam that rise as hot lava hits the ocean waters.

The drive along the Hamakua Coast to Hilo, the island's county seat and the fourth-largest city in the state, brings attention to modern developments on the island. Fields of sugar cane still wave in the breeze, but these are rapidly being replaced by orchards of macadamia nut trees. With such major companies as C. Brewer turning to macadamias, the nuts have become big business on the Big Island, supplying 90% of the state's yield. Kona coffee, anthuriums and orchids, and *pakalolo* (marijuana—at one time said to be the state's biggest income-producing, though illegal, crop)—are adding a new chapter to the agricultural history of the state.

Hilo is a town of modern and rustic buildings, stretching from the banks of the Wailuku River to Hilo Bay, where a few major hotels rim stately Banyan Drive. Nearby, the 31-acre Liliuokalani Garden, a Japanese-style park with arched bridges and waterways, was established as a safety zone after a devastating tidal wave swept away businesses and homes on May 22, 1960, killing 60 people. Residents don't worry much about a tidal wave recurring, but they haven't built anything except hotels, the park, and a golf course in that area, either.

Though it is the center of business, shipping, and government for the island, Hilo is primarily a residential town. Indications of the weather and the character of the residents are provided by the perfectly kept yards with tree ferns and the lush tropical foliage surrounding older wooden houses with rusty red and green corrugated roofs. Bring your umbrella—the rainfall averages 139 inches per year—but do plan to spend a day absorbing the charm of Hilo. It's a friendly community, populated primarily by descendants of the contract laborers—Japanese, Chinese, and Portuguese—brought in to work the sugar cane fields in the 1800s.

You'll have fun experiencing the culture of this town. Try to interpret the bidding at the Suisan fish auction at the end of Banyan Drive any morning at about 7:30 or 8. The combination of dialects, called *pidgin*, might seem like a foreign language, but the fish get sold in good time. At the Malamalama and Haili churches, the choirs still sing Hawaiian hymns, while the annual luau at Haili is a feast of authentic ethnic foods.

The island of Hawaii—with all the diversity and activity it offers—is just beginning to attract hordes of visitors. In the past, hotel occupancy has often dropped to only 50%. Perhaps there's confusion over its name. Sometimes it's called the Orchid Isle or the Volcano Isle (both apt descriptions, by the way), but residents always say "the Big Island of Hawaii," since the entire chain—Kauai, Oahu, Molokai, Lanai, Maui, Hawaii, Kahoolawe, Niihau—is called Hawaii as well. Perhaps it's the silly rumor that good beaches are scarce, or the fact that the nightlife is a little low-key. The fact remains that the Big Island of Hawaii excites the senses and inspires the adventurer. Here you can hike into a crater; catch marlin weighing hundreds of pounds; discover another universe from the top of Mauna Kea; and outstare a shark from the safety of a submarine's viewing port.

Essential Information

Arriving and Departing by Plane

Airports The Big Island has two main airports. Visitors whose accommodations are on the west side of the island, at Keauhou, Kailua-Kona, or the Kohala Coast, normally fly into Kona's **Ke-ahole Airport** (tel. 808/329–2484; visitor information tel. 808/329–3423), 6.8 miles from Kailua. Those staying on the eastern side, in Hilo or near the town of Volcano, fly into **Hilo International Airport** (tel. 808/933–4782; visitor information tel. 808/935–1018), just 2 miles from Hilo's Banyan Drive hotels. In addition, one Oahu-based airline, Aloha IslandAir, has a schedule of regular flights into **Waimea-Kohala Airport** (tel. 808/885–4520), called Kamuela Airport by residents. Located midway between Hilo and Kailua-Kona, Kamuela Airport is used primarily by residents of Waimea-Kamuela to commute between islands. Another airstrip, at Upolu Point, services small private planes only.

Flights from the Mainland U.S. **Hawaiian** (tel. 800/367–5320) and **United Airlines** (tel. 800/241–6522) are the only two carriers that fly daily from the mainland to the Big Island. United flies to both Ke-ahole and Hilo International airports (with about an hour layover in Honolulu) from Los Angeles, San Francisco, and Chicago. Hawaiian Airlines flies from San Francisco and Seattle to Ke-ahole. Both flights make Honolulu and Maui stops. Flying time from the West Coast to Honolulu is about 4½ hours.

Flights from Honolulu Between the Neighbor Islands, both **Aloha Airlines** (tel. 800/367–5250) and **Hawaiian Airlines** offer jet flights, which take about 45 minutes from Honolulu to Hilo International Airport and 34 minutes from Honolulu to Ke-ahole. In addition, Hawaiian operates a Dash prop, which adds a few minutes to the flight times. Fares are approximately $60, though both Aloha and Hawaiian discount their first (6 AM) and last (8 or 9 PM, depending on the airline) flights of each day. Complaints about any airline often have to do with being on time. In general, the earlier in the day you fly interisland, the better assurance you have of departing and arriving on time.

Aloha Airlines owns **Aloha IslandAir** (tel. 808/833–3219), the former Princeville Airlines, which flies from Honolulu to Kamuela Airport three times daily and returns two times daily.

Between the Airport and Hotels The distance from Ke-ahole Airport to Kailua, the resort area on the western side of the Big Island, is 6.8 miles, or a 10-minute drive, while the Keauhou resort area stretches another 6 miles to the south beyond Kailua. Visitors staying at the upscale resorts along the Kona–Kohala coast north of Ke-ahole Airport should allow 30–45 minutes driving time to reach their hotels.

On the eastern side of the island, Hilo International Airport is situated just 2 miles, or a five-minute drive, from Hilo's Banyan Drive hotels. If you've chosen Volcano Lodge or a bed-and-breakfast accommodation near the little mountain town of Volcano, plan on a half-hour drive from Hilo International Airport.

The adventuresome souls who have booked out-of-the-way accommodations near Waimea might want to fly into Kamuela Airport, but be sure to arrange your rental car in advance (*see*

Getting Around, *below*), as few auto-rental companies service that airport.

Unfortunately, no buses operate from the airports.

By Shuttle There is no regularly scheduled shuttle service from either main airport, although a private service is offered by four major Kohala-coast resorts to the north of Ke-ahole Airport. Mauna Kea, Mauna Lani, the Hyatt Regency Waikoloa, and the Royal Waikoloan offer lei greetings and transportation to their hotels for about half the cost of a taxi. The rates vary depending on the distance each resort is from the airport. Arriving guests must simply check in at the Kohala Coast Resort Association counters at the Aloha and Hawaiian Airlines arrival areas.

Guests staying in Kailua or at the Keauhou resort area to the south of the airport should check with their individual hotels upon booking to see if shuttle service is available.

By Taxi Taxis are generally on hand for plane arrivals at both major airports. Some services from Hilo's Airport include **A-1 Bob's** (tel. 808/959–4800), **Ace** (tel. 808/935–8303), and **Hilo Harry's** (tel. 808/935–7091). Taxis from Hilo International Airport to Hilo charge about $7.50 for the 2-mile ride to the Banyan Drive hotels. Often individual drivers will charge an extra $1 for large bags.

A number of taxis service Ke-ahole Airport. The following also offer guided tours: **Kona Airport Taxi Company** (tel. 808/329–7779), **Island Taxi** (tel. 808/325–5381), and **Marina Taxi** (tel. 808/329–2481). From Ke-ahole Airport to the Hotel King Kamehameha, taxi fares are about $15; to the Kona Surf in Keauhou, the cost is about $27. Taxis to South Kohala from Ke-ahole are even more expensive: approximately $32 to the Royal Waikoloan and $45 to the Mauna Kea Beach Hotel.

By Limousine For real luxury, limousine service with a chauffeur who will act as your personal guide is between $55–$60 an hour, with a two-hour minimum. **Luana's** (tel. 808/326–5466) in Kona provides all the extras—TV, bar, and narrated tours, plus Japanese-speaking guides. **Roberts** offers service in both Kailua-Kona (75–5626 Alapa St., tel. 808/329–1688) and Hilo (Hilo International Airport, tel. 808/935–2858).

By Car The best way to see the Big Island is by car, if you want to explore beaches and trails and don't mind driving across wide open stretches of lava that can sometimes become a bit monotonous. Especially in the summer, when temperatures can hit 90 degrees, you'll want to travel in air-conditioned comfort. Though there are perhaps two dozen companies to choose from (*see* Getting Around, *below*, for specific car-rental information), cars can be scarce during holiday weekends and peak seasons—from mid-December through mid-March and sometimes during August. If you haven't reserved a car far in advance for the October Gatorade Ironman Triathlon or for the Merrie Monarch Festival the first week in April, chances are you'll end up walking. Major rental agencies at both Ke-ahole Airport and Hilo International Airport have service desks across the street from the baggage-claim areas. Others furnish free shuttle service to their car yards.

From Ke-ahole Airport, the main road is Highway 19, or Queen Ka'ahumanu Highway. Turn right, or south, as you leave the airport to reach Kailua-Kona. To the left, or north, along this highway are the major resorts of Kona Village, Royal Waikoloan, Hyatt Regency Waikoloa, Aston Shores at Waikoloa (an elegant condo-resort), Mauna Lani Resort, Ritz-Carlton, Mauna Lani, Aston Bay Club at Waikoloa, and Mauna Kea Resort. Highway 19 turns inland to Waimea, then emerges along the northeastern Hamakua Coast, eventually terminating in Hilo (96 miles from Kailua-Kona via this northern route), on the east side of the island. South from Hilo, Highway 11 bypasses Hilo International Airport, angling inland as the Hawaii Belt Road through the volcano area and continuing around the south and southwest coasts of the island as Mamalahoa Highway to Kailua-Kona (126 miles from Hilo via this southern route). From Kailua-Kona, Mamalahoa Highway is the older, more curvy, up-country route to Waimea, while Queen Ka'ahumanu is a straight, well-paved highway that follows a coastal route to Kawaihae and then turns inland to Waimea.

Arriving and Departing by Ship

From Honolulu   **American Hawaii Cruises** also runs seven-day excursions departing Honolulu Harbor every Saturday on two ships, the SS *Constitution* and the SS *Independence*. You have the option of choosing a four-day cruise and disembarking on the island of Hawaii, where special rates can be arranged at the Kona Surf, Aston Shores at Waikoloa, or Aston Royal Sea Cliff resorts. Pre- and postcruise hotel packages are offered at a variety of rates. *American Hawaii Cruises, 530 Kearny St., San Francisco, CA 94108, tel. 800/765–7000 for information or a free brochure about cruises or cruise-and-land packages.*

Getting Around

By Car   An automobile is necessary to see the sights of the Big Island in any reasonable amount of time. Even if you're solely interested in relaxing at your self-contained megaresort, you may still want a car, simply to travel to Kailua-Kona or Waimea so you can try cuisine other than hotel fare.

If you pick up an auto at either airport and drop it off at the other, be aware that it could cost you as much as $30 extra. If you decide to return a car to the original pickup point, allow 2¼ hours to drive the 96-mile Hamakua Coast route. To get the best rate on a rental car—and surprisingly, Hawaii's rates are often better than mainland rates—book it in conjunction with a round-trip interisland Hawaiian or Aloha Airline flight, or ask your travel agent to check out room and car packages for you.

The national car-rental firms represented on the Big Island are: **Alamo** (tel. 800/327–9633), **Avis** (tel. 800/831–8000), **Budget** (tel. 800/527–7000), **Dollar** (tel. 800/800–4000), **Hertz** (tel. 800/654–3131), **National** (tel. 800/227–7368), and **Thrifty** (tel. 808/935–1936 in Hilo, tel. 808/329–1730 in Kailua). The Hawaii-based companies are **Harper's** (tel. 808/969–1478), **VIP Car Rentals** (tel. 808/329–7328), **Sunshine** (tel. 800/367–1977 or 808/329–2926), and **Tropical** (tel. 800/678–6000). Harper's (at Hilo airport only) is the only agency with a rental contract that allows its four-wheel-drive vehicles to be taken on Saddle Road (a rough, winding shortcut from Hilo to Waimea), although a number of other agencies have four-wheel-drives in their fleets. (You'll need a four-wheel-drive to reach some rugged shoreline sites.)

By Bus/Shuttle A locally sponsored **Hele-On Bus** (*hele* translates roughly as "go") operates Monday–Saturday between Hilo and Kailua-Kona. The bus goes from Kailua-Kona to Hilo and back again, at $6 each way. For luggage and backpacks that do not fit under the seat, an additional $1 is charged per piece. Hele-On (tel. 808/935–8241) departs from Mokuaikaua Church, on Alii Drive in Kailua-Kona at 6:43 AM arriving in Hilo at 9:45 AM. It leaves from the Mooheau Bus Terminal, between Kamehameha Avenue and Bayfront Highway in Hilo, at 1:30 PM to arrive in Kailua-Kona at 4:30 PM. In Hilo, a Hele-On operates between downtown and the shopping malls for 75¢ (exact fare required).

Within Keauhou, a free shuttle (tel. 808/322–3500 or 808/322–3000) runs from hotels and condos to Keauhou Shopping Village and the Kona Country Club golf course.

By Taxi Several companies advertise guided tours by taxi, but it is an expensive way to travel, with a trip around the island totaling about $300. Meters automatically register $2 on pickup, and most click off another $1.60 with each passing mile. If you've got the urge to splurge, in Hilo call **Ace Taxi** (tel. 808/935–8303) or **Hilo Harry's** (tel. 808/935–7091). In Kona, try **Kona Airport Taxi Company** (tel. 808/329–7779), **Island Taxi** (tel. 808/325–5381), or **Marina Taxi** (tel. 808/329–2481).

By Moped Mopeds and scooters can be rented in Kailua-Kona from **Ciao! Activities Center** (tel. 808/326–2426) and from **Alii Moped Rentals** (tel. 808/329–0112). Some words of warning: Big Island roads often have narrow shoulders, and the drafts from over-size tour buses swooping by can double the excitement of a simple Sunday ride. Helmets are advised but not mandatory in Hawaii.

By Plane **Big Island Air** (tel. 800/367–8047, ext. 207, or 808/329–4868) offers charter flightseeing from Ke-ahole Airport in an eight-passenger Cessna 402 at a basic hourly rate of $475. "Wait time" (for example, if you fly to Kamuela for lunch and the plane sits on the ground for several hours while you dine) is charged at a lower rate.

Important Addresses and Numbers

Tourist Information The minute you step off the plane at any Hawaii airport, grab a handful of the free brochures that describe attractions, restaurants, scheduled events, and tours and often contain free discount coupons. At the Big Island's airports, brochures are dispensed at the **Hawaii Visitors Bureau** (HVB) booths, and you can ask the booth attendent anything you need to know. In addition, if you rent a car, be sure to get a "Drive Guide," as these handy little booklets have all the maps you'll probably need to navigate the island. *HVB office in Hilo: Hilo Plaza, 180 Kinoole St., Suite 105, tel. 808/961–5797; in Kailua-Kona: 75-5719 W. Alii Dr., Kailua-Kona 96740, tel. 808/329–7787. Open weekdays 8–noon and 1–4:30.*

Before you go, you can write HVB for its accommodation and restaurant guides. Another helpful source of information is the **Kohala Coast Resort Association** (HC02, Box 5300, Waikoloa 96743, tel. 808/885–4915), a group of resorts and luxury hotels cooperating to promote the Kohala Coast as a resort destination. For visitors staying in Keauhou, the **Keauhou Visitors Association** (78-6831 Alii Dr., Suite 234, Kailua-Kona 96740, tel. 808/322–3866) is a source of information. For questions about east Hawaii, write **Destination Hilo,** Box 1391, Hilo 96721. For general information about the entire island, write **Big Island Group,** HCO 2, Box 5900, Kamuela, Hawaii 96743, or call 808/885–5900 or 800/648–BIG1.

Emergencies **Police** (tel. 808/329–3311).
Kailua-Kona **Hospital. Kona Hospital** (Hwy. 11, Box 69, Kealakekua 96750, tel. 808/322–9311).
Dentist. West Hawaii Dental Associates (tel. 808/322–9355).
Pharmacy. Long's Drug Store (Lanihau Center, 75-5595 Palani Rd., tel. 808/329–1632; open Mon.–Sat. 8:30–9, Sun. 8:30–5).
Help Line Crisis Center (tel. 808/329–9111).

Hilo **Police** (tel. 808/935–3311).
Hospital. Hilo Hospital (1190 Waianuenue Ave., tel. 808/969–4111).
Dentist. Ask the hospital to call a dentist who will take emergency patients.
Pharmacy. Long's Drug Store (555 Kilauea Ave., tel. 808/935–9075; open Mon.–Thurs. and Sat. 8:30–6, Fri. 8:30–7, Sun. 8:30–5).
Help Line Crisis Center (tel. 808/969–9111).

For All Areas **Ambulance or fire** (tel. 808/961–6022).
Poison Control Center (tel. 800/362–3585).
Volcano watchers (tel. 808/967–7977 for 24-hr recorded information).

Parks and **County:** Tel. 808/961–8311. Open weekdays 7:45–4:30. **State:**
Recreation Tel. 808/933–4200. Open weekdays 8–4:15.

Weather Tel. 808/961–5582.

Opening and Closing Times

Banks are open Monday through Thursday 8:30–3:30 and Friday 9–6.

In general, major stores and shopping centers on the Big Island open at 9 or 9:30 and close by 4:30 or 5. Hilo's Prince Kuhio Shopping Center (111 E. Puainako, tel. 808/959–3555) stays open until 9 PM on Thursday and Friday. In Kona, most of the stores at the Kona Coast Shopping Center (Palani Rd., no tel.) are open until 7 PM, though the KTA Super Stores outlet (a supermarket) is open from 6 AM to midnight. Many small grocery stores also maintain longer hours, as do the shops along Kona's main Alii Drive that are geared to tourism.

Guided Tours

Orientation Tours At least four established companies offer circle-island orientation tours at fares of approximately $45. Tours are 9–11 hours long from pickup to drop-off at your hotel or the airport. The circle-island tours generally include Waimea, the Hamakua Coast, Hilo, and Volcanoes National Park. All the companies use air-conditioned vehicles, but only **Akamai** (tel. 800/922–6485 or 808/329–7324) limits tours to a maximum of 12 people in a van. Akamai also has shorter North Kohala scenic tours and Kona scenic tours, and it furnishes transportation and makes arrangements so you can join a Waipio Valley tour. Other companies drive motor coaches or minibuses, depending on the number of bookings. **Gray Line Hawaii** (tel. 800/367–2420 or 808/833–8000) has a circle-island tour originating in Kailua-Kona, a Hilo/Volcano/Kalapana tour, a Hilo/Volcano/Kona tour, and a Kona historical tour. **Roberts Hawaii** (680 Iwilei Rd., Honolulu 96817, tel. 808/523–7750) offers a Hilo/Volcano/Kona tour for about $30 and a Hilo/Volcano/Hilo tour, which takes eight hours. **Hawaii Resorts Transportation** (Box 183, Honoka‘a 96727, tel. 808/885–7484 or 808/775–7291) offers adventures to Waipio and Mauna Kea.

Aerial Tours Hovering over a waterfall that drops a couple of thousand feet into multiple pools is absolutely breathtaking—never mind the noise. You can fly above the lava lake on Kilauea, then follow the flow to the ocean, where huge clouds of steam billow into the air. (Currently the flow is mostly underground, through a lava tube, but that can change, so ask exactly what you'll see when you book your flight.) Some passengers have a tendency to feel woozy in a helicopter, so if you're prone to car, sea, or air sickness, you might want to take a shorter flight, or try the new wristbands we've seen in pharmacies. They work on pressure points and are said not to induce such side effects as drowsiness.

Volcano Heli-Tours (Box 626, Volcano 96785, tel. 808/967–7578) is the only helicopter that departs from the Volcano area (right near the golf course), and since flying time over the lava lake and to the ocean is minimized, the 45-minute flights are somewhat cheaper than other helicopter tours. You must make reservations in advance, however, as the flights are well booked. Countless other tour companies are available: **Mauna Kea Helicopters** (tel. 808/885–6400) pilot Scott Shupe has plenty of experience, while **Io Aviation** (tel. 808/935–3031) takes off from Hilo International Airport, and **Hilo Bay Air** (tel. 808/969–1545 or 800/776–6137) is equipped to accommodate disabled passengers. From Kamuela Airport, **Lacy Helicopters** (tel. 808/885–7272) flies over Waipio Valley. From the Waikoloa Helipad, **Papillon Helicopters** (tel. 800/367–7095 or 808/329–0551) is reputable. Ask at your hotel desk for additional operators. Flight tours range vastly in price. **Kainoa Aviation** (tel. 808/961–5591) advertises a 60-minute volcano tour from Hilo International Airport for $99, Papillon Helicopters describes a longer flight from Kona-coast hotels over Kilauea and Volcanoes National Park for less than $300.

Big Island Air (tel. 800/367–8047, ext. 207, or 808/329–4868) flies two-hour circle-island tours with a minimum of four passengers on its nine-passenger twin-engine Cessna jet for $150 per person. Flights depart from Ke-ahole Airport at 8 AM, 11 AM, and 2 PM seven days a week. Weight is critical on these smaller planes, so be prepared to divulge your true body weight.

Special-Interest Tours
Garden Tours So far, tour agencies have not specialized in offering garden tours, perhaps because most nurseries welcome visitors free of charge in order to sell and ship their orchids and anthuriums on the spot. Most of the nurseries that sell tropical flowers are on the Hilo side near Puna or on the way to Volcano. Close to the center of Hilo, **Nani Mau Gardens** has 100 varieties of tropical fruit trees and 2,000 varieties of ginger, orchids, and anthuriums. Established in 1970, the 53-acre gardens were redeveloped in 1990 to include a Hawaiian cultural garden, a volcano, waterways, and waterfall, as well as palm, orchid, and rose

gardens. Trams and golf carts ensure easy access. The light and airy Nani Mau Gardens restaurant (tel. 808/959–9591) is open daily for lunch and offers catering for weddings held in the gardens. *421 Makalika St., Hilo, tel. 808/959–3541. Admission: $5 adults, $2.50 children 13–18. Open daily 8–5.*

Hawaii Tropical Botanical Garden is an extensive botanical garden, with plants imported from around the world (*see* Tour 4 in Exploring the Big Island, *below*). *Box 415, Hilo, tel. 808/964–5233. Taxdeductible admission: $12 adults, children 16 and younger free. Open daily 8:30–4:30.*

On Volcano Highway 11 you will see signs indicating anthurium gardens, as well as a Hawaiian-warrior sign 22 miles from Hilo pointing the way to **Akatsuka Orchid Gardens** (tel. 808/967–8234; open daily 8:30–5). Also off Highway 11, **Rainbow Tropicals** grows 62 acres of anthuriums (ranging from the green-white obake to the deep red beefsteak), orchids, and other tropical blooms that you can purchase and have shipped home. Little water-filled balloons around their stems keep them fresh. *Box 4038, W. Mamaki St., Hilo, tel. 808/959–4565. Visitor Center open daily 10–4:30.*

In West Hawaii, **Wakefield Garden** is an easy stop and a self-guided walk, appropriate if you want to stretch your legs and have a cool drink at the casual restaurant, but not particularly impressive as far as plants. *Hwy. 160 at Honaunau, tel. 808/328–9930. Open daily 8–sunset. Lunch daily 11–3.*

The **Fuku Bonsai Center** is a visitor center with nine different bonsai gardens. Educational exhibits of these miniature plants show the differences in the cultivation and training of Japanese, Chinese, and Hawaiian bonsai. Fuku is the largest bonsai center and the only one of its kind outside Japan. *78–6767 Mamalahoa Hwy., Holualoa 96725, tel. 808/322–9222. Admission: $5 adults, $2.50 children 4–17, under 4 free. Open daily.*

Mauna Kea The clearest place in the world for viewing the heavens is reputedly the summit of 13,796-foot Mauna Kea. The trick is getting there. It takes a four-wheel-drive vehicle to reach the top, and you must traverse Saddle Road on the way. Driving on Saddle Road is restricted by most car-rental companies, because it twists and turns and has no gas stations or emergency phones from Waimea to Hilo. **Harper's Car Rental** (1690 Kamehameha Ave., Hilo 96720, tel. 808/969–1478) allows use of its $60-a-day Isuzu Trooper IIs and Broncos on Saddle Road.

If you decide to strike out on your own, follow the access road off Highway 20 between Hilo and West Hawaii to reach Onizuka Center for International Astronomy, about 30 miles from Hilo. Every Saturday and Sunday four-wheel-drive vehicles caravan for free tours to the Mauna Kea observatories, which sprout like mushrooms from the otherworldly landscape. Departure is from Onizuka Visitor Center at 2 PM Saturday and Sunday and at 6:30 Saturday evenings. Information and reservations can be obtained by calling **Mauna Kea Support Services** (tel. 808/935–3371). Freezing temperatures are common at the summit, even when the heat is high at the seashore, so you must take along warm parkas.

Three companies take all the worry out of a trip to the top. You may book a day or evening van tour with knowledgeable Pat Wright of **Paradise Safaris** (Box AD, Kailua 96745, tel. 808/322–

2366). He supplies lunch for the day excursion as well as hotel pickup and warm parkas. **Waipio Valley Shuttle** tours (Box 5128, Kukuihaele 96727, tel. 808/775–7121) conduct Mauna Kea summit tours that leave from Parker Ranch Shopping Center in Kamuela with a minimum of four passengers. **Hawaii Resorts Transportation Company** (Box 183, Honokaa 96727, tel. 808/ 775–7291) furnishes transportation by four-wheel drive jeep. Prices among the various companies are $50–$85.

Parker Ranch **Parker Ranch** (*see* Tour 3 in Exploring the Big Island, *below*) attracts not only art lovers, but also those interested in the history of the Parkers and the *paniolos* (cowboys) on the Big Island. At the Parker Ranch Visitor Center at Parker Ranch Shopping Center in Waimea, a video orientation to the ranch—founded in 1847—is presented. Admittance to the adjacent Duke Kahanamoku Museum is included in the ticket price. At the ranch, Mana, the original, koa-wood residence of ranch founder John Palmer Parker, is open, as is Puuopelu, the century-old residence of the late Richard Smart, the ranch's most recent owner and a sixth-generation Parker. Smart was also an avid collector of art: Venetian glass, antique Chinese vases, bronze sculptures, and oils by a variety of artists, including Maurice Utrillo, Lloyd Sexton, and Pierre Auguste Renoir, are all on view at Puuopelu. *Box 458, Kamuela-Waimea 96743, tel. 808/885–7655. Admission to museums and video: $5 adults, $3.75 children 4–11; admission to Mana and Puuopelu: $7.50 adults, $5 children; combined admission: $10 adults, $7.50 children. Shuttle service between 2 locations.*

Walking Tour You can take a self-guided walking tour of downtown Hilo with the help of a "Discover Downtown Hilo" map from the **Lyman House Memorial Museum.** Points of interest are indicated at Kalakaua Park and at 15 historic buildings (*see* Tour 4 in Exploring the Big Island, *below*). *276 Haili St., tel. 808/935–5021. Map $1.25. Open Mon.–Sat. 9–5.*

Exploring the Big Island

If you have only three or four days on the Big Island and you want to reserve some time for relaxing as well as sightseeing, you should look over a map before or upon your arrival and choose the highlights you want most to see. For three- or four-day stays, you might choose to book a hotel along the west coast, in Kailua-Kona or Keauhou, or at one of the resorts on the Kohala Coast in order to be near the best restaurants, beaches, and suntanning weather.

If, on the other hand, your schedule allows a week or 10 days on the island, you might want to spend a night or two in the county seat of Hilo, a night at the Volcano House, and another in Waimea before finishing up your vacation at a resort on the sunny side of the island. It's best to follow this east-coast–to–west-coast order for accommodations so you won't go home with memories of Hilo's often gray skies.

To orient yourself, divide the island into sightseeing sections roughly corresponding to its six official districts: Hilo on the eastern side; Hamakua, the northeast seacoast; Kohala, the northern mountainous region, and the northwestern coastline; Kona, the western seaside village of Kailua-Kona, and the upcountry coffee region; Ka'u and the vast stretches of lava and desert to the south; and Puna, which is east of Volcano.

Reserve Hilo and the rugged Hamakua Coast to Waipio Valley for one or two days of exploring. Another day (more for hikers and outdoor types) could be spent investigating Hawaii Volcanoes National Park, which is slightly east of the center of the island; you could follow Chain of Craters Road to the point where lava blocks it, then retrace your route and continue through the Puna District, with its ebony lava flows and black-sand beaches, to where the road is again blocked by recent flows. On a third or fourth day you might journey all the way around to the southern tip, through the Ka'u district, to a new base at one of the tourist centers on the west coast—the Kona district. The seaside village of Kailua (generally referred to as Kailua-Kona to distinguish it from the Kailuas on Oahu and Maui) is a mecca for shoppers but should also be explored for its historical significance (*see* Tour 2, *below*). From here, day trips can easily be made to cowboy country in Waimea, and you can return via a circle route through the Kohala Mountains to Upolu Point at the northern tip, past Kawaihae, and back.

Make reservations with a tour agency for another day or evening to go stargazing from the top of Mauna Kea, where 10 observatories sprout like mushrooms in the barren cinder and lava landscape. Access to Mauna Kea is via Saddle Road, the most direct route between Hilo and the Kohala Coast; however, nearly all car-rental contracts prohibit driving on this remote, winding, and sometimes rough track. Finally, you'll want a day to get off the beaten track in up-country Kona, simply to enjoy the riot of tropical flora: The bougainvillea, poinsettias, breadfruit, impatiens, and shiny-leaved coffee trees delight the eye. You might make Holualoa (*see* The Arts, *below*) the destination for this day, as this little town houses the Kona Arts Center and a number of fine art galleries for browsing.

If you are short of time, give Hilo a once-over-lightly look, then see Volcanoes National Park on your first day, traveling the Hamakua Coast route and making your new base in Kailua-Kona that night. This unfortunately eliminates the 126-mile drive around the southern end of the island, which gives a wonderful sense of space, history, and isolation with its miles of macadamia nut orchards, lava flows, and ranch lands; however, this area needs correspondingly bigger stretches of time to explore adequately.

For this guide, the island is divided into a car trip from Hilo to the volcano area; a walking tour of Kailua-Kona; a trip around the northwest section, including Waimea and the Kohala Mountains; and a tour of the Hamakua Coast. Later in this chapter, we've included a section on beaches you won't just want to drive past. Generally, in addition to this book, you will find the Drive Guides furnished by car-rental agencies helpful; they are marked with major sightseeing stops. If you want detailed street maps, **Basically Books** (46 Waianuenue Ave., Hilo 96720, tel. 808/961–0144) is a complete map shop. Maps are also available at the **Middle Earth Bookshoppe** (75-5719 Alii Dr., Kailua-Kona, tel. 808/329–2123). Each of the following tours can be divided into two separate trips, but they can also be shortened to one day, if you have plenty of stamina and limited time.

Highlights for First-time Visitors

Akaka Falls State Park, Tour 4
Chain of Craters Road, Tour 1
Devastation Trail, Tour 1
Halemaumau Fire Pit in Kilauea Crater, Tour 1
Hawaii Volcanoes National Park, Tour 1
Hulihee Palace, Tour 2
Lava Tree State Park, Tour 1
Lyman Museum and House, Tour 4
Mokuaikaua Church, Tour 2
Parker Ranch Visitor Center and Museum, Tour 3
Puukohola Visitor Center and Heiaus, Tour 3
Suisan Fish Market, Tour 4
Thurston Lava Tube, Tour 1
Waipio Valley, Tour 4

Tour 1: From Hilo to Hawaii Volcanoes National Park and Puna

Numbers in the margin correspond to points of interest on the Tour 1: Hawaii Volcanoes National Park and Puna map.

The most popular attraction on the Big Island, Hawaii Volcanoes National Park, is home to most of the Kilauea volcano. If you're lucky enough to be visiting when lava is flowing from Kilauea, you'll want to make the park your top-priority destination. Kilauea's recent series of eruptions began in 1983.

Even if you don't witness a fiery display, you'll have plenty to see in the park, which also includes the summit caldera and gently sloping northeast flank of the 13,680-foot Mauna Loa volcano. You'll also be impressed with the lush greenery of the tree ferns and other tropical plants, the lava tubes, cinder cones, odd mineral formations, and trails beside steam vents, and the vast barren craters of Chain of Craters Road. Don't forget to take a sweater (or a jacket in winter), as temperatures can get nippy at the park's 3,700-foot elevation. Also take a flashlight if you'll be in the park after sunset, and a water bottle if you plan to visit the shoreline lava flow.

Start from Hilo's Banyan Drive and continue out on Highway 11—or Kanoelehua Avenue—which takes you directly to Hawaii Volcanoes National Park, 30 miles to the southeast. You can cover the distance from Hilo to the park in a quick 45-minute drive along the smooth divided highway. You might also choose to start early in the day, take your time, and perhaps visit sights along the way.

On Highway 11, keep your eyes peeled for the Hawaiian-warrior markers, the distinctive red-and-white signs installed by the Hawaii Visitors Bureau, that designate visitor attractions. To

❶ the right of the road you'll see the sign for the **Panaewa Rain Forest Zoo**. Turn right at the Hawaiian-warrior sign, and you'll find the zoo just off the Stainback Highway. Children love the monkeys and tigers here. The trails tend to get muddy because of the rain-forest location, so you and your children shouldn't wear good shoes if you plan to come here. *Administrative office: 25 Aupuni St., Hilo, tel. 808/959-7224. Admission free. Open daily 9–4. Closed Christmas and New Year's Day.*

Tour 1: Hawaii Volcanoes National Park and Puna

Saddle Rd.

Saddle Rd.

200

Powerline Rd.

SOUTH HILO

Tree Planting Rd.

Olaa Flume Rd.

Stainback Rd.

Stainback Hwy.

Kulani Honor Camp

Ola'a Rainforest

11

Glenwood

Volcano Art Center

5

Volcano Golf and Country Club

Kilauea Visitor Center

Sulfur Banks

8

4

Hawaii Belt Rd.

Kipuka Puaulu

19

18 17

Volcano Store

20

Tree Molds

Mauna Loa Rd.

9

6

3

Hawaii Volcanoes National Park

Steam Vents

Thomas A. Jaggar Museum

10

7

Volcano House

Kilauea Caldera

13

Thurston Lava Tube

12

Devastation Trail

11

Halemaumau Overlook

Hilina Pali Rd.

Chain of Craters Road

14

Chain of Craters Rd.

Hawaii Volcanoes National Park

11

KAU DESERT

15

Pu'u Loa Petroglyphs

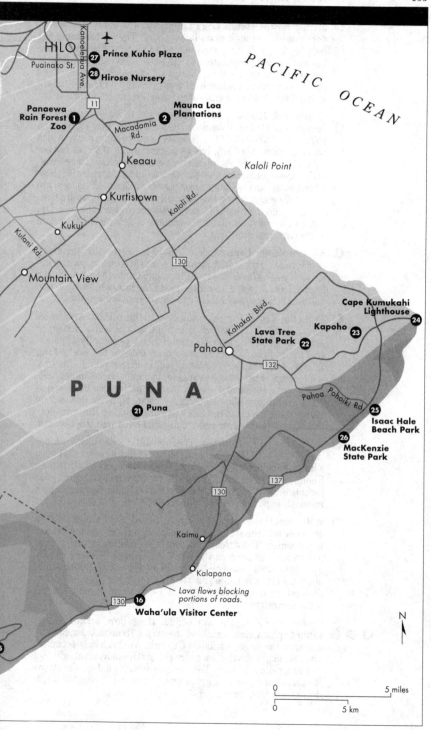

② About 5 miles south of Hilo on Highway 11 on the left is the marker for the **Mauna Loa Plantations.** The entry road meanders 3 miles through macadamia trees. The processing plant here has large viewing windows, and a videotape describes the harvesting and preparation of the nuts. Kids can run off their energy on the nature trail; there's also a place to buy snacks or enjoy your own picnic lunch. *Macadamia Rd. on Hwy. 11 south of Hilo, tel. 808/966-8612. Admission free. Open daily 9-5.*

③ Continue on Highway 11 and turn left at the sign marking the entrance to **Hawaii Volcanoes National Park** (Box 52, Volcano 96718, tel. 808/967-7311). The 344-square-mile park, which was established in 1916, has an admission fee of $5 per car between 8 AM and 5:30 PM; an annual permit costs $15. Those on bicycles or on foot are charged $2, while a Golden Age pass for those 62 and older, and Golden Access passes for disabled visitors, are free. Once you're inside the park, all visitor attractions are free. The park and the Chain of Craters Road are open 24 hours a day, but visitors must obtain a back-country hiker's permit to remain in the park area overnight.

④ **Kilauea Visitor Center** (open 7:45-5) is just beyond the entry booth to the right. Displays and a movie focus on past eruptions; if you can't see the real thing, don't miss the movie shown hourly from 9 to 4. The center posts the latest information on volcanic activity, and hikers can obtain trail information.

⑤ From the Visitor Center, walk over to the **Volcano Art Center** (tel. 808/967-7511), which was built as a Volcano House, or lodge, in 1877. The first Volcano House was actually a thatch-roof hut built in 1846. The art center features the work of Big Island photographers, artists, and craftspeople. Items in a wide range of prices are available, including rice paddles, cutting boards, boxes, and jewelry made of native woods, as well as framed batik-on-silk paintings by Phan Nguyen Barker. Be sure to take a look at the block prints depicting Hawaiian legends by Dietrich Varez and the unusual hand-painted T-shirts.

⑥ Across the street from the art center is today's **Volcano House** (tel. 808/967-7321), a charming old lodge dating from 1941 with a huge stone fireplace, 37 rooms for rent, the Ka Ohelo Dining Room, and a snack bar. The restaurants attract tour groups at lunchtime, but dinner at the Ka Ohelo Dining Room can be a romantic experience (*see* Dining, *below*).

⑦ Walk right through the snack bar to the edge of **Kilauea Caldera** and peer into the steaming fire pit, called **Halemaumau Crater,** at its center. The volcano currently is erupting not from here but from a rift zone on the flanks of Kilauea. Visitors can fly over that area (*see* Guided Tours in Essential Information, *above*). From the lodge you can hike around or into the crater; then return to your car for the 11.1-mile drive around the crater's circumference.

⑧ ⑨ ⑩ Scenic stops along the way include the yellow, acrid-smelling **sulfur banks, steam vents,** and the park's **Thomas A. Jaggar Museum,** on the edge of Kilauea Caldera. At this hands-on museum, seismographs that measure the earth's movement will also record a child's footfall. You can also see fascinating filmstrips of current and previous eruptions. *Museum tel. 808/967-7643. Admission free. Open 8:30-5.*

Note: Pregnant women and anyone with heart or respiratory problems should avoid both the sulfur banks and the fumes emitted from the center of Halemaumau Crater.

Rangers escort groups on scenic walks—ask for information about these at the Kilauea Visitor Center—or you can follow **⑪** the walks on your own: a 10-minute walk to the **Halemaumau Overlook,** with another view of the crater; a 30-minute stroll **⑫** along **Devastation Trail;** and a 20-minute jaunt through a fern **⑬** forest and into the **Thurston Lava Tube.**

On Devastation Trail, a boardwalk leads you through an eerie, barren landscape that may make you feel you're on another planet; this area was created after a 1959 eruption, when fiery lava from the smaller, adjacent Kilauea Iki Crater (*iki* means little) burned the surrounding ohia forest.

The walk to the Thurston Lava Tube takes you to a natural tunnel about 10 feet high that formed when the cooling top and sides of a lava flow hardened and the lava inside drained away. You can walk 450 feet into the tube.

Next, if you still have the time and the stamina, drive from the **⑭** center of the park to **Chain of Craters Road** (you'll understand how it got its name when you see all the huge depressions), which descends 3,700 feet in 24 miles to the Kalapana coastal district of the park. No food or gasoline is available until you return, so be sure to top off both the tank and your appetite before you go; the round-trip can take two hours or more, depending on how often and how long you stop to gawk. The road offers a breathtaking ocean view, while the historic lava flows are awesome to behold. At road's end, rangers direct parking, and you can walk (2–5 miles, depending on where you park) to where the lava flows into the ocean. Bring water: It's hot, you have to walk back to your car, and there are no facilities.

⑮ A sign on the left marks a trail across the lava to the **Pu'u Loa petroglyphs,** about a 25-minute walk inland. Etchings of people, boats, and animals made by early Hawaiians are spread over a vast area of black lava. The round depressions are *piko* holes, where umbilical cords of newborns were burned. Along the Kohala Coast, other easily accessible petroglyph sites may be found, so don't be disappointed if you don't have time for these.

Approximately 28 miles from the Kilauea Visitor Center on the *makai* (ocean) side of Chain of Craters Road is the site where **⑯** **Waha'ula Visitor Center** was demolished by lava in June 1989. Park rangers try to maintain the 1½-mile hiking trail to Waha'ula, however. From time to time Hawaii's oldest sacrificial temple ruin is also in danger of being covered with lava. Constructed in the 13th century, the huge stone platform, enclosed by a thick stone wall, once contained house sites and a *luakine* (sacrificial) heiau, where human sacrifices were made to appease the gods. Check at Kilauea Visitor Center to see if guided walks to some of the world's youngest lava flows and newest black-sand beaches are still being offered in the area. Lava has overflowed the road just beyond the center repeatedly since 1984; the road is now closed.

When hiking in the Waha'ula area, do not go beyond established barriers, as coastal regions do collapse and the ground can be unstable. Years ago, there was another site worth visiting just

off a narrow dirt road just beyond the park boundaries in the
Puna district. **Queen's Bath,** or Punalu'u, once ostensibly reserved for Hawaiian *alii* (royalty), was a freshwater pool about
10 feet deep that was a favorite swimming hole for neighborhood kids. The pool was buried in lava in 1988—another recent
reminder that the Big Island is still a brash, rumbling, changing land.

Return via Chain of Craters Road to exit the park; turn right
onto Highway 11 if you are ready to go back to Hilo, and left if
you are game for some more sightseeing. Then, if you need a
🟊 bite to eat, make the first right turn, which leads to **Volcano
Golf and Country Club** (Box 46, Volcano 96718, tel. 808/967–
7331).

Time Out   **Volcano Country Club Restaurant** (tel. 808/967–8228), at the
golf course, has big plate-glass windows that afford a view of
mist-shrouded greens, rare golden-blossomed lehua trees, and
an occasional nene goose, Hawaii's state bird. Coffee and a
steaming bowl of *saimin* (noodle soup) can be a soul-saver on a
cool, wet Volcano day.

Return to Highway 11, continue in a southwesterly direction to
the next right, and turn onto Mauna Loa Road. Then stop at the
🟊 sign on the right that says **"Tree Molds."** These molds were created when molten lava hardened around a tree and burned it
away in the process. Farther on is a little park with picnic tables, and at the end of the road you can take a self-guided mile-
🟊 long walk around **Kipuka Puaulu.** A *kipuka* is a green, forested
island surrounded by a sea of lava. Here you'll discover a koa
tree and other endemic plants and (if you've got sharp eyes) native birds, such as the *apapane* or the *elepaio*. (You can pick up
a written guide with numbers that correspond to sites along
the kipuka's trail at Volcano National Park's Kilauea Visitor
Center.)

Return toward Hilo by driving back on Highway 11 through
Volcano. The old volcano highway runs parallel to Highway 11,
🟊 and it's fun to take a side trip to the **Volcano Store** (turn left
about a mile from the park entrance to Volcano Village at the
sign; tel. 808/967–7210). The shop has excellent bargains in cut
flowers; when in stock, charming little orchid corsages are only
a couple of dollars.

Continuing back to Hilo on Highway 11, notice the yellow and
white ginger (the aromatic flower prized for leis) and tiny purple wild orchids that grow in profusion along the sides of the
road. Nobody minds if you stop to pick a blossom or two, or you
might prefer to stop at any of the anthurium nurseries along
the road to see how the bright red, pink, white, and varicolored
"little boy" flowers (notice the stamen at the flower's center)
grow. You'll see round wooden water tanks beside weathered
houses until you draw nearer to Mountain View and Kurtistown, where the city supplies water.

🟊 Take a side trip to **Puna** (or, if you prefer, save this excursion
for another day). Turn right onto Highway 130 at Keaau; a new
stretch of Highway 130 bypasses Pahoa, but it is worth turning
right and driving the 11 miles to this little town with wooden
boardwalks and rickety buildings reminiscent of the Wild
West. The restaurants outnumber the art galleries in the
quaint old buildings that are fun to wander through. After

㉒ Pahoa, angle left onto Highway 132 and continue to **Lava Tree State Park.** Tree molds formed here in 1790 when a lava flow swept through the ohia forest. These molds rise like blackened smokestacks 6 or more feet into the cool, damp air. *Admission free. Open 24 hours.*

Keeping to the left, continue on Highway 132 toward the coast ㉓ to **Kapoho**—if you can find it, as today it is simply a place where two roads cross. In 1960 the entire town was covered with lava. Luckily, everyone was safely evacuated. Near the coast, after 2 ㉔ miles on an unpaved road, you'll come across **Cape Kumukahi Lighthouse,** directly in the path of lava that stopped 6 feet away, splitting into two fingers to encircle the lighthouse and tumble into the sea, as if the quixotic goddess Pele had suddenly changed her mind about its destruction. Returning to the Kapoho crossroads, turn left to follow Highway 137 along the ㉕ ㉖ coast, stopping at either **Isaac Hale Beach Park** or **MacKenzie State Park** to take time out for picnicking or to use the facilities.

The Puna area has many black-sand beaches. The black sand is formed when hot 'a'a (chunky, cinder-type lava) hits the cold ocean water, bursting into tiny black granules that are broken down even further by wave action. The most famous of the black-sand beaches, Kaimu, was covered by lava in 1990. Since 1977, nearly 200 homes have been destroyed or moved as a result of the longest lava eruption in recorded history.

In 1990 the **Star of the Sea Painted Church** (Hwy. 130, Pahoa), built in 1931, had to be moved when lava inundated Kalapana. The little white steepled structure contains religious frescoes painted in vivid blue, red, yellow, and green on the walls and ceiling. Lava flows came close to destroying the church in 1977 and again in 1986 and 1987, when lava closed Chain of Craters Road (Hwy. 130), which joins Highway 137 less than a mile inland. At press time the church sat on blocks beside Highway 130, near where the road is closed because of lava.

The return to Hilo via Pahoa and Keaau on Highway 130 to Highway 11 will take about 45 minutes. As you enter town you might want to pick up souvenirs or snacks at Hilo's most mod- ㉗ ern shopping center, **Prince Kuhio Plaza** (11 E. Puainako at Hwy. 11, tel. 808/959–3555), where such fine stores as **Liberty House** also carry muumuus and resort wear. If you would like to ㉘ avoid packing souvenirs, visit **Hirose Nursery** (2212 Kanoelehua Ave., tel. 808/959–4256), near Prince Kuhio Plaza. You can order flowers to be sent to your friends on the Mainland; the owners will even present you with a complimentary blossom to tuck behind your ear when you go out to dinner.

Tour 2: Kailua-Kona

Numbers in the margin correspond to points of interest on the Tour 2: Kailua-Kona map.

The touristy seaside village of Kailua-Kona rests at the base of the 8,271-foot Mt. Hualalai. With the Hotel King Kamehameha at the northern end of Alii Drive, the village has restaurants and shops laid out along a mile strip of oceanfront that culminate in the new Waterfront Row complex at the southern end. You can walk the whole length of "downtown" Kailua-Kona and back again in 45 minutes, or else spend an entire day here, taking time to browse in the shops, do the historical tours, and simply breathe in the atmosphere. Just beyond the new Waterfront Row shopping and dining complex, the Kona Hilton and Tennis Resort marks the beginning of the 6 miles of hotels and condos along Alii Drive that ends at the Kona Surf Resort in Keauhou.

For visitors who are driving, the easiest place to park (and parking fees are not out of line) is at the Hotel King Kamehameha, but free parking is available if you enter Kailua via Palani Road, or Highway 190. Turn left onto Kuakini Highway; in half a block turn right and then immediately left into the parking lot. Walk *makai* (toward the ocean) on Likana Lane half a block to Alii Drive.

Cross Alii Drive to the **seawall,** where fishermen cast their lines. If the *lau hala* weavers are set up on their mats, stop to "talk story" (chat) and they will explain the technique of weaving hats and mats; perhaps they'll weave a bird for you. Pranksters delight in telling visitors that hala trees, which produce the long flat leaves for weaving lau hala items, are actually pineapple trees, because the fruit of the tree is similarly shaped.

Angle to the left, keeping the ocean on your right until you come to the wrought-iron gate that fronts **Hulihee Palace** and museum. The two-story palace was built in 1838 by the island's governor, John Adams Kuakini, and served as King David Kalakaua's summer palace in the 1880s. Tour guides at the restored palace talk about the artifacts and the royal lifestyle and furnish a good basis for appreciating the history of the Big Island. Oversize doors and koa-wood furniture in the elegant home graphically illustrate how huge some of the Hawaiian people were. *75-5718 Alii Dr., tel. 808/329-1877. Admission: $4 adults, $1 children 12–18, 50¢ children under 12, $3 senior citizens. Open daily 9–4. Closed Christmas and New Year's Day.*

Return along the seawall, where fishermen daily cast their lines, past **Kailua Pier.** You may want to return here to watch the fishing fleet come in at dusk, especially during marlin tournament season in August and September. Regular daily catches of the big game fish are now generally weighed in at Honokohau Harbor, north of Kailua-Kona.

Beyond the pier, enter the **Hotel King Kamehameha** for a stroll through the high-ceilinged, extensive lobby, reminiscent of a covered shopping mall. Some of the nicest shops in town, including **Liberty House** department store, **Jafar** clothing boutique, **Lalana's** (for hand-painted silks and cottons), **Mynah Bird Fabrics,** the **Shellery,** and **Trader's Hawaiian Gifts** are side by side with museum-quality displays of Hawaiian artifacts and trophies and mounted marlin from past Hawaiian International Billfish Tournaments. You'll see the 1986 winner of the Hawaiian Billfish Tournament, which weighed in at 1,062 pounds.

Exit the hotel on the makai (ocean) side past the swimming pool and **Kona Beach Restaurant** and continue on the pathway past Kamakahonu Beach and the lagoon. This is where King Kamehameha I lived between 1813 and 1819. **Ahuena Heiau** has been restored with thatched houses, so be sure you have your camera ready. Built by early Hawaiians, heiaus often had grass huts on top. Many heiaus can be found in the Islands; only a few have been restored. *75-5660 Palani Rd., tel. 808/329-2911. The*

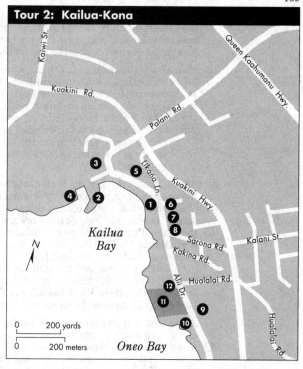

Tour 2: Kailua-Kona

hotel offers free historic tours of its grounds and the heiau Sat.–Thurs. at 1:30 and Fri. at 3, beginning at the mural across from the registration desk. Free ethnobotanical tours identifying and discussing the uses of endemic plants are offered Tues., Thurs., and Sun. at 10 and 11.

Retrace your steps through the hotel, crossing Palani Street to Kona Square, the first of many shopping villages and lanes that lead off Alii Drive.

⑤ If you continue on the *mauka* (mountain) side of the street, you'll find **Kona Arts and Crafts** (75-5699 Alii Dr., tel. 808/329–5590) at the Kailua Bay Inn Shopping Plaza. Everything in this shop is locally produced—petroglyph earrings, iridescent volcano-glass necklaces, pictures made of banana bark, and blown-glass dolphins on coral bases that have been painted black to resemble lava. (A coral substitute is used for lava because it is widely believed that anyone taking lava from Hawaii risks incurring the wrath of the volcano goddess Pele.)

⑥ Farther along Alii Drive, past Ocean View Inn and across the street from Hulihee Palace, is **Mokuaikaua Church** (tel. 808/329–0655), or the Church of the Chimes, which sound on the hour. The present church was built in 1836, though the original Mokuaikaua Church was founded in 1820 by Hawaii's first missionaries and was the earliest Christian church in the Islands. When the Congregationalists arrived on the brig *Thaddeus*, the old Hawaiian religion with all its *kapus* (taboos) had just been banned by the new king, Liholiho, at the insistence of his mother, Keopuolani, and Queen Ka'ahumanu. Many of the kapus governed the behavior of women; for instance, they could not eat certain foods, such as bananas, nor could they eat with men. The Islands were ripe for a new religion, and Queen Ka'ahumanu helped to pave the way for the Protestants.

Mokuaikaua Church is built of black stone from an abandoned heiau, which has been mortared with white coral and topped by an impressive steeple. Inside are pews, balconies, and at the back a panel of gleaming koa wood, behind which is a model of the *Thaddeus* and a reproduction of a page written by Lucy Thurston (a missionary wife), detailing her early impressions. Church employees are not tour guides, but they're happy to tell you about the artifacts and as much as they know about Hawaiian language and history.

At this point, you might opt to return to your car to drive along the waterfront, or you can continue browsing through the shopping plazas that extend off Alii Drive. At the **Kona Shopping Arcade,** behind the Crazy Shirts store and the pink awnings of the second-floor Rusty Harpoon Restaurant, is the **Hawaii Visitors Bureau** (75-5719 Alii Dr., tel. 808/329–7787). HVB has maps and brochures you won't find at the airports, and most publications are free. Ask the staff anything—until *pau hana* (closing) time at 4:30. Maps of the Big Island and Kailua-Kona are sold at the **Middle Earth Bookshoppe** (75-5719 Alii Dr., tel. 808/329–2123), around the corner in the same arcade.

At the next shopping arcade, the **Kona Marketplace,** rest rooms are located upstairs, and next door, clear at the back, is the movie theater. **World Square Theater** (75-5719 Alii Dr., tel. 808/329–4070) shows recent movies at 6 and 8:15 PM. In the marketplace, golfers can check out **Golf USA,** while gift shoppers may want to pick up wallets, coin purses, handbags, and even earrings at **Exotic Skins,** where the leathers range from crocodile to snake and lizard. **Kathy's Incredibles** has locally designed and made clothing and gifts of exceptional quality at reasonable prices.

Time Out   A few steps up the street at **Uncle Billy's Kona Bay Hotel** (75-5739 Alii Dr., tel. 808/329–1393), strollers can stop by the poolside **Banana Bay Restaurant** for an all-you-can-eat buffet breakfast or lunch.

Next you'll find a grotto shrine constructed of coral that holds a statue of the Virgin Mary at the pink **St. Michael's Church** (Alii Dr., tel. 808/329–0655), half a block up the street. To the left of the church, a small thatch structure at the entrance to a poorly maintained graveyard marks the site of the first Catholic church built in Kona in 1840.

At this point, it's time to stroll across the street to the new **Waterfront Row** (75-5770 Alii Dr.), which has more restaurants, and begin the return walk. Alii Drive continues for 6 more miles along the oceanfront, past Disappearing Sands Beach, the tiny blue-and-white St. Peter's Catholic Church, the ruins of a heiau, and Kahaluu Beach Park. Elegant condos with beautifully landscaped grounds, the Kona Country Club (golf course), and the Keauhou Shopping Center are all part of the scenery before the road ends at the **Kona Surf Resort.**

For the footsore, the benches under the trees at the ocean's edge in front of the **Hale Halawai** recreational pavilion furnish a welcome respite, or you can continue your return through the **Kona Inn Shopping Village** (75-5744 Alii Dr.). The boardwalk, with still more shops and restaurants, takes you all the way back along the waterfront to your point of origin. You might decide the Kona Inn Shopping Village deserves a return visit just for the shopping. **Noa Noa** offers hand-dyed silk and batik clothing (all one-size) designed by C. Marie. **Big Island Hat Company** has great tropical toppers, and **Hobey's Sporting Goods** is filled with ocean-going necessities, including surf boards. The **Volcano Shop** has nifty gifts, as does **Alley Geckos,** where you'll find items from around the world.

Children (if they've tagged along this far) deserve a break at **Mrs. Barry's Kona Cookies,** nestled alongside an espresso bar and sandwich stand in Kona Inn Shopping Village. Mrs. Barry won the baking contest at the 1978 Macadamia Nut Festival, and this is the only place in the world where you can buy her prize-winning Mac Nut Cookie (or nine other varieties). This will give mom and dad the chance to walk through **Fisherman's Landing Restaurant** (tel. 808/326–2555) just to enjoy the tropical foliage at the entrance and the lagoons inside. A saltwater pool lies between the restaurant and the ocean.

Time Out   Pause next door at the **Kona Inn Restaurant** (75-5744 Alii Dr., tel. 808/329–4455), where cocktails at sunset are a local tradition. Some visitors bring lawn chairs and stretch out with a good book in the afternoon beneath the coconut trees on the lawn between the restaurant and the ocean.

Near the exit of the arcade, **Moto Photo** (tel. 808/329–2080) offers one-hour film developing. Then cross the street and return to your car via Likana Lane.

Tour 3: The Kohala District

Numbers in the margin correspond to points of interest on the Tour 3: The Kohala District map.

If you're staying in Kona, you can begin this tour early in the morning by driving north on Queen Ka'ahumanu Highway 19. You'll pass both brightly colored bougainvillea along the roadside and white coral rocks carefully arranged by local youths to spell out names and messages on the black lava. Speed on by the glamorous luxury resorts along the Kona–Kohala coast; you can save those to inspect on another day. This is big country we're covering, and you can't see it all in a single swoop. Most of the lava flows that stretch from the mountains to the sea, which are interrupted only by the green oases of irrigated golf courses, resulted from the last eruptions of **Mt. Hualalai** in 1800–1801. You should be able to see the looming mountain to your right clearly in the morning light, though often mist descends later in the day. If you start late, you may not have time to take in every attraction on the Kohala Loop.

When you get to the split in the road 33 miles from Kailua-Kona, go left on Highway 270 toward Kawaihae and stop at **Puukohola Visitor Center.** The National Park Service ranger at this National Historic Site will tell you the history of the three heiaus (stone temples), two large ones on land and a third submerged just offshore, that King Kamehameha I had his men rebuild from 1790 to 1791. A prophet had told him to rebuild

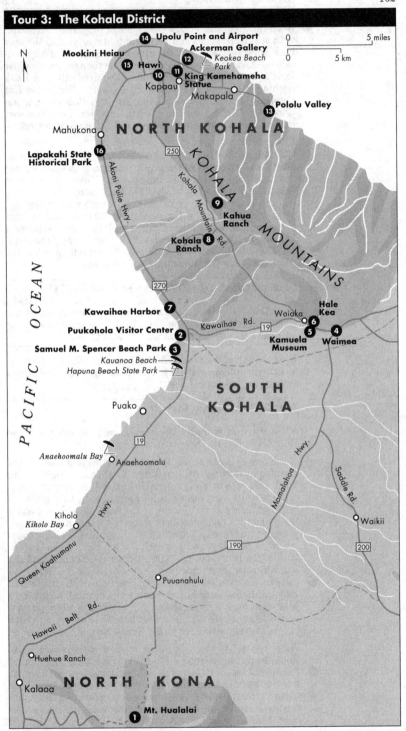

162

Puukohola Heiau (originally constructed about 1550) and dedicate it to the war god Kukailimoku by sacrificing his principal Big Island rival, Keoua Kuahuula, on the temple so that Kamehameha could fulfill his goal of conquering the Hawaiian Islands. The sacrifice was made, and the prophecy was finally fulfilled in 1810. Weather permitting (the trail is closed on windy days), it is a short, downhill walk over arid landscape from the visitor center to Puukohola Heiau and then across the road to the smaller **Mailekini Heiau** for a snapshot that will include both of the stone structures. *Box 44340, Kawaihae 96743, tel. 808/882–7218. Admission free. Open 7:30–4.*

③ You can also get a photo of the two heiaus by driving a bit farther down the road and turning into **Samuel M. Spencer Beach Park** (tel. 808/882–7094; *see* Beaches, *below*).

④ Retrace your route and continue up Highway 19 through Parker Ranch land toward Waimea-Kamuela. You can actually call this town by either part of the name. The community is generally called **Waimea,** but in the past it was affectionately named Kamuela, the Hawaiian word for Samuel, after Samuel Parker, the son of the founder, and mail to the town should be addressed to Kamuela.

⑤ Right where the road splits and Kohala Mountain Road (Hwy. 250) makes a sharp left, you'll find **Kamuela Museum.** Parker descendants Albert and Harriet Solomon have amassed fascinating artifacts from Hawaii and around the world. The Solomons don't worry that the things on display are too eclectic; instead, they think people will be attracted to whatever interests them, whether it's a satiny-smooth koa table that once graced Iolani Palace or a stuffed black bear from British Columbia. Most of the items are neatly labeled, and there's an impressive number of antique poi pounders, calabashes, and bone fishhooks. *At the junction of Hwys. 19 and 250, Box 507, Kamuela 96743, tel. 808/885–4724. Admission: $5 adults, $2 children under 12. Open daily 8–5.*

⑥ Continue inland on Highway 19 (Kawaihae Rd.) to pause again at the shopping complex called **Hale Kea,** to the left of the main road. This area was the ranch of Laurance Rockefeller (the same mogul who built the Mauna Kea Resort). During 1989 the ranch house and outbuildings were remodeled, and now they house wonderful little shops, art galleries, and Hartwell's Restaurant.

You'll also want to take some time to poke around and shop at **Parker Square** (those red buildings with white trim to the right of Kawaihae Rd. as you enter town, tel. 808/885–7178). Take a look at the fine art, Oriental antiques, finely crafted milo- and koa-wood sculptures, bowls, and boxes, and Japanese kimonos in the **General Store.** If you're lucky enough to be in Waimea on a Saturday or Sunday before 11:30 AM, drop by the tiny swap meet (flea market) called **Mother's Den** across from the public school to pick up cookies, cut flowers, or any number of secondhand finds that residents offer for sale.

Waimea has attracted a surprising number of fine restaurants run by chefs who have defected from the luxury resorts on the coast or from the Neighbor Islands. You'll want to make a point of coming back here to dine at **Merriman's, Hartwell's,** or the established standby, **Edelweiss** (*see* Dining, *below*).

Time Out For now, however, a quick lunch at the **Bread Depot** (Hwy. 19, Waimea, tel. 808/885–6354) in Opelo Plaza should suffice, or ask for a picnic lunch to go. The Depot bakes cinnamon rolls and all the breads for its fabulous sandwiches; you can also get soup and a daily special, often pasta or curry.

If Italian food is your passion, the pastas, eggplant, pizza, and hot sandwiches at **Aloha Luigi** (tel. 808/885–7277), at the intersection of Kawaihae Road and Highway 190, are very popular.

The traditional visitor attraction in Waimea is the **Parker Ranch Visitor Center and Museum,** which was opened in 1975 by Richard Smart, a ranch owner and an heir of John Palmer Parker. The latter founded Parker Ranch in 1847, when King Kamehameha I gave the newcomer two acres of land. The museum delves into the history of ranching by the Parkers with life-size replicas and a slide show detailing the growth of the ranch.

A few years later Smart opened **Mana,** the original koa-wood residence of the ranch founder, as well as the century-old Smart family home, **Puuopelu,** so the public could view an extensive private art collection. *At Parker Ranch Shopping Center, junction of Hwys. 19 and 190, Box 458, Kamuela 96743, tel. 808/885–7655. Admission to museum: $5 adults, $3.75 children 4–11. Open Mon.–Sat. 9–4:30. Admission to Historic Homes: $7.50 adults, $5 children 4–11. Open Mon.–Sat. 9:30–4:30.*

If you leave Parker Ranch Visitor Center and drive northeast on Highway 19, you'll pass the **Keck Control Center** on the left (it is the headquarters for the Keck Observatory, containing the world's largest mirrored telescope, at the top of Mauna Kea). Then drive by the first church on the left, but stop to peek into the cream-color church called **Imiola Congregational** (Box 669, Kamuela 96743, tel. 808/885–4987). The entrance of the church, which was built in 1832, is behind the pulpit (be careful not to walk in while a service is in progress). Note the all-koa interior and the very unusual wooden calabashes hanging from the ceiling.

Return through town and turn right on **Kohala Mountain Road** (Hwy. 250) for a scenic ride through the Kohala Mountains to Hawi. An overlook affords a view of the entire coastline; see if **7** you can pick out the protective breakwater at **Kawaihae Harbor** directly below. This harbor is second in size only to Hilo Harbor on the east coast. Farther on, through the ironwood trees that act as windbreaks along the road, you'll see white-board fences that extend across the emerald pastures. These fences divide into 3-, 5-, and 10-acre lots an exclusive country-home subdivi-**8** sion called **Kohala Ranch.** Here the impressive new Arena Polo and Equestrian Center sets the stage for frequent exhibition polo matches, which visitors are welcome to attend. You can arrange at your hotel desk for guided horseback rides through this country with **Ironwood Outfitters** (tel. 808/885–4941). The air is crisp and clear, until the mist sets in and all you can see are the outlines of horses or cattle appearing and disappearing on the pastures.

9 Across the road you will see **Kahua Ranch,** a 23,000-acre operation with progressive cowboys who round up the cattle astride horses or motorcycles and spend part of their days tending sheep and long-stem carnations. Owner Monte Richards realized that the best way to remain economically viable was to diversify his ranching efforts. Sunset in the Kohala Mountains turns the hills into a muted watercolor in shades of mauve, wheat, and cerulean blue.

The road drops gradually from 3,564 feet, and after about 20 miles it rejoins Highway 270 at the dilapidated old sugar village of **Hawi.** Turn right to Kapaau, where on the right of Highway 270 you'll see the original **King Kamehameha Statue** (which is just like the one in front of the Judiciary Building on King Street in Honolulu). This statue was cast in Florence in 1880 but was lost at sea when the German ship that was transporting it sank near the Falkland Islands. A replica was ordered and shipped to Honolulu, and two years later an American sea captain found the original in a Port Stanley (Falkland Islands) junkyard and brought it to the Big Island. The legislature voted to erect it near Kamehameha's birthplace.

Across the street, painter Gary Ackerman and his wife, Yesan, have a fine collection of local gifts and artifacts for sale in their **Ackerman Gallery** (Box 961, Kapaau 96755, tel. 808/889–5971).

Time Out If riding and history have made you hungry, **Tropical Dreams** (tel. 808/889–0505), a little restaurant one block down the street from Ackerman Gallery in Kapaau, dishes out freshly made ice cream.

The road ends at an overlook at **Pololu Valley.** A hiking trail for the very hardy leads into the valley and over several ridges beyond. The trail eventually reaches Waipio Valley. On the return via Highway 270, feel free to pass up **Kapaa Beach Park** and **Mahukona Beach Park;** you've earned the break, and these parks do not have particularly enticing swimming beaches.

But we do recommend you take the turnoff to **Upolu Point** and the **Upolu Airport** if you have a four-wheel-drive vehicle and are truly intent on not missing anything historically important. At the airport a rough lane to the left leads to the **Mookini Heiau.** Few people seem to seek out this isolated *luakine* (sacrificial) heiau, but it is so impressive in size it will give you "chicken skin" (the local equivalent of goosebumps), especially when you think that it was built about AD 480.

The final stop off is **Lapakahi State Historical Park,** if it's not too late in the afternoon, as this beach park closes at 4 PM. It's a healthy walk down an arid hillside to take the self-guided tour through the ruins of an ancient fishing village. Displays illustrate early Hawaiian fishing, salt gathering, legends, games, shelters, and crops. A tour guide hands out maps with sites (and walking distances) marked. You might want to take only part of the trail— unless, of course, you've driven the Kohala Loop in the opposite direction and are ready for some fine snorkeling and a bit of feasting on a picnic lunch. *Box 100, Kapaau 96755, tel. 808/889–5566. Admission free. Open daily 8–4.*

Return to Kona via Highway 270 and perhaps have dinner or drinks at Harrington's or Café Pesto at Kawaihae Harbor (*see* Dining, *below*).

**Tour 4: Hilo and the Hamakua Coast
to Waipio Valley**

*Numbers in the margin correspond to points of interest on the
Tour 4: Hilo Vicinity map.*

Hilo When the sun shines and the snow glistens on Mauna Kea 25
miles in the distance, Hilo is truly beautiful. In the rain, the
town becomes an impressionist painting, with the brilliant
greenery muted alongside the weather-worn brown, red, and
blue buildings. In the last couple of years, these buildings have
been the focus of a $1.4 million refurbishment, undertaken in
hopes of revitalizing the downtown area by attracting more
businesses and visitors. The whole town has only 1,200 hotel
rooms, most of them strung along Banyan Drive, right on Hilo
Bay. In comparison, a single hotel on the west coast, the Hyatt
Regency Waikoloa, has 1,240 rooms.

Nonetheless, Hilo (with a population of 40,000) is the fourth-
largest city in the state: it is home to a branch of the University
of Hawaii. Often the rain blows away by noon, and a colorful
arch will appear in the sky. Some people nickname Hilo "the
City of Rainbows."

❶ From the **Hawaii Naniloa Hotel** (93 Banyan Dr., tel. 808/969–
3333), go southwest on Banyan Drive, keeping to the right with
Hilo Bay to your right. Those banyan trees along the drive, by
the way, were planted in the 1930s by visiting celebrities; you
will find such names as Amelia Earhart and Franklin Delano
Roosevelt on plaques on the trees.

Time Out For a pleasant breakfast, try **Queens Court** at the **Hilo Hawaiian Hotel** (71 Banyan Dr., tel. 808/935–9361). Both the window
seats and the raised booths that are set back from the windows
have a good view of Hilo Bay. Hilo hosts most of the island's in-
trastate business travelers, so prices here are not exorbitant
for a hotel restaurant.

Next, you might want to meander across the footbridge to
❷ **Coconut Island** to watch children play in the tidal pools while
fishermen try their luck. The wide green expanse on either
side of Banyan Drive housed Hilo businesses until a *tsunami*,
or tidal wave, in 1960 swept them away and took the lives of 60
❸ people in the process. Today, **Liliuokalani Gardens**, with its
fish-stocked streams and oriental bridges, pagodas, and cere-
monial teahouse, is a favorite Sunday destination for residents.

Banyan Drive turns left onto Lihiwai Street. This is where the
most action in town takes place Monday through Saturday,
starting at about 7:30 or 8 AM. A fishing fleet arrives sometime in
the wee hours with its catch to be auctioned to retailers at the
❹ **Suisan Fish Market** (85 Lihiwai, tel. 808/935–8051). Take your
camera (and a flash) to get pictures of the bright red aweoweo,
aku, ahi, marlin, and other fish as buyers and sellers do their
thing, generally in unintelligible pidgin.

Leaving Lihiwai Street, turn right onto Kamehameha Avenue,
unless construction forces you to partially retrace your route.
Ignore the connecting Bayfront Highway, which is the fast
way to bypass town to drive to the Hamakua Coast. In three
blocks, turn left on Pauahi Street and left again after 1 block
onto Piopio Street. Park and walk across Liliuokalani Park be-

167

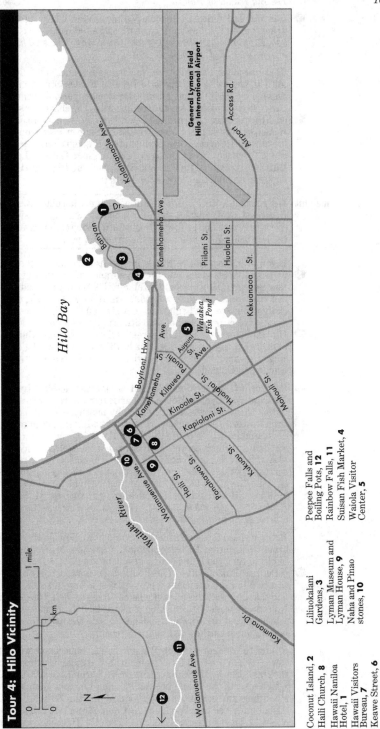

Tour 4: Hilo Vicinity

Coconut Island, **2**
Haili Church, **8**
Hawaii Naniloa
Hotel, **1**
Hawaii Visitors
Bureau, **7**
Keawe Street, **6**

Liliuokalani
Gardens, **3**
Lyman Museum and
Lyman House, **9**
Naha and Pinao
stones, **10**

Peepee Falls and
Boiling Pots, **12**
Rainbow Falls, **11**
Suisan Fish Market, **4**
Waiola Visitor
Center, **5**

❺ side Waiola Pond to the **Waiola Visitor Center,** where a photographic exhibit shows the aftermath of the 1960 tidal wave. *Box 936, Piopio St., tel. 808/961-7360. Open Mon., Tues., Thurs., Fri. 8-4:30; Wed. noon-8:30; Sat. 9-3.*

Continue along Pauahi Street to Kilauea Avenue, and follow it until it angles to the right to become Keawe Street and is crossed by Haili Street. For inveterate shoppers, it is time to park the car and take out the credit cards. The charming shops
❻ on **Keawe Street** are your goal. While away time at **Basically Books,** or browse in the **Most Irresistible Shop in Town** (containing an eclectic array of items, including English china cups, ceramic fireplaces, and handbags), **Cunningham Gallery, Louise Dumaine Antiques, Da Ceramic Shop,** and the **Big Island Gallery,** showcasing the work of local artists.

Time Out We guarantee that a few minutes at the **Chocolate Bar** (98 Keawe St., tel. 808/961-5088), topped off with a few sips of fresh-brewed Kona coffee at **Bear's Coffee Shop** (110 Keawe St., tel. 808/935-0708), will revive the tired shopper.

If you walk from Keawe Street mauka (toward the mountains)
❼ on Haili Street, you'll find the Hilo branch of the **Hawaii Visitors Bureau** (180 Kinoole St., tel. 808/329-7787), marked by a red and white Hawaiian warrior sign. It's worth a visit, especially if you are just beginning your stay on the Big Island and don't have every detail of your itinerary nailed down. Where
❽ Ululani Street crosses Haili Street is the historic **Haili Church,** built by Protestant missionaries in 1859. On Sunday the choir sings Hawaiian hymns, and services are conducted in both Hawaiian and English.

❾ Farther up the block on the right are two attractions, **Lyman Museum** and **Lyman House,** of particular interest to history buffs. The house was built in 1839 by missionaries who came from Boston to run a school for boys. The adjacent museum was dedicated in 1973 to house the museum's unique acquisitions— wooden cuspidors carved by Hawaiians, the world's only display of Hawaiian land shells (snails), and historical dress representing Hawaii's various ethnic groups. A walking-tour map of old Hilo Town, explaining the significance of historic sites and buildings, is available in the museum's gift shop for $1.25. *276 Haili St., tel. 808/935-5021. Admission (includes guided tours): $4.50 adults, $2.50 ages 6-17. Open Mon.-Sat. 9-5.*

Retrace your steps half a block to go along Kapiolani Street and around the corner to 300 Waianuenue Avenue. In front of the public library you'll find two large oblong stones, the legendary
❿ **Naha and Pinao stones.** The Pinao stone is reportedly an entrance pillar of an ancient temple that stood on this site. Legend decreed that the person who could move the 5,000-pound Naha stone would become king of all the islands. Kamehameha I, who united the Hawaiian Islands, is said to have moved the Naha stone when he was still in his teens.

Return to your car to follow Waianuenue Avenue a mile west of town. (When the road forks, remain on Waianuenue Avenue to the right. The left fork, Kaumana Drive, becomes Saddle Road, which bisects the island between Mauna Loa and Mauna Kea mountains and continues on to Waimea and the Kohala Coast. Also, be advised that Waianuenue Avenue from 7:15 to 8 AM is a one-way street entering Hilo.) You'll see the Hawaiian-warrior

⑪ marker for **Rainbow Falls,** which thunders into Wailuku River Gorge. If the sun peeks out in the morning hours, a rainbow forms above the mist.

Continue another 2 miles or so up the road, keeping to the right; you may think you've gotten lost, but eventually you'll
⑫ see a green sign for **Peepee Falls.** The falls drop in four streams of water into a series of circular pools, and the resultant turbulent action of the water has earned the name **Boiling Pots.**

Numbers on the map correspond to points of interest on the Tour 4: Hamakua Coast map.

Hamakua Coast Return along Waianuenue Avenue through Hilo and turn left onto Bayfront Highway if you're still interested in sightseeing along the Hamakua Coast, or if you prefer, save the farther reaches of this drive for another day. You'll be traveling north on Highway 19. It is 95 miles to Kona via this shorter of the two coastal routes and approximately 50 miles to Waipio Valley, the turnaround point of this excursion.

Seven miles out of town, turn right onto a **4-mile scenic drive.** Lush vegetation, flowers, bridges over rushing, tumbling streams, and stunning coastline views appear around each curve. On the left you'll see an old church, now a partially
❶ burned ruin, and a small office, the headquarters of **Hawaii Tropical Botanical Garden.** Tickets are available at the office, where you also catch a van to visit the 17-acre nature preserve just down the hill on Onomea Bay. Pathways lead through more than 1,000 species of plants and flowers, including palms, bromeliads, ginger, heliconia, and ornamentals. You'll see waterfalls and, in the lily lake, the fish called koi, prized by many Japanese collectors. Allow yourself enough time to explore the grounds at a leisurely pace. *Box 415, Hilo, tel. 808/964–5233. Admission (tax deductible, as the nature preserve is a nonprofit organization): $12 adults, children under 17 free. Open daily 8:30–4:30.*

When the scenic drive rejoins Highway 19, turn left at Honomu
❷ to travel 5 miles inland to **Akaka Falls State Park.** On the way to the park you pass through the old plantation town of **Honomu,** home of a little gift shop and gallery, but mostly you'll see fields of sugar cane on both sides of the car and perhaps a loaded cane truck or two.

There are two falls at the park, **Akaka** and **Kahuna;** you have to be willing to walk perhaps 20 minutes total to see them. If you follow the easier downhill trail to your right, you'll pass the 100-foot Kahuna Falls first. Akaka Falls drops more than 420 feet, tumbling far below into a pool drained by Kolekole Stream amid a profusion of fragrant white, yellow, and red torch ginger. *Admission free. Open all day.*

Enjoy the ride through sleepy little towns with music in their names: Honohina, Ninole, Papaaloa. If you say every letter and pronounce *i* as "ee" and *e* as in "hey," you'll come close to the correct pronunciation. Drive off Highway 19 on the ocean side
❸ when you see the sign for **Laupahoehoe Point Park.** It's not a place for swimming, but it is a stunning point of land dotted with ironwood trees and overlooking the pounding surf and the jagged black rocks of the northeast coastline. Still vivid in the minds of longtime Hilo residents is the April 1, 1946, tragedy when 20 schoolchildren and four teachers were swept to sea by

Tour 4: Hamakua Coast

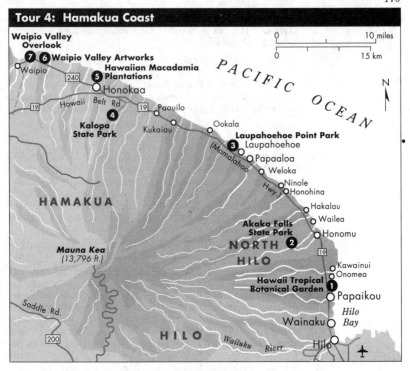

Waipio Valley Overlook

Waipio Valley Artworks

Hawaiian Macadamia Plantations

Waipio

Honokaa

Hawaii Belt Rd.

Paauilo

Kalopa State Park

Kukaiau

Ookala

Laupahoehoe Point Park

Laupahoehoe

Papaaloa

(Mamalahoa)

Weloka

Ninole

Honohina

Hakalau

Wailea

Akaka Falls State Park

Honomu

NORTH HILO

Kawainui

Onomea

Hawaii Tropical Botanical Garden

Papaikou

HAMAKUA

Mauna Kea (13,796 ft.)

Saddle Rd.

HILO

Wailuku River

Hilo Bay

Wainaku

Hilo

PACIFIC OCEAN

N

0   10 miles

0   15 km

a tidal wave that struck here. In 1988 the state constructed **Laupahoehoe Harbor,** and today the area accommodates visitors with bathrooms, showers, picnic tables (open and covered), and stone barbecue pits. *Admission free. Open all day.*

Highway 19 will lead you to the old plantation town of **Paauilo;** past the town is a side road to the left that leads up the hill to **Kalopa State Park,** in a cool, lush, forested area with picnic tables, rest rooms, and cabins. *Tel. 808/775-7114. Admission free. Open all day.*

Waving sugar cane turns to macadamia orchards as you near Honokaa.

Time Out   A quick stop on Highway 19 at **Tex Drive Inn** (191 Hualani St., tel. 808/775-0598) will give you a chance to taste the snack it is famous for: a *malasada*, a puffy, doughy Portuguese doughnut (sans hole), deep-fried and rolled in sugar and best eaten while it's hot. For lunch with a little local flavor, turn right down the hill onto Highway 240 to Honokaa, stopping at the dilapidated old **Hotel Honokaa Club** (Manane St., Honokaa, tel. 808/775-0678 or 808/775-0533). This may well be the only place in town with a salad bar, and the prices are certainly right. After being owned by the same family for umpteen years, the establishment changed hands in 1990, and the new proprietor has done some refurbishing both in the restaurant and in the hotel rooms.

The town of **Honokaa** marks the place where the first macadamia nut trees were planted in Hawaii in 1881 by an Australian named William Purvis. Today Honokaa is hailed as the macadamia capital of the world, mostly by the public-relations department of **Hawaiian Macadamia Plantations,** which may be reached by following Highway 240 through Honokaa and turning right at the sign. *Tel. 808/775–7734. Open for tours and nut purchases daily 9–6.*

If you continue through Honokaa on Highway 240 for about 8 miles, to the end of the road, you'll reach Waipio. A sign on the way out will take you to the right on a loop with no street name off the main road; here you'll find the **Waipio Valley Artworks** (Box 5091, Kukuihaele, tel. 808/775–0958). Finely crafted wood bowls, *ipus* (gourds), art by local artists, jewelry, and stitchery items are for sale. Make arrangements here or at the **Waipio Valley Overlook** for a tour (*see* Off the Beaten Track, *below*) to the floor of the valley, bounded by 2,000-foot cliffs. Nicknamed "the Valley of the Kings," Waipio was once a favorite retreat of Hawaiian royalty. Waterfalls drop 1,200 feet from the Kohala Mountains. A few residents still operate taro farms in the pastoral valley, and horses roam among the flowers and fruit, lotus ponds, and freshwater rivers.

If you have stopped to explore the sleepy plantation towns that look like relics from the past, with wood boardwalks and dogs dozing in backyards, night is undoubtedly falling. Don't worry, the return to Hilo via Highway 19 will take only about an hour, or you can continue on the same road to Waimea (20 minutes) and then to the Kohala Coast resorts (another 40 minutes).

The Big Island for Free

Hawaii compares very favorably cost-wise with any popular resort destination in the world. However, in the interest of economy, we are including a listing of fabulous freebies, just in case you've reached your credit limit but not your departure day.

Gardens. Photographers will revel in these opportunities to snap exotic tropical plants and flowers. At **Akatuska Orchid Garden,** stroll on a self-guided garden tour among orchids and other plants sheltered from the frequent showers. *Located on Hwy. 11, 22½ mi from Hilo, tel. 808/967–8234. Open daily 8:30–5.*

Closer to Hilo is **Hilo Tropical Gardens,** where visitors are welcome to wander through 2½ acres of tropical flowers. *1477 Kalanianaole Ave., tel. 808/935–4957. Open daily 9–4.*

Hikiau Heiau. Unless you take a snorkeling cruise or go hiking, this is the closest you can get to where Britain's Captain Cook landed in 1778. He was warmly welcomed the first time he arrived, as it was the *makahiki* season, a festival time when war was suspended, taxes in the form of food and goods were paid to the king and distributed to the chiefs, and games of strength and swiftness were the order of the day. It is today considered doubtful that the Hawaiians thought Cook was the returning festival god, Lonokamakahiki. At any rate he was greeted with abundant gift-giving, and he gladly accepted the chance to restock his ships, going so far as to take the wooden railing from the heiau (temple) dedicated to Lono to use for firewood.

When he was forced to return a short month later to repair the foremast of the *Resolution*, the makahiki season was over. One Hawaiian stole a longboat from the accompanying British ship, the *Discovery*. Fighting broke out when Cook and his men tried to hold a chief hostage to exchange for the boat, and Cook was killed. His bones were stripped of their flesh to be kept for their *mana* (spiritual power) and taken to another heiau near the bay. When Cook's sailing master, Captain William Bligh of HMS *Bounty* fame, asked for the return of Cook's body, he was given only the skull, hands, arms, and legs.

If you look across Kealakekua Bay from Hikiau Heiau you can see the 27-foot obelisk erected by the British Commonwealth as a memorial in 1874. Today the heiau is a large barren black stone platform. Grass houses once stood on the site. A small beach is beyond the heiau. *Drive south on Hwy. 11 to Captain Cook. Turn right on Napoopoo Rd. for a scenic drive to Kealakekua Bay and Hikiau Heiau.*

Kailua Candy Company. Here's a place on the Big Island where you are welcome to indulge in a free dessert. Take the tour, or bypass it and go straight to the salesroom if you're trying to make a departing plane. In 1977 Jack and Ginny Smoot started producing chocolates using fresh ingredients and no preservatives. They conduct personalized tours of their tiny plant (even if you're a family of only three or four). *A Hawaii Visitor Bureau sign marks the entrance, in the industrial area of Kailua-Kona. 74-5552 C Kaiwi St., tel. 808/329-2522. Open weekdays 9-6, Sat. 9-noon. Tours are weekdays 9-3.*

Macadamia Nut Factories. The best factory visitor center is at the **Mauna Loa Plantations,** 5 miles south of Hilo off Route 11 (*see* Tour 1 in Exploring the Big Island, *above*). Two other factories that welcome the public behind the scenes are the **Hawaiian Macadamia Plantations** in Honokaa (*see* Tour 4 in Exploring the Big Island, *above*) and **Mrs. Field's Macadamia Nut Factory** (Halekii St. off Hwy. 11, Kealakekua, tel. 808/322-9515). A guide at the latter factory leads the way every half hour 9-3. Products are always for sale at the above locations, but often you can buy the same boxes of chocolate-covered macadamia nuts on sale at Long's or Pay'n Save Drug stores for less. One other place that deserves mention is the old **Kona Coast Nut and Candy Factory** (tel. 808/328-8141) on Middle Keei Road, between Highway 11 and Honaunau. The methods and machinery here are old-fashioned, but you can crack a nut yourself at one display, and the little shop sells off-grade, unsalted nuts that are great to use in your own home-baked cookies.

Mauna Kea Royal Kona Coffee Mill and Museum. Sip freshly brewed coffee while you wander through the photo gallery that illustrates 150 years of coffee growing in Hawaii. The Big Island, with orchards at about the 1,200-foot elevation, is the only place in the United States that grows coffee commercially. School vacations in Kona used to be timed to coincide with the harvesting of the ripe beans so the children of family-owned plantations could help with the picking. *Above Kealakekua Bay, 3.3 mi off Hwy. 11 near Captain Cook, tel. 808/328-2511. Open daily 8-4:30.*

Puako Petroglyph Park. Watch for the turnoff from Queen Ka'ahumanu Highway 19 to Mauna Lani Resort. Take the first right at the traffic circle toward the Ritz-Carlton Mauna Lani Hotel and another right through the golf course, to reach Puako Petroglyph Park. Signs point the way to an area where visitors can make petroglyph rubbings of figures carved in stones specially for that purpose. Bring your own white cloth or paper and chalk or charcoal. Beyond the rubbing area, Malama Trail, used by Hawaiians of old to circle the island, has been cleared for ⁷⁄₁₀ of a mile, so hikers can view a lava bed covered with ancient rock carvings of animals, sailing canoes, and people. It's a good idea to take drinking water and to allow an hour or more for leisurely walking and viewing.

Punaluu Village Museum displays old photos of C. Brewer's history in raising cane—for sugar, that is. As the industry became less and less profitable, with a lack of trade restrictions allowing the importation of sugar from other countries, C. Brewer began replanting fields in vast orchards of macadamia nuts in this area. A mural painted by Big Island artist Herb Kane is also at the museum. *Hwy. 11, Punaluu, tel. 808/928–8528. Open daily 10:30–3.*

What to See and Do with Children

In the last few years, the major resorts have become aware that children do travel with parents, particularly during the summer months and the Christmas season—so special activities are planned with the younger set in mind during those times. Sometimes an additional charge is assessed, with the amount based on how long the *keiki* (children) will be in the program and whether meals will be included. Supervised activities cover a broad spectrum, from lei making to fishing with a bamboo pole to sailing to dabbling with the crawly things in tide pools. **Mauna Lani Bay Hotel** offers Camp Mauna Lani; **Kona Village, Mauna Kea Beach Resort,** the **Ritz-Carlton Mauna Lani,** and the **Royal Waikoloan** also sponsor children's programs.

Astronaut Ellison S. Onizuka Space Center. Opened in 1991 as a tribute to Hawaii's first astronaut, who was killed in the 1986 *Challenger* disaster, the Space Center at Keahole Airport features computer interactive exhibits. Visitors can launch a miniature rocket and rendezvous with an object in space, feel the effects of gyroscopic stabilization, and view educational films in the 20-seat theater. *Keahole Airport, Kailua-Kona, tel. 808/329–3441. Open daily 8:30–4:30. Admission: $2 adults, 50¢ children.*

Atlantis Submarine. A boat shuttles passengers from Kailua Pier to the 65-foot *Atlantis IV* submarine, which is so clean and new it feels more like an amusement-park ride than the real thing. A large glass dome in the bow and 13 viewing ports on the sides allow up to 48 passengers clear views of the watery world outside. A scuba diver feeds fish along a coral reef, keeping the viewing ports filled with the colorful finned creatures of the deep. Night dives to view nocturnal fish are also available. *Sign up at the Hotel King Kamehameha, 75-5660 Palani Rd., Kailua-Kona, tel. 808/329–6626. Cost: $75 adults, $50 children.*

Fishing. Youngsters seem to like to try their luck casting at the seawall right in Kailua-Kona. A bamboo pole and hook are easy to come by in the village, and plenty of locals are willing to give pointers.

Hiking at Hawaii Volcanoes National Park. Kids will run off excess energy on **Devastation Trail** or through the **Thurston Lava Tube.** If you are in the park for a full day or more, a hike into

Kilauea Iki Crater is exhilarating and can be accomplished in less than half a day. Hiking information and maps are available at the Kilauea Visitor Center (*see* Tour 1 in Exploring, *above*).

Hyatt Regency Waikoloa. This hotel has free train and boat rides; small children will probably find the monorail a nifty experience. Swimming with the dolphins is done through a special lottery—adult winners pay $65 for the privilege, but a 30-minute children's encounter, available by reservation on Tuesday and Saturday, is $40. *HCO 2, Box 5500, Waikoloa, tel. 808/885–1234 or 800/228–9000.*

Panaewa Zoo. *See* Tour 1, *above*.

Puuhonua o Honaunau. This 180-acre national historic park is perfect for a painless dose of education. In early times, kapu (taboo) breakers, criminals, and prisoners of war who escaped and reached this "city of refuge" were allowed to live and to escape punishment upon purification by the priests who lived within the walls. On the site, Hale-o-Keawe Heiau, built in 1650, has been restored, and the wood images of Hawaiian gods have been replaced along its outer boundaries. Proceed at your own pace with a map for self-guided tours. Demonstrations of Hawaiian skills, games, poi pounding, canoe making, and more are frequently scheduled. Tidal pools and a picnic area with showers and bathrooms lie just beyond Puuhonua o Honaunau. *Follow Hwy. 11 south of Kailua-Kona to Keokea, turn right and follow Hwy. 160 3.6 mi to Puuhonua o Honaunau. Box 129, Honaunau 96726, tel. 808/328–2326. Admission: $1 adults, free under 17. Seniors in a car enable all passengers to get in free. Open daily 7:30–5:30.*

Thomas A. Jaggar Museum, Volcanoes National Park. *See* Tour 1, *above*.

Whale Watching. The season for watching these gentle giants is roughly from December through April, when the humpbacks migrate from the north to Hawaiian waters. Pacific Whale Foundation runs 2½-hour cruises from Kailua Pier daily. All profits go to benefit research and conservation of whales. Other pluses: The guides are knowledgeable, hydrophones allow you to hear the whales, and if the whales don't surface, you receive a "Just a Fluke" coupon for another trip. Take your own binoculars to save a rental fee. *Pacific Whale Foundation, 101 N. Kihei Rd., Kihei, Maui 96753, tel. 800/WHALE–1–1. Cost: $25 adults, $15 children 3–12.*

Off the Beaten Track

South Point   The southernmost point of land in the United States, South Point (Ka Lae) is easily accessible by car, but unless you have ample time for exploring all aspects of the Big Island, it is one destination you might choose to pass up. If you do take the 3½-hour, 126-mile Highway 11 route from Hilo to Kona, Ka Lae is slightly farther than midway. The turn to South Point is just beyond Naalehu, the southernmost U.S. town; you go 12 miles down a narrow road to treeless, windswept Ka Lae, where you'll find the small Kalalea Heiau and abandoned structures once used to lower cattle and produce to ships anchored below the cliffs. Old canoe-mooring holes were carved through the rocks, possibly by settlers from Tahiti as early as AD 750.

If you're determined to get even farther into the outback and lucky enough to be driving a four-wheel-drive vehicle, follow 3 miles along the shoreline to Mahana, or Green Sand Beach. The beach is at the base of a low sea cliff. There are no facilities, and the rip current is dangerous. The beach has a distinct green tint from the glassy olivine formed by the minerals that combine when hot 'a'a (chunky) lava hits the sea.

If you continue on Highway 11 to Kailua-Kona, **Manuka State Park** (tel. 808/933–4720) is a cool picnic stop on the long route. The botanical park is between Hookena and Naalehu and has signs naming the plants and trees. The picnic tables and covered pavilion are always open.

Waipio Valley At 6 miles deep, **Waipio Valley** in the north of the Big Island at the end of Highway 240 is the largest valley on the island. In 1823, the first white visitors found 1,500 inhabitants living in this Eden-like environment, amid wild fruit trees, banana patches, taro fields, and fish ponds. Dubbed the Valley of the Kings because it was once a vacation spot for Hawaiian royalty, the area today is home to only a handful of families. Here, in 1780, Kamehameha I was singled out as a future ruler by reigning chiefs. In 1791, he fought Kahekili in his first naval battle at the mouth of the valley. Now as then, waterfalls frame the landscape; one of them drops from a 2,000-foot cliff to the valley floor.

The no-name hotel (no electricity or private baths, either)—although sometimes it's called the Waipio Hotel—is the only hotel-like accommodation for overnighters. Arrangements for the hotel must be made in advance. Hikers or outdoor types need to pack their own food and bring mosquito repellent and mosquito punks. You can walk into the valley or arrange to be dropped off by one of the four-wheel-drive tours that run daily. *For the hotel, write to Tom Araki, 25 Malana Pl., Hilo 96720, tel. 808/775–0368. 5 rooms. Facilities: kerosene lamp, community kitchen and bath. No credit cards.*

Hawaii Resorts Transportation Company (Box 183, Honokaa 96727, tel. 808/885–7484) hosts a trip into Waipio Valley and includes a stop at Hawaiian Macadamia Plantation in Honokaa. (Cost: $26 adults from Kohala Coast hotels.)

Waipio Na'alapa Trail Rides (Box 992, Honoka'a 96727, tel. 808/ 775–0419) arranges horseback rides in Waipio.

Waipio Valley Shuttle leaves Waipio Valley Artworks daily on 1½-hour tours. *Box 5128, Kukuihaele 96727, tel. 808/775–7121. Cost: $25 adults, $12.50 children under 12.*

Waipio Valley Wagon Tours departs from the Last Chance Store in Kukuihaele for two-hour excursions. *Box 1340, Honokaa 96727, tel. 808/775–9518. Cost: $35 adults, $17.50 children under 13. Private tours in a deluxe sport-cart: $45 adults, $22.50 children.*

Shopping

Residents like to complain that there isn't much to shop for on the Big Island. However, unless you're searching for career clothes or sweaters or a formal ball gown, you'll find plenty to deplete your pocketbook. Kailua-Kona has a range of souvenirs from farflung corners of the globe, such as Hong Kong, the

Philippines, Taiwan, India, and Tahiti. Destination resorts along the Kohala Coast offer quality goods. The **Mauna Lani Bay Hotel and Bungalows,** for example, has **Collections,** an exclusive apparel shop that is a subsidiary of Liberty House. The **Mauna Kea Beach Resort** has a gift and jewelry shop that offers museum-quality objets d'art and unusual jewelry from around the world.

Everybody in the family can find at least one thing to take home from the **Kona Country Fair.** You'll find local produce, flowers, island crafts, and gifts of crystals, eelskin wallets and purses, sea urchin jewelry, T-shirts, and towels, all dispensed with a dash of aloha spirit, not to mention reasonable prices. *Look for the tree house and new visitor center on Hwy. 11 in Honaunau, tel. 808/328–8088. Open daily 8–4.*

In general, major stores and shopping centers on the Big Island open at 9 or 9:30 and close by 4:30 or 5. Hilo's Prince Kuhio Shopping Plaza (*see below*) stays open until 9 on Thursday and Friday. In Kona, most of the stores at the Kona Coast Shopping Center (*see below*) are open until 7, though the KTA Super Stores outlet (a supermarket) is open from 7 AM to 11 PM. Many small grocery stores also maintain longer hours, as do the shops along Kona's main Alii Drive, which are geared toward tourists.

Shopping Malls

In Hilo the most comprehensive mall, similar to mainland malls, is **Prince Kuhio Shopping Plaza** (111 E. Puainako, at Hwy. 11, tel. 808/959–3555). Here you'll find **Liberty House** and **Sears** for fashion, **House of Adler** and the **Diamond Company** for jewelry, **Safeway** for food, and **Long's Drugs** and **Woolworth** for just about everything else. There is a one-hour photo store, in case you want to send home a really current photo. A smattering of specialty shops includes **The Puka** and **Once Upon a Time.**

The older **Hilo Shopping Center** (70 Kekuanaoa St. at Kilauea Ave., tel. 808/935–6499) has more than 40 air-conditioned shops and restaurants and plenty of free parking, and the centrally located **Kaiko'o Mall** (777 Kilauea Ave., tel. 808/935–3233) has 27 shops, including **JC Penney, Singer's,** and **Kinney Shoe Store.**

On the western side of the island, **Keauhou Shopping Village** (78-6831 Alii Dr., tel. 808/322–3000) offers an attractive steak and seafood restaurant, **Drysdale's Two** (tel. 808/322–0070), and upscale boutiques: **Small World** for children, **Showcase Gallery** for works by Hawaiian artists and imaginative feather jewelry, **Collector's Cottage** for the unusual gift, and a post office so you can drop a card and make the folks back home envious.

Right in Kailua-Kona, there are so many shopping malls along Alii Drive that they tend to blend into one another. Virtually all of them offer merchandise to appeal to visitors. On the ocean side of Alii Drive, extending an entire block, is **Kona Inn Shopping Village** (75-5744 Alii Dr., no phone), while the major mall across the street is **Kona Marketplace** (tel. 808/329–3539). A block off Alii Drive, **Lanihau Center** (75-5595 Palani Rd., tel. 808/329–9333) houses **Long's Drug Store** and 21 other stores, or you might want to stop across the street at **Kona Coast Shopping Center** (no phone) to pick up groceries or a bottle of wine at **KTA Super Stores.**

In Waimea, the **Parker Ranch Shopping Center** (at the junction of Hwys. 19 and 190, tel. 808/885–7655) houses 35 shops and the Parker Ranch Visitor Center. **Parker Square** (Kawaihae Rd., tel. 808/885–7178) and **Opelo Plaza** (Hwy. 19, Waimea) have galleries and specialty boutiques. The new **Waimea Center,** with the area's first McDonald's, was completed in 1990.

Hawaiian Arts and Crafts

For souvenirs that truly characterize the Big Island, visitors should take home either foods or crafts and artwork by local artisans. Local artists seem to draw inspiration from the almost spiritual beauty of their island. You'll find gifts and galleries in the most out-of-the-way spaces, as well as in Kailua-Kona and at Keauhou Shopping Village. Finely crafted wood bowls and boxes and beautiful drawings and paintings are not inexpensive, but they can enhance your home for years to come, and they are authentically Big Island. Following are galleries we've oohed and ahhed our way through:

At **Kona Arts and Crafts** (75-5699-0 Alii Dr., tel. 808/329–5590), absolutely everything is handcrafted in Hawaii. It's right on Kailua-Kona's main waterfront street, next to McGurk's blue awning. You'll find koa- and milo-wood carvings, crystal sculptures, scrimshaw, coral and sea urchin jewelry, and prints of ocean scenes by James H. O'Neil.

Six miles down the road at **Keauhou Shopping Village** (78-6831 Alii Dr., tel. 808/322–2007), check out **Alapaki's Hawaiian Gifts.** Here you'll find fine original art work, Hawaiian hula instruments, feather leis, genuine kukui nut jewelry, koa wood jewelry and bowls, ceramics, and wooden *konane* game boards (a Hawaiian board game reminiscent of checkers played with white and black stones).

In Hilo, you can go through the workshop of **Dan DeLuz's Woods, Inc.** (760 Kilauea Ave., tel. 808/935–5587), where master bowl-turner Dan DeLuz creates works of art from 50 types of exotic woods grown on the Big Island; his wares are sold in the adjoining shop.

Big Island Gallery (95 Waianuenue Ave., tel. 808/969–3313), just off Keawe Street, shows *raku* (dark Japanese earthenware), baskets, acrylics and oil paintings, and jewelry by local artists. Be sure to amble down Keawe Street (it's only a few blocks long) as well. Shops like the **Futon Connection** (104 Keawe St., tel. 808/935–8066), with attractive bedroom furnishings, **Louise Dumaine Antiques** (140 Keawe St., tel. 808/935–9604), **Cunningham Gallery** (116 Keawe St., tel. 808/935–7223), and the **Most Irresistible Shop in Hilo** (110 Keawe St., tel. 808/935–9644) are hard to pass up.

Within Volcanoes National Park, the **Volcano Art Center** (tel. 808/967–7511) remains a favorite with everyone. The Dietrich Varez block prints that depict Hawaiian legends are recommended. Unframed, these come in two sizes, both for less than $25. Cutting boards, rice paddles, and finely crafted bowls and boxes are made of a variety of Hawaiian woods. The Art Center represents more Hawaii Island artists than any other gallery, and it carries a selection of fine art prints and oils as well. Here, too, are tie-dyed *pareus* (the colorful strips of material that can be tied in a variety of ways to become all-purpose wearing apparel), handpainted 100% cotton T-shirts ($20–35), and funky Trashface jewelry, which is made of exactly what the name implies (one person's trash is another's treasure).

One other locale deserves special mention for its fine art galleries, and that's Waimea (*see* Tour 3 in Exploring, *above*). This is such an artsy community that even the old fire station has been turned into an arts center. Don't pass up the **Hale Kea** (tel. 808/885–6094) restaurant and boutique complex. At **Parker Square** (the red buildings on Kawaihae Rd., tel. 808/885–7178), in the **Gallery of Great Things,** (tel. 808/885–7706), you'll drool over the Ni'ihau shell leis ($200–$4,000) and bowls by Jack Straka ($300–$700), but there are attractive mirrors and wooden earrings for much less. Artist Kathy Long does charcoal sketches of Hawaiian dancers that are so detailed they capture more than a photo could, and the oils by her mother, Mary Koski, are superb and a branch of **Kamaaina Woods** (tel. 808/885–5521) are at **Opelo Plaza** on Highway 19 in Waimea; stop by if you didn't have time to visit the main branch of this factory and gift shop on Lehua Street in Honokaa (tel. 808/775–7722).

Resort Wear

Hotel shops generally offer the most attractive and original resort wear. **Kona Inn Shopping Village** (75-5744 Alii Dr.), that long boardwalk on the ocean side of Alii Drive, is stuffed with intriguing shops. Here, two places that have creatively hand-painted clothing are **Noa Noa** (also across from Hulihee Palace on Alii Dr., tel. 808/329–1902) and **Cottage Crafted in Hawaii** (no phone), which has 100% cotton hand-painted and silk-screened Aloha fashions.

Up-country in the one-street town of Kainaliu, **Paradise Found** (Mamalahoa Hwy. 11, tel. 808/322–2111) has hand-painted raw silk and cropped pants. Or, if you'd rather take home some of Hawaii's splashy material to make your own, also on Kainaliu's main street is **Kimura's Fabrics** (Mamalahoa Hwy. 11, 808/322–3771).

Across the island in Hilo, **Sig Zane** (140 Kilauea Ave., tel. 808/935–7077), a popular designer of dance costumes for the Merrie Monarch Festival, sells his designer fabrics and aloha shirts.

Hilo Hattie is such an old standby, it has to be mentioned (though most people who live in Hawaii would prefer to buy their muumuus from **Liberty House** at the Prince Kuhio Shopping Plaza in Hilo, the Hotel King Kamehameha in Kona, or the LH outlet, **The Penthouse,** at Keauhou Beach Hotel in Keauhou). The styles are bright, cool, and loose-fitting, and if matching his-and-her aloha wear is your thing, Hilo Hattie is the place to go (933 Kanoelehua St., Hilo, tel. 808/961–3077; 75-5597A Palani Rd., Kailua-Kona, tel. 808/329–7200 for free transportation).

Menswear

Virtually every golf course has a logo shop; even the casual **Volcano Golf Course** (tel. 808/967–7331) has a monogrammed line of golf shirts, shorts, and visors. But men shouldn't forgo shopping just because the prices look high on this logo leisure wear. In Kona, you'll find **Kona Gift Shop** (75-5703 Alii Dr., tel. 808/329–3259) distributing Ironman Triathlon T-shirts, towels, and aloha wear, as well as pocketknives with scrimshaw decorating the handle.

For those men who need a little top-level protection from the tropic sun, the old-time, family-run **Kimura Lauhala Shop** (Holualoa Rd., Hwy. 182, tel. 808/324–0053) in the up-country town of Holualoa has authentic made-in-Hawaii lauhala hats. While hat buyers admire their new looks, others will have time to browse here among the baskets, purses, table mats, hot pads, etc. You can also order wonderful Christmas wreaths custom-made of natural Hawaiian materials.

Beaches

Don't believe it if anyone tells you the Big Island lacks beaches. It actually has 80 or more, and new ones appear—and disappear—regularly. In 1989 a new black-sand beach, Kamoamoa, formed when molten lava shattered as it hit cold ocean waters. Kamoamoa was the largest of the black-sand beaches, more than half a mile long and 25 yards wide, until it was closed by new lava flows in 1992. Some beaches are just a little hard to get to—several are hidden behind elaborate hotels or down unmarked roads for which you'll want a four-wheel-drive vehicle or dauntless hiking spirit (or both)—and others have dangerous undertow and should be used for suntanning and fishing rather than swimming. In 1990 two of the Big Island's most popular beach parks—Harry K. Brown and Kaimu—were covered by lava flows from Kilauea. In Kailua-Kona and even in Keauhou, it's true, there are not broad expanses of coral sand. The most beautiful, swimmable white-sand beaches stretch along the Kohala coastline. The surf tends to get rough during the winter months; to be safe, swim only when you see or otherwise know that local people swim in the area. The tropical sun can be deceptive. Even on a cloudy day, it's wise to take along a sunscreen with a SPF (protection rating) of 15 or more and reapply it often, as saltwater and perspiration reduce its effectiveness. Public transportation to beaches does not exist. Few public beaches have lifeguards or manned beach centers. Beaches are listed in a counter-clockwise direction around the island, starting from the northern tip.

Keokea Beach Park. Driving back from the end of Highway 270 at the Pololu overlook to the north, you'll see a curvy road angle off to the right. Follow it for a mile, pass the cemetery with the weathered old stones, and you'll come upon the green lawns and large picnic pavilion of Keokea Beach Park. The black-boulder beach is suited for fishing and snorkeling in the calm summer months, but heavy surf in the winter makes this a hazardous swimming beach. A shallow, protected cove on the northeastern side of the bay is great for kids to float around on boogie boards and inner tubes. Some of the picnic tables are under cover, others are in the open; rest rooms, showers, drinking water, electricity, and a camping site make this a popular weekend destination for local folks.

Mahukona Beach Park. Located next to the abandoned Port of Mahukona in the Kohala district, where sugar was once shipped by rail to be loaded on boats, Mahukona Beach has old docks and buildings that are a photographer's treat. Divers and snorkelers can view both marine life and remnants of shipping machinery in the clear water. Heavy surf makes water activities off-limits in the winter, however. Boats can be launched with the chain hoist and winch on the old dock. It's a pleasant picnicking spot, with rest rooms, showers, and a camping area, but there is no sandy beach.

Samuel M. Spencer Beach Park. This park is popular with local families because its gently sloping white-sand beach is reef-protected, making it safe for swimming year-round. There are cooking and camping facilities, showers, tennis courts, and a large covered pavilion with electrical outlets. Mynah birds and sparrows make their homes in large shade trees on the grounds. You can walk to see the Puukohola and Mailekini heiaus, midway between the park and Kawaihae Harbor, which is a mile to the north. *The entry road is off Hwy. 270, just up the hill from Kawaihae Harbor, tel. 808/882-7094.*

Kauna'oa Beach at Mauna Kea Beach Resort. It's a toss-up whether this or neighboring Hapuna is the most beautiful beach on the island. Kauna'oa is long and white, and it slopes very gradually. In winter months, when the surf is high, swimmers should consult beach attendants before taking a dip, as the powerful waves can be dangerous. Hotel guests generally congregate near the hotel's beach facilities. Near the public-access end, there's plenty of shady and sunny beach if you prefer to stay away from the action. The amenities are hotel-owned. *Access is through the gate to Mauna Kea Beach Resort off Queen Ka'ahumanu Hwy. 19, which furnishes 30 public parking stalls.*

Hapuna State Recreation Area. The beach is a half-mile crescent of glistening sand guarded by rocky points at either end. The surf can be hazardous in winter, but in summer months the gradual slope of a beach that stretches as wide as 200 feet into a perfectly blue ocean makes it ideal for swimming, snorkeling, and scuba diving. Children enjoy the shallow cove with tidal pools at the north end, while at the southern end, adventuresome swimmers like to jump from the sea cliffs into the ocean. Signs restrict the use of surfboards and similar beach equipment. State cabins and public facilities are available nearby, and there is a conveniently located snack bar. There are no lifeguards to rescue swimmers from rough seas in winter, so keep out of the water at that time. *Between the Mauna Kea Beach and Mauna Lani resorts off Hwy. 19, tel. 808/882-7995.*

Holoholokai Beach Park. Turn off Queen Ka'ahumanu Highway 19 to Mauna Lani Resort taking the first right at the traffic circle toward the Ritz-Carlton Mauna Lani Hotel, and another right through the golf course, to reach this nicely maintained beach park with bathrooms, picnic tables, and barbecue grills. A rocky beach of black lava formations and white coral clinkers is fine for surfers and snorkelers, while a small grassy area is available to sunbathers. Just before the beach park, be sure to explore historic Puako Petroglyph Park. From signs that theorize about the mysterious figures carved in rock, Malama Trail meanders 7/10 of a mile through brush and kiawe trees to an area of lava covered with the ancient etchings of Hawaiian figures and animals. (*See* The Big Island for Free, *above.*)

Anaehoomalu Beach, at the Royal Waikoloan Resort. This expansive beach on the west coast is perfect for swimming, windsurfing, snorkeling, sailing, and scuba-diving. Equipment rental and instructors can be arranged at the north end. Be sure to wander around the ancient fish ponds and petroglyph fields that the hotel has preserved. *Take Waikoloa Beach Rd. to the Royal Waikoloan Resort. Follow the signs to the park and beach right-of-way to the south.*

Kiholo Bay. Don't try to find the unmarked road branching off to the west on the makai (ocean) side from Queen Ka'ahumanu Highway 19 unless you have a four-wheel-drive. The road seems to disappear into nowhere across the lava, but it actually leads to homes built along the oceanfront and to Kiholo Bay. The huge, spring-fed Luahinewai Pond anchors the south end of the bay, while the three black-pebble beaches are fine for swimming in calm weather. At the northern end, Wainanalii Pond (a 5-acre lagoon) is a feeding site for green sea turtles. Kamehameha I had a well-stocked fish pond here that was destroyed by lava in 1859. The two ponds are posted off-limits to swimmers. Secluded areas of the 2-mile bay are sometimes sought out by nude sunbathers although nudity is officially illegal on all Big Island beaches. You'll find good swimming, fishing, and hiking here, but no facilities.

Honokohau and Alula. These two beaches are down the road to Honokohau Harbor. Alula is just a slip of white sand a short walk over the lava to the left of the harbor entrance. Honokohau Beach is north of the harbor (turn right at Gentry Marina and go past the boat-loading dock). Follow the trail to the right through the bush until you come upon the ¾-mile beach and the rocky ruins of ancient fish ponds. The center portion of the beach is comparatively rock-free, though a shelf of lava along the water's edge lines most of the shore. The Aimakapa fish pond is directly inland. At the north end of the beach a trail leads mauka (toward the mountains) across the lava to a freshwater pool. The only public facilities are at the boat harbor. *Off Queen Ka'ahumanu Hwy. 19, 1 mi north of Kailua-Kona.*

Old Kona Airport Recreation Area. The unused runway is still visible above this beach at Kailua Park, which has showers, bathroom facilities, and palm trees strung out along the shore. The beach has a sheltered, sandy inlet with tide pools for children, but for adults it's better for snorkeling and scuba than it is for swimming. An offshore surfing break known as Old Airport is popular with Kona surfers. *Follow Hwy. 11 north to where it ends just outside of Kailua, tel. 808/329–6727.*

White Sands, Magic Sands, or Disappearing Sands Beach Park. Now you see it, now you don't. Overnight, winter waves wash away this small white-sand beach on Alii Drive just south of Kailua-Kona. In summer, you'll know you've found it when you see the body- and board-surfers. Rest rooms, showers, a lifeguard tower, and a coconut grove create a favorite and convenient summer hangout, but this isn't a great beach for swimming. *Go south on Alii Dr. about 1 mi past the Kona Hilton in Kailua-Kona. The beach is just before the small seaside St. Peter's Catholic Church.*

Kahaluu Beach Park. The swimming and snorkeling are fine here, and this spot was a favorite of King Kalakaua, whose summer cottage is on the grounds of the Keauhou Beach Hotel next door. Kahaluu is popular with commoners, too, and on weekends there are just too many people. A strong rip current during high surf pulls swimmers away from the beach. Facilities include a pavilion, rest rooms, showers, a lifeguard tower, and limited parking. *Beside Alii Dr. between Kailua-Kona and Keauhou.*

Hookena Beach Park. You'll feel like an adventurer when you come upon Hookena, at the northern corner of Kauhako Bay, after the 2-mile drive off the main road (Hwy. 11), about 23 miles south of Kailua-Kona. When Mark Twain visited, 2,500 people populated the busy seaport village. You can still find gas lampposts dating back to the 1900s. Good swimming, bodysurfing, fishing, and hiking can be accomplished here, but there's no drinking water at this gray coral-and-lava-sand beach. Rest rooms, showers, and picnic tables are available at the park.

Napo'opo'o Beach Park at Kealakekua Bay. The best way to see this black-sand beach and marine preserve is to take a snorkel, scuba, or glass-bottom boat tour from Keauhou Bay. A 27-foot white obelisk indicates where Captain James Cook was killed in 1779. This 6-acre beach park has a picnic pavilion, tables, showers, rest rooms, and a basketball court.

Green Sand (or Papakolea) Beach. You have to have a four-wheel-drive vehicle to get to this beach, whose greenish tint is caused by an accumulation of the olivine that forms in volcanic eruptions. You can get to South Point (where you'll find ruins of a heiau and the winches once used to load cattle and produce onto boats from the cliffs) in a regular car, but it's another 2½ rough miles northeast to where the beach lies at the base of Pu'u o Mahana, a cinder cone formed during an early eruption of Mauna Loa. Swimming can be hazardous when the surf is up in this windy, remote area. There are no facilities and no shade trees.

Punaluu Beach Park. Turtles swim in the bay (you can watch them surface and submerge), nest, and lay their eggs in the black sand of this beautiful beach. Fish ponds are just inland, and you can find the ruins of a heiau and a flat sacrificial stone at the northern end of the beach near the boat ramp. Sugar was shipped by rail to this former port town, and in 1941 Army troops were stationed here. The tsunami (tidal wave) of 1946 destroyed the Army buildings. The offshore currents here can be dangerous, though you'll see a few local surfers riding the waves. There are rest rooms across the road and also at the **Punaluu Black Sand Restaurant** (tel. 808/928–8528), located inland from the ponds. Here a visitor center houses artifacts from the area, and you'll see a memorial to Henry Opukahaia. In 1809, when he was 17, Opukahaia swam out to a fur-trading ship in the harbor and asked to sail as a cabin boy. When he reached New England, he entered the Foreign Mission School in Cornwallis, Connecticut, but he died of typhoid fever in 1818. His dream of bringing Christianity to the Islands inspired the American Board of Missionaries in 1820 to send the first Protestant missionaries to Hawaii. *26.7 mi beyond Volcanoes National Park on Hwy. 11.*

MacKenzie State Recreation Area. This spacious 13-acre park, shaded by ironwoods, is good for picnicking and camping. You can't swim here, but there are rest rooms, fresh water, and plenty of free parking. *In the Puna district between Hwy. 137 and the sea cliff.*

Onekahakaha Beach Park. A white-sand beach protected by a point of land makes this a favorite for Hilo families with small children. Lifeguards are on duty year-round. The park has picnic pavilions, rest rooms, and showers. *Follow Kalanianaole Ave. east along the water about 3 mi south of Hilo.*

Leleiwi Beach Park and Richardson Ocean Center. Near Hilo, this tiny beach just beyond the seawall allows entry to the water for good snorkeling, swimming, bodysurfing, board surfing, and net fishing. Richardson Ocean Center is a recreation and interpretive center with free marine displays for public viewing. Showers, rest rooms, paved walkways, covered picnic pavilions, and lifeguard service are available. *2349 Kalanianaole Ave., tel. 808/935–3830.*

Reeds Bay Beach Park. Rest rooms, showers, drinking water, and the proximity to downtown Hilo are the enticements that this cove has to offer. The waters are calm and safe. Most swimmers take a dip in the Ice Pond adjoining the head of Reeds Bay. Cold freshwater springs seep from the bottom of the pond and rise in the saltwater. *Banyan Dr. and Kalanianaole Ave., Hilo.*

Sports and the Outdoors

Participant Sports

The Big Island attracts active people. You'll see them running, bicycling, hiking, sailing, and even skiing. Any number of guides and services make it easy to be a joiner. In general, water-sports activities center on the Kailua-Kona area because of its calmer waters.

Biking Although pedalers should be fairly physically fit for extended bicycling tours, there seems to be no typical rider. Everyone from college students to retirees has completed tours of a week or longer, and how much you ride is up to you, as generally the support van that carries gear will also stop to pick up tired riders. Many Big Island roads have narrow shoulders and are traveled by large tour buses and sugar cane hauling trucks. No law requires the wearing of a helmet, but it is strongly recommended, and some operators do require them. Also, sheepskin seat covers and bicycle riding pants add greatly to personal comfort on long trips.

Backroads Bicycle Touring (1516 5th St., Berkeley, CA 94710–1740, tel. 415/527–1555) has been pedaling the blacktop in Hawaii since 1985, offering 10-day, 220-mile circle-island trips. Hotel accommodations (sometimes in such out-of-the-way places as Naalehu and Captain Cook) and meals are included, but the bicycle and airfare are extra.

On the Loose Bicycle Vacations (1030 Merced St., Berkeley, CA 94707, tel. 415/527–4005) offers a 10-day circle–Big Island trip and a 7-day Big Island/3-day Maui combination.

Vermont Bicycle Touring (Box 711, Bristol, VT 05443, tel. 802/453–4811) hit Hawaii's highways in 1988, though the company has been pedaling for 20 years in Vermont.

For those hardy souls who want to strike out on their own, bicycles can be rented in Kailua at **B&L Bike and Sports** (74-5576

B Pawai Pl., Kailua-Kona, tel. 808/329–3309). **Hawaiian Pedals Bicycle Rentals** (Kona Inn Shopping Village, 75–5744 Alii Dr., Kailua-Kona, tel. 808/329–2294) has mountain, touring, and tandem bicycles for rent.

Fitness Centers On the Hilo side, exercise addicts might try **Spencer Health and Fitness Center** (96 Keawe St., tel. 808/969–1511). The **Hawaii Naniloa Hotel** (93 Banyan Dr., Hilo, tel. 808/969–3333 or 800/367–5360) has a beautiful and complete spa and fitness center with such extra services as herbal wraps and massages available. In Kona, the **Club** (75-5722 Hanama St., Kona Center, tel. 808/326–2582) advertises high-tech fitness with child-care facilities as well. Three major hotels, the Mauna Lani, the Mauna Kea, and the Hyatt Regency Waikoloa on the Kohala Coast, have spa facilities.

Of these, the **Hyatt Regency Waikoloa** (HCO 2, Box 5500, Waikoloa 96734, tel. 808/885–1234) has the finest facilities, with the 17,500-square-foot Anara health spa. You can tone up in weight rooms and the aerobics room; relax in saunas, steam baths, Jacuzzis, or the club room; and have a facial, an herbal wrap, a loofah treatment, or a massage.

Mauna Lani Bay Hotel and Bungalows (Box 4000, Kohala Coast 96743, tel. 808/855–6622) has a spa (with weight and aerobics rooms and a Jacuzzi) that is completely adequate but on a much smaller scale than the Hyatt's.

The use of the fitness center at the **Mauna Kea Beach Hotel** (1 Mauna Kea Beach Dr., Kohala Coast 96743, tel. 808/882–7222) is complimentary to hotel guests. The center has 10 Nautilus machines and two Lifecycles, the latest in computerized stationary bicycles. Fitness instructors offer daily counseling sessions. The resort also has a scenic 2-mile jogging trail.

The Ritz-Carlton Mauna Lani (1 North Kaniku Dr., Kohala Coast 96743, tel. 808/885–2000) has a complete fitness center with crystal chandeliers and leaded-glass mirrors. The center offers massages, herbal wraps, and aroma therapy to soothe you mentally as well as physically.

Golf If there is one thing the Big Island is known for, it's the beautiful golf courses that appear like green oases in the black, arid landscape of lava. Costs are very reasonable at the municipal golf courses. On the east side of the island, the **Hilo Municipal Golf Course** (340 Haihai St., Hilo 96720, tel. 808/959–7711) assesses greens fees of only $6 for nonresidents on weekdays, $8 on weekends. The public course most convenient to Hilo's major hotels is the nine-hole **Naniloa Country Club Golf Course** (120 Banyan Dr., Hilo 96720, tel. 808/935–3000). Farther afield, the 18-hole, par 72 course at **Volcano Golf and Country Club** (Box 46, Volcanoes National Park 96718, tel. 808/967–7331) is comfortably cool and countrified, though sometimes a bit soggy in winter. Rates are $45 per player.

About 30 miles south of Volcano Village is **Sea Mountain Golf Course** (at Punaluu, Box 85, Pahala 96777, tel. 808/928–6222), which stretches from the Pacific Coast up the slopes of Mauna Loa. Play is $36 at the 18-hole, par 72 course. At **Discovery Harbor Golf and Country Club** (Box Q, Naalehu 96772, tel. 808/929–7353) you can play 18 holes, par 72, for $20. **Hamakua Country Club** (Honokaa 96727, tel. 808/775–7244) is a nine-hole private course open to the public with greens fees of $10.

On the west coast, golf gets a bit more expensive at the **Kona Country Club** (78-7000 Alii Dr., Keauhou 96740, tel. 808/322–2595), but free shuttle service is available from Keauhou hotels and condos to this 27-hole course, which is par 36 for nine holes. Rates (anywhere from $70 to $100) are less expensive for Kona-area guests and also vary according to season. Don't confuse the two Robert Trent Jones, Jr.–designed Waikoloa courses: **Waikoloa Village Golf Course** (Waikoloa 96743, tel. 808/883–9621), is inland, in South Kohala, while the **Waikoloa Beach Golf Course** (tel. 808/885–6060) is affiliated with the Royal Waikoloan Resort and the Hyatt Regency Waikoloa on the Kohala Coast. A 72-par Tom Weiskoph/Jay Morrish–designed course, the **Kings' Course** (tel. 808/885–4647), featuring four large lakes, opened adjacent to the Hyatt Regency Waikoloa in 1989.

Off Highway 19 are two gems that receive award after award from golf magazines: the **Mauna Kea Beach Resort's** par 72, 18-hole course (1 Mauna Kea Beach Dr., Kohala Coast 94743, tel. 808/882– 7222), designed by Robert Trent Jones, Sr.; and the **Francis H. I'i Brown Golf Course at the Mauna Lani Resort** (Box 4959, Kohala Coast 96743, tel. 808/885–6655), restructured into two 18-hole courses (the North and South) with the opening of the Ritz-Carlton Mauna Lani Resort in 1991. Mauna Kea charges $115 at its championship course. The men's tee at the fifteenth hole of the Mauna Lani's Francis H. I'i Brown South Course is famous among golfers because the ball must soar over a stretch of open ocean to complete play. Rates are $75 for guests, $150 for nonguests. All golfing fees are subject to change.

Hiking and Camping For the hardy and fit adventurer, hiking is a great way to explore the Big Island's natural beauty. In addition to hiking on Mauna Kea and into Kilauea Iki Crater (*see* Tour 1 in Exploring the Big Island, *above*), a little-known trek to the top of 13,680-foot **Mauna Loa**, with overnight stops at two cabins, one at 10,000 feet and the other at the summit, can be arranged. *Write to the superintendent, Hawaii Volcanoes National Park, Volcano 96743. The cabins are free but must be reserved well in advance.*

Namakani Paio Cabins, at the 4,000-foot level 3 miles beyond the Volcano House, are managed by Volcano House, a concession of the state of Hawaii. Each cabin has a double bed, two bunk beds, and electric lights. *Write to: Volcano House, Hawaii Volcanoes National Park, Box 53, Volcano 96718-0053, tel. 808/967–7321. A $15 refundable deposit allows guests to pick up bedding and keys (for the cabins and separate bath facilities) at Volcano House. Guests should bring extra blankets, because it gets cold. Rates: $24 single or double.*

For information on cabins at state parks, including Hapuna Beach Park and the three campgrounds at Kilauea, write to the **Department of Parks and Recreation** (25 Aupuni St., Hilo 96740, tel. 808/961–8311).

Two Oahu-based companies offer a variety of guided hikes on all islands: **Pacific Quest** (Box 205, Haleiwa 96712, tel. 808/638–8338 or 800/776–2518) and **Wilderness Hawaii** (Box 61692, Honolulu 96839, tel. 808/737–4697), which specializes in Big Island back-packing trips and hiking in Volcanoes National Park.

Horseback Riding Some hotels, such as **Mauna Kea Beach Hotel** (1 Mauna Kea Beach Dr., Kohala Coast 96743, tel. 808/885–4288), maintain stables for their guests' use, while others offer transportation to commercial stables. Ask at your hotel Activities Desk. From the Kohala Coast and Kailua-Kona, excellent guided rides are offered by:

Ironwood Outfitters at Kohala Ranch (take Hwy. 250 to the 11-mi marker; Box 832, Kamuela 96743, tel. 808/885–4941). This group offers daily rides at 8 and 10 AM on a 30,000-acre mountain ranch in the Kohala Mountains. Groups are kept small, and the views are of the misty highlands trailing down to the blue Pacific.

King's Trail Rides O'Kona, Inc. (Box 1366, Kealakekua 96750, tel. 808/323–2388 or 808/323–2890). Kealakekua Ranch, located 20 minutes from Kailua-Kona at the 111-mile marker on Highway 11, offers one- and two-hour rides and a 4½-hour excursion (two hours of riding the range, lunch, and exploring the historic dairy and original owner's cabin are included). Prices range from $50 to $79. Custom rides can be arranged.

Waikoloa Village Stables (Box 3466, Waikoloa Village 96743, tel. 808/883–9335) gives riding lessons.

Hunting Among its fantasy-vacation offerings, the Hyatt Regency Waikoloa offers guests the chance to hunt in paradise, but on the Big Island, hunting is not a fantasy. Anyone can make their own arrangements by contacting **Hawaii Hunting Tours** (Box 58, Paauilo 96766, tel. 808/776–1666) or **McCandless Ranch Gentleman's Hunt** (Kai Malino, tel. 808/328–2389). Game in Hawaii includes pheasant, turkeys, wild boar, and sheep. Hunting licenses are issued annually by the **State Department of Land and Natural Resources** (75 Aupuni St., Hilo, tel. 808/961–7291). Permits for birds and mammals are issued daily during the season, generally from the first weekend in November to the third weekend in January. The season is set by the Forestry and Wildlife Division and fluctuates according to game availability.

Skiing Skiing on Mauna Kea is for experienced adventure skiers only. Currently there are no equipment-rental facilities, nor does the ski area have a lodge or lifts. Christopher Langan of Mauna Kea Ski Corporation runs **Ski Guides Hawaii** (Box 1954, Kamuela 96743, tel. 808/889–6398, or in ski season, tel. 808/885–4188), which is licensed to furnish transportation, guide services, and ski equipment on Mauna Kea. Snow might fall from Thanksgiving through June, but the most likely months are February and March. For an eight-hour day trip for up to six people, Langen charges $100 to $150 per person, including refreshments and a mountaintop lunch. On an Alii Tour, for $250 he'll take you to places accessible by snowmobile where few have ever skied.

Tennis School and park courts are free and open to anyone who wishes to play, though students have first priority during school hours at high school courts. In Hilo, you will find courts at the **University of Hawaii–Hilo campus** (333 West Lanikaula St.); there are four free, lighted courts at **Lincoln Park** (Kinoole and Ponahawai Sts.). The eight courts (three lighted for night play) at **Hilo Tennis Stadium** (Piilani and Kalanikoa Sts.) charge a small fee. **Waiakea Racket Club** (400 Hualani St., Hilo 96720, tel. 808/961–5499) is also open to the public for a reasonable fee.

Across the island, the Keauhou-Kona resorts have become renowned for their beautiful tennis courts. **Holua Stadium** is a headquarters for exhibition tennis. One of the few courts where not-so-heavy hitters can play free is at **Kailua Playground**—the wait may be long, however. Nonguests can play for a fee at the **Kona Surf Hotel's Racquet Club** and on the four courts at the **Kona Hilton Beach and Tennis Resort** (*see* Lodging, *below*). At the **Hotel King Kamehameha** (*see* Lodging, *below*) nonguests may purchase memberships to play. Farther afield, there are two free, lighted courts at **Waimea Park** (on Hwy. 19) in Waimea, while courts at the **Royal Waikoloan, Waikoloa Village,** and **Sea Mountain Resort** (*see* Lodging, *below*) are open at an hourly charge. **Ritz-Carlton Mauna Lani's** 10 courts and one exhibition court, and **Mauna Kea Beach Resort's** 13 courts in a beautiful 12-acre tennis park, are also open to the public for a fee.

Resorts offering tennis for guests only include: **Mauna Lani Bay Resort, Hyatt Regency Waikoloa,** and **Kona Village Resort** (*see* Lodging, *below*). Closer to the town of Kailua-Kona, the following also have courts for guests only: **Kona Makai** (75-6026 Alii Dr., Kailua-Kona 96740, tel. 808/329–1511), **White Sands** (77–6469 Alii Dr., Kailua-Kona 96740, tel. 808/329–1264), **Kanaloa** (78-261 Manukai St., Kailua-Kona 96740, tel. 808/322–2272), and the **Keauhou-Kona Surf and Racquet Club** (78-6800 Alii Dr., Keauhou 96740, tel. 808/322–9131).

Water Sports
Deep-Sea Fishing

In Kona, excitement about game fishing hits a peak in July, August, and September, when a number of tournaments are held, but charter fishing goes on year-round. You don't have to be in a tournament to experience the thrill of landing a big Pacific blue marlin or a mahi, tuna, wahoo, or other game fish. More than 50 charter boats, averaging 36 to 42 feet, are available for hire, most of them out of Honokohau Harbor, just north of Kailua. Prices for a full day of fishing begin at about $300 and average $450, though there are a few luxury boats in the $500–$700 range. Half-day charters are also available in the $200 range and might be preferable if you've never experienced dawn-to-dusk fishing. Tackle and soft drinks are furnished. Most boats do not allow you to keep your catch, although it doesn't hurt to ask. Ask your hotel to pack a box lunch or purchase one at the Kona Marlin Center at Honokohau Harbor. If you want to bring stronger refreshments, most boats allow beer or liquor on board.

The biggest of the fishing tournaments is the **Hawaiian International Billfish Tournament** at the beginning of August, which attracts teams from around the world. During the HIBT, the Richard Boone Award is given by participating anglers. This award lists in order the boats on which tournament participants would most prefer to fish; the listing can serve as a helpful guide in choosing which boat to charter. In addition, be sure to describe your expectations when you book your charter so the booking agent can match you with a captain and a boat you will like.

Tournament catches are often weighed in at the pier adjacent to the Hotel King Kamehameha in Kailua-Kona, which, because of its central location, is a popular headquarters for tournament participants and viewers. Both old and young head for either the Kailua Pier or Honokohau Harbor's Fuel Dock between 4 and 5 PM to watch the weigh-in of the day's catch. *Make* arrangements for deep-sea fishing at your hotel Activities Desk or call the Kona Activities Center (tel. 808/329–3171 or 800/367–5299) for information. At Honokohau Harbor, book charters or get information on tournaments from the Kona Marlin Center, 74-381 Kealakehe Pkwy., Kailua-Kona 96740, tel. 808/329-7529 or 800/648-7529.

Diving Two-tank dives should cost from $65 to $75, depending on whether they are in one or two locations and if they are dives from a boat or from the shore. Many dive outfits have underwater cameras for rent, in case you're lucky enough to glimpse humpback whales and their calves during the winter months or simply want to capture colorful reef fish on film. Instruction with PADI certification in three to five days is approximately $100 per day. The Kona Coast has calm waters for diving, and dive operators there are helpful about suggesting dive sites. A 24-page guidebook giving the top 40 scuba and snorkeling sites on all islands and a listing of dive businesses is available for $2 from **University of Hawaii** (Seagrant Extension MSB, 1000 Pope Rd., Honolulu, HI 96822). Reputable scuba charters to consider in Kailua are: **Big Island Divers** (74–425 Kealakehe Pkwy #7, Kailua-Kona 96740, tel. 808/329–6068); **Gold Coast Divers** (75-5744 Alii Dr., Kailua-Kona 96740, tel. 808/329–1328), which offers classes, night and shore dives, and free snorkeling maps; and **Fair Wind Sailing and Diving Adventures** (78-7128 Kaleopapa Rd., Kailua-Kona 96740, tel. 808/322–2788). At Anaeho'omalu Bay at Waikoloa Resort, the friendly operators at **Red Sail Sports** (1 Waikoloa Beach Dr., Waikoloa 96743, tel. 808/885–2876) organize scuba dives from the 38-foot *Lanikai.* First-time divers might want to ask about **Snuba,** which alleviates the apprehension and discomfort of scuba novices by having divers breathe through an air hose connected to an overhead raft that carries the cumbersome air tanks.

Dive Sites **Aquarium,** in Kealakekua Bay, is a state underwater park with depths from 15 to 110 feet, and is a popular place for introductory boat dives. A variety of tame fish that can be fed by hand hang around here.

Pine Trees, in North Kona, is an area that includes sites such as Carpenter's House, Golden Arches, and Pyramid Pinnacles— two underwater lava towers with tubes, arches, and large schools of butterflyfish and false moorish idols. Depths run from 10 to 50 feet.

Plane Wreck Point, off Keahole Point, is for expert divers only. A Twin Beechcraft airplane lies broken in half on a sand bottom 115 feet down. Damselfish, fantail, filefish, and menpachi hover around in the shadows.

Red Hill, near Kainaliu, encompasses six different sites of large caverns and lava tubes. Sites include Boat Wreck Reef, Long Lava Tube, and Fantasy Reef. Sea life in the area includes encrusting sponges, octopus, shells, sleeping reef sharks, and abundant tropical fishes. Depths range from 25 to 70 feet.

Parasailing/ Windsurfing These are two of the newer water sports, and both are generally considered quite safe. Parasailers sit in a harness attached to a parachute that lifts off from the boat deck until they are sailing aloft. Call **Kona Water Sports** (75-56956 Alii Dr., Kailua-Kona 96745, tel. 808/329–1593) to make arrangements for parasailing.

One of the best windsurfing locations on the Big Island is at Anaehoomalu Bay, on the beach in front of the Royal Waikoloan Resort. You can take lessons or rent equipment right at the resort's beach services desk (Waikoloa Rd., Kohala Coast, tel. 808/885–6789).

Sailing/Snorkeling Among the Big Island's wet and wild offerings is the **Captain Zodiac Raft Expedition** (Box 5612, Kailua 96740, tel. 808/329–3199) along the Kona Coast. The four-hour trip begins at Honokohau Harbor, pokes into gaping lava-tube caves, and drifts through Kealakeua Bay where passengers can enjoy snorkeling and a light tropical lunch. Arrangements can be made for a six-hour land/sea trip that also includes a van ride to a macadamia nut factory, a Kona coffee plantation, and St. Benedict's Painted Church. St. Benedict's was originally painted at the turn of the century by its priest, who wanted it to look like a European cathedral; it was recently restored. Other excursions are shorter: January through April you might see the humpback whales, and private charters can be arranged. If you love water and crave adventure, sit at the front edge of the inflatable raft for an exciting, bouncy, wind-in-your-hair ride. Wear a bathing suit (you'll get a chance for snorkeling) and take a towel, sunscreen, and camera. Captain Zodiac furnishes a plastic bag to keep your possessions high and dry.

For a more sedate daytime cruise, the **Captain Cook VIII** (Hawaiian Cruises Ltd., 74-5543 Kaiwi Bay 11; Kailua-Kona 96740, tel. 808/329–6411) takes more than a look through its glass bottom at the fishy underworld. The boat departs from Kailua Pier, and its destination is historic Kealakekua Bay, where Captain Cook met his death at the hands of Kamehameha's men in 1779. Today the bay is a snorkeler's paradise. The glassbottom boat picks up passengers at 8:30 AM for a 4½-hour cruise; the cost is $40. Hawaiian Cruises' *Hawaiian Princess* is also available for charter groups.

Polynesian entertainers liven the decks of Captain Beans' 150-foot *Tamure* (Captain Beans' Kona Voyagers, 74–5626 Alapapa St., B–17, Kailua-Kona 96740, tel. 808/329–2955) as it departs Kailua Pier headed for Kealakekua Bay. A 4½-hour swim and snorkel sail departs at 8:30 AM, or you might opt for the one-hour sail leaving at 1:30 PM *(see* Dinner Cruise in Nightlife, *below).*

The family-owned and operated **Fair Wind Sail and Diving Adventures** sails for 4½ hours from Keauhou Bay at 8:30 AM to Kealakekua Bay. The 50-foot glass-bottom trimaran has a super water slide, inner tubes, and snorkel and scuba gear. *78-7128 Kaleopapa Rd., Kailua-Kona 96740, tel. 808/322–2788. Lunch and gear are included for $54 adults, $30 children 5–12. The 3½-hour afternoon sail departs at 1 PM.*

Romantics might choose **Discovery Charters** (75–293 Aloha Kona Dr., Kailua-Kona 96740, tel. 808/326–1011) for a half-day, full-day, sunset, or overnight cruise on the 45-foot luxury yacht, *Discovery.* Owners Bob and Carol Hogan fill all kinds of special requests, supplying chartered meals, kayaking, and stops at deserted bays. Rates range from $275 to $1,250 for two to six passengers.

Many snorkel and scuba cruises are available. Shop for prices, ask the size of the boat, make sure you know what is included and how much the extras (e.g., underwater cameras) cost.

Spectator Sports

Ample opportunities for celebrity-spotting exist at a growing number of golf tournaments held at resort golf courses in the Kohala area. The biggest and best attended is the **Senior Skins Game** at Mauna Lani Resort, which attracts competitors the caliber of Arnold Palmer, Jack Nicklaus, Lee Trevino, Chi Chi Rodrigues, and Gary Player, all competing for their share of $450,000 in prizes. Open only to PGA members, this tournament kicks off the year in January, usually on Super Bowl weekend. For information, call 808/885–6655.

With the University of Hawaii–Hilo campus the only major college on the Big Island, such spectator sports as football and baseball exist only at the high school level. Volleyball is popular on the University of Hawaii–Hilo campus and the school plays Division 1 baseball. Information about scheduled competition can be obtained by calling tel. 808/961–9520. The Gatorade Ironman Triathlon and polo attract record-breaking crowds.

Gatorade Ironman Triathlon. We call this a spectator sport because it is getting more and more difficult to get into the event. The Ironman is limited to 1,250 competitors, who do a 2.4-mile open-water swim, run a 26.2-mile marathon, and bicycle 112 miles, and most entrants must qualify by doing well in other international competitions, though a few slots are awarded by lottery. The annual competition begins with a swim from Kailua Pier at 7 AM on a Saturday at the beginning of October. Spectators cheer on their favorite contestants from vantage points along Alii Drive and the Queen Ka'ahumanu Highway. The course closes at midnight. *75-5737 Kuakini Hwy., Suite 208, Kailua-Kona 96740, tel. 808/329–0063.*

Waiki'i Ranch Polo. Games are on Sunday, from September through December. *Just off Saddle Road, 6½ mi from Mamalahoa Hwy., tel. 808/885–0538. For information about summer games, polo lessons, and polo vacations, contact Suite 125, Box 111333, Kamuela, HI 96743. Admission: $3.*

Dining

Choosing a place to eat in the western part of the Big Island has become more difficult than in the past—not because of a lack of fine restaurants, but because there are many good, established restaurants and several more new and exciting places to try. In 1989, the dining/shopping complex called Waterfront Row opened on Alii Drive. Waterfront Row is built to reflect Kailua's seafaring past, with antiques and ship models displayed along the wooden decks. A 45-foot observation tower, accessible by glass elevator, is equipped with telescopes for whale watching. Within the complex, the old Spindrifter Restaurant has been remodeled and renamed the Jolly Roger, the two-story oceanfront Chart House is the Row's outstanding showplace, and Phillip Paolo's dishes up fabulous pastas and other Italian specialties. Watch for additional restaurants to open at this oceanfront food arcade.

Little Waimea also has an array of restaurants. With the Kohala Coast resorts established, more and more visitors are willing to make the 40-minute drive inland for a change from hotel dining. Merriman's and the Edelweiss are the ventures of two respected hotel chefs who have gone into business for themselves in Waimea. Hartwell's at Hale Kea offers a choice of settings (the Library, the Paniolo Room, the Sun Room, and the Pa'u Room) in which to enjoy its imaginative cuisine.

Hilo's dining scene, in contrast, has remained fairly stable. Hilo's restaurants are generally lower-priced family places where the food makes up for any lack in atmosphere. Fast-food restaurants can be found along Hilo's Kilauea Avenue, while near Kailua-Kona McDonald's golden arches are beside Kuakini Highway 11 and a Burger King is on Palani Road (Hwy. 190).

Highly recommended restaurants in each area are indicated by a star ★.

Category	Cost*
Very Expensive	over $60
Expensive	$40–$60
Moderate	$20–$40
Inexpensive	under $20

per person, without sales tax (4%), service, or drinks

Hilo

American **Harrington's.** A popular and reliable steak and seafood
★ restaurant with 27 tables right on Reeds Bay, Harrington's has a dining lanai that extends over the water. The fresh ono or mahimahi meunière, served with browned butter, lemon, and parsley, and the Slavic steak, thinly sliced and slathered with garlic butter, are two outstanding dishes. *135 Kalanianaole St., tel. 808/961–4966. Reservations advised. Dress: neat but casual. MC, V. Closed Christmas Day. Inexpensive–Moderate.*

Dick's Coffee House. The locals line up for breakfast on weekends at this old-fashioned coffee shop with its rows of low-backed booths—the price is right and everyone knows everyone else. Wall lamps and a big collection of football pennants set the mood for standard coffee shop fare. Try the "local boy favorite," fried rice topped with an egg and three crisp wonton on the side, or go for the chicken cutlet or chop steak Hawaiian, topped off with a hot fudge sundae. *Hilo Shopping Center, 1235 Kilauea Ave., tel. 808/935–2769. No reservations. Dress: casual. MC, V. No lunch or dinner Sun. Inexpensive.*

Fiasco's. Booths with floor-to-ceiling dividers permit complete privacy in this cheerful restaurant that has something for everyone, from tasty fajitas and snacks to a garden-fresh fruit and salad bar. Porterhouse steak at $14 is Fiasco's most expensive item. Margarita specials and 23 varieties of domestic and imported beer liven the menu—not to mention the imbibers. *200 Kanoelehua Ave., tel. 808/935–7666. Weekend reservations advised. Dress: casual. MC, V. Closed Labor Day and Christmas Day. Inexpensive.*

Ken's Pancake House. For years, this 24-hour coffee shop has been a gathering place for Hilo residents for breakfast. Situated between the airport and the Banyan Drive hotels, Ken's serves good pancakes and omelets—they're cheap, too. Local

The Batik at Mauna Kea Beach Hotel, **8**

Café Pesto, (a.k.a.) We're Talking Pizza, **2**

The Canoe House at the Mauna Lani Bay Hotel, **13**

Cascades at the Hyatt Regency Waikoloa, **18**

Cattleman's Steakhouse, **5**

Chart House at Waterfront Row, **27**

d' Angoras, **41**

Dick's Coffee House, **40**

The Dining Room, **12**

Donatoni's at the Hyatt Regency Waikoloa, **16**

Edelweiss, **6**

Fiasco's, **42**

Fisherman's Landing, **25**

Gallery at Mauna Lani Resort, **11**

The Garden at Mauna Kea Beach Hotel, **9**

The Grill and Lounge, **12**

Hale Samoa at Kona Village Resort, **19**

Harrington's, **44**

Hartwell's Restaurant at Hale Kea, **3**

Hele Mai at Kona Hilton Beach and Tennis Resort, **29**

Huggo's, **31**

Imari at the Hyatt Regency Waikoloa, **17**

Jameson's by the Sea, **33**

Jolly Roger, **28**

Ka Ohelo Room, **38**

Kana Zawa-Tei, **32**

Ken's Pancake House, **43**

Knicker's at the Mauna Lani Resort, **14**

The Kona Beach Restaurant at Hotel King Kamehameha, **20**

Kona Inn Restaurant, **24**

Kona Provision Company at Hyatt Regency Waikoloa, **15**

Kona Ranch House, **21**

La Bourgogne, **34**

Lehua's Bay City Bar and Grill, **46**

Le Soleil at Mauna Lani Bay Hotel, **10**

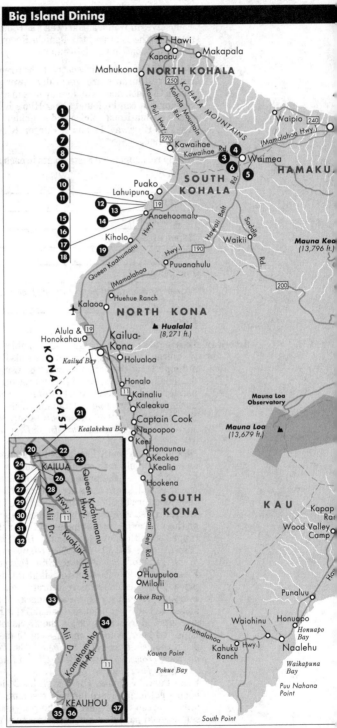

Big Island Dining

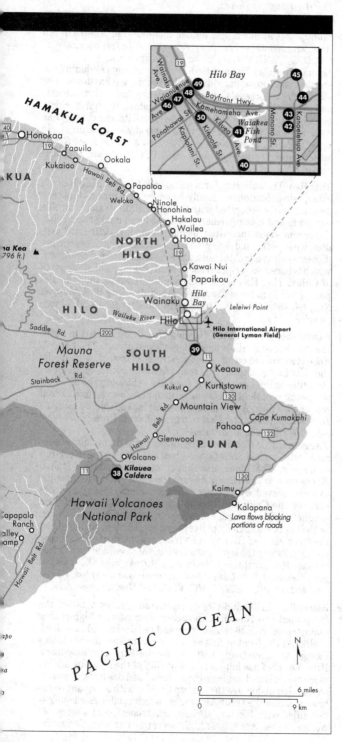

Makee Restaurant at the Kona Surf Resort, **35**

Merriman's, **4**

Ocean View Inn, **22**

Palm Cafe, **30**

Pavilion at Mauna Kea Beach Hotel, **7**

Pescatore's, **49**

Phillip Paolo's at Waterfront Row, **26**

Players, **49**

Restaurant Fuji at the Hilo Hotel, **47**

Roussel's, **48**

Royal Siam, **50**

Rusty Harpoon, **23**

Sandalwood Room at the Naniloa Hotel, **45**

Teshima's, **37**

Ting Hao, **39**

Tres Hombres Beach Grill, **1**

favorites, such as hot and cold sandwiches, steaks, and fish, round out the lunch and dinner menus. *1730 Kamehameha Ave., tel. 808/935–8711. No reservations. Dress: casual. AE, CB, D, DC, MC, V. Open 24 hours. Inexpensive.*

Lehua's Bay City Bar and Grill. Popular among residents (diners all seem to know each other), this restaurant has doubled its seating area. A casual California ambience, live entertainment, and good food—crisp salads, shrimp scampi, fresh fish, chicken, ribs, steak, and rich homemade chocolate and cheese cake desserts—are all served up in this centrally located, funky old wood building. *11 Waianuenue Ave., tel. 808/935–8055. Reservations accepted for 5 or more. MC, V. Closed Sun. Inexpensive.*

Chinese **Ting Hao.** The only Mandarin restaurant in town, Ting Hao is a clean, air-conditioned, family-oriented restaurant that has been modestly decorated with Chinese paintings and fans. The Szechuan and Hunan dishes may be ordered mild or spicy hot; the scrumptious specialties include dumplings, stir-fried noodles with pork, and spicy noodles with seafood. Vegetarian dishes, such as eggplant with garlic sauce, round out the menu, which is based on recipes from Taiwan, Peking, and other parts of China. Ting Hao is conveniently located near the Hilo airport. *Puainako Town Center (Kilauea Ave. and W. Kahaopea St.), tel. 808/959–6288. Dress: neat but casual. MC, V. Inexpensive.*

Continental **Sandalwood Room at the Naniloa Hotel.** Remodeled in 1990, this has become Hilo's most elegant restaurant. The Sandalwood Room opens on one side to a stretch of lawn that overlooks the Hilo Bay coastline. The menu features such local items as Hawaiian spiny-back lobster, fresh fish, chicken yakitori, and, on special occasions, a Hawaiian luau plate served in a carved monkeypod dish. An extensive wine list is available. *93 Banyan Dr., tel. 808/969–3333. Reservations advised. Dress: informal. AE, CB, DC, MC. Moderate.*

d'Angoras. This Continental restaurant and nightclub is decorated with etched and stained glass and blue and rose colored wallpaper. The lunch and dinner menus emphasize Italian dishes such as *capellini d'Angora* (thin spaghetti with marinara sauce served with Italian sausage and meatballs). For dinner, try the Cajun escargot followed by *pesto Genovese* (thin spaghetti with oysters, mussels, shrimp, clams, and scallops) or the captain's seafood platter (oysters, shrimp, scallops, and the fresh catch of the day deep fried in a thin batter). Dancing starts at 9 PM to the strains of a live band or disco, and there's free karaoke Monday through Wednesday. *101 Aupuni St., Hilo Lagoon Center, tel. 808/934–7888. Reservations accepted. Dress: neat but casual. AE, DC, MC, V. Closed Mon. Inexpensive.*

Creole **Roussel's.** This Cajun-Creole restaurant brings a bit of the ★ Deep South to Hawaii with arched doorways, a high-ceiling dining room with 16 tables, gray and red decor, and cane-back chairs. At the front of Roussel's, the cocktail lounge has tables facing the attractively restored Keawe Street in downtown Hilo. The chef has improved the quality of the menu by adding more specials and baking his own bread and desserts. Two recommended dishes are the shrimp Creole, with a piquant tomato sauce, and the trout Alexander, which combines a boneless fish fillet with lobster, shrimp, mushrooms, and sherry. *60 Keawe St., tel. 808/935–5111. Reservations advised. Dress: in-*

formal. AE, DC, MC, V. Closed the fourth of July, Christmas Day, and New Year's Day. Moderate.

Italian **Pescatore's.** Situated in downtown Hilo, Pescatore's achieves a friendly, intimate atmosphere with lace curtains on the windows, a miniature waterfall, and, to set the Italian mood, a display of pastas at the entrance. In addition to such traditional dishes as eggplant parmigiana and lasagne del Girono, Pescatore's serves a delicious *Fra Diavolo* (a combination of shrimp, clams, and fresh fish with spicy marinara sauce aromatic with garlic and basil). *235 Keawe St. at Haili St., tel. 808/ 969–9090. Reservations accepted. Dress: casual. DC, MC, V. Inexpensive.*

Japanese **Restaurant Fuji at the Hilo Hotel.** At this plain, rather noisy Japanese *teppan-yaki* restaurant, diners can stir-fry marinated steak or chicken right at the table on their personal grill or order from a regular menu. Tempura and teriyaki dishes are particularly well-prepared. Fuji has excellent service and caters to Big Island families. *142 Kinoole St., tel. 808/961–3733. Reservations advised on holidays. Dress: casual. AE, DC, MC, V. Closed Mon. Inexpensive–Moderate.*

Thai **Royal Siam.** Mild, medium, or hot and spicy are the choices for more than 50 Thai dishes based on chicken, beef, seafood, pork, and vegetables. Appetizers, daily specials, and delicious curries round out the menu at this small dining spot. *68 Mamo St., tel. 808/961–6100. Reservations accepted. Dress: casual. Closed Sun. MC, V. Inexpensive.*

Kohala-Kona-Keauhou

American★ **The Grill and Lounge.** Rich koa wood paneling and a long koa bar give this restaurant the feeling of an established club, and the food gives it a top-notch reputation. Choose from fresh asparagus and pastas to precede such grilled specialties as porterhouse steak, mahimahi with chili salsa, and fillet of onaga with mushroom-tomato sauce. There's dancing and entertainment nightly. *Ritz-Carlton, Mauna Lani, 1 N. Kaniku Dr., Kohala Coast, tel. 808/885–2000. Reservations advised. Dress: jackets for men; skirts or evening pants for women. AE, CB, D, DC, MC, V. Expensive.*

Makee Restaurant at the Kona Surf Resort. An uplifting setting with polished wood decor and garden and bay views enhances the Pacific Rim Cuisine. The chef recommends the lobster wonton soup flavored with a dash of sesame and garnished with snow peas and onions, or the warm salad of Hawaiian seafood— ono, opakapaka, mahimahi, crab, and prawns—served with lettuce and vegetables and a shallot and macadamia nut dressing. *78–128 Ehukai St., Keauhou, tel. 808/322–3411. Reservations advised. Dress: casual. AE, CB, D, DC, MC, V. Expensive.*

Chart House at Waterfront Row. This spectacular two-story restaurant in the shopping and dining complex on Alii Drive overlooks the ocean. Koa-wood booths, a waterfall, and floral arrangements complement the fine artwork displayed in the restaurant. Dinners of thickly sliced prime rib, fresh local fish, and Alaskan king crab come with unlimited salad service and squaw (sourdough) bread. *75-5770 Alii Dr., Kailua-Kona, tel. 808/941–6669. Reservations accepted. Dress: casual. AE, DC, MC, V. Moderate.*

The Pavilion at the Mauna Kea Beach Hotel. Whether you have a macadamia-waffle breakfast, or dinner from the menu, featuring lighter, California-style cuisine, the spectacular view of Kauna'oa Bay at this restaurant is mesmerizing. The spacious, airy interior, with arrangements of orchids and other tropical flowers, encourages diners to linger over coffee. Local seafood, veal scallopini on crisp risotto cake, and a selection of kiawe-grilled meats are artfully presented with good health in mind. The Pavilion is in a resort hotel on Highway 19 on the Kohala coast, a half hour from Ke-ahole Airport. *1 Mauna Kea Beach Dr., Kohala Coast, tel. 808/882–7222. Reservations advised. Dress: casual. AE, DC, MC, V. Moderate.*

Fisherman's Landing. Cobblestone paths lead to an elaborate display of fresh fish on ice at the entrance. Inside you'll find tropical foliage and saltwater ponds with reef fish and fountains. Five open-air dining rooms, divided by water and walkways, overlook the ocean in a relaxing, romantic setting that is more inspiring than the seafood and Oriental and Polynesian entrées served here. However, the steak and lobster, fresh fish, and shrimp Louis are *ono* (good). *75-5739 Alii Dr., Kailua-Kona, tel. 808/326–2555. Dress: informal. AE, CB, D, DC, MC, V. Moderate.*

Huggo's. The open windows look out over the rocks at the ocean's edge, so you can actually feed the fish, if you wish. Fresh local seafood (mahimahi, shrimp scampi) is the safest bet on the menu, though the prime rib is also recommended. *75-5828 Kahakai St., Kailua-Kona, tel. 808/329–1493. Reservations advised for parties of 6 or more. Dress: informal. AE, D, DC, MC, V. Moderate.*

Jameson's by the Sea. Sit outside next to the ocean or just inside the picture windows for glorious sunset views over Magic Sands Beach. The co-owner and chef serves three or four island fish specials daily, plus a tasty baked shrimp stuffed with crab and garnished with hollandaise sauce. *77–6452 Alii Dr., Kailua-Kona, tel. 808/329–3195. Reservations advised. Dress: casual. AE, DC, MC, V. Closed Christmas Day. Moderate.*

Knicker's at the Mauna Lani Resort. This open-air restaurant, opened in 1989, overlooks the Francis H. I'i Brown Golf Course. Mahogany paneling, 26 teak tables in the restaurant, and nine in the lounge, which is highlighted by a massive koa bar, create a comfortable clubhouse atmosphere. Dinner entrées include sautéed island snapper with artichokes and mushrooms in a brown butter sauce, and a bouillabaise of fish, lobster, shrimp, and shellfish enchanced with saffron and pernod. *Off Hwy. 19, ½ hour from Ke-ahole Airport, 1 Kaniku Dr., Kohala Coast, tel. 808/885–6699. Reservations advised. Dress: casual. AE, MC, V. Moderate.*

The Kona Beach Restaurant at the Hotel King Kamehameha. At this centrally located major hotel in the Kailua-Kona area, the tables, positioned near large windows, look out on a torch-lit lawn; beyond is the beach, with outrigger canoes and a thatch house built on a restored heiau (temple). Some of the tantalizing entrées served here are the mixed grill for two (with baby back ribs, Kona broil, and chicken breast), kiawe-grilled prime rib and fresh local catch, and Maine lobster. The Sunday champagne brunch is served from 9 to 1. *75-5660 Palani Rd., Kailua-Kona, tel. 808/329–2911. Reservations advised. Dress: informal. AE, D, DC, MC, V. Moderate.*

Kona Provision Company at the Hyatt Regency Waikoloa. You'll have a spectacular view of the Kona-Kohala coastline as you sample excellent salad selections, broiled and grilled steak, or seafood at this restaurant. Tables along the lanai open to sea breezes, while ceiling fans cool the rest of the dining room, which seats 189 people. Before or after dinner, sip cocktails on the lanai that overlooks the resort's impressive waterfall and swimming pool. The fresh fish include all the Hawaiian favorites: opakapaka (pink snapper), ono, onaga, mano, and more, and you can order it sautéed, grilled, poached, or blackened. *HCO 2, Box 5500, Waikoloa, tel. 808/885–1234. Reservations advised. Dress: informal. AE, DC, MC, V. Moderate.*

Kona Inn Restaurant. This open-air restaurant, which faces a wide lawn with the ocean beyond, has been a longtime favorite for cocktails at sunset. The fresh fish and chicken entrées are consistently delectable. Burgers at lunch are generously sized and reasonably priced, while the most expensive dinner item is a shellfish platter of scampi, scallops, and lobster. *75-5744 Alii Dr., Kailua-Kona, tel. 808/329–4455. Reservations advised. Dress: informal. AE, MC, V. Inexpensive–Moderate.*

Jolly Roger. This restaurant with a nautical theme and pink-and-gray decor sits right at the ocean's edge, though some of the 100 tables are set back from the water. We recommend the Jolly Roger for a leisurely breakfast rather than for dinner. Try the 4-ounce steak and a half order of eggs Benedict with a papaya wedge. Smaller appetites opt for the bargain-priced breakfast special described on the signboard out front. *75-5776 Alii Dr., tel. 808/329–1344. No reservations. Dress: informal. AE, DC, MC, V. Inexpensive.*

Kona Ranch House. This reliable dining spot is known in the area for its reasonable prices and pleasant service. The Kona Ranch House has two sections; the Plantation Lanai is preferable, with its turn-of-the-century Hawaiian wicker furniture, tablecloths, and candles. The adjoining Paniolo Room serves food from the same kitchen, but the decor is simple café-style, with booths and no tablecloths. The fresh local fish and big barbecue platters warrant the short walk up the hill from the Hotel King Kamehameha. *75-5653 Olioli St., Kailua-Kona, tel. 808/329–7061. Reservations advised for the Plantation Lanai. Dress: neat but casual. AE, MC, V. Inexpensive.*

Ocean View Inn. If you're on a tight budget, this local hangout with an ocean view is a lifesaver for breakfast, lunch, and dinner. Chinese, American, and Hawaiian food are on the plate-lunch menu. Although there's no atmosphere, the servings are ample. *Alii Dr. near Palani Rd., Kailua-Kona, tel. 808/329–9998. Dress: casual. No credit cards. Closed Mon. Inexpensive.*

Tres Hombres Beach Grill. Featuring lanai dining as well as tables set beside open windows that overlook the fishing fleet at Kawaihae Harbor, this cute, clean, and casual Mexican restaurant offers a good and less expensive lunch and dinner alternative for those who are staying at Kohala Coast resorts. Mexican beer and specialty drinks (some are non-alcoholic) promote conviviality in the lounge, which has a '50s Surf City look, with a thatch roof over surfboard tables. Burgers, sandwiches, and huevos rancheros are served at lunch. Dinner items include Tex-Mex combinations, sashimi, Caesar salad, and gazpacho, and a "Fit-for-life" menu offers tofu and black bean tacos, and other low-fat entrées. *Wharf Rd. and Mahukona Hwy., Kawaihae Center, tel. 808/882–1031. Reservations accepted. Dress: casual. AE, DC, MC, V. Inexpensive.*

Continental **The Batik at the Mauna Kea Beach Hotel.** For a very special
★ night out, capture the spirit of Sri Lanka at the Batik, with its
furnishings of tangerine and pink tapestries, Ceylonese batiks,
brass service plates, and an *houdah* (used by the Asian upper
class when riding on the back of an elephant). Chef Jean Marc
Heim sprinkles the menu with Indian curries, as well as Continental and regional dishes that satisfy the most discriminating
palates. Enticing choices include roasted duck served with papaya and honey-lime sauce, and grilled tiger prawns with red-
pepper coulis. The extensive wine list includes French Bor-
deaux and burgundies and good California wines. The Batik
overlooks Kauna'oa Bay. *1 Mauna Kea Beach Dr., Kohala
Coast, tel. 808/882–7222. Reservations advised. Jacket and tie
required. AE, D, DC, MC, V. Expensive.*

The Dining Room. Chef Amy Ferguson-Ota presides over this
formal French dining room with upholstered furniture, blue
tapestry draperies, and tables decked in spotless linen. Exquisite presentation of imaginative cuisine—tender salmon appetizer, braised kumu fillet with woodland mushrooms, venison
accompanied by mashed sweet potato, walnut-garnished goat
cheese with vinaigrette dressing, and for dessert, strawberry
sunburst with almond cream and fresh mint—make dining
here a gourmand's pleasure. *Ritz-Carlton, Mauna Lani, 1 N.
Kaniku Dr., Kohala Coast, tel. 808/885–2000. Reservations
advised. Jacket required. AE, D, DC, MC, V. Expensive.*

★ **The Garden at Mauna Kea Beach Hotel.** This restaurant features beautiful Polynesian decor with table settings of Hawaiian koa and teak alongside French and Belgian crystal. Every
item on the menu is grown or raised in Hawaii. Ohelo-berry-
glazed wild boar, breast of pheasant, and Pacific lobster and
prawns with melon and ginger sabayon are among the imaginative offerings guaranteed to please. The Garden is in a resort
hotel overlooking Kauna'oa Bay on the Kohala Coast (on Hwy.
19, a half hour north of Ke-ahole Airport). *1 Mauna Kea Beach
Dr., Kohala Coast, tel. 808/882–7222. Reservations advised.
Jacket and tie required. AE, CB, D, DC, MC, V. Expensive.*

★ **Gallery at Mauna Lani Resort.** Apart from the hotel at the tennis complex and surrounded by a golf course, the Gallery has a
cozy, cheerful atmosphere that is enhanced by a friendly staff.
A huge picture window on one side overlooks an exhibition tennis court. The restaurant has gained a reputation for unique
cuisine with Pacific Rim touches. The chef is continuing a tradition of using fresh, island ingredients in new and creative ways,
and you can make personal requests as well. The attractive
menu includes tasty appetizers, such as grilled chicken with
macadamia nut sauce and shrimp in phyllo, and such entrées as
sautéed scallops with *lilikoi* (passion fruit) and cilantro sauce
and fillet of steak *kiana* with shiitake mushrooms and cream
sauce. *Off Hwy. 19, Kalahuipuaa, Kohala Coast, tel. 808/885–
7777. Reservations advised. Dress: informal. AE, MC, V.
Moderate.*

Hele Mai at the Kona Hilton Beach and Tennis Resort. This
open-air dining room overlooks Kailua Bay; at dusk, when the
sun outlines the boats bobbing offshore, you'll have a lovely,
peaceful view. Jumbo prawns, fresh fish, and scallops are all
winning choices. Big eaters can go for the 22-ounce rib-eye-
steak special. *Within walking distance of central Kailua-
Kona; 75-5852 Alii Dr., Kailua, tel. 808/329–3111. Reservations required. Dress: neat but casual. AE, CB, D, DC, MC, V.
No dinner Sun., Mon. Moderate.*

Palm Café. Opened in 1991 by Daniel Thibaut, the chef who gained renown at the Mauna Kea Beach Hotel with his Pacific Rim cookery, this restaurant is one to seek out. Open-air views to the ocean, rattan chairs, and a carpet patterned with palm trees give a tropical feel. The French-Asian cuisine is imaginative: One tempting appetizer spreads scallops and shrimp between two thick layers of puff pastry with Hawaiian chile curry sauce. Fresh wok-fried sea scallops, Keahole koho salmon with Maui onion confit, roasted loin of veal, and spiny lobster with black-bean sauce are popular entrées. This is one of the few places that serves hot desserts—try fruit gratin in a glazed custard. White chocolate and ginger ice cream is a Palm Café exclusive. *75–5819 Alii Dr., Kailua-Kona 96740, tel. 808/329–7765. Dress: casual. AE, MC, V. Moderate.*

Rusty Harpoon. The pleasant peach decor, matched with natural oak and highlighted with the work of local artists, makes this second-floor restaurant, which overlooks Kailua-Kona's main street, the prettiest in the village center. Breakfast features waffles and French toast; lunch offers special soups. Baked or broiled fresh fish offerings are highlighted by stuffed ono; for traditionalists, the prime rib is certified Black Angus beef, cooked in rock salt to seal in the flavor. Top off dinner with amaretto cake. *75-5719 N. Alii Dr., Kailua-Kona, tel. 808/329–8881. Reservations advised for parties of 8 or more. Dress: informal. AE, D, DC, MC, V. Open for breakfast, lunch, and dinner. Inexpensive.*

French **Le Soleil at the Mauna Lani Bay Hotel and Bungalows.** This ele-
★ gant restaurant with 21 tables overlooks a tropical garden with waterfalls and fish ponds. The waiters wear tuxedos and pamper you as they serve such sumptuous delicacies as grilled veal chop stuffed with Big Island goat cheese or grilled ono (fish) and sundried tomato aioli, but it's the desserts that will do you in. Even if you order a pastry or flambé dessert specialty, every diner receives the Pele flambé bonbons (dry ice is used in a beautiful presentation) and finger bowls; footstools and roses for the ladies add to the delight of dining here. *Off Hwy. 19, ½ hour from Ke-ahole Airport, Box 4000, Hwy. 19, Kohala Coast, tel. 808/885–6622. Jacket required. AE, D, DC. Very Expensive.*

La Bourgogne. A genial husband-and-wife team owns this relaxing, country-style French restaurant with dark wood walls and blue velvet booths; it's just 4 miles out of town. Classic French cooking at its best keeps the 10 tables filled six nights a week. Chef Guy Chatelard is particularly proud of his sweetbreads of veal with Madeira sauce and his roast saddle of lamb with mustard sauce. *Kuakini Plaza S on Hwy. 11, 77-6400 Nalani St., Kailua-Kona, tel. 808/329–6711. Reservations advised (to be safe, call a couple of days in advance). Dress: informal. AE, CB, D, DC, MC, V. Closed Sun. Moderate.*

Italian **Donatoni's at the Hyatt Regency Waikoloa.** Lighter cuisine, shellfish, and the more subtle sauces of Italy, as well as specialty pizzas made to suit your personal tastes, are served in this romantic restaurant, complete with an accordion player during dinner. Reminiscent of an Italian villa overlooking a lagoon, Donatoni's seats 192 on multilevels so no view is obstructed. Prices on the extensive Italian wine and champagne list range from $14 to $39. *1 Waikoloa Beach Resort, HCO 2, Box 5500, Waikoloa, tel. 808/885–1234. Reservations advised. Dress: casual. AE, CB, D, DC, MC, V. Moderate.*

Phillip Paolo's at Waterfront Row. Portions are generous at this Italian (with a French flair) restaurant. Dining is on two levels in a Mediterranean setting by the water. The Giuseppe fettucine is a wonderful blend of fresh snow crabmeat sautéed in fresh basil and oregano and garnished with bacon and olives. Or you might try the osso bucco (veal), or the opakapaka with crab, shrimp, mushrooms, and capers served on oglio pasta. *75-5770 Alii Dr., Kailua-Kona 96740, tel. 808/329–4436. Reservations advised. Dress: casual. AE, MC, V. Inexpensive–Moderate.*

Café Pesto (a.k.a.) We're Talking Pizza. Even people who don't like pizza like the pizza made here. The chef uses fresh island ingredients in his version of nouvelle cuisine. Hint: You can have pizza al pesto, with sun-dried tomatoes, eggplant, and fresh basil pesto, delivered right to your hotel room. Twenty tables seat 65 at this harborside restaurant with a contemporary art-deco decor. *Wharf Rd. and Mahukona Hwy., Kawaihae Center, 1st Floor, Kawaihae, tel. 808/882–1071. Reservations advised for large groups. Dress: casual. Closed Thanksgiving and Christmas. MC, V. Inexpensive.*

Japanese **Imari at the Hyatt Regency Waikoloa.** The teriyakis and tempuras aimed to please mainland tastes are about the only way you can distinguish this Japanese restaurant, complete with waterfalls and a teahouse, from the most elegant of those in Japan. Beyond the display of Imari porcelain at the entrance, you'll find beef and chicken *shabu shabu* cooked at your table, complete teppan-yaki dinners prepared on a grill, and an outstanding sushi bar. Impeccable service by kimono-clad waitresses and modern, uncluttered Japanese decor (lacquer, bamboo, cloisonné vases, and Imari dinnerware in spotless, light surroundings) add to your dining pleasure. The restaurant seats 136. *1 Waikoloa Beach Resort, HCO 2, Box 5500, Waikoloa, tel. 808/885–1234. Reservations advised. Dress: informal. AE, DC, MC, V. Moderate.*

Kana Zawa-Tei. Located across the street from the Kona Hilton and within walking distance of the central hotels, Kana Zawa-Tei has the only sushi bar (seats 11) in Kailua. Traditionally clad waitresses serve patrons in this authentic Japanese restaurant, which is decorated with black lacquer booths, 18 oak tables, and lanterns. The *bento* specials come in a lacquer serving dish and allow you to sample tempura, sashimi, eel, lobster, and other items. Kana Zawa-Tei serves 32 varieties of sushi. *75-5845 Alii Dr., Kailua-Kona, tel. 808/326–1881. Dress: informal. AE, DC, MC, V. Moderate.*

Teshima's. The local lawyers and doctors show up at Teshima's whenever they're in the mood for some Big Island Japanese-American cooking. Don't expect a soothing ambience; Teshima's is on the dark and questionably clean side, with scarred booths and clattering dishes. Service is so-so, but residents come for the sashimi, sukiyaki, and puffy shrimp tempura. You might also want to try a *teishoku* (tray) of assorted Japanese delicacies. The teriyaki steak is under $10. *15 min. from Kailua-Kona on Mamalahoa Hwy. in Honalo, tel. 808/322–9140. Dress: casual. No credit cards. Open for breakfast, lunch, and dinner. Closed Christmas Day and New Year's Day. Inexpensive.*

Mixed Menu **Hale Samoa at Kona Village Resort.** Ferns, tapa screens, hurricane lamps, and mounted marlin and other fish, all bathed in the glow of sunset, set a magical mood at this Kona Village signature restaurant, with 18 tables. The escargots and artichokes, baked in Boursin cheese with garlic sauce, are heavenly, as are the Malaysian prawns stir-fried in black-bean sauce, both dreamed up by James Balanay, the Chinese-Filipino chef. The Hale Samoa serves Asian, French, and Hawaiian cuisines, while the prix fixe dinner includes appetizer, soup, salad, entrée, dessert, and coffee. The entry road to Kona Village is 7 miles out Highway 19 from Kailua; you'll see the thatch guard shack. *Box 1299, Kalipulehu, tel. 808/325-5555. Reservations required. Dress: informal. AE, CB, DC, MC, V. No lunch. Closed Wed., Fri., and 1 week in Dec. when resort is closed. Expensive.*

The Canoe House at the Mauna Lani Bay Hotel and Bungalows. This open-air, beachfront restaurant, surrounded by fishponds, was a welcome addition to the Kohala Coast dining scene in the fall of 1989. An enormous koa canoe is the focal point of this restaurant serving Pacific Rim cuisine; entrées include wok-fried sesame shrimp on crispy noodles with lilikoi glaze and bamboo-steamed mahimahi with ginger-scallion salsa and baby Chinese cabbage. *1 Mauna Lani Dr., Kohala Coast, tel. 808/885-6622. Reservations advised. Dress: casual. AE, D, DC, MC, V. Moderate.*

Players. This gem of a fine dining restaurant, located in a condominium complex at Keauhou, is worth seeking out for its intriguing, Japanese, Thai, Chinese, French, and Greek inspired flavors. Whether you choose blackened fish served with bechamel, basil, and lobster sauces; moussaka (lamb and eggplant); or roasted game hen with feta cheese, spinach, and garlic stuffing; you'll find that fresh Island ingredients highlight all entrées. A fine variety of wines, particularly Californian, is available. Diners may sit indoors or on a terrace overlooking a tennis stadium. *78-7190 Kaleleopapa Rd., Mauna Loa Village at Keauhou, tel. 808/322-2727. Reservations advised. Dress: informal. AE, MC, V. Closed Mon. Inexpensive–Moderate.*

Polynesian **Cascades at the Hyatt Regency Waikoloa.** This open-air restaurant, next to a cascading waterfall and a pond with swans floating by, seats 337. Cascades is open for breakfast and lunch (American-style omelets, etc.) and offers theme buffet dinners, such as a Polynesian buffet that includes curried veal, kalua pig, teriyaki beef, and seafood. *HCO 2, Box 5500, Waikoloa, tel. 808/885-1234. Dress: neat but casual. AE, DC, MC, V. Moderate.*

Waimea-Kamuela, Honokaa

American **Hartwell's Restaurant at Hale Kea.** Built in 1897 and named for a Parker Ranch manager who once lived here, this house is the centerpiece of the boutiques and shops at Hale Kea. Various rooms of the house—the Library, the Sun Room, the Pa'u Room, and the Paniolo Room—restored with period furnishings make Hartwell's seem like many restaurants in one. Parties of 12 or more can reserve a private room. Chef Dallas Nutter presents "Upcountry" cuisine, flavored with herbs grown on the property. Roast duckling with lilikoi sauce served with wild rice pancakes and a tenderloin in two sauces draw raves. A light dinner menu is available from 5 to 6:30. *Near entrance to Waimea on Kawaihae Rd., Box 982, Kamuela 96743, tel. 808/885-6095. Reservations advised. Dress: casual. AE, D, MC, V. Brunch and dinner on Sun. Moderate.*

Cattleman's Steakhouse. This steakhouse is fronted by a popular cocktail lounge with a bar and polished redwood tables. The dining room with white-topped tables and pink linen napkins overlooks a grassy field and the Kohala foothills. A great salad bar, shrimp scampi, and a variety of steaks make this an all-American choice for lunch or dinner. *Adjacent to Waimea Center on Hwy. 190, Waimea, tel. 808/885-4077. Dress: casual. MC, V. No lunch Sat. and Sun. Inexpensive.*

Continental **Merriman's.** Peter Merriman opened his restaurant in 1988, after winning rave reviews as the chef at the Mauna Lani's Gallery Restaurant. It's worth the 20-minute drive from the Kohala Coast hotels to cowboy country in Waimea to sample his imaginative cuisine. The menu includes vegetarian selections along with beef and veal dishes named for local ranches. Decorated in bright, playful colors, Merriman's brings to mind the steamship days in Hawaii—a sort of Hawaiian art-deco decor features an exhibition kitchen that allows diners to watch the chef create. *Opelo Plaza II, corner of Rte. 19 and Opelo Rd., Kamuela, tel. 808/885-6822. Reservations advised. Dress: informal. AE, MC, V. Moderate.*

★ **Edelweiss.** Faithful local diners and visitors alike flock to this relaxed family-oriented restaurant with rustic redwood furnishings. The chef's rack of lamb is still excellent. The varied menu includes 14 daily specials (such as a sausage platter), many with a European flavor. Go early—5:30–6:30—to avoid a long wait for one of the 14 tables. *Hwy. 19 entering Waimea-Kamuela, tel. 808/885-6800. No reservations. Dress: informal. MC, V. Closed Mon., New Year's Day, and lunch on Christmas Day. Inexpensive.*

Volcano

American **Ka Ohelo Room.** A new chef and recent remodeling have improved the appeal of the Ka Ohelo Room. Smaller and more intimate, with red-checked tablecloths, the restaurant is perched right at the edge of Kilauea Crater in a mountain-lodge setting. Breakfast and luncheon buffets accommodate tour groups during the day, but at night it's lovely and romantic. A new banquet room for parties seats 150. Recommended for dinner are the mahi Florentine or prime rib, topped off with pie made from Ohelo berries picked on the mountainside. *Volcano House, Volcanoes National Park, tel. 808/967-7321. Reservations advised. Dress: informal. AE, DC, MC, V. Moderate.*

Lodging

The types of accommodations vary tremendously on the Big Island: from hot and sunny resorts to condominiums on cool mountaintops and bed-and-breakfasts in damp, beautifully green little towns geared more toward fishing and farming than vacationing. That, in fact, is the beauty of a trip to this island: You can sample that elusive thing people like to call "the real Hawaii," yet complete your stay at a resort designed for fun and fantasy—or, if you're limited for time, opt only for the fantasy and never leave your "total destination resort." If you decide to spend an entire week or 10 days in more than one location on the Big Island, you'll need to plan the order of your moves. If, for example, you begin with fun and sun in Kailua-Kona or along the Kohala Coast, you might be disappointed to end with a night or two in Hilo, particularly if it rains (and in

Hilo that's very likely). Accommodations are listed by area in the order in which you might plan your stay. If you have only three nights on the Big Island, go directly to Keauhou, Kailua-Kona, or the Kohala Coast and bask in the sun. Condominiums, like bed-and-breakfasts and small out-of-the-way hotels, are listed in separate categories.

Generally, you'll always be able to find a room on the Big Island; however, you might not get your first choice if you wait until the last minute to make reservations at the top resorts during the winter season, which runs from December 15 through April 15. Amazingly enough, you will not be able to find a room in Hilo during the first week in April, when the Merrie Monarch Festival *(see* The Arts, *below)* is in full swing. Hula *halau* (schools) from all Islands converge on Hilo to compete in the week-long contests staged to honor Hawaii's last monarch, King David Kalakaua. Across the island, Kailua-Kona bursts at the seams in mid-October, when athletes and their support teams fill the hotels, the ocean waters, and the highways during the Gatorade Ironman World Triathlon Championships. An even bigger problem than finding a room at these times is finding a rental car. Be sure to make reservations well in advance—six months to a year—if your stay coincides with the festival, the triathlon, or any major holiday.

Room and car packages are often available in all price categories. A reputable travel agent should be able to furnish up-to-date information on these packages. The more expensive hotels offer special packages for tennis players, golfers, or honeymooners—but no one minds if you pretend to be a honeymooner to take advantage of the deal. Included in the package price are such things as lei greetings, perhaps a meal or two, free court time for tennis buffs, or carts and complimentary greens fees for golfers. We have indicated when hotels offer an American plan, meaning meals included. Otherwise, hotel rates are for a double room only.

Generally, all large hotels and condos have outdoor swimming pools—a particularly nice amenity to have if you're staying in Kailua-Kona, where the beaches are limited. Some of the older hotels do not have air-conditioning, but these will almost always be equipped with ceiling or room fans, which should be adequate except during the hot summer and early fall seasons. All rooms have a television set and telephone unless otherwise indicated.

Highly recommended hotels in each price category are indicated by a star ★.

Category	Cost*
Very Expensive	over $120
Expensive	$90–$120
Moderate	$60–$90
Inexpensive	under $60

All prices are for a standard double room, excluding 9¼% tax and service charges.

Hilo

★ **Hawaii Naniloa Hotel.** Renovations in 1990 made this one of the most comfortable hotels in Hilo. Be sure to ask for a room with a harbor view when you book into this hotel. The rooms are done in soft tones of beige and rose. Coffee makers in all rooms are a bonus. The 7- and 12-story towers are connected by a lobby area with shops, and on the lower level are the Sandalwood Dining Room; the Polynesian Room; Nihon Saryo, an authentic Japanese restaurant with a sushi bar; a fully equipped spa with weight and steam rooms, aerobics classes, Jacuzzi, massages, and a beauty salon; and the Karaoke Bar for poolside cocktails. An executive golf course, the Naniloa Country Club, is just across Banyan Drive. *93 Banyan Dr., Hilo 96720, tel. 808/969–3333 or 800/367–5360, fax 808/969–6622. 325 air-conditioned rooms with bath. Facilities: pool, shops, cocktail lounges, restaurants, free parking. AE, DC, MC, V. Expensive–Very Expensive.*

★ **Hilo Hawaiian Hotel.** One of the most pleasant hotels on the shores of Hilo Bay, the Hilo Hawaiian has a lanai terrace and bayfront rooms with spectacular views of Mauna Kea, the bay, and Coconut Island. Streetside rooms have a view of the golf course. The rooms were redone in 1990 with new carpets and rattan furniture; most have private lanais, and several are designed for guests in wheelchairs. Kitchenettes are available with one-bedroom suites. The Queen's Court Dining Room has reasonable prices for a hotel restaurant; it has a beautiful view of Hilo Bay and serves breakfast, lunch, and dinner buffets. The Menehune Lounge serves up cocktails and entertainment seven days a week. *71 Banyan Dr., Hilo 96720, tel. 808/935–9361 or 800/367–5004. 285 large, air-conditioned rooms with bath. Facilities: shops, pool, Monarch banquet room, restaurant, cocktail lounge, free parking. AE, DC, MC, V. Expensive.*

Waiakea Villas Hotel. Aku the macaw greets visitors and residents alike at the entry to the airy lobby. The hotel stands on 14 acres, surrounded by foliage, waterways, and carp ponds. Spacious rooms and one-bedroom suites are tropically decorated with rattan furniture and have bathtubs with showers. If not recently aired, the rather dark units can have a musty aroma, but they are clean; ask for a room that has been recently refurbished. Waiakea Villas is located next to Waiakea Fish Pond and Wailoa State Park, near Hilo and shopping centers. *400 Hualani St., Hilo 96720, tel. 808/961–2841 or 800/367–7042. 141 of 292 condominium apartments in 3-story walk-up buildings available for daily rental. Facilities: golf, 2 tennis courts, pool, air-conditioning, John Michael's Restaurant and Ohana Bar (American), Miyo's Restaurant (Japanese), Hale Inu Sports Bar, meeting rooms. AE, DC, MC, V. Moderate–Expensive.*

Arnott's Lodge. Designed as a budget lodge for backpackers, bicyclists, and other active visitors, this plain but spotless lodge offers dormitory-style accommodations with up to four people per room; semiprivate, double, and private rooms; and suites. It is minutes from the airport and the coastline in a lush wilderness setting. *98 Apapane Rd., Hilo 96720, tel. 808/969–7097, fax 808/961–0645. 9 2-bedroom apartments with bath. Facilities: shared kitchen, laundry and TV room, free parking. DC, MC, V. Inexpensive.*

Dolphin Bay Hotel. All rooms have kitchens in this clean, homey hotel in a lovely, green Hawaiian garden setting. The rooms do not have phones, but they do have desk fans to stir the air. The hotel is away from the beach in a residential area called Pueo. *333 Iliahi St., Hilo 96720, tel. 808/935-1466. 4 blocks from Hilo Bay. 18 units. Facilities: free parking. MC, V. Inexpensive.*

Hilo Bay Hotel, Uncle Billy's. Small- to average-size rooms in this low-rise hotel on Hilo Bay were recarpeted in 1991 and come equipped with showers (but no bathtubs). It's a popular stopover for Neighbor Islanders, who enjoy proprietor Uncle Billy Kimi's Hawaiian hospitality. A nightly hula show and entertainment during dinner are part of the fun. *87 Banyan Dr., Hilo 96720, tel. 808/935-0861 or 800/367-5102. 146 rooms, 38 with kitchenettes, some with refrigerators. Facilities: shops, pool, cocktail lounge, meeting rooms, air-conditioning, free parking. AE, D, DC, MC, V. Inexpensive–Moderate.*

Hilo Hotel. Favored by Japanese travelers and economy-minded visitors, this centrally located hotel has spotlessly clean studios and two-bedroom family suites that sleep up to six. The communal sitting room has a television, while the Fuji Japanese Restaurant is popular among residents. *142 Kinoole St., Hilo 96720, tel. 808/961-3733. 30 spartan rooms in downtown Hilo. Facilities: pool, cocktail lounge, restaurant, room and car packages, complimentary Continental breakfast. AE, DC, MC, V. Inexpensive.*

Hilo Seaside Hotel. The pleasant, clean rooms in the two- and three-story walk-up buildings were redone in 1991. The nicest rooms have lanais and overlook the lagoon or are situated around the pool. Lots of foliage along the walkways and friendly local personnel create a very Hawaiian ambience. A peaceful place, except when planes take off and land, as the hotel is near the airport's flight path. *126 Banyan Dr., Hilo 96720, tel. 808/935-0821 or 800/367-7000. 145 rooms with bay and garden views. Facilities: ceiling fans, shops, pool, meeting rooms, restaurant, cocktail lounge, free parking. AE, DC, MC, V. Inexpensive.*

Kailua-Kona and Keauhou

Kona Hilton Beach and Tennis Resort. Of the major hotels, the Kona Hilton is nearest to Kailua on the south side of town. It has a distinctive profile (built to resemble an early Hawaiian *holua* slide dropping toward the sea) that is easy to pick out from downtown. Rooms have coffee makers, safes, refrigerators, and standard rattan furniture. Corner rooms in the Beach Building are the best, because they have huge lanais that overlook the ocean. Full and modified American plans can be booked. A complimentary shuttle is available to Kailua Village. *75-5852 Alii Dr., Kailua-Kona 96740, tel. 808/329-3111 or 800/452-4411. 445 rooms in a main building, a beach building, and a village building. Facilities: Hele Mai dining room (Continental), cocktail lounges, pool, shops, meeting and banquet rooms, 4 Laykold tennis courts, free parking. AE, D, DC, MC, V. Very Expensive.*

Kona Surf Resort. Owned by a Japanese firm, Otaka, Inc., and catering to Japanese tour groups, this large, easy-to-getconfused-in hotel is the last property at the end of the road in Keauhou. Ask for a hotel map. The pink-stucco rooms, with separate dressing areas and private lanais, are large almost to the point of feeling bare. A charming copper-roofed wedding

Big Island Lodging

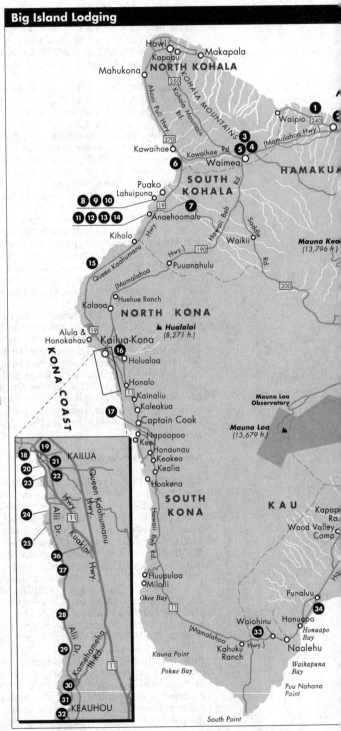

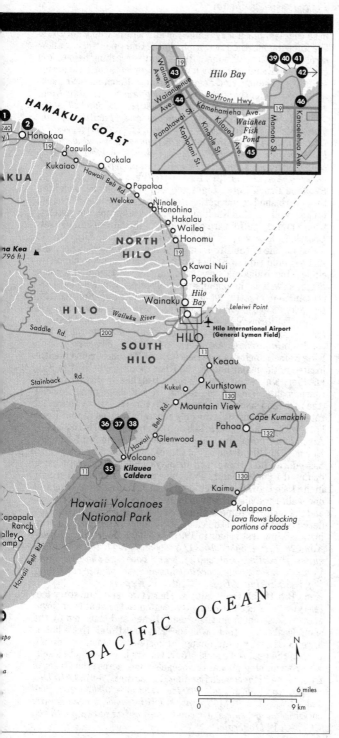

chapel beside peaceful koi (carp) ponds caters mainly to Japanese couples, but it's available for all visitors who want to tie the knot during their vacation. Paths and open spaces allow strolls along the cliff edge with the waves crashing below. You can walk to Keauhou Bay, where arrangements can be made for sailing, snorkeling, and deep-sea fishing. Room-and-car packages are frequently offered. *78-128 Ehukai St., Kailua-Kona 96740, tel. 808/322-3411 or 800/367-8011, fax 808/329-4602. 530 rooms available in 3 wings and one tower. Facilities: freshwater and saltwater pools, 3 tennis courts, golf course, restaurants, including the Makee Restaurant (steaks and seafood), Poi Pounder Showroom (comedy club), cocktail lounges, shops, meeting rooms, air-conditioning, refrigerators, free parking. AE, DC, MC, V. Expensive–Very Expensive.*

Keauhou Beach Hotel. Light and airy color schemes brighten the refurbished rooms in the ocean wing of this oceanfront hotel, as well as the Kuakini Terrace restaurant downstairs, whose nightly buffets are popular with the all-you-can-eat set. Location, however, is the hotel's real plus: Adjacent to Kahaluu, one of the Big Island's best snorkeling beaches, and just a 5-mile ride to Kailua town, the hotel's own grounds include King Kalakaua's restored summer cottage and a small heiau, as well as the popular open-air Makai Bar with local entertainment nightly. *78-6740 Alii Dr., Kailua-Kona 96740, tel. 800/367-6025 or 808/322-3441. 310 rooms including 6 suites. Facilities: 2 pools, sauna, exercise and weight room, 6 tennis courts, restaurant, lounge, shops, meeting room, air-conditioning, refrigerators. AE, DC, MC, V. Expensive.*

★ **King Kamehameha's Kona Beach Hotel.** The most conveniently located of the major hotels, the King Kam is right next to Kailua Pier, where big game fish are weighed in during fishing tournaments. Though the rooms are not particularly special (the fifth- and sixth-floor oceanfront rooms are best), this hotel rates a star because it is the only centrally located Kailua-Kona hotel with a white-sand beach and a shopping mall in the lobby. Among the numerous shops is the only branch of Liberty House (a quality department store) in Kailua. The lobby also has educational Hawaiiana displays and fishing trophies; a mounted 1,062½-pound Pacific blue marlin, which set a record in the 1986 Hawaii International Billfish Tournament, hangs on one wall. Free historically oriented tours explore the grounds and the restored Ahuena Heiau, which King Kamehameha I ordered constructed in the early 1800s. New beds and TVs were installed in guest rooms in 1991. *75-5660 Palani Rd., Kailua-Kona 96740, tel. 808/329-2911 or 800/367-2111. 460 rooms and suites. Facilities: pool, sauna, tennis courts, Kona Beach and Veranda restaurants, cocktail lounges, shops, air-conditioning, free parking. AE, D, DC, MC, V. Expensive.*

Kona Bay Hotel, Uncle Billy's. These two- and four-story motel-type units are conveniently located in the center of town, across the street from the ocean. Owned and managed by the same local family that owns the Hilo Bay Hotel, these hotels have a friendly, fun-loving atmosphere. Open-air dining around the pool is a casual affair. Guests have access to a saltwater swimming pool at the ocean's edge, across the street in front of the Fisherman's Landing Restaurant. *75-5739 Alii Dr., Kailua-Kona 96740, tel. 808/329-1393 or 800/367-5102, 800/423-8733, ext. 220. 146 rooms. Facilities: pool, 2 restaurants, cocktail lounge, shops, air-conditioning, free parking. AE, D, DC, MC, V. Moderate.*

Kona Islander Inn. Its close-to-the-village location and turn-of-the-century plantation-style architecture in a setting of palms and torch-lit paths make this pleasant but older apartment-style hotel a good value. Studios, some with built-in sofas, are located across the street from Kailua Bay. *75-5776 Kuakini Hwy., Kailua-Kona 96740, tel. 808/329–3181 or 800/922–7866, fax 808/326–9339. 59 hotel units. Facilities: pool, air-conditioning, free parking. AE, DC, MC, V. Moderate.*

Kona Seaside Hotel. The old Hukilau Hotel and the adjoining Kona Seaside have been combined and renovated, with 155 rooms in four price categories (according to size and location). This hotel has the best central location in the area, across the street from Kailua Bay. Rooms nearest the main street are built around a pool with a grassy courtyard. The Garden Wing is set back, and the Tower Pool Wing opens onto Palani Road on the opposite side. The small rooms have tiny bathrooms and showers but are completely adequate for the budget traveler. *75-5646 Palani Rd., Kailua-Kona 96740, tel. 808/329–2455 or 800/367–7000. 155 rooms. Facilities: restaurant, cocktail lounge, 2 pools, meeting rooms, air-conditioning and/or ceiling fans, free parking. AE, MC, V. Inexpensive–Moderate.*

Kona Tiki Hotel. The best thing about this simple, older 3-story walk-up hotel about a mile south of Kailua-Kona is that all the units have lanais right next to the ocean. All the rental units have refrigerators, and others have kitchens for an extra $5. Recarpeted and decorated in off-white and pastels in 1991, the rooms are not luxurious, but the proximity to the ocean is a definite asset. Guests can sunbathe by the pool. A Continental breakfast is provided. No in-room TV or phones are available. *Box 1567, Kailua-Kona 96745, tel. 808/329–1425. 15 rental units. Facilities: pool, ceiling fans, free parking. No credit cards. Inexpensive.*

Kohala Coast and Waikoloa

★ **Hyatt Regency Waikoloa.** The guest rooms in this fantasy resort are large, beautifully appointed, and decorated in soft beige and sand colors; the works of such well-known local artists as Yvonne Cheng grace the walls. Each room has its own small lanai, minibar, ample walk-in closet, couch, dining table, and chairs. Guests at this resort on 62 acres of rocky ocean shoreline can swim with dolphins (for a fee) in a protected area of a man-made 4-acre lagoon, bordered on one side by a man-made sunning beach. No natural sand beach is available. A swimming pool nearly an acre in size has water slides; two other pools are connected by a river pool; and a third swimming pool is located in the Ocean Tower atrium. For vacationers who are not in a rush to make an early tee-time or the last interisland flight of the day, this resort is an adventure. Otherwise, one tends to grow weary of the advance planning and the waiting involved to get places via the Disneyesque trams and boats. It's no wonder a one-time fee of $12.50 is automatically added to your bill for luggage handling. The hotel is known for its fine restaurants, including Casa Marabella, Donatoni's, Imari, and the Kona Provision Company. Spats Disco is one of the few places where the nightlife is actually lively along the Kohala Coast. *HCO2, Box 5500, Waikoloa 96743, tel. 808/885–1234 or 800/233–1234. 1,241 rooms in 3 buildings. Facilities: 7 restaurants and adjoining bars, luau grounds, Spats Disco, 6 additional bars, 3 pools, 8 tennis courts, health spa, 2 racquet-*

ball courts. A Tom Weiskopf–Jay Morrish golf course and a Robert Trent Jones, Jr., course adjoin the resort. AE, D, DC, MC, V. Very Expensive.

★ **Kona Village Resort.** The winner of Condé Nast *Traveler's* Best Tropical Resort in the world in 1991, this is the ultimate retreat for privacy and peaceful surroundings. It's easy to feel you are part of an extended Polynesian *ohana* (family) with your own thatch-roof *hale* (house) beside the sea. Houses are available in various island designs, such as Hawaiian, Tahitian, New Caledonian, Fijian, Samoan, and Marquesan. Access to the resort, with its crescent of sparkling beach, is down a narrow road leading off Queen Ka'ahumanu Highway, 15 miles north of Kailua. No phones, televisions, or radios are available in any of the hales, but you might have your own hammock right outside the door. The extra-large rooms are cooled by ceiling fans and decorated with bright tropical prints, many silk-screened or hand-painted by local artists. Families seem to return again and again; an added enticement is that the full American plan includes nearly everything: Meals, tennis, sailing, outrigger canoeing, kayaking, snorkeling, volleyball, shuffleboard, and rides in the glass-bottom boat are at no additional charge. In keeping with the Polynesian mood, jackets and ties are not worn at dinner, even in the resort's finest restaurant, the Hale Samoa. *Box 1299, Kaupulehu-Kona 96745, tel. 808/325–5555 or 800/367–5290, fax 808/325–5124. 125 bungalows. Facilities: limited meeting and banquet space, "flightseeing" from the grounds, tennis, masseuse, scuba and sailing lessons, 2 pools, beach, 2 dining rooms, bars, general store, free airport transfers, village goldsmith. AE, DC, MC, V. Closed 1 week in Dec. Very Expensive.*

★ **Mauna Kea Beach Hotel.** This discreetly low-key, world-class resort, featuring a museum-quality art collection, is located on what is possibly the most beautiful, gently sloping, white-sand beach on the island; some guests are out and swimming by 7 AM. The peaceful hotel is not known for its nightlife, though dancing is offered in The Batik most evenings. The rooms, which can be completely darkened by closing off the spacious lanais with sliding louvered doors, have tropical furnishings, with refrigerators, clock radios, and safes. The dressing rooms feature his-and-hers closets, complimentary cotton *yukatas* (robes) to wear during your stay, and the biggest, softest towels ever seen in a hotel. Rooms do not have televisions, on the premise that Mauna Kea guests prefer the serene "away-from-it-all" ambience. The hotel, which is known for its fine dining, particularly at The Batik and The Garden, offers modified American-plan rates (two meals included) as well as European plan (accommodations only). The Mauna Kea, developed by Laurance S. Rockefeller, opened its doors in 1965. *1 Mauna Kea Beach Dr., Kohala Coast 96743–9706, tel. 808/882–7222 or 800/882–6060, fax 808/822–7757. 310 mountain- and ocean-view rooms and suites. Facilities: golf on the award-winning Robert Trent Jones, Sr., Mauna Kea Beach Golf Course (famous for its signature "over-the-water" third hole), 13 oceanside tennis courts, sailing, scuba diving, fitness center, exercise trail, shops, movies, sauna, 6 restaurants, luau garden. Sportfishing is available from nearby Kawaihae Harbor. Hunting and horseback riding are also within a short distance. AE, DC, MC, V. Very Expensive.*

★ **Mauna Lani Bay Hotel and Bungalows.** Almost all the spacious rooms in this exquisite modern hotel have views of the ocean. Soft chairs, a couch, a marble coffee table, and an oversize television are the comfortable furnishings in rooms decorated in whites and natural tones with linen, cotton, and teak. The rooms, with big, sunny lanais, are equipped with a dry bar and refrigerator, a clock radio, and a safe. The resort is especially known for its two spectacular golf courses and its signature fifteenth hole, where golfers tee off over a wide expanse of ocean. Oceanfront dining can be enjoyed at the Canoe House, which features Pacific Rim cuisine, or try the award-winning Le Soleil Restaurant. Gourmands will want to time a visit to the Mauna Lani during the annual Cuisines of the Sun celebration in June. Chefs and vintners from other sunny climes present a week of food and beverage workshops and dinner parties that are a gastronomic delight. *1 Mauna Lani Dr., Kohala Coast 96743, tel. 808/885–6622 or 800/367–2323. 350 hotel rooms and suites. Facilities: golf, pool, 10 tennis courts, restaurants, bars, shops, air-conditioning. AE, DC, MC, V. Very Expensive.*

★ **Ritz-Carlton, Mauna Lani.** This Ritz-Carlton, set on 32 acres of secluded beachfront property, adds island touches to the chain's high standards. The rooms are furnished warmly and traditionally with marble-top side tables and massive highboys with carved pineapple posts (the fruit of friendship). Marble bathrooms include both a tub and a separate shower and such amenities as hair dryers, terry robes, and scales. Lanais afford views of the ocean and magnificent gardens. Red Sail Sports offers sailing, snorkeling, and scuba activities; less-adventurous guests dip into a protected swimming lagoon or loll on the white-sand beach. For hard-core landlubbers, the Ritz-Carlton has the island's finest tennis facilities and golf at the adjacent Francis I'i Brown course—or aromatherapy massage in the hotel spa. Resort restaurants include the signature Dining Room and the popular Grill. *1 N. Kaniku Dr., Kohala Coast 96743, tel. 808/885–2000 or 800/845–9905. 542 rooms, 54 suites. Facilities: pool, 10 tennis courts and 1 exhibition court, 2 golf courses, health club, sauna. AE, D, DC, MC, V. Very Expensive.*

Royal Waikoloan. The emphasis is on Hawaiiana in this hotel with its updated lobby and conference facilities. The lobby features demonstrations of Hawaiian quilting and other crafts. While the majority of rooms have an ocean view, all of them have private lanais, radios, and air-conditioning. The Royal Waikoloan also features 20 plush cabanas near the ocean. The resort is situated on 15.7 acres, bordered by royal fish ponds with a white-sand crescent beach and Anaehoomalu Bay just beyond. The bay is perfect for windsurfing and snorkeling. Luaus, *hukilaus* (communal fishing parties), and other special dining nights are regularly scheduled. *HC02, Box 5300, Waikoloa 96743-5000, tel. 808/885–6789 or 800/537–9800. 550 guest rooms in a multiwing, 6-story hotel and 20 cabanas. Facilities: 2 18-hole golf courses, pool, fitness center, shops, 6 tennis courts, conference facilities, free parking, petroglyph park and trails, guest laundry. AE, DC, MC, V. Expensive–Very Expensive.*

Bed-and-Breakfast and Out-of-the-Way Hotels

It is practically imperative that you have a car if you choose to stay overnight at any of the places that follow. Generally, the hotels are small, family-run affairs that furnish a clean bed but little luxury. Many visitors are also beginning to "wake up and smell the coffee" when it comes to bed-and-breakfast lodgings, and on the Big Island a demand for less-expensive accommodations is being fulfilled by B&B hosts (usually outside the resort areas), who are opening their doors to guests.

Hawaii's Best Bed and Breakfasts (Box 563, Kamuela 96743, tel. 808/885-4550 or 800/BNB-9912), **Go Native Hawaii** (65 Haulaulani Place, Box 11418, Hilo 96721, tel. 808/935-4178 or 800/662-8483), and **My Island B&B** (Box 100, Volcano 96785, tel. 808/967-7216 or 808/967-7110) are Big Island-based bed and breakfast networks that will help you find the B&B to meet your needs. Explain your expectations fully and ask plenty of questions before booking. For example, many B&Bs are located within a few miles of Volcanoes National Park, a haven for lovers of the great outdoors, though not the perfect location for beach and sun worshipers. Some require stays of two or three days. When booking, ask about car-rental arrangements, as many B&B networks can offer discounted rates.

Hamakua Coast **Waipio Wayside Bed and Breakfast.** This former plantation manager's home, located near Honokaa on the way to Waipio Valley, has five sparkling clean rooms (two with full bath) decorated with special touches that include light, airy curtains handpainted on silk by a local artist. One room is furnished with Chinese antiques, another (with private bath) has an early American theme, with blond wood paneling and a patchwork quilt. A sundeck and gazebo overlook fields of cane to the ocean. The B&B is about 15 minutes from Waimea (where at least four fine restaurants are located) and about 45 minutes from the Kohala Coast resorts. Gourmet breakfast is included. *Box 840, Honokaa 96727, tel. 808/775-0275 or 800/833-8849. 5 rooms, 2 with bath. Facilities: handicapped accessible. DC, MC, V. Inexpensive-Moderate.*

Hotel Honokaa Club. A funky bargain place to stay in a pinch, but definitely not for luxury. This old, wood-frame hotel, which had been owned by the same family since 1908, changed hands in 1990. The new owners painted and recarpeted the rooms. The second-story rooms are more appealing for their views, if you don't mind the walk upstairs. The lunches are reasonably priced in the downstairs restaurant, which has a tiny salad bar. *Box 185, Honokaa 96727, tel. 808/775-0678. 14 hotel units. Facilities: desk fans, restaurant, bar. MC, V. Inexpensive.*

Up-country **Holualoa Inn.** A suite and three rooms, each with private bath,
Kona District are available in this cedar estate home. Situated in up-country Kona, amid coffee trees and bucolic fields above Kailua Bay, the artsy town of Holualoa is only 4 miles from Kailua-Kona. Each guest room is named for its decorating theme: Tahiti Suite, Bali Room, Oriental Room, and Polynesian Room. Constructed in 1978, the 5,000-square-foot inn features a rooftop gazebo. *Box 222, Holualoa 96725, tel. 808/324-1121. 3 rooms and 1 suite. Facilities: pool, ping-pong and pool tables. AE, DC, MC, V. Expensive-Very Expensive.*

Waimea Gardens Cottage B&B. These particularly charming country streamside cottages come complete with window boxes spilling over with flowers, lace-curtained double French doors, and New England and Hawaiian antique accents in the decor. Guests can awake in the cool, upcountry mornings to collect their own fresh eggs from the hen's nest outside. Hosts Charles and Barbara Campbell make sure every amenity is available—including a fully stocked kitchen with your preference of breakfast items, warm robes, and Hawaiian reading material. *Box 563, Kamuela 96743, tel. 808/885–4550 or 800/262–9912. 2 cottage units. Facilities: private entrances, TV. Moderate–Expensive.*

Manago Hotel. You'll get a great view high above the Kona Coast in the newer wing of this older, but clean, family-run hostelry. The rooms are reminiscent of a mainland motel, except for one—a Japanese-style room with *tatami* (sleeping mats) instead of beds and a *furo* (deep bathtub), which the proprietor has kept in remembrance of his grandparents, who built the main hotel in 1917. If you seek something unusual, ask for this room; otherwise, request a room in the newer wing, as those in the main building share bathrooms. Large groups can arrange a Japanese dinner (leave your shoes at the door and sit on the floor) in a special dining room. *Box 145, Captain Cook 96704, tel. 808/323–2642. 42 rooms with bath in the newer wing. Facilities: restaurant, bar, free parking, shared TV. MC, V. Inexpensive.*

Volcano/South Point

Volcano House. The charm of the Volcano House is its location at the edge of Kilauea Caldera, so if you choose to stay, plan on paying a bit extra to book one of the rooms with a crater view. Refurnished in 1990 with beige floral rugs and new beds, the clean and comfortable rooms still boast period koa furniture. Dinner at the Ka Ohelo Room can stir romance, as can a walk in the cool, crisp air, topped off with a nightcap sipped while nestling in commodious leather chairs by the ohia-wood fire in the lobby's stone fireplace. *Box 53, Hawaii Volcanoes National Park 96718–0053, tel. 808/967–7321. 42 rooms. Facilities: restaurant, shops, Volcano Golf Course. AE, DC, MC, V. Moderate–Very Expensive.*

Kilauea Lodge. A mile from the Volcanoes National Park entrance, this is possibly the most romantically appealing place to stay in the area. Remodeled and opened in March 1988, the lodge has added seven rooms to its original four rooms and a cottage; several have fireplaces. The rooms are slickly decorated to reflect a theme. Kimura has Oriental touches, while Noekolo, Paina, and Hapuu have a Hawaiian ambience. Set amid tree ferns and forests, the lodge offers cool mountain air and opportunities for brisk walks along the peaceful back roads of Volcano. A country-style restaurant, also with a fireplace, has earned a reputation for good food. A big breakfast is included in the price of the room. *Box 116, Volcano Village 96785, tel. 808/967–7366. 11 rooms and a cottage with bath. Facilities: restaurant, fireplaces, near Kilauea General Store, Volcano Golf Course. AE, MC, V. Moderate.*

My Island Bed and Breakfast. Gordon and JoAnn Morse opened their historic three-story, 100-year-old house to visitors four years ago. The house is the oldest in Volcano, built in 1886 by the Lyman missionary family (Hilo has the Lyman Museum). Three rooms are available in the house (one sleeps up to six), and you will definitely want a tour with the genial host. However, if you seek privacy and a brand-new, uncluttered haven, you might be happier in either the newly opened studio apartment with a kitchenette or in one of two new studios that are separate from the house. A full breakfast is included. *Box 100, Volcano 96785, tel. 808/967–7216. 6 rooms and studios. No credit cards. Inexpensive.*

Shirakawa Motel. In the remote Kau District, midway between Kona and Hilo near Naalehu, the southernmost town in the

United States, this bare, basic, and clean motel has been run by the same family since 1921. Families can get connecting units with cooking facilities, though there are two snack shops and Na'alehu Coffee Shop in town. *Box 467, Naalehu 96772, tel. 808/929–7462. 13 double rooms, 4 with kitchenettes. Facilities: shower stalls. No credit cards. Inexpensive.*

Volcano Bed and Breakfast. Twelve years ago, Jim and Sandy Pedersen bought their 1930s-vintage house, about a mile from the park entrance, but they waited to complete extensive rebuilding and remodeling before opening their doors to guests in June 1988. The Pedersens live on the ground level of the three-story house, which has its main entrance on the second level, where there is a sun room, living room, dining room, fireplace, and one bedroom. A bathroom is shared with two other bedrooms on the third level. *Box 22, Volcano 96785, tel. 808/967–7779 or 800/733–7713. 3 double rooms. Facilities: Continental breakfast, bicycles, shared TV, VCR, piano. MC, V. Inexpensive.*

Waimea-Kamuela **Kamuela Inn B&B.** You might choose to spend a night in Waimea-Kamuela just to stay at this nicely decorated country inn. Every room is attractively designed, but the penthouse suite, which sleeps six, is the pièce de résistance, with sunset lanai and full kitchen with microwave. A new wing containing two executive suites with full kitchens was added in 1990. Continental breakfast is served at the cheery breakfast lanai. The inn has a peaceful, lush, country setting, yet it's near shops, a theater, restaurants, and a museum. *Box 1994, Kamuela 96743, tel. 808/885–4243. 31 rooms, 2 executive suites and a penthouse suite. Facilities: private baths, pay phone in office, breakfast, free parking. AE, DC, MC, V. Inexpensive–Expensive.*

Parker Ranch Lodge. In cool up-country, the lodge has rustic rooms that look out onto green pastures. All rooms have heaters and some have kitchenettes. The lodge is suitable for an overnight stay, but you wouldn't particularly want to spend a 10-day honeymoon here. *Box 458, Kamuela 96743, tel. 808/885–4100. 20 rooms. Facilities: free parking. AE, MC, V. Moderate.*

Condominiums

Kailua-Kona and **Aston Kona by the Sea.** Complete modern kitchens and tile la-
Keauhou nais can be found in every suite in this comfortable oceanfront condo. The spacious rooms were tastefully redecorated in 1990 in mauve and gray with new furniture. An open-air lobby and a helpful reception desk add to the friendly atmosphere. There's no sandy beach, but the pool is situated next to the ocean. *75-6106 Alii Dr., Kailua-Kona 96740, tel. 808/327–2300 or 800/367–5124. 80 1- and 2-bedroom units. Facilities: 2 pools, restaurant, air-conditioning. AE, DC, MC, V. Very Expensive.*

Aston Royal Sea Cliff. This is a Mediterranean-style condominium resort on 7 coastal acres with pleasantly tree-shaded grounds. Plushly furnished one- and two-bedroom apartments, decorated in soft, tropical colors, have large lanais and kitchen/dining areas. *75-6040 Alii Dr., Kailua-Kona 96740, tel. 808/329–8021 or 800/922–7866. 150 rental units. Facilities: 2 pools, sauna, hot tub, tennis, free parking, air-conditioning, health spa, laundry. AE, DC, MC, V. Very Expensive.*

★ **Kona Coast Resort.** The beautifully decorated rooms with contemporary soft rose and gray decor have modern wood-and-tile kitchens. This 12-acre, low-rise resort is across Alii Drive from the Keauhou Shopping Center. Units have every amenity you could ask for: Jennair ranges, microwaves, washers and dryers, hair dryers in the master bathrooms, and more. Lanais have views of the ocean or golf course. *78-6842 Alii Dr., Kailua-Kona 96740, tel. 808/324–0412 or 800/745–5662. 68 1-, 2-, and 3-bedroom rental units. Facilities: pool and spa with waterfall, VCRs, room safes, barbecues, recreation pavilion. AE, MC, V. Very Expensive.*

★ **Kanaloa at Kona.** The 13-acre grounds provide a lovely setting for this low-rise condominium bordering the Keauhou-Kona Country Club. Large one-, two-, and three-bedroom apartments have wall-to-wall carpeting, koa-wood cabinetwork, and tile and marble decor. The fully equipped kitchens have microwave ovens. Oceanfront suites are furnished with private Jacuzzis; the bathroom showers are big enough for two. The Terrace Restaurant has a romantically tropical atmosphere, in addition to serving reasonable and good American cuisine with local flavor. *78-261 Manukai St., Kailua-Kona 96740, tel. 808/322–2272 or 800/777–1700. 166 rooms and villa apartments (condominiums) in 37 buildings. Facilities: 3 outdoor pools, hot tub, 2 tennis courts, ceiling fans, laundry, meeting area, free parking. AE, DC, MC, V. Expensive–Very Expensive.*

Kona Bali Kai. These older, family-style units midway between Kailua-Kona and Keauhou Country Club were decorated with new furnishings and carpeting in 1988. All units have kitchen/dining areas. The property is divided, so ask for a place on the ocean side rather than the mountain side of the road. *76-6246 Alii Dr., Kailua-Kona 96740, tel. 808/329–9381 or 800/388–3800. 91 condo units available for daily rental. Facilities: pools, sauna, laundry, some rooms have air-conditioning. AE, D, DC, MC, V. Expensive–Very Expensive.*

Hale Kona Kai. This small vacation condominium on the ocean's edge next door to the Kona Hilton requires a three-day minimum stay. Units are furnished differently, because they are privately owned; the corner units have the best views. Hale Kona Kai is within walking distance of Kailua-Kona restaurants and shopping. *75-5870 Kahakai Rd., Kailua-Kona 96740, tel. 808/329–2155 or 800/421–3696. 39 1-bedroom rental units. Facilities: pool, full kitchens, air-conditioning, free parking. AE, MC, V. Moderate.*

Kona Magic Sands. A three-day minimum stay is required in this small beachside condominium, which has maid service on request. The studios do not have telephones, but they do have kitchenettes. Units vary, because they are individually owned, but all are oceanfront. Some have enclosed lanais to give more living space. The condo is located near Disappearing Sands Beach, which is a plus for swimmers and sunbathers when the sand is there in the summer months (it washes away in winter). *77-6452 Alii Dr., Kailua-Kona 96740, tel. 808/329–6488 or 800/367–5168. 26 hotel units. Facilities: pool, Jameson's by the Sea seafood restaurant, cocktail lounge, free parking. AE, MC, V. Moderate.*

Kohala Coast and Waikoloa **Aston Bay Club at Waikoloa.** New in 1991, this luxury condominium resort sits on 15 acres surrounded by Waikoloa's championship Beach and Kings' golf courses. The spacious and serene one- and two-bedroom suites have gourmet kitchens with microwave ovens, air conditioning, wet bars, private lanais, and daily maid service. *HCO2, Box 5525, Waikoloa Beach Dr., Waikoloa 96743, tel. 808/885–7979 or 800/922–7866. 24 rooms. Facilities: 2 tennis courts, 2 championship golf courses, pool, jet spa and saunas, barbecue, entertainment area, free parking. AE, DC, MC, V. Very Expensive.*

★ **Aston Shores at Waikoloa.** These red-tile-roof units won *Condo Vacations* "Condominium of the Year for 1992." The spacious one-bedroom/one-bath and two-bedroom/two-bath condominiums have been decorated in muted shades, such as rose and light green. The plush carpets are even vacuumed in a shell pattern. Units all have kitchens and dining areas, as well as daily maid service. Oversize tubs and separate large glassed-in showers add to the luxury. Sliding glass doors in both the bedrooms and the living room open onto large lanais. The villas are landscaped with lagoons and waterfalls at the edge of the championship Waikoloa Golf Course. *HC02, Box 5460, Waikoloa Beach Dr., Waikoloa 96743, tel. 808/885–5001 or 800/922–7866. 72 villas. Facilities: pool, hot tub, tennis, golf, equestrian center, air-conditioning and ceiling fans, free parking. AE, DC, MC, V. Very Expensive.*

Mauna Lani Point Condominiums. These elegant and roomy suites are set off by themselves on one of the world's most beautiful oceanside golf courses, a few steps away from the Mauna Lani Bay Hotel and its fine restaurants. This is the only condominium in Hawaii that offers full concierge services. Fans on the vaulted ceilings cool the rooms, which have a modern tropical decor in soft pink and eggshell colors. Kitchens, microwave ovens, and washer/dryers are in every unit, and daily maid service is standard. *2 Kaniku Dr., Kohala Coast 96743, tel. 808/885–5022 or 800/642–6284. 55 hotel units. Facilities: pool, Jacuzzi, sauna, golf and tennis, laundry, jogging trails, free parking. AE, DC, MC, V. Very Expensive.*

Waikoloa Villas at Waikoloa Resort. This is just about the only place to stay in the Waikoloa area (relatively near the Kohala Coast resorts) that is more modestly priced—and it's 6 miles inland. Individually owned condominium units are all decorated differently, but they each meet standards set by the rental agency. Two-night minimum stays are required, and maid service is on a weekly basis. The wide open spaces of cowboy country attract golfers and the horsey set. *Box 3498, Lua Kula Dr., Waikoloa 96743, tel. 808/883–9144 or 800/367–7042. 55 1-bedroom rental units. Facilities: golf, tennis, horseback riding, pools, air-conditioning, free parking, restaurant at golf club. AE, DC, MC, V. Expensive.*

Volcano/ South Point **Sea Mountain at Punaluu.** Avid golfers will enjoy the spacious Colony One condominiums, bordered on one side by the ocean and on the other by fairways. Units are not ultraplush but have a country feel, with comfortable wicker and rattan furnishings and complete kitchens. Owned by SaZale Corporation, the property includes the Aspen Institute, a think-tank retreat. Plans for construction of a new hotel are in the works. *Box 460, Pahala 96777, tel. 808/928–6200 or 800/344–7675. 35 rental units. Facilities: pool, nearby Broiler Restaurant and Punaluu Black Sands Restaurant, cocktail lounge, tennis courts, golf course, meeting rooms, free parking, weekly maid service. 2-day minimum stay. MC, V. Moderate–Expensive.*

The Arts

Artwork

Big Island residents rank second to none in artistic creativity, as becomes apparent by the number of galleries tucked in out-of-the-way places *(see* Shopping, *above)*. Two hamlets are especially noted for their art communities. Just up-country of Kailua, the little town of Holualoa, on Highway 180, is a nest of artists, possibly because many years ago a California couple, Bob and Carol Rogers, moved to town and opened the **Kona Arts Center** (tel. 808/322–2307) in an old coffee mill. To this day they give classes, and their doors are open to curious drop-in visitors or aspiring students. Classes at the Kona Arts Center were what originally encouraged Hiroki Morinoue, who then studied in California and Japan and returned to Holualoa to open his own gallery, **Studio 7** (tel. 808/324–1335), a half block from the Kona Arts Center. You'll also want to investigate Holualoa Gallery's raku ceramics and other local work, **Kim Starr's Gallery** (tel. 808/324–1769), and **Hale o Kula Goldsmith Gallery** (tel. 808/324–1688).

In Waimea, the **Waimea Arts Council** (Box 1818, Kamuela 96743, tel. 808/885–7671 or 808/969–2400) is dedicated to promoting the arts in Waimea, Hamakua, Kohala, and Waikoloa. The council sponsors free *kaha ki'is* (one-man shows) at the Art Center Gallery, located in the old fire station near the stoplight in Waimea (open Tues., Thurs., Sat. 10–2).

When it comes to art for viewing, three collections deserve mention. **Puuopelu,** the private home of Parker Ranch's last owner Richard Smart, is open for public viewing of his vast collection of paintings, Venetian glass, antique Chinese vases, and sculpture *(see* Guided Tours, *above)*. For guests, the **Mauna Kea Beach Hotel** (tel. 808/882–7222) conducts free tours of its Pacific Rim collection on Monday and Friday at 11:30 AM. The **Hyatt Regency Waikoloa** (tel. 808/885–1234) also offers free tours of its vast art collection for those who make reservations with the Aloha Services desk in the lobby.

Hula

For dance lovers, the biggest wingding of the year is the **Merrie Monarch Festival** (400 Hualani, Apt. 8-279, Hilo 96270, tel. 808/935–9168), staged in Hilo during the first week in April. Hula *halau* (schools) converge on the town to honor King David Kalakaua, Hawaii's last king, in a dance competition that names the best male, female, group, and so on. The Waiakea Villas Hotel *(see* Lodging, *above)* recently became the headquarters for the dancers; if you want to stay anywhere in Hilo, or even get tickets for the competition, it is best to make reservations as much as a year in advance.

Film

When you ask about cultural outings on the Big Island, you're just as likely to get directions to the nearest movie theater as anyplace else:

Kailua-Kona **Hualalai Theaters 1, 2, and 3** (Hualalai Center, Kuakini Hwy. and Hualalai St., tel. 808/329–6641) and **World Square Theater** (Kona Marketplace, 75-5719 Alii Dr., tel. 808/329–4070).

Hilo **Prince Kuhio Theaters 1 and 2** (Prince Kuhio Plaza, 111 E. Puainako Ave., tel. 808/959–4595) and **Waiakea Theaters 1, 2, and 3** (Waiakea Kai Shopping Plaza, 88 Kanoelehua Ave., tel. 808/935–9747).

Pahoa **Akebono Theater and Playhouse** (Pahoa on Hwy. 130, tel. 808/965–9943) sometimes shows special engagement movies, such as surfing films, and occasional plays by the fledgling Hawaii Island Theater.

Theater

For legitimate theater, the little town of Waimea is your best bet. The **Kihulu Theater Foundation** (Kamuela, tel. 808/885–6017) produces plays and imports entertainment on a fairly regular basis. Nearer the resort areas, if you're dying to see a play, check with the **Aloha Community Players** (Aloha Theatre Café, Hwy. 11, Kainaliu, tel. 808/322–9924) for its next production.

Nightlife

Clubs and Cabarets

If you're the kind of person who doesn't come alive until after dark, you're going to be pretty lonely on the Big Island. In Hilo, the streets roll up at dusk.

d'Angoras (101 Aupuni St., tel. 808/934–7888) offers dancing to live bands or disco from 9 PM. Bands change frequently, and a disk jockey at **Fiascos** (200 Kanoelehua Ave., Hilo, tel. 808/935–7666) plays music from the 1950s, '60s, and '70s. The remodeled lounge **Stratton's** at the Country Club Hotel and Condominium (121 Banyan Dr., Hilo, tel. 808/961–6815) also provides disco music for revelers.

Even on the visitor-oriented Kona–Kohala coast, there's not a lot doing after dark. Blame it on the plantation heritage (people did their cane-raising in the morning) or the fact that life is lived to the fullest during the daylight hours, but it has taken a newcomer to turn on the bright lights. The hottest place—actually half an hour out of town—is **Spats Disco,** at the Hyatt Regency Waikoloa (1 Waikoloa Rd., off Queen Ka'ahumanu Hwy., tel. 808/885–5737). This is a high-energy, Toulouse-Lautrec-theme club for the young at heart. In Kailua, the **Eclipse Restaurant** (75-5711 Kuakini Hwy., tel. 808/329–4686) turns disco at 10 PM, except on Thursday, when country music is featured. Earlier in the evening, this is a pleasant place to dine, with Continental cuisine and attentive service for about $15–$20 per person.

Dinner Cruise

Captain Beans' Kona Voyagers is the ever-popular standby in sunset dinner cruises. You can't miss it. As the sun sets in Kailua, look out over the water and you'll see a big, gaudy, orange-and-brown boat with distinctive orange sails. This cruise is corny, and you would get a better full-course dinner in a restaurant for less, but it's an experience. *74–5626 Alapa St., B–17, Kailua-Kona 96740, tel. 808/329–2955. Cost: $55, adults only, for 5:15 sail with dinner, entertainment, and open bar.*

Luaus and Polynesian Revues

Four luaus are recommended in the Kohala Coast and Waikoloa area:

The **Hyatt Regency Waikoloa** seats 750 outdoors at the Kamehameha Court for its "Legends of Polynesia" show, which features a buffet with samplings of Hawaiian food, as well as fish, beef, and chicken to appeal to all tastes, and two cocktails. *HC02, Box 5500, Waikoloa, tel. 808/885–1234. Cost: $55 adults, $27.50 children 5–12. Fri. from 6 PM.*

Everybody knows **Kona Village Resort** has the best luau of the Big Island resorts, if you are judging by authenticity, atmosphere, and attitude—and they don't even use too much salt in the seasoning. Mainland taste buds might reject some items, such as *opihi* (a limpet, considered a chewy delicacy in Hawaii, that sells for about $24 a pound), but don't worry, there's plenty to appeal to everyone. A Polynesian show on a stage over a lagoon creates magic. *7 mi north of Ke-ahole Airport, off Queen Kaʻahumanu Hwy.; Box 1299, Kapulehu-Kona 96745, tel. 808/325–5555. Cost: $49 adults, $24.50 children 6–12. Fri. from 6:15 PM.*

Gourmet magazine called the **Mauna Kea Beach Resort's** Tuesday *paʻina* (luau) "a Hawaiian feast elevated to haute cuisine." The menu includes traditional luau specialties, kalua (roasted) pig, grilled steaks, and more. A culturally sensitive show features an exciting fire dance. *Half hour north of Ke-ahole Airport off Queen Kaʻahumanu Hwy., near Kawaihae; 1 Mauna Kea Beach Dr., Kohala Coast, tel. 808/882–7222. Cost: $47.50 adults, $29 children 5–8. Tues. 6 PM.*

The **Royal Waikoloan** does a nice job with its Sunday-night luau at the Luau Grounds, where the Polynesian review showcases a local hula halau (dance school) presenting the entertainment, and island artisans demonstrating and selling their products. *Box 5000, Waikoloa Rd., Waikoloa, tel. 808/885–6789. Cost: $40 adults, $20 children 4–12. Sun. 6–9 PM.*

In Kailua, two luaus fill the bill, with Polynesian entertainment, an *imu* ceremony (placing and removing the pig from the underground oven), pageantry, and an open bar:

King Kamehameha's Kona Beach Hotel. *75-5660 Palani Rd., Kailua-Kona, tel. 808/329–2911. Cost: $42 adults, $15 children under 13. Tues., Thurs., Sun. at 6 PM.*

The **Kona Hilton Beach and Tennis Resort** also lights luau torches three times a week. *Alii Dr., Box 1179, Kailua-Kona, tel. 808/329–3111, ext. 4. Cost: $44 adults, $25 children under 12. Mon., Wed., Fri. at 6 PM.*

5 Maui

Maui, say the locals, is *no ka oi*—the best, the most, the top of the heap. To those who know Maui well, there's good reason for the superlatives. The second-largest island in the Hawaiian chain, Maui has made an international name for itself with its tropical allure, heady nightlife, and miles of perfect-tan beaches. Maui magic weaves a spell over the 2 million people who visit its shores each year and leaves them wanting more. Often visitors decide to return for good.

In many ways, Maui comes by its admirable reputation honestly. The island's 729 square miles contain Haleakala, a 10,023-foot dormant volcano whose misty summit beckons the adventurous; several villages where Hawaiian is still spoken; more millionaires per capita than nearly anywhere else in the world; three major resort destinations that have set new standards for luxury; Lahaina, an old whaling port that still serves as the island's commercial crossroads; and more than 80,000 residents who work, play, and live on what they fondly call the Valley Isle.

Maui residents have quite a bit to do with their island's successful tourism story. In the mid-1970s, savvy marketers on Maui saw a way to increase their sleepy island's economy by positioning it as an island apart. Maui was tired of settling for its meager 50,000 or so visitors each year and decided it didn't want to be one of the gang anymore. So community leaders started advertising and promoting their Valley Isle separately from the rest of the state. They nicknamed West Maui "the Golf Coast," luring in heavy-weight tournaments that, in turn, would bring more visitors. They went after the upscale visitor, renovating their finest hotels to accommodate a clientele that would pay more for the best. And they became the state's condominium expert, so that condos no longer meant second-best accommodations. Maui's visitor count swelled, putting it far ahead of that of the other Neighbor Islands.

That quick growth has led to its share of problems. During the busy seasons—from Christmas to Easter and then again during the summer—West Maui can be overly crowded. Although the County of Maui has seen success in its attempts to widen the two-lane road that connects Lahaina and Kaanapali, the stop-and-go traffic during rush hour reminds some visitors of what they face at home. It's not that residents aren't trying to do something about it—the Kapalua-West Maui Airport, with its free shuttle to and from Kaanapali, has alleviated some of the heavy island-circling traffic.

The explosion of visitors seeking out the Valley Isle has also created a large number of businesses looking to make a fast buck from the high-spending segment. Most of the time, the effect is harmless: Lahaina could easily be called the T-shirt capital of the Pacific (in close competition with Waikiki), and the island has nearly as many art galleries and cruise-boat companies as T-shirts. As in other popular travel destinations, the opportunity to make money from tourists in Maui has produced its fair share of schlock.

But then consider Maui's natural resources. The island is made up of two volcanoes, one now extinct and the other dormant, that both erupted many years ago and joined into one island. The resulting depression between the two is what gives Maui its nickname, the Valley Isle. West Maui's 5,788-foot Puu Kukui was the first volcano to form, a distinction that gives the area's mountainous topography a more weathered look. Rainbows seem to grow wild over this terrain as gentle mists move quietly from one end of the long mountain chain to the other. Sugarcane gives the rocky region its life, with its green stalks moving in the trade winds born near the summit.

The Valley Isle's second volcano is the 10,023-foot Haleakala, a mountain so enormous that its lava filled in the gap between the two volcanoes. You can't miss Haleakala (House of the Sun), a spectacle that rises to the east, often hiding in the clouds that cover its peak. To the Hawaiians, Haleakala is holy, and it's easy to see why. It's a mammoth mountain, and if you hike its slopes or peer into one of its craters, you'll witness an impressive variety of nature. Desertlike terrain butted up against tropical forests. Dew-dripping ferns a few steps from the surface of the moon. Spiked, alien plants poking their heads out of the soil right near the most elegant and fragrant flowers.

In fact, the island's volcanic history gives Maui much of its beauty. Rich red soil lines the roads around the island—*becoming* the roads in some parts. That same earth has provided fertile sowing grounds for the sugarcane that has for years covered the island's hills. As the deep blue of ocean and sky mingle with the red and green of Maui's land, it looks as if an artist had been busy painting the scenery with his favorite colors. Indeed, visual artists love Maui. Maybe it's the natural inspiration; maybe it's the slower pace, so conducive to creativity.

Farmers also appreciate the Valley Isle. On the slopes of Haleakala, the volcanic miracle has wrought agricultural wonders, luring those with a penchant for peat moss to plant and watch the lush results. Sweetly scented flowers bloom large and healthy, destined later to adorn a happy brow or become a lovely lei. Grapes cultivated on Haleakala's slopes ripen evenly and deliciously, then are squeezed for wine and champagne. Horses graze languidly on rolling meadows of the best Upcountry grasses, while jacaranda trees dot the hillsides with spurts of luscious lavender. As the big brute of a volcano slides east and becomes the town of Hana, the rains that lavishly fall there turn the soil into a jungle. Ferns take over the forest, waterfalls cascade down the crags, and moss becomes the island's carpeting.

The Valley Isle is full of people ready to share the friendly aloha spirit. If you take the drive to Hana, around dozens of hairpin curves, across bridges, and past waterfalls, you'll find a gentle folk who still speak the Hawaiian language. On a stroll through the streets of Wailuku, you'll meet elderly Filipino men who can remember their parents' stories of the old country. Or if you relax on the wharf in historic Lahaina, you can watch transplanted Californians have a great time surfing—most of them find West Maui the best place in the world to work and live. All these residents love their island and will gladly help you have a good time.

By all means, make the effort. Although a fantastic time can be had simply by bronzing on the silky-soft, white-sand beaches, the wonder of Maui is that much, much more awaits your discovery. Don't be surprised if quite a few of your fantasies are actually fulfilled. The Valley Isle hates to let anyone down.

Essential Information

Tour Groups

Package tours to Hawaii usually include airfare, accommodations, transfers, some sightseeing, and plenty of free time for the beach. Choosing a tour comes down to how inclusive you want it to be: Do you want to know all your meals are paid for before you leave, or would you rather hunt out a local eatery? Would you prefer to arrange a private sail, or is a group outing on a catamaran fine with you?

When considering a tour, be sure to find out (1) exactly what expenses are included—particularly tips, taxes, side trips, additional meals, and entertainment; (2) ratings of all hotels on the itinerary and the facilities they offer; (3) cancellation policies for both you and the tour operator; (4) the number of travelers in your group; and (5) if you are traveling alone, the cost of the single supplement. Note whether the tour operator reserves the right to change hotels, routes, or even prices after you've booked, and check out the operator's policy regarding cancellations, complaints, and trip-interruption insurance. Most tour operators request that bookings be made through a travel agent—in most cases there is no additional charge for doing so.

Arriving and Departing by Plane

Airports Maui's major airport, in Kahului, at the center of the island, has undergone a $100 million renovation, which began in 1982. Its new terminal opened in late 1990, making **Kahului Airport** (tel. 808/872–3800 and 808/372–3830) efficient and remarkably easy to navigate. Its major disadvantage is its distance from the major resort destinations in West Maui and Wailea. It will take you about an hour, with traffic in your favor, to get to a hotel in West Maui and about 20 to 30 minutes to go to Wailea. However, Kahului is the only airport on Maui that has direct service from the mainland.

If you're staying in West Maui, you might be better off flying into the new **Kapalua–West Maui Airport** (tel. 808/669–0228), an $8.5 million facility that opened in 1987. The only way to get to the Kapalua–West Maui Airport is on an interisland flight, however, since the short runway allows only small planes to land there. The little airport is set in the midst of a pineapple field with a terrific view of the ocean far below and provides one of the most pleasant ways to arrive on the Valley Isle. It was built by a locally based carrier, Hawaiian Air, which years ago had purchased small planes, giving it exclusive rights in West Maui. Before long, however, competitor Aloha Airlines figured out a way to fly into the Kapalua facility: It simply purchased commuter carrier Princeville Airways—which already flew the requisite-size prop planes—and renamed it Aloha IslandAir. Several major rental-car companies have courtesy phones inside the terminal. Shuttles also run between the airport and the Kaanapali and Kapalua resorts.

The only other airport on Maui is **Hana Airport** (tel. 808/248–8208), which is not much more than a landing strip. Only commuter Aloha IslandAir flies there, landing about once an hour.

When there is no flight, the tiny terminal usually stands eerily empty, with no gate agents, ticket takers, or other people in sight. If you are staying at the Hotel Hana-Maui, your flight will be met; if you have reserved a rental car, the agent will usually know your arrival time and meet you. Otherwise you can call **Dollar Rent A Car** to pick you up (tel. 808/248–8237).

Flights from North America **United Airlines** (tel. 800/241–6522) flies directly to Kahului from Los Angeles, Chicago, and San Francisco while **American Airlines** (tel. 800/433–7300) also flies into Kahului, with one stop in Honolulu, from Los Angeles, Chicago, Detroit, Houston, St. Louis, New York, and Dallas. **Delta** (tel. 800/221–1212) has through service to Maui daily from Salt Lake City, Atlanta, Dallas, and Los Angeles.

Maui is part of the world's most isolated chains of islands, so even if you fly directly to the Valley Isle, be prepared for a lengthy flight. From the West coast, Maui is about 5 hours; from the Midwest, expect about an 8-hour flight; and coming from the East coast will take about 10 hours. If you have to connect with an interisland flight in Honolulu, add at least another hour.

Maui is two hours behind Los Angeles, three hours behind Salt Lake City, four hours behind Chicago, and five hours behind New York. Hawaii doesn't turn back its clocks for daylight savings time, however, so add an extra hour to the time difference during the summer.

Flights from Honolulu In addition, **Continental** (tel. 800/525–0280), **Hawaiian** (tel. 800/367–5320), **Northwest** (tel. 800/225–2525), **America West** (tel. 800/247–5692), and **TWA** (tel. 800/221–2000) fly from the mainland to Honolulu, where Maui-bound passengers can connect with a 20- to 30-minute interisland flight. Interisland flights generally run about $50 one-way between Honolulu and Maui and are available many times each day from **Hawaiian Airlines** (tel. 800/367–5320), **Aloha Airlines** (tel. 800/367–5250), and **Aloha IslandAir** (tel. 800/323–3345). In fact, Maui is the most visited of the Neighbor Islands and therefore the easiest to connect to on an interisland flight. Flying a commuter carrier like Aloha IslandAir can take a few minutes longer, since the planes are generally small prop planes. Flights on all carriers usually stop running around 8 PM and begin again at about 6:30 the next morning.

Between the Airport and Your Destination *By Bus/Shuttle* If you're staying at the Kaanapali Beach Resort and fly into the Kapalua–West Maui Airport, you can take advantage of the resort's free shuttle and go back to the airport later to pick up your car. During daylight hours, the shuttle passes through the airport at regular intervals. Likewise, a **Gray Line-Maui** bus (tel. 808/877–5507) operates between Kahului and Kaanapali every hour between 7 AM and 5 PM. If you book the Hotel Hana-Maui, the charge for pickup at Hana Airport is included in the rate.

By Taxi You could also opt for a taxi. Maui has more than two dozen taxi companies, and they make frequent passes through the airport. If you don't see a cab, you can call **Yellow Cab** (tel. 808/877–7000) or **La Bella Taxi** (tel. 808/242–8011) for islandwide service from the airport, or **Kihei Taxi** (tel. 808/879–3000) if you're staying in the Kihei, Wailea, or Makena areas. Charges from Kahului Airport to Kaanapali run about $35; to Wailea, about $20; and to Lahaina, about $30.

By Car   Frankly, the best way to get from the airport to your destination is in your own rental car. You're going to need it for the rest of the trip; you might as well get it right away. Most major car-rental companies have conveniently located desks at each airport (*see* Getting Around, *below*).

Arriving and Departing by Ship

From Honolulu   Approaching the Valley Isle from the deck of a ship is a great orientation. Watching the land loom ever larger conjures up the same kinds of feelings the early Polynesians probably had on their first voyage—except they didn't get the kind of lavish treatment those on board a luxury cruise ship routinely receive. If this is an option that appeals to you, you can book passage through **American Hawaii Cruises** (550 Kearny St., San Francisco, CA 94108, tel. 800/765–7000), which offers seven-day interisland cruises departing from Honolulu on the SS *Constitution* and the SS *Independence*. Both have recently been renovated.

Getting Around

By Car   Maui, the second-largest island in the state of Hawaii, with 729
Driving   square miles, has some 120 miles of coastline, not all of which is accessible. Less than one-quarter of its land mass is inhabited. To see the island your best bet is a car, because there is no reliable public transportation.

Maui has several major roads. Highway 30, or the Honoapiilani Highway, goes from Wailuku in Central Maui around the south of the West Maui mountains and up past Lahaina, Kaanapali, and Kapalua. The road from the Kahului Airport to Kihei, Wailea, and Makena is called Highway 350, or the Mokulele Highway. When you reach Kihei, you can take Kihei Road to reach all the lodgings in that town, or you can bypass them on Highway 31 (the Piilani Highway) if you're staying in Wailea or Makena. The latter road is the best on the island in terms of driving because it is wide and sparsely traveled. Another main thoroughfare is Highway 37, or the Haleakala Highway, which goes between Kahului and Haleakala. Most of the island's roads have two lanes.

If you're going to attempt the dirt roads between Kapalua and Wailuku or from Hana to Makena, you'll need a four-wheel-drive vehicle, but be forewarned: Rental-car companies prohibit travel off the pavement, so if you break down, you're on your own for repairs. The only other difficult road on Maui is Highway 36, or the Hana Highway, which runs 56 miles between Kahului and Hana and includes more twists and turns than a person can count. Take it slow and you should have no problems.

Car Rentals   During peak seasons—summer and Christmas through Easter—be sure to reserve your car well ahead of time. Although you'll generally pay a higher price in the peak seasons, you'll find Maui one of the cheapest U.S. destinations for renting an auto. Expect to pay about $35 a day for a compact car from one of the major companies. You can get an even more inexpensive deal from one of the locally owned budget companies. For these, you'll probably have to call for a shuttle from the airport since they often don't have rental desks there.

Budget (tel. 800/527–0707 or, in Canada, 800/268–8900), **Dollar** (tel. in the U.S. and Canada, 800/800–4000), and **National** (tel. 800/CAR–RENT) have desks at the Kapulua–West Maui Airport, while **Hertz** (tel. 800/654–3131 or, in Canada, 800/263–0600), **Alamo** (tel. 800/327–9633), **Thrifty** (tel. 800/367–2277), and **Tropical** (tel. 800/678–6000) are nearby. All the above, plus **Avis** (tel. 800/331–1212 or, in Canada, 800/879–2847), have desks at or near Maui's major airport in Kahului. **Roberts Tours** (tel. 808/871–6226) offers car rentals through package tours. In addition, quite a few locally owned companies rent cars on Maui, including **Rent-A-Jeep** (tel. 808/877–6626), **Payless Car Rental** (tel. 800/345–5230), and **Trans-Maui** (tel. 800/367–5228). They are near the Kahului Airport and will pick you up only from there.

By Shuttle If you're staying in the right hotel or condo, there are a few shuttles that can get you around the area. The **Kaanapali–Lahaina Shuttle** runs daily from the Royal Lahaina Hotel in Kaanapali to the Wharf Shopping Center in Lahaina every half hour between 8 AM and 10:25 PM with stops at all Kaanapali hotels. The cost is $1.50. The **Kaanapali Shuttle** runs within the resort between 7 AM and 11 PM and stops automatically at all hotels and at condos when requested. It also goes to and from Lahaina at 55-minute intervals. It's free. All Kaanapali hotels have copies of schedules, or you can call the Kaanapali Beach Operators Association (tel. 808/661–3271). The free **Aston Hotels Shuttle** in the Kaanapali area runs from 8 AM to 6 PM for guests who want to go to the Whalers Village Shopping Center and Lahaina. You can get schedules at Aston hotel desks. The **Wailea Shuttle** and the **Kapalua Shuttle** run within their respective resorts and are free; schedules are available throughout each resort.

By Taxi For short hops between hotels and restaurants, this can be a convenient way to go, but you'll have to call ahead. Even busy West Maui doesn't have curbside taxi service. **West Maui Taxi** (761 Kumukahi, Lahaina, tel. 808/667–2605) and **Yellow Cab of Maui** (Kahului Airport, tel. 808/877–7000) both service the entire island, but you'd be smart to consider using them just for the areas where they're located. **Alii Cab** (475 Kuai Pl., Lahaina, tel. 808/661–3688) specializes in West Maui, while **Kihei Taxi** (Kihei, tel. 808/879–3000) serves Central Maui.

By Limousine **Arthur's Limousine Service** (Box 11865, Lahaina 96761, tel. 800/345–4667) provides a chauffeured superstretch Lincoln complete with two TVs, three bars, and two sunroofs for $60 per hour. **Inlanda Inc.** (91 Alo Alo Pl., Lahaina 96761, tel. 808/669–7800) has Cadillacs and Lincolns from $50 an hour. Both companies are based in or near Lahaina but serve the entire island. There's a minimum time requirement—usually two hours—but the companies have put together personalized sightseeing tours just to make it easy for you.

By Moped Mopeds from **A&B Moped Rental** (3481 Lower Honoapiilani Hwy., Lahaina, tel. 808/669–0027) go for about $25. Be especially careful navigating the roads on Maui, since there are no designated bicycle or moped lanes.

Important Addresses and Numbers

Tourist Information **Maui Visitors Bureau** (250 Alamaha St., Suite N–16, Kahului 96732, tel. 808/871–8691).

Maui Chamber of Commerce (26 Puunene Ave., Kahului 96732, also in the industrial district, tel. 808/871–7711).

Emergencies **Police, fire,** or **ambulance** (tel. 911).

Doctors **Doctors on Call** (Hyatt Regency Maui-Napili Tower #1, Kaanapali, tel. 808/667–7676) and **Maui Physicians** (3600 Lower Honoapiilani Rd., Lahaina, tel. 808/669–9600) are doctors serving West Maui. Another walk-in clinic at Whalers Village, **West Maui Healthcare Center** (2435 Kaanapali Pkwy., Suite H-7, Kaanapali, tel. 808/667–9721) also serves West Maui. Created by two doctors in 1980 to treat tourists, the clinic is open daily 7 AM–11 PM. **Kihei Clinic** and **Wailea Medical Services** (1993 S. Kihei Rd., Kihei, tel. 808/879–1440 or 808/879–7447) are based in the more central part of the Valley Isle. All of the above groups are geared toward working with visitors.

Hospitals **Hana Medical Center** (Hana Hwy., Hana, tel. 808/248–8294).

Kula Hospital (204 Kula Hwy., Kula, tel. 808/878–1221).

Maui Memorial Hospital (221 Mahalani, Wailuku, tel. 808/244–9056).

Pharmacies Maui has no 24-hour pharmacies but several where you can get prescriptions filled during daylight hours. The least expensive are the island's two **Longs Drug Stores** (Maui Mall, corner of Kaahumanu and Puunene Aves., Kahului, tel. 808/877–0068; Lahaina Cannery Shopping Center, Honoapiilani Hwy., tel. 808/667–4390; both open daily, 8:30 AM–9 PM). **Kihei Drug** is in the Kihei Town Center (1881 S. Kihei Rd., Kihei, tel. 808/879–1915; open weekdays 8:30–7, Sat. 8:30–5:30, Sun. 10–3).

Road Service On Maui, the one **AAA** garage that offers 24-hour islandwide service is **Sunset Towing** (Bldg. 30, Halawai Rd., Kaanapali, tel. 808/667–7048). It specializes in serving West Maui and Kahului but will travel anywhere on Maui with a tow truck.

Grocers Three major groceries are open 24 hours a day. **Safeway** (Hanoapiilani Hwy., Lahaina, tel. 808/667–4392), at the Lahaina Cannery Shopping Center, serves West Maui, while **Foodland** (1881 S. Kihei Rd., Kihei, tel. 808/879–9350), in the Kihei Town Center, and **Safeway** (170 E. Kamehameha Ave., Kahului, tel. 808/877–3377) operate on the island's other side.

Weather **National Weather Service/Maui Forecast** (tel. 808/877–5111). **Haleakala Weather Forecast** (tel. 808/871–5054).

Others **Coast Guard Rescue Center** (tel. 808/244–5256).

Suicide and Crisis Center Help Line (tel. 808/244–7407).

Opening and Closing Times

Banks on the island are generally open Monday–Thursday 8:30–3, Friday 8:30–6.

Shops are generally open seven days a week, 9–5. Shopping centers tend to stay open later (until 9 on certain days).

Guided Tours

If getting yourself oriented on an island doesn't come easy, try taking one of a variety of guided tours offered on Maui. This is a perfect opportunity to benefit from the services of an expert who can point out the sights you're most interested in and explain what it all means. Basically, you have your choice of getting oriented from the ground or from the air.

By Land **Circle Island Tour.** This is a big island to tour in one day, so several companies combine various sections of it—either Haleakala, Iao Needle, and Central Maui, or West Maui and its environs. Some stops include the historical sections of the county seat of Wailuku, while others focus on some of the best snorkeling spots. Call a selection of companies to find the tour that suits you. The cost is usually $35–$65 for adults, half that for children.

Haleakala Sunrise Tour. This tour starts before dawn so that visitors get a chance to actually make it to the top of the dormant volcano before the sun peeks over the horizon. Some companies throw in champagne to greet the sunrise. Cost of the six-hour tour: about $45.

Haleakala/Upcountry Tour. Usually a half-day excursion, this tour is offered in several versions by different companies. The trip often includes stops at a protea farm and at Tedeschi Vineyards and Winery, the only place in Hawaii where wine is made. Cost: about $40 adults, $20 children.

Hana Tour. This tour is almost always done in a van, as the winding road to Hana just doesn't provide a comfortable ride in bigger buses. Of late, Hana has so many of these one-day tours that it seems as if there are more vans than cars on the road. Still, it's a more relaxing way to do the drive than behind the wheel of your own car. Guides decide where you stop for photos. Cost: about $60.

Tour Companies Ground-tour companies are usually statewide and have a whole fleet of vehicles. Some use air-conditioned buses, while others prefer smaller vans. Then you've got your minivans, your microbuses, and your minicoaches. The key is how many passengers each will hold. Be sure to ask how many stops you'll get on your tour, or you may be disappointed to find that all your sightseeing is done through a window.

Most of the tour guides have been in the business for years; some were born in the Islands and have taken special classes to learn more about their culture and lore. They expect a tip ($1 per person at least), but they're just as cordial without one.

There are many ground-tour companies. Here are some of the most reliable and popular ones, with their mailing addresses:

Gray Line Hawaii (273 Dairy Rd., Kahului 96732, tel. 800/367–2420 or 808/877–5507) uses air-conditioned motor coaches, limos, and vans.

No Ka Oi Scenic Tours (Box 1827, Kahului 96732, tel. 808/871–9008) specializes in a Hana tour.

Maui Fun Centers (2191 S. Kihei Rd., Kihei 96753, tel. 808/874–3773) offers van, bicycle, and hiking tours.

Polynesian Adventure Tours (536 Keolani Pl., Kahului 96732, tel. 800/622–3011 or 808/877–4242) has guides that keep up an amusing patter. The talk can get annoying, however, if you're more interested in the serious stuff.

Roberts Hawaii Tours (Box 247, Kahului 96732, tel. 808/871–6226) and **Trans Hawaiian Services** (3111 Castle St., Honolulu 96815, tel. 800/533–8765) are two of the largest companies in the state, but each manages to keep its tours personal.

By Air **Circle Island Tour.** Helicopter companies handle this in different ways. Some have fancy names, such as Ultimate Experience or Circle Island Deluxe. Some go for two hours or more. Cost: about $185–$200.

Hana/Haleakala Crater Tour. This takes about 90 minutes to travel inside the volcano, then down to the Hawaiian village of Hana. Some companies stop in secluded areas for refreshments, but local residents have had moderate success in getting this stopped. Cost: about $130.

Tour Companies About seven helicopter companies regularly offer air tours over Maui. If you're at all nervous, ask about the company's safety record, although most are reliable. The best Maui operators include **Hawaii Helicopters** (Kahului Heliport, Hangar 106, Kahului 96732, tel. 808/877–3900 or 800/346–2403 from the Mainland), **Maui Helicopters** (Box 1002, Kihei 96753, tel. 808/879–1601 or 800/367–8003 from the Mainland), **Papillon Hawaiian Helicopters** (Box 1478, Kahului 96732, tel. 808/669–4884 or 800/367–7095), and **Kenai Helicopters** (Box 685, Puunene 96784, tel. 808/871–6483 or 800/622–3144).

Special-interest Tours Once you have your bearings, you may want a tour that's a bit more specialized. For example, you may have a hankering for hunting but not know where to go. You might want to bike down a volcano or visit artists. Here are some options:

Crater Bound Tours. Groups assemble at a Haleakala ranger station at 7:30 AM, then walk 4–10 miles to where Craig Moore (Box 265, Kula 96790, tel. 808/878–1743) and his crew have unpacked the horses, set up the campsite, and organized cocktail hour. A second day is spent exploring the crater; the third day is a hike back out of the crater. Gourmet breakfasts and dinners are served. A basic 3-day, 2-night package is $300 per person, or talk to Moore about special arrangements and interests.

Haleakala Downhills. It started back in 1983 with **Cruiser Bob's Original Haleakala Downhill** (99 Hana Hwy., Box B, Paia 96779, tel. 808/579–8444), which now has competition from **Maui Downhill Bicycle Safaris** (199 Dairy Rd., Kahului 96732, tel. 800/535–2453) and **Maui Mountain Cruisers** (Box 1356, Makawao 96768, tel. 800/232–MAUI). All three companies will put you on a bicycle at the top of Haleakala and let you coast down. Safety precautions are top priority, so riders wear helmets and receive training in appropriate bicycle-bell ringing. Meals are provided. Cost: $85–$100.

Hiking Tours. Hike Maui (Box 330969, Kahului 96733, tel. 808/879–5270) is owned by naturalist Ken Schmitt, who guides some 50 different hikes himself. Prices range from $60 for a 4-mile, five-hour hike to $990 for a week-long trek with accommodations and all meals. **Maui-Anne's Island Photography Tours** (Box 2250, Kihei 96753, tel. 808/874–3797) offers hiking trips with a focus on photography. A wide variety of tours and prices is available upon request.

Horseback Tours. At least two companies on Maui now offer horseback riding that's far more appealing than the typical hour-long trudge over a boring trail with 50 other horses. Mauian Frank Levinson started **Adventures on Horseback** (Box 1771, Makawao 96768, tel. 808/242–7445) a few years back with five-hour outings into secluded parts of Maui. The tours traverse ocean cliffs on Maui's north shore, along the slopes of Haleakala, as they pass by streams, through rain forests, and near waterfalls. The $125-per-person price includes breakfast, lunch, and refreshments. **Charley's Trail Rides & Pack Trips** (c/o Kaupo Store, Kaupo 96713, tel. 808/248–8209) requires an even more stout physical nature, as the overnighters go from Kaupo—a *tiny* village nearly 20 miles past Hana—up the slopes of Haleakala to the crater. For parties of four to six, the per-person charge is $150, including meals and cabin or campsite equipment, or $125 without meals. Charges are higher for fewer people.

Hunting Adventures of Maui (645-B Kaupakalua Rd., Haiku 96708, tel. 808/572–8214). This is a guided excursion on more than 100,000 acres of private ranch land on Maui, a "fair chase" hunt for Spanish mountain goats and wild boar. Maui has a year-round hunting season, so this tour is always available. Cost: $400 for the first person, $200 for each additional hunter. Cost includes transportation, food, beverages, clothing, boots, packs, and meat storage and packing for shipping. Nonhunters can accompany the tour free.

Maui Art Tours (Box 1058, Makawao 96768, tel. 808/572–7132). Maui publisher Barbara Glassman produces a book every year that catalogues and pictures Maui artists and their work in exchange for an entry fee. That project has been successful, so Glassman now offers a tour that takes creative types into artists' homes for tea and conversation. Limo transportation and an elegant lunch are provided, as is the opportunity to buy art directly from the artists. This is a very enjoyable, refined tour that costs $150. Maui Art Tours will customize each tour, letting clients choose the type of art they want to see and even how many artists they want to visit.

Star-gazing. Take a star-studded trip with **Astronomy Tours Maui** (1597 Aa St., Lahaina 96761, tel. 808/667–9080). An astronomer leads this tour to Haleakala's summit to view the sunset and stars. Dinner at Kula Lodge is included in the $85 package; $50 for children 12 and under.

Personal Guides **Local Guides of Maui** (333 Dairy Rd., Kahului 96732, tel. 800/ 228–6284). This is *the* best way to see Maui through the eyes of the locals. Started by Laurie Robello, who is part-Hawaiian, the company now has more than a dozen guides. Your guide will come to your hotel, but then transportation is in your car, which he or she will drive. Local Guides of Maui tailors its tours to your particular interests. Local Guides of Maui charges $165 for two people all day; each additional person is $20.

Temptation Tours (RR1, Box 454, Kula 96790, tel. 808/877– 8888). At the other end of the spectrum is this company, which leads you around luxuriously. Company president Dave Campbell has targeted members of the affluent older crowd (though almost anyone would enjoy these tours) who don't want to be herded into a crowded bus. He provides exclusive tours in his plush, six-passenger limo-van and specializes in full-day tours to Haleakala and Hana. Prices vary depending on the degree of customization; the average Hana tour, with a picnic lunch, however, runs about $105, plus tax, per person.

Walking Tours The **Lahaina Restoration Foundation** (Baldwin Home, 696 Front St., Lahaina, tel. 808/661–3262) has published a walking-tour map for interested visitors. The map will guide you to the most historic sites of Lahaina, some renovated and some not. Highlights of the walk include the Jodo Mission, the Brig *Carthaginian II*, The Baldwin Home, and the old Court House. These are all sights you could find yourself, but the map is free, and it makes the walk easier.

Exploring Maui

A visitor to Maui has plenty of things to see and do besides spending time on the beach. To help you organize your time, this guide divides the island into four tours—West Maui, Central Maui, Haleakala and Upcountry, and the Road to Hana (East Maui). Each tour lasts from a half day to a full day, depending on how long you spend at each stop. All tours require a car, but they include opportunities for walking.

Highlights for First-time Visitors

Alexander & Baldwin Sugar Museum, Tour 2
Baldwin Home, Tour 1
Brig *Carthaginian II*, Tour 1
Hale Hoikeike, Tour 2
Haleakala, Tour 3
Hana, Tour 4
Helani Gardens, Tour 4
Hookipa Beach, Tour 4
Iao Valley, Tour 4
Lahaina, Tour 1
Paia, Tour 4
Tedeschi Vineyards and Winery, Tour 3

Tour 1: West Maui

Numbers in the margin correspond to points of interest on the Maui map.

Drive about as far north as you can on the Honoapiilani Highway (Hwy. 30), and make a left on Bay Drive at the Kapalua sign. We'll start this tour at the **Kapalua Bay Hotel** (1 Bay Dr., tel. 808/669–5656), set in a beautifully secluded location in upper West Maui. Surrounded by pineapple fields, this classy hotel was built in 1978 by Maui Land & Pineapple Company, joined in 1992 by a dazzling **Ritz-Carlton,** and now hosts dedicated golfers, celebrities who want to be left alone, and some of the world's richest folks. The nearby Kapalua Villas are expansive condominiums on the resort property that start at $275 a night. Kapalua's shops and restaurants are some of Maui's finest, but expect to pay big bucks for whatever you purchase (*see* Lodging, *below*).

Back in the car, return from the hotel to Honoapiilani Highway and make a left. Drive north, and in less than a mile the road is less well maintained. This used to be the route to Wailuku. It was never a good road, and storms now and then make it partly impassable. However, you'll discover some gorgeous photo opportunities along the road, and if you go far enough, you'll come to **Kahakuloa,** a tiny fishing village that seems lost in time. It is one of the oldest towns on Maui. Many remote villages that were similar to Kahakuloa used to be tucked away in the valleys of this area. This is the wild side of West Maui; true adventurers will find terrific snorkeling and swimming here, as well as some good hiking trails.

Kahakuloa is about as far as you can go on the "highway" that alternates between being called 30 and 340. From Kahakuloa, turn around and go back in the direction from which you came—south toward Kaanapali and Lahaina. Along the way to

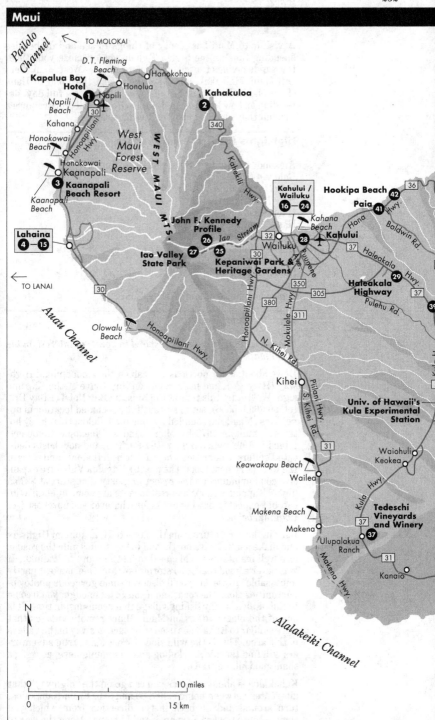

Maui

Pailolo Channel

← TO MOLOKAI

D.T. Fleming Beach

Hanokohau

Kapalua Bay Hotel ❶

Napili

Napili Beach

Kahana

Kahakuloa ❷

Honokowai Beach

Honoapiilani Hwy.

Honokowai

Kaanapali

Kaanapali Beach Resort ❸

Kaanapali Beach

Lahaina ❹–❿

WEST MAUI FOREST RESERVE

WEST MAUI MTS.

Kahekili Hwy. 340

West Maui Forest Reserve

← TO LANAI

Auau Channel

John F. Kennedy Profile ❷❻

Iao Valley State Park ❷❼

Iao Stream

Kepaniwai Park & Heritage Gardens ❷❺

Kahului / Wailuku ❶❻–❷❹

Kahana Beach

Hookipa Beach ❹❷

Paia ❹❶ Hana Hwy. 36

Kahului

Wailuku 32 ❷❽

Puunene Ave. Baldwin Rd.

350

305

380

311

Haleakala Hwy. 37

Haleakala Highway ❷❾

Pulehu Rd.

Kula Hwy.

Olowalu Beach

Honoapiilani Hwy.

Honoapiilani Hwy.

N. Kihei Rd.

Mokulele Hwy.

Kihei

Piilani Hwy.

S. Kihei Rd.

Univ. of Hawaii's Kula Experimental Station

31

Waiohuli

Keokea

Keawakapu Beach

Wailea

Kula Hwy.

Makena Beach

Makena

Tedeschi Vineyards and Winery ❸❼

37

Ulupalakua Ranch

31

Makena Hwy.

Kanaio

N

Alalakeiki Channel

0   10 miles

0   15 km

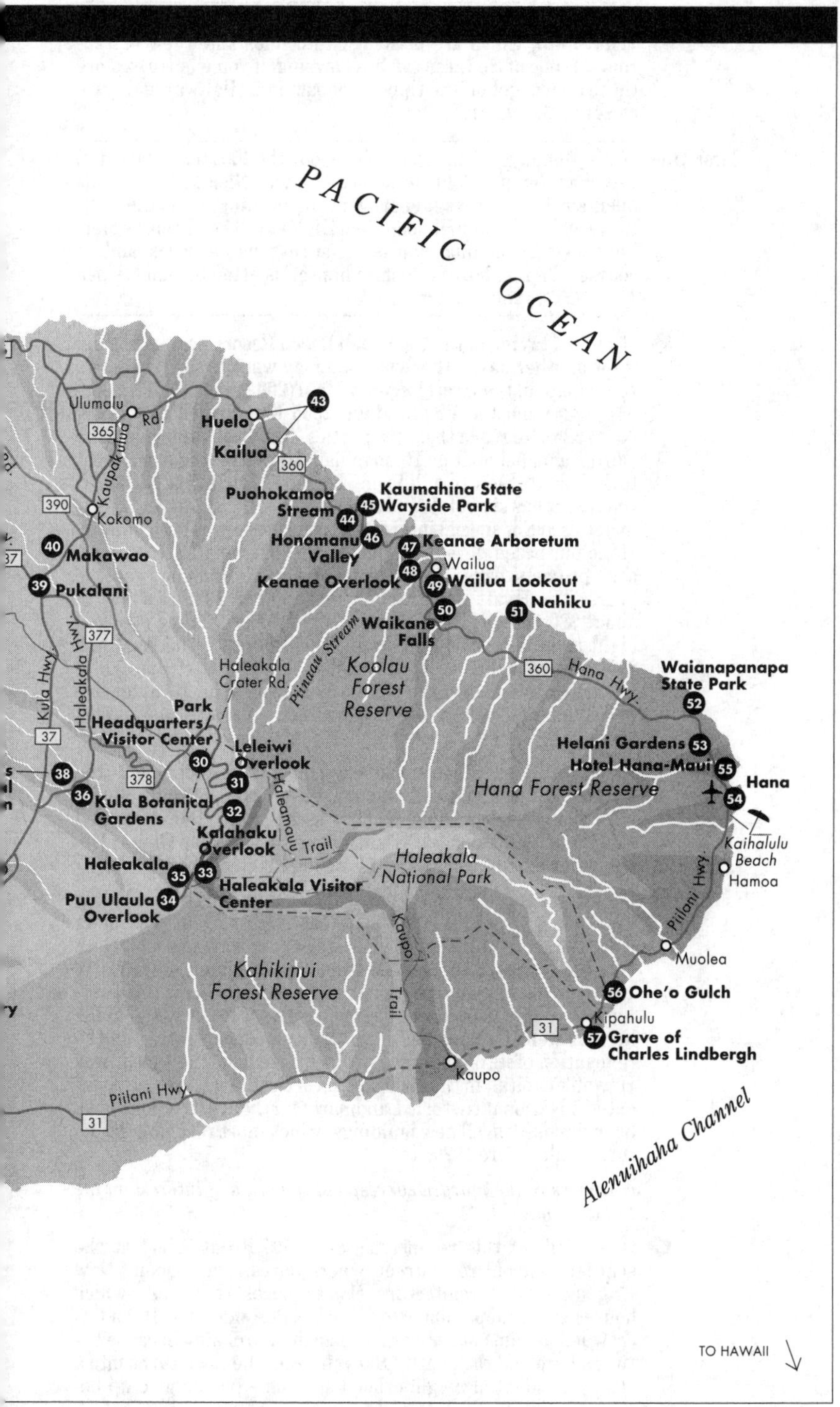
PACIFIC OCEAN
Ulumalu
Rd.
365
Kaupakalua
Huelo
43
Kailua
360
390
Kokomo
Puohokamoa Stream
44
45
Kaumahina State Wayside Park
46
Honomanu Valley
47
Keanae Arboretum
48
Keanae Overlook
Wailua
49
Wailua Lookout
50
Waikane Falls
51
Nahiku
40
Makawao
39
Pukalani
377
Kula Hwy.
Haleakala Hwy.
37
Haleakala Crater Rd.
Piinaau Stream
Koolau Forest Reserve
360
Hana Hwy.
Waianapanapa State Park
52
Park Headquarters/ Visitor Center
30
Leleiwi Overlook
31
Haleamau
38
378
36
Kula Botanical Gardens
32
Helani Gardens
53
Hotel Hana-Maui
55
Hana
54
Hana Forest Reserve
Kalahaku Overlook
Trail
Haleakala National Park
Kaihalulu Beach
Hamoa
Haleakala
35
33
Haleakala Visitor Center
Puu Ulaula
34
Overlook
Kaupo
Trail
Piilani Hwy.
Muolea
Kahikinui Forest Reserve
56
Ohe'o Gulch
31
Kipahulu
57
Grave of Charles Lindbergh
Kaupo
Piilani Hwy.
31
Alenuihaha Channel
TO HAWAII

Kaanapali, you'll pass the beach towns of **Napili, Kahana,** and **Honokowai,** which are packed with condos and a few restaurants. Some of this area can be charming; if you wish to explore these towns, get off the Upper Honoapiilani Highway and drive closer to the water.

Time Out If it's Monday or Thursday, check out the **Farmer's Market** in Kahana. County Council member Wayne Nishiki sets up his open-air fruit-and-veggie show in the parking lot at the ABC Store at 3511 Lower Honoapiilani Highway. The Farmer's Market specializes in quality produce at reasonable prices, and, of course, the flamboyant Nishiki himself is often on hand. *Open Mon. 12:30–4:30, Thurs. 9–noon.*

❸ If you're staying at the **Kaanapali Beach Resort,** save exploring it for another day. Otherwise, you may want to see two hotels at Kaanapali, the **Hyatt Regency Maui** (200 Nohea Kai Dr., 808/661–1234) and the **Westin Maui** (2365 Kaanapali Pkwy., 808/667–2525). To reach these properties, from Kahakuloa take the third Kaanapali exit on Honoapiilani Highway (the one closest to Lahaina), then turn left on Kaanapali Parkway. Although the resort has six hotels and seven condos, the Hyatt and Westin hotels are of special interest because they were both built by Honolulu-based developer Christopher Hemmeter, whose resort projects have grown more and more opulent over the years. The Hyatt, for example, was built in 1980 at a cost of about $80 million. It has a waterfall in the swimming pool and eight more falls scattered around the property. The Westin, a $155 million makeover of the much older Maui Surf Hotel, also has waterfalls all over the place—15 at last count. Its extensive art collection, worth about $2 million, includes work from around the world, with an emphasis on Asian and Pacific art.

Kaanapali Beach Resort also has some decent shopping at the **Whalers Village** (2435 Kaanapali Pkwy., tel. 808/661–4567), with such trendy mainland shops as ACA Joe, Benetton, and Esprit, as well as such Hawaiian boutiques as Blue Ginger Designs, Paradise Clothing, and Lahaina Printsellers.

❹ Back in the car, it's time to head for **Lahaina.** This little whaling town has a notorious past; there are stories of lusty whalers who met head-on with missionaries bent on saving souls. Both groups journeyed to Lahaina from New England in the early 1800s. To get oriented, take a drive down **Front Street.** At first, Lahaina might look touristy, but there's a lot that's genuine here as well. Lahaina has recently been concentrating on the renovation of its old buildings, which date from the time it was Hawaii's capital, in the 1800s. Much of the town has been designated a National Historic Landmark; further restrictions have been imposed on all new buildings, which must resemble structures built before 1920.

Numbers in the margin correspond to points of interest on the Lahaina map.

❺ One result of this reconstruction is **505 Front Street** at the southern end of Front Street, where you can park. Quaint New England–style architecture characterizes this mall, which houses small shops connected by a wooden sidewalk. It isn't as crowded as some other areas in Lahaina, probably because between here and the nearby Banyan Tree, the town turns into a sleepy residential neighborhood and some people give up be-

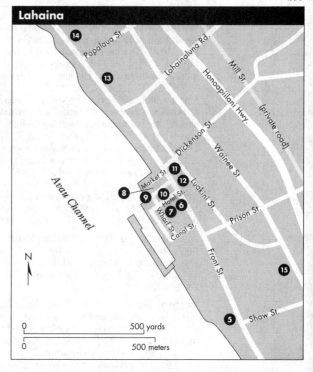

fore reaching the mall. A local hangout called **Sam's Pub,** how-ever, seems to lure its fair share of fun-lovers.

6 The **Banyan Tree,** which is a short walk from 505 Front Street, was planted in 1873. It is the largest of its kind in the 50th state and provides a welcome retreat for the weary who come to sit under its awesome branches. When the sun sets each evening, mynah birds settle in for a screeching symphony (which can be

7 an event in itself). Next to the tree is the **Court House,** which now houses two art galleries—one upstairs and one in what was an old prison in the basement. The Court House was origi-nally built in 1857 and rebuilt in 1925. *649 Wharf St., tel. 808/ 661–0111. Admission free. Open daily 10–4.*

8 About a half block northwest, you'll find the site of a **Brick Pal-ace** built by King Kamehameha I, as well as the four cannons he used to protect it. Don't waste time looking for a building. All that's left is a space with several holes sectioned off in front of the Pioneer Inn. Hawaii's first king lived only one year in the palace because his favorite wife, Kaahumanu, refused to stay there. After 70 years, it collapsed.

9 The **Brig *Carthaginian II*** is anchored at the dock nearby and is open as a museum. It was made in Germany in the 1920s and is a replica of the type of ship that brought the missionaries around the Horn to Hawaii in the early 1800s. The Brig *Carthaginian II* is the only authentically restored square-rigged brig in the world. A small museum below deck features a film and exhibit about whaling. *At the harbor, tel. 808/661–3262. Admission: $3. Open daily 9–4:30.*

Time Out If you're in the mood for some local color, stroll into the **Pioneer**
⓾ **Inn** (658 Wharf St., tel. 808/661–3636) for a refreshment. This
hotel, built in 1920, has a few inexpensive rooms upstairs and a
restaurant. The inn's ambience capitalizes on Lahaina's whaling era, during the 19th century. Cruise-boat captains, fishermen, and scores of tourists hang out here during the afternoon.

If you walk from the *Carthaginian II* to the corner of Front and
⓫ Dickenson streets, you'll find the **Baldwin Home.** An early missionary to Lahaina, Ephraim Spaulding, built this plastered
and whitewashed coral stone home in 1834–35; in 1836 Dr.
Dwight Baldwin—also a missionary—moved in with his family. The home is now run by the Lahaina Restoration Foundation and has been restored and furnished in a decor that reflects
the period. You can view the living room with the family's
grand piano, the dining room, and Dr. Baldwin's dispensary,
including his Hawaiian medical license. *696 Front St., tel. 808/
661–3262. Admission: $2. Open daily 9–4:30.*

Next door is the **Master's Reading Room,** Maui's oldest building, constructed in 1833. In the early days, the ground floor
was a mission's storeroom, while the reading room upstairs was
for sailors. The **Lahaina Restoration Foundation** is housed in
the building.

Continue north or south on **Front Street** for Lahaina's commercial side. Shops abound here; some are funky, a few are exquisite. Several little malls go back off the street, and some of the
unique stores can be found there. Lahaina also boasts so many
fine art galleries that it's occasionally referred to as SoHo West
(*see* Shopping, *below*). At the Wharf Cinema Center (658 Front
⓬ St.), you can see the **Spring House,** which was built by missionaries over a freshwater spring. The building is now home to a
huge Fresnel lens once used in a local lighthouse that guided
ships to Lahaina.

Time Out Dockside ambience given you a yen for a big beefy burger?
Head for **Cheeseburgers in Paradise** (Front St. at Lahainaluna
Rd., tel. 808/661–4855). Up-country locals, who raise their own
beef, travel to Lahaina for these $5 behemoths, topped with
cheddar, mozzarella, or Swiss cheese.

⓭ If you continue north on Front Street, you'll pass the **Wo Hing**
Society, originally built as a temple in 1912. It now contains
Chinese artifacts and a historic theater that features Thomas
Edison films of Hawaii, circa 1898. Upstairs is the only public
Taoist altar on Maui. *858 Front St., tel. 808/661–3262. Admis-
sion free. Open daily 9–4:30.*

⓮ Head another block north and you'll find the **Seamen's Hospital,**
which was built in the 1830s as a royal party house for King Kamehameha III. It was later turned over to the U.S. government, which used it as a hospital for whaling men. Now within
the building, **Lahaina Printsellers** sells antique maps and
charts. *1024 Front St., tel. 808/661–3262. Admission free.
Open daily.*

Time Out There's nothing like watching the sun sink in the western sky
while you sit near the ocean. In Lahaina, a couple of restaurants have situated their lanais right over the water. Try
Kimo's (845 Front St., tel. 808/661–4811). Here, you can have

simple food and a relaxing drink while you watch the parasailors, the cruise boats, and other water fanatics work in the last minutes of another great day.

If you're finished walking before dusk with a hankering for just one more stop, try the **Waiola Church** (535 Wainee St., tel. 808/661–4349) and the **Waiola Cemetery**. To reach the church and cemetery, walk south down Front Street, make a left onto Dickenson Street, then make a right onto Wainee Street and walk another few blocks. The cemetery is the older of the two sites, dating from the time when Kamehameha's sacred wife Queen Keopuolani died and was buried there in 1823. The church was erected next door in 1832 by Hawaiian chiefs and was originally named Ebenezer by the queen's second husband and widower, Governor Hoapili. It was later named Wainee, after the district in which it is located. After a few fires and some wind damage, the current structure was put up in 1953 and named Waiola Church.

Tour 2: Central Maui

Numbers in the margin correspond to points of interest on the Kahului–Wailuku map.

This tour begins in **Kahului**, which looks nothing like the lush tropical paradise most people envision when they think of Hawaii. This industrial and commercial town is home to many of Maui's permanent residents, who find their jobs and the center of commerce close by. Kahului was built in the early 1950s as the answer to Alexander & Baldwin's problems. This large company was tired of playing landlord to its many plantation workers and sold land to a developer who promised to create affordable housing. The scheme worked, and Kahului became the first planned city in Hawaii. Most tourists spend little time here, merely passing through on their way to and from the airport. Kaahumanu Avenue (Hwy. 32) is Kahului's main street and runs east and west.

Kahului does have Maui's largest shopping mall, the **Kaahumanu Center** (275 Kaahumanu Ave., tel. 808/877–3369). You might want to stop in at **Camellia Seed Shop** for what the locals call "crack seed," a delicacy that's made from dried fruits, nuts, and sugar. Other places to shop at Kaahumanu Center include **Shirokiya**, a major department store brought to Hawaii from Japan, and such American standards as Mrs. Field's Cookies, Sears, Kay-Bee Toys, and Kinney Shoes.

Next take a detour to visit the **Alexander & Baldwin Sugar Museum**. Get on Kaahumanu Avenue from the shopping center and take a right onto Highway 350 (Puunene Ave.). Look for the museum just off Highway 350 as you drive into the town called Puunene (pronounced *Poo-oo-NAY-nay*) in the direction of Wailea. You'll be heading toward **Haleakala**, a 10,023-foot dormant volcano, which you should save most of a day to explore (*see* Tour 3, *below*). Alexander & Baldwin, Maui's largest landowner, opened this museum in 1988 to detail the rise of sugarcane in the Islands. Alexander & Baldwin was one of five companies, better known as the Big Five, that spearheaded the planting, harvesting, and marketing of the valuable agricultural product. Although Hawaiian sugar has been supplanted by cheaper foreign versions—as well as by less costly sugar

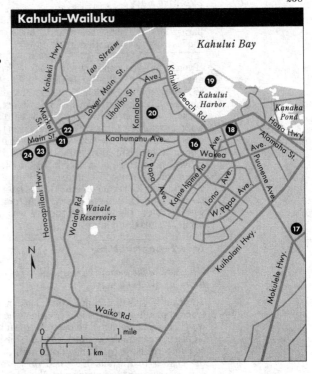

Kahului–Wailuku

beets—for many years, the crop was the mainstay of the Hawaiian economy.

The museum is located in a small, restored plantation-manager's house next to the post office and the still-operating sugar mill. At the refinery, black smoke billows up when cane is burning; from the outside, the whole operation looks dirty and industrial. Inside the museum, you'll find historic photos, artifacts, and documents that explain the introduction of sugarcane to Hawaii and how plantation managers brought in laborers from other countries, thereby changing the Islands' ethnic mix. This fascinating exhibit is well worth your time. *3957 Hansen Rd., Puunene, tel. 808/871–8058. Admission: $3 adults, $1.50 students 6–17. Open Mon.–Sat. 9:30–4:30.*

Time Out   As you return to Kahului, head toward the Kaahumanu Center. When you reach the corner of Puunene and Kaahumanu **18** avenues, you'll be at the **Kahului Shopping Center**. Here you'll find **Ah Fook's Super Market** (tel. 808/877–3308), a local-style grocery where you can also get genuine Japanese, Chinese, and Hawaiian food. There are no tables, but the shady mall offers a quiet stopping spot.

Return to Kaahumanu Avenue, head toward Wailuku, and take a right onto Kahului Beach Road. Here you can see any ships in **19** port at **Kahului Harbor**. This is Maui's chief port, since it's the island's only deep-draft harbor. Cruise ships call here, as do large freighters and tugboats. Surfers sometimes use this spot as a castoff to catch some good waves, but it's not a good swimming beach.

Continue on the beach road until you reach Kanaloa Avenue, **20** make a left and soon you'll find **Maui Zoological and Botanical Gardens.** This is a great spot for kids, since there's a small children's zoo that includes peacocks, African pygmy goats, spider monkeys, and lots more. The gardens of native Hawaiian plants actually take a much smaller role in this attraction than the name implies. *Kanaloa Ave. off Kaahumanu Ave., tel. 808/243-7337. Admission free. Open daily 9–4.*

Press on to Wailuku by turning right from Kanaloa Avenue back onto Kaahumanu Avenue. (Kaahumanu eventually be- **21** comes Wailuku's Main Street.) You'll soon reach **Wailuku's Historical District,** mostly concentrated on High Street, as well as around Vineyard and Market streets. Much of the area is in the Register of Historic Places, and many of the old buildings are being preserved with their wooden facades intact. Overall, the little town is sleepy and belies its function as Maui's county seat. Wailuku is where you'll see the County Court House (on the corner of Main St. and Honoapiilani Hwy.), from which Maui's first woman mayor, Linda Lingle, runs the county that includes the islands of Maui, Molokai, Lanai, and Kahoolawe.

In ancient times, Wailuku was a favored place for the inhabitants of Maui, who maintained two *heiaus* (temples) on the hills above. They used these heiaus primarily to watch for intruders, and villages grew up around the temples to support the cause. But the town really began to grow when the first missionaries arrived in the 1820s.

To get a closer look at this historical area, turn right at Market **22** Street from Main Street, where you'll see the **Iao Theater** (68 N. Market St., tel. 808/242-6969), one of Wailuku's most photographed landmarks. This charming movie house went up in Wailuku in 1927 and acted as a community gathering spot. A few years ago, several ambitious developers almost had the community convinced that the theater should be gutted and replaced with brand-new shops and offices. But then the Maui Community Theatre started using it as its headquarters. The art deco–style building is now the focus of the Wailuku Main Street Program. Unless there's a play or concert on, you can't usually get inside the theater.

Time Out Stop off at **Hazel's** (2080 Vineyard, tel. 808/244-7278). Owner Hazel Yasutomi serves no-nonsense food here—such specialties as Spam and eggs, pork chops, and burgers. This is where the locals hang out to enjoy the relaxed environment. You'll see the Wailuku Grand Hotel nearby.

23 Next visit **Kaahumanu Church** (tel. 808/244-5189), which is on High Street around the corner from Main Street and across the way from the County Court House. It's said that Queen Kaahumanu attended services on this site in 1832 and requested that a permanent structure be erected. Builders first tried adobe, which dissolved in the rain, then stone. The present wooden structure, built in 1876, is classic New England style, with white exterior walls and striking green trim. You won't be able to see the interior, however, unless you attend Sunday services. The church features a Hawaiian service—completely in Hawaiian—each Sunday at 9 AM.

Return to Main Street and drive away from Kahului. After a few blocks, on your left, you'll see Hale Hoikeike (House of Display). Locals (and the sign out front) call this structure the
㉔ Bailey House, and it was the home of Edward and Caroline Bailey, two prominent missionaries who came to Wailuku to run the first Hawaiian girls' school on the island, the Wailuku Female Seminary; this school's function was mainly to train the girls in the "feminine arts."

Hale Hoikeike's construction between 1833 and 1850 was supervised by Edward Bailey himself. The Maui Historical Society has opened a museum in the plastered stone house, with displays of a small artifacts collection from before and after the missionaries' arrival, and Mr. Bailey's paintings of Wailuku. Some rooms are decorated with missionary-period furniture. The Hawaiian Room has exhibits on the making of tapa cloth, as well as samples of pre–Captain Cook weaponry. Unfortunately, the girls' school is no longer standing. *2375A Main St., tel. 808/244-3326. Suggested optional donation: $2 adults, 50¢ children. Open Mon.–Sat. 10–4:30.*

Numbers in the margin correspond to points of interest on the Exploring Maui map.

Back on Main Street, drive toward the mountains for this tour's last destination, Iao Needle. If you go straight, Main Street turns into Iao Valley Road. Before you're even out of town, the air cools and the hilly terrain gets more lush. Soon you'll come
㉕ to **Kepaniwai Park and Heritage Gardens.** This county park is now a memorial to Maui's cultural roots, with picnic facilities and ethnic displays dotting the landscape. There's an early Hawaiian shack, a New England saltbox, a Portuguese villa with gardens, and dwellings from other cultures, such as China, the Philippines, and Portugal.

However, the peacefulness here belies the history of the area. During his quest for domination, King Kamehameha I brought his troops to the Valley Isle in 1790 and engaged in a particularly bloody battle near Kepaniwai Park. He succeeded in his plan to defeat Maui and thereby take over the entire group of islands, but the result was mass murder. Bodies blocked Iao Stream, so that the village downstream was given the name Wailuku, which means "bloody river."

As you drive toward the needle, you'll come to a landmark
㉖ called **John F. Kennedy Profile.** The Hawaiians, it seems, can see something in every rock formation throughout the Islands. But this one does uncannily resemble the profile of the late president.

㉗ Iao Valley Road ends at **Iao Valley State Park.** When Mark Twain saw this park, he dubbed it the Yosemite of the Pacific. Here you'll find the erosion-formed gray and moss-green rock called **Iao Needle,** a spire that rises 1,200 feet from the valley floor. You can take one of several easy hikes from the parking lot across Iao Stream and explore the junglelike area. This park offers a beautiful set of well-maintained walks, where you can stop and contemplate by the edge of a stream or look at some of the native plants and flowers. Mist occasionally rises if there's been a rain, making the spot look even more magical. *Admission free. Open daily 7–7.*

Tour 3: Haleakala and Upcountry

The fertile western slopes leading up to majestic **Haleakala** are called Upcountry. This region is responsible for much of Hawaii's produce. Lettuce, tomatoes, and sweet Maui onions are some of the most popular crops grown here, but the area is also a big flower producer. As you drive along you'll notice plenty of natural vegetation, as clumps of cacti mingle with purple jacaranda, wild hibiscus, and towering eucalyptus trees. Carnations are the number one flower in the area, but the exotic-looking protea are rapidly gaining in popularity.

Upcountry is also fertile ranch land, with such spreads as the 30,000-acre Ulupalakua, long famous for raising cattle, and the 20,000-acre Haleakala Ranch, which throws its well-attended rodeo each July 4th. In addition, Tedeschi Vineyards and Winery dominates Hawaii's only wine-producing region, just a few acres of Ulupalakua land.

28 Start this tour of Haleakala in **Kahului.** Before setting out, call 808/871–5054 for Haleakala's weather conditions. Extreme gusty winds, heavy rain, and even snow in winter are not uncommon—even if it is paradise as usual down at beach level. Because of the high altitude, the mountaintop temperature is often as much as 30 degrees cooler than in sea-level Maui. If you didn't pack a warm jacket or can't borrow one, skip watching the sunrise until the next trip and settle for a morning or midday visit.

29 After you've checked out the weather conditions, drive on **Haleakala Highway,** or Highway 37, toward the big mountain of Haleakala (House of the Sun) in the center of the island. On this road, you'll travel from sea level to an elevation of 10,023 feet in only 38 miles—a feat you won't be able to repeat on any other car route in the world. It's not a quick drive, however; it'll take you about two hours. We recommend that you start fairly early in the morning, since the clouds move over the top of the mountain as soon as 11 AM.

Try to make the drive up Haleakala without stopping, since you'll want the best views possible. Watch the signs, because Haleakala Highway will diverge in two directions. If you go straight, the road becomes Kula Highway, which is still Highway 37. If you veer to the left, the road becomes Highway 377. You want this latter road. After about 6 miles, make a left onto Haleakala Highway. The switchbacks begin here. With the ascent, you'll notice the weather getting a bit chilly. As you near the top, there's a
30 **Park Headquarters/Visitor Center,** where you can stop and orient yourself to the volcano's origins and eruption history. Haleakala is the centerpiece of the 27,284-acre Haleakala National Park, which was dedicated in 1961 to preserving the area. The "crater" is actually an "erosional valley," created by centuries of wind and rain chipping away at the mountain's summit (where there may have once been a small crater), sculpting the dramatic landscape you see today. The small hills within the valley are volcanic cinder caves, each with a small crater at its top, and each the site of an eruption. At the gift shop, you can get maps, as well as some nice posters and other memorabilia. *At the 7,000-ft elevation on Haleakala Hwy., tel. 808/572–9306. Cost: $3 car fee, $1 per person for hikers, senior citizens free. Visitor Center open daily 7:30–4.*

Several lookout areas are located within the park itself. The first you'll come to as you continue your ascent on Haleakala **③** Crater Road is **Leleiwi Overlook,** at about 8,800 feet elevation. There's parking here and the beginning of the Haleamauu Trail, which leads into the valley. If you happen to be at this point in the late afternoon, it's possible you'll experience a phenomenon called the Brocken Specter. Named after a similar occurrence in East Germany's Harz Mountains, the "specter" allows you to see yourself reflected on the clouds and circled by a rainbow. Don't wait all day for this, because it is not an everyday thing.

③ Next is **Kalahaku Overlook,** a particularly interesting stop at about the 9,000-foot level. The famous silversword plant grows here amid the desertlike surroundings; in fact, the endangered flowering plant grows in only one other place in the park, along the Halemauu Trail, within the crater. The silversword looks like a member of the yucca family and produces a stalk some 3 to 8 feet tall with several hundred yellow and purple flower heads. At this lookout, the silversword is kept in an enclosure to protect it from nibbling wildlife.

③ Next you'll come to **Haleakala Visitor Center,** at about 9,800 feet. By now you're about 10 miles from park headquarters, but a ranger is on duty here as well. The center has exhibits inside and a trailhead that leads to White Hill, a small crater nearby. This is a short, easy walk that will give you an even better view of the valley. Shortly after noon each day, the ranger gives an informative lecture on Haleakala geology. In the summer, a 90-minute walk with a ranger guide that goes partly down Sliding Sands Trail starts daily at 9. *Center open sunrise–3.*

③ Continue on to reach the highest point on Maui, the **Puu Ulaula Overlook.** Here you'll find a glass-enclosed lookout that boasts a 360-degree view from the 10,023-foot summit. People gather here for the best sunrise view, as the building's open 24 hours a day. Sunrise generally begins between 5:45 and 7, depending on the time of year. On a clear day, you can see the islands of Molokai, Lanai, Kahoolawe, and the Big Island. On a *really* clear day, you can even spot Oahu glimmering in the distance.

On a small hill above, you'll see **Science City,** a research and communications center that looks like it's straight out of an espionage thriller. You can't visit the center, unfortunately, since the University of Hawaii and the Department of Defense don't allow visitors. The university maintains an observatory, while the Defense Department tracks satellites.

Now head back down the way you came and see the lower nooks **③** and crannies of **Haleakala.** When you reach Highway 377 again, make a right.

Time Out Within about a quarter mile on Highway 377, you'll see **Kula Lodge** (Haleakala Hwy., tel. 808/878–2517). The lodge is a popular post–Haleakala-sunrise spot; it offers a hearty breakfast of the best eggs Benedict you'll find this side of the Rockies. The views are spectacular since the lodge has windows all around, which allows you to see all the way to the ocean. The flower fields outside are an added benefit.

Backtrack and stay on Highway 377 and then go past the 378 **③** intersection for about 2 more miles, where you'll come to **Kula**

Botanical Gardens on your left. Specimens grow somewhat naturally here, and you'll see all kinds of flora that may be unfamiliar. There are koa trees, often made into finely turned bowls and handcrafted furniture, and kukui trees (ancient Hawaiians used the tree's nuts, which are filled with oil, for lighting). In addition, the gardens have the requisite protea, varieties of ginger, and stands of bamboo orchid. *RR 2, Box 288, Upper Kula Rd., tel. 808/878–1715. Admission: $3 adults, 50¢ children 6–12. Open daily 9–4.*

Continue on Highway 377 away from Kahului and you'll soon join Highway 377 again. In about 8 miles, you'll come to **37** **Tedeschi Vineyards and Winery,** where you can sample Hawaii's only homegrown wines: a pleasant Maui Blush, the Maui Brut-Blanc de Noirs Hawaiian Champagne, and Tedeschi's annual Maui Nouveau. You can also get a tour of the winery and purchase whatever wines you like. The most unusual wine, Maui Blanc, is made from pineapple concentrate; the winery owners started their operation by buying juice from their neighbor, Maui Land & Pineapple Company.

You'll want to taste Maui Blanc before you buy—it's not for everyone. The winery's tasting room is unusual because it once served as the jail for James Makee's Rose Ranch, where the old-time farmer grew sugarcane back in the 1860s. A large plantation house perches on the slope above, dominating the scenery. Tedeschi is definitely worth a visit. *Ulupalakua Ranch, Haleakala Hwy., tel. 808/878–6058. Admission free. Open daily 9–5.*

Now return the way you came and head toward Kahului on Highway 37. When you get to the Highway 37/377 fork, bear to the left to stay on Highway 37. You're now on Kula Highway, which eventually turns back into Haleakala Highway (this isn't as confusing as it sounds). Within about 2 miles, you'll see a turnoff to the right called Copp Road. About ½ mile later, turn **38** left onto Mauna Place. Here you can visit the **University of Hawaii's Kula Experimental Station.** The station planted the first protea here in the mid-'60s and since then has become the world's foremost protea research and development facility.

Within the gates, you'll see as many as 300 varieties of the exotic bloom, most with names to match: Rickrack Banksia, Veldfire Sunburst, Pink Mink, Blushing Bride, and Safari Sunset, to name just a few. You can talk to the growers to find out more about the plants, which were brought to Maui from Australia in 1965 by Dr. Philip Parvin, a University of Hawaii horticulture professor. Then you can proceed to one of Upcountry Maui's many commercial outlets and buy your favorite blooms. *Mauna Pl. in Upcountry Maui, tel. 808/878–1213. Admission free. Open weekdays 7–3:30, but you must stop at the office and sign a sheet releasing the station from any liability. You'll then be given a map to help you find your way.*

Retrace your steps to Kula Highway and, again, head toward **39** Kahului. In about 4 miles, you'll come to the town of **Pukalani,** essentially an Upcountry bedroom community for Kahului. If you're pressed for time, this is the point from which you can take Highway 37 back to Kahului.

Otherwise, take a right onto Highway 400, which you'll find right in Pukalani, and head toward the *paniolo* (Hawaiian cowboy) village of **Makawao.** This tiny town was settled long ago by **40** Portuguese immigrants who were brought to Maui to work the sugar plantations. After their contracts ran out, many of them moved Upcountry, where their descendants now work the neighboring Haleakala and Ulupalakua ranches. Once a year on the Fourth of July, the paniolos come out in force for the Makawao rodeo.

Time Out   One of Makawao's most famous landmarks is **Komoda Store & Bakery** (3674 Baldwin Ave., tel. 808/572–7261), where you can get a delicious cream puff. They sell hundreds each day, as well as offering all the other trappings of a general store.

Besides the annual rodeo, Makawao also provides an opportunity to browse through unusual shops. You can find casual attire at **Collections** (3677 Baldwin Ave., tel. 808/572–0781); original children's toys and books at **Maui Child Toys & Books** (3643 Baldwin Ave., tel. 808/572–2765); and trinkets, souvenirs, and collectibles at **Goodies** (3633 Baldwin Ave., tel. 808/572–0288) or **Coconut Classics** (3647 Baldwin Ave., tel. 808/572–7103). **Glassman Galleries** (3682 Makawao Ave., tel. 808/572–0395) is the newest enterprise of Barbara Glassman, who brings us Maui Art Tours (*see* Guided Tours, *above*).

From Makawao, it's a short drive down toward the ocean on Baldwin Avenue to the Hana Highway. Make a left on the Hana Highway to head back to Kahului.

Tour 4: The Road to Hana

Don't let anyone tell you the Hana Highway is impassable, frightening, or otherwise unadvisable. Because of all the hype, you're bound to be a little nervous approaching it for the first time. But once you try it, you'll wonder if maybe there's somebody out there making it sound tough just to keep out the hordes. Certainly the road is challenging, spanning some 55 miles of turns and bridges. But it's not a grueling, all-day drive. The road isn't a freeway, but it has been resurfaced to make it a pleasant drive.

①   Start your trip to Hana in the little town of **Paia** by having breakfast at one of the restaurants that line the main street. **Charley's** (142 Hana Hwy., tel. 808/579–9453) is recommended; you can get a good meal here and watch the locals go by. We suggest you also stop at **Picnics** (30 Baldwin Ave., tel. 808/579–8021) to buy a lunch for the road.

If you want to do some shopping as well, Paia is a friendly little town. You can find clothing and keepsakes in shops run by retailers who'll stop and chat, ask where you're from, and, most likely, give you their card in case something doesn't fit or you'd like to return. Here you'll find artists, windsurfers, and some folks who've lived in these parts all their lives.

Paia was once a sugar-growing enclave, an operation complete with a mill and plantation camps. Shops opened by shrewd immigrants quickly sprouted to serve the workers, who probably found it easier to buy supplies near home. The town boomed during World War II when the Marines set up camp nearby. After the war, however, sugar grower Alexander & Baldwin closed its Paia operation, many workers moved on, and the town's population began to dwindle. Many residents took off for the new city of Kahului, where they were able to purchase their own homes.

In the 1960s, Paia became a hippie town as dropouts headed for the sunny shores of Maui to open ethnic shops, bizarre galleries, and unusual eateries. By the late 1970s, windsurfers had **42** discovered nearby **Hookipa Beach,** and soon Paia was the windsurfing capital of the world. You can see this in the youth of the town and in the budget inns that have cropped up to offer cheap accommodations to those who windsurf for a living. Paia is certainly a fun place.

As you begin your drive to Hana, remember that many people—mostly those who live in Hana—make this trip frequently. You'll recognize them because they're the ones who'll be zipping around every curve as if they had a death wish. They don't; they've just seen this so many times before that they don't care to linger. With stops, this drive should take you between two and three hours. Locals will do it in about 45 minutes. Pull over and let them pass.

About 10 miles from Paia, the famous road really begins to twist and turn (as it will for the next 40 miles or so). About 3 miles later, you'll come to the first of the Hana Highway's approximately 65 bridges. All along this stretch of road, waterfalls are abundant. Turn off the radio and the air conditioner and open the windows to enjoy the sounds and smells. There are plenty of places to pull off and park; all are ideal spots to stop and take a picture. You'll want to plan on doing this a few times, as the road's curves make driving without a break difficult. When it's raining (which is often), the drive is particularly beautiful: there are waterfalls everywhere.

43 As you drive on, you'll pass the small villages of **Huelo,** with its two quaint churches, and **Kailua,** home to Alexander & Baldwin's irrigation employees. At about mile marker 11, you can **44** stop at the bridge over **Puohokamoa Stream,** where there are more pools and waterfalls. If you walk up to the left of the first pool, you'll find a larger pool and waterfalls. Picnic tables are available at Puohokamoa Stream, so many people favor this as a stopping point.

If you'd rather stretch your legs *and* use a flush toilet, continue **45** on another mile to the **Kaumahina State Wayside Park,** which has a picnic area and a lovely overlook to the Keanae Peninsula. Hardier souls can camp here with a permit. *Admission free. No set hours.*

A mile past the park, you'll see an enormous valley to your **46** right. This is **Honomanu Valley,** carved by erosion during Haleakala's first dormant period. At the canyon's head, there are 3,000-foot cliffs and a 1,000-foot waterfall, but don't try to reach them. There's not much of a trail, and what does exist is practically impassable.

47 Another 4 miles brings you to the **Keanae Arboretum,** where you can admire many plants and trees that are now considered native to Hawaii. The meandering Piinaau Stream adds a graceful touch to the arboretum and provides a swimming pond besides. You can take a fairly rigorous hike from the arboretum, if you can find the trail at one side of the large taro patch. Be careful not to lose the trail once you're on it. A lovely forest waits at the end of the hike. *Admission free. No set hours.*

48 Near mile marker 17, you'll find the **Keanae Overlook.** From here, you'll notice the patchwork-quilt effect the taro farms create below. The ocean provides a dramatic backdrop, while in the other direction you have some awesome views of Haleakala through the foliage. This is a good spot for photos.

Coming up is the **halfway mark to Hana.** If you've had enough scenery, this is as good a time as any to turn around and head back to civilization. The scenery from here is essentially the same. Once you get to Hana, don't expect a booming city. It's the road that's the draw. Diehards will want to stick with us.

Time Out   Just past Keanae, you can pull over at **Uncle Harry's** (tel. 808/248–7019), a refreshment stand run by Uncle Harry Mitchell. Uncle Harry and his family also have souvenirs for sale, and they've opened a small museum next door, including a grass house to demonstrate how their ancestors lived. The Mitchells have some Hawaiian food available, as well as fruit, home-baked breads, and beverages.

49   Turn off the Hana Road at mile marker 18, and take the Wailua Road for about ¾ mile to **Wailua Lookout.** From the parking lot, you can see Wailua Canyon, but you'll have to walk up steps to get a view of Wailua Village. The landmark in Wailua Village is a church made of coral, built in 1860. Once called St. Gabriel's Catholic Church, the current Our Lady of Fatima Shrine has an interesting legend surrounding it; as the story goes, a storm washed just enough coral up onto the shore to build the church, but then took any extra coral back to sea.

50   Back on the Hana Road, after another ½ mile, you'll hit the best falls on the entire drive to Hana. **Waikane Falls** are not necessarily bigger or taller than the other falls, but they're dramatic just the same. That's partly because the water is not diverted for sugar irrigation; the taro farmers in Wailua need all the run-off. Here is another good spot for photos.

51   At about mile marker 25, you'll see a road that heads down toward the ocean and the village of **Nahiku.** This was a popular spot in ancient times, providing a home to hundreds of natives. Now Nahiku's population numbers about 80, consisting mostly of native Hawaiians and some back-to-the-land types. Like so many other Hawaiian villages, Nahiku was once a plantation town. A rubber grower planted trees there in the early 1900s. The experiment didn't work out, so Nahiku was essentially abandoned.

52   As you continue on toward Hana, you'll pass **Waianapanapa State Park,** which has state-run cabins where you can stay with a permit for between $14 and $30 a night, depending on the number of people. The park is right on the ocean, and it's a lovely spot to picnic, hike, or swim. An ancient burial site is located nearby, as well as a heiau, or temple. Waianapanapa also boasts one of Maui's only black-sand beaches and some caves for adventurous swimmers to explore. *Hana Hwy., tel. 808/248–8061. Admission free. No set hours.*

53   Closer to Hana, you'll come to **Helani Gardens,** a 60-acre enclave of plants collected and grown by Hana native Howard Cooper. Cooper is the crusty old guy you'll find wandering the place or hanging out in his treehouse. His wife, Nora, is editor of the *Maui News* in Kahului, but Howard just couldn't bear to leave his beloved Hana, so Nora commutes. Howard's philosophy of life crops up all over the garden in delightful, hand-painted signs. A tour of Helani Gardens is a self-guided one, but if Howard's around, he'll be glad to show you his favorite plants. *No street address; you can write to Helani Gardens, Box 215, Hana 96713, tel. 808/248–8274. Admission: $2 adults, $1 children 6–16. Open daily (weather permitting) 10–4.*

54 **55** **Hana** is just minutes away from Helani Gardens. It's a blink-and-you'll-miss-it kind of place, with only a couple of roads and clusters of houses. In Hana, a high spot is the **Hotel Hana-Maui** (Hana Hwy., tel. 808/248–8211), one of the best hotels in the state—if not the world (*see* Lodging, *below*).

Time Out **Tutu's** (tel. 808/248-8224) is a snack shop down by the bay. Aside from the Hotel Hana-Maui and its two eating establishments, this is the only place for a meal in the entire town. Although nothing is fancy here (burgers are the typical fare), the prices are lower than those at the hotel restaurants. You'll also get a view of fishing boats bringing in their catch in the late afternoon.

As you wander around Hana, keep in mind that this is a company town. Although sugar was once the mainstay of Hana's economy, the last plantation shut down in the 1940s. In 1946, rancher Paul Fagan built the Hotel Hana-Maui and stocked the surrounding pastureland with cattle. Suddenly, it was the ranch and its hotel that were putting food on the most tables.

The Cross you'll see on the hill above the hotel was put there in memory of Fagan. After Fagan died in the mid-1960s, ranch-and-town ownership passed into the hands of 37 shareholders, most of whom didn't care about their property. Then the Rosewood Corporation came along and purchased most of Hana's valuable land. The company put megamillions into restoring the Hotel Hana-Maui and began teaching the *paniolos* (cowboys) all the latest techniques in grazing and breeding. Recently, however, Rosewood sold its Hana holdings to a Japanese company, which appointed Sheraton as manager. Sheraton has restored the old hotel and added the plantation-look Sea Ranch health spa across the road, and the isolated resort has become a favorite hideaway for health-conscious celebrities.

Because of the town's size, most of the townspeople are the hands-on suppliers of the services and amenities that make hotel guests happy. Moreover, many locals have worked at the hotel for years; a fascinating family tree that hangs near the lobby shows the relationships of all the employees. If you're at all adventurous, you'll no doubt be able to talk to several of the people who live and work in Hana. They're candid, friendly, and mostly native Hawaiian—or at least born and raised in Hana.

56 Once you've seen Hana, you might want to drive past the town for a dip in the pools at **Ohe'o Gulch.** Called the Piilani Highway once past Hana, the road that spans the 10 miles to the gulch is truly bad—rutted, rocky, and twisting. You're just sure you've passed the pools because the terrain is so awful, but don't give up. These refreshing pools are worth the drive.

From the paved parking lot, you can walk a short way to the first of the pools. Rocks are available for sunbathing, and caves may be explored. In the spring and summer, it can get quite crowded here, and it doesn't even thin out when it rains.

57 A lot of people come this far just to see the **Grave of Charles Lindbergh,** the world-renowned aviator. Lindbergh chose to be buried here because he and his wife, writer Anne Morrow Lindbergh, spent a lot of time living in the area in a home they built. His grave is very difficult to spot, which is probably intentional. It's about a mile past Oheo Gulch on a road that goes toward the ocean. On this road you'll find **Hoomau Congregational Church,** next to which Lindbergh was buried in 1974. Remember, this is a churchyard, so be considerate and leave everything exactly as you found it.

Unless you've decided to drive completely around east Maui and end up at Makena (which isn't advisable unless you have a four-wheel-drive vehicle), this is the place to turn around. The drive back isn't nearly as much fun, so you might want to plan on spending a night in Hana (*see* Lodging, *below*).

Maui for Free

Hale Paahao/Old Lahaina Prison. Here you can see the original coral-block walls that were once the jail for rowdy sailors and whalers. This prison was built between 1852 and 1854 by the prisoners themselves; the small, brown building looks like a chapel. The rock for the coral prison came from the walls of an old fort, which Hale Paahao replaced. *Prison Rd. just off Wainee St., Lahaina, tel. 808/661–3262. Open daily 9–5.*

Hale Pai/Old Print Shop. Located on the grounds of Lahainaluna School in Lahaina, this print house was opened in 1837 and put out the first Hawaiian-language newspaper. Founded by the missionaries, it now houses the Lahaina Restoration Foundation's extensive archival collection and exhibits depicting Maui's early whaling and missionary days. *At the mountain end of Lahainaluna Rd., Lahaina, tel. 808/661–3262. Open Mon.–Fri. 10–4.*

Hui Noeau Visual Arts Center. This nonprofit cultural center is set in the Upcountry town of Makawao in the old Baldwin estate. There are regular exhibitions, as well as audiovisual presentations. *2841 Baldwin Ave., Makawao, tel. 808/572–6560. Open daily 10–4.*

Jodo Mission. The Lahaina Jodo Mission Cultural Park is one of the town's busiest tourist attractions, sitting on a parcel of land called Puunoa Point just off Front Street near Mala Wharf. The park's centerpiece is the largest Buddha outside Japan, placed there to commemorate the arrival of the first Japanese immigrants in 1868. The park includes the shrine, graveyards, a crematorium, and an extensive outdoor meeting area. *12 Ala Moana, Lahaina, tel. 808/661–4304. No set hours.*

Lahaina Whaling Museum. Crazy Shirts' owner, Rick Ralston, has opened this repository of more than 800 pieces of whaling memorabilia in his Front Street store. His collection includes carved ivory, harpoons, and old photos. *865 Front St., tel. 808/661–4775. Open Mon.–Sat. 9 AM–10 PM, Sun. 9–9.*

Maui Zoological and Botanical Gardens (Kanaloa Ave. off Kaahumanu Ave., Kahului, tel. 808/243–7337). *See Tour 2, above.*

Muumuu Factory. Famous muumuu manufacturer **Hilo Hattie** advertises all over Maui. Owned by the same company that

American Express offers Travelers Cheques built for two.

American Express® Cheques *for Two*. The first Travelers Cheques that allow either of you to use them because both of you have signed them. And only one of you needs to be present to purchase them.

Cheques *for Two* are accepted anywhere regular American Express Travelers Cheques are, which is just about everywhere. So stop by your bank, AAA* or any American Express Travel Service Office and ask for Cheques *for Two*.

runs the Maui Tropical Plantation, Hilo Hattie stocks aloha wear made on the premises, as well as souvenirs aplenty. The company will pick you up if you're staying in the Kaanapali or Lahaina area, or you can drive there yourself. Be forewarned that the clothing isn't much cheaper or better quality than what you'll find in the stores, but if you're determined to buy all your souvenirs in one place, this could be it. *Lahaina Center, Lahaina, tel. 808/661–8457. Open daily 8:30–5.*

Pacific Brewery. Look for this operation on the grounds of the old Wailuku Sugar Mill. You can get 15-minute tours of this Maui Lager beer plant, which recently began shipping its product to the Mainland. The tour acquaints you with brewing and bottling techniques and ends with a taste test. *Imi Kala St., Wailuku, tel. 808/244–0396. Open weekdays 10–4.*

Reach Out to the Stars. Astronomy buffs can get their fill of stargazing at a unique nightly program at the Hyatt Regency Maui. A constellation slide show is followed by a look through giant binoculars and a deep-space telescope. The program is run by a real astronomer. *Hyatt Regency Maui's Lahaina Tower, 200 Nohea Kai Dr., Kaanapali, tel. 808/661–1234, ext. 3143. Wed.–Sun. 8 and 9 PM.*

Sandcastle Exhibition. Billy Lee is getting a reputation. The master sandcastle builder has set up his pails and shovels on the beach in front of 505 Front Street in Lahaina, and between 9 AM and sunset he sculpts whatever comes to mind—mermaids, castles, towers, lions, you name it.

Upcountry Protea Farm. On the slopes of Haleakala, Upcountry Protea Farm grows exotic blossoms and offers views of the gardens to all who stop by. You can also purchase protea here, or have them shipped home. *One mi off Hwy. 37, at the top of Upper Kimo Dr., tel. 808/878–2544. Open daily 8–4:30.*

Whalers Village Museum. On the shore at the Kaanapali Beach Resort, this museum's exhibits explore whaling history. The museum contains a 30-foot sperm whale skeleton, with information about whale biology, photos, and artifacts from 1825 to 1860. A video theater shows films, and an authentic whaling boat is displayed in the outdoor pavilion. Lectures and special tours are available. *2435 Kaanapali Pkwy., tel. 808/661–5992. Open daily 9:30 AM–10 PM.*

What to See and Do with Children

Lahaina–Kaanapali & Pacific Railroad. Affectionately called the Sugarcane Train, this choo-choo is Hawaii's only passenger train. It's an 1890s-vintage railway that once shuttled sugar but now moves sightseers between Kaanapali and Lahaina. This quaint little attraction is a big deal for Hawaii but probably not much of a thrill for those more accustomed to trains. The kids will like it. You can also get a package that combines a ride and lunch in Lahaina or a historic Lahaina tour. *1½ blocks north of the Lahainaluna Rd. stoplight on Honoapiilani Hwy., Lahaina, tel. 800/661–0080. Cost for round-trip ride: $10 adults, $5 children; one-way: $7 adults, $3.50 children. Open daily 9–4.*

Maui Tropical Plantation. This visitor attraction used to be a huge sugarcane field, but when Maui's once-paramount crop declined severely in importance, a group of visionaries decided to open an agricultural theme park. The 120-acre preserve now ranks as Hawaii's third most popular tourist attraction. Located on Highway 30 just outside Wailuku, the plantation offers a 30-minute tram ride through its fields with an informative narration of growing processes and plant types.

Kids will also probably enjoy a historical-characters exhibit, as well as fruit-testing, coconut-husking, and lei-making demonstrations and bird shows. There's a restaurant on the property and a souvenir shop that sells fruits and vegetables. At night, the Maui Tropical Plantation features a country barbecue. *On Honoapiilani Hwy. right outside Wailuku toward Kaanapali, tel. 808/244-7643. Admission free to the Marketplace; cost of narrated tour, $8 adults, $3 children 6-12. Open daily 9-5.*

Whale-watching. Appealing to both children and adults, whale-watching is one of the most exciting activities in the United States. During the right time of year on Maui—between November and April—you can see whales breaching and blowing just offshore. The humpback whales' attraction to Maui is legendary. More than half the North Pacific's humpback population winters in Hawaii, as they've been doing for years. At one time, thousands of the huge mammals existed, but the world population has dwindled to about 1,500. In 1966, they were put on the endangered-species list, which restricts boats and airplanes from getting too close.

Experts believe the humpbacks keep returning to Hawaiian waters because of the warmth. Winter is calving time for the behemoths, and the whale babies, born with little blubber, probably couldn't survive in the frigid Alaskan waters. No one has ever seen a whale give birth, but the experts studying whales off Maui know that calving is their main winter activity, since the one- and two-ton babies suddenly appear while the whales are in residence.

Quite a few operations run whale-watching excursions off the coast of Maui. This allows you to get a closer view; it gives the whale a better vantage point, too. Sometimes, in fact, a curious whale can get so close that it makes the passengers downright nervous. **Pacific Whale Foundation** (Kealia Beach Plaza, Kihei 96753, tel. 808/879-8811) pioneered whale-watching back in 1979 and now runs two boats.

Also offering whale-watching in season are the following: **Ocean Activities Center** (1325 S. Kihei Rd., Suite 212, Kihei 96753, tel. 808/879-4485), **Leilani Cruises** (505 Front St., Suite 225, Lahaina 96761, tel. 808/661-8397), **Captain Zodiac Raft Expeditions** (Box 1776, Lahaina 96761, tel. 808/667-5351), **Seabern Yachts** (Box 1022, Lahaina 96767, tel. 808/661-8110), and **Trilogy Excursions** (Box 1121, Lahaina 96767, tel. 808/661-4743). Ticket prices average about $30 adults, $15 children.

Off the Beaten Track

Kaupo Road. This stretch of road beyond Charles Lindbergh's grave is located near where the pavement stops 10 miles past Hana. Kaupo Road is rough, with more than a few miles of rocky, one-lane terrain not unlike that of the moon. Drop-offs plunge far down to the sea and washouts are common. It's a beautiful drive, however, and probably the closest to Old Hawaii you'll find. Along the way, the little Kaupo Store, about 15 miles past Hana, sells a variety of essential items, such as groceries, fishing tackle, and hardware; it's also a good place to stop for a cold drink. You'll also pass the renovated Hui Aloha Church, a tiny, wood-frame structure surrounded by an old Hawaiian graveyard. You will want a four-wheel-drive vehicle for this road. You'll eventually wind up near Makena.

Maui Swap Meet. The Maui Swap Meet flea market is the biggest bargain on Maui, with crafts, gifts, souvenirs, fruits, flowers, jewelry, antiques, art, shells, and lots more. *At the Kahului Fairgrounds, Hwy. 35, just off Puunene Ave. Admission: $2 per car. Open Sat. 8–1.*

Yee's Orchard. If you're up for a little local shopping, look for Wilbert Yee's Orchard, near the Azeka Shopping Center (1280 S. Kihei Rd.) in Kihei. The Yee family has farmed the same 20-acre plot for more than half a century, raising mangoes, papayas, bananas, guavas, and tomatoes. You can also purchase certain livestock, such as chickens and peacocks. *Open Wed. 10–4 and Sun. 9–5.*

Shopping

Whether you head for one of the malls (*see below*) or opt for the boutiques hidden around the Valley Isle, one thing you should have no problem finding is clothing made in Hawaii. The Hawaiian garment industry is now the state's third-largest economic sector, after tourism and agriculture.

Maui has an abundance of locally made arts and crafts in a range of prices. In fact, a group that calls itself Made on Maui exists solely to promote the products of its members—items that range from pottery and paintings to Hawaiian teas and macadamia caramel corn. Made on Maui has a booth at the Kaahumanu Shopping Center, or you can identify the group by its distinctive Haleakala logo.

You'll find some of the same merchandise in gift shops at museums and historic sites. And there's a crafts fair somewhere (check newspapers) almost every weekend on Maui. These have their share of kitsch, but you can almost always find high-quality woodcrafts, jewelry, and aloha wear at attractive prices—and talk story with the artists. Maui also boasts plenty of food choices besides the usual pineapple or macadamia nuts. Maui onions, sweet bread, and potato chips are only a few of the possibilities.

Business hours for individual shops on the island are usually 9–5, seven days a week. Shopping centers tend to stay open later (until 9 on certain days).

Shopping Centers

Maui now has three major shopping centers: the Kaahumanu Center in Kahului, and the Lahaina Cannery Shopping Center and Lahaina Center in Lahaina. Newest of the three is the Lahaina Center, which opened in mid-1990.

Kaahumanu Center, in the heart of Kahului, takes up an entire block and boasts more than 60 shops and restaurants. The mall also has free parking. Its anchor stores are **Liberty House** (tel. 808/877–3361), **Sears** (tel. 808/877–2221), and the popular Japanese retailer **Shirokiya** (tel. 808/877–5551). Shirokiya's owners came to Hawaii long before the recent influx of Japanese businesses; their store is worth visiting for its electronic gadgets, kitchen utensils, toys, and other Japanese specialties.

Kaahumanu Center has other interesting shops, including the **Center for Performing Plants** (tel. 808/877–3655), which stocks a variety of greenery; **Lace Secrets** (tel. 808/871–6207), one of Maui's best lingerie stores; and the **Coffee Store** (tel. 808/871–6860), the place for a rich cup of java and good conversation. You can also find such recognizable Mainland stores as **Casual Corner, Kay-Bee Toys,** and **Radio Shack.** *Kaahumanu Center, 275 Kaahumanu Ave., Kahului, tel. 808/877–3369. Open Mon.–Wed. and Sat. 9–5:30, Thurs. and Fri. 9–9, Sun. 10–3.*

Time Out While shopping at Kaahumanu Center, stop at **Ma-Chan's Okazu-ya** (tel. 808/877–7818), a delicatessen-like place where you can choose from Japanese snacks displayed behind a glass case. Dishes consist of bite-size portions of food, such as fish and rice, as well as chopped steak and chicken cutlets. The service here is friendly.

Lahaina Cannery Shopping Center is set in a building reminiscent of an old pineapple cannery. Unlike many shopping centers in Hawaii, the Lahaina Cannery isn't open-air; it is air-conditioned. The center has some 50 shops, including **Arabesque Maui** (tel. 808/667–5337), with classy fashions for women; **Dolphin Galleries** (tel. 808/661–5000), featuring sculpture, paintings, and other Maui artwork; **Superwhale** (tel. 808/661–3424), with a good selection of children's tropical wear; and **Kite Fantasy** (tel. 808/661–4766), one of the best kite shops on Maui. *Lahaina Cannery Shopping Center, 1221 Honoapiilani Hwy., Lahaina, tel. 808/661–5304. Open daily 9:30–9:30.*

Time Out **Sir Wilfred's** (tel. 808/667–1941) at the Lahaina Cannery is a charming spot to stop for coffee and croissants. The little eatery, a branch of a similar place in Central Maui, also sells tobacco and other gift items.

In West Maui, Lahaina has several shopping centers besides the Cannery. The newly opened **Lahaina Center** (corner of Front and Papalaua Sts.) houses the local **Hard Rock Cafe** (900 Front St., tel. 808/667–7400) and several small shops. The **Wharf Cinema Center** (658 Front St., tel. 808/661–8748) boasts 31 air-conditioned shops and restaurants within a wooden building. Smaller centers include **505 Front Street** (tel. 808/667–2514), with its New England–style architecture, and **Lahaina Market Place** (corner of Front St. and Lahainaluna Rd., tel. 808/667–2636), a brick-paved area with 14 quality boutiques and eateries. North of Lahaina, at the Kaanapali Beach Resort, the upscale **Whalers Village** (2435 Kaanapali Pkwy., Kaanapali, tel. 808/661–4567) combines a shopping mall with a museum and has 31 galleries, shops, and restaurants.

In Central Maui, Kahului has one other large shopping center besides the Kaahumanu Center—the **Maui Mall Shopping Center** (corner of Kaahumanu and Puunene Aves., tel. 808/877–5523), with 33 stores.

In East Maui, Kihei offers the large and bustling **Azeka Place Shopping Center** (1280 S. Kihei Rd., tel. 808/879–4449) and the

smaller **Kamaole Shopping Center** (2463 S. Kihei Rd., tel. 808/
879–5233) and **Rainbow Mall** (2439 S. Kihei Rd., tel. 808/879–
6144). South of Kihei, the Wailea Resort has the **Wailea Shopping Village** (tel. 808/879–4474), with 25 gift shops, boutiques,
and restaurants.

For specific stores within shopping centers, consult the categories below.

Art

Maui has more art per square mile than any other Hawaiian Island—maybe more than any other U.S. county. Artists love
Maui, and they flock there to live and work. There are artists'
guilds and co-ops, as well as galleries galore. Moreover, the
town of Lahaina hosts Art Night every Friday starting at 6;
galleries open their doors, musicians stroll the streets, and
Chinese lions parade along the main drag.

The **Old Jail Gallery,** located in the basement of the old Lahaina
Court House (649 Wharf St., across the street from the Pioneer
Inn and Lahaina Harbor), sells work by artists who belong to
the Lahaina Arts Society (tel. 808/661–0111). The artists range
from watercolorists to specialists in oil and sculpture. Down
the street, **Sunset Galleries** (758 Front St., Lahaina, tel. 808/
667–9112 and 156 Lahainaluna Rd., Lahaina, tel. 808/661–
3371) has exclusive rights in Hawaii to sell the work of famous
American Indian artist R. C. Gorman, among other artwork.
Martin Lawrence Galleries (Lahaina Market Place, tel. 808/
661–1788) represents noted mainland artists, including Andy
Warhol and Keith Haring, in a bright gallery opened in 1991.

As for exclusivity, **Wyland Galleries** (697 Front St., Lahaina,
tel. 808/661–7099; 711 Front St., Lahaina, tel. 808/667–2285;
136 Dickenson St., Lahaina, tel. 808/661–0590) is the only Maui
shop to sell the work of Wyland, the marine artist whose favorite technique is a simultaneous look at scenes from under and
above the water. **Coast Gallery** in the Maui Inter-Continental
Wailea (3700 Wailea Alanui Dr., Wailea, tel. 808/879–2301) has
an attractive selection of marine-related paintings and sculptures by such well-known artists as Richard Pettit, George
Sumner, and Robert Lyn Nelson.

A popular Maui art enclave, **Village Gallery,** now has three locations—one in Lahaina (120 Dickenson St., tel. 808/661–
4402), one at the Lahaina Cannery Shopping Center (tel. 808/
661–3280), and one in the Embassy Suites (104 Kaanapali
Shores Pl., tel. 808/667–5115) —featuring such local artists as
Betty Hay Freeland, Wailehua Gray, and Margaret Bedell.
Lahaina Galleries has three locations (728 Front St., Lahaina,
tel. 808/667–2152; Whalers Village, Kaanapali Beach Resort,
tel. 808/661–5571; Kapalua Resort, tel. 808/669–0202). One of
the most interesting galleries on Maui is the **Maui Crafts Guild**
(43 Hana Hwy., Paia, tel. 808/579–9697), on the road to Hana.
Set in a two-story wooden building alongside the highway, the
Guild is crammed with work by local artists; the best pieces are
the pottery and sculpture. Upstairs, antique kimonos,
handpainted silks, and batik fabric are on display.

Clothing

Aloha Wear To find the kind of aloha wear, such as colorful shirts and muumuus, worn most by the people who live year-round on Maui,
check out **Liberty House.** The store has six locations on the island, including shops in the Maui Marriott, Stouffer Wailea,
and Maui Inter-Continental hotels and in Azeka Place Shopping Center (1280 S. Kihei Rd.) in Kihei, Whalers Village (2435
Kaanapali Pkwy.) in the Kaanapali Beach Resort, and
Kaahumanu Center in Kahului. The largest Liberty House
store is the one at Kaahumanu Center (tel. 808/877–3361).

Also in the Kaahumanu Center, **Sears** (tel. 808/877–2221) sells
some decent muumuus and aloha shirts, as does **Andrade,** with
its authentic, high-quality aloha wear in several hotel locations,
including the Royal Lahaina, Sheraton Maui, Kapalua Bay,
Maui Marriott, and Maui Inter-Continental. **Reyn's,** at the
Kapalua Bay Hotel (tel. 808/669–5260) and the Lahaina Cannery Shopping Center (tel. 808/661–5356), and **Watumull's** (tel.
808/661–0528), at the Lahaina Market Place, also have tasteful
selections. **Islandwear on the Beach** (505 Front St., Lahaina,
tel. 808/661–8897) has choice selections from such Hawaiian-
wear clothiers as Reyn Spooner and Malia.

If you want something a bit more brazen—as in louder prints,
definitely not what the locals would wear, but something that
might work better at a wild party at home—try **Island Muumuu Works** (180 Dickenson St., Lahaina, tel. 808/661–5360; and
Maui Mall Shopping Center, corner of Kaahumanu and
Puunene Aves., Kahului, tel. 808/871–6237). Also visit
Luana's, with two Lahaina locations (869 Front St., tel. 808/
667–2275; and 658 Front St., at the Wharf, tel. 808/661–0651),
as well as the **Maui Muumuu Factory** (111 Hana Hwy., tel. 808/
871–6672). Prices are generally cheaper at the above-men-
tioned outlets.

Resort Wear You can find lots of casual, easygoing clothes at Liberty House
or any of the hotel shops. Whalers Village in the Kaanapali
Beach Resort has several good resort-wear shops, including
Foreign Intrigue (tel. 808/667–6671) and **Paradise Clothing** (tel.
808/661–4638).

Although stores for women's resort wear are easy to find on
Maui, stores for men's resort wear are scarcer. Some recom-
mended shops for men's clothing are: **Chapman's,** at the Hyatt
Regency (tel. 808/661–4121) and at the Wailea Shopping Vil-
lage (tel. 808/879–3644); **Kramer's Men's Wear,** at the Lahaina
Cannery Shopping Center (tel. 808/661–5377) and Kaahumanu
Center (tel. 808/871–8671); and **Reyn's,** in Kapalua (tel. 808/
669–5260).

Food

Many visitors to Hawaii opt to take home some of the local
produce: pineapples, papayas, guavas, coconut, or Maui onions. You can find jams and jellies—some of them Made on Maui
products—in a wide variety of tropical flavors. Cook Kwee's
Maui Cookies have gained quite a following, as have Maui Potato Chips. Both are available in most Valley Isle grocery stores.
Maui has just started growing its own macadamia trees—but it
takes seven years before nuts can be harvested! Still, macadamia nuts are a favorite gift back home.

Remember that fresh fruit must be inspected by the U.S. Department of Agriculture, so it's safer to buy a box that's already passed muster. **Paradise Fruit** (1913 Kihei Rd., Kihei, tel. 808/879–1723) sells ready-to-ship pineapples, Maui onions, and coconuts, while **Take Home Maui** (121 Dickenson St., Lahaina, tel. 808/661–8067) will deliver produce free to the airport or your hotel.

Gifts

You may be looking for a unique gift—expensive and unlike anything already sitting on your recipient's dusty bookcase. On the grounds of the Kapalua Bay Hotel, look for two fine shops guaranteed to fit the bill: **By the Bay** (107 Bay Dr., Kapalua, tel. 808/669–5227), which specializes in shells, coral, and hand-crafted jewelry; and **Distant Drums** (125 Bay Dr., Kapalua, tel. 808/669–5522), a boutique that has put together a collection of primitive arts and crafts. **Maui on My Mind** (tel. 808/667–5597) at the Lahaina Cannery Shopping Center offers fine arts and crafts made right on Maui. **Maui's Best,** with its three locations—Kaahumanu Center, Wailea Shopping Village, and its own Kahului Warehouse (tel. 808/877–4831)—also has a wide selection of locally made gifts.

Hawaiian Arts and Crafts

Some visiting shoppers are determined to buy only what they can't get anywhere else. Some of the arts and crafts native to Hawaii can be just the thing. Woods such as koa and milo grow only in certain parts of the world, and because of their increasing scarcity, prices are rising. In Hawaii, craftsmen turn the woods into bowls, trays, and jewelry boxes that will last for years. One of the best places to find Hawaiian crafts on Maui is in the Upcountry town of Haiku, at **John of Maui & Sons** (100 Haiku Rd., Haiku, tel. 808/575–2863). If you're driving east from Kahalui, you'll need to turn right up Baldwin Avenue in Paia and drive for about 15 minutes. This little family operation turns out some of the most exacting wood products in the Islands.

Quilts may not sound Hawaiian, but the way they're done in the 50th state is very different from anywhere else in the world. Missionaries from New England were determined to teach the natives their homespun craft, but—naturally—the Hawaiians adapted quilting to their own style. **Lahaina General Store** (829 Front St., Lahaina, tel. 808/661–0944) and **Tutu's Palaka** (76 Hana Hwy., Paia, tel. 808/579–8682) have a few of these precious coverlets.

If you're looking for a unique experience while you're shopping for Hawaiian-made crafts, try the **Maui Rehabilitation Center** (95 Mahalani, Wailuku, tel. 808/244–5502). You won't find the world's most expert craftsmanship, but the prices are reasonable and you can meet some local folks who are just breaking into this segment of the visitor industry.

Jewelry

In Lahaina, a visit to **Claire the Ring Lady** (858-4 Front St., tel. 808/667–9288) can be a worthwhile jewelry-buying expedition. The somewhat eccentric craftswoman will make an original piece of jewelry for you while you wait. **Jack Ackerman's The Original Maui Divers** (640 Front St., tel. 808/661–0988) is a company that's been crafting gold and coral into jewelry for about 20 years. You can buy Hawaiian heirloom jewelry and tiny carved pendants from **Lahaina Scrimshaw** (tel. 808/661–3971) in the Lahaina Cannery Shopping Center or at two locations on Front Street. **Haimoff & Haimoff Creations in Gold** (tel. 808/669–5213), located at the Kapalua Resort, features the original work of award-winning jewelry designer Harry Haimoff, and **Olah Jewelers** (839 Front St., Lahaina, tel. 808/661–4551) displays Australian black opal jewelry designed by Yvette and George Olah.

Beaches

Maui has more than 100 miles of coastline. Not all of this is beach, of course, but Maui's striking white crescents do seem to be around every bend. All of Hawaii's beaches are free and open to the public—even those that grace the front yards of fancy hotels—so you can feel free to make yourself at home on any one of them.

While they don't appear often, be sure to pay attention to any signs on the beaches. Warnings of high surf or rough currents should be noted. Before you seek shade under a swaying palm tree, watch for careening coconuts. Though the trades seem gentle, the winds are strong enough to knock the fruit off the trees and onto your head. Also be sure to diligently apply that sunscreen. Maui is closer to the equator than the beaches to which you're probably accustomed, so although you may think you're safe, take it from those who've gotten a beet-red burn in 30 minutes or less—you're not. Drinking alcoholic beverages on beaches in Hawaii isn't allowed.

West Maui boasts quite a few beach choices. If you start at the northern end of West Maui and work your way down the coast in a southerly direction, you'll find the following beaches:

D. T. Fleming Beach is one of West Maui's most popular beaches. This charming, mile-long sandy cove is better for sunbathing than for swimming, because the current can be quite strong. There are rest-room facilities, including showers; picnic tables and grills; and paved parking. *Take Hwy. 30 about 1 mi north of the Kapalua Resort.*

The lovely **Napali Beach** is located right outside the **Napili Kai Beach Club,** a popular little condominium for honeymooners. This sparkling white crescent makes a secluded cove perfect for strolling. No facilities are available here unless you're staying at the condo, but you're only a few miles south of Kapalua. *5900 Honoapiilani Hwy. From the upper highway, take the cutoff road closest to the Kapalua Resort.*

Honokowai Beach is a bust if you're looking for that classic Hawaiian stretch of sand. Still, kids will enjoy the rocks here that have formed a pool. This beach does have showers and picnic tables. *Across from the Honokowai Superette at 3636 Lower Honoapiilani Rd.*

Fronting the big hotels at Kaanapali is one of Maui's best people-watching spots, **Kaanapali Beach.** This is not the beach if you're looking for peace and quiet, but if you want lots of action, lay out your towel here. Cruises, windsurfers, and parasails exit off this beach while the beautiful people take in the scenery. Although no facilities are available, the nearby hotels have rest rooms. You're also close to plenty of shops and concessions. *Take any one of the three Kaanapali exits from Honoapiilani Hwy. Park at any of the hotels.*

South of Lahaina at mile marker 14 is **Olowalu Beach,** a secluded snorkeling haven. There's no parking here—except right on the road—and no facilities, but it's one of Maui's best sandy spots. With mask and fins, you'll see yellow tangs, parrot fish, and sometimes the state fish, the humuhumunukunukuapuaa. You can call it a humu, if you like.

Farther south of Olowalu, you'll find **Wailea's five crescent beaches,** which stretch for nearly 2 miles with relatively little interruption by civilization. Several hotels call Wailea home, and more condominiums are under construction. So far, the buildings haven't infringed on the beaches in a noticeable way. With any luck, the population boom won't affect this area either. Swimming is good here—the crescents protect the shoreline from rough surf. Few people populate these beaches—mostly hotel guests who have briefly forsaken the pools of the nearby lodgings—which makes Wailea a peaceful haven.

Just south of Wailea is **Makena,** with two good beaches. **Big Beach** is 3,000 feet long and 100 feet wide. The water off Big Beach is fine for swimming and snorkeling. If you walk over the cinder cone at Big Beach, you'll reach **Little Beach,** which is used for nude sunbathing. Officially, nude sunbathing is illegal in Hawaii, but several bathers who've pushed their arrests through the courts have found their cases dismissed. Understand, though, that you take your chances if you decide to partake of a favorite local pastime at Little Makena.

The beaches in Central Maui are far from noteworthy, but if you're staying in the area, try **Kanaha Beach** in Kahului. A long, golden strip of sand bordered by a wide grassy area, this is a popular spot for windsurfers, joggers, and picnicking Maui families. Kanaha Beach has toilets, showers, picnic tables, and grills. *In Kahului, take Dairy Rd. toward the airport. At Koeheke, make a left and head toward Kahului Bay.*

If you want to see some of the world's finest windsurfers, stop at **Hookipa Beach** on the Hana Highway. The sport has become an art—and a career, to some—and its popularity was largely developed right at Hookipa. Waves get as high as 15 feet. This is not a good swimming beach, nor the place to learn windsurfing yourself, but plenty of picnic tables and barbecue grills are available. *About 1 mi past Paia on Hwy. 36.*

In East Maui, **Kaihalulu Beach** was once a favorite spot of privacy-seeking nudists. Now, however, Hana's red-sand beach has gotten a little less secluded as more people have discovered it, but this is still a gorgeous cove, with good swimming and snorkeling. To get there, start at the Hana Community Center at the end of Hauoli Road and walk along the outside of Kauiki Hill. The hike won't be easy, but it's worth the effort. No facilities are available.

Sports and the Outdoors

Participant Sports

Bicycling   Maui's roads are narrow, which can make bicycling a harrowing experience. Some visitors rent a bike just to ride around the resort where they're staying, but to go anywhere else requires getting on a two-lane highway. If it looks like something you'd like to try anyway, **A & B Moped Rental** (3481 Lower Honoapiilani Hwy., Lahaina, tel. 808/669–0027) is about your only choice. Bikes rent for $10 an hour.

Camping   Like the other Hawaiian islands, Maui is riddled with ancient
and Hiking   paths. These were the roads the Polynesians used to cross from one side of their island home to another. Most of these paths today are too difficult to find. But if you happen to stumble upon something that looks like it might have been a trail, chances are good it was used by the ancients.

In fact, most trails on Maui are not well marked. Only three areas have clearly marked trailheads. Luckily, they're some of the best hikes on the island.

In Maui's center, **Haleakala Crater** in Haleakala National Park is an obvious hiking haven, boasting several trails. As you drive to the top of the 10,023-foot dormant volcano on the Haleakala Highway, you'll first come to **Hosmer Grove,** less than a mile after you enter the park. This is a lovely forested area, with an hour-long nature trail. You can pick up a map at the trailhead and camp without a permit in the campground. There are six campsites, pit toilets, drinking water, and cooking shelters. There's also **Halemauu Trail,** near the 8,000-foot elevation. The walk to the crater rim is a grassy stroll, then it's a switchback trail nearly 2 miles to the crater floor. Nearly 4 miles from the trailhead, you'll find **Holua Cabin,** which you can reserve—at least three months in advance—through the National Park Service (Box 369, Makawao 96768, tel. 808/572–9306). Nearby, you can pitch a tent, but you'll need a permit that's issued on a first-come, first-served basis at Haleakala National Park Headquarters/Visitors Center (Haleakala Crater Rd., 7,000-ft elevation, tel. 808/572–9306. Open daily 7:30–4).

If you opt to drive all the way to the top of Haleakala, you'll find a trail called **Sliding Sands,** which starts at about the 10,000-foot elevation, descending 4 miles to the crater floor. The scenery is spectacular; it's colorful and somewhat like the moon. You can reach the abovementioned Holua Cabin in about 7 miles if you veer off to the left and out of the crater on the Halemauu Trail. If you continue on the Sliding Sands Trail, however, you'll come to **Kapalaoa Cabin** within about 6 miles, and at about 10 miles you'll hit **Paliku Cabin,** both also available from the park service with at least three months' notice. All three cabins have bunks, firewood, water, and a stove and are limited to 12 people. They can be reached in less than a day's walk. Paliku Cabin has tent camping nearby with toilets and drinking water. Tent permits, again, are issued at park headquarters on the day you want to use them.

Maui's second hiking area, in East Maui, is called **Oheo Gulch.** The gulch is part of Haleakala National Park, but it's very different from the crater. That's because it's over on the Hana side of the park—which actually extends far beyond the mountain you see in the clouds. This is a lush, rainy, tropical area. You can reach Oheo Gulch by continuing on the Hana Highway about 10 miles past Hana. Oheo Gulch includes the Seven Pools, where the two major trails begin. The first trail is **Makahiku Falls,** a half-mile jaunt from the parking lot to an overlook. You can go around the barrier and get closer to the falls if you want. From here, you can continue on the second trail for another 1½ miles. You'll dead-end at **Waimoku Falls.** There's camping in this area, with no permit required, although you can stay only three nights. Toilets, grills, and tables are available here, but no water.

Another camping and hiking area is located on the southern slope of Haleakala. Called **Polipoli Forest,** this place will remind you of a Walt Disney movie. It was once heavily forested, until cattle and goats chewed away most of the natural vegetation. Starting in about 1930, the government began a program to reforest the area, and soon redwoods, cedar, pine, and cypress took hold. Because of the elevation, it's a bit cooler here and sometimes wet and misty. But you'll appreciate the peace and quiet.

To reach the forest, drive on Highway 377 past Haleakala Road to Waipoli Road. Go up the hill until you reach the park. Next to the lot, you'll see a small campground and a cabin you can rent from the Division of State Parks (write far in advance for the cabin to: Box 1049, Wailuku 96793, tel. 808/244–4354; for the campground, you can wait until you arrive in Wailuku, then visit the State Parks office at 54 High St.). Once you're at Polipoli, there are three trails from which to choose.

Fitness Centers There are more fitness centers in hotels than anywhere else on Maui, and those will probably be the most convenient for you. The **Grand Hyatt Wailea's** Spa Grande is the largest (and grandest) in Hawaii. At the Kaanapali Resort, the **Hyatt Regency** has a guests-only health spa with all the trimmings and daily aerobics classes; the **Maui Marriott** boasts a weights room and aerobics with a $3 charge for nonguests; and the **Westin Maui** has a health club with weights, aerobics, and massage. At Wailea, the Grand Hyatt, Maui Inter-Continental, and Stouffers offer aerobics daily.

Outside the resorts, the **Lahaina Nautilus Center** (180 Dickenson St., Suite 201, tel. 808/667–6100) has a complete fitness center as does **World Gym** (845 Wainee St., Lahaina, tel. 808/667–0422), which specializes in weights. The **Kahana Gym** (4310 Lower Honoapiilani Hwy., Kahana, tel. 808/669–7622) specializes in free weights. There are other clubs as well, but they are simply not convenient unless you want to drive to Kahului or Wailuku—about an hour from West Maui and 45 minutes from Wailea.

Golf How do you keep your mind on the game in a place like Maui? It's very hard, because you can't ignore the view, but Maui has become one of the world's premier golf-vacation destinations. The island's three major resorts all have golf courses, each of them stunning. They're all open to the public as well.

The **Royal Kaanapali Golf Courses** (Kaanapali Beach Resort, Lahaina, tel. 808/661–3691) are two of Maui's most famous, due to television exposure. The layout consists of two 18-hole courses, which are each celebrities in their own right. The

North Course was designed by Robert Trent Jones, Sr., while the South Course architect was Arthur Jack Snyder. Greens fees run about $90 for guests and nonguests.

The **Kapalua Golf Club** (300 Kapalua Dr., Lahaina, tel. 808/669–8044) has three 18-holers—the Village Course and the Bay Course, designed by Arnold Palmer, and the Plantation course designed by Ben Crenshaw. Kapalua is also well known among television sports watchers. One of the Kapalua Bay Hotel owners is Mark Rolfing, who's made a name for himself as a producer of sporting events (he founded the Kapalua International) and as an announcer on ESPN. Greens fees at Kapalua are $75 for nonguests, $45 for guests. Carts go for $15 and clubs for $25.

The **Wailea Golf Club** (120 Kaukahi St., Wailea, tel. 808/879–2966) also has two courses—the Orange and the Blue—which were designed by Arthur Jack Snyder. In his design, the golf architect incorporated ancient lava-rock walls and *heiaus* (temples) for an even more unusual golfing experience. Greens fees are $105 for nonguests and $60 for guests.

The island's newest resort at Makena has a golf course as well, the lovely **Makena Golf Course** (5415 Makena Alanui Rd., Kihei, tel. 808/879–3344), designed by Robert Trent Jones, Jr. Of all the resort courses, this one is the most remote. At one point, golfers must cross a main road, but there are so few cars that this poses no problem. Greens fees are $100 per person, including a cart.

Maui has municipal courses as well, where the fees are lower. Be forewarned, however, that the weather can be cooler and wetter, while the locations may not be as convenient as you are used to at home. The **Waiehu Municipal Golf Course** (tel. 808/243–7400) is set on the northeast coast of Maui a few miles past Wailuku off Highway 340. Greens fees are $25; carts are $13. Up the hill from Kihei, the **Silversword Golf Course** (1345 Piilani Hwy., Kihei, tel. 808/874–0777) charges $50 including a cart.

Tennis   The state's finest tennis facilities are at the **Wailea Tennis Club** (131 Wailea Ike Pl., Kihei, tel. 808/879–1958), often called "Wimbledon West" because of its grass courts; there are also 11 Plexipave courts and a pro shop. You'll pay between $10 and $12 an hour per person for the hard courts, and between $40 and $60 per court per hour for the grass numbers. At the Makena Resort, just south of Wailea, the **Makena Tennis Club** (5415 Makena Alanui Rd., Kihei, tel. 808/879–8777) has six courts. Rates are $5 per person per hour for guests, $8 for nonguests. After an hour, if there's space available, there's no charge.

Over on West Maui, the **Royal Lahaina Tennis Ranch** (2780 Kekaa Dr., tel. 808/661–3611, ext. 2296) in the Kaanapali Beach Resort offers 11 courts and a pro shop. Guests pay $6 a day per person, while nonguests are charged $9. The **Hyatt Regency Maui** (200 Nohea Kai Dr., Kaanapali, tel. 808/661–1234, ext. 3174) has five courts, with rentals and instruction. Courts go for $12 an hour for singles, $15 for doubles. Farther north, **Kapalua Tennis Garden** (100 Kapalua Dr., Kapalua, tel. 808/669–5677) serves the Kapalua Resort with 10 courts and a pro shop. You'll pay $9 a day if you're a guest, $10 if you're not.

There are other facilities around the island, usually one or two courts in smaller hotels or condos. Most of them, however, are open only to their guests. The best free courts are the five at the **Lahaina Civic Center** (1840 Honoapiilani Hwy., Lahaina, tel. 808/661–4685), near Wahikuli State Park; they're available on a first-come, first-served basis.

Water Sports
Deep-sea Fishing If fishing is your sport, Maui is the place for it. You'll be able to throw in hook and bait for fish like *ahi* (yellowfin tuna), *aku* (a skipjack tuna), barracuda, bonefish, *kawakawa* (bonito), mahi-mahi (a dolphin fish—*not* the mammal), Pacific blue marlin, *ono* (wahoo), and *ulua* (jack crevalle). On Maui, you can fish throughout the year, and you don't need a license.

Plenty of fishing boats run out of Lahaina and Maalaea harbors. If you charter a boat by yourself, expect to spend in the neighborhood of $600 a day. But you can share the boat with others who are interested in fishing the same day for about $100. While there are at least 10 companies running boats on a regular basis, these are the most reliable: **Finest Kind Inc.** (Slip 7, Box 10481, Lahaina 96767, tel. 808/661–0338), **Hinatea Sportfishing** (Slip 18/Lahaina Harbor, Lahaina 96761, tel. 808/667–7548), and **Luckey Strike Charters** (Box 522, Lahaina 96767, tel. 808/661–4606). **Ocean Activities Center** (1325 S. Kihei Rd., Suite 212, Kihei 96753, tel. 808/879–4485 or 800/367–8047, ext. 448) can arrange fishing charters as well. You're responsible for finding your own transportation to the harbor.

Sailing Because of its proximity to the smaller islands of Molokai, Lanai, Kahoolawe, and Molokini, Maui can provide one of Hawaii's best sailing experiences. Most sailing operations like to combine their tours with a meal, some throw in snorkeling or whale-watching, while others offer a sunset cruise. If you want to really sail—as opposed to cruising on a motorized catamaran or other vessel—try **Genesis Sailing Charters** (Box 10697, Lahaina 96761, tel. 808/667–5667), **Maui–Molokai Sea Cruises** (831 Eha St., Suite 101, Wailuku 96793, tel. 808/242–8777), **Sail Hawaii** (Box 573, Kihei 96753, tel. 808/879–2201), **Scotch Mist Charters** (Box 831, Lahaina 96767, tel. 808/661–0386), and **Seabern Yachts** (Box 1022, Lahaina 96767, tel. 808/661–8110).

Scuba Diving Believe it or not, Maui is just as scenic underwater as it is above. In fact, some of the finest diving spots in Hawaii lie along the Valley Isle's western and southwestern shores. If you're a certified diver, you can rent gear at any Maui dive shop simply by showing your PADI or NAUI card. Unless you're familiar with the area, however, it's probably best to hook up with a dive shop for an underwater tour. Additionally, the only really decent shore dive is at Honolua Bay, a marine reserve above Kapalua Resort. The water is usually rough during the winter.

Popular Maui dive shops—stores that deal exclusively in the sale and rental of diving equipment, as well as lessons and certification—include **Capt. Nemo's Ocean Emporium** (150 Dickenson St., Lahaina, tel. 808/661–5555), **Central Pacific Divers** (780 Front St., Lahaina, tel. 808/661–8718), **Dive Maui** (Lahaina Market Place, Lahaina, tel. 808/667–2080), **Ed Robinson's Diving Adventures** (Box 616, Kihei, tel. 808/879–3584), and **Lahaina Divers** (710 Front St., Lahaina, tel. 808/667–7496). All provide equipment with proof of certification, as well as introductory dives for those who aren't certified. Introductory boat dives generally run about $60.

Dive Sites   **Honolua Bay,** in West Maui, is a marine preserve with many varieties of coral and tame tropical fish, including large ulua, kahala, barracuda, and manta rays. With depths of 20 to 50 feet, this is a popular spot for introductory dives. Dives are generally given only during the summer months.

Molokini Crater, at Alalakeiki Channel, is a crescent-shaped islet formed by the top of a volcanic crater. This marine preserve's depth range (10–80 feet), combined with the attraction of the numerous tame fish dwelling here that can be fed by hand, make it a popular introductory dive site.

Snorkeling   The same dive companies that take scuba aficionados on tours will take snorkelers as well—for a lot less money. One of Maui's most popular snorkeling spots can be reached only by boat: Molokini Crater, that little bowl of land off the coast of the Makena Resort. For about $55, you can spend the day at Molokini, with meals provided. **Ocean Activities Center** (1325 S. Kihei Rd., Suite 212, Kihei 96753, tel. 808/879–4485) does the best job, although other companies also do this tour.

You can find some good snorkeling spots on your own. Secluded **Windmill Beach** (take Hwy. 30 3½ mi north of Kapalua, then turn onto the dirt road to the left) has a superb reef for snorkeling. A little more than 2 miles south, another dirt road leads to **Honolua Bay;** the coral formations on the right side of the bay are particularly dramatic. One beach south of the Kapalua Resort, you'll find **Napili Bay,** also quite good for snorkeling.

Almost the entire coastline from Kaanapali south to Olowalu offers fine snorkeling. Favorite sites include the area just out from the cemetery north of Wahikuli State Park, near the lava cone called **Black Rock,** on which Kaanapali's Sheraton Maui Hotel is built (tame fish will take bread from your hand there), and the shallow coral reef south of **Olowalu** General Store.

The coastline from Kihei to Makena is also generally good for snorkeling. The best is found near the rocks of **Kamaole Beach III** in Kihei and the rocky fringes of Wailea's **Mokapu, Ulua, Wailea,** and **Polo** beaches.

Between Polo Beach and Makena Beach (shortly before the turnoff to Ulupalakua) lies **Five Caves,** where you'll find a maze of underwater grottoes below offshore rocks. This spot is recommended for experienced snorkelers only, since the tides can get rough. At Makena, the waters around the **Puu Olai** cinder cone provide great snorkeling.

If you need gear, **Snorkel Bob's** (5425 Lower Honoapiilani Rd., Napili, tel. 808/669–9603), in the Napili Village Hotel, will rent you a mask, fins, and snorkel, and throw in a carrying bag, map, and snorkel tips for $15 a week.

Surfing   Although on land it may not look as if there are seasons on Maui, the tides tell another story. In winter, the surf's up on the northern shores of the Hawaiian Islands, while summer brings big swells to the southern side. Near-perfect winter waves on Maui can be found at **Honolua Bay,** on the northern tip of West Maui. To get there, continue 2 miles north of D. T. Fleming Park on Highway 30 and take a left onto the dirt road next to a pineapple field; a path takes you to the beach.

Next best for surfing is **Hookipa Beach Park** (off Hwy. 36 a short distance east of Paia), where the modern-day sport began on Maui. This is the easiest place to watch surfing, because there are paved parking areas and picnic pavilions in the park. A word of warning: The guys who come here are pros, and if you're not, they may not take kindly to your getting in their way.

You can rent surfboards and boogie boards at many surf shops, such as **Indian Summer Surf Shop** (193 Lahainaluna Rd., Lahaina, tel. 808/661–3794), **Second Wind** (111 Hana Hwy., Kahului, tel. 808/877–7467), **Lightning Bolt Maui** (55 Kaahumanu Ave., Suite E, Kahului, tel. 808/877–3484), and **Ole Surfboards** (1036 Limahana Pl., Lahaina, tel. 808/661–3459).

Maui Surfing School (tel. 808/875–0625) guarantees one two-hour lesson is all it takes to have "anyone who can walk" standing on a surfboard and riding the gentle waves of Lahaina Harbor. Costs are $55 per person (maximum class size of 6), including equipment rental; group discounts are available.

Waterskiing Only one company tows water-skiers off the coast of Maui: **Lahaina Water Ski** (104 Wahikuli Rd., Lahaina, tel. 808/661–5988). For $30 per 15 minutes for one person, $50 per 30 minutes for one to three people, or $90 an hour for one to five people, Lahaina Water Ski provides the boat, driver, and equipment.

Windsurfing It's been more than a dozen years since Hookipa Bay was discovered by boardsailors, but in those years since 1980, the windy beach 10 miles east of Kahului has become the windsurfing capital of the world. The spot boasts optimal wave-sailing wind and sea conditions and, for experienced windsurfers, can offer the ultimate experience. Other locations around Maui are good for windsurfing as well—Honolua Bay, for example—but Hookipa is absolutely unrivaled.

Even if you're a windsurfing aficionado, chances are good you didn't bring your equipment. You can rent it—or get lessons—from these shops: **Kaanapali Windsurfing School** (104 Wahikuli Rd., Lahaina, tel. 808/667–1964), **Maui Magic Windsurfing School** (520 Keolani Pl., Kahului, tel. 808/877–4816), **Ocean Activities Center** (1325 S. Kihei Rd., Kihei, tel. 808/879–4485), and **Maui Windsurfari** (Box 330254, Kahului, tel. 808/871–7766). Lessons range from $30 to $60 and can last anywhere from one to three hours. Equipment rental also varies—from no charge with lessons to $20 an hour. For the latest prices and special deals, it's best to call around once you've arrived.

Spectator Sports

Golf **Tournaments** Maui has a number of golf tournaments, many of which are televised on ESPN. Especially popular during the last two months of each year, Maui's golf tourneys are of professional caliber and worth watching. The **Isuzu Kapalua International Championship of Golf** held each November at the Kapalua Resort is the granddaddy of them all and now draws big names competing for a $600,000 purse. Also at Kapalua is the **Kirin Cup World Championship of Golf,** with teams representing the U.S. Professional Golf Association (PGA) tour, the European PGA tour, the Japan PGA Tour, and the Australia/New Zealand PGA tour. Golfing greats play on Kapalua's Bay Course for a $1.1 million purse each December. At Kaanapali, the **GTE Kaanapali Golf Classic** pits senior duffers in a battle for a $300,000 purse each

December. Over in Wailea, the **Annual Asahi Beer Kyosan Golf Tournament** has a $100,000 purse, and the **LPGA Women's Kemper Open** moved from Kauai to Wailea starting with the February 1990 tournament. For more information and tournament dates, call Rolfing Productions, tel. 808/669-4844.

Windsurfing Not many places can lay claim to as many windsurfing tournaments as Maui. The Valley Isle is generally thought to be the world's preeminent windsurfing location, drawing board-sailing experts from around the globe who want to compete on its waves. In April, the **Marui/O'Neil Invitational** lures top windsurfers from at least a dozen countries to vie for a $30,000 purse. The **Hawaiian Pro-Am Speed Slalom Windsurfing Competition** and **Wailea Speed Crossing** take place in September, and the **Maui Grand Prix** and the **Aloha Classic Wave Sailing World Championships** are held in October. The **Junior World Wave Sailing Championships,** for kids under 18 from around the world, is in May. All events are held at Hookipa Bay, right outside the town of Paia, near Kahului.

Dining

Maui cuisine consists of a lot more than the poi and pineapple you'll find at a local luau. It's also more than the burgers and fries doled out at the ubiquitous fast-food chains that in some towns seem to post a store on every other corner. Maui continues to attract fine chefs, some of whom have initiated the trend some call "nouvelle Hawaiian." This growing movement uses fruits and vegetables unique to Hawaii in classic European or Asian ways—spawning such dishes as ahi carpaccio, breadfruit soufflé, and papaya cheesecake. Sometimes a touch of California is added as well.

Of course, you can find plain old local-style cooking on the Valley Isle—particularly if you wander into the less touristy areas of Wailuku or Kahului, for example. Greasy spoons abound, and some of those places are where you can get the most authentic local food, or what residents call "plate lunch," for very little expense. A good plate lunch will fulfill your daily requirement of carbohydrates: macaroni salad, two enormous scoops of rice, and an entrée of, say, curry stew, teriyaki beef, or *kalua* (roasted) pig and cabbage.

Some of the island's best restaurants are in hotels—not surprising, considering that tourism is the island's number one industry. In the resorts, you'll find some of Maui's finest Continental restaurants and some good coffee shops as well. In addition, because many of the upscale hotels sit right on the beach, you'll often have the benefit of an oceanfront ambience. Few restaurants on Maui require jackets. An aloha shirt and pants for men and a simple dress or pants for women are acceptable in all but the fanciest establishments.

Restaurants are open daily unless otherwise noted.

Highly recommended restaurants in each price category are indicated by a star ★.

Category	Cost*
Very Expensive	over $60
Expensive	$40–$60
Moderate	$20–$40
Inexpensive	under $20

*per person, excluding drinks, service, and sales tax (4%)

West Maui

American
★ **David Paul's Lahaina Grill.** Owners David Paul and Michelle Johnson doubled the size of this place and it still fills up every night; the imaginative menu is one reason (ahi carpaccio, tequila shrimp with "firecracker" rice—chili and vanilla bean-flavored—or Kona coffee-roasted lamb). When David's not concocting innovative food combinations, he's guest-chefing at overseas food and wine fêtes, gathering ideas, and searching out special wines for the Grill's cellar. The Grill has a wine and cheese hour weekdays at 5. *127 Lahainaluna Rd., Lahaina, tel. 808/667–5117. Reservations advised. Dress: casual. AE, MC, V. Moderate.*

Lahaina Provision Co. This small place, located in the Hyatt Regency, serves a tasty lunch buffet, as well as sandwiches, steak, and seafood; there's also a well-stocked salad bar. At 6 PM for dinner, it also opens its Chocoholic Bar, and until 10:30, you can get chocolate treats of every variety. *Hyatt Regency Maui, 200 Nohea Kai Dr., Kaanapali, tel. 808/661–1234. Dress: casual. AE, DC, MC, V. Moderate.*

★ **Longhi's.** Proprietor Bob Longhi has gotten a lot of notoriety for the way his young waiters and waitresses pull up a chair and recite the day's menu. But what makes this establishment worth a visit is the food and the award-winning wine list of more than 600 selections. Homemade pasta and pastry—whipped up by the full-time pastry chef—as well as fresh-squeezed orange juice, fresh fish, and sandwiches you can't get your mouth around are only some of the choices here. Longhi's is an open-air establishment; on its first floor, tile floors and casual wood tables invite celebrities, as well as more run-of-the-mill diners, to stop and watch the world go by while supping on Pasta Sicilian (calamari in a spicy red sauce), New York prime rib, shrimp Longhi, or live Maine lobster. This is a good choice for breakfast and opens at 7:30. At night, the upper floor offers a fancier version of dinner. *888 Front St., Lahaina, tel. 808/ 667–2288. No reservations. Dress: casual. AE, V. Moderate.*

Continental
★ **The Bay Club.** Here's just the place to have lunch or a candlelight dinner. This restaurant is situated on a lava-rock promontory overlooking the bay at the far end of Kapalua Beach, within the Kapalua Resort. Set in an open-air room, with richly paneled walls and rattan furniture, the Bay Club has an excellent wine list and nouvelle cuisine menu; the roasted veal chop, sautéed breast of duck with Frangelico and roasted pecans, and fresh catch of the day from the Molokai Channel are all superior choices. *At the Kapalua Bay Resort, 1 Bay Dr., Kapalua, tel. 808/669–5656. Reservations suggested. Jackets optional. AE, DC, MC, V. Expensive.*

The Grill. The new Ritz-Carlton's showcase restaurant starts serving dinner early enough (6 PM) for sunset to be a major part

Maui Dining

Hanokohau

Honolua

Kahakuloa

1
2

Napili

Kahana

3

Honokowai

Kaanapali

Honoapiilani Hwy.

340

W E S T   M A U I   M T S .

4
5

6
7 LAHAINA
8
9
10

*Iao Valley
State Park*

30

11

Olowalu

Honoapiilani Hwy.

N

0   5 miles

0   5 km

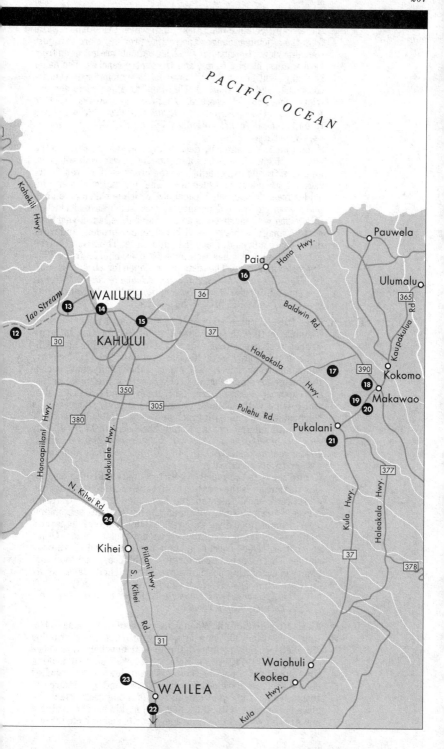

of the meal—especially if you're seated in the lanai just outside the elegant, clublike main room, into which piano music wafts from the adjoining lounge. The setting provides more than just romantic views; the cuisine's fresh ingredients are gathered from local waters, nearby farms, and Upcountry ranches. The menu helpfully identifies its "light" (lower-fat) selections for the calorie-conscious, and for those who'll want to allow room for the white chocolate cheesecake. *Ritz-Carlton, Kapalua, One Ritz-Carlton Dr., Kapalua, tel. 808/669–6200. Reservations recommended. Jacket optional. AE, D, DC, MC, V. Moderate–Expensive.*

Swan Court. You enter by descending a grand staircase to the edge of a lagoon in which swans glide by. A waterfall splashes, and palm fronds sway slightly in the breeze—the Swan Court radiates grandeur and elegance. The international menu includes fresh Island fish Eichenholz, which is baked on an oak plate with capers and mushroom garnish; breast of chicken filled with wild mushrooms and a champagne sauce; veal chop sauté Armagnac, in cream with morrel mushrooms; and roast duck, chateaubriand, fresh fish, and more. The Swan Court's extensive wine list has won awards of excellence from *Wine Spectator* magazine. The restaurant is open for a breakfast buffet. *Hyatt Regency Maui, Kaanapali Beach Resort, 200 Nohea Kai Dr., tel. 808/661–1234. Reservations advised. Dinner jacket optional. AE, DC, MC, V. Expensive.*

French **Chez Paul.** A mere wide spot in the road, 4 miles south of
★ Lahaina in Olowalu, provides the setting for this intimate French restaurant that's made a name for itself since 1975. Chez Paul has only 14 tables, each set with linen tablecloths, china, and fresh flowers. The menu changes daily, but specialties include scampi Olowalu, cooked with white wine, herbs, and capers; poisson beurre blanc, fresh island fish poached in white wine with shallots, cream, and capers; and veal à la Normande, sautéed with green apples in a Calvados sauce. If you're still hungry, try the Kahlua cheesecake. *On Hwy. 30, 4 mi south of Lahaina, tel. 808/661–3843. Reservations required. Dress: casual chic. AE, MC, V. 2 dinner seatings nightly, at 6:30 and 8:30. Expensive.*

★ **Gerard's.** Set in the romantic, Victorian-style Plantation Inn, this restaurant is the creation of owner Gerard Reversade, one of Hawaii's most talented and award-laden chefs. Gerard's serves French cuisine, with a menu that changes seasonally. Two recommended dishes are rack of lamb and veal chops with basil butter, fresh pasta topped with a tomato sauce. Other specialties include fresh fish, lamb, beef, veal, and 75 wine varieties. This place has a comfortable ambience, great food, and plenty of stargazing possibilities—it's a celebrity favorite. *At the Plantation Inn, 174 Lahainaluna Rd., Lahaina, tel. 808/ 661–8939. Reservations suggested. Dress: casual. AE, DC, MC, V. Dinner only. Expensive.*

Italian **Alex's Hole in the Wall.** When Alex and Tom Didio came to Ha-
★ waii more than 30 years ago, they brought their grandpa Marchetti's family recipes, determined to put them to good use someday. In 1971, Alex's Hole in the Wall started making Grandpa proud. Look for the restaurant down a narrow alley behind the Tom Barefoot Discount Travel and up a staircase. Inside, you'll think you're in an Italian living room, since the place is crammed with knickknacks of all kinds. The brothers make their own pasta and sausage; favorite dishes include *pollo*

e'salsicca (chicken with garlic and sausage) and lasagne *imbottita* (with meat and four cheeses). The desserts are to die for. *834 Front St., Lahaina, tel. 808/661-3197. Reservations advised. Dress: casual. AE, MC, V. Dinner only. Inexpensive–Moderate.*

Japanese **Nikko.** This is Japanese food *teppan* style. That means you'll be seated with other diners at a table that has a built-in grill. Together you'll watch the chef and his slicing, dicing, and chopping knives. He can perform amazing feats—and the best part is you get to eat the creations he prepares. Vegetables, such as green peppers, eggplant, and squash, as well as bite-size chicken, pork, and beef, are grilled to perfection. A lot of Japanese visitors find their way to Nikko—and you know what that says about a place. *Maui Marriott Hotel, Kaanapali Beach Resort, 100 Nohea Kai Dr., tel. 808/667-1200. Reservations required. Dress: casual. AE, DC, MC, V. Moderate.*

Seafood **Erik's Seafood Grotto.** This award-winning restaurant and oyster bar in the Kahana Villas Condominiums offers a netful of fresh island fish daily, plus such flavorful house specialties as cioppino and seafood curry. The fresh Hawaiian spiny or slipper lobster is filled with seafood stuffing and flame-broiled, while you can get your *opakapaka* (pink snapper) sautéed with butter. The mahimahi is especially delicious baked in vermouth with macadamia nuts. Five daily specials are priced between $10.95 and $11.95. Erik's also offers *keiki* dinners—a petite steak or medley of chicken, fish, and shrimp at $9.95 for children under 12. Erik's has a nautical feel to it, with a rustic open-beam ceiling and lots of hanging plants. *Kahana Villas, 4242 Lower Honoapiilani Hwy., Kahana, tel. 808/669-4806. Reservations advised. Dress: casual. AE, MC, V. Dinner only. Moderate.*

Tropical/ Continental
★ **Avalon Restaurant and Bar.** This is one of Maui's trendiest restaurants. Mark Ellman is a young Californian who came to Maui and opened his first commercial venture in 1988, with Ellman himself in the kitchen. The decor at the Avalon is Hawaiian 1940s, with bright tropical prints on the chairs and tables, reminiscent of the days when you had to cruise to the Islands and, once there, would find a paradise of swaying palms and hula girls. Oversize dishware brings the Hawaiian Regional food to the table—and what food it is! Ellman's inventive menu mixes and matches the cuisines of California, Hawaii, Indonesia, Thailand, Vietnam, and Japan. Signature items include roast duck with plum sauce and Chinese steamed dumplings; and giant prawns in a garlic black-bean sauce. For dessert, try the caramel Miranda—fresh exotic fruits in a homemade caramel sauce with macadamia nut ice cream. *Mariner's Alley, 844 Front St., Lahaina, tel. 808/667-5559. Reservations advised. Dress: casual. AE, DC, MC, V. Expensive.*

★ **Lahaina Coolers.** This surf bistro specializes in unusual food at reasonable prices. Try the pepper chicken linguini in a sauce of roasted bell peppers, or a spinach and feta quesadilla. *180 Dickenson St., Lahaina, tel. 808/661-7082. Reservations advised. Dress: casual. AE, MC, V. Inexpensive.*

Central Maui

American **Mark Edison's.** A romantic dining spot, Mark Edison's boasts one of Maui's most unusual locations. With views of the West

Maui mountains and Iao Valley Park, this restaurant has a lush, tropical ambience unlike that of any other eating establishment. Specialties include chicken, steak, pasta, and fish, with a well-stocked salad bar. Each day from 5:30 to 6:30, you can order prime rib and teriyaki chicken at $8.95. Mark Edison's has a large local following, especially at lunch. It also brings in good entertainment at least once a week. *Iao Valley Rd., just beyond Kepaniwai Park at the Iao Needle, tel. 808/242–5555. Reservations advised. Dress: casual. AE, MC, V. Moderate–Expensive.*

Chinese **Ming Yuen.** This place is low-key, with unassuming decor, but
★ locals love it and will line up to prove it. The menu is extensive and features mostly Cantonese cuisine, plus a few Szechuan dishes. The lemon chicken has made it famous, but you might try the hot-and-sour soup to start and then go for the Kung Pao chicken: chicken stir-fried with chili peppers, garlic, peanuts, and chopped vegetables. The mu-shu pork is also recommended. Ming Yuen's most unusual dish is a minced squab cooked in a Chinese mushroom sauce and served in lettuce pockets. *162 Alamaha St., Kahului, tel. 808/871–7787. Reservations advised. Dress: casual. MC, V. Inexpensive.*

Steakhouse **The Chart House.** This dining spot is about as close to the ocean as you can get in a Kahului restaurant. Model ships, boat hulls, and surf prints contribute to the nautical decor. The menu includes steaks grilled to order; fresh fish baked, broiled, or cooked in herbs and spices; and a well-stocked salad bar. One of the nicest dining establishments for both food and ambience in Kahului, the Chart House is very popular with the local after-work crowd. *500 N. Puunene Ave., Kahului, tel. 808/877–2476. Reservations advised. Dress: casual. AE, MC, V. Moderate.*

Thai **Siam Thai.** This is one of the best places to sample Thai cuisine in the Islands—and such celebrities as Robert Redford (whose picture adorns the wall) will probably vouch for it. There are about 70 selections on the menu, including some fine vegetarian dishes. The specialties are the curries, which come in red, green, or yellow, and hot, medium, or mild. Plants grace the interior, while white tablecloths add a touch of class. *123 Market, Wailuku, tel. 808/244–3817. Reservations advised. Dress: casual. AE, MC, V. Inexpensive–Moderate.*

East Maui

American **Bullock's.** The large Moonburgers here are terrific, so it's easy to see what attracts the locals. The shakes are recommended, too, particularly the ones featuring such tropical fruits as guava and papaya. A lot of people stop here on their way to or from Haleakala, because it's located in Pukalani, about 10 miles up the Haleakala Highway. *3494 Haleakala Hwy., Pukalani, tel. 808/572–7220. Dress: casual. MC, V. Closed for dinner. Inexpensive.*

Maui Onion. Set out by the pool at the ocean-front Stouffer Wailea Hotel, this award-winning lunch spot has a small menu that includes salads and sandwiches. Maui Onion made it onto this list, however, because of its mouth-watering Maui onion rings. If you love onion rings, we recommend you make a special trip here. *Stouffer Wailea Hotel, Wailea Resort, 3550 Wailea Alanui Dr., Wailea, tel. 808/879–4900. Dress: casual. AE, DC, MC, V. Inexpensive.*

Continental

★ **Raffles.** The pride and joy of the Stouffer Wailea Beach Resort, Raffles is a luxurious, award-winning room that pays homage to British colonial elegance. In fact, the name was inspired by Sir Thomas Stamford Raffles (1781–1826), founder of the city of Singapore; the Raffles Hotel in that city is world renowned. Wall-to-wall carpeting and hanging brass lamps provide an Old World ambience. The sophisticated Pacific Rim cuisine includes opakapaka in lobster broth with baby leeks and chavril; roast rack of lamb with Molokai herbs; and sautéed veal medallions with a ginger scallion buerre blanc. The signature dessert souffle changes daily. Raffles also has an extravagant Sunday brunch that features, among other things, omelets and strawberries dipped in chocolate. *Stouffer Wailea Beach Resort, 3550 Wailea Alanui Dr., Wailea, tel. 808/879–4900. Reservations required. Dress: casual but chic. AE, DC, MC, V. Very Expensive.*

★ **Prince Court.** This fine-dining restaurant, located in the Maui Prince Hotel, has made a name for itself with the help of its innovative chef, Roger Dikon. Although it bills itself as an American restaurant, it seems to belong in the Continental category, with the other classy establishments. The view of the ocean is marvelous at this romantic place, which offers exquisite candlelit dining on two levels, and excellent service in a long room decorated with bamboo-cushioned chairs, island plants, and tropical flowers. The chef puts together a delectable prix-fixe menu, usually featuring fish specialties and luscious desserts, such as Strawberry Bombe in Chocolate. Although the chef's creativity with the island's fresh seafood is most notable, you'll also find such dependable Continental fare as veal, rack of lamb, and local fish, complemented by an extensive wine list. The restaurant also features a wonderful Sunday brunch from 10 to 2. *Maui Prince Hotel, Makena Resort, Makena, tel. 808/874–1111. Reservations advised. Jacket optional at dinner. AE, DC, MC, V. Dinner and Sun. brunch only. Expensive.*

Italian

Casanova Italian Restaurant & Deli. Owned by three young native Italians—and a German brought up in Italy—this Upcountry establishment has expanded into a real restaurant offering the best Italian food on Maui. A wood-fired pizza oven produces a variety of yummy pies; try the salsiccia with mozzarella, ham, and broccoli in a tomato sauce. You can also order pasta, chicken, or fresh fish. *1188 Makawao Ave., Makawao, tel. 808/572–0220. Reservations advised. Dress: casual. AE, MC, V. Moderate.*

Mexican

★ **Polli's.** Who would've thought you could find a world-class vegetarian Mexican restaurant on Maui? Native Arizonan Polli Smith and her husband started La Familia 10 years ago, sold it, then opened a lively Mexican cantina called Polli's in Upcountry Makawao. They've always offered meat dishes on the menu, but their meatless tacos, burritos, and enchiladas are just as good. Everything's offered à la carte, but you can get complete lunches and dinners, too. Polli's margaritas are the best in the state—take it from us. *1202 Makawao Ave., Makawao, tel. 808/572–7808. Dress: casual. MC, V. Inexpensive.*

Seafood

★ **Mama's Fish House.** For the best seafood on Maui put your car on the Hana Highway and head toward Paia. About 1½ miles past Paia, you'll see an oceanfront building on your left— Mama's, an Old Hawaiian–style restaurant serving honest food. This is a lovely spot, well landscaped and well tended. The fresh fish here has the reputation of being the best you can find in the area, and you can get it sautéed in butter, poached in white-wine sauce with mushrooms, or broiled with lemon butter. One recommended dish is the fresh fish fillet baked with Mama's bread and shrimp stuffing in a champagne sauce. Mama's also serves meat and chicken. *799 Kaiholo Pl., Paia, tel. 808/579–8488. Reservations recommended at dinner. Dress: casual. AE, MC, V. Moderate.*

Steakhouse   **Makawao Steak House.** This popular Upcountry dinner house is arguably one of the best steak joints on the island—a tender filet mignon or Porterhouse goes for less than $25. The fresh fish, and fresh-baked bread are just as good. If you really decide to splurge, you can get scampi and lobster. But meat lovers shouldn't miss the steak. *3612 Baldwin Ave., tel. 808/572–8711. Dress: casual. AE, MC, V. Dinner only, with specials offered nightly. Moderate.*

Tropical/   **Haliimaile General Store.** This delightful restaurant was a
Continental   camp store in the 1920s, but you'd never know it now. From the
★   outside, its white, green, and peach tin exterior looks a little out of place, sitting proudly in a pineapple field in Upcountry Maui, literally in the middle of nowhere. Owner Beverly Gannon has done wonders with this place, turning it into a charming outpost that serves some of the best food in the state. The contemporary menu uses Island products that change with the seasons. One of Haliimaile's staples is duck prepared in a variety of ways, such as duck smoked with pineapple chutney. Other specialties include the dynamite barbecued ribs, lobster pasta with fresh tarragon, and spicy shrimp Diane. Mrs. Gannon intended to open a deli with only 32 seats—although it grew to 80 within one week—and there's a stainless steel deli case featuring all the different specials. A corner of this restaurant looks like an old general store, with items for sale. Since its opening in 1988, this has become one of Maui's most magnetic restaurants, repeatedly attracting celebrities and a host of other see-and-be-seen types. *Haliimaile Rd., 2 mi before Pukalani, tel. 808/572–2666. Dress: casual. MC, V. Open daily. Moderate–Expensive.*

Lodging

Maui has the state's highest concentration of condominium units. More than half of the island's rental units, in fact, are condos. Don't be put off by this; it's not what you're thinking. For the most part, Maui's condos are not the tacky high rises that boast thin walls and cheap appliances. These are top-of-the-line units with all the amenities. Many are oceanfront and offer the ambience of a hotel suite without the cost.

Maui also boasts the highest percentage of luxury hotel rooms in the state. According to a national hotel-research firm, a full 50% of the Valley Isle's hotel rooms can be placed in the stratosphere when it comes to elegance. And although the figure for luxury condominiums is lower, you can nonetheless find some outrageously upscale condos on the Valley Isle.

Of course, the price you'll pay to stay on Maui reflects this attention to luxury. The island has the highest average accommodation cost of any Hawaiian island, and hoteliers here have tended in the past to raise rates with abandon. In recent years, this has created a greater willingness on the part of visitors to try other islands, which is one reason Kauai and the Big Island visitor counts and occupancy rates have improved. The average lodging rate on Maui can run as much as $70 more a night than on the other islands. Most lodgings come equipped with swimming pools, all of them outdoors to take full advantage of the gentle year-round climate.

What you'll pay depends in part on where you want to stay. West Maui is the center of tourism. More rooms are available on this part of the Valley Island than anywhere else, and most are high quality, and expensive. Two major resort areas anchor West Maui: the Kaanapali Beach Resort, with its six hotels and seven condominiums, and the Kapalua Bay Resort, with its two hotels and several condo complexes.

East Maui is a mixed bag when it comes to accommodations. You can find just about any rate and just about any degree of comfort. That's partly because the area is so huge, encompassing the Wailea and Makena resorts along the southwestern shore; Kihei, a hodgepodge strip running north from Wailea; Upcountry Maui, the area that rises into the clouds of Haleakala; and Hana, secluded in the easternmost part of Maui.

Condominiums and bed-and-breakfasts are listed in separate categories following the hotels.

Highly recommended hotels in each price category are indicated by a star ★.

Category	Cost*
Very Expensive	over $175
Expensive	$125–$175
Moderate	$75–$125
Inexpensive	under $75

All prices are for a standard double room, excluding 9¼% tax and service charges.

West Maui

Very Expensive **Embassy Suites.** The Hawaiian Islands' first all-suite hotel opened north of Kaanapali in late 1988 with one- and two-bedroom apartments. The units are spacious, with a blue-and-beige decor that gently insists on being trendily tropical. Each suite has two phones (with separate phone lines), ceiling fans, air-conditioning, a refrigerator, a microwave oven, and a coffee maker, as well as a 36-inch color television with a VCR. Fine touches have been added, such as an inviting wicker chaise longue perched next to an open window. The rates include a full breakfast each morning and a two-hour cocktail party with manager Gary Ettinger each evening. *104 Kaanapali Shores Pl., Lahaina 96761, tel. 808/661–2000 or 800/462–6284, fax 808/667–5821. 413 units. Beachfront. Facilities: sauna, health club, pool, tennis, golf, A/C, color TV. AE, DC, MC, V.*

Hyatt Regency Maui. Want to stay in a fantasyland? This lavish property was built in 1980 by Chris Hemmeter, a developer with a penchant for water fantasies and expensive art, and the hotel shows his biases. There are nine major waterfalls and sev-

Maui Lodging

Aloha Cottages, **26**
Aston Kamaole
Sands, **18**
Embassy Suites, **6**
Four Seasons
Resort, **24**
Grand Hyatt
Wailea, **23**
Hana Kai-Maui, **28**
Heavenly Hana
Inn, **27**
Hotel Hana-Maui, **29**

Hyatt Regency
Maui, **12**
Kaanapali Alii, **9**
Kaanapali Beach
Hotel, **8**
Kapalua Bay Hotel, **3**
Kapalua Bay Villas, **2**
Kula Lodge, **17**
Lahaina Hotel, **13**
Mana Kai-Maui, **19**
Maui Inter-
Continental Wailea, **22**
Maui Lu Resort, **16**

Maui Marriott, **11**
Maui Prince, **25**
Napili Kai Beach
Club, **4**
Papakea Beach
Resort, **5**
Pioneer Inn, **15**
Plantation Inn, **14**
Ritz-Carlton,
Kapalua , **1**
Royal Lahaina, **7**
Stouffer Wailea Beach
Resort, **20**

Wailea Villas, **21**
Westin Maui, **10**

eral smaller ones. The 750,000-gallon pool is something every honeymooning couple should have access to—there's a secret, romantic grotto made more secluded by a waterfall cascading over the opening, as well as a 130-foot water slide, a swinging rope bridge, and a swim-up cocktail bar. A $12 million renovation has made the rooms better than ever. *200 Nohea Kai Dr., Lahaina 96761, tel. 808/661–1234 or 800/233–1234, fax 808/667–4498. 815 rooms with bath. Beachfront. Facilities: 5 restaurants, 7 cocktail lounges, golf, tennis, color TV, A/C, library, health spa. AE, DC, MC, V.*

★ **Kapalua Bay Hotel.** Part of the Kapalua Bay Resort, this is one of the finest hotels in the state, winner of numerous awards and accolades. Built in 1978, the hotel has a California feel to it: the exterior is all understated white and natural wood. The open lobby, filled with flowering vanda and dendrobium orchids, has a fine view of the ocean beyond. The rooms are spacious and have recently been renovated. The impeccable staff is always ready to fill any need, and for the price, you certainly won't be disappointed. Although it's isolated from other resort areas, Kapalua has some of the island's finest restaurants and shops to make up for it. *1 Bay Dr., Kapalua 96761, tel. 808/669–5656 or 800/367–8000, fax 808/669–4694. 194 rooms with bath. Beachfront. Facilities: pool, restaurants, shops, color TV, A/C, golf, and tennis. AE, DC, MC, V.*

Maui Marriott. The Marriott sits on the same impressive Kaanapali beach as the Hyatt and Westin, but its rooms and service offer a lot less flash. The rooms are large—90% have ocean views—decorated in shades of mauve and mint with floral-pattern drapes and bamboo furniture, while the lobby is open and airy and filled with cascading orchids. The best thing about the Marriott, however, is the service. Most hotels talk about a guest-oriented staff; the Marriott lives the notion. These people are genuinely friendly and helpful. You almost think they'll invite you home for a visit. One of Maui's best Japanese restaurants, Nikko, is on the ground floor. The Lokelani specializes in fish entrées, while the cheerful Mauna Terrace features open-air dining and more casual fare. *100 Nohea Kai Dr., Lahaina 96761, tel. 808/667–1200 or 800/228–9290. 720 rooms with bath. Beachfront. Facilities: A/C, 4 restaurants, 3 lounges, tennis, disco, color TV, golf, pool. AE, DC, MC, V.*

Ritz-Carlton, Kapalua. Kapalua's newest beachfront hotel features spacious, comfortable rooms with oversize marble bathrooms, lanais overlooking the three-level pool, and all the grace, elegance, and service that this classy hotel chain is known for. Most rooms have ocean views. Guests on the Club floors have a private concierge and lounge with complimentary snack and beverage service all day long. *One Ritz-Carlton Dr., Kapalua, tel. 808/669–6200 or 800/241–3333. 550 rooms with bath. Facilities: air-conditioning, 4 restaurants, lounges, shops, health club, beauty salon, golf, tennis, water sports, pool, whirlpool, children's center. AE, D, DC, MC, V.*

Westin Maui. The Westin is another property from the developer of the Hyatt Maui. Opened in the fall of 1987, the Westin is a make-over of a lower-end hotel called the Maui Surf. The design restrictions inherent in a renovation, unfortunately, have limited the room size, which is rather small for the price. This, however, is a hotel for active people who like to be out and about and won't spend all their time in their rooms. *2365 Kaanapali Pkwy., Lahaina 96761, tel. 808/667–2525 or 800/228–3000. 761 rooms with bath. Beachfront. Facilities: A/C, 8 restaurants,* *lounges, shops, Jacuzzis, health club, beauty salon, 5 pools. AE, DC, MC, V.*

Expensive **Kaanapali Beach Hotel.** This property is right in the middle of all the Kaanapali action and offers much more reasonable rates than its neighbors. Instead of glitz and flash, you'll find a comfortable hotel with a friendly Hawaiian staff. The hotel conducts complimentary classes in hula, lei making, ukulele playing, and more. *2525 Kaanapali Pkwy., Lahaina 96761, tel. 808/661–0011 or 800/657–7700, fax 808/661–1025. 430 rooms with bath. Beachfront. Facilities: pool, golf, shops, color TV, A/C, restaurants, lounge. AE, DC, MC, V.*

★ **Napili Kai Beach Club.** Owner Dorothy Millar and her late husband created a homey little place on one of the finest beaches in Maui; it attracts a loyal following each year. The clean, Japanese-style rooms with shoji doors open onto your lanai, with the beach and ocean right outdoors. Most rooms have kitchens; all have refrigerators and coffee makers. This place is particularly popular with honeymooners and Canadians. The weekly cocktail party Mrs. Millar hosts encourages a friendly atmosphere. *5900 Honoapiilani Hwy., Lahaina 96761, tel. 808/669–6271 or 800/367–5030. 163 rooms with bath. Beachfront. Facilities: A/C in most rooms, 4 pools, Jacuzzi, tennis courts, putting green. No credit cards. Advance payment or traveler's checks required.*

Royal Lahaina. The lanais at this Outrigger Hotels property have stunning ocean or golf-course views, which are worth the price of the room. What distinguishes the Royal Lahaina are the two-story ocean cottages, each divided into four units. Lushly decorated, the bedrooms open to the trade winds on two sides. The upstairs units have private lanais, while the downstairs share. *2780 Kekaa Dr., Lahaina 96761, tel. 808/661–3611 or 800/44–ROYAL. 512 rooms with bath. Beachfront. Facilities: 3 pools, shops, 3 restaurants, tennis, golf, color TV, A/C. AE, DC, MC, V.*

Moderate **Lahaina Hotel.** This once derelict hotel has reopened after more than $3 million in renovations by Honolulu businessmen Rick Ralston and Alan Beall. Ralston, also responsible for the rebirth of the Manoa Valley Inn on Oahu, has stocked the 13-room Maui property with antique beds, wardrobes, and chests, as well as delightful country print curtains and spreads. Downstairs, the trendy David Paul's Lahaina Grill, near the lively corner of Front Street and Lahainaluna Road, attracts diners. *127 Lahainaluna Rd., Lahaina 96761, tel. 808/661–0577 or 800/669–3444. 13 rooms with bath. MC, V.*

★ **Plantation Inn.** The charming Plantation Inn is one of those places you just won't find everywhere else. The newly constructed inn resembles a renovated Victorian home on a quiet country street in the heart of Lahaina, within walking distance of the ocean and all the down-to-earth bars, restaurants, and shops in the old whaling port. Each room at the inn is decorated differently, with exquisite attention to detail. The owners have stocked the place with antiques, stained glass, brass beds, and ceiling fans and polished up the hardwood floors, wood trim, and wide verandas. Downstairs is one of Hawaii's best French restaurants, Gerard's, whose candlelit ambience definitely adds to the romantic European charm of the place. The Plantation Inn also offers meal, airfare, car, and dive packages. *174 Lahainaluna Rd., Lahaina 96761, tel. 808/667–9225 or 800/433–6815, fax 808/667–9293. 18 rooms with bath. Facilities:*

*restaurant, refrigerators, pool, A/C, ceiling fans, color TV.
AE, MC, V.*

Inexpensive **Pioneer Inn.** You want fancy? Don't check into the Pioneer Inn. If, however, you'd like to try a taste of old Lahaina, then this is the place for you. Downstairs is the boisterous saloon, where tourists and locals alike hang out—if you get a room over the bar, forget about sleeping until the bartender rousts the last revelers at about 1 AM. Rooms are on the second floor. In the older section up front, they're nothing fancy: smallish and rather dim, with ceiling fans and no air-conditioning. Ask about the Spencer Tracy–Katharine Hepburn suite in the newer section, which is brighter and quieter, with air-conditioning. In this newer wing, some rooms overlook the small hotel pool and courtyard, while others face Front Street. What you get at the Pioneer Inn is history—and plenty of it. *658 Wharf St., Lahaina 96761, tel. 808/661–3636, fax 808/667–5708. 48 rooms with bath. Near the ocean. Facilities: 2 restaurants, cocktail lounge, small pool. AE, DC, MC, V.*

East Maui

Very Expensive ★ **Four Seasons Resort.** Opened in mid-1990, the Four Seasons has quickly become a favorite Maui hotel. Part of the reason is its location: smack dab on one of the Valley Island's finest beaches with all the amenities of the well-groomed Wailea Resort. The property itself is no less a stunner, with terraces, courtyards, gardens, waterfalls, and fountains. Nearly all the rooms have an ocean view and combine traditional style with tropical touches. You'll find terry-cloth robes and Japanese yukatas in each room and the best service in Hawaii. *3900 Wailea Alanui, Wailea 96753, tel. 808/874–8000 or 800/334–MAUI, fax 808/ 874–2222. 380 rooms with bath. Facilities: 3 restaurants, cocktail lounges, tennis, golf, nearby shopping, pool, health club. AE, DC, MC, V.*

★ **Grand Hyatt Wailea.** Sunny opulence and luxury are everywhere at this $60 million, 42-acre resort opened in late 1991. Elaborate water features, including a 2,000-foot, multilevel "canyon riverpool" with its own water slides and grottos, meander through magnificent gardens dotted with quiet enclaves that would seem an accident of nature were it not for the hotel-provided swing settees. The Spa Grande cossets guests with relaxing and rejuvenating offerings from regular aerobics classes to exotic water-and-massage therapies that could turn even a marathoner into a Sybarite. The feeling of luxury extends to the spacious ocean-view rooms, beautifully appointed and outfitted with such amenities as an overstuffed chaise longue, a comfortable writing desk, natural-wood dining furniture on the private lanai, in-room coffee service, minibar and cable TV stashed inside a graceful armoire, three telephones, and a marble tub and separate shower (both oversize). *3850 Wailea Alanui Dr., Wailea 96753, tel. 808/875–1234, fax 808/ 874–5143. 787 rooms with bath. Beachfront. Facilities: 6 restaurants, 12 cocktail lounges, pools, spa, shops, children's day-camp, chapel, cable TV. AE, DC, MC, V.*

★ **Hotel Hana-Maui.** One of the best places to stay in Hawaii—if not the Western Hemisphere—is this small, secluded hotel in Hana. A few years ago, the Rosewood Corporation of Dallas purchased the hotel and the 7,000-acre ranch that surrounds it. It then proceeded to invest an additional $25 million or so in upgrading the hotel before selling it to a Japanese investor. The original buildings now boast white plaster walls and trellised verandas, while inside, the rooms have bleached wood floors, overstuffed furniture in natural fabrics, and such decorator touches as art and orchids. The Plantation-look Sea Ranch Cottages across the road surround a state-of-the-art health spa. Sheraton Hotels now manages this hotel, and they have continued to upgrade amenities and decor. *Box 8, Hana 96713, tel. 808/248–8211 or 800/321–HANA, fax 808/248–7202. 97 large units with bath. Facilities: shuttle to secluded beach, pool, shops, restaurant, cocktail lounge, health spa, tennis, stables, library, jogging paths. Optional American plan includes all meals. AE, DC, MC, V.*

Maui Inter-Continental Wailea. Many repeat guests swear an undying loyalty to the Inter-Continental, coming back year after year to prove it. Luxurious without being overwhelming, this is a genuine hotel—upscale, unpretentious, and expertly run, with its share of amenities, including a set of rooms right on the beach. All the quietly elegant rooms are decorated in subtle tones of white, peach, or lavender and have private lanais and spacious bathrooms. The grounds are beautiful, with walks along paths through jungles of palm, banana, and torch ginger. Activities abound here, and award-winning restaurants are located within the hotel. *3700 Wailea Alanui Dr., Wailea 96753, tel. 808/879–1922 or 800/367–2960, fax 808/874–8331. 516 rooms with bath. Beachfront. Facilities: golf, tennis, restaurants, pools, Jacuzzi, shops. AE, DC, MC, V.*

Maui Prince. The Prince is a low-key luxury hotel, quietly attending to upscale hospitality since its opening in 1986. The attention to service, style, and presentation are apparent from the minute you walk into the delightful open-air lobby of the hotel, which is owned and managed by a Japanese company. Rooms on three levels surround the courtyard, which is home to a Japanese garden with carefully tended plants and a bubbling stream. Each evening a three-piece string ensemble performs classical music in the courtyard. Room decoration is understated, in tones of mauve and beige. Unfortunately, there's an earth berm between the hotel and the beach—part of the agreement the hotel had to make with the zoning commission and local residents—so an ocean view isn't possible from the first floor. *5400 Makena Alanui Rd., Makena 96753, tel. 808/874–1111 or 800/321–MAUI, fax 808/879–0082. 310 rooms with bath. Beachfront. Facilities: 4 restaurants, pool, golf, tennis, shops, color TV, A/C. AE, DC, MC, V.*

★ **Stouffer Wailea Beach Resort.** This is the first hotel you'll come to once you enter the stylish Wailea Beach Resort. Nothing here is lean. Situated on fantastic Mokapu Beach, most of the hotel's luxury rooms are contained in a seven-story, T-shape building, and the Mokapu Beach Club—26 cottagelike suites—is right on the water. Guest rooms, decorated in beige, burgundy, and blue, have refrigerators. The hotel emphasizes Hawaiian flavor, with gigantic contemporary tapestries and gorgeous carpets in the public areas; outside, you'll find gardens of exotic flowers, waterfalls, and reflecting ponds. Plenty of activities and award-winning restaurants are available right on the property. *3550 Wailea Alanui Dr., Wailea 96753, tel. 808/879–4900 or 800/9–WAILEA, fax 808/874–5370. 347 rooms with bath. Beachfront. Facilities: pool, Jacuzzi, restaurants, shops, cocktail lounges, color TV with HBO, A/C. AE, DC, MC, V.*

Moderate **Kula Lodge.** The Kula Lodge isn't your typical Hawaiian place, for two reasons: (1) it looks like a chalet property that should grace the Swiss Alps; and (2) three of its five units come with a fireplace. But the lodge is charming and cozy in spite of its non-tropical ambience. It's a perfect spot for a romantic interlude or reading a good book next to a roaring fire. The five units are in two wooden cabins; four have lofts in addition to the ample bed space downstairs. Set on 3 wooded acres, the lodge has a view of the valley and ocean, enhanced even more by the forest that surrounds it. Other amenities include a restaurant and lounge, as well as a gift shop and a protea co-op that will pack the unusual flowers for you to take home. The rates include breakfast. *RR1, Box 475, Kula 96790, tel. 808/878–1535. 5 units with bath. Facilities: restaurant. No phones or TVs. MC, V.*

★ **Mana Kai-Maui.** This lodging is a real find in Kihei, partly because of the property itself and partly because it sits on the end of one of the nicest beaches in the state, just down the strip from the Stouffer Wailea. Here you can get a studio without a kitchen, or a one- or two-bedroom unit with a kitchen. The decor is modest—what people in the Islands might call typical tropical—but the view of the ocean right outside the lanai overcomes any reservations you might have about the rooms' interiors. What's more, the rates usually include a car. The Mana Kai has a very good beachfront restaurant, open for all meals. *2960 S. Kihei Rd., Kihei 96753, tel. 808/879–1561 or 800/525–2025, fax 808/248–7482. 134 rooms. Beachfront. Facilities: pool, restaurant, lounge, shopping arcade, cable color TV, ceiling fans. AE, DC, MC, V.*

Maui Lu Resort. The first hotel in Kihei, this place reminds one of a rustic lodge. The main lobby was the summer home of the original owner, and over the years, the Maui Lu has added numerous wooden buildings and cottages to its 28 acres. Of the 129 rooms, 50 are right on the beach, in their own secluded area. The rest are across Kihei Road, on the main property. In addition, 16 large, one-bedroom cottages have a garden setting and screened-in lanais. The decor isn't fancy, but it isn't motel-tacky either. *575 S. Kihei Rd., Kihei 96753, tel. 808/879–5881 or 800/92–ASTON. 129 rooms with bath. Facilities: restaurant, lounge, pool, shops, color TV, A/C, tennis. AE, DC, MC, V.*

Inexpensive **Aloha Cottages.** If you want to meet the people in little Hana town, check into one of these cottages, run by Fusae Nakamura. Tourism is Mrs. Nakamura's way of earning extra money for her family now that she's retired, and she takes it seriously. The three two-bedroom units and one studio all have kitchens. The rooms are sparsely furnished but clean and adequate. A special touch is the carefully tended fruit trees on the neighboring property—Mrs. Nakamura often supplies her guests with the harvest, which includes papaya, bananas, and avocados. *Hana 96713, tel. 808/248–8420. 4 cottages with bath. No credit cards.*

Heavenly Hana Inn. Whether you fly or drive to Hana, you'll pass the Heavenly Hana Inn and probably wonder what it is. An impressive Japanese gate flanked by two lions guards the property, making it look like a temple of sorts. Inside, the rustic and quiet inn goes in for eccentric decor, with knickknacks everywhere. You can rent one of four two-bedroom units, each with a kitchenette and decorated with Japanese shoji screens, antique furniture, and Asian art. If the location, 2 miles from town, seems too remote (although, let's face it, all of Hana is remote), the inn also has a one-bedroom beach cottage and a family cottage near the center of town. *Box 146, Hana 96713, tel. 808/248–8442. 4 rooms, plus 1 cottage on Hana Bay and 1 in town. Kitchenettes, lanais, TVs. No credit cards.*

Bed-and-Breakfasts

Maui also has quite a few homes available for bed-and-breakfast rentals. Many have their units in separate guest houses, which allows privacy while still giving you a chance to get to know your hosts. Rates range from $30 a night to as much as $150. For more information about Maui B&Bs, write or phone: **Bed & Breakfast Hawaii** (Box 449, Kapaa 96746, tel. 808/822–7771 or 800/733–1632). Headquartered on Kauai, this organization has listings throughout the state and handles about 35 B&Bs on Maui. A directory is available for $10.95.
Bed & Breakfast Honolulu (3242 Kaohinani Dr., Honolulu 96817, tel. 800/595–7533 or 800/288–4666). This organization has statewide listings, with about 50 B&Bs on Maui.
Bed & Breakfast Maui-Style (Box 98, Kihei 96784, tel. 808/879–7865 or 800/848–5567). This organization has listings for about 25 B&Bs in Maui.

Condominiums

West Maui **Kaanapali Alii.** This is a condominium, but you'd never know it; the four 11-story buildings are put together so well, you still have the feeling of seclusion. Instead of tiny rooms, you can choose from one- and two-bedroom apartments. Each features lovely amenities: a chaise in an alcove, a bidet, a sunken living room, a whirlpool, oak kitchen cabinets, and a separate dining room. Run by a company called Classic Resorts, the Kaanapali Alii is maintained like a hotel—with daily maid service, an Activities Desk, and a 24-hour front desk. If you can afford the nightly rate, it's well worth the price. *50 Nohea Kai Dr., Lahaina 96761, tel. 808/667–1400 or 800/642–MAUI. 264 1- and 2-bedroom units with bath. Beachfront. Facilities: sauna, pools, lighted tennis courts, golf, A/C, color TV. AE, DC, MC, V. Very Expensive.*
Kapalua Bay Villas. Privately owned and individually decorated one- and two-bedroom units may be rented through the Kapalua Bay Hotel. Condos are assigned to one of five luxury categories. Renters enjoy a free shuttle to the hotel, guest rates for golf, tennis, and other hotel amenities. *1 Bay Dr., Kapalua 96761, tel. 808/669–5656 or 800/367–8000. 125 units. Very Expensive.*
Papakea Beach Resort. This resort is an active place to stay if you consider all the classes held here, such as swimming, snorkeling, and pineapple cutting. Located in Honokowai, Papakea has built-in privacy because its units are spread out among 11 low-rise buildings on some 13 acres of land. You aren't really aware that you're sharing the property with 363 other rooms. Bamboo-lined walkways between buildings and fish-stocked ponds create a serene mood. *3543 Honoapiilani Hwy., Lahaina 96761, tel. 808/669–9680 or 800/367–5637. 364 units with bath, including studios and 1- and 2-bedrooms. Beachfront. Facilities: 2 pools, whirlpool, spas, saunas, color TV, tennis, putting green. 2-day minimum stay. AE, MC, V. Expensive.*

East Maui **Wailea Villas.** The Wailea Resort has built three fine condominiums, calling them—appropriately—Wailea Ekahi, Wailea Elua, and Wailea Ekolu (Wailea One, Two, and Three). All three have beautifully landscaped grounds, large units with exceptional views, and access to one of the island's best beaches. Wailea Elua is usually considered the nicest of the three, with more expensive furnishings and rates to match. We recommend all three. It's an expansive property, with all the amenities of the fine Wailea Resort, including daily maid service and a concierge. *3750 Wailea Alanui Dr., Wailea 96753, tel. 808/879–1595 or 800/367–5246. 598 units in 3 complexes, 2 of them beachfront. 1-, 2-, and 3-bedroom apartments with bath available. Facilities: pools, color TV, hotel restaurants and lounges nearby. MC, V. Expensive.*

Aston Kamaole Sands. This is a huge property for Kihei—10 four-story buildings wrap around a grassy slope on which are clustered swimming and wading pools, a small waterfall, Jacuzzis, and barbecues. All units have laundry facilities and air-conditioning. Managed by the well-run Aston Hotels & Resorts, this condominium property boasts a 24-hour front desk, an Activities Desk, and on-property food and beverage. *2695 S. Kihei Rd., Kihei 96753, tel. 808/874–8700 or 800/92–ASTON. 440 1-, 2-, and 3-bedroom condo units with bath. Across the road from Kihei Beach. Facilities: pool, jet spa, wading pool, tennis. AE, DC, MC, V. Moderate–Expensive.*

★ **Hana Kai-Maui.** This small condominium is the only true beachfront property in the tiny town of Hana. The large and simply furnished units are set on lush, manicured grounds. One added benefit is the spring-fed swimming pool on one side of the property: Built with lava rock, it looks almost too unusual to swim in. *Box 38, Hana 96713, tel. 808/248–8426 or 808/248–7742. 17 units with bath. Beachfront. AE, MC, V. Moderate.*

Rental Agents

Besides the properties listed above (which operate like hotels and offer hotel-like amenities), Maui has condos you can rent through central booking agents. Most agents represent more than one condo complex (some handle single-family homes as well), so be specific about what kind of price, space, facilities, and amenities you want.

Multi-property agents include: **Ameri Resort Management, Inc.,** 5500 Honoapiilani Rd., Kapalua, Maui 96761, tel. 808/669–5635 or 800/SUNSETS; **Aston Hotels & Resorts,** 2255 Kuhio Ave., 18th Fl., Honolulu 96815, tel. 800/342–1551; **Condofree Resorts Hawaii,** 2155 Kalakaua Ave., St. 706, Honolulu 96815, tel. 800/535–0085; **Destination Resorts,** 3750 Wailea Alanui Dr., Wailea, Maui 96753, tel. 800/367–5246; **Hawaiian Apartment Leasing Enterprises,** 479 Ocean Ave. #B, Laguna Beach, CA 92651, tel. 714/497–4253 or 800/854–8843; **Hawaiian Resorts, Inc.,** 1270 Ala Moana Blvd., Honolulu 96814, tel. 800/367–7040 or (in Canada) 800/877–7331; and **Vacation Locations–Hawaii,** Box 1689, Kihei, Maui 96753, tel. 808/874–0077 or 800/522–2757.

The Arts

Most of Maui's cultural activities are community efforts, with theater, film, and symphony productions held in the island's central towns of Kahului and Wailuku. For more specific information, check the daily newspaper, the *Maui News*.

Film

International Film Festival. This acclaimed salute to celluloid used to be restricted to Honolulu, but now festival films are also presented in Maui. Each year in late November and early December, the festival, sponsored by East-West Center, brings together filmmakers from Asia, the Pacific Rim, and the United States to view feature films, documentaries, and shorts. The films are shown at the Holiday Theaters at the Kaahumanu Center. Related activities take place at resort hotels. To find out about specific films and dates, phone the East-West Center's International Film Festival Office (tel. 808/944–7200) in Honolulu.

Music

Kapalua Music Festival. Since 1982, the music festival has brought some of the world's finest musicians to Maui for several days each summer. Representatives from Juilliard and the Chicago and New York philharmonics and the Tokyo String Quartet have performed here in recent years. Kapalua usually has special room rates during the festival. *J. Walter Cameron Center, 95 Mahalani St., Wailuku 96793, tel. 808/244–3771. Tickets: $10 adults, $6 children 6–12.*
Maui Philharmonic Society. The Society has presented such prestigious performers as Ballet Hispanico, Shostakovich String Quartet, and the new-age pianist Philip Glass. Performances take place in various spots around the island. *J. Walter Cameron Center, 95 Mahalani St., Wailuku 96793, tel. 808/244–3771.*
Maui Symphony Orchestra The symphony orchestra performs five season concerts and a few special musical sensations as well, including a July 4th concert on the Kaanapali Golf Course, complete with fireworks. The regular season includes a Christmas concert, an opera gala, a classical concert, and two pops concerts outdoors at Wailea. *Tel. 808/244–5439. Season tickets: $12 adults, $8 students; tickets for the July 4th concert: $3 adults, $1 children.*

Theater

Baldwin Theatre Guild. Dramas, comedies, and musicals for the entire island are presented by this group about eight times a year. The guild has staged such favorites as *The Glass Menagerie*, *Brigadoon*, and *The Miser*. Musicals are held in the Community Auditorium, which seats 1,200, while all other plays are presented in the Baldwin High School Mini Theatre. *1650 Kaahumanu Ave., Kahului, tel. 808/242–5821. Tickets: $6 adults, $4 seniors, $3 students.*
Maui Community Theatre. Now staging about six plays a year, this is the oldest dramatic group on the island, started in the early 1900s. Recent productions included *Fiddler on the Roof*,

Amadeus, and *Dracula: The Musical?* Each July, the group also holds a fund-raising variety show, which can be a hoot. *Iao Theatre, 68 N. Market, Wailuku, tel. 808/242-6969. Tickets for musicals: $12 adults, $11 seniors, $6 children under 17. Nonmusicals are $1 less.*

Maui Youth Theatre. This theater program for children is one of the largest arts organizations in Hawaii; it takes plays into the schools around the county but also performs about 10 productions a year for the entire community. Plays have included name shows, such as *Mame,* and original plays and ethnic dramas. Performances are held in various locations around the island. *Box 518, Puunene 96784, tel. 808/871-7484; box office 808/871-6516. Tickets: $3-$8.*

Nightlife

Nightlife on Maui can be of the make-your-own-fun variety. As on all the Neighbor Islands, the pace is a bit slower than what you'll find in Waikiki. Watching the sunset from a tropical perch, taking a moonlight stroll along one of the island's near-perfect crescent beaches, or dining in a meadow can be some of the best nightlife you'll find.

Dancing, luaus, dinner cruises, and so on are found mainly in the resort areas. Kaanapali in particular can really get hopping, with myriad activities for visitors of all ages. The old whaling port of Lahaina also parties with the best of them, and attracts a younger, often tow-headed crowd who all seem to be visiting from towns on the West Coast. Overall, Wailea and Kapalua appear more sedate, but Wailea's Maui Inter-Continental boasts one of the island's most lively discos, the Inu Inu Lounge, which always seems jammed.

Bars and Clubs

Comedy **Comedy Club** (Maui Marriott, Kaanapali Beach Resort, tel. 808/667-1200). Every Sunday evening is laugh night at the Marriott now that the owners of the Honolulu Comedy Club have set up a weekly Valley Isle venue. Although the show starts at 8 PM in the Lobby Bar, it's better to get there early since comedy has caught on in a big way. Tickets are $10.

Contemporary **El Crab Catcher** (Whalers Village, Kaanapali, tel. 808/661-
Music 4423). In addition to seafood, you'll find live music here nightly, 5:30-7:30. Often a contemporary Hawaiian duo or trio performs.

Lost Horizon (3550 Wailea Alanui Dr., Wailea, tel. 808/879-4900). This popular spot in the Stouffer Wailea Beach Resort features live easy-listening music, often Hawaiian. There's some dancing here, but it's on the slow side.

Molokini Lounge (Maui Prince Hotel, Makena Resort, tel. 808/874-1111). This is a pleasant bar with an ocean view, and you can even see Molokini Island before the sun goes down. Live music is presented, often Hawaiian in theme. There's a dance floor for late-night revelry.

Discos **Banana Moon** (Maui Marriott, Kaanapali Beach Resort, tel. 808/667-1200). This is a lively spot in the Maui Marriott Hotel, open nightly from 9 to 2. It has high-tech decor and good music. Banana Moon is an enjoyable place to meet other young tourists and hotel employees out for a night on the town.

Inu Inu Lounge (Maui Inter-Continental Wailea, Wailea Resort, tel. 808/879–1922). There's dancing nightly here starting at 9, with live music—rock, big bands, or golden oldies. This is a very active spot for young crowds from Wailea, Kihei, and Makena. It also lures groups who are visiting the resort.

Moose McGillycuddy's (844 Front St., Lahaina, tel. 808/667–7758). The Moose has only recorded music, but it's played so loud you would swear it's live. This entertaining place tends to draw an early-20s crowd, who come for the burgers and beer and to meet one another.

Spats II (Hyatt Regency Maui, Kaanapali Beach Resort, tel. 808/667–7474). This club is open for disco dancing Sunday through Thursday 10 PM –2 AM and Friday and Saturday until 4. (Spats is a Travel-Holiday Award–winning Italian restaurant from 6:30 to 9:30.) There's a cover charge on Friday and Saturday nights.

Jazz **Blackie's Bar** (Blackie's Boat Yard, on the mountain side of Honoapiilani Hwy. in an orange octagonal building, Lahaina, tel. 808/667–7979). Even without the finest jazz on Maui, Blackie's would be an interesting place to go. Take Blackie himself; the crusty proprietor often cruises the joint, making sure everyone's behaving, and chastising those who put their feet on the chairs or spit or break some other rule he has set forth for his establishment. The jazz is terrific, featuring the Gene Argel Trio and other guest performers. The music starts up at 5:30 PM, but stops at 8:30 PM, because that's when Blackie goes to bed.

Dinner and Sunset Cruises

Stardancer. This 150-foot luxury yacht is the largest to sail the Lahaina waters, serving nightly a gourmet buffet in its elegant dining room. The three-level boat also has a disco. *Lahaina Harbor, Lahaina 96761, tel. 808/871–1144. Cost: $50.*

Genesis **Sailing Charters.** This dinner sail goes for 2½ hours and includes a gourmet catered meal on the 48-foot luxury sailing yacht *Genesis.* The cruise is limited to 20 passengers at a time. *Box 10697, Lahaina 96761, tel. 808/667–5667. Cost: $56 adults.*

Pardner **Sailing Charters.** Six passengers at a time are taken for a two-hour sunset sail with champagne, mai tais, and snacks on the 46-foot ketch the *Pardner. Pier 21, Lahaina Harbor, Lahaina 96767, tel. 808/661–3448. Cost: $30 adults.*

Scotch Mist **Charters.** A two-hour champagne sunset sail is offered on the 19-passenger Santa Cruz 50 sloop *Scotch Mist II. Box 831, Lahaina 96767, tel. 808/661–0386. Cost: $30 adults.*

Windjammer Cruises. This cruise includes a sit-down meal and live entertainment on the 65-foot, 110-passenger *Spirit of Windjammer*, a three-mast schooner. *505 Front St., Suite 229, Lahaina 96761, tel. 808/667–6834. Cost: $49 adults.*

Luaus and Polynesian Revues

Drums of the Pacific. The Hyatt presents a fine Polynesian revue on the hotel's Sunset Terrace. The all-you-can-eat buffet dinner includes such fare as fresh fish, prime rib, chicken, and a native luau pupu platter. Afterward, the show features traditional dances and chants from such countries as Tahiti, Samoa, and New Zealand. *Hyatt Regency Maui, Kaanapali, tel. 808/*

661–1234, ext. 4420. Tickets: $42 adults, $34 children 6–12. Mon.–Wed., Fri., Sat. Dinner seating begins at 5:30.

Luau at the Maui Lu. Held on Saturday evenings only on the grounds of the Maui Lu Resort, this standard Maui event includes an imu ceremony, a Polynesian buffet dinner, all the drink you want, and a Polynesian revue. *Maui Lu Resort, 575 S. Kihei Rd., Kihei, tel. 808/879–5881. Cost: $35 adults, $20.50 children 7–12.*

Maui's Merriest Luau. The Inter-Continental's oceanfront lawn is certainly a beautiful spot to hold a luau. The traditional feast begins with a rum punch welcome and imu ceremony, and the evening includes colorful Polynesian entertainment. *Maui Inter-Continental Wailea, Wailea, tel. 808/879–1922. Tues., Wed., and Thurs. 5:30.*

Old Lahaina Luau. This is the best luau you'll find on Maui—it's small, personal, and authentic. The Old Lahaina Luau is held on the beach at 505 Front Street in Lahaina, presumably the former Hawaiian entertainment grounds of the royals. You'll get all-you-can-eat traditional Hawaiian luau food: kalua (roasted) pork, long rice, lomilomi salmon, haupia cake, and other items, such as fresh fruit and salad. You'll also get all you can drink. Guests sit either on tatami mats or at tables. Then there's the entertainment, featuring a musical journey from Old Hawaii to the present with hula, chanting, and singing. Four young men started the Old Lahaina Luau in 1986, and their attention to detail is remarkable. *505 Front St., Lahaina, tel. 808/667–1998. Tickets: $45 adults, $25 children under 13, infants free.*

Stouffer Wailea Beach Resort Luau. A five-star hotel, the Stouffer puts on its excellent Hawaiian luau each Monday and Thursday evening, featuring an open bar, an imu ceremony, a luau buffet, music by a Hawaiian band, and a show called "Memories of the Pacific," featuring dancers performing pieces from around the Pacific—including one wielding a "fire knife." *Stouffer Wailea Beach Resort, 3550 Wailea Alanui Dr., tel. 808/879–4900. Cost: $38 adults, $21 children under 12.*

Shows

Maui Tropical Plantation's Hawaiian Country Barbecue & Buddy Fo Revue. This Hawaiian country evening with a *paniolo* (cowboy) theme starts with a narrated tram ride through about half of the 120-acre showcase of Hawaii's leading agricultural crops; then it moves to an all-you-can-eat barbecued steak dinner and open bar. After, Buddy Fo and his lively entertainers put on a Hawaiian country-and-western variety show; the audience can join in for some square dancing. *Maui Tropical Plantation, Waikapu, tel. 808/244–7643. Tickets: $46.95 adults, $23.50 children 5–12, $10 children under 5. Mon., Wed., Fri. 5–8 PM.*

6 Molokai

By Marty Wentzel

Nicknames for Molokai have come and gone. In ancient times it was called Molokai of the Potent Prayers, for the island's powerful *kahuna* (priests) practiced their worship in solitude. During the late 1800s, it was dubbed the Forbidden Isle, because Hawaii's lepers were banished to a remote peninsula on its northern shore. Only in the last few decades has it worn a new nickname, the Friendly Isle.

Today Molokai is indeed friendly, and those who visit its shores quickly become aware of the down-to-earth charm of its 263 square miles. As other Neighbor Islands become increasingly crowded with high-rise hotel developments and visitor activities, Molokai quietly greets its guests with a handful of basic accommodations and unusual sightseeing alternatives.

Something else about Molokai makes it stand out from the other Neighbor Islands. You can smell it in the fresh mangos along the trail to Halawa Valley, where the earliest community on the island once lived (AD 650). You can see it in the way the sun hits the water in the ancient south-shore fish ponds, which date back to the 13th century. You can hear it in the crashing of the waves as they rush up to 3-mile-long Papohaku Beach. All of these things evoke a mysterious sensuality that springs from the land and its past and that inspires its people in the present.

Most of the attractions of the Friendly Isle are to be found in the great outdoors. For a walk back through time, take the switchback trail down a steep mountain to Kalaupapa. There you tour the historic colony once reserved for sufferers of Hansen's disease (leprosy), in a pristine town set at the base of dramatic sea cliffs. On a wildlife safari ride you can see rare African and Asian animals roaming in their preserve on 1,500 acres of the west end of the island. A horse-drawn-wagon tour takes you to Hawaii's largest *heiau* (outdoor shrine) and through enormous mango and coconut groves. And in the island's highest reaches you can explore the Kamakou Preserve, a 2,774-acre refuge for endangered birds, plants, and wildlife.

Molokai appeals to the visitor who enjoys adventuring at a personal pace. Plenty of opportunities are available for snorkeling, swimming, hiking, and sunbathing, but fewer possibilities exist for such organized sports as fishing, horseback riding, tennis, and golf. The more creative you are, the more you will enjoy Molokai, for it doesn't shout at you with things to do. Instead, it gently whispers, "Come play with me."

Big-city shoppers find little to rave about on the island. However, the one-road former plantation town of Maunaloa offers eclectic shops with such unique creations as homemade kites and hand-dyed shirts. The main town of Kaunakakai is equally unimpressive, but if you dig around you'll find such one-of-a-kind delights as Molokai bread from Kanemitsu's Bakery and local carvings at the Molokai Gallery.

The dining scene on Molokai is, once again, limited, which is why many visitors to the island stay in condominiums and cook their own food. There are, however, some great little local eateries where a slice of Molokai life is served up with every meal.

One of the best things one can say about the Friendly Isle is that it is uncluttered. You can drive your rental car down any road and take your time looking around without fear of someone honking at you to maintain the speed limit. Sometimes yours is the only car on the road! There are no buildings higher than three stories, no elevators, no traffic jams, no stoplights, and no movie theaters. The fanciest hotels are bungalow-style low-rises. Molokai also has miles and miles of undeveloped countryside, like the rolling farmlands of the 52,000-acre Molokai Ranch (the island's largest local landholder) and the acres of abandoned pineapple fields, which once did big business for Dole and Del Monte but have now been phased out of the island's economy.

Ten miles wide and 38 miles long, Molokai is the fifth-largest island in the Hawaiian chain. As you drive along its roads you can see how its two main volcanic mountains are connected by a plain. To the west is Maunaloa, which is 1,381 feet high and the home of an ancient hula school. This dormant volcano overlooks dry, rolling countryside and hosts the island's only resort, Kaluakoi, with 6,700 acres. To the east is Mt. Kamakou, which at 4,961 feet is the highest peak on the island. Kamakou's rain forests house a gentle system of plants and animals found nowhere else in the world.

At night, from the western shores of the island on the beach fronting Kaluakoi Resort, you can see the twinkling lights of Oahu, 25 miles across the channel. In spirit, however, Molokai is much, much farther away from its highly developed neighbor. With its slow pace of life and simple beauty, it is drowsing in another era; if its 6,700 proud people have their way, it's likely to remain so.

Essential Information

Arriving and Departing by Plane

Airports/Airlines The center of air traffic for Molokai is called **Hoolehua Airport** (tel. 808/567–6140), a tiny airstrip located just west of the island's center. It is 8 miles west of Kaunakakai and about 15 miles east of Kaluakoi Resort. Plans to construct a new 24,000-square-foot terminal have been stop-and-go for several years, but at press time the project was slated for completion sometime in the 1990s.

If you want to fly from the mainland United States to Molokai, you must first make a stop in Honolulu; from there, it's a 25-minute trip to the Friendly Isle. **Hawaiian Airlines** (tel. 800/367–5320) offers the most flights daily between Oahu and Molokai aboard its 50-passenger Dash-7 aircraft, at a round-trip cost of $138 per person. **Aloha Island Air** (tel. 800/323–3345) flies 18-passenger deHaviland Dash-6 Twin Otters at a round-trip cost of $138. **Air Molokai** (tel. 808/521–0090) has daily flights between Honolulu and Molokai for $99.90 round-trip. Its fleet includes 9-passenger Cessna 402s.

An even smaller airstrip serves the little community of **Kalaupapa** (tel. 808/567–6331), the former Hansen's-disease colony on the north shore. **Island Air** flies directly into that town from Honolulu for about $138 round-trip. However, you must first have a land-tour confirmation for Kalaupapa, and your arrival should coincide with one of the authorized ground tours of the area (*see* Guided Tours, *below*). Otherwise you'll be asked to leave.

Between the   By van, taxi, or rental car, a drive from Hoolehua Airport to
Airport and Hotels   Kaunakakai takes about 10 minutes. To the hotels and condominiums of Kaluakoi Resort, your driving time from the airport
is 25 minutes. Since there's no rush hour on the Friendly Isle,
you can count on an easy drive.

When arranging transportation from the airport to your accommodations, check to see if your hosts offer free airport
shuttle service.

By Bus   There is no public bus service on the island of Molokai.

By Taxi   **T.E.E.M. Cab-Molokai** (tel. 808/553–3433), run by David and
Cookie Robins, charges $1.40 at the meter drop and $1.40 for
each additional mile, plus 25¢ for each piece of luggage. Discounts are available for senior citizens and students. It costs
about $14 from Hoolehua Airport to Kaunakakai, and about $25
to Kaluakoi Resort. Drivers are on call 24 hours a day. You can
also call **Molokai Off-Road Tours and Taxi** (tel. 808/553–3369) or
Kukui Tours and Limousines (tel. 808/553–5133).

By Car   After renting a car at the Hoolehua Airport, it's easy to find
your way around the island roads. Simply turn right on the
main road (Hwy. 460) to reach Kaluakoi Resort and left if
you're staying in Kaunakakai. **Avis, Budget, Dollar,** and **Tropical** are the four car-rental companies that serve Molokai. Their
offices are located at the Hoolehua Airport (*see* Getting
Around, *below*, for further car-rental information).

Getting Around

By Car   You'll most likely want to get out and explore the island from
one end to the other. However, options for guided tours are
quite limited, so it's advisable to rent a car.

Driving   Driving is a snap on Molokai, because there are just a few main
roads to choose from. Highway 460, also known as Maunaloa
Highway, is a wide, well-paved route running from Kaunakakai west to Maunaloa. Kaluakoi Road runs off it to the north
and leads you to the accommodations of Kaluakoi Resort. Highway 450, or Kamehameha Highway, runs east to Halawa Valley, becoming narrower and extremely bumpy for the last 5
miles. Highway 470 runs north to Kalaupapa Lookout.

Gas stations are located in Kaunakakai and Maunaloa. Please
note that most gas stations are closed on Sunday on Molokai. If
you park your car somewhere, be sure to lock it. Even on the
Friendly Isle, thefts have been known to occur. When driving,
buckle your seat belt, because there's a $15 fine for noncompli-
ance. Children up to age three must be seated in a federally approved car safety seat, which you can lease from your car-rental
agency. When you rent a car, you will receive the small but
helpful *Molokai Drive Guide.*

Car Rentals   Four car-rental agencies are available on Molokai, all of which
have offices right at Hoolehua Airport. They are **Avis** (tel. 800/
331–1212), **Budget** (tel. 800/527–0700), **Dollar** (tel. 800/367–
7006), and **Tropical** (tel. 800/367–5140). Expect to pay around
$24.95 per day for a standard compact car, and $29.95 for one
with air-conditioning. Rates are seasonal, however, and can
run up to $45 per day during peak seasons, such as Christmas
vacation and the winter months. Advance car reservations are
usually necessary. If you're flying on Hawaiian Airlines, ask in

advance if the airline has a fly/drive deal available. Sometimes it will offer you cheaper rates (around $15 per day) on a car from Avis, Dollar, or Tropical.

By Taxi **T.E.E.M. Cab** (tel. 808/553–3433) offers rates of $1.40 for the first meter drop and $1.40 for each additional mile. The company also offers exclusive tours (from 2½ hours to a full day) to various points of interest in seven-passenger minivans. Or try **Molokai Off-Road Tours and Taxi** (tel. 808/553–3369) for personalized service to any point on the island.

Important Addresses and Phone Numbers

Tourist Information **Destination Molokai Association** (Box 960, Kaunakakai 96748, tel. 808/553–3876) or **Visitor Information** on Maui (tel. 808/877–4636) can offer advice on accommodations and tours and other visitor information.

Emergencies **General emergencies** (tel. 911).
Police (tel. 808/553–5355).
Ambulance (tel. 808/553–5331).
Fire (tel. 808/553–5601 in Kaunakakai, tel. 808/567–6525 at Hoolehua Airport).
Coast Guard (tel. 808/244–5626).

Doctors Round-the-clock medical attention is available at **Molokai General Hospital** (Box 408, Kaunakakai 96748, tel. 808/553–5331).

Pharmacy **Molokai Drugs** (tel. 808/553–5790) in Kaunakakai is the most reliable source for filling prescriptions. Open Monday–Saturday 8:45–5:45.

Opening and Closing Times

Banks are open Monday–Thursday 8:30–3, Friday 8:30–6.

Most stores are open Monday–Saturday 9–6; they are generally closed on Sunday.

Guided Tours

Wildlife Tours **Molokai Ranch.** This relatively new tour program combines a camera safari through the Molokai Ranch Wildlife Park (*see* Tour 1, *below*) with a west end beach excursion. Highlights include a visit with giraffes, a look at a rare white stripeless zebra born at the park in 1991, a variety of water sports, and a picnic on one of the pristine, isolated beaches for which Molokai is prized. This is a great choice for families. *Box 8, Maunaloa 96770, tel. 808/552–2767. Tour lasts 5½ hours. Cost: $105 adults, $88 children; includes picnic and use of surfing, snorkeling, and fishing gear.*

Four Wheel Drive Tours **Molokai Off-Road Tours and Taxi.** Fully narrated tours of Molokai are provided by Pat and Alex Puaa. In an air-conditioned 4×4 Cherokee Jeep or a 4×4 Ford Ranger pickup you see Halawa Valley, ancient fishponds, churches, flower farms, Kalaupapa Lookout, macadamia nut farms, Maunaloa town, and more. They can even help you mail a coconut back home. *Box 747, Kaunakakai 96748, tel. 808/553–3369. Pickup at 7 AM, return at 1 PM. Cost: $50 adults, $40 children.*

Kalaupapa Tours **Damien Molokai Tours.** Founded in the 1860s and now a National Historical Park, Kalaupapa was once a community of about

1,000 people who were banished from other parts of Hawaii due to their medical plight, Hansen's disease (leprosy). A caring priest named Father Damien committed himself to the care of the sufferers until he died there of the same disease in 1889. **Damien Tours** is the only tour service owned and operated by long-time residents of Kalauapapa, who are well-versed in the history of the area. They take guests on a fascinating four-hour van tour of the former settlement. Tours begin and end at Kalaupapa Airport if you arrive by air or at the foot of the trail if you hike down the mountain. Departing at 10:15 AM you get a look at such historic sites as Father Damien's Church. *Box 1, Kalaupapa 96742, tel. 808/567–6171. Cost: $20 for 4 hours. Bring your own lunch.*

Exploring Molokai

Since Molokai is long and slipper-shaped, it takes at least two days to explore it: one day for the "heel" or western reaches, and one for the "toe" to the east. The imaginary dividing line is in the town of Kaunakakai, which is set right in the center of the island's southern shore. This guide divides the island into two car trips. On a third day, you might want to head on a short excursion north, which leads you to a spectacular overlook.

The eastern end of Molokai is flanked by Mt. Kamakou, the island's highest point at 4,961 feet. Kamakou presides over miles of rain forests burgeoning with fresh tropical fruit, misty valleys tickled with waterfalls, and ancient lava cliffs that rise above the sea as high as 3,000 feet. To the west is Maunaloa, a smaller dormant volcano that rises above rolling pastures, farmlands, and a town of the same name. The western portion of the island is much drier than the east, and boasts some magnificent long beaches by Kaluakoi Resort.

You'll have the most fun if you explore the island at your own pace in a rental car. Most of the highlights are natural landmarks—waterfalls, valleys, overlooks, and the like—and it's nice to get out of your car and wander around an area at your leisure without missing the tour bus.

Directions on the island are often referred to as *mauka* (toward the mountains) and *makai* (toward the ocean). You'll find these terms used in this chapter.

Highlights for First-time Visitors

Halawa Valley, Tour 2
Kalaupapa Lookout, Tour 3
Kalokoeli Fish Pond, Tour 2
Kamakou Preserve, Tour 2
Kaunakakai, Tour 1
Maunaloa, Tour 1
Molokai Ranch Wildlife Safari, Tour 1

Tour 1: West Molokai

Numbers in the margin correspond to points of interest on the Molokai map.

The western portion of the island is warm, sunny, breezy, and basically untouched. Its two areas of "civilization" are Kaluakoi

Resort and the sleepy town of Maunaloa. This driving trip includes a stop at a glorious sunbathing beach, so bring along your bathing suit and allow some time to linger there.

① Begin the tour at **Kaluakoi Resort,** located on Kaluakoi Road. Molokai's only major resort development, it sprawls over approximately 6,700 acres of beachfront property and looks tame and manicured next to the surrounding wilds of Molokai Ranch. Commanding 5 miles of coastline, Kaluakoi was developed in 1968 by Kaluakoi Corporation, and in 1987 it was sold to Tokyo Kosan Company, Ltd. The area is home to three bungalow-style condominiums and a hotel, plus residences, ranch properties, a 10-acre beach park, and the 18-hole Kaluakoi Golf Course.

② Kaluakoi Resort is the starting point for the **Molokai Ranch Wildlife Safari,** hailed as one of the world's finest natural game preserves, with 1,000 acres of wildlife open to guided camera safaris. In comfortable 14-passenger vans that depart from the resort, passengers take the bumpy 1¾-hour trek through a landscape that resembles African plains. Nearly 1,000 animals roam the area, including sika and axis deer, Barbary sheep, Indian black buck, oryx, greater kudu, eland, rheas, and wild turkeys. The safari chief stops along the way and calls to the animals, some of which come right up to the van in hopes of a snack. At one point your tour guide lets you feed the giraffes from the safety of a "people pen." Both adults and children enjoy this tour. *Wildlife Park Reservations Desk, Box 8, Maunaloa 96770, tel. 808/552–2555, ext. 7553. Cost: $30 adults, $20 children under 12. 4 tours daily.*

③ Continue west on Kaluakoi Road, which runs along the shoreline past a number of lovely beach parks. Turn right at the sign for **Papohaku Beach,** park in the parking lot, and walk over the dunes to the beach, which is 3 miles long. The largest white-sand beach in the islands, Papohaku is a splendid place for walking and sunbathing; in the calm summer months, it is also fine for swimming.

④ Return to Kaluakoi Road and follow it uphill to Highway 460. Turn right and drive 2 miles to **Maunaloa,** a former sugar plantation town built in 1923. The layout and size of each house and garden indicate the hierarchy of the plantation when it was in full swing. Today this is essentially a one-road town whose pineapple fields are now overgrown. Interspersed among the town's houses are an attractive collection of shops run by a colorful assortment of local characters.

Time Out **Jojo's Cafe** (mauka [mountain] side of Maunaloa Hwy., tel. 808/552–2803). While in Maunaloa, stop by this local eatery run by Jojo Espaniola and her family. An antique bar adds to the funky, down-home atmosphere. The menu is the same every day, and the place is open for lunch and dinner. You get good burgers, hot dogs, salads, *saimin* (a Hawaiian noodle soup), and ribs, plus fresh tuna and butterfish.

The main road in Maunaloa is a dead-end street, so turn around at Jojo's and head east on Highway 460 for about 10 miles. As you drive along this section you get a view of how the island is laid out: two dormant volcanoes connected by a vast plain. Past the airport, follow the signs to Highway 450.

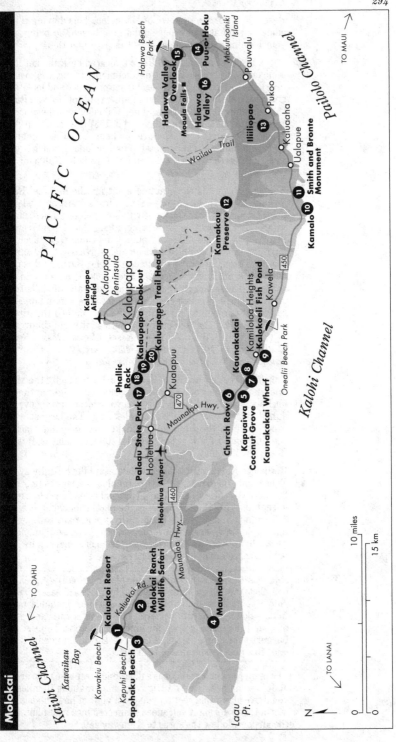

Molokai

PACIFIC OCEAN

Kaiwi Channel

← TO OAHU

Kawaihau Bay

Kawakiu Beach

Kepuhi Beach

Papohaku Beach

Laau Pt.

← TO LANAI

Kaluakoi Resort **1**

Kaluakoi Rd.

Molokai Ranch Wildlife Safari **2**

3

Maunaloa **4**

Maunaloa Hwy.

Hoolehua Airport

Hoolehua

Maunaloa Hwy.

460

470

Kualapuu

Maunaloa Hwy.

Palaau State Park **17**

Phallic Rock

Kalaupapa Lookout **18 19 20**

Kalaupapa Trail Head

Kalaupapa

Kalaupapa Airfield

Kalaupapa Peninsula

Church Row **6**

Kapuaiwa Coconut Grove **5**

7 8 Kaunakakai

9 Kalokoeli Fish Pond

Kamiloloa Heights

Kaunakakai Wharf

Onealii Beach Park

Kawela

450

Kamakou Preserve **12**

Kamalo **10**

11 Smith and Bronte Monument

Iliiliopae **13**

Ualapue

Kaluaaha

Kalae

Pukoo

Pauwalu

Makuhooniki Island

Halawa Beach Park

Halawa Valley Overlook **15**

Moaula Falls ■

Puuo-Hoku **14**

Halawa Valley **16**

Wailau Trail

Kalohi Channel

Pailolo Channel

TO MAUI →

N

0   10 miles

0   15 km

About a mile farther, look on the makai (ocean) side of the road for what seems, at first glance, to be a sea of coconut trees ❺ standing tall and close together. This is the **Kapuaiwa Coconut Grove**, one of the last surviving royal groves planted by Prince Lot, whose nickname was Kapuaiwa. Prince Lot lived on Molokai and eventually became Hawaii's King Kamehameha V in 1863.

Across the street from the coconut grove, you'll see several ❻ houses of worship along the road. This is called **Church Row**, and the parishioners of its congregations are primarily Hawaiian. You can see the unadorned, boxlike style of architecture, reminiscent of missionary homes, of each of the buildings, which are built adjacent to Hawaiian Homelands. On these lands, persons of at least half-Hawaiian blood can lease the sites at a nominal fee.

If you're interested in boats, turn makai (toward the ocean) at the intersection of Highway 450 and Ala Malama Street. This ❼ takes you to **Kaunakakai Wharf**, the docks that were once bustling with pineapple exports and that now primarily send out honey, watermelons, cattle, and herbs. The wharf is home to deep-sea fishing boats, some of which offer sailing, snorkeling, whale watching, and diving excursions.

At the junction of Highway 450 and Ala Malama, head mauka to ❽ reach the center of **Kaunakakai**, Molokai's "big" city. As the island's commercial hub, it leaves something to be desired when compared to cities on other Hawaiian islands. What Kaunakakai does have is character; it looks like an Old West movie set. Along its one block is a cultural grab bag of restaurants, plus one of everything you're looking for: a gift shop, crafts store, sporting goods shop, bakery, supermarket, liquor store, bank, and so on. Its people are generally friendly and willing to give you directions, and you'll never see anyone dressed in anything fancier than a muumuu or aloha shirt—more often, the preferred dress of Kaunakakai is shorts and a T-shirt.

Time Out **Kanemitsu Bakery and Restaurant** (mauka [mountain] side, Ala Malama St., tel. 808/553–5855). Anyone who has ever been to Molokai will tell you to stop by this bakery for a taste of its round Molokai bread, a pan-style white loaf that makes excellent French toast and cinnamon toast. In its glass display cases, Kanemitsu also shows off a calorie-laden assortment of rolls, buns, doughnuts, pies, and cakes. Try the *haupia* (coconut) jelly roll cake, the recipe for which is a guarded family secret. While there, you can sit right at the counter and have a diner-style breakfast or lunch.

Tour 2: East Molokai

This driving tour takes you through countryside that has been largely untouched. The road from Kaunakakai is 30 miles long, and much of it runs along the coast. It changes from a two-lane paved road to a narrow, bumpy track that dead-ends at Halawa Valley. You just might want to explore the valley on foot. In that case, bring shoes that you don't mind getting dirty, because the valley gets plenty of rain, which muddies up the trail.

Begin this tour heading east on Highway 450 out of Kaunakakai. After passing the **Pau Hana Inn**, **Molokai Shores**, and

Hotel Molokai, you will see fewer houses and more natural countryside. About 6 miles out of Kaunakakai, look on the ❾ makai (ocean) side for the **Kalokoeli Fish Pond,** one of the many narrow ocean walls connecting two points of the shore. Kalokoeli is typical of the numerous fish ponds that line the southern shore, many of which were built around the 13th century. This early type of aquaculture is unique to Hawaii, and the fish ponds are examples of man's early ingenuity.

Six miles farther on the makai side, look for a natural harbor ❿ called **Kamalo,** which was a stopping place for small ships carrying cargo along the coast in the 19th century. Here you'll also see one of the two churches built by Father Damien in the late 1800s.

In this vicinity, there is a monument on the makai side of the road. This is the **Smith and Bronte Monument,** dedicated to Er-❶ nest Smith and Emory Bronte, who crash-landed here in 1927. They were the first civilians to complete a transpacific flight from California, a noteworthy feat even if it did have a bumpy ending.

Time Out **Wavecrest General Store** (Hwy. 450, entrance to Wavecrest condominiums, 13 miles east of Kaunakakai, tel. 808/558–8335). This is the last "major" store if you're heading east, and the best place to stock up on picnic supplies, including ice, small coolers, film, and video tape.

By now you are at the base of Mt. Kamakou, the island's highest ❶ peak. Hidden within the mountain is **Kamakou Preserve,** which harbors endangered birds and plants amid its lush 2,774 acres. Kamakou Preserve is a dazzling natureland full of wet ohia forests, rare bogs, native trees, and indigenous wildlife, which you can explore on a hike with the Nature Conservancy of Hawaii. *Contact Ed Misaki, Box 220, Kualapuu 96757, tel. 808/553–5236. Cost: $5 members, $25 non-members. Hikers are picked up at Hoolehua Airport at 9 AM and returned by 4. Hikes are limited to 15 people. Approximately 12 hikes are held each year, and reservations in writing are required well in advance.*

Five miles east of Kamalo and ½-mile inland on the mauka ❸ (mountain) side of the road is **Iliiliopae,** a major heiau (outdoor shrine) that is listed in the National Registry of Historic Places. You can't miss it; it's as long as a football field. Treat this area with great respect, for it is the site of ancient human sacrifices and is said to hold great power to this day. It is also private property, so don't wander off the designated trail. *Park on the side of the road, look for the Wailau Trail sign, and walk about 10 minutes toward the mountains. A sign on the left will point you to the heiau. Admission free. Open all day.*

Time Out **Neighborhood Store and Snack Bar** (Kamehameha Hwy., Pukoo, tel. 808/558–8933). Less than a mile past the Iliiliopae heiau is this little family-run store. It's your last chance to get food and drink before the end of Highway 450. A Filipino clan named the Quinones has run this slice of local life for years, and their chicken papaya is worth sampling. Check out the pictures on the wall, which detail the rise of this modest business.

Now the coastline changes from rocks to white sandy beaches, and there are several bays where you may want to stop and take a breather. More and more potholes appear in the road, which hugs the shore as it twists and turns. Ten miles from Pukoo you ⑭ make an ascent up 1,200-foot **Puu-o-Hoku** (Hill of Stars), where you get panoramic views of West Maui. The small island off this coast is **Mokuhooniki,** where the United States military practiced its bombing techniques during World War II.

⑮ The road takes a hairpin turn left at **Halawa Valley Overlook**. By all means stop here and enjoy the vista of the mountains, the ⑯ sea, and historic **Halawa Valley** (AD 650), the oldest recorded habitation site on Molokai. A busy community grew fruit and taro and fished here until it was struck by a fierce tidal wave in 1946. Now the valley is overrun with lush vegetation, although the remains of house platforms and garden walls are visible.

The road descends to a small church parking lot, where you can get out and hike the trail to **Moaula Falls.** It takes a muddy and mosquito-ridden hour one-way to reach the 250-foot cascade, but the effort pays off when you dive into the refreshing mountain pool at its base. Enjoy the hike back past taro patches, sweet-smelling forests of ginger and guava, and a freshwater stream that follows you back to your car.

Tour 3: A Short Excursion North

This easy morning or afternoon trip takes you to the cooler highlands of the island, so you might want to bring along a light jacket.

From Kaunakakai, follow Highway 460 west and turn mauka on ⑰ Highway 470. This leads you to **Palaau State Park,** one of the island's few formal recreation areas. At a 1,000-foot elevation, it sits in the center of the island on 233 acres. Forests of ironwood beckon to nature lovers. The park is well maintained, with camping facilities, washrooms, and picnic tables. *Admission free. Open daily 24 hours.*

Park in the lot at the end of the road, and follow the trail straight ahead to a distinctive formation jutting up from the ⑱ ground. This is the **Phallic Rock,** also known as Kauleonanahoa by the ancient Hawaiians. Barren women would sit here to absorb its strength and gain fertility.

From the parking lot, follow the trail to the right that points to ⑲ **Kalaupapa Lookout**. After walking for several minutes through a heady pine forest, you reach this magnificent overlook, which offers views of the tiny Hansen's-disease settlement, its airport, its main buildings, and the 2,000-foot-high sea cliffs protecting it. A series of informative plaques have been set up at the lookout with facts about Hansen's disease, Father Damien, and the colony itself.

Turn around in the parking lot and drive about ½ mile, until you ⑳ reach a clearing on the right. This is the **trail-head** of the steep path 1,600 feet down to Kalaupapa (*see* Guided Tours in Essential Information, *above*).

Two miles below Kalaupapa Overlook on the right is the **Meyer Sugar Mill,** built in 1878 and reconstructed to teach visitors about sugar's importance in Molokai's agricultural history. *Box 986, Kaunakakai 96748, tel. 808/567–6436. Cost: $2.50 adults, $1 students. Open Mon.–Sat. 10–2.*

Molokai for Free

Purdy's All-Natural Macadamia Nut Farm. Molokai's only working macadamia nut farm is open to visitors for casual tours. This family business on Hawaiian homestead land takes up 1½ acres, and its flourishing grove of 45 trees is more than 60 years old. You learn how the trees are grown, how the nuts are harvested, and what makes them one of Hawaii's top products. *Box 84, Hoolehua Homestead 96729, tel. 808/567–6601; 808/567–6495 evenings. Open Mon.–Sat. 9–1, Sun. 10–1, or call for an appointment.*

Kite Flying. Big Wind Kite Factory owner Jonathan Socher provides free lessons and fun conversation. Call ahead to arrange a time. *Maunaloa Rd., Maunaloa, tel. 808/552–2364. Open Mon.–Sat. 8:30–5, Sun. 10–2.*

Off the Beaten Track

Maupulehu Glass House. Ellen Osborne runs this unusual attraction: a massive glass structure that she has converted into a hothouse. Tour it to see tropical flowers like heliconia and pink ginger, and perhaps buy a fruit basket or flower arrangement while you're here. *Milepost 15, Hwy. 450, Maupulehu, tel. 808/ 558–8160. Admission free.*

Molokai Wagon Ride. Island-born Larry Helm takes folks on a scenic and informative amble in a horse-drawn wagon. First you stop at the Iliiliopae heiau, the largest outdoor place of worship in Hawaii. Next you tour the largest mango grove in the world. Afterward, you are regaled with a beach barbecue, coconut husking, fishing, and traditional Hawaiian net throwing, on an exotic south-shore beach with views of Maui, Kahoolawe, and Lanai. *Box 56, Hoolehua 96729, tel. 808/567–6773 or 808/558–8380. Cost: $37 adults, $18.50 children under 13. Tours daily.*

Shopping

The shopping scene on the Friendly Isle can be divided into two districts: along Ala Malama Street in Kaunakakai and along Maunaloa Road in Maunaloa. Mind you, neither of these strips is a Rodeo Drive. Neither town has department stores or shopping malls, and the fanciest clothes you can find on the island are pretty muumuus and aloha shirts.

However, in each tiny hamlet you will find shops with flair and diversity. Some of the best bargains can be found in the stores that sell locally made goods, such as artwork and jewelry. For the most part, you can skip the small and insignificant emporia of Molokai's hotels, which sell high-priced clothing and gifts of little distinction.

Most stores are open Monday through Saturday between 9 and 6, but fewer stores open their doors on Sunday. You might want to call ahead to make sure of the particular store's hours.

Kaunakakai

It takes about five minutes to walk from one end of the main street, Ala Malama, to the other. Here are some of the charming, family-run establishments you'll find along the way or right nearby:

Clothing The **Molokai Gift Shop** (tel. 808/553–5801), in the lobby of the Hotel Molokai, carries a little something for everyone: women's, men's, and children's aloha wear, hand-painted Molokai designer T-shirts, sportswear, and swimwear.

A small selection of casual wear, such as Levi's jeans and Nike shoes, is also for sale at the **Imports Gift Shop** (tel. 808/553–5734), across from the post office. **Molokai Island Creations** (tel. 808/553–5926) has unique designs in Hawaiian swimwear and tank tops that are made exclusively for the shop.

Pharmacy **Molokai Drugs, Inc.** (tel. 808/553–5790) is a well-stocked, full-service pharmacy that's been in business since 1935. *Open Mon.–Sat. 8:45–5:45.*

Grocery/Beverage Stores If you're staying in a condominium, you'll appreciate the services of the best-stocked supermarket on the island, the **Friendly Market Center** (tel. 808/553–5595). Its slogan is "Your family store on Molokai," and it lives up to the promise with hats, T-shirts, and other vacation needs as well as fresh produce, meat, groceries, liquor, and sundries. *Open weekdays 8:30–8:30, Sat. 8:30–6:30.*

Kaunakakai's other full-service grocery is **Misaki's Inc.** (tel. 808/553–5505). Misaki's traces its beginnings back to 1922, so it's a real island tradition. You can pick up liquor and dry goods here, as well as meat and produce. Its main advantage over the Friendly Market Center is that it's open on Sunday 9–noon.

Don't let the name **Molokai Wines 'n' Spirits** (tel. 808/553–5009) fool you. Along with a good selection of fine wines and liquors, it also carries gourmet foods and quality cuts of meat. *Open daily 8AM–10 PM.*

Jewelry Along with casual clothing, the **Imports Gift Shop** (tel. 808/553–5734), also features a decent collection of 14-karat-gold chains, rings, earrings, and bracelets, plus freshwater pearl jewelry. They also carry Hawaiian heirloom jewelry, which is unique to the islands. These stunning gold pieces are made to order with your Hawaiian name inscribed in Victorian-style black letters.

Leis Donald Gutierres runs **Kuualoha Flowers and Leis** (tel. 808/553–3455) and creates leis from such island flowers as ginger and pikake. The shop specializes in the traditional circular *haku* lei, which is worn on the head.

Locally Produced Goods **Molokai Island Creations** (tel. 808/553–5926) carries original Molokai glassware, exclusive Hawaiian notecards, jewelry made from coral right out of Hawaii's waters, and books on such Molokai subjects as history and fishing. It also sells authentic Molokai-design blouses and tank tops.

Outdoor Gear **Molokai Fish and Dive** (tel. 808/553–5926) is Molokai's main source of sporting goods, from snorkeling rentals to free and friendly advice. Owner Jim Brocker knows the island inside out and can recommend the best spots for fishing and diving. Ask to see his Molokai T-shirts, an original design available nowhere else on the island. *Open weekdays 8:30–6, Sat. 8–6, Sun. 8–2.*

Video Rentals When you're ready to document your island adventures, **Molokai Sight and Sound** (tel. 808/553–3600) can restock you with tape and batteries, or even rent you a CamCorder.

Maunaloa

The solitary shopping street in this old plantation town plays host to a handful of family-run businesses. Their owners are always happy to welcome a visitor through their doors.

Arts and Crafts The **Plantation Gallery** (tel. 808/552–2364) is an arts and crafts emporium crammed with local works and goods from Bali, from sculptures and clothes to jewelry and musical instruments.

Grocery Store The essentials are available at the **Maunaloa General Store** (tel. 808/552–2868), run by the same owners as the Friendly Market Center in Kaunakakai. This supermarket is convenient for guests who are staying at the condominiums of the Kaluakoi Resort. It carries meat, vegetables, fruit, dry goods, drugs, and liquor.

Kites The **Big Wind Kite Factory** (tel. 808/552–2364) features custom-made kites to fly and display. In stock is a wide variety of kite kits, paper kites, minikites, and wind socks.

Shirts Also at the **Big Wind Kite Factory** (tel. 808/552–2364) are the popular Red Dirt Shirts, one-of-a-kind Molokai T-shirts with Hawaiian graphics and other images unique to the Friendly Isle.

Beaches

On Molokai, don't be surprised if you're the only person sunbathing for miles. That's because the island has numerous beaches to choose from, many of them quite remote and undisturbed. You'll find the most spacious and beautiful beaches along the west coast, although you shouldn't venture into the high winter waves. Beaches fronting the Kaunakakai hotels and condominiums are narrow and less appealing, but the shallow waters are almost always calm for wading. At the extreme east end of the island is the beach fronting Halawa Valley, a nice place for relaxing after the long drive getting there.

All of the beaches on Molokai are free and open to the public. None of them has a telephone number, so if you want to find out more about them, contact the **Department of Parks, Land and Natural Resources,** Box 153, Kaunakakai 96746, tel. 808/567–6083.

West Side **Kawakiu Beach.** One of the best swimming beaches on Molokai, this is part of the Kaluakoi Resort. It has also been set aside as a beach park in honor of its archaeological sites, including house platforms and structures from an ancient Hawaiian settlement. Outdoor showers are available at the resort. *At the northern end of the bay fronting Kaluakoi Resort, on Kaluakoi Rd.*

Kepuhi Beach. Looking for a romantic sunset-watching spot? This is it! Ideal for strolling and sunbathing, this white-sand beach stretches about ½ mile in front of Kaluakoi Resort. However, it is fairly windy here all year long, which makes the swimming somewhat dangerous when the waves come up. There are outdoor showers at the resort, but no lifeguards. *Kaluakoi Resort, Kaluakoi Rd.*

Papohaku Beach. Perhaps the most sensational beach on the island, Papohaku is a 3-mile-long strip of white-sand glory, the longest of its kind in the state. It's also quite wide, so you can relax in privacy. Some places are too rocky for swimming; look carefully before entering the water, and go in only when the waves are small (generally the summer months). Between the parking lot and the beach are outdoor showers, picnicking facilities, and a rest room. There are no lifeguards. *Kaluakoi Rd., 2 mi beyond the Kaluakoi Resort. Look for the big sign on the makai (ocean) side of the road.*

Pohakuloa Beach. Parents like to bring their children here, because a protective cove makes the waters calm and swimmable most of the year. As a result, it can get pretty busy with families during the weekends. An outdoor shower is available, but there are no lifeguards. *Drive about 1½ mi beyond Papohaku Beach to the end of the coastal road on the northwest end of the island. There is a sign on the makai side of the road pointing you to the parking lot.*

Central **Onealii Beach Park.** Visit this beach for its smashing views of Maui, and Lanai, 8 miles across the channel. It's also the only decent beach park on the island's south-central shore. The narrow and long beach has adequate swimming in calm waters year-round. Onealii has rest rooms, outdoor showers, and picnic tables under the trees. There are no lifeguards. *On Hwy. 450, just east of Hotel Molokai.*

East Side **Halawa Beach Park.** Halawa's picnic facilities are some of the nicest on the island, making this an ideal beach for a family outing. The long, curving beach at the head of Halawa Valley has safe swimming during the calm summer months, but watch out for the hazardous rip currents and high surf during winter. Outdoor showers are available, but there are no lifeguards. *Drive to the eastern end of Hwy. 450 until it dead-ends at the beach.*

Sports and the Outdoors

Molokai's untouched beauty and sunny skies make it a wise choice for the active-minded vacationer. Some sporting options can be arranged through the travel desk of your hotel, but in many cases you should call the companies directly for information and reservations.

Participant Sports

Fishing Based at the Kaunakakai docks, the **Alyce C.** (Box 825, Kaunakakai 96748, tel. 808/558–8377) runs excursions on a 4-passenger 31-foot twin diesel cruiser. If you go in a group, the shared cost is about $150 a day, or $100 a half day for excellent sportfishing. On an exclusive basis, the full-day cost runs approximately $350, and $225 for a half day. Your host is Capt. Joe Reich.

Golf Compared to the more commercialized Neighbor Islands, Molokai has a relatively mellow golf scene. The place to play is the **Kaluakoi Golf Course** (Kepuhi Beach 96770, tel. 808/552–2739) at the Kaluakoi Resort. At par 72, it features 18 holes on a 6,559-yard course designed by Ted Robinson, and its 160 manicured acres include five holes next to the beach. Greens fees and a cart cost $70 for nonguests, $50 if you're staying at the resort. There's also community duffing at the **Ironwood Hills**

Golf Course (Box 182, Kualapuu 96757, tel. 808/567–6000), located in upcountry Kalae. Greens fees are $10; carts are $7 per person for 18 holes.

Hiking Hardy visitors can make a day of **hiking to Kalaupapa** and back along the 2½-mile, 26-switchback trail once used for the Molokai Mule Ride. The National Park Service, which maintains the steep trail, planned to restore it in 1993, including repaving it with rough stones. You will need a permit to hike the trail, as well as a confirmed reservation to tour Kalaupapa with Damien Tours (*see* Guided Tours in Essential Information, *above*). For further information contact the National Park Service in Kalaupapa (Box 2222, Kalaupapa 96742, tel. 808/567–6102).

For a free hike, try the trek into **Halawa Valley** on the east coast. It's a muddy but magnificent hike through groves of fruit trees and past taro patches and the remains of stone walls from centuries ago. The trail ends at Moaula Falls, a 250-foot cascade with refreshing swimming. The hike takes about 3 hours round-trip. (For detailed maps and information about this hike, consult Robert Smith's *Hawaii's Best Hiking Trails*, Wilderness Press.)

Horseback Riding **Molokai Horse and Wagon Ride** (Box 56, Hoolehua 96729, tel. 808/567–6773 or 808/558–8380) offers guided trail rides at $33 per person for an hour and a half.

Hunting **Molokai Ranch** (Ala Malama St., Kaunakakai 96748, tel. 808/552–2767) provides guides and transportation for outings on private lands. Hunts for axis deer take place from February through October. During bird-hunting season, from November through January, you can look for ring-necked and green pheasant, quail, and wild turkeys. Occasionally, hunting for axis deer, Indian black buck, and audad sheep is also allowed at Molokai Ranch Wildlife Park. The cost is $400 a day for axis deer and $1,000 for black buck and audad. Nonguided hunts are allowed at $150 a day, plus $250 for any trophy animals taken ($600 for a trophy buck).

Before you do any hunting in Hawaii, you must obtain a hunting license from the **Division of Forestry and Wildlife** (1151 Punchbowl St., Room 330, Honolulu 96813, tel. 808/587–0077). You also must pass a hunter education course. A one-year license costs $20.

Sailing The 42-foot Cascade sloop *Satan's Doll* is your craft when you sign up with **Molokai Charters** (Box 1207, Kaunakakai 96748, tel. 808/553–5852). The company offers two-hour sunset sails for $30 per person. Half-day sailing trips cost $40 per person, including soft drinks and snacks. A minimum of four people is required, but shared charters can be arranged.

Snorkeling and Scuba Diving **Molokai Charters** (Box 1207, Kaunakakai 96748, tel. 808/553–5852) takes people on full-day snorkeling sails, including soft drinks and a picnic lunch, for $75 per person. In addition, you can rent your own equipment at the main hotels of the island, including Kaluakoi Resort and Hotel Molokai. Or, you can go through **Molokai Fish and Dive** (Ala Malama St., Kaunakakai, tel. 808/553–5926) for equipment rentals. It costs less than $10 for a set of snorkel, fins, and mask. The shop will be happy to give you information on good snorkeling and diving spots around the island.

Dive Sites **Mokuhooniki Rock,** at the east end of the island, was once a military bombing target, and artifacts from World War II are scattered throughout the many pinnacles and drop-offs. The area is home to barracuda, gray reef sharks, and large ulua; black coral is also found here. Depths range from 30 to 100 feet.

Tennis The **Kaluakoi Hotel and Golf Course** (tel. 808/552–2555 or 800/777–1700) provides the best facilities for a round of tennis on Molokai. It has four courts, which are lighted for night play, and equipment rentals are available. Guests play free; nonguests pay $5 per hour singles, and $7 doubles. Also at Kaluakoi, **Ke Nani Kai** (tel. 808/552–2761) has two courts for guests only at no charge. **Wavecrest** (tel. 808/558–8101), a condo to the east, also has two free courts for guests only.

Spectator Sports

When it comes to cheering from the sidelines, there's really only one event for which Molokai is known: the **Molokai-to-Oahu Canoe Race.** This is the world's major long-course event in the sport of outrigger canoeing, and the best in the field turn up on the Friendly Isle to participate. It begins on the southwest coast near the harbors of Halelono. After paddling across the rough Kaiwi Channel in traditional Hawaiian canoes, participants finish at Fort DeRussy Beach in Waikiki. The event takes place each September for the women and October for the men. Diehard fans watch the start on Molokai, hop on a plane, and fly to Oahu for the finish. Consult newspapers for date.

Dining

The choices for eating and drinking on Molokai are limited. In fact, during a week's vacation you can easily hit all the restaurants worth trying and return to your favorite places for a second round. Nevertheless, the dining scene is fun because it is a microcosm of Hawaii's diverse cultures. You'll find freshly baked Molokai bread, natural vegetarian foods, spicy Filipino cuisine, and Hawaiian-style fish all in the same block of Ala Malama Street in Kaunakakai. What's more, the price is right at Kaunakakai's eateries: All of them fall into the Inexpensive category.

In addition, you can choose from one moderately priced establishment at the Kaluakoi Resort, one local-style gathering place in Maunaloa (*see* Tour 1 in Exploring, *above*), and a dining room at the Hotel Molokai. If these options don't sound appetizing, you had better rent a condominium and cook your own food.

Restaurants on Molokai do not require a jacket. They are open daily unless otherwise noted.

Highly recommended restaurants in each price category are indicated by a star ★.

Category	Cost*
Moderate	$20–$40
Inexpensive	under $20

*per person, excluding drinks, service, and 4% sales tax

Kaunakakai and Kualapuu

Holo Holo Kai. Because of its diversified menu and pleasant surroundings, one might dare to say that this is Kaunakakai's fanciest restaurant. However, the atmosphere remains strictly casual. Set on the beach, Holo Holo Kai has a South Seas decor and views of the Pacific. Meals include such seafood as sautéed mahimahi and baked cod, generally prepared without fancy sauces. Other entrées include shrimp tempura, top sirloin, and teriyaki chicken or steak. Beef stew is a favorite here, as are the Molokai prawns, and there's an all-you-can-eat soup-and-salad buffet with delicious Molokai bread. You'll see a lot of visitors eating at Holo Holo Kai, since it's part of the town's main hotel. *Hotel Molokai, tel. 808/553-5347. Reservations not necessary. Dress: casual. AE, DC, MC, V. Inexpensive.*

★ **Kualapuu Cookhouse.** This cozy, casual restaurant is fast catching on because of its excellent homemade pies. Set in a small plantation house, it's also the *only* eatery in rural Kualapuu, so it usually draws a crowd. The menu offers a mix of cuisines, like teriyaki plate, honey-dipped chicken, stir-fried beef, tropical chile, pizza, and a variety of sandwiches. *Box 174, Kualapuu, tel. 808/567-6185. No reservations. Dress: casual. No credit cards. Closed Sun. Inexpensive.*

Molokai Drive Inn. If take-out food is what you're craving, try this simple eatery in the heart of Kaunakakai. It's Molokai's answer to McDonald's, with burgers and fries as well as local food like Japanese-style bento and plate lunches. *Ala Malama St., tel. 808/553-5655. No credit cards. Closed Sun. Inexpensive.*

Outpost Natural Foods. Vegetarian cuisine has made its way to Kaunakakai in the form of this unpretentious and carry-out. Located on an unmarked side street off Ala Malama, it features good salads (taco, chef's, and fruit) as well as vegetarian burritos, tempe burgers, and a daily special hot entrée such as curried vegetables over brown rice. Their fruit shake smoothies are delicious. Call for directions. *Kaunakakai, tel. 808/553-3377. No reservations. Dress: casual. No credit cards. Closed Sat. Inexpensive.*

Oviedo's. As the main city of the island, Kaunakakai may seem lacking in many ways, but it does have good Filipino food at Oviedo's. The waitresses treat you like family, with a pat on the back, a wink, or a smile. The restaurant offers cheap prices on tasty lunch and dinner plates. Oviedo's specializes in *adobos* (stews) with a variety of traditional Filipino spices and sauces. Try the tripe, pork, or beef adobo for a real taste of tradition. A mixed plate comes with vegetables and rice. You can eat in or take out. *Ala Malama St., tel. 808/553-5014. Reservations not necessary. Dress: casual. No credit cards. Inexpensive.*

Pau Hana Inn Restaurant. This open-air restaurant is set by the sea, and its big doors open onto picturesque ocean views. The restaurant has been expanded onto the oceanview Banyan Tree Terrace underneath a 100-year-old banyan tree. The cuisine is American, including honey-dipped chicken, roast beef, New York strip steak, catch of the day, barbecued beef short ribs, and teriyaki steak. All entrées come with a starch and a beverage. In the evening, locals love to party here, and live bands provide loud music for dancing on weekends. *Pau Hana Inn, Kamehameha Hwy., tel. 808/553-5342. Reservations not necessary. Dress: casual. AE, DC, MC, V. Inexpensive.*

The West End

★ **Ohia Lodge.** The most sophisticated restaurant on Molokai, the Ohia Lodge offers Continental dining by the sea. Its oversize doors add an informal touch to an otherwise elegant decor, and through its large open doors you get lovely views of the sea and the lights of Oahu across Kaiwi Channel. Menus change nightly, with fresh fish spotlighted each evening. Cashew chicken, filet mignon béarnaise, and seafood tempura are regular features. The salad bar is especially good here, big enough to make a meal in itself, and you also have your choice of vegetarian platters, prime rib, prawns, and pasta dishes. *Kaluakoi Resort, Maunaloa, tel. 808/552-2555. Reservations advised. Dress: neat but casual. AE, DC, MC, V. Moderate.*

Lodging

A visit to Molokai is an enriching experience, in part because the island is still highly undeveloped. While hotels and condos spring up like weeds on the more popular Neighbor Islands, Molokai has maintained an even keel with its accommodations. Its major resort area, Kaluakoi, will eventually expand to add the new multimillion-dollar luxury Kaiaka Rock Hotel, but it has been on the drawing board for so long that one wonders if even that will ever materialize.

Instead, Molokai appeals less to those who like impeccable furnishings and swanky amenities and more to those who appreciate genuine Hawaiian hospitality and relaxation in down-home surroundings. Hotel and condominium properties on Molokai range from the fine to the funky. Pools are outdoors. Kaluakoi Resort boasts the best hotel, while the condominiums of Kaunakakai are great for families, due to their proximity to the island's calmest, shallowest waters. None of the accommodations falls into the Very Expensive category, which is good news for the budget vacationer. Molokai hotel prices usually follow a European plan, meaning no meals are included.

Highly recommended lodgings in each price category are indicated by a star ★.

Category	Cost*
Expensive	$90–$120
Moderate	$60–$90
Inexpensive	under $60

All prices are for a standard double room, excluding 9¼% tax and service charge.

Kaunakakai and Vicinity

Moderate ★ **Hotel Molokai.** Polynesian-style architecture graces a series of three-unit cottages at this laid-back hotel just a mile from the center of town. The furnishings are rustic, with basket swings on the lanais and wood beams on the ceiling. Although the hotel is somewhat run-down, each room is kept clean, right down to the wall-to-wall carpet. Hotel Molokai is on the beach, but the swimming pool is a welcome addition since the waters in front of the property are shallow and not always good for swimming. The hotel often offers overnight deals in conjunction with airlines and rental-car companies; ask about this when you make your reservation. *Box 546, Kaunakakai 96748, tel. 808/553–5347 or 800/423–MOLO. 51 rooms with bath. Facilities: pool, shops, restaurant, lounge. AE, DC, MC, V.*

Molokai Shores. Located between the Pau Hana Inn and the Hotel Molokai, this three-story condominium is also oceanfront, and each room offers a view of the water. Your condo also comes with a color TV and a fully equipped kitchen. The furnished lanais look out to 4 acres of tropical gardens. One-bedroom/one-bath units and two-bedroom/two-bath units are available. In addition, picnic tables and barbecue areas are on hand for outdoor family fun. *Box 1037, Kaunakakai 96748, tel. 808/553–5954 or 800/367–7042. 102 condominiums with kitchen. Facilities: pool, shops. MC, V.*

Wavecrest. Another condominium set right on the shore near Kaunakakai, the Wavecrest offers one- and two-bedroom apartments equipped with electric kitchens and color TV. The decor is your basic tropical design, with rattan furniture and a pastel color scheme. Each unit has a furnished lanai from which you have views of the islands of Maui and Lanai. The shallow water here is bad for swimming but great for fishing. Car and room rates are available. *Star Rte., Kaunakakai 96748, tel. 808/558–8101 or 800/367–2980. 126 condominium units with kitchen. Facilities: pool, shops, tennis. AE, DC, MC, V.*

Inexpensive– Moderate ★ **Pau Hana Inn.** The somewhat funky accommodations of this good-time hotel should be reserved for those who like to rough it. It's composed of a ramshackle set of cottages with clean but uninspired furnishings reminiscent of motels on the mainland. It can get noisy here on weekend evenings, when there's live entertainment. On the plus side, a nice swimming pool makes up for the poor swimming beach fronting the property. Rooms with a kitchenette fall into the Moderate price category. *Box 860, Kaunakakai 96748, tel. 808/553–5342 or 800/423–MOLO. 40 rooms with bath. Facilities: pool, restaurant, lounge. AE, DC, MC, V.*

The Kaluakoi Resort

Expensive **Colony's Kaluakoi Hotel and Golf Club.** The only combination hotel/condo at Kaluakoi, this property does its best to provide a sense of laid-back elegance for its guests. A series of two-level complexes are spread across ultragreen lawns, which are shaded by immense palm trees and brightened by bougainvillea bushes. Rooms have high ceilings with exposed wood beams, rattan furnishings, and bright tropical colors. Each unit has a kitchenette and furnished lanai. *Box 1977, Maunaloa 96770, tel. 808/552–2555 or 800/777–1700. 179 rooms with bath. Facilities: pool, shops, restaurant, lounge, snack bar, tennis, golf. AE, DC, MC, V.*

Kaluakoi Villas. Charming studios and one-bedroom oceanview suites are decorated island-style, with rattan furnishings, private lanai, color television, and refrigerator, but without telephones. Guests can take advantage of Kaluakoi Hotel's many activities. *Box 200, Maunaloa 96770, tel. 808/555–2721 or 800/525–1470. 100 condominium units with bath and kitchen. Facilities: pool, shops, restaurant, lounge, snack bar, tennis, golf. AE, DC, MC, V.*

Ke Nani Kai. This is a decent condominium complex with two-story buildings set back from the water. Your views are primarily of the gardens and golf courses, but the beach is a mere five-minute walk away. Sliding screen doors open onto furnished lanais with flower-laden trellises, and the spacious interiors are done in tropical rattans and pastels. Each unit has a washer and dryer and a completely equipped kitchen. *Box 126, Maunaloa 96770, tel. 808/552–2761 or 800/888–2791. 120 condominium units with bath and kitchen. Facilities: pool, golf, spa, tennis, whirlpool. AE, DC, MC, V.*

★ **Paniolo Hale.** Considered by many to be Molokai's best condominium property, this one is perched high on a ledge overlooking the beach, right next to the Kaluakoi Hotel. Paniolo Hale has units with spectacular ocean-view and nice garden views as well, with an option for studios or one or two bedrooms. The units have screened lanais, some of which even have hot tubs for an additional charge. Kitchens are well stocked, and the tidy decor is appropriately casual, to match the tropical surroundings. Adjacent to the greens of the Kaluakoi Golf Course, the property is sometimes a playground for wild turkeys and deer at night. *Box 190, Maunaloa 96770, tel. 808/552–2731 or 800/367–2984. 77 condominium units with bath and kitchen. Facilities: paddle tennis, pool, golf. AE, DC, MC, V.*

Alternative Accommodations

Moderate–Expensive **Hale Kawaikapu.** Weekly or longer rentals are available at two homes located 17 miles east of Kaunakakai, set on a 250-acre oceanfront site. The fully furnished two-bedroom home sleeps six, while the Polynesian cottage can accommodate four. *Box 939, Honolulu 96808, tel. 808/521–9202.*

Moderate **Honomuni House.** This vacation rental cottage boasts a tropical garden setting complete with a freshwater stream and waterfalls. It's located 17.4 miles east of Kaunakakai. *Star Route 306, Kaunakakai 96748, tel. 808/558–8383.*

Palm Cove Bed & Breakfast. On the ocean, just three miles east of Kaunakakai, this one-bedroom suite is part of a home, but it has a private entry and sundeck. *Star Route 53-B, Kaunakakai 96748, tel. 808/553–5894.*

The Arts and Nightlife

Molokai has limited options for cultural activity. Most people who live on Molokai must fly to a neighboring island if they wish to hear a symphony performance or see a first-run movie or a community play. As for organized evening entertainment, most residents enjoy simply sitting around with friends and family, sipping a few cold ones, strumming ukuleles and guitars, singing old songs, and "talking story" (conversing).

Still, a handful of opportunities are offered for visitors to kick up their heels in the evening. Go into Kaunakakai, pick up a copy of the *Molokai Dispatch* or the *Molokai News* (the local papers, published every other week), and see if there's a church supper or square dance taking place. If you're looking for still more to do in the evening, why not take a walk on the beach and let the evening stars entertain you?

Festivals

The **Molokai Ka Hula Piko.** Translated, this festival's name means "A Celebration of the Birth of Hula on Molokai." The annual, day-long event in May features performances by some of the state's best hula troops, musicians, singers, lecturers, and storytellers. It's all in tribute to Kaana, on the slopes of Maunaloa Mountain, which is reputed to be the birthplace of the hula. *Contact Destination Molokai, Box 960, Kaunakakai 96748, tel. 808/553-3876 or 800/367-4753.*

Films

The **Kaluakoi Resort** (tel. 808/552-2555) shows one movie nightly to its guests. The films are generally about three to five years old, or sometimes black-and-white classics; you sit on folding chairs in a recreation hall to watch them. It's free, so don't complain.

Bars and Clubs

Hotel Molokai. The bar is poolside and offers views of the ocean, Lanai, and Maui. What better place to relax with a drink or two? Once in a while the hotel also presents hula shows, but there's no set schedule. *Kamehameha Hwy., Kaunakakai, tel. 808/553-5347. Live music nightly for listening, 6:30–9.*

Ohia Room. Live bands take over the cozy lounge of this breezy seaside restaurant and play Top 40, pop, and Hawaiian numbers for dancing. *Kaluakoi Resort, tel. 808/552-2555. Nightly 8–10:30.*

Pau Hana Inn. This is the island's liveliest forum for local music. The regulars can get pretty rowdy here on the weekends, but visitors are more than welcome to join in the fun. *Kamehameha Hwy., Kaunakakai, tel. 808/553-5342. Happy hour 4–6 PM; dance music Fri. and Sat. nights 9–1.*

7 Lanai

By Marty Wentzel

For decades, Lanai was known as the Pineapple Island, with hundreds of acres of fields growing the golden fruit. Today, however, this 140-square-mile island has been renamed "Hawaii's Private Island," as developers attempt to replace pineapples with people. The island, which was once rarely visited, is now joining most of its sister islands in the tourism business. In the past five years, Castle & Cooke, the company that owns 98% of the island, has opened two upscale hotels, the luxurious 102-room Lodge at Koele and the 250-room Manele Bay Hotel. Despite these new additions, Lanai—third smallest of the islands—still remains the most remote and intimate destination in Hawaii.

Lanai's one population center is called Lanai City, an old plantation town whose tiny houses have colorful facades, tin roofs, and tidy gardens. With its well-planned grid of paved roads and small businesses, Lanai City adds one of the few hints of civilization to an otherwise wild island.

Though the weather across much of the island is hot and dry, the Norfolk pines that line Lanai City's streets create a cool refuge. While there, you'll encounter some of the people who came from the Philippines to work in Lanai's pineapple fields. You'll also be exposed to the many other races of Hawaii, from Korean, Chinese, and Japanese to transplanted mainland *haoles* (Caucasians).

Lanai City has a few family-run shops and stores, but its options are limited. It also offers a couple of diner-style eateries as well as the charming old Hotel Lanai, a 10-room hostelry that serves as a gathering place for locals and tourists alike.

But Lanai City is not the real reason for coming to Lanai. Visitors should be prepared to spend a lot of time outdoors, because Lanai has no commercial attractions, no movie theaters, and no bowling alleys. Instead you can visit such sights as the Garden of the Gods, where rocks and boulders are scattered across a crimson landscape as if some divine being had placed them there as his own sculpture garden. You can spend a leisurely day at Hulopoe Beach, where the waters are so clear that within a minute of snorkeling you can see fish the colors of turquoise and jade. And then there's the top of Lanaihale, a 3,370-foot-high, windswept perch from which you can see every inhabited Hawaiian island, except Kauai and Niihau.

While today it is an island that welcomes visitors with its friendly, rustic charm, Lanai has not always been so amiable. The earliest Polynesians believed it to be haunted by evil ghosts who gobbled up unsuspecting visitors. In 1836 a pair of missionaries named Dwight Baldwin and William Richards came and went after failing to convert the people of Lanai to their Christian beliefs. In 1854 a group of Mormons tried to create the City of Joseph on Lanai, but they, too, retreated in 1857 after drought forced them to abandon their endeavors.

One of Lanai's more successful visitors was a man named Jim Dole. In 1922, Dole bought the island for $1.1 million and began to grow pineapples on it. He built Lanai City on the flatlands where the crater meets the mountains. Then he planned the harbor at Kaumalapau, from which pineapples would be shipped. Four years later, as he watched the first harvest sail away to Honolulu, this enterprising businessman could safely say that Lanai's Dole Plantation was a success.

Today, a visit to Lanai can be simple or elegant. You can be all alone simply by leaving your hotel. That is, unless you encounter the deer on the hillsides, or the spirits that linger amid the ancient fishing village of Kaunolu, or the dolphins that come into Manele Bay to swim with you. On the other hand, you can rub elbows with sophisticated travelers during a game of croquet at the Lodge at Koele or a round of golf at the Greg Norman–designed golf course. Bring casual clothes, because many of your activities will be laid-back, whether you're riding the unpaved roads in a four-wheel-drive vehicle or having a drink on the front porch of the Hotel Lanai. Then change into something dressy for a gourmet meal at the Manele Bay Hotel.

Plans for Lanai call for a second golf course, new condominiums, and road improvements. Despite the changes, however, everything on Lanai is leisurely and lovely, especially its people. Come, take your time, and enjoy yourself before the island changes too much more.

Essential Information

Arriving and Departing by Plane

Airport To meet the growing numbers of visitors to the island, the state has been upgrading the Lanai airport (tel. 808/565–6757). Improvements include a new $7.5 million passenger terminal building with gift shops, food concessions, and better parking. Work was scheduled for completion in late 1993.

Airlines In order to reach Lanai from the mainland United States, you must first stop at Oahu's Honolulu International Airport; from there, it takes about a half hour to fly to Lanai. **Hawaiian Airlines** (tel. 800/367–5320) offers round-trip flights twice daily between Honolulu and Lanai. A round-trip on one of its 50-seat Dash 7s costs $140. **Aloha IslandAir** (tel. 800/323–3345) has 13 flights daily on its 18-passenger Twin Otters and its new Dornier 228s, also at a round-trip cost of $140. **Aloha Airlines** (tel. 800/367–5250) flies jets to Lanai, twice each Saturday, Sunday, and Monday at $140 round-trip.

Between the Airport and Hotels Lanai's airport is a 10-minute drive from Lanai City. If you're staying at the Hotel Lanai, the Lodge at Koele, or the Manele Bay Hotel, you will be met by a complimentary shuttle that will take you to your accommodations. Don't expect to see any public buses at the airport, because there are none on the island.

By Taxi **Lanai City Service** (tel. 808/565–7227) covers the market for taxi transfers to and from the airport. The charge to Lanai City is $7.

By Car There is a distinct advantage to renting your own vehicle on Lanai, because public transportation is nonexistent and attractions are far apart. Make your car- or jeep-rental reservation way in advance of your trip, because Lanai is small and its fleet of vehicles is limited.

Only one company on Lanai rents vehicles to visitors. Contact **Lanai City Service** (Box N, Lanai City 96763, tel. 808/565–7227), which is the Dollar Rent-a-Car affiliate on the island. You'll pay from $50 a day for cars and $100 a day for four-wheel-drive jeeps and vans. The company offers complimentary airport pickup and drop-off for car renters.

Getting Around

Some sort of private transportation is advised on Lanai, unless you plan to stay in one place during your entire visit. Avoid that urge, because the island has natural splendors from one end to the other.

By Car Driving around Lanai isn't as easy as on other islands, because
Driving most roads outside of Lanai City aren't marked. From town, the streets extend outward as paved roads with two-way traffic. Keomuku Highway runs north to Shipwreck Beach, while Highway 440 leads south down to Manele Bay and Hulopoe Beach and west to Kaumalapau Harbor. The rest of your driving takes place on bumpy and muddy dirt roads, which are best navigated by a four-wheel-drive jeep or van.

The island has no traffic lights, and you'll never find yourself in a traffic jam. However, heed this word of caution: Before heading out on your explorations, ask at your hotel desk if you're headed in the right direction. There are no signs by the major attractions, and it's easy to get lost.

Car Rentals *See* Between the Airport and Hotels, *above,* for information on renting a vehicle.

By Taxi It costs up to $10 for a cab ride from Lanai City to almost any point on the paved roads of the island. Call **Lanai City Service** (tel. 808/565–7227).

By Bicycle A mountain bike is a fun way to explore the pineapple fields and back roads of Lanai. The Lodge at Koele provides them free to guests.

Important Addresses and Numbers

Tourist The two major hotels—the Lodge at Koele and the Manele Bay
Information Hotel—have information desks. In addition, you should write ahead of time to **Destination Lanai** (Box 700, Lanai City 96763, tel. 808/565–7600). The **Maui Visitors Bureau** (250 Alamaha St., Suite N-16, Kahului 96732, tel. 808/871–8691) offers information about Lanai as well as Maui.

Emergencies **Police, fire,** or **ambulance** (tel. 911).

Hospital The **Lanai Community Hospital** (628 7th Ave., Lanai City, tel. 808/565–6411) is the center of health care for the island. It offers 24-hour ambulance service and a pharmacy.

Opening and Closing Times

Lanai City basically shuts down on Sunday. **First Hawaiian Bank** (644 Lanai Ave., tel. 808/565–6969) is open Monday through Thursday 8:30–3, Friday until 6. Shops open Monday through Saturday between 9 and 10 and close between 5 and 6.

Guided Tours

Off-Road Tours. Many of the highlights of Lanai are accessible only from the unpaved back roads of the island. On a guided tour you can leave the navigation to a driver who knows what he's doing, while you simply hang on and enjoy the ride in a Jeep Wrangler. Along the way you will see petroglyphs, the Garden of the Gods, and the Munro Trail. Tours are at least two hours long and are limited to three people. **Oshiro Tour & U-Drive** (Box 516, Lanai City 96763, tel. 808/565–6952) offers tours daily at $33 per hour per person. In addition, **The Lodge at Koele** (tel. 808/565–7300) offers off-road tours for guests.

Hiking Tours. The **Lodge at Koele** (tel. 808/565–7300) hosts free two-hour morning walks for its guests through the eucalyptus-covered hillsides of the island on Monday, Wednesday, and Saturday. The concierge desk can provide you with information and reservations.

Horticultural Tours. The **Lodge at Koele** (tel. 808/565–7300) was designed to incorporate a lush landscape that is an attraction in itself. On Tuesday at 2:30 and Saturday at 8:30 a horticulturalist takes hotel guests on a free tour of the colorful gardens of Koele, including a stop at the Orchid House, an ornamental glass greenhouse shipped from England. In the orchard, guests are invited to pick ripe mangoes, cherries, plums, bananas, apples, guava, passion fruit, coconuts, and avocados.

Exploring Lanai

Lanai is small enough to explore in a couple of days of leisurely travel, depending on how you want to experience it. If you're a hiker, you'll want a day just to enjoy the splendors of Lanaihale, the mountain that rises above Lanai City. If you're a fan of water sports, you'll want to take time to jump into the water at Hulopoe Beach to the south or Shipwreck Beach to the north.

Most of the sights are out of the way; that is, you won't find them in Lanai City or along paved roads. You'll have to look to find them, but the search is worth it. Remember to ask directions at your hotel desk before setting out, because Lanai attractions aren't usually marked. Bring along a cooler with drinks and snacks for your explorations, because there are no places to stop for refreshments along the way—unless you return to your hotel or Lanai City.

All of the sights mentioned in this chapter are free.

Highlights for First-time Visitors

Garden of the Gods, Tour 3
Hulopoe Beach, Tour 1
Keomuku, Tour 2
Lanaihale, Tour 2
Manele Bay, Tour 1
Shipwreck Beach, Tour 2

Tour 1: Heading South

Numbers in the margin correspond to points of interest on the Lanai map.

Begin this tour in Lanai City. Head south on Highway 440 for about a mile, until you see an unmarked dirt road that heads left through some pineapple fields. At the end of that road, get out of the car and climb up another unmarked trail to the **❶ Luahiwa Petroglyphs,** ancient rock carvings. These simple stick figures represent man, nature, and life on Lanai as drawn by the Hawaiians of the early 19th century.

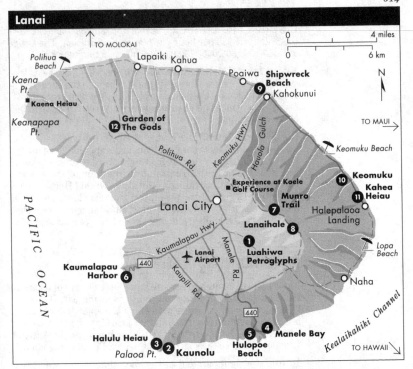

Lanai

Return to Highway 440 and continue south by making a left;
the highway is now called Manele Road. When this road makes
a sharp left turn, continue straight on Kaupili Road, which
leads you through pineapple fields. When you come to the
fourth dirt road, take it toward the ocean until you reach

2 **Kaunolu,** an old fishing village once inhabited by King Kamehameha I. The Bishop Museum excavated these ruins, which include stone floors and platforms where 86 houses and 35
shelters once stood. You can also see house sites and terraces,
all set atop the island's highest sea cliffs. In this area you can
also find some petroglyphs, a series of intricate carvings that
have been preserved in tribute to this once-thriving community. Just to the west of Kaunolu are the remnants of a sacred

3 gathering place called **Halulu Heiau.**

4 Return to Manele Road and follow it downhill to **Manele Bay.**
Flanked by lava cliffs that are hundreds of feet high, the bay
hosts a regular influx of small boats whose owners are generally from other Neighbor Islands. To the right of the harbor are
the foundations of some old Hawaiian houses.

The road winds to the right and passes the new Manele Bay Hotel on the right. To your left is a sparkling crescent called

5 **Hulopoe Beach,** whose broad expanse is one of the best beaches
in all of Hawaii. It's an ideal spot for a picnic lunch, a dip in the
water, and relaxing under the trees. The waves are gentle
enough for beginning bodysurfers, and the waters are full of
fish that are easily visible to snorkelers, since it is a marine life
conservation area.

Retrace your route back up Manele Road to Highway 440, and take the highway until it meets up with Highway 440 west (Kaumalapau Highway). Turn left and drive about 7 miles to the ocean. This is **Kaumalapau Harbor,** a busy port that has been used to ship millions of crates of pineapples. The cliffs flanking the western shore are as high as 1,000 feet.

Tour 2: Heading North

Begin this tour at the Lodge at Koele. Head north on Keomuku Highway for about 1¼ miles, and turn right onto a smaller, tree-lined road. A half mile past the cemetery on your right is the trailhead of the **Munro Trail,** an 8-mile route. From here only a jeep or your feet will get you up to **Lanaihale,** the high point of the island, at 3,370 feet. From its peak you'll get spectacular views of nearly all the Hawaiian islands. You can also see 2,000 feet down into Lanai's deepest canyon, Hauola Gulch. The trail, which winds through a lush tropical rain forest, was named after George Munro, a New Zealand naturalist who planted the pine trees in Lanai City in 1910.

Return to the highway and continue north about 8 miles until the pavement ends. Turn left on a dirt road and drive one mile. Park your car and walk another mile to **Shipwreck Beach,** so named because of the tricky winds that have caused many boats to crash on the reef. You can still see the remains of a World War II vessel here, not to mention sensational views of Molokai across the channel.

There's more excitement awaiting you if you feel adventurous. A word of caution: Do not continue on this tour unless you have a four-wheel-drive vehicle. The going is rough and often muddy.

From the end of the paved road, go to the right (east) along the very bumpy dirt road. Five miles later you will come to an area where there are dozens of tall coconut trees. This is **Keomuku,** once a busy Lanai community, which was abandoned in 1901 after the collapse of the Maunalei Sugar Company. You can still go into the ramshackle old church, the oldest on the island. There's an eerie beauty about Keomuku, with its once-stately homes now reduced to weed-infested sites and crumbling stone walls.

A mile and a half farther down the road, you can see the ruins of a temple called **Kahea Heiau,** whose stone formations are visible amid overgrown shrubs and bushes. The dirt road ends 3 miles later, at the remnants of the old Hawaiian village of **Naha,** and the often-deserted Lopa Beach. Here you must turn around and retrace your route—back to Keomuku Highway.

Tour 3: Garden of the Gods

Once again, heed this advice: Ask for directions at your hotel before heading off on this excursion. It could very well be the most sought-after attraction on the island, yet it is also one of the most difficult to find.

From the Lodge at Koele, turn right on Keomuku Highway. Turn left on the road that runs between the stables and the tennis courts. This leads you to a dirt road, which cuts through hay fields for a couple of miles. At the crossroad, turn right. This road heads upward through an ironwood forest and eventually takes you to your destination, 1½ miles beyond: the **Garden of the Gods,** a heavily eroded canyon scattered with boulders of different sizes, shapes, and colors that seem to have been placed there with some purpose. Stop and enjoy this eerie scenery for a while, for its lunar appearance is unmatched in Hawaii. Anyone who's a geology buff will want to take photos of the area, and there are also magnificent views of the Pacific Ocean.

Shopping

Except for the specialty boutiques at the Lodge at Koele and Manele Bay Hotel, Lanai City is the only place on the island to buy what you need. Its main streets, 7th and 8th avenues, offer a small scattering of shops that look as if they're out of the 1920s. Each offers personal service and congenial charm.

Stores open their doors Monday through Saturday between 8 and 9 and close between 5 and 6. Some shops are closed on Sunday and between noon and 1:30 PM on weekdays.

General Stores

In the most literal sense, the four main businesses in town are what you would call general stores. That means they try to carry whatever customers need, and no business has a specialty.

You can get everything from cosmetics to canned vegetables at **Pine Isle Market** (356 8th Ave., tel. 808/565–6488).

In 1946, Richard Tamashiro founded **Richard's Shopping Center** (434 8th Ave., tel. 808/565–6047), which is run today by his sons. Among other things, the store has a fun selection of Lanai T-shirts, which make great souvenirs.

You may not find everything the name implies at **International Food and Clothing Center** (833 Ilima Ave., tel. 808/565–6433). However, Andrew de la Cruz, whose parents started the store in 1952, does carry a good supply of everyday needs at this modest emporium.

If you're still looking for groceries and general necessities, go to **S.&T. Properties** (419 7th Ave., tel. 808/565–6537).

Beaches

Only a few beaches on Lanai are worth seeking out. All of them have good swimming in protected waters. None has a phone number, so if you need more information, try **Destination Lanai** (Box 700, Lanai City 96763, tel. 808/565–7600) or ask at your hotel desk. The beaches below are listed clockwise from the south.

Hulopoe Beach is the island's only easily accessible white-sand beach. The snorkeling here is ideal, and the scuba diving, swimming, and bodysurfing are fine as well. Residents enjoy spending the day here, cooking over the grills, swimming, and watching the sunset. The beach has certainly become more crowded with the opening of the new Manele Bay Hotel, but its broad, long stretch of sand is able to accommodate everyone. There are changing rooms, outdoor showers, picnic tables, grills, and lifeguards. *On the south shore of Hulopoe Bay, 10 mi south of Lanai City on Manele Rd.*

Polihua Beach. Due to its more obscure location and frequent high winds, this beach is often deserted. It is spectacular all the same, with a long white-sand beach and glorious views of Molokai. Swimming is good when the wind dies down. You need a four-wheel-drive to get there. *On the northwest shore, 11 mi from Lanai City, past the Garden of the Gods (see Tour 3 in Exploring, above). Ask at your hotel desk for directions.*

Shipwreck Beach. Don't let the name scare you away. This is a nice beach for exploring as well as swimming. More isolated and rustic than Hulopoe Beach, Shipwreck is a popular spot for snorkeling in shallow waters, thanks to the reef 200 yards offshore. Many people dive here for lobsters. The beach has no lifeguards, no changing rooms, and no outdoor showers. *On the north shore, 10 mi north of Lanai City at the end of Keomuku Hwy.*

Sports and the Outdoors

Golf **Experience at Koele** is an 18-hole championship course designed by Greg Norman, with Ted Robinson as architect, at the **Lodge at Koele** (tel. 808/565–7300). Rates including carts: $95 guests, $140 nonguests. The lodge also has an 18-hole executive putting course, free for guests.

In addition, an 18-hole waterfront golf course has been designed by Arnold Palmer for the **Manele Bay Hotel** (tel. 808/565–7700). The course should be open by 1994.

Hiking The most popular Lanai hike is the **Munro Trail,** a strenuous 8-mile trek that takes about eight hours. There is an elevation gain of 1,400 feet leading you to the lookout at Lanai's highest point, Lanaihale. You can also hike as far as 8 miles along **Shipwreck Beach,** if you're up for it. Along the way you'll see a whimsical assortment of seashells and ship debris. No permission is needed to venture along either of these routes.

Before taking off, fill a water bottle and arm yourself with provisions in case you get a little off the track. Also, look at Craig Chisholm's paperback, *Hawaiian Hiking Trails* (Touchstone Press, 1977), and Robert Smith's *Hawaii's Best Hiking Trails* (Wilderness Press, 1987).

Hunting The **Koele Company** (Lanai City 96763, tel. 808/565–7233) provides hunting information for Lanai.

Scuba Diving Ask at your hotel's activities desk about renting dive equipment or arranging a dive.

Dive Sites **Cathedrals,** off the south shore, gets its name from the numerous pinnacles that rise from depths of 60 feet to just below the water's surface, with spacious caverns creating a cathedral effect. Within these beautiful chambers live friendly spotted moray eels, lobster, and ghost shrimp.

Sergeant Major Reef, also on the south shore, is made up of three parallel lava ridges, a cave, and an archway, with rippled sand valleys between the ridges. Several large schools of sergeant major fish that live here give the site its name. Depths range from 15 to 50 feet. Other nearby sites include Lobster

Rock; Menpachi Cave; Grand Canyon; Sharkfin Rock; and Monolith, home to Stretch, a five-foot-long moray eel.

Snorkeling **Hulopoe Beach** is one of the most outstanding snorkeling destinations in all of Hawaii. It attracts brilliantly colored fish to its protected cove, in which you can also marvel at underwater coral and lava formations. Ask at your hotel's activities desk about renting equipment.

Tennis The **Lodge at Koele** (tel. 808/565–7300) and **Manele Bay Hotel** (tel. 808/565–7700) each have 3 tennis courts.

Dining

Although Lanai's restaurant choices are limited, the menus are wide ranging. If you dine at the Lodge at Koele or Manele Bay Hotel, you'll be treated to unique preparations of ingredients from an organic garden, served in upscale surroundings.

Dining in Lanai City is a different story; its restaurants have simple food, homey atmospheres, and friendly service.

Highly recommended restaurants in each price category are indicated by a star ★.

Category	Cost*
Expensive	$40–$60
Moderate	$20–$40
Inexpensive	under $20

per person, excluding drinks, service, and sales tax (4%)

★ **The Dining Room.** Reflecting the elegant country atmosphere of the Lodge at Koele, the hotel's main restaurant has hefty wood beams, gleaming crystal, a roaring fireplace, and hand-painted stencils on the walls. Inventive gourmet island cuisine is created by a chef who works closely with the garden manager to keep the ingredients fresh. Try the marble of *ahi* (yellowfin tuna) with radish, fennel, and mustard seed or the chilled roasted red banana and Kona coffee bisque with cinnamon croutons for an appetizer. Entrées include roasted axis deer marinated with *lilikoi* (passion fruit). *Lodge at Koele, tel. 808/565–7300. Reservations advised. Jacket and tie required. AE, DC, MC, V. Dinner only. Expensive.*

Hotel Lanai. Don't overlook this charming spot where the locals go out for dinner. Banana pancakes and specialty omelets are offered at breakfast, soups and sandwiches at lunch, and American cuisine at dinner (steaks, chicken, and fish prepared simply). The pretty room is just off the hotel's lanai and features large wood tables, a fireplace at one end, and stunning paintings and photographs by island artists. *828 Lanai Ave., tel. 808/565–7211. Reservations advised. Dress: casual. AE, MC, V. Moderate.*

★ **Hulopoe Court.** Designed along a Mediterranean theme, this bayview restaurant serves a mix of cuisines: Italian, French, Spanish, Portuguese, and Greek. Drawing from Rockresorts' organic garden, the menu includes such fresh flavors as fennel-cured salmon with green lentil salad, tiger prawns in tangerine olive oil with garlic and Italian parsley, and buckwheat pasta with vegetable vermicelli and lemon butter sauce. *Manele Bay*

Hotel, tel. 808/565–7700. Reservations advised. Dress: casual. AE, DC, MC, V. Moderate.

Blue Ginger Cafe. Formerly Dahang's Pastry Shop, this small eatery looks as funky as ever, but the menu has been expanded to appeal to the new breed of visitors on the island. There's even some art on the wall. At breakfast enjoy a custom-made omelet or a big plate of eggs, toast, and hash browns. Lunchtime brings more selections, including the best hamburgers on the island and croissant sandwiches. Pizza, plate lunches, and saimin are other menu offerings. This is a real diner, with Formica-top tables, plastic chairs, and mismatched silverware. Try the Filipino-style doughnuts coated with granulated sugar; freshly made, they're a real treat. *409 7th Ave., tel. 808/565–6363. No reservations. Dress: casual. No credit cards. Inexpensive.*

S.&T. Properties. Occupying part of a general store, this place has an old-fashioned soda fountain with a counter and swivel stools. The food is classic breakfast and lunch diner fare, such as burgers, fries, and sundaes. *419 7th Ave., tel. 808/565–6537. No reservations. Dress: casual. No credit cards. Open 6:30 AM–1 PM. Inexpensive.*

Lodging

Until recently, the only accommodation on the island was the comfy old Hotel Lanai in Lanai City. Now two swanky alternatives for the discriminating traveler have opened. Let your tastes and your budget determine which place you choose.

Category	Cost*
Very Expensive	over $120
Moderate	$60–$90

*All prices are for a standard double room, excluding 9¼% tax and service charges.

Very Expensive

Lodge at Koele. One of the new additions to the hotel scene, the lodge resembles a luxurious private mountain retreat. Sprawled over 21 acres, it sits on the edge of Lanai City, in the highlands, where the temperature is cool and the pine trees are plentiful. The two-story lodge features a reception building and a main hall with unusual furnishings and rare Pacific artifacts. The porch is a generous space in which guests may enjoy the view and take refreshments, and the interiors have high beamed ceilings, natural stone fireplaces, and works by island artists. In the Hawaiian fruit garden, visitors can pick and sample fruits from a variety of trees, and there is more than a mile and a half of pathways through orchid gardens, macadamia forests, and palm landscapes. *Box 774, Lanai City 96763, tel. 808/565–7300 or 800/223–7637. 102 rooms and suites with bath. Facilities: golf, tennis, croquet, lawn bowling, horseback riding, restaurant, 2 lounges, pool. AE, DC, MC, V.*

Manele Bay Hotel. Opened May 1, 1991, this elaborate beachfront property offers suites that command views of Hulopoe Bay, the coastline, and the island of Maui. Design is reminiscent of traditional Hawaiian architecture, with lots of open-air lanais. Three two-story buildings overlook a courtyard, and a reception building houses the lobby and specialty boutiques. Ground- and second-level guest rooms feature private lanais and are surrounded by courtyards, waterfalls, ponds, and lawns landscaped with bromeliads, canopy trees, and other exotica. *Box 774, Lanai City 96763, tel. 808/565-7245 or 800/ 223-7637. 250 rooms and suites with bath. Facilities: golf, tennis, croquet, 3 restaurants, lounge, pool, spa. AE, DC, MC, V.*

Moderate

Hotel Lanai. First built to house visiting plantation executives, this quaint 10-room inn was once the only accommodation on the island. Today, even though two new hotels have opened up, you shouldn't overlook this Lanai institution. The old front porch with the big wicker chairs has long been a meeting place for residents and locals alike, who gather to read the paper, order a drink, and "talk story" (converse). The renovated rooms are simple, with single or twin beds, flowered wallpaper, and sometimes mismatched furniture, offering the feeling that you're in an eccentric great-aunt's country home. The grounds are well-maintained, with flower gardens and enormous Norfolk pines, and you can get three meals a day here (not included in the room fee). *Box A119, Lanai City 96763, tel. 808/565-7211 or 800/624-8849. 10 rooms with bath. Facilities: restaurant. AE, MC, V.*

Nightlife

The locals entertain themselves by gathering on the front porch of the **Hotel Lanai** for drinks and "talk story" sessions.

The **Lodge at Koele** (tel. 808/565-7300) features music in its Great Hall. Entertainment is offered by Lanai residents who share songs, dances, and chants of the island. In addition, the Music Room occasionally offers live entertainment.

The **Manele Bay Hotel** (tel. 808/565-7700) has after-dinner dancing in a romantic garden setting next to a fountain and reflecting pool.

8 Kauai

By Marty Wentzel

Nicknamed "the Garden Isle," Kauai is Eden epitomized. In the mountains of Kokee, lush swamps ring with the songs of rare birds, while the heady aroma of ginger blossoms sweetens the cool rain forests of Haena. Time and nature have carved elegant spires along the remote northern shore, called the Pali coast, while seven powerful rivers give life to the valleys where ancient Hawaiians once dwelled. Visitors can become one with that Eden on land and sea or in the air, by hiking along the Kalalau Trail, or paddling a kayak along the Hanalei River, or taking an exhilarating helicopter ride above Mt. Waialeale, the wettest spot on earth.

Still, even Eden has its drawbacks. In September 1992, a fierce hurricane named Iniki devastated most of the island, packing winds up to 175 miles per hour and causing hundreds of millions of dollars' worth of damage to homes, hotels, and the island's infrastructure. Almost immediately, the tourism industry got to work replanting, repairing, and rebuilding, and visitors were expected to begin returning to Kauai in mid-1993. While much of Kauai should be back to normal in 1994, guests will doubtless continue to notice some effects of the storm, such as houses with tarps for roofs, palms without fronds, and beaches that have been reconfigured.

It's important to note that hurricanes are rare in Hawaii, the last one hitting Kauai in 1982. The more appropriate portrait of the Garden Isle is that of a laid-back, restful retreat. Indeed, this is an island that appeals most to those with a love of the great outdoors.

During your days, you can take a boat trip up the Pali coast and go snorkeling. You can ride in a horse-drawn coach around a plantation-era sugar estate called Kilohana. You can play golf on the world-class greens of Princeville Resort, with views of the mountain ridge nicknamed Bali Hai. You can even saddle up and go on a horseback ride into Waimea Canyon, called the "Grand Canyon of the Pacific."

One road runs almost all the way around the circumference of the island, although it dead-ends on either side of the 15-mile stretch of rugged Pali coast. Driving from one end to the other takes you past emerald blankets of sugarcane, an important economic force on the island since Hawaii's first sugar mill was built in Koloa in 1836. You pass the taro patches of Hanalei Valley, where the long-time staple of the Hawaiian diet is grown for its root (used to make a paste called *poi*) as well as its leaves (used to wrap and cook food). You see such movie backdrops as Lumahai Beach, where *South Pacific* was filmed, and the Huleia River, where Indiana Jones made his daring escape at the beginning of *Raiders of the Lost Ark*. More recently, the island has been featured in the films *Honeymoon in Vegas* and *Jurassic Park*.

Kauai is the fourth-largest island of the Hawaiian chain, and its capital is Lihue, a town whose governmental buildings look like something out of a little New England village. Lihue is the commercial center of the Garden Isle, yet its collection of businesses—a pair of banks, a library, a school, a museum, some family-run restaurants, and hotels—is small enough to keep the pace slow and relaxed. During rush hour, Lihue becomes citified, for its narrow roads have a hard time accommodating the traffic of residents as well as tourists. Some contemporary shopping complexes are also gently pushing Lihue into a more modern-day pace.

To the south of the island is the major resort of Poipu, whose sunny beaches and clear skies have spawned a crop of condos and hotels. The eye of Hurricane Iniki passed directly over Poipu, and there are still some hotels, homes, and businesses yet to be rebuilt there. Heading west beneath the slopes of the Hoary Head Mountains, you encounter such storybook plantation villages as Hanapepe, Kalaheo, and Waimea, where Captain James Cook made his first Hawaiian landing back in 1778. Beyond Waimea, you'll find the long, idyllic sands of Polihale Beach, above which are the cool highlands of Kokee.

From the southwestern portion of the island you can see the island of Niihau, 17 miles off the southern coast. Until 1987, no uninvited guests were allowed to visit this family-owned island. Today most people who live in Hawaii still consider it off-limits, although this mysterious cay is now open to Kauai-based helicopter tours, which touch down on two Niihau beaches.

To the north of Lihue, the climate becomes cooler and wetter, and everything has grown back quickly since the hurricane. The towns of Wailua and Kapaa offer several resort complexes along a picturesque shoreline. This area is called the Royal Coconut Coast due to its proliferation of palms. As you head farther north to Anahola, Kilauea, and Hanalei, a kaleidoscope of vines and flowers takes over. At the end of the road in Haena, you'll encounter a misty otherworldliness conjuring up the legends of the ancients.

More myths are attached to the natural landscape of Kauai than to that of any other Hawaiian Island. A favorite among locals is the story of the legendary *menehune*, a community of tiny yet industrious workers who are said to have lived on Kauai before the Polynesians. Few people actually saw the menehune, because they worked in privacy at night. However, their stoneworks were impressive, and today you can see the bridges, walls, and structures that have been attributed to this mysterious race. It's still uncertain whether the menehune really existed, but no one has come up with an alternative regarding the source of the stoneworks.

Kauai may not be cosmopolitan, but as the sun sets on your day of play, the lights come up on a number of first-rate restaurants. Most of them are centered in the tourist resorts, including Poipu on the south shore and along the east coast from Wailua and Kapaa to Princeville and Hanalei. You can also catch a couple of luaus in which performers take you back in time with the chants of Kauai's earliest inhabitants.

The oldest of the Hawaiian Islands, Kauai's 350,000 acres are ripe with natural history and reflections of past cultures. Nowadays, it boasts tourist attractions, commercial activities, and award-winning accommodations. With a sensitive eye toward the preservation of its rural charm, Kauai is always open to change.

As it drifts in the Pacific just 95 miles northwest of Honolulu, Kauai makes no excuses for being less glamorous than Oahu. With unaffected natural beauty, it calmly welcomes all who step off the plane at the Lihue Airport and wraps them in a lei of ancient Hawaiian hospitality. With some 8,200 hotel rooms, condominium units, and bed and breakfasts on the island, it's no surprise that tourism is Kauai's number-one industry. The people involved in that business are working hard to keep its guests satisfied, and the aloha spirit is highly apparent. In fact, many think that Kauai's people are the friendliest in all of Hawaii.

The fact that Kauai's visitor industry has bounced back so quickly from the hurricane is a credit to these people, who demonstrated their strength during the drama of Iniki, the storm only enhancing their love of the island. Now more than ever, Kauai deserves a visit, not only to witness its tremendous rebirth, but to appreciate the triumph of the human spirit over adversity.

Essential Information

Arriving and Departing by Plane

Airports The **Lihue Airport** (tel. 808/246–1400) handles most of the air traffic in and out of Kauai. Located 3 miles east of the town of Lihue, the terminal is spacious, clean, contemporary, and friendly and easily accommodates the growing number of visitors to the Garden Isle. Arriving passengers walk through automatic revolving doors to enter the baggage claim area, and gift and snack shops are available with essentials for the road. Once you arrive, if you have any immediate questions, stop by the **Lihue Airport Visitor Information Center** (tel. 808/246–1440), located at each baggage claim area. It's open daily.

To the north of Lihue is **Princeville Airport** (tel. 808/826–3040), a tiny strip in the middle of rolling ranch lands and sugarcane fields. The open-air design and single check-in counter of its terminal impart a distinctly easygoing atmosphere. Two car-rental counters are located right at the terminal.

Princeville Airport is just a five-minute drive from the Princeville development area, which plays home to condos and a luxurious accommodation called the Princeville Hotel. The airport is also about a 15-minute drive from the shops and accommodations of sleepy Hanalei.

Flights from the **United Airlines** (tel. 800/241–6522) discontinued its direct serv-
Mainland U.S. ice from the mainland to Lihue following Iniki, but airline officials said that the flights from San Francisco may be reinstituted in the near future. Call the airline for an update.

Flights from Carriers flying from Oahu to Lihue Airport include **Aloha Air-**
Honolulu **lines** (tel. 800/367–5250) and **Hawaiian Airlines** (tel. 800/367–5320). Each offers approximately 30 flights a day. The rates go up and down depending on which airline is trying to outdo the other, but the one-way, per-person fare generally is $69. When you call to make a reservation, ask if there are reduced rates for traveling on the first or last flight of the day. Sometimes that price drops to as low as $49.95 one-way. It's a 25-minute flight between Honolulu and Lihue.

Flights from Honolulu to Princeville Airport are offered by **Island Air** (tel. 800/323–3345), formerly Princeville Airways. The cost per person from Honolulu is $69 one-way, and the flight takes about 45 minutes.

Lei Greetings Receiving a garland of fresh flowers as you step off the plane is a wonderful way to arrive at a new destination. You may decide to set up such a greeting for yourself or, better yet, for your traveling partner. Companies that cover the Lihue Airport include **Roberts Hawaii** (Honolulu International Airport, 96819, tel. 808/831–1134), **Aloha Lei Greeters** (Box 29133, Honolulu 96820, tel. 808/836–0249), **Greeters of Hawaii** (Box 29638, Honolulu 96820, tel. 800/736–5665), **Hawaii 800** (Box 89696, Honolulu 96830-0810, tel. 800/367–5270), **Kamaaina Leis, Flowers & Greeters** (3159-B Koapaka St., Honolulu 96819, tel. 800/367–5183), and **Trans Hawaiian Services** (3111 Castle St., Honolulu 96815, tel. 800/533–8765). Leis range from $6.95 for the simple orchid lei to $25 for the deluxe treatment. Some companies will also put together fruit baskets, bouquets, liquors and wines, champagne, and other special orders.

Between the Airport and Hotels The driving distance from Lihue Airport to the town of Lihue is a mere five minutes. If you're staying in Wailua or Kapaa, your driving time from Lihue is 15 minutes, and to Princeville and Hanalei it takes about an hour behind the wheel. If you're staying in Hanalei, try to fly into Princeville Airport to save on driving time.

To the south, it's a 30–45-minute drive from Lihue to Poipu, the major resort of that area. If you choose the rustic accommodations in the hills of Kokee, allow a good two hours of driving time from Lihue.

Before you look into one of the following methods of transportation to your lodgings, check with your hotel or condo to see if it offers free shuttle service from the airport.

By Bus Kauai has no public bus system. From Princeville Airport, you can catch the free shuttle service (tel. 808/826–3040) offered by the Princeville Resort to its hotels and condos.

By Van **Polynesian Adventure Tours** (tel. 808/246–0122) provides a shuttle service that takes you from the airport to various hotels around the island in 17-passenger air-conditioned mini-buses. Charges differ according to distance; for instance, the round-trip, per-person cost from the airport to Poipu is $10, to Kapaa $7.50. Polynesian Adventure Tours doesn't charge for your bags. There's no set schedule; just call the service one day ahead of your arrival.

By Taxi Fares around the island are $2 at the meter drop plus $2 per mile. That means a taxicab from Lihue Airport to Lihue town runs about $6, and to Poipu costs $36, excluding tip. Two taxi companies that will take you to Lihue and Poipu are **Hanamaulu Taxi** (tel. 808/245–3727) and **Kauai Cab** (tel. 808/246–9554).

From the Princeville Airport to Hanalei, you'll pay about $12 when you ride with the **North Shore Cab Company** (tel. 808/826–6189), which serves only the northeast portion of the island.

By Limousine For luxurious transportation between the airport and your accommodations, contact **Carey Limousine of Hawaii** (1314 S. King St., Suite 1553, Honolulu 96814, tel. 800/336–4646), whose hourly rates begin at $45 with a two-hour minimum. Another possibility for luxury travel is **Limo Limo Limousine Service of Kauai** (Box 636, Kapaa 96746, tel. 808/822–0393). Its rates are $66 to $75 per hour, with a two-hour minimum. **Rob-**

erts Hawaii (Box 3389, Lihue 96766, tel. 808/245–9558) also provides formal airport pickup, as does **Al's Koloa-Poipu VIP Taxi** (Box 374, Poipu 96756, tel. 808/742–1390). **North Shore Limousine** (Box 757, Hanalei 96714, tel. 808/826–6189) can pick you up at Princeville Airport.

By Car Unless you plan to do all of your sightseeing as part of guided van tours, you will want a rental car on Kauai. The vast beauty of the island begs to be explored, and its attractions are sprinkled from one end to the other.

The main road north from Lihue Airport is Route 56 (also known as Kuhio Highway), which ends 38 miles later in Haena. From Lihue south and west, the coastal highway is called Highway 50 (Kaumualii Highway), which ends about 40 miles later near Polihale Beach State Park. Highway 52 (Maluhia Road) runs south off Highway 50 to Poipu. On the west side, Highway 55 (Kokee Road) heads north from Kekaha up to the wilds of Kokee State Park.

Right across from the baggage claim area at Lihue Airport you'll find several rental-car firms, as well as vans that will shuttle you to offices nearby. These include **Alamo, Avis, Budget, Dollar, Hertz, National, Sunshine,** and **Tropical.** There are also several lesser-known and local companies that offer slightly lower rates (*see* Getting Around, *below*, for specific car-rental information).

Arriving and Departing by Ship

From Honolulu A romantic way to visit Kauai for a short time is to book passage on an interisland cruise ship. These massive white "love boats" leave Honolulu each Saturday night and stop at Kauai, as well as Maui and the Big Island. At each port of call, you may get off the ship and sightsee for a day, sometimes two. **American Hawaii Cruises** (550 Kearny St., San Francisco, CA 94108, tel. 800/227–3666) has been presenting these successful excursions for several years on board the 800-passenger SS *Independence* and SS *Constitution*. Give one of the ships a whirl if you have the time and the money (weekly rates begin at $1,195 during low season, including meals).

Getting Around

Although Kauai is relatively small, its sights reach from one end of the island to the other. Often you can walk to the stores and restaurants in your resort area, but the important attractions of the island are generally not within walking distance of each other. As a result, you'll probably want to rent a car, unless you plan to do all your sightseeing with tour companies.

By Car It's easy to get around on Kauai, for it has one major road that
Driving almost encircles the island. Your rental-car company will supply you with a map with enlargements of each area of the island. The traffic on Kauai is pretty light most of the time, except in the Lihue area during rush hour (6:30–8:30 AM and 3:30–5:30 PM). The major attractions are indicated on the side of the road by a Hawaiian-warrior marker.

As is the case throughout Hawaii, a seat-belt law is enforced on Kauai for front-seat passengers. Children under the age of three must be in a car seat, which you can get from your car-rental company.

Although Kauai looks like paradise, it has its fair share of crime. Play it safe and lock up your car whenever you park it. Don't leave valuables in the car, and pay attention to parking signs, particularly in Lihue.

Car Rentals It is advisable to reserve your vehicle before you arrive, especially if you will be on Kauai during the peak seasons of summer, the Christmas holidays, and February.

Daily prices for a car from the major-name companies begin at $23. A fly/drive deal can sometimes reduce that cost to $17. If you sign up with a small or lesser-known local renter, prices range from $15 to $20.

Car-rental companies with offices at or near Lihue Airport are **Alamo** (tel. 800/327–9633), **Avis** (tel. 800/331–1212), **Budget** (tel. 800/527–7000), **Dollar** (tel. 800/367–7006), **Hertz** (tel. 800/654–3011), **National** (tel. 800/227–7368), **Sunshine** (tel. 800/367–2977), and **Tropical** (tel. 800/678–6000).

Companies with Princeville Airport offices are **Avis** and **Hertz**. Several companies also operate reservation desks at the major hotels on the island. These include **Avis** (Stouffer Waiohai Beach Resort, tel. 800/426–4122, and Hyatt Regency Kauai, tel. 800/233–1234), and **Hertz** (Kauai Lagoons Resort, tel. 800/228–3000).

You can get some good deals on a car if you book with one of Kauai's budget or used-rental-car companies. These include **Rent-A-Wreck of Kauai** (tel. 808/245–6411) and the reliable **Westside U-Drive** (tel. 808/332–8644), which rents cars from $19.95 and jeeps from $59.95. They keep their vehicles in good shape.

By Bus Kauai has no public bus system. There are, however, private buses that take visitors to such specific commercial attractions as Fern Grotto, Waimea Canyon, Spouting Horn, the Russian Fort, Opaekaa Falls, and Menehune Fish Pond (*see* Guided Tours, *below*).

By Taxi A taxicab will take you islandwide, but you'll pay dearly for that luxury. The cost for each mile is $2, after a $2 meter drop. So, from Lihue to Poipu the price is $36; from Lihue to Princeville, $50, excluding tip. Your best bet is to call a cab for short distances only (to a restaurant, for instance). A 5-mile cab ride will run you about $12, excluding tip. The drivers are often from Kauai, which means they'll give you information about the island. Two reliable taxicab companies on the island are **Hanamaulu Taxi** (tel. 808/245–3727) and **Kauai Cab** (tel. 808/246–9544). Based in Princeville is the **North Shore Cab Company** (tel. 808/826–6189), which provides complete ground handling services for the north and east sections of the island.

By Limousine One doesn't see a lot of limousines cruising the country roads of Kauai, but if the idea intrigues you, contact **Carey Limousine of Hawaii** (1314 S. King St., Suite 1553, Honolulu 96814, tel. 800/336–4646), whose hourly rates begin at $45 with a two-hour minimum. Among its options are airport service, charters, touring, wedding packages, lei greetings, and complete ground handling. Another possibility for luxury travel is **Limo Limo Limousine Service of Kauai** (Box 636, Kapaa 96746, tel.

808/822–0393). Its rates are $66–$75 per hour, with a two-hour minimum, and it operates Lincoln and Cadillac custom stretch limousines, a classic Rolls Royce "Princess," and presidential stretches with VCRs, bars, and a sunroof.

By Moped/ Motorcycle/ Bicycle A two-wheeler is an exciting way to cruise around the Garden Isle. Its country roads are generally uncrowded and safe, so you can ride along at your own pace and enjoy the views. This is a safe island to explore by bicycle, as long as you exercise caution on the busier thoroughfares. **Pedal and Paddle** (tel. 808/826–9069) charges $30 a day (24 hours) for mopeds, $20 for bicycles. Hourly and weekly rates are also available. **Ray's Rentals and Activities** (tel. 808/822–5700) offers a two-for-one bike rental deal for $75 a week. You can also rent bikes from the activities desks of certain hotels around the island. Check with your concierge or front desk.

Important Addresses and Numbers

Tourist Information The **Hawaii Visitors Bureau** has its headquarters at 3016 Umi Street, Lihue Plaza, Suite 207, Lihue 96766, tel. 808/245–3971. Umi Street runs off of Rice Street, Lihue's main thoroughfare, right near the Kauai Museum. The bureau has a good selection of brochures and other visitor's literature, including three free weekly visitor's magazines, *Spotlight Kauai, This Week on Kauai,* and *Kauai Beach Press.*

The **Kauai Visitor Center** (Coconut Plantation Market Place, Waipouli, tel. 808/822–5113; Kauai Village, Kapaa, tel. 808/822–7727) is another good source of information about the Garden Isle. It handles reservations for a variety of activities and has current brochures and schedules on hand.

Several activity centers will help visitors book tours, arrange sporting excursions, rent cars, reserve rooms in hotels and condos, and even plan weddings. These centers include **Aloha Destinations** (Box 1386, Koloa 96756, tel. 808/742–7548), **Kauai 800** (Box 640, Koloa 96756, tel. 800/443–9180), and **Paradise Club Activities** (Box 3477, Princeville 96722, tel. 808/826–7581).

Emergencies For police, ambulance, or fire department, dial 911.

Hospital Emergency Rooms **Wilcox Memorial Hospital** (3420 Kuhio Hwy., Lihue 96766, tel. 808/245–1100).
Kauai Veterans Memorial Hospital (4643 Waimea Canyon Dr., Waimea 96796, tel. 808/338–9431).

Doctors The **Kauai Medical Group** (KMG) offers 32 specialties to handle all medical problems. It features lab and X-ray facilities, physical therapy, optometry, and emergency rooms. The main clinic is located at 3420-B Kuhio Highway, Lihue 96766, tel. 808/245–1500. Other KMG clinics can be found in Kilauea (tel. 808/828–1418), Princeville (tel. 808/826–6300), Kukui Grove (tel. 808/246–0051), Koloa (tel. 808/742–1621), and Kapaa (tel. 808/822–3431). *Open Mon., Thurs., Fri. 10:30–1:30; Sat. noon–6; Sun. 10–4. Physicians are on call 24 hours (tel. 808/245–1831 after hours).*

Shiatsu International Massage Clinic deals with stress, back pain, arthritis, injuries, headaches, fatigue, and the aches and pains of having too much fun on your vacation. Licensed staff members practice this ancient and respected system of pressure-point massage therapy. *1592 Kuhio Hwy., Kapaa 96746, tel. 808/822–9779. Open daily 9–9.*

Late-Night The **Kauai Medical Group** (3420-B Kuhio Hwy., Lihue 96766,
Pharmacies tel. 808/245–1500) offers an extensive pharmacy and features offices around the island. In Lihue, try **Long's Drugs** (Kukui Grove Center, Hwy. 50, tel. 808/245–7771), and in Kapaa, try **Shoreview Pharmacy** (4–1177 Kuhio Hwy., Suite 113, tel. 808/822–1447).

Opening and Closing Times

Most Kauai banks are open Monday through Thursday between 8:45 and 3 or 4:30, Friday until 6. Most financial institutions are closed on weekends and holidays.

Kauai attractions have their own specific hours, usually Monday through Saturday from 9 or 10 to 4:30 or 5. For instance, the Kauai Museum is open weekdays from 9 to 4:30, Saturday from 9 to 1. Most museums are closed on Christmas Day.

Kauai's major shopping centers are open daily from 10 to 5, although some close later. In Kapaa, Kinipopo Shopping Village is open daily from 9 to 9, while Princeville Center's hours are 9 to 5.

Guided Tours

There are three major methods for getting a good look at the Garden Isle: by land, by sea, and by air. You can book these tours through the travel desk of your hotel or call directly.

Tour Companies The companies that take you on guided ground tours of Kauai use big air-conditioned buses and stretch limousines as well as smaller vans. The latter seem to fit in more with the countrified atmosphere of Kauai. Whether you choose a bus or van tour, the equipment will be in excellent shape, because each of these companies wants your business. When you make your reservations, ask what kind of vehicle you'll be riding in and which tours let you get off and look around. The guides are friendly and generally know their island inside out. It's customary to tip them $2 or more per person for their efforts.

The helicopter and boat touring companies also use top-of-the-line equipment. If you're interested in a north shore sea excursion, be forewarned that environmentalists have been trying to ban all boat tours out of Hanalei. At press time the debate was still raging, so call first to find out if the company you're interested in is even operating. The best-known and most reliable land, sea, and air tour companies on Kauai include the following:

Captain Zodiac Raft Expeditions (Box 456, Hanalei 96714, tel. 800/422–7824 or 808/826–9371) has long been known for its boat trips along the Pali coast.
Gray Line Hawaii (Box 1551, Lihue 96766, tel. 800/367–2420) features tours by motor coach as well as by smaller vans.
Kauai Island Tours (Box 1645, Lihue 96766, tel. 800/733–4777) takes you around Kauai in 14-, 25-, and 57-passenger vans and 5- and 6-passenger Cadillacs.
Na Pali–Coast Cruise Line (Box 869, Eleele 96705, tel. 808/335–5078 or 246–1015) tours the northern coastline in the 150-passenger *Na Pali Queen*. It departs from the south shore.

Papillon Hawaiian Helicopters (Box 339, Hanalei 96714, tel. 800/367–7095) gives you a birds-eye view from a 6-passenger whirlybird.

Polynesian Adventure Tours (4254 Rice St., Lihue 96766, tel. 800/622–3011) specializes in an all-day Kauai tour.

Roberts Hawaii Tours (Box 3389, Lihue 96766, tel. 808/245–9558) has top-of-the-line equipment, including stretch limos.

Trans Hawaiian Services (3111 Castle St., Honolulu 96815, tel. 800/533–8765) offers multilingual tours.

Round-the-Island Tours Sometimes called the Wailua River/Waimea Canyon Tour, this offers a good overview of the island, because you get to see all the sights, including the Russian Fort, Queen Victoria's Profile, Opaekaa Falls, and Menehune Fish Pond. Guests are transported in air-conditioned 17-passenger minivans. The trip includes a boat ride up the Wailua River to Fern Grotto, then a drive around the island to scenic views above Waimea Canyon. The tour stops at a casual restaurant for a no-host lunch. Companies offering round-the-island ground tours include Gray Line Hawaii, Polynesian Adventure Tours, and Roberts Hawaii Tours (*see* Tour Companies, *above*).

Best of Kauai Tour. This whirlwind five-hour tour, sponsored by the North Shore Cab Company, focuses on the highlights of the east and north shores. It starts with a visit to Kilohana, a refurbished plantation mansion in Lihue, followed by a boat ride to Fern Grotto. After lunch at Coco Palms Resort, you take a tour of Kilauea Lighthouse and end up with a helicopter tour out of Princeville Airport. Ground transportation is in 15-passenger, air-conditioned vans. *Box 757, Hanalei 96714, tel. 808/ 826–6189. Cost: $109 per person with a minimum of 12 people. North Shore Cab will pick you up at your hotel if you are staying on the north or east side of the island. It will also pick you up at Lihue Airport.*

Helicopter Tours Kauai from the air is mind-boggling. In an hour you can see waterfalls, craters, and places that are inaccessible even by hiking trails. Companies include **Kenai Air Hawaii** (Box 3270, Lihue 96766, tel. 800/622–3144), which costs $135 per person for a 50–55 minute tour. Or try **Bali Hai Helicopters** (Box 1052, Kalaheo 96741, tel. 808/325–TOUR), a $130, round-island, photographer's delight. **Will Squyre's Helicopter Tours** (Box 1770, Lihue 96766, tel. 808/245–8881) has group rates and charters.

Great Outdoors Tours **Kayak Kauai.** Hawaii's forests and marshes are the home of rare and exceptional flora and fauna, which often go unseen by visitor and resident alike. Kayak Kauai takes inquisitive visitors on three-hour tours along the Hanalei River in open-cockpit canoes with a stop for snorkeling in Hanalei Bay. It also offers a five-day camping/kayaking adventure—including transportation, boats, meals, and gear—for groups of 4 to 12 people. Or explore the Na Pali Coast with Kayak Kauai between May and September. *Box 508, Hanalei 96714, tel. 808/ 826–9844. Cost: Hanalei River, $45 with snorkeling; camping/ kayaking, $150 per day; Na Pali, $115 with lunch.*

North Shore Bike, Cruise, and Snorkel. This is a great all-day tour for the ultimate outdoors person. Hotel pickups and drop-offs take place along the northeastern coast only. The company sponsors a bicycling tour plus a 6-mile cruise to two snorkel sites. Two guides and a support van accompany the group, which ranges from 6 to 13 people. Snorkeling instruction is included, as is a barbecue lunch. *Box 1192, Kapaa 96746, tel. 808/ 822–1582. Cost: $99.*

Historical Tours   **History, Myth, and Legend Tour.** This 2½-hour tour, sponsored by **North Shore Cab Company,** focuses on the facts and fiction that spring from the lush north-shore landscape. The folks who put it together did plenty of research, and the guides are highly qualified to point out locations of historical value. You're driven around in 15-passenger air-conditioned vans, and along the way you learn about the myths associated with the north shore's natural formations. *Box 757, Hanalei 96714, tel. 808/ 826–6189. Cost: $29 per person with a minimum of 6 people. Departs daily at 11:30 and 2. North Shore Cab Company will pick you up at your hotel if you are staying on the north or east side of the island. It will also pick you up at Lihue Airport.*

Niihau Tours   Once the "Forbidden Isle," this area off Kauai's southern coast is now accessible to tourists, but only on a one- or two-hour tour with Niihau Helicopters (*see* Tour 4 in Exploring, *below*).

Exploring Kauai

The main road that runs along the edges of the island takes you past a variety of landscapes and attractions that can easily be explored in two or three full days. If you follow the road north from Lihue, you'll encounter green pasturelands, lush valleys, and untamed tropical wilderness. This area is rich in history and legend, for it was one of the primary communities of the first Polynesians, who settled here more than 1,000 years ago.

If you follow the road south from Lihue, the air feels warmer and dryer. This is Poipu, where the sun shines steadily on the populated beaches. A string of condos and hotels (some still under repair after Iniki) lines the sparkling coastline, and an impressive variety of water sports is available for the asking.

Head west and you feel as if you're stepping back in time as you pass through one former plantation town after the next, each with its own story to tell: Waimea, home of the Menehune Ditch, which was supposedly built by a mysterious race of little people; Hanapepe, whose salt ponds have been farmed since ancient times; and in the middle of nowhere, Fort Elizabeth, from which an enterprising Russian tried to take over the island in the early 1800s.

From Waimea you can drive upland to the crisp, cool climate of Kokee, 3,000 feet above sea level, where you'll see yet another side of this most ancient of the Hawaiian Islands. Here sequoia forests and swamplands provide a home for fascinating indigenous birds and plants, while a mountain lodge welcomes guests with old-style hospitality.

Each of the following driving tours can easily fill a day of sightseeing. If you need to cut your time short, allow one day for the north and east portion of the island and another day for sights to the south and west.

Mauka means on the mountain side of the road, while *makai* means on the ocean side. These terms will be used throughout this touring section.

Highlights for First-time Visitors

Fern Grotto, Tour 1
Fort Elizabeth, Tour 3
Kalalau Lookout, Tour 3
Kamokila, Tour 1
Kauai Museum, Tour 2
Kilauea Lighthouse, Tour 1
Kilohana, Tour 2
Opaekaa Falls, Tour 1
Spouting Horn, Tour 2
Waimea Canyon, Tour 3

Tour 1: The Heavenly Northeast

Numbers in the margin correspond to points of interest on the Kauai map.

Begin this tour by driving north on Highway 56 out of Lihue. If you're ready for an immediate scenic diversion, in about 10 minutes turn left on Highway 583 (Maalo Rd.), at the bottom of the ❶ hill in Kapaia. Drive 4 miles to reach **Wailua Falls,** an impressive cascade that you might recognize from the opening sequences of the old "Fantasy Island" television show.

❷ Another 10-minute drive on Highway 56 takes you to **Wailua,** which means "two waters" in Hawaiian. Kauai's first communities were built along the Wailua River, and tucked away along its banks are remnants of some *heiau* (sacred stone platforms for the worship of the gods).

In Wailua, turn mauka (toward the mountains) onto Highway 580 (Kuamoo Rd.). This is nicknamed the King's Highway, for in ancient times monarchs were carried along this road because their feet were not supposed to touch the ground. On your im- ❸ mediate left is **Pohaku Ho'Ohanau**—a collection of rocks comprising a revered heiau. Oahu's Bishop Museum and the Kauai Historical Society joined forces to restore this sacred landmark, where sacrifices were once made to the gods.

Continue for 1 mile along Highway 580 to a lookout on the right. ❹ Here you see a dramatic vision called **Opaekaa Falls,** plunging hundreds of feet to the pools below. Opaekaa means "rolling shrimp," which refers to the little creatures that once tossed and turned at the base of the falls.

Across the street from the falls is a red sign with a Hawaiian ❺ warrior on it, pointing you to **Kamokila,** a restored Hawaiian village that sits on the banks of the peaceful Wailua River surrounded by taro and banana patches. Guests are invited to take guided tours of the houses and learn ancient crafts and games. Authentic luaus are also held here. It's a great place to take the whole family. *6060 Kuamoo Rd., Kapaa 96746, tel. 808/822–1192. Admission: $8 adults, $5 children 6–12. Open Mon.–Sat. 9–4.*

Return to Highway 56 and continue heading north. On the ❻ mauka side awaits **Wailua Marina,** a pretty little set of docks from which cruise boats depart for **Fern Grotto.** This 3-mile trip up the Wailua River culminates at a yawning lava tube that is decorated with enormous fishtail ferns, an 80-foot waterfall, and other natural delights. On 150-passenger flat-bottom riverboats, the trip takes 1½ hours to reach the grotto, which is truly a tropical masterpiece. During the boat ride, good-natured musicians strum guitars and ukuleles and regale you with up-beat Hawaiian melodies. Fern Grotto is the setting for hundreds of weddings each year, and when you take a look at this romantic fairyland, you'll understand why. *Two companies offer several trips daily to Fern Grotto. One is Waialeale Boat Tours, Wailua Marina, Kapaa 96746, tel. 808/822–4908. Cost: $10 adults, $5 children 3–12. Also featured is a 2-hr. evening barbecue cruise. Call for rates. The other company is Smith's Motor Boat Service, 174 Wailua Rd., Kapaa 96746, tel. 808/822–4111. Cost: $10 adults, $5 children under 12.*

7 Proceed north on Highway 56 and look makai (toward the ocean) for **Lydgate State Park.** Here is a lovely coconut grove that was once a city of refuge for Hawaiian fugitives. If they made their way to this beachfront haven, their lives were saved (*see* Beaches, *below*).

8 About 10 minutes farther north you reach **Waipouli,** the little town where the Coconut Marketplace holds forth. This overwhelming conglomeration of shops and restaurants offers just about anything a traveler might need, from tacky souvenirs to elegant strands of Niihau shells. If you're not in the mood for shopping, keep driving.

9 On the mauka (mountain) side you soon see a mountain ridge resembling a **Sleeping Giant.** This formation is said to be the giant Puni, who has dozed undisturbed since doing fierce battle with an island enemy. The next town you come to is **Kapaa,** Kauai's largest town with some 5,000 people. Here you can see quaint storefronts and buildings that have been restored to house souvenir shops, clothing boutiques, and eateries. You will also probably see homes and other structures which haven't been repaired since Hurricane Iniki.

Time Out **Ono Family Restaurant** (4-1292 Kuhio Hwy., Kapaa tel. 808/822–1710) is a family-style eatery that draws big crowds with its homemade Portuguese bean soup, gourmet hamburgers, and freshly baked pies. It's a great slice of local color, whether you stop here for breakfast or lunch. Get daring and order a buffalo burger, a specialty of the house, which is made with meat from the herds of Hanalei.

10 After the town of **Kealia,** you reach **Anahola,** best known as the home of **Anahola Beach Park.** This sleepy spot offers rest for the weary, shade for the overheated, and calm waters for the swimmers among you (*see* Beaches, below).

11 Continue north on Highway 56, and in about 7 miles you encounter **Kilauea,** another former plantation town. Today Kilauea is known for its aquacultural successes, especially with prawns. It has also distinguished itself with its guava plantation (*see* Kauai for Free, *below*). Turn right on Kolo Road when you see the post office, next to which is **Christ Memorial Episcopal Church** (2518 Kolo Rd., tel. 808/828–1791), which dates back to 1941. This church is constructed of native lava rock, and its stained-glass windows come from England.

12 Take the first left off Kolo Road, on Kilauea Road, and follow it to the end. This takes you to **Kilauea Lighthouse,** a beacon for passing air and water traffic since it was built in 1913. Once it boasted the largest lens of any lighthouse in the world. Now it

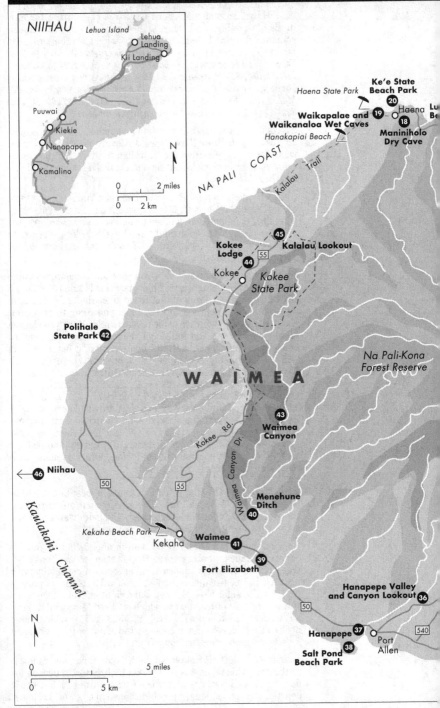

Kauai

NIIHAU

Lehua Island

Lehua Landing

Kii Landing

Puuwai

Kiekie

Nonopapa

Kamalino

N

0   2 miles

0   2 km

Haena State Park

Ke'e State Beach Park 20

Waikapalae and Waikanaloa Wet Caves 19   Haena 18

Hanakapiai Beach

Lu
Be

Maniniholo Dry Cave

NA PALI COAST

Kalalau Trail

Kokee Lodge 44

Kokee

55

Kalalau Lookout 45

Kokee State Park

Polihale State Park 42

W A I M E A

Na Pali-Kona Forest Reserve

43 **Waimea Canyon**

Niihau 46 ←

50

55

Kekaha Beach Park

Kekaha

Kokee Rd.

Waimea Canyon Dr.

Menehune Ditch 40

Waimea 41

39 **Fort Elizabeth**

Kaulakahi Channel

N

0   5 miles

0   5 km

50

Hanapepe Valley and Canyon Lookout 36

540

Hanapepe 37

Port Allen

38 **Salt Pond Beach Park**

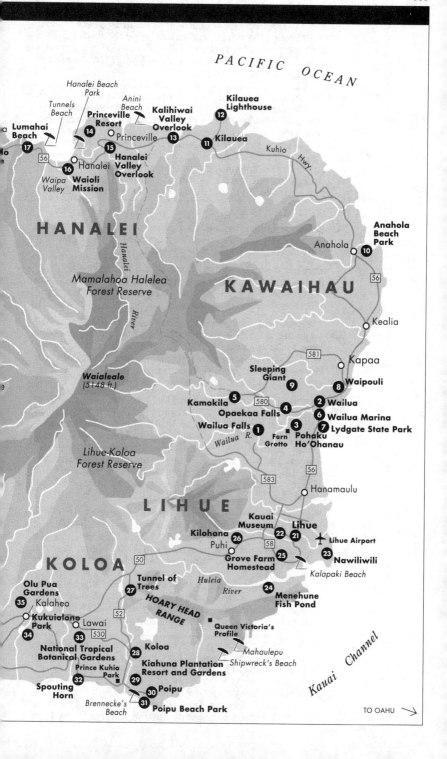

PACIFIC OCEAN

Hanalei Beach
Park

Tunnels
Beach

**Lumahai
Beach**
17

Anini
Beach

**Princeville
Resort**
14

O Princeville

**Kilauea
Lighthouse**

**Kalihiwai
Valley
Overlook**

12

13

11 **Kilauea**

Kuhio Hwy.

56

16 O Hanalei

15

**Hanalei
Valley
Overlook**

**Waioli
Mission**

Waipa
Valley

HANALEI

Hanalei River

*Mamalahoa Halelea
Forest Reserve*

River

**Anahola
Beach
Park**

O Anahola

10

56

KAWAIHAU

O Kealia

*Waialeale
(5148 ft.)*

581

O Kapaa

**Sleeping
Giant**

9

8 **Waipouli**

Kamokila **5**

580

4

2 **Wailua**

Opaekaa Falls

6 **Wailua Marina**

Wailua Falls **1**

3

7 **Lydgate State Park**

Wailua R.

**Pohaku
Ho'Ohanau**

Fern
Grotto

*Lihue-Koloa
Forest Reserve*

56

583

O Hanamaulu

LIHUE

**Kauai
Museum**

Kilohana **26**

O Puhi

22

Lihue

21

✈ **Lihue Airport**

58

25

**Grove Farm
Homestead**

23 **Nawiliwili**

Kalapaki Beach

KOLOA

50

**Tunnel of
Trees**

27

*Huleia
River*

24 **Menehune
Fish Pond**

*HOARY HEAD
RANGE*

**Olu Pua
Gardens**

35

O Kalaheo

52

O Lawai

530

■ **Queen Victoria's
Profile**

**Kukuiolono
Park**

34

33

**National Tropical
Botanical Gardens**

28 **Koloa**

Mahaulepu

Shipwreck's Beach

Prince Kuhio Park

32

**Kiahuna Plantation
Resort and Gardens**

29

30 **Poipu**

**Spouting
Horn**

31 **Poipu Beach Park**

*Brennecke's
Beach*

Kauai Channel

TO OAHU →

is better known as the landmark of the **Kilauea Wildlife Refuge,** home to eight species of endangered seabirds. There are foot trails around the refuge, and guides inside the Visitor Center can fill you in on the various wildlife you may be lucky enough to spot. *Kilauea Rd., Kilauea, tel. 808/828–1413. Admission free. Open weekdays 10–4.*

Time Out On the mauka side of Highway 56 just past the center of Kilauea sits **Banana Joe's Tropical Fruit Farm** (5-2719 Kuhio Hwy., Kilauea, tel. 808/828–1092), a rustic shelter with a distinctly Polynesian look to it. This is the home of Banana Joe, whose fresh, ripe, Kauai-grown fruits are the perfect energy booster. He also sells fresh corn and other vegetables in season. If you're staying in a condo, pick up something for dinner. Joe also specializes in fruit smoothies, fruit salads, and delicious dehydrated tropical fruit, which you can eat here or take with you.

When you reach the 25-mile marker of Highway 56, you'll be at **13** **Kalihiwai Valley Overlook.** There is room on the side of the road to pull over. This is a splendid vantage point for photographing the valley and its glimmering waterfall.

Turn right onto Kalihiwai Road on the northern side of the bridge, and take the left fork onto Anini Road. This will take you to **Anini Beach,** a good spot for beginning windsurfers and snorkelers (*see* Beaches, *below*).

The next highlight of Highway 56 is Princeville Airport, a small **14** commuter airport on the mauka side of the road. **Princeville Resort** follows on the right, with its two Robert Trent Jones, Jr. golf courses and tidy shopping center. Turn right on Princeville Road only if you're interested in seeing some fancy hotels and condominiums. Otherwise, skip it.

Directly across the street from the Princeville Shopping Cen- **15** ter is the **Hanalei Valley Overlook,** identified by a Hawaiian-warrior marker. Here, in the 1850s, Robert Wyllie once attempted to establish a coffee plantation. After that failed, the Chinese planted rice here until the early 1900s. Now the valley floor is filled with taro, the staple plant of the Hawaiian diet. From this panoramic overlook you can see more than a half mile of taro, plus the 900 acres that comprise a National Wildlife Refuge for endangered waterfowl.

Highway 56 now descends and crosses a rustic, arched one-lane bridge dating back to 1912, then swings into the town of **16** **Hanalei.** This is the site of the 1837 **Waioli Mission,** once the home of missionary teachers Lucy and Abner Wilcox. Its prim and proper koa wood furniture and other furnishings are straight out of missionary Hawaii, and its tidy architecture feels like it belongs back in New England, from which the missionaries came. *Kuhio Hwy., Hanalei, tel. 808/245–3202. Admission free, although donations are accepted. Open Tues., Thurs., Sat. 9–3. Half-hour guided tours are available.*

Time Out Tahiti Nui (Kuhio Hwy. at Aku Rd., Hanalei, tel. 808/826–6277). This landmark was hit hard by Hurricane Iniki, and no reopening date had been announced at press time. If it is open, check it out, because it's a favorite with locals; they love to gather on its funky front porch or inside the colorful bar to "talk story" (chat), have a few drinks, and eat pupus (hors d'oeuvres). Owned and operated by the Marston family from

Tahiti, this restaurant is known in the area for its affordable meals, including fresh fish from the north shore and smoked ribs.

Highway 56 north of Hanalei winds its way between the mountains and the sea and crosses a series of old one-lane bridges. The driving pace here is slow, so if you see a car coming the other way, just take your time and let him cross first. (It's the Kauai spirit!) As the road rises and curves left, look for the marker
17 to **Lumahai Beach.** You can park on the makai side of the road and walk down the steep (and sometimes muddy) path to the beach, which was the setting for the film *South Pacific.* This ivory, mile-long strand is one of Kauai's best beaches, particularly for its spectacular setting of majestic cliffs, black lava rocks, and hala trees (*see* Beaches, *below*).

Back on the road going west, look for the 36-mile marker on Highway 56. A little farther, you'll see a right turn through a grove of trees. This takes you to **Tunnels Beach,** a well-protected swimming beach (*see* Beaches, *below*).

18 A little farther on the mauka (mountain) side is **Maniniholo Dry Cave,** an eerie grotto said to have been dug by a menehune chief who was looking for an evil spirit. This cave was a site of ancient worship, and today you can walk back into it about 75 yards . . . if you dare. Across from the dry cave is **Haena State Park,** a fine beach for swimming when there's no current. A lunch wagon stands ready to feed hungry surf bums and sightseers (*see* Beaches, *below*).

19 Also on the mauka side, just north of the dry cave, are **Waikapalae** and **Waikanaloa wet caves,** said to have been dug by the volcano goddess Pele. These watering holes used to be clear, clean, and great for swimming. Now stagnant, they're still photogenic and an example of the many haunting natural landmarks of Kauai's north shore.

20 When you reach the end of Highway 56 in Haena, you'll be at **Ke'e Beach State Park,** an idyllic beach for viewing the spectacular Na Pali coastline. This is where you'll find the start of the 11-mile Kalalau Trail (*see* Beaches, *below*). From the beach, a path to the left leads to an open, grassy meadow with a stone altar called **Lohiau's Hula Platform.** They say that Laka, goddess of the hula, did most of her dancing on this very spot, and today's hula practitioners sometimes leave offerings here. Treat this beautiful site with reverence, for it is full of historical and spiritual *mana* (power).

Tour 2: Lihue and Southward

21 Begin this tour on Rice Street, the main road of **Lihue.** This town is the commercial and political center of both Kauai and
22 Niihau. It is also the home of the **Kauai Museum,** whose exhibits present an informative overview of the Garden Isle. On permanent display at the museum is "The Story of Kauai," tracing the island's geological, natural, cultural, and mythological history and featuring a 20-minute aerial movie. Works by local artists are on display in the Plantation Gallery, and the gift shop offers a good selection of books and souvenirs. *4428 Rice St., Lihue 96766, tel. 808/245–6931. Admission $3 adults, children under 18 free. Open Mon.–Fri. 9–4:30, Sat. 9–1.*

Time Out   If you're looking for a decent breakfast to fuel you for the day,
The Eggbert's (4483 Rice St., Lihue, tel. 808/245–6325), a rambling two-story restaurant, is your spot. Family fare at reasonable prices is the attraction here, with specialty omelets in two
sizes (one huge), banana pancakes, fruits, juices, and such local
taste treats as Portuguese sausage. The eggs Benedict are an
insider's favorite. Breakfast is served through mid-afternoon,
and the place also offers lunch and dinner.

Follow Rice Street east until it dead-ends. Turn right on Waapa
㉓ Road, which takes you to **Nawiliwili,** Kauai's major port. Here
you will see a host of little fishing and recreational boats, as
well as tour boats that offer snorkeling and sightseeing adventures along the east and south coasts. In addition, Nawiliwili is
where the weekly luxury liners dock, as do container ships and
U.S. Navy vessels. **Kalapaki Beach** is nearby for protected
swimming and sunbathing by the glitzy Westin Kauai (*see*
Beaches, *below*).

From Waapa Road, turn right on Mokihana Street, which becomes Halemalu Road. Here you follow the Huleia River, site of
㉔ the **Menehune Fish Pond.** Secretive little workers are said to
have built these intricate walls 4 feet long and 5 feet high for a
princess and prince. Today the structures rise above the water
like a masterwork of engineering. Mullet are raised in the fish
pond as they were in ancient times.

Return to Nawiliwili, take a left on Nawiliwili Road (Route 58),
㉕ and begin to look on your right for **Grove Farm Homestead.** One
of Kauai's oldest plantation estates, it was founded in 1864
by George Wilcox; today it offers a look at 19th-century life on
Kauai. On the 80 acres comprising this living museum are the
original family mansion (filled with turn-of-the-century memorabilia), workers' quarters, and elaborate gardens of tropical
flowers and tall palm trees. *Box 1631, Nawiliwili Rd., Lihue
96766, tel. 808/245–3202. Admission: $3. Guided 2-hour tours
are available Mon., Wed., and Thurs. at 10 AM and 1 PM. Advance reservations required.*

At the intersection of Nawiliwili Road and Highway 50 turn
left and head west on Highway 50. Two miles farther, turn
㉖ right at the entrance to **Kilohana.** Dating from 1935, this is the
site of the old Wilcox sugar plantation, which has been transformed into a 35-acre visitor attraction. There are agricultural
exhibits, local arts and crafts, horse and carriage rides, specialty shops, and a pleasant restaurant called Gaylord's in the
back courtyard. The estate is a beautiful showpiece from plantation days. *3–2087 Kaumualii Hwy., Lihue 96766, tel. 808/
245–5608. Admission free. Open daily 9–5.*

Continue west on Highway 50, past the majestic slopes of the
Hoary Head Mountains. On the top of the range is a formation called **Queen Victoria's Profile,** indicated by a Hawaiian-
warrior marker. Some folks see a resemblance between the
monarch and the mountain.

When you get to the intersection of Highways 50 and 52, you
have reached **Koloa Gap,** which is the natural pass between Mt.
Waialeale on your right and the Hoary Heads on your left. Turn
㉗ left on Highway 52 (Maluhia Rd.), also called the **Tunnel of
Trees** because of the long stretch of protective eucalyptus trees
on either side of the road. For many months after the hurri-

cane, they formed less of a tunnel than usual as their branches recuperated from damaging winds, but thanks to Kauai's tropical climate, they are gradually returning to their full beauty.

28 Highway 52 takes you to **Koloa,** site of Kauai's first sugar mill, dating back to 1835. You can see the remains of the mill on the right side of the road, where its old stone smokestack still stands. Adjacent to that is a sculpture depicting the various ethnic groups that made their mark on the sugar industry on Kauai. The main street of Koloa is lined with old buildings that have been beautifully restored to house expensive boutiques, an old general store, and a selection of restaurants.

Time Out Fourteen kinds of hot dogs, burgers made with such fresh fish as ono and mahimahi, and a big condiment bar make **Mustard's Last Stand** (corner of Hwy. 50 and Koloa Rd., Lawai, tel. 808/ 332–7245) an appropriate snack-time stop while you're touring the south of the island. The place also serves Lappert's Ice Cream, which is made in the Islands and features plenty of gourmet flavors. After you eat, why not play a round on the miniature golf course?

Head south on Highway 52, which now is also called Poipu Road. At the fork, stay to the left. Look for a sign on the right
29 to **Kiahuna Plantation Resort and Gardens,** which was damaged by the hurricane but which was scheduled to reopen by the end of 1993. The estate is known for its Hawaiian orchids, African aloes, lava-rock pools, and 4,000 varieties of plants, which has earned it a listing in the book *Great Gardens of America.* You can also visit a Hawaiian garden and learn how herbs and plants were used by early settlers. *2253 Poipu Rd., Poipu 96756, tel. 808/742–6411. Admission free. Open daily 9–6, with a 40-minute tour at 10.*

Poipu Road runs into Hoowili Road, which takes you through
30 the heart of sunny **Poipu,** the major resort of Kauai's south shore. The boogey-boarding and swimming at some of these beaches is spectacular, although you need to look out for occasional patches of coral, which can make a nasty cut on the foot when stepped on.

31 On the makai (ocean) side of the road is **Poipu Beach Park,** where you can park the car and look for the petroglyphs on sandstone ledges at the far end of the beach. Here, too, is **Brennecke's Beach,** well-known for its bodysurfing action. If you follow Poipu Road to the end, it becomes a cane road. Turn right on the first well-traveled byway and you'll find **Shipwreck's Beach.** Around the point is an even quieter stretch of sand called **Mahaulepu** (*see* Beaches, *below*). On Poipu Road, head back to the fork and turn left on Lawai Road. This takes you past **Prince Kuhio Park,** honoring the birthplace of one of Hawaii's most beloved congressmen.

32 At the end of this road is **Spouting Horn,** a waterspout that shoots up out of an ancient lava tube like Old Faithful. Be sure to follow the paved walkways around this area, because the rocks are slippery and people have been known to fall in. You will encounter a group of souvenir vendors along this walkway. Their wares are basically second-rate, so pass them by.

Time Out On your way back through Koloa, pull up to an open-air establishment called **Koloa Broiler** (Old Koloa Rd., Koloa, tel. 808/

742–9122), where you can help yourself to the best *mai tai* on the island. The left side of the restaurant is the bar, a rustic wood-paneled room. Sit by one of the huge open windows if you can, and watch the world go by as you recap the day's events. The dining room is on the right when you're ready for dinner.

Tour 3: The Western Route and Kokee

The west side of the island offers a look at the sleepiest, as well as the most dramatic, sections of Kauai. Begin this tour by heading west on Highway 50 out of Lihue. The first town you come to is called **Lawai,** once the home of the Kauai Pineapple Cannery. Although that operation has long since closed its doors, Lawai has become a prolific producer of tropical fruits and plants.

A good example of Lawai's green thumb can be found by turning left on Hailima Road, which takes you to the **National Tropical Botanical Gardens,** a 186-acre scientific research center and estate property for botany and horticulture. The visitor center presents a showcase of 2,600 different plant species. There's a gift shop, too. *Box 340, Hailima Rd., Lawai 96765, tel. 808/332–7361. Admission: $15. Open daily. An escorted 2½-hour, 2-mile narrated shuttle and walking tour is offered daily at 9 and 1. Advance reservations required.*

The next town along Highway 50 is **Kalaheo,** which means "proud day." Proud it should be, for it features one of Kauai's most scenic park areas. To see it, turn left on Papalina Road, which climbs to **Kukuiolono Park.** Translated "light of the god Lono," Kukuiolono offers serene Japanese gardens, an exhibit of old Hawaii, and spectacular panoramic views, which make this an ideal picnic spot. There is also a golf course spread across a 9-acre expanse (*see* Sports, *below*). *Admission to park free. Open 6–6.*

Time Out **Lawai Restaurant** (2–3687 Kaumualii Hwy., Kalaheo, tel. 808/ 332–9550) is a slice of Kauai life if ever there was one. Lawai serves an eclectic variety of home-cooked Chinese, American, and Hawaiian food, and it's all quite good. You can go local by ordering some noodle soup and shave ice (a snow cone) or take the oriental route with sweet and sour pork topped off with a fortune cookie. Either way, the prices here are very reasonable, and it's open daily for breakfast, lunch, and dinner to suit your sightseeing schedule.

Just past Kalaheo, look on your right for macadamia nut groves and a Hawaiian-warrior marker indicating **Olu Pua Gardens.** If you just can't get enough of beautiful plants, turn right and drive a half mile up the private road to find yet another of Kauai's fine botanical showcases. Encompassing 12 acres, Olu Pua (which means "floral serenity" in Hawaiian) is a 1931 plantation estate. You can wander down shaded paths and enjoy the exotic flowers and plants, plus views of a pond shaped like a hibiscus blossom. *Hwy. 50, Kalaheo, tel. 808/332–8182. Admission: $10 adults, $5 children under 12. Open daily 8:30–5. Closed Christmas and New Year's Day. Guided 1-hour tours at 9:30, 11:30, and 1:30.*

Continue along Highway 50 and soon, to your right, you will
36 see a Hawaiian-warrior marker indicating the **Hanapepe Valley
and Canyon Lookout.** This dramatic divide once housed a thriv-
ing Hawaiian community, and some of its taro patches are still
in existence here. Hanapepe is a historic canyon, for it is the
site of Kauai's last battle, led in 1824 by Humehume, the son of
Kauai's King Kaumualii.

On your right you'll see an old-fashioned sign welcoming you to
37 **Hanapepe,** dubbed by some "the Biggest Little Town on Kauai." As you come down the hill, take a right on Hanapepe Road
to see the street that was used in the filming of the television
miniseries *The Thorn Birds.* Hanapepe is a quiet farming town
that supplies Kauai with much of its produce.

On the west end of Hanapepe, turn makai (toward the ocean) on
38 Lele Road and follow it to the **Salt Pond Beach Park.** Here you
can see how the Hawaiians have made salt for almost 200 years.
They let the sun evaporate the sea water in mudlined drying
beds, which leaves only the salt. This is also a safe area for
swimming (*see* Beaches, *below*).

Near the ponds is **Burns Fields,** Kauai's first airfield and now
the base of operation of several helicopter companies. Before
you return to Highway 50, you might want to explore this
coastal area just a bit more to see **Port Allen Harbor,** the shipping center for the west side of Kauai and the headquarters of
the McBryde Sugar Company. You'll pass the humble Eleele
Shopping Center, which was Kauai's first "modern" shopping
center when it was built.

Return to Highway 50 and look on the makai side of the road for
39 the Hawaiian-warrior marker to **Fort Elizabeth.** What's left of
this stone fort, built in 1816 by an agent of the Imperial Russian
government named Anton Scheffer, recalls the days when
Scheffer tried to conquer the island for his homeland. King
Kaumualii eventually chased the foreigner off the island.

Cross the Waimea River Bridge and take your first right on
Menehune Road, which leads you 2½ miles up the Waimea
40 Valley to **Menehune Ditch.** Archaeologists claim that this aque-
duct was built before the first Hawaiians lived on Kauai, and it
is therefore attributed to the industrious hands of the tiny
menehune. The way the flanged and fitted cut-stone bricks
are stacked and assembled indicates a knowledge of construction that is foreign to Hawaii, and the ditch is inscribed with
mysterious markings. Until someone comes up with a better
suggestion, the menehune once again take credit for this
engineering feat.

41 Next, enter **Waimea** and enjoy a look at the town that first welcomed Captain James Cook to the Sandwich Islands in 1778. An
easy-to-miss monument on the mauka (mountain) side of the
road commemorates his landmark arrival. Waimea was also the
place where Kauai's King Kaumualii ceded his island to the uni-
fying efforts of King Kamehameha.

Waimea played host to the first missionaries on the island, and
if you take a right on Makeke Road you can see their old
Waimea Christian Hawaiian and Foreign Church. Constructed
in 1846, the church was made of huge timbers, which were
brought down from the mountains 8 miles away, as well as lime-

stone blocks from a nearby quarry. Sadly, the church suffered severe damage from Hurricane Iniki, and it may not be rebuilt.

Highway 50 next passes through the sugar town of **Kekaha**, beyond which lies Mana Drag Strip, an extremely straight shoreside road that runs through acres of cane fields. Eventually it passes the **Pacific Missile Range Facility**, an underwater test range for the Navy's antisubmarine-warfare training and weapons firing.

Turn left at the Hawaiian-warrior marker that points you to a dirt road through more sugarcane fields. It dead-ends at **Polihale State Park**, a long and beautiful stretch of unspoiled beach flanked by enormous sea cliffs. There are rest rooms, picnic pavilions, and showers here (*see* Beaches, *below*).

As you return to civilization, you have two choices for visiting **Waimea Canyon**, the "Grand Canyon of the Pacific." From Kekaha, Kokee Road (Highway 55) makes a steep climb, with immediate views of the town and ocean below. The road up from Waimea, Waimea Canyon Drive, is narrower and in worse condition. A few miles up, the roads intersect, and you continue to climb past spectacular panoramas of the canyon, which is 3,600 feet deep, 2 miles wide, and 10 miles long. Created by an ancient fault in the Earth's crust, it has been eroding over the centuries due to weather, rivers, and streams. Its deep reds, greens, and browns are ever-changing in the light. Be sure to stop at the **Puu Ka Pele** and **Puu Hina Hina** lookouts for the most appealing views.

As the road rises to 4,000 feet, it passes through **Kokee State Park**. Here the air is cool and crisp, and the vegetation turns to evergreens and ferns. This 4,345-acre wilderness park is full of wild fruit, heady flowers, and the colorful rare birds that make their home in these forests. A 45-mile network of hiking trails takes you to some of Kauai's most remote places. Before you set off, ask first about trail closures. A few paths were still off-limits at press time due to hurricane damage. *Contact the Division of State Parks, Box 1671, Lihue 96766, tel. 808/335–5871.*

Time Out Treat yourself to a cup of coffee or a cocktail at **Kokee Lodge** (Waimea Canyon Dr., Kokee State Park, tel. 808/335–6061), a homespun mountaintop inn. Since the temperature can be nippy outside, the fireplace inside is almost always going. Afterward, peruse the gift shop, which carries T-shirts, postcards, and lots of Kokee memorabilia.

The road out of Kokee State Park leads you past the **NASA Tracking Station**, where a roomful of computers kept track of the various goings-on in the wild blue yonder from 1960 through the '80s. This station shut down its operations for good a few years ago due to the deployment of a $100-million satellite by the space shuttle *Discovery*.

Waimea Canyon Drive ends 4 miles above the park at the **Kalalau Lookout**, 4,120 feet above sea level. This is the beginning of a beautiful hiking trail. On a clear day at the lookout, you can gaze right down into the gaping valley, with its elegant ridges and waterfalls; if you look closely you can just barely see the shining sands of Kalalau Beach, like a tiny golden thread against the vast blue Pacific.

Tour 4: A Short Excursion to Niihau

Once it was called the Forbidden Isle. Now it takes only 12 minutes to fly from Kauai to **Niihau,** an island that few outsiders have set foot on since Elizabeth Sinclair bought it from King Kamehameha V in 1864. This 72-square-mile island just 17 miles from Kauai is now run by the Robinson family, which raises cattle and sheep on the barren, arid land. The Robinsons continue to preserve Niihau as a last refuge of primitive Hawaii. Residents of the island speak Hawaiian and do not use electricity, plumbing, or telephones; they ride bikes and horses to get around.

Bruce Robinson initiated Niihau Helicopters in 1987 in order to boost the struggling island economy. Tours avoid the western coastline, where Puuwai village—home to the island's 200 residents—is located. Flights depart from and return to Kauai's Burns Airfield near Hanapepe and are conducted in an air-conditioned Agusta 109 twin-engine, 7-passenger, single-pilot helicopter. The first touchdown on the two-stop tour is near the sunken crater of Lehua. The second takes you to a cliff overlooking the beach coves of Keanahaki Bay. It's the perfect tour for those with a yen to explore untrammeled territory. *Niihau Helicopters, Box 370, Makaweli 96769, tel. 808/335–3500. Cost: 3-hour tour with 2 stops, $200. Maximum of 4 flights per day, Mon.–Fri. No ground transportation available. Advance reservations required.*

Kauai for Free

Coconut Plantation Hula Show. In and around its 70 shops and restaurants, Coconut Plantation Market Place hosts a variety of free Hawaiiana demonstrations throughout the day, including songs and dances, lei making, and quilting. Its best-known freebie is the hula show on center stage. *4–484 Kuhio Hwy., Kapaa, tel. 808/822–3641. Mon., Wed., Fri., Sat. at 4:30.*

Guava Kai Plantation. The world's largest commercial guava orchard took a beating from Hurricane Iniki, but it was expected to be back to normal by 1994. Hundreds of acres of the pretty trees are on view. There's a self-guided tour, a video presentation, and samples of products at the Guava Kai Store. *End of Kuawa Rd., Box 693, Kilauea, tel. 808/828–1925. Open daily 9–5.*

Hilo Hattie Fashion Factory Tour. Hawaii's garment industry is booming, and Kauai is keeping in step with the other islands by presenting factory tours of this top fashion company. Here you can see how they make those colorful aloha shirts, muumuus, and other tropical togs. Aloha wear is on sale for the entire family, at factory-outlet values. Free alterations are available while you wait. *3252 Kuhio Hwy., Lihue, tel. 808/245–4724. Open daily 8:30–5. Free hotel pickup in Lihue and Coconut Plantation areas daily at 9, 11, 1, and 3. From Poipu, call for information.*

Kilauea Lighthouse and Wildlife Refuge. *See* Tour 1, *above.*

Kilohana. *See* Tour 2, *above.*

Kokee Natural History Museum. Next door to the Kokee Lodge, this one-room museum presents intriguing displays about the natural wildlife of Waimea Canyon. Here you can learn about the rare birds and plants that are indigenous to the area. The museum also has maps, old photographs, petroglyph rubbings, artifacts, posters, souvenirs, and postcards. *Kokee Rd., Kokee, tel. 808/335–9975. Open daily 9–5.*

Waioli Mission. *See* Tour 1, *above.*

What to See and Do with Children

Kamokila. *See* Tour 1, *above.*

Smith's Tropical Paradise. Right next to Wailua Marina on the east side of the island, Smith's Tropical Paradise is 30 acres of family fun, with orchards, jungle paths, exotic foliage, tropical birds, ethnic village settings, tranquil lagoons, and a tram tour every hour. A luau banquet and live show are offered each evening from 5 to 9. *174 Wailua Rd., Kapaa 96746, tel. 808/822–4654. Admission: $5 adults, $2.50 children under 11. Tram tour: $9 adults, $4.50 children. Luau and show: $43.75 adults, $26 children. Open daily 8:30–4. A free shuttle runs from Wailua. Reservations required for the luau, shuttle, and show.*

Snorkeling with Blue Water Sailing. A fun excursion for all ages, this four-hour snorkeling sail off the southern shores of Kauai includes gear, instruction, swimming, fishing, a gourmet picnic lunch, snacks, and beverages. During the winter season, you might catch glimpses of whales. Your craft is the 12-passenger, 42-foot luxury Pearson sailing yacht the *Lady Leanne II. Box 250, Eleele 96705, tel. 808/822–0525. Cost: $75 adults, $45 children 3–12; full day: $115 adults, $75 children.*

Off the Beaten Track

Kauai By Design. In response to a growing interest in ecotourism among travelers, the Hyatt Regency Kauai provides guests with a choice of environmentally oriented tours presented by rangers, historians, and other island authorities. These tours have been designed for their low impact on the surroundings. Included are hikes to waterfalls, marine-awareness scuba dives, and bicycle excursions to little-known beaches. *Hyatt Regency Kauai, 1571 Poipu Rd., Koloa 96756, tel. 808/742–1234. Prices start at $75 adults, $55 children.*

Kauai Lagoons Visitor Center. You don't need to be a guest of this Nawiliwili Resort to enjoy its unusual tours by land and water. A hand-crafted mahogany launch ferries people through 40 acres of lagoons, past Kauai's only moated zoo, whose islands hold exotic wildlife from around the world. You can also take an outrigger canoe tour or see the 800-acre resort grounds from a 19th-century–style horse and buggy. *Kauai Lagoons Resort, Nawiliwili, tel. 808/245–5050.*

Kauai Mountain Tours. You'll get *way* off the beaten track on this four-wheel-drive excursion through Na Pali-Kona Forest Preserve and the rugged side of Waimea Canyon. *Box 3069, Lihue 96766, tel. 800/452–1113. Cost with Continental breakfast, picnic lunch, and hotel pick-up included: $75 adults, $55 children.*

Niihau Safaris. This recreational tour takes you to a 72-square-mile island that most people never see. Run by the same family that operates Niihau Helicopters (*see* Tour 4, *above*), Niihau Safaris was created to decrease the island's overpopulation of feral pigs and sheep. Hunters are flown from Kauai to Niihau by helicopter, departing early in the morning, hunting at two spots far from civilization, and returning in the evening. Rough terrain and scrub vegetation make this a tough shoot, but a world record for boars taken by rifle has been set on Niihau. *Box 370, Makaweli 96769, tel. 808/335-3500. Cost: $1,200 plus a trophy fee if a record-quality animal is taken. Hunters must have a Hawaii hunting license (see Sports, below).*

Shopping

Kauai certainly doesn't have the myriad shopping alternatives of its cosmopolitan neighbor, Oahu. What the Garden Isle does have, however, is character. Along with a few major shopping malls, Kauai features some of the most delightful mom-and-pop shops and family-run boutiques imaginable.

Kauai also offers one-of-a-kind options for souvenirs, things you'd be better off buying here than on Oahu. For instance, the famous shell jewelry from Niihau is sometimes sold on Kauai for less than it is on other islands, due to the proximity of Kauai to Niihau.

Kauai is also known for its occasional outdoor markets, where you will find bargain prices on various souvenirs and produce and get a chance to mingle with island residents.

Some stores may still be rebuilding from the hurricane, but they'll do their best to help you find what you're after.

Kauai's major shopping centers are open daily from 9 or 10 to 5, although some stay open until 9. Stores are basically clustered around the major resort areas and Lihue.

Shopping Centers

One of Kauai's newer shopping centers is called **Kauai Village** (4–831 Kuhio Hwy., Kapaa, tel. 808/822–4904), whose architecture re-creates the style of 19th-century plantation towns. Its **ABC Store** (tel. 808/822–2115) sells sundries, **Safeway** (tel. 808/822–2464) sells groceries, and **Wyland Gallery** (tel. 808/822–9855) sells an array of island art.

Kauai's largest assemblage of shops is **Kukui Grove Center** (3-2600 Kaumualii Hwy.; tel. 808/245-7784 for free shuttle service), on Highway 50, just west of Lihue. Besides the island's major department stores, it offers a **Long's Drugs** (tel. 808/245–7771) for personal needs and **Star Market** (tel. 808/245–7777) for groceries. You'll find island-inspired garb at **Home Fashions Kauai** (tel. 808/245–2926), Hawaiian heirloom jewelry at **Capricorn Fine Gems** (tel. 808/245–6233), and sundries at **Woolworth** (tel. 808/245–7702).

South of Lihue in Nawiliwili, **Kauai Lagoons Shopping Village** (Westin Kauai, Kalapaki Beach, tel. 808/245–5050) has such boutiques as **Louis Vuitton** (tel. 808/245–7025), home of designer handbags and luggage.

West of Lihue in Puhi, **Kilohana Plantation** (3-2087 Kaumualii Hwy.) offers a unique collection of plantation-style shops, most of which anticipated a 1993 reopening after Iniki. Its **Cane Field Clothing Co.** (tel. 808/245–5020) features cool island fashions, including hand-painted batik. **Sea Reflections** (tel. 808/

245–5210) is a fantasy gift shop, while **Stones at Kilohana** (tel. 808/245–6684) sells artwork collected from craftspeople around the South Pacific.

On the east coast of the island is **Waipouli Town Center** (4-901 Kuhio Hwy.) in Kapaa, a modest assemblage of 10 shops where you can buy a T-shirt at **Waipouli Variety** (tel. 808/822–1014), and then grab a sandwich at **Waipouli Delicatessen** (tel. 808/ 822-9311). Nearby in Waipouli you'll find the **Coconut Plantation Market Place** (4-484 Kuhio Hwy., tel. 808/822–3641), part of a larger complex of resort hotels and restaurants.

On Kuhio Highway in Kapaa is **Kinipopo Shopping Village** (4-356 Kuhio Hwy.), which has created a tropical garden setting for casual shopping. Here you'll find **The Goldsmith's Gallery** (tel. 808/822–4653), featuring handcrafted Hawaiian-style gold jewelry.

Princeville Center (5-4280 Kuhio Hwy., Princeville, tel. 808/ 826–3320) is an upscale little gathering of such trendy shops as **Kauai Kite and Hobby Shop** (tel. 808/826–9144) and such restaurants as **Pizza Burger** (tel. 808/826–6070). Less fancy and more laid-back, **Ching Young Village** (tel. 808/826–7222) in Hanalei draws people to its **Village Variety Store** (tel. 808/826– 6077), with cheap prices on beach towels, macadamia nuts, film and processing, wet suits, you name it.

Heading south, shoppers encounter old **Koloa.** It's not exactly a shopping center, but its main street, Old Koloa Road, concentrates several boutiques and eateries in one handy location. Favorites include **Koloa Ice House** (tel. 808/742–6063), which sells shave ice fantasies laced with tropical syrups, and **Progressive Expressions** (tel. 808/742–6041), which offers surfing and windsurfing accessories, swimwear, and beachwear. Farther south, in Poipu, is the **Poipu Shopping Village** (2360 Kiahuna Plantation Dr., tel. 808/246–0634), which features pricey stores worthy of a window-shopping excursion.

To the west of Kauai is a scattering of stores, including those at the no-frills **Eleele Shopping Center** on Highway 50 near Hanapepe. Waimea is proud of its relatively new **Waimea Canyon Plaza** on Highway 50, which opened in 1988 and includes gift shops, fashion stores, and other family-run businesses.

Department Stores

As is true on the other major Hawaiian Islands, the primary department stores on Kauai are **Sears** (tel. 808/245–3325), **JC Penney** (tel. 808/245–5966), **F. W. Woolworth** (tel. 808/245–7702), and **Liberty House** (tel. 808/245–7751). You can find all of them at **Kukui Grove Center** in Lihue.

Aloha Wear

Hilo Hattie Fashion Factory (tel. 808/245–3404) is the big name in aloha wear throughout the isles, and it creates more than 10,000 different types of garments. You can visit the factory, 1 mile from Lihue Airport, to pick up floral duds at good savings. With three stores in Poipu, Lawai, and Waipouli, **Tropical Shirts** (Coconut Plantation Market Place, tel. 808/822–0203) captures the beauty of Kauai with clothing that has been embroidered or hand-screened by local artists. For colorful aloha togs for tots, try **Traders** (tel. 808/742–7224), located at the Poipu Shopping Village. Kapaa's **Art to Wear** (1435 Kuhio Hwy., tel. 808/822–1125) offers hand-painted, hand-sewn originals decorated with flowers, seascapes, and animal motifs. At Coconut Plantation Market Place, **Tahiti Imports** (tel. 808/822–9342) carries the Polynesian *pareu*, a multicolored wraparound that can be tied in dozens of different ways to suit the occasion.

Books

Several fine books have been written about Kauai, and many more about Hawaii. **Waldenbooks** (tel. 808/245–7162) at Kukui Grove Center presents the island's broadest assortment of reading materials.

Clothing

Liberty House (tel. 808/245–7751) in Kukui Grove Center carries high-quality designer labels as well as nice resort wear. Also at Kukui Grove, **Sears** (tel. 808/245–3325) features reliably handsome men's and women's clothing in mainland designs and some tropical stylings. In East Kauai, **Reyn's** (tel. 808/822–7800) at Coconut Plantation Market Place provides traditional sportswear and classic clothing for men, plus dresses, blouses, slacks, and shorts for women. **M. Miura Store** (4-1419 Kuhio Hwy., Kapaa, tel. 808/822–4401) has a great assortment of clothes for the outdoor fanatic, including tank tops, visors, swimwear, and Kauai-style T-shirts. **Crazy Shirts** (Poipu Shopping Village, tel. 808/742–9000; Anchor Cove, tel. 808/245–7073; Koloa, tel. 808/742–7161; Coconut Marketplace, tel. 808/822–3101) has a wide variety of shirts, from classy to crazy designs. It's a good place for active wear.

Food

Kauai has its own yummy specialties that you won't be able to resist while on the island. Kauai Kookies, taro chips, Kauai boiled peanuts, salad dressings, and jams and jellies from locally grown fruit make delicious gifts to take back home. For ideas, call the **Kauai Products Council** (tel. 808/246–0232).

Near Lihue, you can buy fresh pineapple, sugarcane, ginger, coconuts, local jams, jellies, and honey, plus Kauai-grown papayas, bananas, and mangos in season—all at **Lady Jane's Tropical Products** (3-4684 Kuhio Hwy., tel. 808/245–1814). Special gift packs are available, inspected and certified. At Coconut Plantation Marketplace, the **Nut Cracker Sweet** (tel. 808/822–4811) has a delicious assortment of chocolates, like macadamia clusters.

Macadamia nuts are a must-buy present for friends back home. Some of the best prices are available at **Star Market** (tel. 808/245–7777) in the Kukui Grove Center (*see* Tour 3 in Exploring, *above*). Don't forget to try a big scoop of **Lappert's Ice Cream,** invented by Walter Lappert in Hanapepe in 1983 and now a favorite all over Hawaii. You'll find it just about anywhere you go on Kauai.

Flowers

Flowers Forever (Princeville Center, Princeville, tel. 808/826–7420) can help you ship leis, corsages, and flower arrangements back home, as well as take care of the agricultural inspection.

Shimonishi Orchids (3567 Hanapepe Rd., Hanapepe, tel. 808/335–5562) has a delightful selection of orchids.

Gifts

Eelskin is a popular item in the Islands, and you can buy it wholesale at **Lee Sands' Eelskin** (tel. 808/332–7404) at the intersection of Highway 50 and Koloa Road in Lawai. This unusual store includes such skin lines as sea snake, chicken feet, and frog skin. A lizard card case is available for about $10.

How about a fun beach towel for the folks back home? That's just one of the gifts you can find in the **Village Variety Store** (Ching Young Village, Hanalei, tel. 808/826–6077). It also has eelskin gifts, shell leis, Kauai T-shirts, macadamia nuts, and other great island memorabilia at low prices.

Hawaiian Crafts

Kapaia Stitchery (Kuhio Hwy., tel. 808/245–2281), a red store just north of Lihue, features quilting and other fabric arts, plus kits for trying your own hand at various crafts. Kauai artist Peter Kinney specializes in scrimshaw pocket and army knives, available at **Ye Olde Ship Store & Port of Kauai** (tel. 808/822–1401) in Coconut Plantation Market Place.

Jewelry

At the Outrigger Kauai Beach Hotel (4331 Kauai Beach Dr.) in Hanamaulu, **Remember Kauai** (tel. 808/245–6650) offers mementos of your trip in the form of fashion jewelry. There's a branch in Kapaa as well (4–734 Kuhio Hwy., tel. 808/822–0161). **Kauai Gold** (tel. 808/822–9361) at the Coconut Plantation Market Place presents a wonderful selection of rare Niihau shell leis, strung by women from the Forbidden Isle and ranging from $20 to $200. The store also has a selection of 14K gold jewelry. In Kapaa, **Jim Saylor Jewelers** (1318 Kuhio Hwy., tel. 808/822–3591) showcases a good selection of gems from around the world, with black pearls, diamonds, and unique settings. Its pretty keepsakes are designed right on the premises. **Jen's Jewelry and Gift Shop** (Ching Young Village Shopping Ctr., tel. 808/826–2588) sells fine jade and coral jewelry. Factory-direct pieces are discounted by 20%.

Local Art

Kauai's natural beauty has served as the inspiration for many of Hawaii's best artists, and a painting or sculpture by a local creator can be a very special keepsake indeed. You can purchase the works of many local artists—including seascapes by George Summer and Roy Tabora—at **Kahn Galleries** (tel. 808/822–4277 at the Coconut Plantation; tel. 808/245–5397 in the Anchor Cove Shopping Center). Then there's **The Art Shop** (3196 Akahi St., tel. 808/245–3810) in Lihue, an intimate gallery that sells original oils, photos, and sculptures.

Kauai Images Gallery (937 Kuhio Hwy., tel. 808/822–1950), in Kapaa features original artwork by many of Hawaii's finest artists. Among the treats are hand-painted photographs by Diane Ferry, whose work has won numerous awards in Kauai art shows. Kauai Images also offers a large variety of quality frames, some in the rare and highly prized island wood.

Wyland Galleries (Kauai Village, 4-831 Kuhio Hwy., Kapaa, tel. 808/822–9855) showcases the work of Wyland, a famed artist of marine life. You can buy his original works, lithographs, prints, and sculptures, plus pieces by other island artists.

Beaches

Of all the Hawaiian Islands, Kauai has had the most time to develop—and perfect—its beaches. The Garden Isle is embraced by stretches of magnificent ivory sands, many with breathtaking mountain backdrops. Perhaps Hurricane Iniki's most unexpected effect on Kauai was that it beautified the island's beaches beyond their former glory. The churning waters brought up cleaner sand, making many of Kauai's beaches wider and more inviting than ever.

The south shore is known for its enduring sunshine, which has made beaching in Poipu a popular activity. Here, too, has been some of the island's best swimming, snorkeling, and bodysurfing in waters that are generally safe year-round, although the surf is a bit bigger in the summer. However, Poipu Beach sustained heavy damage from the hurricane, and it remained unclear at press time just how long it would take to restore it.

The north shore is a different story altogether. While some of Kauai's most scenic beaches can be found here, they are treacherous during the winter months. In the summer, however, they are safe for swimming. No matter what time of year it is, be sure to exercise caution, because only a few of these beaches have lifeguards.

The beaches that front the hotels and condominiums along the eastern shore are conducive to seaside strolling but less favorable for swimming. The strong surf and rip currents of the winter months are unpredictable, and it's often quite windy.

If you want beaches with plenty of peace and quiet, drive to the west coast beyond Kekaha. This is where the locals often go to fish and swim, and you'll catch the best sunsets from this vantage point.

The list of beaches below starts from the eastern shore and goes clockwise around the island.

The waters that hug the island are clean, clear, and inviting, but be careful to go in only where it's safe. All of the beaches on Kauai are free, and none has a phone number. For information about beaches around the island, call the **County Department of Parks and Recreation** (tel. 808/245–8821) and the **State Department of Land and Natural Resources** (tel. 808/241–3444).

Lydgate State Park. Depending on the wind, this beach can be a good place for family picnicking and swimming. Any time of year, it's a nice place for beachcombing and reflecting on the days when this was a Hawaiian city of refuge. Rest rooms and showers are available. *In Wailua, on Hwy. 56.*

Kalapaki Beach. This sheltered bay is ideal for swimming, sunning, surfing, and beginning windsurfing in the small waves. It fronts the Westin Kauai, and there are rest rooms, lifeguards, and showers. *In Nawiliwili off Wapaa Rd., which runs east out of Lihue.*

Poipu Beach Park. Once a prime bodysurfing and sunbathing spot, Poipu Beach lost its sand and part of its parking area to Hurricane Iniki. What shape it will be in by 1994 was not known at press time. *On Poipu Rd. on the south shore.*

Brennecke's Beach. A steady stream of small- to medium-size waves makes this a bodysurfer's heaven. The waves are bigger here in the summer than in the winter months. Showers, rest rooms, and lifeguards are on hand, and there are several carry-out-food stands across the street. *On Poipu Rd. on the south shore.*

Kekaha Beach Park. Stretching along the south shore for many miles is this strip of sand recalling the long beaches of California. The latest sport here is dune buggying. If you don't like the noise of those vehicles, stay away. There are no lifeguards, rest rooms, or showers. *Along Hwy. 50 west of Kekaha.*

Salt Pond Beach Park. The waters here are particularly safe for swimming, so this is a real family spot. There are picnic tables, showers, and rest rooms. *Take Lele Rd. makai (toward the ocean) off Hwy. 50 in Hanapepe.*

Polihale Beach Park. This is a magnificent stretch of sand, many miles long, flanked by impressive sea cliffs. Swim here only when the surf is small. Locals dune buggy here on the weekends. Polihale has no lifeguards, but there are showers, rest rooms, and picnic pavilions. *Drive to the end of Hwy. 50 and turn left at the Hawaiian-warrior marker. This takes you several bumpy miles on a dirt road through sugarcane fields.*

Hanakapiai Beach. This crescent of beach changes length and width throughout the year as fierce winter waves rob the shoreline of sand and summer's calm returns it. Be very careful swimming here in the summer, and don't even think of going in during the winter swells. There's a beautiful freshwater stream here, too. *At mi 2 of the Kalalau Trail, which begins at Ke'e State Park, at the northern end of Hwy. 56.*

Haena State Park. This is a good beach for swimming when the surf is down, which means summertime. There are rest rooms, showers, and snack vans. *On the north shore near the end of Hwy. 56.*

Ke'e Beach. In the summer months, this is a fine swimming beach. In the winter, stay out of the water and enjoy the views of the Na Pali Coast. This is where the Kalalau Trail begins. Extensive facilities are available, including showers and rest rooms. *At the northern end of Hwy. 56.*

Lumahai Beach. Here's a beach known for its striking natural beauty, flanked by high mountains and lava rocks. In the movie *South Pacific*, this is where Mitzi Gaynor sang, "I'm Gonna Wash That Man Right Outa My Hair." The swimming here is good only in the summer. There are no lifeguards, showers, or rest rooms. *On the winding section of Hwy. 56 west of Hanalei.*

Park on the ocean side of the road and walk down a steep path to the beach.

Tunnels Beach. Tunnels offers one of Kauai's best-protected beaches for swimming and snorkeling. On the downside, there are no lifeguards, showers, or rest rooms. *Halfway between the 36- and 37-mi markers on Hwy. 56. Turn toward the ocean on a dirt road that runs through a grove of trees.*

Hanalei Beach Park. With views of the Pali coast and shady trees over picnic tables, this is a beach bum's heaven. However, swimming here can be treacherous. Stay near the old pier, where the water is a bit calmer. Rest rooms and showers are available. *In Hanalei, turn toward the ocean at Aku Rd. and right at the dead-end.*

Anini Beach. On the north shore, this is a good place for beginning windsurfers, snorkelers, and swimmers. There are public rest rooms, showers, and picnic tables. *Turn makai (toward the ocean) onto Kalihiwai Rd. on the Hanalei side of Kalihiwai Bridge.*

Anahola Beach Park. This is a quiet stretch of sand on the east shore whose calm waters are good for swimming and snorkeling. The Makalena Mountains are your backdrop here. There are rest rooms and showers. *Hwy. 56 heading north, between Anahola and Kilauea.*

Sports and the Outdoors

Participant Sports

Bicycling **Kauai Downhill** offers group rides down the Waimea Canyon rim. Rides begin at sunrise, with breakfast at the top. *Box 3322, Lihue 96766, tel. 800/234–1774. Cost: $60, including transportation to and from Lihue.*

Golf The Garden Isle has sprouted a healthy crop of golf courses, some with spectacular views. They weathered Hurricane Iniki remarkably well, and all were available for play by early 1993. Best-known is the **Princeville Resort Makai Course** (Box 3040, Princeville 96722, tel. 808/826–3580). Designed by Robert Trent Jones, Jr., it features a pro shop, a driving range, a practice area, lessons, club rental and storage, instruction, restaurants, a lounge, and a bar. Cost: $70 guests, $90 nonguests, including shared carts. The **Princeville Resort Prince Course** has expanded to 18 holes, and it costs $85 guests, $110 nonguests.

At the **Kukuiolono Golf Course** (Box 1031, Kalaheo 96741, tel. 808/332–9151) greens fees are $5 daily; carts are $5 for 9 holes and $10 for 18 holes. In the southern part of the island is the **Kiahuna Golf Club** (2545 Kiahuna Plantation Dr., Koloa 96756, tel. 808/742–9595). Robert Trent Jones, Jr., designed the 18-hole course, and there's a pro shop, rentals, a restaurant, and a bar. Greens fees with shared cart: $75 nonguests, $68 guests; $45 after 2 PM. To the east, **Wailua Municipal Golf Course** (3-5351 Kuhio Hwy., Wailua 96766, tel. 808/245–8092) sits next to the Wailua River and beach. Its 18 holes have hosted national tournaments, and there's a pro shop, a driving range, and a restaurant. Cost: $18 weekdays, $20 weekends.

Hiking While most of the popular trails have been cleared, the extent of Hurricane Iniki's damage to a few specific hiking trails was unknown at press time. Before planning your hike, contact the **Department of Land and Natural Resources** (State Parks Division, Box 1671, Lihue 96766, tel. 808/241–3444) for information on which trails are open. For your safety, bring plenty of water, never hike alone, stay on the trail, and avoid hiking when it's wet and slippery. All hiking trails on Kauai are free.

Kokee State Park is a glorious 45-mile network of hiking trails of varying difficulty, all worth the walk. Its acres of native forests withstood Iniki's fury and today they are a wonder to behold. The Kukui Trail takes hikers right down the side of Waimea Canyon. Awa'awapuhi Trail leads 4 miles down to a spectacular overlook into the canyons of the north shore. All hikers should register at Kokee Park headquarters (tel. 808/335–5871), which offers trail maps and information. *To reach the park, follow Waimea Canyon Rd. 20 mi to reach Kokee.*

Kauai's prize hiking venue is the **Kalalau Trail,** which begins at the northern end of Highway 56 and proceeds 11 miles to Kalalau Beach. With hairpin turns and constant ups and downs, this hike is a true test of endurance and can't be tackled round-trip in one day. For a good taste of it, hike just the first 2 miles to Hanakapiai Beach (*see* Beaches, *above*). For the best trail and weather conditions, hike Kalalau between May and September.

Horseback Riding Kauai's scenic south shore can be explored on escorted rides along panoramic oceanside cliffs and beaches. **CJM Stables** (1731 Kelaukia St., Koloa 96756, tel. 808/742–1392) charges $27 an hour, $47 for two hours. Its three-hour hidden valley beach breakfast ride is $65. Private rides are available on request.

To the north, **Pooku Stables** (Box 888, Hanalei 96714, tel. 808/826–6777) offers guided horseback tours into the less-explored reaches of the island. A one-hour valley ride is $27 per person; a two-hour shoreline-vista ride is $48 per person; a three-hour waterfall picnic ride is $75, including lunch.

Hunting If you want to hunt on Kauai, you need to visit during hunting season, which for game birds runs from November through mid-January. The schedule varies for other animals. You'll also need a license, so contact the **Division of Conservation and Resources Enforcement** (3060 Eiwa St., Lihue 96766, tel. 808/241–4444) for details. You can also hunt on Niihau (*see* Off the Beaten Track in Exploring, *above*).

Tennis Kauai offers 20 lighted public tennis courts and more than 70 private courts at the hotels. Six hard courts at **Coco Palms Resort** (4-241 Kuhio Hwy., Kapaa 96766, tel. 808/822–4921) are open to guests for $10, nonguests $12. The resort also has three clay courts. **Hanalei Bay Resort** (Box 220, Hanalei 96714, tel. 808/826–6522) has eight courts; cost: guests free, $30 per day nonguests. **Princeville Tennis Center** (Box 3040, Princeville 96722, tel. 808/826–9823) has six courts; cost: $7 per hour for guests, $9 nonguests. **Kauai Coconut Beach Resort** (Box 830, Kapaa 96746, tel. 808/822–3455) offers three courts; cost: $5 guests, $7 nonguests. **Stouffer Waiohai Beach Resort** (2249 Poipu Rd., Koloa 96756, tel. 808/742–9511) has six courts; cost: $8 guests, $15 nonguests.

Water Sports No matter which company you choose, plan to spend $125–$150
  Fishing for a full day of charter fishing on a shared basis, $85–$90 for a
half day on a shared basis, $600–$700 for an exclusive full day,
and $400–$450 for an exclusive half day. One reliable enterprise is **Alana Lynn Too Charters** (Box 137, Anahola 96703, tel.
808/245–7446), with a six-passenger, 33-foot Bertram boat.
Gent-Lee Fishing (Box 1691, Lihue 96766, tel. 808/245–7504)
has 32- and 36-foot, six-passenger custom sportfishers, and
Sportfishing Kauai (Box 1195, Koloa 96756, tel. 808/742–7013)
runs a 28-foot, six-passenger custom sportfisher. **Anini Fishing
Charters** (Box 594, Kilauea 96754, tel. 808/828–1285) features a
30-foot sportcruiser that carries up to six passengers.

For freshwater fishing, head for the bass- and trout-filled
streams near Kokee and Waimea Canyon. A 30-day freshwater
fishing license is necessary. You can obtain one from the **Department of Land and Natural Resources** (1151 Punchbowl St.,
Honolulu 96815, tel. 808/587–0777). A permit costs $3.75. **Bass
Guides of Kauai** (Lihue, tel. 808/826–2566) is one outfitter that
specializes in freshwater fishing trips.

  Kayaking **Kayak Kauai** takes you on guided, open-cockpit kayak tours up
the Hanalei River (*see* Guided Tours in Essential Information,
above).

Scuba Diving Kauai's spectacular reef formations suffered extensive damage
from the 1992 hurricane, and they were littered with debris,
according to the Department of Parks and Recreation. Still,
there are some dive sites worthy of exploration. The following
companies have scoped out the optimum options for visitors.
Dive Kauai (4–976 Kuhio Hwy., Kapaa 96746, tel. 808/822–
0452) offers an introductory half-day scuba excursion for $80.
One-tank shore dives for certified divers cost $80, a refresher
course is $65, and a five-day PADI (scuba-diving certification)
course is $395. If you want to go out on a boat dive with two
tanks, it costs $90, including equipment. Other companies offer
night dives for $55, and underwater videotaping can be ar-
ranged.

Similar packages are offered by **Fathom Five Divers** (Box 907,
Koloa 96756, tel. 808/742–6991), **Wet-N-Wonderful Ocean
Sports** (Box 910, Kapaa 96746, tel. 808/822–0211), and **Sea Sage
Diving Center** (4-1378 Kuhio Hwy., Kapaa 96746, tel. 800/659–
DIVE).

  Dive Sites **Cannon's Reef,** on the north shore, drops quickly from the
shoreline forming a long ledge permeated with lava tubes.
Plate coral is found here, and turtles are a common sight. You
may come across white tip shark sleeping in caverns or patrol-
ing the ledge. Depths range from 30 to 60 feet. Summer months
only.

General Store, at Kukuiula, is the site of a 19th-century shipwreck with five large anchors and chain. The horseshoe-shaped
ledge and two caverns teem with schools of lemon butterflyfish
that follow divers around. There are also green moray eels and
black coral under the ledges. Depths of 65 to 80 feet.

Sheraton Caverns, off Poipu, are formed by three immense, parallel lava tubes. There's a lobster nursery in one cavern, turtles
swim in all three, and the occasional white tip shark cruises by.
Depths of 35 to 60 feet.

Snorkeling The following experts operate snorkeling cruises to the reefs which were least damaged by Iniki. **Captain Andy's Sailing Adventures** (Box 1291, Koloa 96756, tel. 808/822–7833) takes up to 40 passengers on its 46-foot catamaran, the *Akialoa*. Rates for the four-hour morning "ultimate adventure" are $65 for adults, $50 for children under 12, including gear and lunch. Captain Andy's also features a two-hour sunset sail ($35 adults, $25 children) and presents whale watches during the winter months. Contact **Blue Water Sailing** (Box 250, Eleele 96705, tel. 808/822–0525), with comparable rates, for fun on a 12-passenger, 42-foot luxury Pearson sailing yacht. **Na Pali Coast Cruise Line** (4402 Waialo Rd., Eleele 96705, tel. 808/335–5078) has a six-hour snorkel and lunch cruise for $95.

Several companies depart from the north shore for snorkeling trips along the scenic Na Pali Coast. However, in recent years their fate has been uncertain due to questions raised by environmental groups. Call in advance to find out if the following boats are in operation. **Hanalei Sea Tours** (Box 1437, Hanalei 96714, tel. 800/733–7997) has a four-hour Na Pali snorkeling tour for $85. **Catamaran Kahanu** (Box 624, Kilauea, tel. 808/826–4596) has a similar package on its 36-foot power catamaran.

Windsurfing This sport is growing in popularity around the islands, and **Hanalei Surf** (Box 790, Hanalei 96714, tel. 808/826–9000) stands ready to help you get started. Hanalei Surf offers private lessons for $65 for 90 minutes and rentals for $45 per day. Six-hour certification course: $120.

Spectator Sports

Golf In recent years, the **Princeville Resort Makai Course** (Box 3040, Princeville 96722, tel. 808/826–3580) has been the setting for the LPGA Women's Kemper Open, including the Helene Curtis Pro-Am. **Kauai Lagoons** (Kalapaki Beach, Lihue, tel. 800/634–6400) has also hosted nationally-televised golf tournaments.

Rodeo In April or May, the **Po'oku Annual Hanalei Stampede** (Box 888, Hanalei 96714, tel. 808/826–6777) takes place. This statewide rodeo, held at Po'oku Stables in Hanalei, includes music and dancing, plus plenty of cowpunching.

Dining

The sugar plantations of 19th-century Kauai brought together a universe of cultures as workers from other countries sought new jobs in Hawaii. With the workers came a delightful assortment of foods, which is reflected in the cuisine found today on Kauai. Depending on your mood, you can find restaurants preparing, among other cuisines, Chinese, Japanese, Thai, Mexican, Spanish, and French specialties, mixed with a heavy dose of traditional Hawaiian food, which is available in just about any town on the island.

The best restaurants are no longer found exclusively in the island's hotels. A growing contingent of independent restaurateurs are stepping beyond the bounds of traditional Continental fare and experimenting with Hawaii Regional Cuisine. They are taking advantage of the many fine products that come from native soil, and on Kauai, there is an especially heavy emphasis on the fruits of its extensive groves. Thanks to the abundance of fish in the waters surrounding Kauai, the catch of the day is always well worth trying.

The ambience of each Kauai restaurant is unique. Many capitalize on splendid views of the waterfront. Some are candlelit and serve meals on the finest china, while others present your food with plastic plates and silverware.

When it's time for a snack, look for the carryout wagons that are often parked at the major beaches. They serve such local food as the plate lunch, in which two scoops of rice are served with every entrée.

Few restaurants require jackets. An aloha shirt and pants for men, and a simple dress or pants for women are acceptable in all but the fanciest establishments.

Restaurants are open daily unless otherwise noted. At press time, a few of the following restaurants were still in some stage of reconstruction after the hurricane, but they expected to open by late 1993. Call first to make sure they've finished rebuilding.

Highly recommended restaurants in each price category are indicated by a star ★.

Category	Cost*
Expensive	$40–$60
Moderate	$20–$40
Inexpensive	under $20

per person without sales tax (4%), service, or drinks

Lihue and Vicinity

American **Oar House Saloon.** The theme here is nautical, with life preservers hanging from the beams and fish nets draped along the walls. The restaurant's owners have created a relaxed setting in which to enjoy the views of Kauai's ever-green mountains. Step outside and you're right at the waterfront, next to the Kauai Lagoons Resort. Broiler offerings include 6-ounce burgers made with your choice of cheese, mushrooms, or bacon. The T-bone steak is a whopping 14 ounces, and the chef's salad comes with ham, turkey, Swiss, Cheddar, hard-boiled eggs, tomatoes, and more. During the afternoon and evening, the Oar House's dart board attracts a colorful local clientele. *Wapaa Rd., Nawiliwili, tel. 808/245-4941. No reservations. Dress: casual. AE, V. Inexpensive.*

Chinese **Club Jetty.** This restaurant's simple Formica tables and chairs are arranged so as not to disrupt the picturesque views of the harbor from the large picture windows. As you dine, you can gaze at the comings and goings of cruise and pleasure boats sailing by. For more than 30 years, the club has been entertaining guests with such Chinese dishes as abalone with black mushrooms, shrimp Canton with fresh pineapple, and sweet and sour fish with fresh island vegetables. Dinner entrées also include steaks and seafood. *Nawiliwili Harbor, Nawiliwili, tel. 808/245-4970. Reservations advised. Dress: casual. AE, DC, MC, V. Dinner only. Inexpensive.*

A Pacific Cafe, **21**

Bali Hai, **23**

Brennecke's Beach
Broiler, **7**

Bull Shed, **17**

Cafe Hanalei and
Terrace, **25**

Casa di Amici, **22**

Charo's, **28**

Chuck's Steak
House, **24**

Club Jetty, **13**

Foong Wong's, **27**

Gaylord's, **9**

Green Garden, **2**

Hanamaulu Cafe, **14**

House of Seafood, **8**

Inn on the Cliffs, **10**

Kapaa Fish &
Chowder House, **18**

Kiahuna Golf Cub, **4**

Kokee Lodge, **1**

La Cascata, **25**

The Lanai, **25**

Norberto's El Cafe, **20**

Oar House Saloon, **12**

Pizza Bella, **3**

Pizza Burger, **24**

Plantation Gardens, **4**

Pancho and Lefty's, **5**

Prince Bill's, **11**

Restaurant
Kintaro, **19**

Seashell, **16**

Tahiti Nui, **26**

Tamarind, **6**

Wailua Marina
Restaurant, **15**

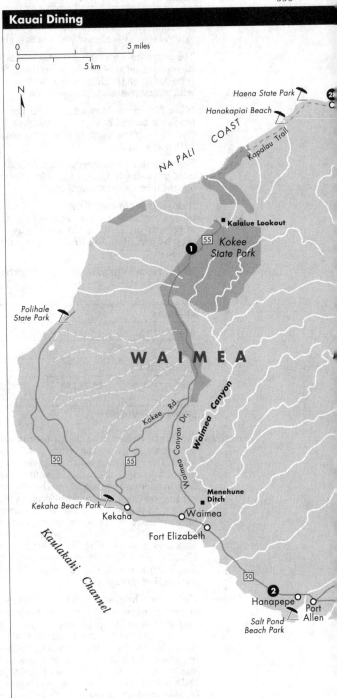

Kauai Dining

0 ———— 5 miles

0 ———— 5 km

N

Haena State Park

Hanakapiai Beach

NA PALI COAST

Kalalau Trail

■ **Kalalue Lookout**

1 55 *Kokee State Park*

Polihale State Park

W A I M E A

Waimea Canyon

Kokee Rd.

Waimea Canyon Dr.

50

55

■ **Menehune Ditch**

Kekaha Beach Park

Kekaha

Waimea

Fort Elizabeth

Kaulakahi Channel

50

2 Hanapepe

Port Allen

Salt Pond Beach Park

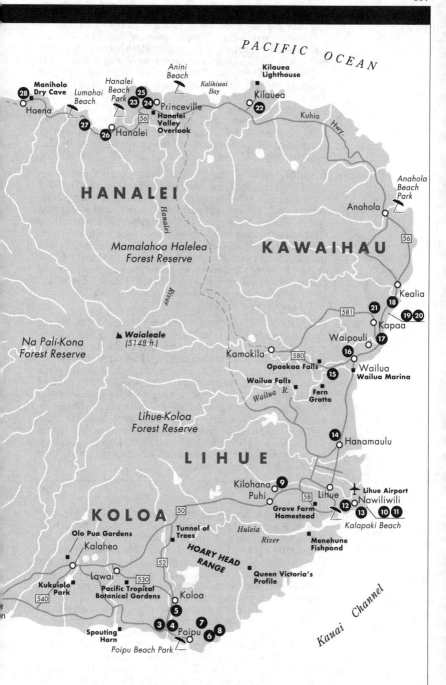

Continental **Gaylord's.** A gracious plantation mansion from the 19th centu-
★ ry is the charming setting of this special restaurant. White
tablecloths and pastel furnishings contribute to the cool
ambience of the alfresco dining room, which opens to extensive
gardens in back. Gaylord's prepares every dish to order, and
each entrée is distinctive. Try the venison in blueberry-juniper
sauce, or the pan-blackened and highly spiced fresh salmon.
The roast duck breast features three sauces—peppercorn,
port wine, and Madeira. For dessert, chef Chris Harris offers a
truly decadent French Silk, which is whipped chocolate laced
with raspberry-wine sauce. *Kilohana Plantation, 3–2087
Kaumualii Hwy., 1 mi south of Lihue, tel. 808/245–9593. Reservations required. Dress: casual. AE, DC, MC, V. Moderate.*

Seafood **Inn on the Cliffs.** Sweeping views of the ocean highlight the decor of this elegant dining room with high ceilings and low-key
furnishings. The chef here prepares fresh island seafood in inventive ways. For an appetizer, she sautées shrimp with spring
onions, Hawaiian ginger, and Chinese parsley. Entrées include
Cajun tiger prawns in a lobster-brandy sauce; soft-shell crab
pan-fried with capers and brown butter; and calamari steak
prepared with sweet Maui onions, peppers, and capers. Catch
of the day usually includes *opakapaka* (pink snapper) and *ono*
(wahoo). *Westin Kauai, Kalapaki Beach, Lihue, tel. 808/245–
5050. Reservations recommended. Dress: casual. AE, DC,
MC, V. Dinner only. Expensive.*

Italian **Prince Bill's.** This penthouse trattoria was named after Hawai-
i's 19th-century King Lunalilo, known as Prince Bill, who favored the high life. Designed in multiple levels, the restaurant
has spectacular views of Kalapaki Bay. Pastas are also spectacular here—fettuccine with shrimp, scallops, mussels, garlic
cream, basil, and romano cheese, for example. The sautéed
breast of chicken is served with prosciutto and *bel paese*
cheese, and the fresh island snapper is baked in parchment paper with *pancetta*, leeks, carrots, fresh herbs, and olive oil. A
buffet of Italian specialty desserts tops off the evening. *Westin
Kauai, Kalapaki Beach, Lihue, tel. 808/245–5050. Reservations recommended. Dress: casual. AE, DC, MC, V. Dinner
and Sun. brunch only. Moderate.*

The East Shore

Asian **Restaurant Kintaro.** A pretty restaurant with sliding *shoji*
screen doors and oriental prints on the walls, Restaurant
Kintaro has gained a favorable reputation for its updated versions of traditional Japanese cuisine. Teppanyaki dinners include tender hibachi shrimp sautéed in lemon butter and
served with bean sprouts and steamed rice. Dinners come with
chilled buckwheat noodles, miso soup, rice, Japanese pickles,
and tea. The tempura combination is a light and crispy assortment of fresh local fish, shrimp, and vegetables. A sushi bar is
also on hand, and you can order complete sukiyaki dinners of
beef and vegetables cooked in soy sauce and served in an iron
pot. *4-370 Kuhio Hwy., Kapaa, tel. 808/822–3341. Dress: casual. AE, MC, V. Dinner only. Closed Sun. Moderate.*
★ **Hanamaulu Cafe.** Three miles north of Lihue is this tranquil
teahouse with interior gardens and carp-filled brooks. The im-
maculate setting creates a serene environment for the two spacious tearooms and authentic sushi bar with seating for 24. The
robatayaki-style (cooked on an open grill) Japanese dishes in-

clude Tokyo steak, soft-shell crabs, and Kauai prawns. Chinese cuisine is also featured, including the chef's special nine-course dinner of pork and vegetable soup, crispy wonton, sweet and sour spareribs, fried shrimp, chop suey with noodles, crab claws with butter sauce, crisp fried chicken, beef with broccoli and tomatoes, and *char siu* (roast pork), plus rice, tea, and fortune cookies. *Hwy. 56, Hanamaulu, tel. 808/245–2511. Reservations required. Dress: casual. MC, V. Inexpensive.*

Mexican **Norberto's El Cafe.** This award-winning family restaurant has been a well-kept secret among locals for some time, but visitors are catching on to the joys of this little gem. Since 1977, Norberto's has prepared meals without lard or animal fat, using the freshest ingredients possible. One specialty is burritos rancheros: toasted flour tortillas rolled and stuffed with seasoned beef, Cheddar cheese, onions, and green chiles, smothered with Spanish sauce and cheeses. Norberto's fajitas are tender slices of prime Kauai steak or chicken sautéed with fresh mushrooms, bell peppers, and onions and served with Spanish rice and flour tortillas. Complete dinners come with soup, beans, and rice, plus chips and salsa. *4–1373 Kuhio Hwy., Kapaa, tel. 808/822–3362. Dress: casual. AE, MC, V. Dinner only. Inexpensive.*

Pacific Rim **A Pacific Cafe.** Chef Jean Marie Josselin's intimate restaurant in the Kauai Village Shopping Center is bright and cheery with Oriental overtones. Josselin combines his love of Asian cooking with his commitment to fresh, home-grown ingredients. In nouvelle fashion he presents lamb with plum-tamarind sauce, scallop-filled ravioli in lemon-ginger sauce, bamboo steamed bass with blue crab bisque, and sizzling squid salad with lime-ginger vinaigrette. The *lilikoi* (passion fruit) chiffon pie is a tangy taste of Hawaii. *Kauai Village Shopping Center, Hwy. 56, Kapaa, tel. 808/822–0013. Dress: casual. AE, MC, V. Dinner only. Moderate.*

Steak and Seafood **Kapaa Fish & Chowder House.** The decor here combines thick hanging ferns and nautical memorabilia. Owners Jan and Glenn Lovejoy like Louisiana-style food and have included some dishes with a Cajun accent on the menu. For instance, the chef quickly sautées fresh shrimp, then coats it with some piquant Cajun spices that are sure to wake up the taste buds. Another unusual entrée served here is Alaskan snow crab legs and claws steamed in beer and served with drawn butter. The seafood fettuccine is recommended; stir-fried shrimp, scallops, clams, and fish are served on a combination of spinach and egg fettuccine blended with a white-wine sauce. Ask for a table in the Garden Room, a veritable Eden. *4-1639 Kuhio Hwy., Kapaa, tel. 808/822–7488. Reservations advised. Dress: casual. AE, MC, V. Dinner only. Moderate.*

Seashell. A tropical garden on a bluff overlooking the sea is the setting of the Seashell, next to Wailua Beach at the Coco Palms Resort. Seafood prepared Island-style is the fare here, including shrimp dim sum (bite-sized dumplings stuffed with the delectable Island shellfish). Opihi wontons use the highly prized, tiny shellfish, which are found on coastline rocks. Entrées include shrimp tempura, *onaga* (red snapper) presented on a sizzling platter, and a fish stew called cioppino. A salad buffet and homemade desserts are featured, and tropical drinks are available during happy hour. *Coco Palms Resort, Hwy. 56, Wailua,* *tel. 808/822–3632. Reservations advised. Dress: casual. AE, DC, MC, V. Dinner only. Moderate.*

★ **Bull Shed.** The A-frame design of this popular restaurant imparts a distinctly rustic feel, as do the exposed wood interior and big, family-style tables. Set on the shoreline and offering views of the ocean, the Bull Shed presents prime rib, teriyaki sirloin, chicken, and Alaskan king crab; the fresh fish is particularly good. The salad bar is a real disappointment, however, so skip it and proceed directly to the entrées, which come with hot rolls and rice. *796 Kuhio Ave., Waipouli, tel. 808/822–3791. Reservations advised. Dress: casual. AE, MC, V. Dinner only. Inexpensive.*

Wailua Marina Restaurant. Technicolor bougainvillea and boats chugging along the charming Wailua River are your views from this dockside eatery, ideal for before or after the boat ride up to Fern Grotto. The open-air dining lanai is perched right on the water, next to shores where ancient Hawaiian communities once stood. For the large number of people it serves, the restaurant has a surprisingly thoughtful menu. For instance, the baked stuffed chicken is cooked in plum sauce and served with a lobster salad, and the baked salmon comes covered with a rich bacon sauce. A variety of steak and fresh seafood dishes are also on the menu. Complimentary transportation is available from Wailua-area hotels and condos in the evenings. *Wailua River State Park, Wailua Rd., Wailua, tel. 808/822–4311. Reservations advised. Dress: casual. AE, MC, V. Inexpensive.*

The North Shore

American **Pizza Burger.** With its tidy little wooden front porch and white railing, Pizza Burger is a fun indoor/outdoor emporium and a great place to watch the world go by. The pizzas here offer a variety of toppings in whatever combination you'd like: salami, Italian sausage, mushrooms, jalapeños, tomatoes, pineapple, and so on. The burgers, too, are interesting, including one made of a quarter-pound of 100% pure buffalo meat from Hanalei Garden Farms. The Fin Burger is four ounces of mahimahi fillet topped with Cheddar cheese, and another quarter-pounder combines pastrami and mozzarella. You pay a little more for your pizza if you carry it out. *Princeville Shopping Center, Hwy. 56, Princeville, tel. 808/826–6070. No reservations. Dress: casual. MC, V. Inexpensive.*

Chinese **Foong Wong's.** One story up in Ching Young Village, Foong Wong presents a striking first impression, with its predominantly red decor. The next thing you notice about the place is its wonderful views of the mountains of Hanalei, right outside the big picture windows. The interior is traditional, as is the presentation of the restaurant's Cantonese and Szechuan dishes. Owner Wing Yuen Leung and his wife, Mi Wah, have assembled a masterful menu of specialties, including three-flavored seafood sizzling plate, hot and sour soup, and chicken with cashew nuts. The abalone soup, enough for four or five persons, is an unexpected treat. *Ching Young Village, Hwy. 56, Hanalei, tel. 808/826–6996. No reservations. Dress: casual. AE, MC, V. Inexpensive.*

Continental **Cafe Hanalei and Terrace.** Using indoor and outdoor tables, Cafe Hanalei takes full advantage of its setting and its panoramic views of Hanalei Bay and the mountains. Breakfast treats include grilled pineapple with palm sugar and coconut syrup, and Hawaiian smoothies made of just about any tropical fruit you desire. Whole-wheat pancakes with macadamia nuts and guava syrup are equally tasty. The luncheon menu boasts grilled salmon fillet with bok choy and mustard-seed sauce, and spiced chicken paillard with pomelo and scallion salad on a sweet curry sauce. Try the grilled opakapaka with black bean butter and crispy leeks at dinner. *Princeville Hotel, Princeville Resort, tel. 808/826–9644. Dress: casual. AE, DC, MC, V. Expensive.*

The Lanai. Princeville has a lush, rolling countryside flanked by cliffs that have inspired generations of Hawaiians. That's the view that surrounds you at this alfresco restaurant. A pair of chefs—Androcles Handy and Mike Daigan—make the Lanai's victuals as memorable as the visuals. They share a keen interest in the preparation of fresh fish from Hawaii's waters and have come up with such crowd pleasers as fillets of *ono* (wahoo) in a sauce of tomato, garlic, shallots, and white wine. The 10-ounce steak is broiled and laced with a peppery sauce, while the scampi are sautéed in butter, garlic, white wine, and parsley and served on rice. Try the Hula Pie made of macadamia nut ice cream, chocolate cookie crumb crust, whipped cream, and toasted almonds. *Makai Clubhouse, Princeville Resort, tel. 808/826–6226. Reservations advised. Dress: casual. AE, DC, MC, V. Dinner only. Moderate.*

Italian **La Cascata.** Terracotta floors, hand-painted murals, and *trompe l'oeil* paintings give La Cascata an Italian villa flair. The views of Hanalei Bay through picture windows are breathtaking. The Mediterranean menu features light sauces and an abundance of fresh seafood. Appetizers include a warm salad of spaghetti, clams, and julienne of vegetables. The tastes of southern Italy are showcased in the Mahi fillet braised with tomato, olives, capers, and oregano. Pasta includes a braised Italian rice casserole with prawns and radicchio, and seafood ravioli in a tomato and basil sauce. The grilled swordfish cutlet is garnished with eggplant compote, and roasted guinea fowl breast is served with spinach, pine nuts, and raisins. Top it off with hazelnut nougat in a chocolate crust. *Princeville Hotel, Princeville Resort, tel. 808/826–9644. Reservations required. Dress: casual chic. AE, DC, MC, V. Expensive.*

★ **Casa di Amici.** A welcome addition to the north-shore dining scene, Casa di Amici means "house of friends," and it feels that way, too. The menu is broken down as it would be if you were dining in Italy; that is, antipasti (starters), *zuppe* (soup), pasta, *insalate* (salads), and *pietanza maggiore* (main courses). You can mix your favorite pasta with your choice of sauce, including pesto (fresh basil, pine nuts, garlic, and Romano cheese) and *salsa di noci* (walnut sauce with fresh Romano cheese and marjoram in cream). The house scampi is prepared with garlic, capers, fresh tomatoes, and olive oil on a bed of linguine. *2484 Keneke St. at Lighthouse Rd., Kilauea, tel. 808/828–1388. Reservations advised. Dress: casual. AE, DC, MC, V. Moderate.*

Mixed Menu **Charo's.** Famed for her "coochi coochi" act, Charo has adopted Kauai as her second home. Her restaurant and nightclub draws in visitors by the busload. The views of the ocean and magnificent north-shore sunsets are heightened by floor-to-ceiling windows in this high-ceiling restaurant. The entrance is designed with lush plants and bamboo, while the Polynesian-style dining room features aquariums used as room dividers. The food has decidedly Island overtones. The teriyaki New

York steak is marinated in soy sauce, ginger, garlic, and wine, while the large shrimp are lightly breaded with macadamia nuts and deep-fried, then served with cocktail sauce and lemon. Try Charo's super quesadilla platter, a large tortilla stuffed with Cheddar and Monterey Jack cheeses and beef, chicken, or fish. *Colony Resort, Hwy. 56, Haena, tel. 808/826–6422. Reservations advised. Dress: casual. AE, DC, MC, V. Moderate.*

Polynesian **Tahiti Nui.** By 1994, owner Louise Marston hopes to have her landmark restaurant back in business, after it was hard-hit by the hurricane. It's a down-home spot in the heart of Hanalei town and has been a gathering place for locals and residents since 1960. Whether you sit on the rambling porch and enjoy a cocktail or a full dinner, you'll most likely be charmed by the friendliness of your hosts and the casual nature of your surroundings. Tahiti Nui's luau takes place each Wednesday and Friday night, and there's pre-dinner entertainment by members of her family. The lunch menu includes *poisson cru* (fish marinated in lime, lemon, and coconut milk with green onions, tomato, egg, and cucumber). Dinner on nonluau nights includes a fine chicken curry with green pepper, onion, and your choice of pineapple or papaya. *Kuhio Hwy., Hanalei, tel. 808/826–6277. Reservations suggested. Dress: casual. AE, DC, MC, V. Inexpensive.*

Steak and Seafood **Bali Hai.** The views of the bay are as memorable as the cuisine at the signature restaurant of the Hanalei Bay Resort. Completely refurbished after Hurricane Iniki, it has an open-air, tropical ambience. The fresh seafood is particularly good, such as the appetizer of charbroiled scallops served with prosciutto and papaya salsa. The restaurant's specialty is baked salmon stuffed with cream cheese, spinach, and capers and wrapped in puff pastry. Steaks, chicken, lamb, veal, and vegetarian offerings are also on the menu. For breakfast, Bali Hai serves poi pancakes and fried taro along with the more traditional eggs and griddle fare. *Hanalei Bay Resort, 5380 Honoiki Rd., Princeville, tel. 808/826–6522. Reservations advised for dinner. Dress: casual. AE, DC, MC, V. Moderate.*

Chuck's Steak House. A *paniolo* (cowboy) feeling permeates this place, right down to the saddles and blankets that hang from the open-beamed ceiling and the planters made out of wagon wheels. Choose from a very good salad bar with any entrée you order. From the land, try chunks of beef marinated in teriyaki sauce and showered with pineapple and bell peppers. From the sea, a good bet is the sea scallops sautéed in white wine with lime wheels and Canadian bacon. The barbecued beef ribs, lobster, chicken, and Alaskan king crab are also good. For dessert, Chuck's special mud pie is a winner, made with coffee ice cream and a chocolate and walnut crust, topped with cream. *Princeville Shopping Center, Princeville, tel. 808/826–6211. Reservations advised. Dress: casual. AE, DC, MC, V. Moderate.*

The South and West

Continental **Tamarind.** The centerpiece of the Stouffer Waiohai Hotel, the
★ Tamarind lives up to the standards of the finest signature restaurants. It's decorated in soft earth tones, highlighted by elegant mirrors and chrome finishings, and the comfortable seats invite you to linger over your meal. A specialty of the house is the lamb, which is marinated in mustard and garlic. A different

pâté is offered each night, and the duckling and lobster are good choices for entrées. As a sweet after-dinner touch, each diner receives a small chocolate cup filled with liqueur. *Stouffer Waiohai Hotel, 2249 Poipu Rd., Poipu, tel. 808/742-9511. Reservations advised. Jacket required. AE, DC, MC, V. Dinner only. Expensive.*

Kiahuna Golf Club. Set practically on the green, this resort restaurant has a spacious alfresco ambience that's perfect for the consistently sunny clime of Poipu. The breakfasts are decadent in an Island fashion, especially the thick Hawaiian French toast, topped with macadamia nuts and strawberries. Lunch features sandwiches and salads with golf-oriented names; try the Birdie, half a strawberry papaya filled with chicken or tuna salad and topped with bay shrimp. If you're planning a private party, the staff is happy to help. They also do catering. *Kiahuna Shopping Village, 2360 Kiahuna Plantation Dr., Poipu, tel. 808/742-6055. Reservations advised. Dress: casual. AE, DC, MC, V. Breakfast and lunch only. Inexpensive.*

Mexican **Pancho and Lefty's Cantina and Restaurante.** It's hard to describe the decor here, except to say it's colorful and fun. What first catches your eye is a vintage gas pump by the front door, followed by papier-mâché parrots, hanging plants, a neon Pegasus by the bar, and chile pepper salt shakers. The menu, created by chefs from Guadalajara, is equally unusual. Start with *calientita* (mild jalapeño peppers stuffed with cheese, then deep fried) and progress to *pechuga pollo relleno* (chicken breast stuffed with Jack cheese and chiles, dipped in egg batter and pan fried, and finished with a blanket of enchilada sauce). *Koloa Rd., Old Koloa Town, tel. 808/742-7377. Reservations not necessary. Dress: casual. AE, DC, MC, V. Inexpensive.*

Mixed Menu **Green Garden.** With orchids on every table and an assortment of hanging and standing plants throughout the place, this family-run restaurant is aptly named. Formerly a five-bedroom home, it has been a favorite dining spot for Kauai residents and visitors since 1948. The Green Garden is very low-key, and the waitresses treat you like you're old friends. The food is no-frills local fare; you come here for the atmosphere first and the meals second. Dinner, which includes some 30 items, might consist of the Chinese plate, with pork chow mein, sweet and sour spareribs, and *char siu* (roast pork). The seafood special is breaded mahimahi fillet, scallops, oysters, and deep-fried shrimp. The homemade desserts are something special. Be sure to try the *lilikoi* (passion fruit) chiffon pie. *Hwy. 50, Hanapepe, tel. 808/335-5422. Reservations advised for dinner. Dress: casual. AE, DC, MC, V. Closed Tues. nights. Inexpensive.*

Kokee Lodge. Set midway between Waimea Canyon and the Kalalau Lookout, this mountaintop lodge is protected on one side by a grove of pines. On the other side, picture windows open up to a rolling green lawn and clear blue Kokee skies (when the clouds haven't rolled in). This environment is a different slice of Kauai indeed. The food at the lodge consists of several types of cuisine, including Cornish game hen with mushroom and rice stuffing. The vegetarian fettuccine is quite good, or you can order steak, Island fish, or ribs. At breakfast, the pancakes sometimes come with tropical-flavored syrups. Try some mud pie for dessert; it's a chocolate lover's dream come true. *Kokee Rd., Kokee State Park, tel. 808/335-6061. No reservations. Dress: casual. AE, DC, MC, V. Breakfast and lunch daily, dinner Fri. and Sat. only. Inexpensive.*

Pacific Rim **Plantation Gardens.** Pacific Rim cuisine is all the rage in Hawaii these days. It involves using only the freshest local ingredients and preparing them in styles that draw on both classical and oriental preparations. Plantation Gardens serves such dishes in a tropical setting, with hanging gardens and carp ponds surrounding an outdoor terrace. Starters include spring rolls, Chinese pot stickers, and escargots in puff pastry. For entrées, order the flame-grilled ahi served with papaya and chili salsa, or the Thai-style chicken with shiitake mushrooms, red and yellow peppers, and lemon basil with somen noodles. *Kiahuna Plantation, Poipu Beach, tel. 808/742–1695. Reservations advised. Dress: casual. AE, DC, MC, V. Dinner only. Moderate.*

Pizza **Pizza Bella.** A friendly place in Poipu Shopping Village, Pizza Bella offers sit-down, take-out, and delivery service. Its pizzas are made with white flour crust covered with sauce and cheese; then you top it off with your own choice of additional ingredients, from traditional pepperoni, mushrooms, and bell peppers to zucchini, black olives, and Portuguese sausage. You can also order ten-inch gourmet pizzas such as the Cajun Seafood with shrimp, clams, two cheeses, onions, bell peppers, chopped tomatoes, and spicy sauce. Hot sandwiches include chicken parmesan, deep fried and covered with melted provolone and marinara sauce. Also on the menu are soups, salads, and pastas. *Poipu Shopping Village, Poipu Beach, tel. 808/742–9571. No reservations. Dress: casual. MC, V. Inexpensive.*

Steak and Seafood **House of Seafood.** Owners Don Kubisch and John Borales run
★ this pretty restaurant, which overlooks the Poipu Resort tennis courts. Inside, the ceilings are so high that you feel you're dining outside, and tropical vines wrap themselves around the handsome exposed beams. The name says it all: This is a fine place to try island seafood, from *ahi* (tuna) to *weke* (goatfish). Preparations vary from night to night, and your server will tell you your options. A variety of shellfish dishes are available, including Oriental shrimp and scallops, lobster and shrimp Cantonese, and lobster tail. All entrées come with a cup of chowder or salad, fresh vegetables, almond rice pilaf, and freshly baked rolls. *1941 Poipu Rd., Poipu, tel. 808/742–6433. Reservations advised. Dress: casual. AE, DC, MC, V. Dinner only. Expensive.*

★ **Brennecke's Beach Broiler.** Situated right across from Poipu Beach Park, this place has been around for years, and happily so. The names of Island fish are inscribed in big bold letters on the white walls, and pretty flower boxes brighten up the windows. You also have a view of the chef, who specializes in *kiawe*-broiled foods ("kiawe" is a mesquite-type wood). Along with the standard burgers, Brennecke's serves fresh clams, catch of the day, and exceptional homemade desserts, such as guava and mango sherbet. Ask to sit on the second floor so you can get better views of the ocean. *Ho'one Rd., Poipu, tel. 808/742–7588. Reservations advised. Dress: casual. MC, V. Moderate.*

Lodging

Part of the appeal of the Garden Isle is its range of hotel properties, which cover the gamut from swanky and stuffy resorts to rustic mountaintop cabins to the bare-bones accommodations whose main appeal is the rock-bottom price. Since they had to shut down and make repairs after the hurricane anyway, many hotels on the island took the opportunity to upgrade their appearance and services. Here are some basic guidelines to help you make a choice.

Those seeking the sunshine often head south to the shores of Poipu, where high rises line the coast and the gentle surf offers ideal swimming. The hotels and condominiums of Poipu are in the Moderate to Very Expensive price range, although several shoreside cottages are in demand with the budget traveler.

Guests who are interested in the more historical and sacred sections of Kauai often stay on the east coast near the Wailua River, home of Kauai's first inhabitants. Many of the hotels here place an emphasis on the legends and lore of the area. Shops and restaurants are within walking distance of most accommodations, and the beaches are so-so for swimming but nice for sunbathing.

Farther north are the swanky hotels and condominiums of the Princeville Resort, generally reserved for the island's wealthiest patrons. You can't go wrong with a room here, because just about any accommodation offers views of Hanalei Bay, the Pali coast, or the chiseled mountain peaks of Hanalei. This is a duffer's paradise, for panoramic vistas are seen from every hole of the resort's two golf courses.

Bed-and-breakfasts are becoming a more attractive option for the many visitors to Kauai who wish to get a resident's point of view. These private homes are scattered around the island, and a good booking service can help you locate one.

You'll have no trouble finding a place to stay on Kauai if you make your reservations beforehand. Allow extra time during the peak months of February and August. When making your booking, ask about such extras as special tennis, golf, honeymoon, and room-and-car packages.

Highly recommended hotels in each price category are indicated by a star ★ .

Category	Cost*
Very Expensive	over $120
Expensive	$90–$120
Moderate	$60–$90
Inexpensive	under $60

All prices are for a standard double room excluding 9¼% taxes and service.

Lihue and Vicinity

Very Expensive **Outrigger Kauai Beach Hotel.** Formerly the Kauai Hilton, this resort was designed with sensitivity to the history and scenery of the nearby Wailua River area. This explains why the low-rise, horseshoe-shape structure surrounds a pool complex with rock-sculptured slopes, waterfalls, bright tropical flowers, and a cave resembling Fern Grotto. Each night at sunset, people in native dress light 100 tiki torches around the pools. Guest rooms and public areas are decorated in muted tones of peach, mauve, and teal against an off-white background, and each

Aston Kauai Beachboy, **16**

Coco Palms Resort, **13**

Garden Isle Cottages, **3**

Hale Lihue Motel, **9**

Hanalei Bay Resort, **21**

Hotel Coral Reef, **18**

Hyatt Regency Kauai, **8**

Kapaa Sands, **17**

Kauai Resort, **12**

Kauai Sands, **15**

Kay Barker's Bed & Breakfast, **14**

Kiahuna Plantation, **6**

Kokee Lodge, **1**

Koloa Landing Cottages, **4**

Kuhio Shores, **2**

Outrigger Kauai Beach Hotel, **11**

Poipu Beach Hotel, **7**

Princeville Hotel, **19**

Sandpiper Village, **20**

Sheraton Kauai Hotel, **5**

Westin Kauai, **10**

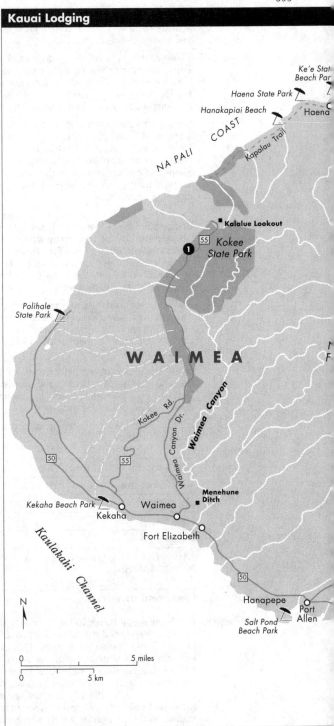

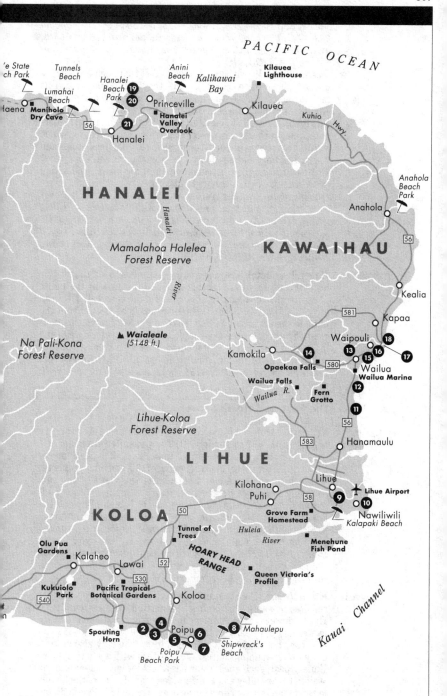

room has a lanai and views of mountains, gardens, or the sea. *4331 Kauai Beach Dr., Lihue 96766, tel. 808/245–1955 or 800/ 733–7777. 350 hotel rooms and 135 condominiums with bath, on the beach. Facilities: 4 pools, 2 restaurants, 2 lounges, tennis, golf. AE, DC, MC, V.*

★ **Westin Kauai.** While some residents feel that such opulence is out of place on a rural island, they do admit that this megaproperty can be very impressive. Guests are met at Lihue Airport in a limousine and driven on the resort's private road. The lobby boasts a $2.5 million art collection, and hotel amusements include horse-drawn-carriage rides and outrigger-canoe tours. Five towers of guest rooms have colonial furnishings and floor-to-ceiling sliding doors for ocean or mountain views. Rooms include robes, stocked minibars, big lanais, and a king or twin double beds. Although this property had planned on reopening by early 1994, reconstruction had been stalled over ownership disputes at press time. *Kalapaki Beach, Lihue 96766, tel. 808/245–5050 or 800/228–3000, fax 808/245–5049. 850 rooms with bath, on the beach. Facilities: Jacuzzis, health spa, golf, tennis, horse-drawn carriages, 12 restaurants and lounges, shops. AE, DC, MC, V.*

Inexpensive **Hale Lihue Motel.** There are two advantages to staying at this hotel. First, it is located smack-dab in Lihue, making the sights of the north, south, and west portions of the island all within an easy hour's drive. Second, the price can't be beat. From the outside the low-rise building looks run-down, but the inside is clean. The rooms are very simple, with cinder-block walls and utilitarian furnishings. Kitchenettes are available. Ask in advance for one of the air-conditioned rooms. *2931 Kalena St., Lihue 96766, tel. 808/245–3151. 18 rooms with bath. No credit cards.*

The East and North Shores

Very Expensive **Princeville Hotel.** After extensive remodeling, this property ★ had its grand re-opening in 1991. Then, it suffered a major setback when the winds and rains of Iniki caused it major damage. Plans called for a late-1993 reopening of this splendid property, which drapes down a cliff to maximize the views of the surrounding scenery. Rooms have marble counters and goldplated fixtures. Ocean-side views look to Hanalei Bay and the peaks known as Bali Hai; the lobby now looks straight out to the bay through a wall of glass. Princeville Resort's top-ranked golf course is right outside the front door. *Box 3069, Princeville 96722, tel. 808/826–9644 or 800/325–3535. 252 rooms with bath. Facilities: pool, tennis, golf, shops, 3 restaurants, 3 lounges, in-house cinema. AE, DC, MC, V.*

Expensive **Kauai Resort.** The constant care lavished on this property has resulted in a hotel that is clearly dedicated to its surroundings. Exotic flowers grace interiors and exteriors, and rooms feature pastel colors, rattan furnishings, and large windows. A Hawaiian story hour is available for children, who may also enter a daily flower-naming contest. For visitors with a yen to explore Kauai's past, each guest room has a booklet with legends of the Wailua River Valley and a self-guided tour of some of the historic Hawaiian temple ruins in the area. The hotel's Pacific Room features contemporary island entertainers each weekend. *3- 5920 Kuhio Hwy., Kapaa 96746, tel. 808/245–3931 or 800/74–*

KAUAI. 242 rooms with bath. Facilities: pool, shops, restaurant, lounge. AE, DC, MC, V.

★ **Coco Palms Resort.** The Coco Palms has a long history of hospitality. The queen of Kauai once owned these 45 acres, and the place is now done up like a Polynesian village, with lagoons, fish ponds, and thatched huts that keep alive the past. The lobby mirrors its cool, serene surroundings with soft sea colors and rattan furnishings. A white-on-pastel Pacific-colonial theme is the guest-room motif, and each bathroom has a giant clamshell washbasin. The resort also features the first clay tennis courts ever built in Hawaii, plus an eight-person Jacuzzi next to a lava-rock waterfall. *Box 631, Lihue 96766, tel. 808/822–4921 or 800/542–2626. 390 rooms with bath. Facilities: pools, tennis, shops, 3 restaurants, lounges. AE, DC, MC, V.*

★ **Hanalei Bay Resort.** Part of the Princeville community, this resort has a clifftop location and offers accommodations in 16 low-rise buildings overlooking Hanalei Bay and Kauai's north shore. After the hurricane, all guest rooms were completely renovated. Each unit is extremely spacious, some with as much as 2,000 square feet. What's more, the rooms have high, sloping ceilings and large private lanais with mountain or bay views. Rattan furniture and Island art add a casual feeling to each room, which comes with a fully equipped kitchen, a large dressing area, a color TV, daily maid service, and 24-hour switchboard service. *Box 220, Hanalei 96714, tel. 808/826–6522 or 800/827–4427. 287 condominiums with bath. Facilities: pool, tennis, golf, restaurant, lounge, laundry facilities. AE, DC, MC, V.*

Moderate **Aston Kauai Beachboy.** Eight miles north of Lihue Airport, the Kauai Beachboy is well situated for east- and north-shore sightseeing. It's also a five-minute drive from the Wailua Golf Course and within walking distance of the Coconut Market Place shopping complex. The four-building, three-story hotel is set along an uncrowded, mile-wide stretch of Waipouli Beach. Rooms have large sliding screen doors, which open onto private lanais. The furnishings are heavy-handed in the Hawaiian motif department, with loud-colored bedspreads and gaudy prints on the white walls. On the plus side, guest rooms come with air-conditioning, color TV, daily maid service, and a refrigerator. *4–484 Kuhio Hwy., #100, Kapaa 96746, tel. 808/822–3441 or 800/922–7866, fax 808/822–0843. 243 rooms with bath. Facilities: pool, shops, restaurant, tennis, lounge. AE, DC, MC, V.*

Inexpensive **Hotel Coral Reef.** An older hotel that has been well maintained, the Coral Reef is right on the sand's edge, although the swimming in front of the hotel is not as good as at the public beaches nearby. Colorful bedspreads liven up the somewhat stark furnishings of the rooms, which are clean and freshly painted. The upper floors have carpeting in each unit, while the ground-level rooms are done in terrazzo tile. Oceanfront accommodations feature private lanais and refrigerators. The property is ideally situated, near plenty of shopping, dining, and sightseeing, and the rates are attractive to budget travelers. *1516 Kuhio Hwy., Kapaa 96746, tel. 808/822–4481 or 800/843–4659. 26 rooms with bath. Facilities: refrigerators, laundromat within walking distance. AE, MC, V.*

Kauai Sands. Another good bet for money-saving beachfront accommodations is the Kauai Sands, where the green and blue decor of the rooms is a reflection of the ocean right outside the windows. Each unit is carpeted and air-conditioned, and you can get one with a kitchenette for a few extra dollars. The restaurant and lounge offer up-close views of the sea. *420 Papaloa Rd., Kapaa 96746, tel. 808/822–4951 or 800/367–7000. 200 rooms with bath. Facilities: pool, shops, restaurant, lounge. AE, DC, MC, V.*

The South and West

Very Expensive **Hyatt Regency Kauai.** Opened in November of 1990, Hyatt's
★ Kauai property is done in classic Hawaiian architecture reminiscent of the 1920s and '30s, with no building taller than a coconut tree. Extensive gardens, open-air courtyards, and Hawaiian artwork highlight the public areas. Room decor furthers the plantation theme with bamboo, wicker, and Island paintings, and most rooms have ocean views. Five acres of meandering saltwater swimming lagoons feature islands—each with its own private beach; an "action pool" has waterfalls, slides, water volleyball, Jacuzzis, and an area for children. The extensive fitness facility covers 25,000 square feet. *1571 Poipu Rd., Koloa 96756, tel. 808/742–1234 or 800/233–1234, fax 808/742–1577. 600 rooms and suites with bath. Facilities: 4 tennis courts, shops, 2 saltwater pools, chlorinated pool, golf, health club, 3 restaurants, 2 lounges, nightclub. AE, DC, MC, V.*

★ **Sheraton Kauai Hotel.** Stretching across 20 acres of prime Poipu Beach property, the recently remodeled Sheraton Kauai is comprised of low-rise Polynesian buildings that were designed to complement the surrounding beach, tropical gardens, and waterways. At press time, it was uncertain when the Sheraton's Ocean Wing would reopen; fronting Poipu Beach, it was severely damaged by the hurricane. The Garden Wing, however, weathered the storm well, with its tropical foliage and lagoons intact. Each room has a lanai, refrigerator, color TV, radio, telephone, and air-conditioning. Furnishings are appropriately Hawaiian, and rooms are very spacious. *2440 Hoonani Rd., Koloa 96756, tel. 808/742–1661 or 800/325–3535. 456 rooms with bath. Facilities: pools, shops, restaurants. AE, DC, MC, V.*

Expensive **Poipu Beach Hotel.** One of the smaller facilities on Poipu Beach, this low-rise hotel predicted a fall 1993 reopening after Iniki. It is particularly appropriate for families, since the swimming nearby is usually safe for beginners. Each room has a small refrigerator. The decor is no-frills, with dark tile floors and simple Island-style furnishings. Rooms all have a lanai with patio tables and chairs, plus a color television, air-conditioning, maid service, and a telephone. *2251 Poipu Rd., Koloa 96756, tel. 808/742–1681 or 800/426–4122. 138 rooms with bath. Facilities: swimming pool, shops, tennis, restaurant, lounge. AE, DC, MC, V.*

Inexpensive **Garden Isle Cottages.** Here you'll find oceanside accommoda-
★ tions at budget prices. The theme of each interior is Hawaiian, and tropical flower gardens surround the cottages for an exotic yet homespun touch. Rooms have no telephones or televisions. Some do include kitchens, so ask in advance if you wish to reserve one. It's a five-minute walk to the restaurants of nearby Poipu. *2666 Puuholo Rd., Koloa 96756, tel. 808/742–6717. 13 cottages with bath. No pool. MC, V.*

★ **Kokee Lodge.** This may not fit the image of real Hawaiian lodgings held by first-time visitors: it's up in the mountains, where the air is considerably cooler than around the beachfront properties. Instead of palm trees there are pines, and accommodations are individual cottages rather than Poipu-style high rises. However, the Kokee Lodge offers the outdoors-oriented visitor a chance to experience the rare flora and fauna of Kauai's highlands. Housing is in 12 cabins that are rustic inside and out. Each has a fireplace (you pay a few dollars extra for wood) and comes with a fully equipped kitchen. The eight older wooden cabins are cheaper than the four newer, log-cabin-type structures. Many Kauai residents head for Kokee for the weekend, so make your reservations in advance. *Box 819, Waimea 96796, tel. 808/335–6061. 12 cabins with bath. Facilities: shop, restaurant. AE, MC, V.*

Alternative Accommodations

Bed and Breakfasts

Bed & Breakfast Hawaii. This booker offers inexpensive single and double accommodations in family homes around the islands. The advantage here is that you get your morning meal as part of the deal, and you usually get an insider's view of Kauai from your congenial hosts. *Box 449, Kapaa 96746, tel. 808/822–7771 or 800/733–1632.*

Kay Barker's Bed & Breakfast. Kay Barker is a sprightly woman in her 80s who opens her home to guests and serves them a Continental breakfast in the morning. Four inexpensive bedrooms are available, each with a private bath, and guests are invited to relax in the common rooms of the house as Kay shares her recollections of life on Kauai. *Box 740, Kapaa 96746, tel. 808/822–3073. 4 bedrooms with bath. Facilities: living room, TV room, library. No credit cards.*

Condominiums

Kiahuna Plantation. With its reliably warm temperatures and ocean breezes, the southern coast is the perfect setting for a vacation in one of Kiahuna's one- or two-bedroom cottages, many of which are right on the shoreline. Interiors are done in green and yellow and furnished with rattan-style chairs and couches. There's no television in the rooms, but you won't really need it, because the great outdoors beckons with the beaches, golf courses, swimming pools, shops, and restaurants of the bustling Poipu area. Each unit has a fully equipped electric kitchen and daily maid service. *2253 Poipu Rd., Koloa 96756, tel. 808/742–6411 or 800/367–7052. 333 rooms with bath. Facilities: pool, restaurant, tennis, golf. AE, DC, MC, V. Very Expensive.*

Kuhio Shores. An ideal waterfront location and an ingenious design allow this condominium building to make a promise you won't hear from many other properties: Every unit in the complex will offer a view of the water. Some of the large, clean windows and spacious lanais look out to the Pacific Ocean while others offer harbor views. Accommodations are large here, with rattan furniture in the living rooms. The fully equipped kitchens come with microwaves, garbage disposals, and dishwashers. Each unit is individually owned and has its own personality. *5050 Lawai Beach Rd., Koloa 96756, tel. 808/742–7555 or 800/367–8022. 75 one- and two-bedroom condominiums with bath and kitchen. No pool. AE, MC, V. Expensive.*

Kapaa Sands. With only 22 condominium units, the Kapaa Sands is an intimate, off-the-beaten-track gem. On the eastern coast right by the sea, it's on the site of an old Japanese Shinto temple, and today an old rock etched with Japanese characters graces the gardens. The small rooms come with full kitchen plus telephone and TV, and some have dishwashers and garbage disposals. Furnishings are done in rustic wood with ceiling fans, appropriate for a beachside bungalow. Ask for an oceanfront room, because they offer great open-air lanais with gorgeous Pacific views. The landscaping around the eight two-story buildings is lush and lovely, with meandering pathways lined with palms, gingers, gardenias, and other tropicana. *380 Papaloa Rd., Kapaa 96746, tel. 808/822–4901 or 800/222–4901. 22 condominiums with bath and kitchen. Facilities: pool. AE, DC, MC, V. Moderate.*

Vacation Rentals **Koloa Landing Cottages.** Just five accommodations are available in this garden complex near Poipu Beach, so advance reservations are a must. Once here, guests are treated like family by the owners, who invite their visitors to partake of fresh fruit picked from the trees right outside the door and who offer knowledgeable sightseeing advice. Koloa Landing has two-bedroom cottages and studios available for rent. Each has open-beamed ceilings, which keep the interiors cool, and batiks are used for decoration. Each cottage has a fully equipped kitchen with microwave, color cable television, and telephone. Family swimming beaches and restaurants of all ilk are located within walking distance. *2704-B Hoonani Rd., Koloa 96756, tel. 808/742–1470. 5 cottages with private bath. Facilities: laundry, barbecue. MC, V. Moderate.*

Sandpiper Village. If you want your own separate dwelling in the Princeville area, check out the Sandpiper Village, which rents two-bedroom/two-bath cottages. The garden setting is shaded and quiet, and picture windows in each unit offer views of the mountains of the Hanalei area. Inside each condo are high ceilings with ceiling fans, dark bamboo furnishings, and a recreation and barbecue area for guest use only. *4770 Pepelani Loop, Princeville 96722, tel. 808/826–9613 or 800/367–5205. 74 condominiums with bath. Facilities: pool, sauna, golf, spa. AE, DC, MC, V. Moderate.*

The Arts

Very little classical arts activity happens on laid-back Kauai. The island doesn't have its own symphony, but the **Honolulu Symphony Orchestra** (tel. 808/537–6191) does perform on the Garden Isle from time to time. For a specific schedule, call the **Kauai Concert Association** (tel. 808/245–7464).

In Lihue, the **Kauai Regional Library** (4344 Hardy St., tel. 808/245–3617) often plays host to films, storytelling, musical presentations, and arts and crafts events.

Nightlife

People on Kauai take great pride in their culture, and they like to share their unique traditions with those who come to call. As a result, on the Garden Isle you will find more traditional Hawaiiana and less Las Vegas–style glitz than on neighboring Oahu.

Because tourists are extremely important to Kauai's economy, most of the island's dinner shows and luaus take place within a hotel or resort. You will also find some pretty entertaining options on board the cruise boats. Hotel lounges and restaurant bars offer live music with no cover charge, and often they have discount drinks during happy hour. Stand-up comedy is the latest craze to hit Kauai, with a club on the east side doing record business.

Check the local newspaper, *The Garden Island Times*, for listings of weekly happenings. Three free magazines—*Spotlight Kauai, This Week on Kauai*, and *Kauai Beach Press*—also offer listings of entertainment events. You can pick them up at the Hawaii Visitors Bureau and at Lihue Airport.

Bars and Clubs

For the most part, discos just don't fit into the serenity of Kauai, and the bar scene is extremely limited. The major resorts generally host their own live entertainment and happy hours.

The drinking age in Hawaii is 21, and if you look younger than that, you may be asked to show some identification. All bars and clubs that serve alcohol must close at 2 AM, except for those with a cabaret license, which close at 4 AM.

The following establishments present dance music on a regular basis.

Buzz's Steak & Lobster (Coconut Plantation Market Place, Kapaa, tel. 808/822–7491). The lounge area of this visitor-oriented restaurant features Hawaiian music and Top 40 tunes. Happy hour daily 3–5, entertainment nightly 8:30–11:30.

Club Jetty Restaurant and Cabaret (Nawiliwili Harbor, Nawiliwili, tel. 808/245–4970). This disco by the sea attracts crowds both young and old. Along with taped music, it hosts live bands from time to time. Wednesday–Saturday nights 10–3:30.

Kuhio's Nightclub (Hyatt Regency Kauai, tel. 808/742–1234). This is the south shore's newest hot spot. High energy entertainment and late-night dancing are the drawing cards in this very '90s nightclub. You'll find it at the new Hyatt Regency Kauai in Poipu. Music nightly 9–2.

Paddling Club (Westin Kauai, Kalapaki Beach, Nawiliwili, tel. 808/246–5048). This high-energy, five-level, adult-entertainment discotheque features music from the past and present. It attracts the upscale resort crowd. Nightly 9–1.

Legends Nightclub (Harbor Village Shopping Center, 3501 Rice St., Nawiliwili, tel. 808/245–5775). With the largest dance floor on the island, this fast-paced disco features Top 40 tunes in a garden setting. It caters to the under-30 age group. Happy hour on Wednesday lasts until midnight. Music nightly 9:30–4.

Dinner and Sunset Cruises

Choose a cruise along the north shore or the south. Either way, sunset is a magical time to watch Kauai from the water. Prices range from $45 to $75 per person for food and drink.

Captain Andy's Sailing Adventures (Box 1291, Koloa, tel. 808/822–7833). The 46-foot catamaran *Akialoa* takes up to 40 passengers on a two-hour sunset sail along the south shore. Hors d'oeuvres and beverages are included.

Na Pali Coast Cruise Line (4402 Waialo Rd., Eleele, tel. 808/
335–5078). This 2½-hour cruise on the *Na Pali Queen* leaves
Port Allen and serves drinks at twilight. The dinner headlines
either prime rib or fresh fish. The views of the southern coastline make up for the lack of on-board musical entertainment.
Wednesday, Friday, and Saturday 5:30–8.

Luaus

Each of the listings offers its own unique variation on the luau
theme. The cost ranges from $35 to $45 for adults, $15 to $30 for
children under 12.

Kauai Coconut Beach Resort Luau (Coconut Plantation,
Kapaa, tel. 808/822–3455 ext. 651). The music, dance, and food
of Polynesia come together at this hotel-based luau, regarded
by many as the island's best. It takes place in a lovely setting of
flaming tiki torches. Nightly at 6:45.

Smith's Tropical Paradise Luau (Wailua Marina, 174 Wailua
Rd., Wailua, tel. 808/822–4654). Set amid 30 acres of tropical
flora and fauna, this luau begins with the traditional blowing of
the conch shell and *imu* (underground oven) ceremony, followed by cocktails, an island feast, and an international show in
the Lagoon Amphitheater. Weeknights at 6.

Tahiti Nui Luau (Kuhio Hwy., Hanalei, tel. 808/826–6277).
While a post-Iniki reopening date was unavailable at press
time, it is likely that this venerable institution will be operating
in 1994. It's a welcome change from the standard commercial
luau, because it's put on by a family that really knows how to
party. A mood of fun pervades this open-air restaurant. Emcee
Auntie Louise keeps things rolling, with lots of good local entertainment. The menu is a luau with all the trimmings, from
kalua (roasted) pig to *haupia* (gelatinlike dessert made from
coconut). Wednesday and Friday evenings starting at 7.

Shows

Charo's (Colony Resort, Haena, tel. 808/826–6422). After
years as an international dancer and guitarist, this Latin star
has taken up part-time residence on the north shore. Her show
features Latin, flamenco, and island dancing by a well-choreo-
graphed ensemble, and Charo herself puts in an occasional appearance when she's not starring in her Waikiki-based act. The
restaurant setting is lovely, right on the beach. A shuttle service is available from the Princeville area. Price ranges from
$45 to $55 per person, including a cocktail and dinner. Shows
nightly at 8. Dinner 6–9.

Polynesian Revue (Sheraton Kauai Hotel, Poipu Beach, tel.
808/742–1661). Perched next to the ocean with views from every table, the Outrigger Room is an appropriate setting for the
pulsating rhythms and captivating dances of the South Pacific.
This production features a good mix of the old and the new.
Sunday and Wednesday at 6.

Hawaiian Vocabulary

The Hawaiian language is unlike anything heard by the average traveler. But given the chance, say at a traditional church service or a local ritual ceremony, visitors will find the soft, rolling language of the Islands both interesting and refreshing to the ear.

Although an understanding of Hawaiian is by no means required on a trip to the Aloha State, *malihinis*, or newcomers, will find plenty of opportunities to pick up a few of the local words and phrases. In fact, traditional names and expressions are still in wide use, and Governor John Waihee signed a bill in 1992 to encourage authentic Hawaiian spelling, with *Kahakō* (macrons) and *'okina* (glottal stops). With a basic understanding and some uninhibited practice, anyone can have enough command of the local tongue to ask for directions and to order off the neighborhood restaurant menu.

Simplifying the learning process is the fact that the Hawaiian language contains only seven consonants—H, K, L, M, N, P, and W—and the five vowels. All syllables and all words end in a vowel. Each vowel, with the exception of the diphthong double vowels such as *au* (pronounced ow) or *ai* (pronounced eye), is pronounced separately. *A'a*, the word for "rough lava" for example, is pronounced ah-ah. (The 'okina, or glottal stop, is sometimes called the eighth consonant.)

Although some Hawaiian words have only vowels, most also contain some combination consonants as well. Consonants are never doubled, and they always begin syllables, as in Ka-me-ha-me-ha.

The accent in most Hawaiian words falls on the next-to-the-last, or penultimate, syllable. Examples are KO-na, PA-li and KA-na. The exception occurs when the vowels in the second syllable become dipthongized, as in ha-PAI and ma-KAI, which are fundamentally ha-PA-i and ma-KA-i.

Pronunciation is simple. Pronounce *A* "ah" as in father; *E* "ay" as in weigh; *I* "ee" as in marine; *O* "oh" as in no; *U* "oo" as in true.

Consonants mirror their English equivalents, with the exception of W. When the letter begins the last syllable of a word, it is sometimes pronounced as a V. Awa, the Polynesian drink, is pronounced "ava"; Ewa is pronounced "Eva."

What follows is a glossary of some of the most commonly used Hawaiian words. Don't be afraid to give them a try. Hawaiian residents appreciate visitors who at least try to pick up the local language—no matter how fractured the pronunciation.

a'a—rough, crumbling lava, contrasting with *pahoehoe*, which is smooth.
ae—yes.
akamai—smart, clever, possessing savoir-faire.
ala—a road, path, or trail.
alii—a Hawaiian chief, a member of the chiefly class; also plural.

aloha—love, affection, kindness. Also a salutation meaning both greetings and farewell.

aole—no.

auwai—a ditch.

auwe—alas, woe is me!

ehu—a red-haired Hawaiian.

ewa—in the direction of Ewa plantation, west of Honolulu.

hala—the pandanus tree, whose leaves *(lauhala)* are used to make baskets and plaited mats.

hale—a house.

hana—to work.

haole—originally a stranger or foreigner. Since the first foreigners were Caucasian, *haole* now means a Caucasian person.

hapa—a part, sometimes a half.

hapa haole—part *haole*, a person of mixed racial background, part of which is Caucasian.

hauoli—to rejoice. *Hauoli Makahiki Hou* means Happy New Year.

heiau—an ancient Hawaiian place of worship.

holo—to run.

holoholo—to go for a walk, ride, or sail.

holoku—a long Hawaiian dress, somewhat fitted, with a scoop neck and a train. Influenced by European fashion, it was worn at court.

holomuu—a recent cross between a *holoku* and a *muumuu*, less fitted than the former but less voluminous than the latter, and having no train.

honi—to kiss, a kiss. A phrase that some tourists may find useful, quoted from a popular *hula*, is *Honi Kaua wikiwiki:* Kiss me quick!

hoomalimali—flattery, a deceptive "line," bunk, baloney, hooey.

huhu—angry.

hui—a group, club, or assembly. There are church *huis* and social *huis*.

hukilau—a seine; a communal fishing party in which everyone helps to drive the fish into a huge net, pull it in, and divide the catch.

hula—the dance of Hawaii.

ipo—sweetheart.

ka—the definite article.

kahuna—a priest, doctor, or other trained person of old Hawaii, endowed with special professional skills that often included the gift of prophecy or other supernatural powers.

kai—the sea, saltwater.

kalo—the taro plant from whose root *poi* is made.

kamaaina—literally, a child of the soil, it refers to people who were born in the Islands or have lived there for a long time.

kanaka—originally a man or humanity in general, it is now used to denote a male Hawaiian or part-Hawaiian.

kane—a man, a husband. If you see this word on a door, it's the men's room.

kapa—also called *tapa*, a cloth made of beaten bark and usually dyed and stamped with a geometric design.

kapakahi—crooked, cockeyed, uneven. You've got your hat on *kapakahi*.

kapu—keep out, prohibited. This is the Hawaiian version of the more widely known Tongan word *tabu* (taboo).

keiki—a child; *keikikane* is a boy child, *keikiwahine* a girl.

kokua—help.

kona—the south, also the south or leeward side of the islands from which the *kona* wind and *kona* rain come.

kuleana—a homestead or small plot of ground on which a family has been installed for some generations without necessarily owning it. By extension, *kuleana* is used to denote any area or department in which one has a special interest or prerogative. You'll hear it used this way: If you want to hire a surfboard, see Moki; that's his *kuleana*. And conversely, I can't help you with that; that's not my *kuleana*.

lamalama—to go torch fishing.

lanai—a porch, a balcony, an outdoor living room. Almost every house in Hawaii has one.

lani—heaven, the sky.

lauhala—the leaf of the *hala* or pandanus tree, widely used in Hawaiian handcrafts.

lei—a garland of flowers.

luna—a plantation overseer or foreman.

mahalo—thank you.

makai—toward the ocean.

malihini—a newcomer to the Islands.

mana—the spiritual power that the Hawaiians believed to inhabit all things and creatures.

manawahi—free, gratis.

mauka—toward the mountains.

mauna—mountain.

mele—a Hawaiian song or chant, often of epic proportions.

menehune—a Hawaiian pixie. The *menehunes* were a legendary race of little people who accomplished prodigious work, like building fish ponds and temples in the course of a single night.

moana—the ocean.

muumuu—the voluminous dress in which the missionaries enveloped Hawaiian women. Now made in bright printed cottons and silks, it is an indispensable garment in a Hawaiian woman's wardrobe.

nani—beautiful.

nui—big.

pake—a Chinese.

palapala—book, printing.

pali—a cliff, precipice.

panini—cactus.

paniolo—a Hawaiian cowboy.

pau—finished, done.

pilikia—trouble. The Hawaiian word is much more widely used here than its English equivalent.

puka—a hole.

pupule—crazy, like the celebrated Princess Pupule. This word has replaced its English equivalent in local usage.

wahine—a female, a woman, a wife, and a sign on the ladies' room door.

wai—fresh water, as opposed to saltwater, which is *kai*.

wikiwiki—to hurry, hurry up.

Pidgin English is the unofficial language of Hawaii. It is heard everywhere: on ranches, in warehouses, on beaches, and in the hallowed halls (though not in the classrooms) of the University of Hawaii. It's still English and not much tougher to follow than Brooklynese; it just takes a little getting used to.

Menu Guide

Much of the Hawaiian language encountered during a stay in the Islands will appear on restaurant menus and lists of luau fare. Often these menus will also include terms from Japanese, Chinese, and other cultures. Here's a quick primer.

ahi—locally caught tuna.

aku—skipjack, bonito tuna.

ama ama—mullet; it's hard to get, but tasty.

bento—a box lunch.

dim sum—Chinese dumplings.

chicken luau—a stew made from chicken, taro leaves, and coconut milk.

guava—This tasty fruit is most often used in juice and in jellies. As a juice, it's pink and quenches a thirst like nothing else.

haupia—a light, gelatinlike dessert made from coconut.

imu—the underground ovens in which pigs are roasted for luaus.

kalua—to bake underground. A *kalua* pig is the pièce de résistance of a Hawaiian feast.

kaukau—food. The word's derivation is Chinese, but it is widely used in the Islands.

kim chee—pickled Chinese cabbage made with garlic and hot peppers.

kona coffee—coffee grown in the Kona district of the Big Island; prized for its rich flavor.

laulau—literally, a bundle. In everyday usage, laulaus are morsels of pork, butterfish, or other ingredients wrapped along with young taro shoots in *ti* leaves for steaming.

lilikoi (passion fruit)—a tart, seedy yellow fruit that makes delicious desserts, jellies, and sherbet.

lomilomi—to rub or massage; also a massage. Lomilomi salmon is fish that has been rubbed with onions and herbs, commonly served with minced onions and tomatoes.

luau—a Hawaiian feast, also the leaf of the taro plant used in preparing such a feast.

luau leaves—cooked taro tops with a taste similar to spinach.

macadamia nuts—These little round, buttery-tasting nuts are mostly grown on the Big Island, but are available throughout the Islands.

mahimahi—mild-flavored dolphin, not to be confused with porpoise.

mai tai—Hawaiian fruit punch with rum.

malasada—a Portuguese deep-fried doughnut, dipped in sugar, with no hole.

manapua—dough wrapped around diced pork.

mango—a juicy sweet fruit, with a yellowish-red smooth skin and a yellow pulpy interior.

mano—shark.

niu—coconut.

okolehao—a liqueur distilled from the *ti* root.

onaga—pink snapper.

ono (adj.)—delicious.

ono (n.)—a long, slender mackerel-like fish; also called a wahoo.

opakapaka—pink snapper.

opihi—a tiny shellfish, or mollusk, found on rocks; also called limpets.

papaya—This little green or yellow melon-like fruit will grow on you; it's high in vitamin C and is most often eaten at breakfast with a squeeze of lemon or lime.

papio—a young ulua or jack fish.

poha—cape gooseberry. Tasting a bit like honey, the poha berry is often used in jams and desserts.

poi—a paste made from pounded taro root, a staple of the Hawaiian diet.

pupu—Hawaiian hors d'oeuvre.

saimin—long thin noodles and vegetables in a thin broth.

sashimi—raw fish sliced thin, usually eaten with soy sauce.

sushi—a variety of raw fish, served with vinegared rice and Japanese horseradish.

uku—deep-sea snapper.

ulua—crevelle, or jack fish; the giant trevally.

Index

Escape to ancient cities and exotic

islands

with CNN Travel Guide, a

wealth of valuable advice. Host Valerie Voss will take you

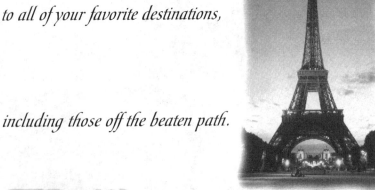

to all of your favorite destinations,

including those off the beaten path.

Tune into your passport to the world.

CNN TRAVEL GUIDE

SATURDAY 10:00 PMᴘᴛ   SUNDAY 8:30 AMᴇᴛ

Announcing the only guide to explore a Disney World you've never seen before:

The one for grown-ups.

This terrific new guide is the only one written specifically for the millions of adults who visit Walt Disney World each year <u>without</u> kids. Upscale, sophisticated, packed full of facts and maps, *Walt Disney World for Adults* provides up-to-date information on hotels, restaurants, sports facilities, and health clubs, as well as unique itineraries for adults, including: a Sporting Life Vacation, Day-and-Night Romantic Fantasy, Singles Safari, and Gardens and Natural Wonders Tour. Get essential tips and everything you need to know about reservations, packages, annual events, banking service, rest stops, and much more. With *Walt Disney World for Adults* in hand, you'll get the most out of one of the world's most fascinating, most complex playgrounds.

At bookstores everywhere, or call 1-800-533-6478

Fodor's

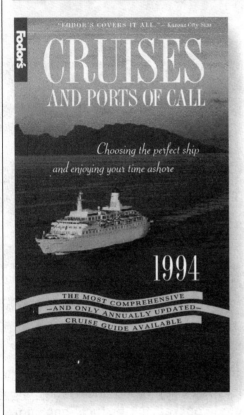
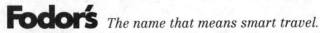

Fodor's Travel Guides

Available at bookstores everywhere, or call 1–800–533–6478, 24 hours a day.

U.S. Guides

Alaska

Arizona

Boston

California

Cape Cod, Martha's Vineyard, Nantucket

The Carolinas & the Georgia Coast

Chicago

Colorado

Florida

Hawaii

Las Vegas, Reno, Tahoe

Los Angeles

Maine, Vermont, New Hampshire

Maui

Miami & the Keys

New England

New Orleans

New York City

Pacific North Coast

Philadelphia & the Pennsylvania Dutch Country

The Rockies

San Diego

San Francisco

Santa Fe, Taos, Albuquerque

Seattle & Vancouver

The South

The U.S. & British Virgin Islands

The Upper Great Lakes Region

USA

Vacations in New York State

Vacations on the Jersey Shore

Virginia & Maryland

Waikiki

Walt Disney World and the Orlando Area

Washington, D.C.

Foreign Guides

Acapulco, Ixtapa, Zihuatanejo

Australia & New Zealand

Austria

The Bahamas

Baja & Mexico's Pacific Coast Resorts

Barbados

Berlin

Bermuda

Brazil

Brittany & Normandy

Budapest

Canada

Cancun, Cozumel, Yucatan Peninsula

Caribbean

China

Costa Rica, Belize, Guatemala

The Czech Republic & Slovakia

Eastern Europe

Egypt

Euro Disney

Europe

Europe's Great Cities

Florence & Tuscany

France

Germany

Great Britain

Greece

The Himalayan Countries

Hong Kong

India

Ireland

Israel

Italy

Japan

Kenya & Tanzania

Korea

London

Madrid & Barcelona

Mexico

Montreal & Quebec City

Morocco

Moscow & St. Petersburg

The Netherlands, Belgium & Luxembourg

New Zealand

Norway

Nova Scotia, Prince Edward Island & New Brunswick

Paris

Portugal

Provence & the Riviera

Rome

Russia & the Baltic Countries

Scandinavia

Scotland

Singapore

South America

Southeast Asia

Spain

Sweden

Switzerland

Thailand

Tokyo

Toronto

Turkey

Vienna & the Danube Valley

Yugoslavia

WHEREVER YOU TRAVEL, *H*ELP IS NEVER FAR AWAY.

From planning your trip to providing travel assistance along the way, American Express® Travel Service Offices* are always there to help.

HONOLULU

1440 Kapiolani Blvd., Suite 104
808-946-7741

223 South King St.
808-536-3377

Hawaiian Regent Hotel
808-924-6555
Hilton Hawaiian Village
808-947-2607
Hyatt Regency Waikiki
808-926-5441
Ilikai Hotel
808-945-2679
Pacific Beach Hotel
808-922-2363
Royal Hawaiian Center
808-922-0575

MAUI

658 Front Street
The Wharf, Shop 174, Lahaina
808-667-4381
Hyatt Regency Maui
808-667-7451
Kaanapali Beach Hotel
808-661-4908
Maui Marriott Hotel
808-667-7991

HAWAII

Hyatt Regency Waikoloa
808-885-7958
The Ritz-Carlton Hotel
808-885-6600
Royal Waikoloan Hotel
808-885-1209

KAUAI

Hyatt Regency Kauai
808-742-2323

© 1993 American Express Travel Related Services Company, Inc.

* Comprises Travel Service locations of American Express Travel Related Services Company, Inc., its affiliates and Representatives worldwide.

INTRODUCING

Fodor's
WORLDVIEW
TRAVEL UPDATE

AT LAST, YOUR OWN PERSONALIZED LIST OF WHAT'S GOING ON IN THE CITIES YOU'RE VISITING.

KEYED TO THE DAYS WHEN YOU'RE THERE, CUSTOMIZED FOR YOUR INTERESTS, AND SENT TO YOU BEFORE YOU LEAVE HOME.

EXCLUSIVE FOR PURCHASERS OF FODOR'S GUIDES...

Introducing a revolutionary way to get customized, time-sensitive travel information just before your trip.

Now you can obtain detailed information about what's going on in each city you'll be visiting <u>before</u> you leave home—up-to-the-minute, objective information about the events and activities that interest you most.

This is a special offer for purchasers of Fodor's guides – a customized Travel Update to fit your specific interests and your itinerary.

Travel Updates contain the kind of time-sensitive insider information you can get only from local contacts – or from city magazines and newspapers once you arrive. But now you can have the same information before you leave for your trip.

The choice is yours: current art exhibits, theater, music festivals and special concerts, sporting events, antiques and flower shows, shopping, fitness, and more.

The information comes from hundreds of correspondents and thousands of sources worldwide. Updated continuously, it's like having your own personal concierge or friend in the city.

You specify the cities and when you'll be there. We'll do the rest — personalizing the information for you the way no guidebook can.

It's the perfect extension to your Fodor's guide and the best way to make the most of your valuable travel time.

Your Itinerary:
Customized reports available for 160 destinations

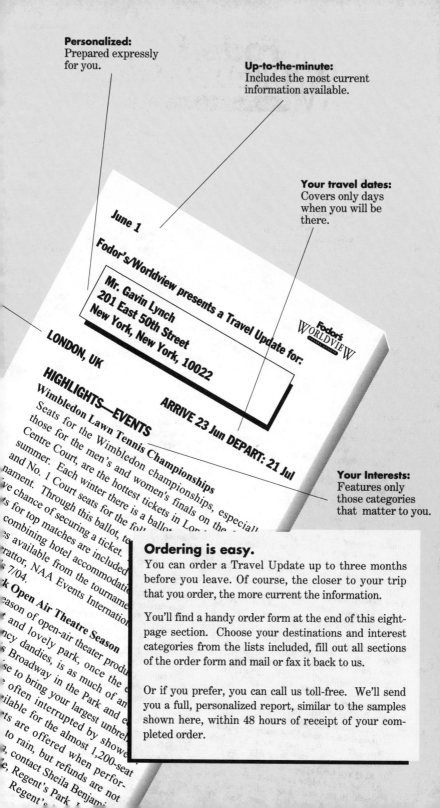

Personalized:
Prepared expressly
for you.

Up-to-the-minute:
Includes the most current
information available.

Your travel dates:
Covers only days
when you will be
there.

June 1

Fodor's/Worldview presents a Travel Update for:

Mr. Gavin Lynch
201 East 50th Street
New York, New York, 10022

Fodor's
WORLDVIEW

LONDON, UK

ARRIVE 23 Jun DEPART: 21 Jul

HIGHLIGHTS—EVENTS

Wimbledon Lawn Tennis Championships

Seats for the Wimbledon championships, especiall
those for the men's and women's finals on the
Centre Court, are the hottest tickets in Lon
summer. Each winter there is a ballo
and No. 1 Court seats for the foll
nament. Through this ballot, te
ve chance of securing a ticket.
s for top matches are included
combining hotel accommodatio
es available from the tourname
rattor, NAA Events Internation
s 7/04.

k Open Air Theatre Season

eason of open-air theater produ
* and lovely park, once the e
ncy dandies, is as much of an
s Broadway in the Park and e
se to bring your largest unbre
 often interrupted by showe
ilable for the almost 1,200-seat
ts are offered when perfor
to rain, but refunds are not
e, contact Sheila Benjami
e, Regent's Park
Regent's

Your Interests:
Features only
those categories
that matter to you.

Ordering is easy.

You can order a Travel Update up to three months
before you leave. Of course, the closer to your trip
that you order, the more current the information.

You'll find a handy order form at the end of this eight-
page section. Choose your destinations and interest
categories from the lists included, fill out all sections
of the order form and mail or fax it back to us.

Or if you prefer, you can call us toll-free. We'll send
you a full, personalized report, similar to the samples
shown here, within 48 hours of receipt of your completed order.

**Special concerts—
who's performing
what and where**

**One-of-a-kind,
one-time-only events**

**Special interest,
in-depth listings**

Children — Events
Angel Canal Festival
The festivities include a children's funfair,
entertainers, a boat rally and displays on the
water. Regent's Canal. Islington. N1. Tube:
Angel. Tel: 267 9100. 11:30am-5:30pm. 7/04.

Blackheath Summer Kite Festival
Stunt kite displays with parachuting teddy
bears and trade stands. Free admission. SE3.
BR: Blackheath. 10am. 6/27.

Megabugs
Children will delight in this infestation of
giant robotic insects, including a praying
mantic 60 times life size. Mon-Sat 10am-
6pm; Sun 11am-6pm. Admission 4.50
pounds. Natural History Museum, Cromwell
Road. SW7. Tube: South Kensington. Tel:
938 9123. Ends 10/01.

Childminders
This establishment employs only women,
providing nurses and qualified nannies to

Music — Jazz & Blues
Tito Puente's Golden Men of Latin Jazz
The father of mambo and Cuban rumba king
comes to town. Royal Festival Hall. South Bank.
SE1. Tube: Waterloo. Tel: 928 8800. 8pm. 7/15.

Georgie Fame and The New York Band
Riding a popular tide with his latest album, the
smoky-voiced Fame and his keyboard are on a
tour yet again. The Grand. Clapham Junction.
SW11. BR: Clapham Junction. Tel: 738 9000.
7:30pm. 7/07.

Jacques Loussier Play Bach Trio
The French jazz classicist and colleagues.
Kenwood Lakeside. Hampstead Lane.
Kenwood. NW3. Tube: Golders Green, then bus
210. Tel: 413 1443. 7pm. 7/10.

Tony Bennett and Ronnie Scott
Royal Festival Hall. South Bank. SE1. Tube:
Waterloo. Tel: 928 8800. 8pm. 7/11.

Santana
Royal Festival Hall. South Bank. SE1. Tube:
Waterloo. Tel: 928 8800. 8pm. 7/12.

Count Basie Orchestra and Nancy Wilson Trio
Royal Festival Hall. South Bank. SE1. Tube:
Waterloo. Tel: 928 8800. 8pm. 7/14.

King Pleasure and the Biscuit Boys
Royal Festival Hall. South Bank. SE1. Tube:
Waterloo. Tel: 928 8800. 6:30 and 9pm. 7/16.

Al Green and the London Community Gospel Choir
Royal Festival Hall. South Bank. SE1. Tube:
Waterloo. Tel: 928 8800. 8pm. 7/13.

BB King and Linda Hopkins
Mother of the blues and successor to Bessie
Smith, Hopkins meets up with "Blues Boy"
Festival Hall. South Bank. SE

Music — Classical
Marylebone Sinfonia
Kenneth Gowen conducts music by Puccini
and Rossini. Queen Elizabeth Hall. South
Bank. SE1. Tube: Waterloo. Tel: 928 8800.
7:45pm. 7/16.

London Philharmonic
Franz Welser-Moest and George Benjamin
conduct selections by Alexander Goehr
Messiaen, and some of Benjamin's own com
positions. Queen Elizabeth Hall. South Bank
SE1. Tube: Waterloo. Tel: 928 8800. 8pm.

London Pro Arte Orchestra and Forest Choir
Murray Stewart conducts selections b
Rossini, Haydn and Jonathan Willcocks.
Queen Elizabeth Hall. South Bank. SE
Tube: Waterloo. Tel: 928 8800. 7:45pm. 7/1

Kensington Symphony Orchestra
Russell Keable conducts Dvorak's Dmit

Here's what you get . . .

Detailed information about what's going on — precisely when you'll be there.

Show openings
during your visit

Reviews by
local critics

Exhibitions & Shows—Antique & Flower

Westminster Antiques Fair
Over 50 stands with pre-1830 furniture and other Victorian and earlier items. Thu-Fri 11am-8pm; Sat-Sun 11am-6pm. Admission 4 pounds, children free. Old Royal Horticultural Hall. Vincent Square. SW1. Tel: 0444/48 25 14. 6-24 thru 6/27.

Royal Horticultural Society Flower Show
The show includes displays of carnations, summer fruit and vegetables. Tue 11am-7pm; Wed 10am-5pm. Admission Tue 4 pounds, Wed 2 pounds. Royal Horticultural Halls. Greycoat Street and Vincent Square. SW1. Tube: Victoria. 7/20 thru 7/21.

Hampton Court Palace International Flower Show
Major international garden and flower show taking place in conjunction with the British ... of floral exhibitions ...

Theater — Musical

Sunset Boulevard
In June, the four Andrew Lloyd Webber musicals which dominated London's stages in the 1980s (Cats, Starlight Express, Phantom of the Opera and Aspects of Love) are joined by the composer's latest work, a show rumored to have his best music to date. The 1950 Billy Wilder film about a helpless young writer who is drawn into the world of a possessive, aging silent screen star offers rich opportunities for Webber's evolving style. Soaring, aching melodies, lush technical effects and psychological thrills are all expected. Patti Lupone stars. Mon-Sat at 8pm; matinee Thu-Sat at 3pm. In-person sales only at the box office; credit card bookings, Tel: 344 0055. Admission 15-32.50 pounds. Adelphi Theatre. The Strand. WC2. Tube: Charing Cross. Tel: 836 7611. Starts: 6/21

Leonardo A Portrait of Love
A new musical about the great Renaissance artist and inventor comes in for a London premiere tested by a brief run at Oxford's Old Fire Station ... autumn. The work explores the relations ... Vinci and the woman ...

Alberquerque • Atlanta • Atlantic City • Ne
Baltimore • Boston • Chicago • Cincinnati
Cleveland • Dallas/Ft.Worth • Denver • De
• Houston • Kansas City • Las Vegas • Los
Angeles • Memphis • Miami • Milwaukee •
New Orleans • New York City • Orlando •
Springs • Philadelphia • Phoenix • Pittsburg
Portland • Salt Lake • San Antonio • San Di
• San Franc... • Seattle • St Louis • Tamp
Oslo • Wash... • Honolulu • Island
Hawaii • Kauai • Maui • ... • Bimini
Express • Ber... Countryside • Hampton • Islan
Antigua & B... • ... • Jvilla
... Gorda • Barbados • Dominica • Forte
...cia • St. Vincent • Trinidad &Tobago • Gren
...ymans • Puerto Plata • Santo Domin
Aruba • Bonaire • Curacao • St. Ma...
...ec City • Montreal • Ottawa • Toron
...ancouver • Guadeloupe • Martiniqu
...helemy • St. Martin • Kingston • Ixta
...o Bay • Negril • Ocho Rios • Ponce
... • Grand Turk • Providenciales • S
St. John • St. Thomas • Acapulco •
& Isla Mujeres • Cozumel • Guadal
... • Los Cabos • Manzanillo • Mazatl
City • Monterrey • Oaxaca • Mazatl
...do • Puerto Vallarta • Veracruz • Puerto
...dam • Athens • ... Ix

Fodor's WORLDVIEW
TRAVEL UPDATE

Spectator Sports — Other Sports

Greyhound Racing: Wembley Stadium
This dog track offers good views of greyhound racing held on Mon, Wed and Fri. No credit cards. Stadium Way. Wembley. HA9. Tube: Wembley Park. Tel: 902 8833.

Benson & Hedges Cricket Cup Final
Lord's Cricket Ground. St. John's Wood Road. NW8. Tube: St. John's Wood Tel: 289 1611. 11am. 7/10.

Business-Fax & Overnight Mail

Post Office, Trafalgar Square Branch
Offers a network of fax services, the Intelpost system, throughout the country and abroad. Mon-Sat 8am-8pm, Sun 9am-5pm. William IV Street. WC2. Tube: Charing Cross. Tel: 930 ...

Interest Categories

For <u>your</u> personalized Travel Update, choose the categories you're most interested in from this list. Every Travel Update automatically provides you with *Event Highlights* – the best of what's happening during the dates of your trip.

1.	**Business Services**	Fax & Overnight Mail, Computer Rentals, Photocopying, Secretarial , Messenger, Translation Services

Dining

2.	**All Day Dining**	Breakfast & Brunch, Cafes & Tea Rooms, Late-Night Dining
3.	**Local Cuisine**	In Every Price Range—from Budget Restaurants to the Special Splurge
4.	**European Cuisine**	Continental, French, Italian
5.	**Asian Cuisine**	Chinese, Far Eastern, Japanese, Indian
6.	**Americas Cuisine**	American, Mexican & Latin
7.	**Nightlife**	Bars, Dance Clubs, Comedy Clubs, Pubs & Beer Halls
8.	**Entertainment**	Theater—Drama, Musicals, Dance, Ticket Agencies
9.	**Music**	Classical, Traditional & Ethnic, Jazz & Blues, Pop, Rock
10.	**Children's Activities**	Events, Attractions
11.	**Tours**	Local Tours, Day Trips, Overnight Excursions, Cruises
12.	**Exhibitions, Festivals & Shows**	Antiques & Flower, History & Cultural, Art Exhibitions, Fairs & Craft Shows, Music & Art Festivals
13.	**Shopping**	Districts & Malls, Markets, Regional Specialities
14.	**Fitness**	Bicycling, Health Clubs, Hiking, Jogging
15.	**Recreational Sports**	Boating/Sailing, Fishing, Ice Skating, Skiing, Snorkeling/Scuba, Swimming
16.	**Spectator Sports**	Auto Racing, Baseball, Basketball, Football, Horse Racing, Ice Hockey, Soccer

Please note that interest category content will vary by season, destination, and length of stay.

Destinations

The Fodor's/Worldview Travel Update covers more than 160 destinations worldwide. Choose the destinations that match your itinerary from this list. (Choose bulleted destinations only.)

United States (Mainland)
- Albuquerque
- Atlanta
- Atlantic City
- Baltimore
- Boston
- Chicago
- Cincinnati
- Cleveland
- Dallas/Ft. Worth
- Denver
- Detroit
- Houston
- Kansas City
- Las Vegas
- Los Angeles
- Memphis
- Miami
- Milwaukee
- Minneapolis/St. Paul
- New Orleans
- New York City
- Orlando
- Palm Springs
- Philadelphia
- Phoenix
- Pittsburgh
- Portland
- St. Louis
- Salt Lake City
- San Antonio
- San Diego
- San Francisco
- Seattle
- Tampa
- Washington, DC

Alaska
- Anchorage/Fairbanks/Juneau

Hawaii
- Honolulu
- Island of Hawaii
- Kauai
- Maui

Canada
- Quebec City
- Montreal
- Ottawa
- Toronto
- Vancouver

Bahamas
- Abacos
- Eleuthera/Harbour Island
- Exumas
- Freeport
- Nassau & Paradise Island

Bermuda
- Bermuda Countryside
- Hamilton

British Leeward Islands
- Anguilla
- Antigua & Barbuda
- Montserrat
- St. Kitts & Nevis

British Virgin Islands
- Tortola & Virgin Gorda

British Windward Islands
- Barbados
- Dominica
- Grenada
- St. Lucia
- St. Vincent
- Trinidad & Tobago

Cayman Islands
- The Caymans

Dominican Republic
- Puerto Plata
- Santo Domingo

Dutch Leeward Islands
- Aruba
- Bonaire
- Curacao

Dutch Windward Islands
- St. Maarten

French West Indies
- Guadeloupe
- Martinique
- St. Barthelemy
- St. Martin

Jamaica
- Kingston
- Montego Bay
- Negril
- Ocho Rios

Puerto Rico
- Ponce
- San Juan

Turks & Caicos
- Grand Turk
- Providenciales

U.S. Virgin Islands
- St. Croix
- St. John
- St. Thomas

Mexico
- Acapulco
- Cancun & Isla Mujeres
- Cozumel
- Guadalajara
- Ixtapa & Zihuatanejo
- Los Cabos
- Manzanillo
- Mazatlan
- Mexico City
- Monterrey
- Oaxaca
- Puerto Escondido
- Puerto Vallarta
- Veracruz

Europe
- Amsterdam
- Athens
- Barcelona
- Berlin
- Brussels
- Budapest
- Copenhagen
- Dublin
- Edinburgh
- Florence
- Frankfurt
- French Riviera
- Geneva
- Glasgow
- Interlaken
- Istanbul
- Lausanne
- Lisbon
- London
- Madrid
- Milan
- Moscow
- Munich
- Oslo
- Paris
- Prague
- Provence
- Rome
- Salzburg
- St. Petersburg
- Stockholm
- Venice
- Vienna
- Zurich

Pacific Rim Australia & New Zealand
- Auckland
- Melbourne
- Sydney

China
- Beijing
- Guangzhou
- Shanghai

Japan
- Kyoto
- Nagoya
- Osaka
- Tokyo
- Yokohama

Other
- Bangkok
- Hong Kong & Macau
- Manila
- Seoul
- Singapore
- Taipei

Fodor's WORLDVIEW **Order Form**

THIS TRAVEL UPDATE IS FOR (Please print):

Name

Address

City	State		ZIP

Country	Tel # ( ) -

Title of this Fodor's guide:

Store and location where guide was purchased:

INDICATE YOUR DESTINATIONS/DATES: Write in below the destinations you want to order. Then fill in your arrival and departure dates for each destination.

			Month	Day		Month	Day
(Sample)	LONDON	From:	6	21	To:	6	30
1		From:	/		To:	/	
2		From:	/		To:	/	
3		From:	/		To:	/	

You can order up to three destinations per Travel Update. Only destinations listed on the previous page are applicable. Maximum amount of time covered by a Travel Update cannot exceed 30 days.

CHOOSE YOUR INTERESTS: Select up to eight categories from the list of interest categories shown on the previous page and circle the numbers below:

1   2   3   4   5   6   7   8   9   10   11   12   13   14   15   16

CHOOSE HOW YOU WANT YOUR TRAVEL UPDATE DELIVERED (Check one):

❑ Please mail my Travel Update to the address above **OR**

❑ Fax it to me at **Fax #** ( ) -

DELIVERY CHARGE (Check one)

	Within U.S. & Canada	Outside U.S. & Canada
First Class Mail	❑ $2.50	❑ $5.00
Fax	❑ $5.00	❑ $10.00
Priority Delivery	❑ $15.00	❑ $27.00

All orders will be sent within 48 hours of receipt of a completed order form.

ADD UP YOUR ORDER HERE. *SPECIAL OFFER FOR FODOR'S PURCHASERS ONLY!*

	Suggested Retail Price	Your Price	This Order
First destination ordered	$13.95	$ 7.95	$ 7.95
Second destination (if applicable)	$ 9.95	$ 4.95	+
Third destination (if applicable)	$ 9.95	$ 4.95	+
Plus delivery charge from above			+
		TOTAL:	$

METHOD OF PAYMENT (Check one):   ❑ AmEx   ❑ MC   ❑ Visa   ❑ Discover
❑ Personal Check   ❑ Money Order

Make check or money order payable to: Fodor's Worldview Travel Update

Credit Card #   **Expiration Date:**

Authorized Signature

SEND THIS COMPLETED FORM TO:
Fodor's Worldview Travel Update, 114 Sansome Street, Suite 700, San Francisco, CA 94104

OR CALL OR FAX US 24-HOURS A DAY
Telephone **1-800-799-9609** • Fax **1-800-799-9619** (From within the U.S. & Canada)
(Outside the U.S. & Canada: Telephone 415-616-9988 • Fax 415-616-9989)

(Please have this guide in front of you when you call so we can verify purchase.)

Offer valid until 12/31/94.